D1084551

HANDBOOK OF STRESS, REACTIVITY, AND CARDIOVASCULAR DISEASE

WILEY SERIES ON
HEALTH PSYCHOLOGY/BEHAVIORAL MEDICINE

Thomas J. Boll, Series Editor

THE PSYCHOLOGIST AS EXPERT WITNESS
by Theodore H. Blau

HEALTH, ILLNESS, AND FAMILIES: A LIFE-SPAN PERSPECTIVE
edited by Dennis C. Turk and Robert D. Kerns

MEASUREMENT STRATEGIES IN HEALTH PSYCHOLOGY
edited by Paul Karoly

HEALTH AND INDUSTRY: A BEHAVIORAL MEDICINE PERSPECTIVE
edited by Michael F. Cataldo and Thomas J. Coates

CHILD HEALTH BEHAVIOR: A BEHAVIORAL PEDIATRICS PERSPECTIVE
edited by Norman A. Krasnegor, Josephine D. Arastch, and
Michael F. Cataldo

HANDBOOK OF STRESS, REACTIVITY, AND CARDIOVASCULAR DISEASE
edited by Karen A. Matthews, Stephen M. Weiss, Thomas Detre,
Theodore M. Dembroski, Bonita Falkner, Stephen B. Manuck, and
Redford B. Williams, Jr.

HANDBOOK OF STRESS, REACTIVITY, AND CARDIOVASCULAR DISEASE

Edited by

KAREN A. MATTHEWS, *University of Pittsburgh*

STEPHEN M. WEISS, *Behavioral Medicine Branch, National Heart, Lung, and Blood Institute*

THOMAS DETRE, *University of Pittsburgh*

THEODORE M. DEMBROSKI, *University of Maryland—Baltimore County*

BONITA FALKNER, *Hahnemann University*

STEPHEN B. MANUCK, *University of Pittsburgh*

REDFORD B. WILLIAMS, JR., *Duke University Medical Center*

A Wiley-Interscience Publication
JOHN WILEY & SONS
New York / Chichester / Brisbane / Toronto / Singapore

Library of Congress Cataloging in Publication Data:

Main entry under title:

Handbook of stress, reactivity, and cardiovascular
  disease.

  (Wiley series on health psychology/behavioral
medicine)
  "A Wiley-Interscience publication."
  Includes indexes.
  1. Cardiovascular system—Diseases—Psychosomatic
aspects—Handbooks, manuals, etc.   2. Stress
(Physiology)—Handbooks, manuals, etc.   3. Stress
(Psychology)—Handbooks, manuals, etc.   I. Matthews,
Karen A.   II. Series.   [DNLM: 1. Cardiovascular
Diseases.   2. Cardiovascular system—physiopathology.
3. Stress—physiopathology.   4. Stress, Psychological—
physiopathology.   WG 100 H236]
  RC669.H285   1986   616.1'08   85-26636

ISBN 0-471-82219-1

Printed in the United States of America

10 9 8 7 6 5 4 3 2 1

List of Contributors

Bruce S. Alpert, M.D., Chief, Division of Cardiology, Le Bonheur Children's Medical Center, Memphis, Tennessee

James C. Buell, M.D., Associate Professor of Medicine, Division of Cardiology, School of Medicine, Texas Tech University Health Sciences Center, Lubbock, Texas

Margaret A. Chesney, Ph.D., Director, Department of Behavioral Medicine, Stanford Research Institute International, Menlo Park, California

Thomas B. Clarkson, D.V.M., Professor and Chair, Department of Comparative Medicine, Bowman Gray School of Medicine, Wake Forest University, Winston-Salem, North Carolina

Theodore M. Dembroski, Ph.D., Professor of Psychology, University of Maryland—Baltimore County, Catonsville, Maryland

Joel E. Dimsdale, M.D., Associate Professor of Psychiatry, University of California at San Diego Medical Center, San Diego, California

Elaine Eaker, Sc.D., Behavioral Epidemiologist, Epidemiology Branch, National Heart, Lung, and Blood Institute, Bethesda, Maryland

Leonard H. Epstein, Ph.D., Associate Professor of Psychiatry, Epidemiology, and Psychology, University of Pittsburgh, Pittsburgh, Pennsylvania

Bonita Falkner, M.D., Professor of Pediatrics, Director, Pediatric Nephrology and Hypertension, Hahnemann University, Philadelphia, Pennsylvania

David S. Goldstein, M.D., Ph.D., Senior Investigator, National Heart, Lung, and Blood Institute, Bethesda, Maryland

Clarence E. Grim, M.D., Professor of Medicine and Director of Hypertension Research, Martin Luther King, Jr. General Hospital, Los Angeles, California

James P. Henry, M.D., Ph.D., Research Professor of Psychiatry, Loma Linda University, Loma Linda, California

J. Alan Herd, M.D., Medical Director, Institute for Preventive Medicine, Methodist Hospital, Houston, Texas

Alan L. Hinderliter, M.D., Fellow in Hypertension, Department of Internal Medicine, University of Michigan Medical Center, Ann Arbor, Michigan

B. Kent Houston, Ph.D., Professor of Psychology, University of Kansas, Lawrence, Kansas

Rolf G. Jacob, M.D., Assistant Professor of Psychiatry, University of Pittsburgh, Pittsburgh, Pennsylvania

J. Richard Jennings, Ph.D., Associate Professor of Psychiatry, University of Pittsburgh, Pittsburgh, Pennsylvania

Stevo Julius, M.D., Professor of Internal Medicine and Physiology, University of Michigan Medical Center, Ann Arbor, Michigan

Jay R. Kaplan, Ph.D., Associate Professor of Comparative Medicine, Bowman Gray School of Medicine, Wake Forest University, Winston-Salem, North Carolina

David S. Krantz, Ph.D., Associate Professor of Medical Psychology, Uniformed Services University of the Health Sciences, Bethesda, Maryland

James D. Lane, Ph.D., Medical Research Assistant Professor of Psychiatry, Duke University Medical Center, Durham, North Carolina

Robert W. Levenson, Ph.D., Professor of Psychology, Indiana University, Bloomington, Indiana

Kathleen C. Light, Ph.D., Research Assistant Professor of Psychiatry and Physiology, University of North Carolina, Chapel Hill, North Carolina

Wallace W. McCrory, M.D., Director, Division of Pediatric Nephrology, New York Hospital—Cornell Medical Center, New York, New York

Robert H. McDonald, M.D., Chief of Clinical Pharmacology and Hypertension, University of Pittsburgh, School of Medicine, Pittsburgh, Pennsylvania

Stephen B. Manuck, Ph.D., Associate Professor of Psychology and Psychiatry, University of Pittsburgh, Pittsburgh, Pennsylvania

Karen A. Matthews, Ph.D., Associate Professor of Psychiatry, Epidemiology, and Psychology, University of Pittsburgh, Pittsburgh, Pennsylvania

Thomas G. Pickering, M.D., D.Phil., Associate Professor of Medicine, Cardiovascular Center, New York Hospital—Cornell Medical Center, New York, New York

Richard J. Rose, Ph.D., Professor of Psychology and Medical Genetics, Indiana University, Bloomington, Indiana

Neil Schneiderman, Ph.D., Professor of Psychology, University of Miami, Coral Gables, Florida

Alvin P. Shapiro, M.D., Professor of Medicine, University of Pittsburgh, School of Medicine, Pittsburgh, Pennsylvania

David Shapiro, Ph.D., Professor of Psychiatry and Psychology, University of California, Los Angeles, California

Richard S. Surwit, Ph.D., Professor of Medical Psychology, Duke University Medical Center, Durham, North Carolina

Laurence O. Watkins, M.D., M.P.H., Private Practice, Fort Lauderdale, Florida

Alan B. Weder, M.D., Assistant Professor of Internal Medicine, University of Michigan Medical Center, Ann Arbor, Michigan

Stephen M. Weiss, Ph.D., Director, Behavioral Medicine Branch, National Heart, Lung, and Blood Institute, Bethesda, Maryland

Redford B. Williams, Jr., M.D., Professor of Psychiatry and Associate Professor of Medicine, Duke University Medical Center, Durham, North Carolina

Rena R. Wing, Ph.D., Assistant Professor of Psychiatry and Epidemiology, University of Pittsburgh, Pittsburgh, Pennsylvania

Series Preface

This series is addressed to clinicians and scientists who are interested in human behavior relevant to the promotion and maintenance of health and the prevention and treatment of illness. *Health psychology* and *behavioral medicine* are terms that refer to both the scientific investigation and interdisciplinary integration of behavioral and biomedical knowledge and technology to prevention, diagnosis, treatment, and rehabilitation.

The major and purposely somewhat general areas of both health psychology and behavioral medicine which will receive greatest emphasis in this series are: theoretical issues of bio-psycho-social function, diagnosis, treatment, and maintenance; issues of organizational impact on human performance and an individual's impact on organizational functioning; development and implementation of technology for understanding, enhancing, or remediating human behavior and its impact on health and function; and clinical considerations with children and adults, alone, in groups, or in families that contribute to the scientific and practical/clinical knowledge of those charged with the care of patients.

The series encompasses considerations as intellectually broad as psychology and as numerous as the multitude of areas of evaluation treatment and prevention and maintenance that make up the field of medicine. It is the aim of the series to provide a vehicle which will focus attention on both the breadth and the interrelated nature of the sciences and practices making up health psychology and behavioral medicine.

THOMAS J. BOLL

The University of Alabama in Birmingham
Birmingham, Alabama

Preface

The purpose of this book is twofold: (1) to present the accumulated data, theoretical underpinnings, and speculations regarding the role of stress-induced reactivity in the etiology, course, and recovery from cardiovascular disease; and (2) to provide a primer of the key research questions for future investigation and suggestions on how to proceed in addressing those questions. *Reactivity* is defined as the magnitude of an array of physiological responses to discrete, environmental stressors, for example, performing a challenging mental task or exercising strenuously. Reactivity is considered to be a relatively stable characteristic of the individual who is responsive to specific challenges and stresses of daily living.

The impetus for this book is derived from at least three sources. First, the enormous interest of the scientific community in Selye's concept of nonspecific physiological response to diverse environmental challenges has led to a more differentiated perspective on human responses to stressors. It is now clear that there are striking individual differences in physiological responses to laboratory stressors and that these responses vary in part as a function of the attributes of the stressors themselves. Moreover, stressors under specific conditions have proven useful to establishing the diagnosis and prognosis of cardiovascular disease, for example, exercise stress testing and salt-loading. Second, accumulating evidence now indicates that "hyperreactivity" is a characteristic of some individuals at high risk for cardiovascular disease (e.g., Type A men and borderline hypertensives) and that psychological stress may precede a clinical event. Thus, an intriguing question is whether or not stress-induced reactivity is a risk factor for cardiovascular disease. Third, an international conference, which is described in Chapter 1, was convened in April 1984 by the National Heart, Lung and Blood Institute and the University of Pittsburgh to evaluate the methodological and theoretical bases of investigations on the relationship between stress-induced reactivity and cardiovascular disease. The present book benefits from this conference in that all its authors were present at the conference and played key roles there. Thus, the book communicates the most recent advances and hypotheses in the field.

The plan of the book is outlined at the end of Chapter 1. Examination of succeeding chapters reveals, for the most part, tentative support for the importance of reactivity in cardiovascular disease. The book freely points out, however, crucial methodologic and conceptual gaps in the hypotheses. This is not an admission of weakness or lack of completeness. Rather, pointing to these gaps arises from the fact that now is a fruitful time to take stock of what we do and do not know and to identify key questions for future investigation. Thus, the present book is not a final accounting of the field, but a progress report.

The book is the collaborative enterprise of editors with diverse training: health psychologists; a psychiatrist; a pediatric nephrologist; and an internist. This diversity has brought to the editing process a collective wisdom greater than each individual's contribution and an appreciation of different perspectives possible only through the cooperation of behavioral medicine scientists. The book benefited enormously from the knowledge and enthusiasm generated at the 1984 Conference on Stress, Reactivity, and Cardiovascular Disease. A special thanks goes to Thomas Detre, M.D., who not only served as an editor of this volume but also chaired the conference, and who has supported rigorous scientific methods and active interchange to evaluate the importance of the reactivity hypothesis. Lori Liller and Karen Campbell performed essential administrative work connected with the project. I thank them for their forbearance and competence. The book was edited while I was an American Heart Association Established Investigator.

KAREN A. MATTHEWS

Pittsburgh, Pennsylvania
April 1986

Contents

PART II DEFINING AND IDENTIFYING INDIVIDUAL DIFFERENCES IN REACTIVITY

PART III ATTRIBUTES ASSOCIATED WITH REACTIVITY

PART IV   STIMULATORS OF STRESS-INDUCED REACTIVITY

PART V   MODULATORS OF STRESS-INDUCED REACTIVITY

1

Introduction and Overview

STEPHEN M. WEISS

Health expenditures in the United States will hover at close to $400 billion in 1985, a figure that accounts for over 11 percent of the gross national product for our country. Since the virtual conquest of the most virulent acute infectious diseases earlier in this century, chronic diseases (cardiovascular disease, cancer, and stroke) have become our major source of death and disability. The largest single portion of those costs noted above are related in one form or another to cardiovascular diseases, which will account for approximately $100 billion of the total health expenditure.

Fortunately for all, cardiovascular disease in the United States has been declining since 1964.[1] However, it continues to be the nation's leading source of morbidity and mortality, claiming nearly 1 million lives per year. The form of cardiovascular disease most responsible for these statistics is coronary heart disease (CHD), in which the development and progression of atherosclerosis appears to be the primary pathogenic agent.

1

Unlike the infectious diseases, in which the identification of a single virus, bacteria, vector, or pathogen has led to the prevention and control of the affliction, the causes of chronic disease appear to be multifactorial, involving a broad spectrum of potential contributors in yet undetermined proportions. In coronary heart disease, genetic, dietary, environmental, behavioral, and sociocultural variables may be contributors, in addition to the traditional risk factors, which account for only approximately 50 percent of the variance associated with the disease.

In addition to investigating the importance of individual factors in terms of their contribution to the disease process, it has become evident that *interaction* among these variables may be of greater and even paramount importance in understanding their impact on the development and progression of coronary heart disease. Although the additive effect of relevant variables can be understood by studying them independently, the potential for synergistic response resulting from the interaction of contributor variables on the disease process must also be considered. This requires more extensive use of multifactorial designs to permit concurrent systematic variation of the variables under consideration. This model is particularly germane to the interaction of biological and behavioral factors, whereby uncontrolled variation of any of the potential contributors could produce spurious and inconsistent findings across studies (ample evidence of such can be found in the recent scientific literature).

Thus, we must understand both the independent and interactive contributions of all implicated variables to apprehend fully the "mosaic" of factors responsible for the development and progression of coronary heart disease. In addition to identifying the epidemiologic relationship of such factors to the disease state, it is particularly important to uncover the *mechanisms* by which behavioral, psychological, and environmental factors alone and in conjunction with biological variables can result in pathogenic consequences.

This issue was highlighted by two working conferences: the Forum on Coronary Prone Behavior[2] and the Review Panel on Coronary Prone Behavior and Coronary Heart Disease.[3] The latter meeting acknowledged that the Type A behavior pattern as developed by Friedman and Rosenman[4] was associated with the occurrence of CHD but cautioned that the diffuse nature of the dichotomous typology required refinement in terms of:

1. Identifying which components of Type A behavior might convey greater risk than others
2. Elucidating the physiological and biochemical pathways by which behavioral and environmental events might influence the disease process

In regard to the latter, the incidence of traditional risk factors has typically been proportionately distributed among the population without regard to Type A or Type B behavior. In consequence, researchers have sought other measures that might better reflect the effects of behavioral factors on the disease process. Recognizing that the majority of individuals' waking hours was spent in acting and reacting to their environment, it was felt that measuring various cardiovascular parameters under conditions of physical and psychological challenge ("stressors") might provide a more dynamic picture of cardiovascular performance than the typical static (resting state) measures currently used as the standard for assessing cardiovascular risk. Recent developments in noninvasive and ambulatory monitoring technology have permitted these researchers to explore the *variability* as well as consistency of various hemodynamic values under experimental and field conditions.

Such measures of "reactivity" to environmental stressors (psychological and physical) have permitted us to better understand individual patterns of neuroendocrine, metabolic, and cardiovascular response. As the basic pathways mediating environmental impact on physiologic arousal are assumed to be neural in origin, both central and peripheral nervous system regulation of cardiovascular and metabolic functions must be considered. Therefore, neurohormonal, cardiovascular, and behavioral/psychological responsivity measures are necessary to adequately characterize the relevant biobehavioral dimensions that may be associated with pathogenesis.

Responsivity measures to environmental stressors are hardly new. Exercise stress testing, glucose tolerance, and isometric strength tests have been routinely used by the biomedical community for many years. Reaction time, problem solving, and various perceptual-motor and performance tests have similarly been employed by psychologists in various social-psychological and psychophysiological studies. The "biobehavioral" perspective, combining the most salient features of biological and behavioral concept and assessment, has stimulated research attempting to categorize individuals according to hyperresponsive/hyporesponsive cardiovascular patterns as being potentially more or less susceptible to disease.

As data have begun to accumulate on differential responsivity to physical and psychological stressors, the study designs have expanded to include the potentiating or inhibiting effects of other variables on this process. As various dietary substances (e.g., caffeine, salt) have been implicated (albeit inconsistently) in the development of hypertension and coronary heart disease,[5] the independent and interactive effects of these substances on reactivity are currently being examined in ongoing research. Preliminary evidence suggests possible synergistic consequences under certain conditions.

Studies of the effects of smoking on stress-induced reactivity have demonstrated both additive and synergistic effects on various cardiovascular parameters.[6] Ongoing research on the effects of alcohol, exercise, and behavioral therapies will further clarify the potential catalyzing, stimulating, inhibiting, and modulating effects of various environmental factors on reactivity.

WORKING CONFERENCE ON STRESS, REACTIVITY, AND CARDIOVASCULAR DISEASE

In an effort to develop a more uniform and coordinated approach to these problems, a working conference entitled "Stress, Reactivity and Cardiovascular Disease," was cosponsored by the National Heart, Lung and Blood Institute and the University of Pittsburgh in April 1984. The objectives of this conference were to:

1. Assess the state of science in the following areas:
    a. Stress and cardiovascular/neuroendocrine reactivity
    b. The relationship of stress-induced hyperreactivity to cardiovascular disease, particularly coronary heart disease
    c. The interactive effects of environmental stress and smoking, caffeine, salt, and similar substances on cardiovascular reactivity
2. Examine the theoretical and conceptual basis for these studies
3. Establish standards and criteria for laboratory stressors
4. Develop a consensus on the most pertinent physiological/biochemical variables to be studied
5. Establish standards of measurement/instrumentation
6. Establish criteria for "hyporesponders" and "hyperresponders"
7. Determine the effect of "modulators" such as exercise, relaxation training, and alcohol on reducing reactivity to environmental challenge

Thus, the conference reviewed different perspectives on the meaning of reactivity and its relationship to behavioral/environmental stressors and attempted to establish consensus on guidelines for research in this area.

This volume was stimulated by the discussions, formal papers, and recommendations of the conference; chapter authors were selected on the basis of their acknowledged capability to produce a scholarly elaboration on the topics covered at the conference.

PLAN OF THIS BOOK

The first part of this volume is devoted to an extensive review of basic concepts and evidence regarding reactivity and risk for cardiovascular disease. As stated earlier, the concept of reactivity is based upon the hypothesis that the range of cardiovascular response to physical and psychological stressors may provide important new information related to cardiovascular risk factors. Although there is preliminary evidence from both basic and clinical research suggesting such an association between hyperreactivity and coronary heart disease,[7-9] whether such reactivity is a cause of, a contributor to, or just a marker for coronary heart disease is not established.

The relationship of reactivity to the development of hypertension remains a much debated topic.[10-12] The evidence linking hypertension to coronary heart disease is essentially epidemiological with little consensus as to mechanism of activity. However, the question as to whether or not reactivity produces hypertension may be less important than the potential status of reactivity as an independent risk factor for the development of coronary heart disease per se. As can be seen from the information presented in later parts, the relationship between cardiovascular, neuroendocrine, and metabolic reactivity and various physical and psychological stressors appears to be positive. What remains to be determined is the precise nature of the linkage between reactivity and cardiovascular disease; what is known about this issue is reviewed in the first part of this volume.

The second part of this volume is devoted to identifying and defining individual differences in reactivity. Within the past five years, research devoted to these questions has employed a wide variety of physical and psychological stressors under both laboratory and field conditions with various levels of instructional challenge in an effort to better define the nature of reactivity in all of its manifestations. It was inevitable that such enthusiasm as would expand the scope of legitimate inquiry would also create a certain amount of redundancy and lack of comparability across studies due to nonstandardized methodologies. Although such happenings appear to be a necessary feature of the early stages of scientific inquiry, at some point in this process it becomes equally necessary to create a degree of coordination and order in the system as one seeks to establish a critical mass of information that confirms or refutes the hypothesis under consideration. Thus, it appeared timely to consider guidelines in terms of the stressors themselves; the experimental conditions under which these stressors would be used; the neuroendocrine, metabolic, and cardiovascular variables to be studied; and the instrumentation and psychometric measurement that appear most likely to yield valid and reliable information about these variables. This would also include assessing appropriate psychological, demographic, and genetic variables that might also influence individual differences in reactivity—the topic of the third part of this book.

The fourth and fifth parts of this book are devoted respectively to stimulators and modulators of reactivity in terms of both their direct relationship to stress and reactivity as well as their relationship to other variables, for example, genetic factors. The basic and epidemiologic research on the roles of such substances as caffeine, nicotine, and salt in the development of coronary heart disease has yielded equivocal results. Typically, one finds in such cases that while the substance in question may play some role in the process, this role becomes obscured by uncontrolled variance from other substances or processes that have not been systematically controlled and/or varied in the investigation. As noted earlier in this chapter, the multifactorial perspective requires "casting a wider net" than one typically finds in the traditional biomedical or behavioral investigations. Biobehavioral research, on the other hand, is not only concerned with the effects of various substances or the effects of stress per se, but also attempts to recognize the *interaction* effects capable of a synergism that cannot be ascertained by a study of these variables individually. For example, studying the effect of salt on blood pressure may yield inconsistent results unless genetic variables are considered.[e.g., 13] Further, both of these variables may be confounded by stress-related circumstances unless these circumstances are either controlled for or systematically varied. Only by taking these and perhaps other variables into account can we begin to tease apart the complexity of the problem associated with prevention and control of cardiovascular disease.

In addition to understanding the contributors involved in stress-related reactivity, one must also understand the modulators or inhibitors of such reactivity to environmental challenge. Again, we see equivocal results in the study of exercise, alcohol, and relaxation therapies, among others, in terms of their direct effects on cardiovascular disease. In our study of the meaning of reactivity, it is extremely important to gain a better understanding how different forms of exercise, different levels of alcohol ingestion, and various forms of behavioral and pharmacologic therapies may affect reactivity, if in fact such studies are to aid us in better understanding the relationship of these various factors to the disease process. The ultimate test, of course, is not only to be able to understand the association and mechanism by which certain factors affect the disease process, but also to devise strategies of intervention to ameliorate the condition as well as the means by which one may prevent the process from occurring at all. The development of guidelines for both stimulators and modulators of reactivity will also provide the necessary basis for enhancing comparability across studies in this area.

Finally, we need to consider the challenges and future directions for this research. These are summarized in the last chapter. Although it is too early to make any final statements on the subject, reactivity research paradigms have created unique opportunities to better understand the processes whereby behavioral factors influence physiologic function. To better understand the role of behavioral factors in the development, progression, treatment, and prevention of cardiovascular disease, it is essential that significant effort be devoted to the question of "mechanism of action." Although a considerable (and growing) body of evidence links behavioral factors as contributors to the disease process (singly and/or through interaction with other putative risk factors), the physiologic and biochemical pathways through which this process occurs remain obscure. And, the subsequent chapters in this volume begin to identify some of the relevant pathways by which behavior may affect disease.

REFERENCES

1. Havlick R, Feinleib M (eds): *Proceedings of the Conference on the Decline in Coronary Heart Disease Mortality*. USDHEW, NIH Publ No 1, 79–1610, 1979.

2. Dembroski T, Weiss SM, et al (eds): *Coronary Prone Behavior*. New York, Springer-Verlag, 1978.

3. Weiss SM, Cooper T, Detre TP (eds): Coronary prone behavior and coronary heart disease: A critical review. *Circulation* 63:1199–1215, 1981.

4. Rosenman RH, Brand RJ, et al: Coronary heart disease in the Western Collaborative Group Study: Final follow-up experience of 8½ years. *JAMA* 223:872–877, 1975.

5. Hennekens CH, Drolette ME, et al: Coffee drinking and death due to coronary heart disease. *N Engl J Med* 294:633–637, 1976.

6. MacDougall JM, Dembroski TM, Herd JA: Selective cardiovascular effects of stress and cigarette smoking. *J Human Stress* 9:13–21, 1983.

7. Manuck SB, Kaplan JR, Clarkson TB: Behaviorally-induced heart rate reactivity and allierosclerosis in cynomolgus monkeys. *Psychosom Med* 45:95–108, 1983.

8. Devereux RB, Pickering TG, et al: Left ventricular hypertrophy in patients with hypertension: Importance of blood pressure response to regularly recurring stress. *Circulation* 68:470–476, 1983.

9. Perloff D, Sokolow M, Cowan R: The prognostic value of ambulatory blood pressures. *JAMA* 249:2792–2798, 1983.

10. Falkner B, Onesti G, et al: Cardiovascular response to mental stress in normal adolescents with hypertensive parents. *Hypertension* 1:23–30, 1979.

11. Julius S, Esler M: Autonomic nervous cardiovascular regulation in borderline hypertension. *Am J Cardiol* 36:685–696, 1975.

12. Obrist PA, Light KC, et al: Behavioral-cardiovascular interaction. In Smith OA, Galosy RA, Weiss SM (eds): *Circulation, Neurobiology and Behavior*. New York, Elsevier, 1982, pp. 57–76.

13. Light KC, Koepka JP, et al: Psychological stress induces sodium and fluid retention in men at high risk for hypertension. *Science* 220:429–431, 1983.

PART I

REACTIVITY AND CARDIOVASCULAR DISEASE

2

Psychophysiologic Reactivity in Coronary Heart Disease and Essential Hypertension

STEPHEN B. MANUCK AND DAVID S. KRANTZ

It is well established that behavioral stimuli often evoke substantial responses of the autonomic and neuroendocrine systems and that the magnitude of such responses varies significantly among individuals. The latter observation, individual differences in psychophysiologic reactivity, reflects a topic of longstanding interest in the investigation of psychosomatic

Portions of this manuscript are adapted from: Manuck SB, Krantz DS: Psychophysiologic reactivity in coronary heart disease. *Behav Med Update* 6:11–15, 1984; and Krantz DS, Manuck SB: Acute psychophysiologic reactivity and risk of cardiovascular disease: A review and methodologic critique, *Psychol Bull* 96:435–464, 1984.

Preparation of this paper was assisted by NIH grants HL29028 and HL31514, and USUHS grant R07233.

disorders. This interest has grown appreciably in recent years, particularly in relation to cardiovascular and catecholamine reactions to psychological stressors. Indeed, it has been proposed that an exaggerated physiologic responsivity to behavioral challenges may be implicated in the development or clinical expression of major cardiovascular disorders, such as coronary heart disease (CHD) and essential hypertension.[1-4] Also, several plausible hypotheses for a reactivity-disease link have now been advanced and much indirect—but suggestive—data collected. The purpose of this chapter is to summarize pathogenetic hypotheses relating individual differences in acute psychophysiologic reactivity to CHD and hypertension and to review briefly available data relevant to such associations.

GENERAL CONSIDERATIONS

It may first be useful to discuss the concept of psychophysiologic reactivity as it may be associated with cardiovascular disease. Most epidemiologic associations are based on assessment of the "casual" or resting levels of suspected risk variables (e.g., clinical evaluations of blood pressure). Measurement of psychophysiologic reactivity, however, involves the assessment of *changes* in physiologic parameters that occur when individuals are exposed to behavioral or psychological challenges. Since the magnitude of such changes usually cannot be inferred from resting (baseline) levels of these variables, reactivity measurements often contribute unique information on the physiologic functioning of the individual. It has been hypothesized further that, insofar as acute reactions observed in the laboratory also reflect responses to challenges encountered in daily life, evaluation of psychophysiologic reactivity may provide additional—and perhaps more useful—indicators of pathophysiologic processes than do measurements recorded under resting or casual conditions.[2]

A critical question underlying the value of *acute* measures of reactivity concerns the extent to which laboratory-based measurements generalize to nonlaboratory settings. That is, do individual differences in cardiovascular and/or neuroendocrine responses to standardized test stimuli predict responsivity to naturally occurring stressors? Unfortunately, this question has not yet been addressed in any detail, either empirically or conceptually. However, such generalization could occur in a number of different ways. One possibility is that persons who show exaggerated physiologic responses to laboratory stressors (so-called hyperreactors) exhibit similarly exaggerated reactions to events occurring in day-to-day activities, whereas individuals who show little reactivity in the laboratory (hyporeactors) may, in life, experience small or only moderate physiological reactions to stress. Thus,

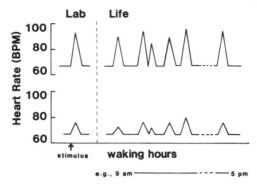

RECURRENT ACTIVATION MODEL

FIGURE 2.1.   Stylized figure depicting the generalization to nonlaboratory settings of individual differences in laboratory-assessed heart rate reactivity, as predicted by the "recurrent activation model." The upper and lower panels illustrate responses of a prototypic hyperreactor and hyporeactor, respectively. Depicted on the left (Lab) are subjects' heart rate responses to a standardized behavioral stimulus (or stressor) in the laboratory. Illustrated on the right (Life) are the predicted heart rate responses of these individuals to naturally occurring events in daily life. (See text.) (From "Psychophysiologic reactivity in coronary heart disease," by S.B. Manuck, D.S. Krantz, *Behavioral Medicine Update* 6:11–15, 1984.)

daily life for the hyperreactor may be accompanied by repeated episodes, or occurrences, of acute physiologic arousal that resemble in their magnitude responses exhibited in the laboratory.

This lab-life relationship—which we will call the *recurrent activation model*—is illustrated in the stylized drawing in Figure 2.1. In the upper and lower panels of this figure are depicted a prototypic hyperreactor and hyporeactor. For illustrative purposes, heart rate is listed on the ordinate as the physiologic parameter of interest, though any other response measure (i.e., blood pressure, plasma epinephrine or norepinephrine) could be placed in its stead. Note that real life in these two individuals is occasioned by repeated episodes of physiologic reactivity, which are similar to their corresponding responses in the laboratory. Although reactions seen out of the laboratory will vary in magnitude, depending on the nature of the precipitating stimulus or environmental event, by this model the ordered relationship between individuals is retained.

"Recurrent activation" is perhaps the most commonly held hypothesis regarding the generalization of individual differences in psychophysiologic reactivity. It is also based, in part, on the assumption that baseline values recorded in the laboratory reflect a common or usual state of the organism. Hence, it follows that daily challenges outside the laboratory will precipitate repeated, transient episodes of reactivity (i.e., acute changes from baseline).

It is possible, however, that baseline, or resting measurements represent the more anomolous states of the individual, and are observable in a labora-

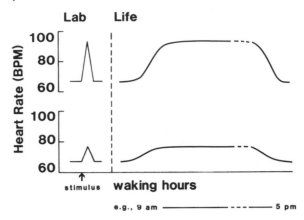

PREVAILING STATE MODEL

FIGURE 2.2.   Stylized figure depicting the generalization to nonlaboratory settings of individual differences in laboratory-assessed heart rate reactivity, as predicted by the "prevailing state model." The upper and lower panels illustrate responses of a prototypic hyperreactor and hyporeactor, respectively. Depicted on the left (Lab) are subjects' heart rate responses to a standardized behavioral stimulus (or stressor) in the laboratory. Illustrated on the right (Life) are the predicted heart rate responses of these individuals to naturally occurring events in daily life. (See text.) (From "Psychophysiologic reactivity in coronary heart disease," by S.B. Manuck, D.S. Krantz, *Behavioral Medicine Update* 6:11–15, 1984.)

tory setting only due to investigators' exceptional efforts to establish a rested condition in their subjects and a relatively stimulus-free environment. Of course, these values still have meaning as baseline measurements, since they indicate what the subject's physiologic "state" tends to be in the absence of notable behavioral stimuli. Yet, this state might occur quite infrequently during the preponderance of waking hours, when individuals are continually engaged in significant activities (e.g., work demands) and interactions with other people.

Seen in this context, measurement of a *reactive* state of the individual in the laboratory might be achieved more easily than baseline evaluations, since the former only requires providing a lifelike behavioral challenge. In turn, this reactive state (as suggested above) may also reflect the condition most frequently experienced in daily life. If so, measurement of psychophysiologic reactivity in the laboratory will be more predictive of physiologic states prevailing throughout the waking, active hours of the day than it is of transient episodes of acute arousal. This relationship is illustrated in Figure 2.2 and labeled the *prevailing state model*.

These two formulations—recurrent activation and prevailing states—are probably oversimplifications, and some combination or neither may reflect the true generalization of laboratory-assessed reactivity. Yet to evaluate reactivity—disease relationships, it is critical to determine how psychophysiologic reactivity finds expression in the lives of individuals; after all, it is during the course of daily activities—and not in the laboratory—that cardiovascular disorders develop. The nature of this generalization from laboratory to life is important, too, for the types of associations we may wish to explore in relating the reactivity construct to disease endpoints. Pathogenetic formulations hypothesizing relatively persistent states of sympathetic arousal,[e.g., 5] for example, are generally more compatible with a prevailing state model than with notions of generalization based on recurrent and transient activation.

In the preceding paragraphs we have focused on one issue that illustrates the assumptions of hypotheses implicating idiosyncratic autonomic and neuroendocrine responses in the pathophysiology of cardiovascular disease. Of course, there are many other such issues, including the stability over time (or reproducibility) of individual differences in reactivity, the importance of situational or task influences on the measurement of psychophysiologic responses, influences of subject characteristics (e.g., age, gender, coping styles) on responsivity, and the applicability of common test protocols to population-based epidemiologic investigations. While substantive consideration of these additional matters is beyond the scope of this chapter, extensive discussions of the various methodologic and conceptual issues relevant to the study of psychophysiologic reactivity can be found elsewhere in this volume. In the remainder of the present chapter we will consider, more specifically, the relationship of individual differences in behaviorally induced physiologic reactivity to risk for coronary artery atherosclerosis, CHD, and essential hypertension.

CORONARY HEART DISEASE

Behavioral Factors in CHD

In addition to the standard risk factors for coronary disease (viz., hyperlipoproteinemia, arterial hypertension, cigarette smoking), psychosocial factors have been implicated in the pathogenesis of CHD. While there is currently some uncertainty regarding the consistency of reported epidemiologic associations,[6] the so-called Type A, or coronary-prone, behavior pattern has figured most prominently among the many psychosocial variables that have been investigated.[7] Briefly, the Type A pattern is characterized by extremes of competitiveness, a chronic sense of time urgency, and easily evoked hostility. A contrasting Type B pattern is defined as the relative absence of these attributes and consists of a different style of coping with challenge.

Regarding the Type A–B construct, a variety of studies—most notably, the Western Collaborative Group Study[8]—has provided evidence that Type A individuals are more likely than Type B individuals to develop clinical CHD. Of the various Type A characteristics, moreover, recent studies suggest that aggressiveness, or a high "potential for hostility," may be especially important.[9–11] Some, though not all, investigators have also demonstrated relationships between these behavioral characteristics (e.g., Type A, hostility) and coronary artery atherosclerosis, as revealed on angiographic examination[e.g., 10–13] and in thallium-201 myocardial perfusion studies during exercise stress testing.[14] A similar association has been reported between Type A behavior pattern and extent of carotid artery atherosclerosis, as measured by a Doppler ultrasonography.[15]

It is commonly thought that behavioral factors influence the development of CHD through the cardiovascular or endocrine correlates of sympathetic-adrenal-medullary and pituitary-adrenal-cortical activity. One proposed mechanism is that repeated physiologic reactions involving excessive heart rate and or pressor responses to behavioral stressors promote arterial "injury" through hemodynamic forces such as turbulence and sheer stress.[16] Alternatively, biochemical sources of injury may follow from an increased output of certain endocrine substances, such as catecholamines and corticosteroids, which may exert toxic influences on the coronary arteries. Additionally, increased levels of circulating catecholamines may affect coronary atherogenesis in an indirect manner, as through influences on platelet aggregation and on the mobilization of serum lipids.[3, 17] Data indicating that acute behavioral stressors can lower thresholds for ventricular fibrillation suggest further that disruption of the central nervous system control of the heart may be implicated in the initiation of arrhythmic activity, and hence, potentially, in precipitation of sudden cardiac death.[3] Comprehensive discussions of the possible neuroendocrine and hemodynamic mechanisms mediating behavioral influences on CHD and atherogenesis can be found in the subsequent chapters of this volume by Herd and by Clarkson, Manuck, and Kaplan.

Psychophysiologic Reactivity in CHD

If the foregoing physiologic mechanisms (i.e., sympathetic and adrenal-cortical activity) contribute to coronary artery disease or its clinical sequelae, this contribution would presumably be greatest among individuals exhibiting the most pronounced psychophysiologic responsivity (i.e., hyperreactors). What is the evidence, then, that individual differences in behaviorally induced autonomic and neuroendocrine reactivity are associated with CHD? In addressing this question, several types of evidence can be marshalled: (1)

data obtained from appropriate animal models; (2) findings of both prospective and case-control investigations involving human subjects; and (3) results of experimental studies examining the physiologic correlates of coronary-prone behaviors.

With respect to animal models, there are currently two studies of specific relevance to individual differences in cardiovascular reactivity. In the first of these investigations[16], male cynomolgus monkeys (Macaca fascicularis) fed a moderately atherogenic diet for 22 months were identified as either "high" or "low" heart rate reactive animals, based on their cardiac responses to a common laboratory stressor (threat of capture). Following necropsy, the "high" heart rate reactive animals were found to have developed nearly twice the coronary artery atherosclerosis of their "low" heart rate reactive counterparts. Interestingly, the "high" and "low" reactors did not differ significantly in resting heart rate, blood pressure, or serum lipid concentrations, suggesting that the heart rate reactivity–atherosclerosis association was largely independent of influences of other risk variables commonly associated with atherogenesis. In the second study in this series,[18] female cynomolgus macaques were exposed to the same experimental procedures and divided similarly into groups of "high" and "low" heart rate reactors. As in male animals, high heart rate reactive females had significantly more coronary artery atherosclerosis than did females that showed a less pronounced cardiac responsivity to stress. "High" and "low" reactors again did not differ in baseline heart rate, blood pressure, or serum lipids. Finally, it should be noted in relation to these studies that since heart rate measurements were recorded on only a single occasion and at a time shortly prior to the termination of the animals (i.e., after many months on atherogenic diet), the preceding findings are basically retrospective.

There is, however, one published prospective study bearing on the reactivity-CHD relationship in human beings.[19] In this study it was found that the magnitude of subjects' diastolic blood pressure responses to cold immersion (the cold pressor test) was associated significantly with development of CHD at a 23-year follow-up. Indeed, the prediction of subsequent disease from subjects' diastolic reactivity to the cold pressor test in this investigation exceeded associations based on many of the more traditional risk factors.

Several retrospective, or case-control, studies contrasting the psychophysiologic responses of persons with and without CHD have also been reported.[e.g., 20–25] Most of these investigations demonstrate a heightened reactivity to laboratory stressors—usually, increased blood pressure responses—in patients with histories of angina or previous infarction, when these subjects are compared with noncoronary patient samples or nonpatient controls. The experimental tasks employed have generally involved either interpersonal challenge (e.g., the structured interview for Type A assessment) or relatively demanding tests of subjects' cognitive abilities (e.g., mental arithmetic, Raven's progressive matrices). However, a number of these studies may be faulted on methodologic grounds, such as failure to control for the medication status of coronary patients and for the presence of other chronic disorders known to affect vascular responses (e.g., essential hypertension). Also, virtually no association between behaviorally elicited cardiovascular reactivity and extent of coronary atherosclerosis is reported in one recent study of patients undergoing diagnostic angiography.[22] Overall, then, case-control studies provide suggestive evidence, yet findings reported in this literature are not entirely consistent, and the studies themselves are few in number and of variable quality.

As noted, a final source of data concerns the autonomic and neuroendocrine response characteristics of persons at behavioral risk for CHD—that is, Type A individuals. This line of investigation is encouraged by the observation that influences of Type A behavior on CHD have been largely independent of the concomitant effects of other major risk factors, such as serum cholesterol, hypertension, smoking, and age.[7] There are now approximately 50 published studies comparing the physiologic responses of Type A and Type B subjects to diverse psychological and physical stressors. Subjects employed in these investigations range from children, adolescents, and college students to working class and professional adults and coronary disease patients. In the majority of studies, Type A subjects are found to exhibit larger increases in blood pressure, heart rate, and plasma catecholamines and/or cortisol, relative to Type B subjects, when exposed to appropriately stressful laboratory tasks. These effects are seen most consistently where subjects are faced with threat of failure, harassment, or competitive task demands; during interpersonal interactions; and when instructional sets are designed to assure high levels of task involvement.[2]

Still, there are several well-conducted studies that fail to replicate associations between Type A behavior and indices of reactivity. In this regard, differing methods of assessing the Type A pattern seem to be of some importance; this is especially true of adult samples, where response differences between Type A and Type B subjects have emerged most frequently in studies employing the interview technique for Type A evaluation rather than more commonly used questionnaires.[20] Other factors, such as the presence or absence of a family history of cardiovascular disease, various demographic variables, and the gender-appropriateness of experimental tasks, also appear to modulate Type A reactivity associations[26,27] and may account, in part, for inconsistencies in this literature. Nonetheless, it is reasonable to conclude from existing findings that Type A individuals do experience somewhat greater autonomic and neuroendocrine responses than their noncoronary-prone, Type B counterparts, at least when encountering some types of laboratory stimuli. A more thorough discussion of the Type A reactivity association is included in the chapter by Houston.

ESSENTIAL HYPERTENSION

Behavioral Factors in Essential Hypertension

Arterial hypertension contributes importantly to the development of a number of serious cardiovascular diseases, including heart failure, CHD, and stroke. Hypertension is also widespread among the industrialized nations, with an estimated prevalence in the United States of 15 percent or more of the adult population.[28] Although in some patients this condition may be traced to identifiable renal, endocrine, or other disorders (secondary hypertension), in the great majority of cases the elevated blood pressure remains of indeterminate origin and is termed "essential hypertension." Most authorities also agree that essential hypertension is a "multifactorial" disorder, of considerable heterogeneity, and possessing a complex pathogenesis.

Due to the well-established association between behavior and influences of the autonomic nervous system on blood pressure regulation, it is not surprising that the role of psychosocial factors in essential hypertension has been a focus of longstanding research interest.[29] Despite several decades of active investigation, though, no clear behavioral precursor of essential hypertension as yet been documented. On the other hand, there is much suggestive evidence that at least certain hypertensive individuals experience difficulties in the expression of feelings, especially those of anger and hostility. Indeed, since Alexander's initial hypothesis that "inhibited aggressive impulses" give rise to hypertension,[30] numerous investigators have sought links between elevated blood pressure and a variety of aggression-related constructs, such as "suppressed hostility," "inwardly directed anger," and "inhibited power motivation." A number of positive associations have been reported in cross-sectional studies involving diverse subject populations (e.g., young adults, middle-aged adults, and patient populations), and more recently, in two prospective investigations.[e.g., 31–42] When subjects' overt behaviors have been observed directly, as in simulated interpersonal encounters in a laboratory setting, hypertensive patients have often been described as reacting in an inappropriately submissive, deferential, and inhibited manner in comparison to normotensive controls.[37,43–47] Yet, many other investigations have failed to establish such relationships[48–52] and in some studies hypertensive subjects have been found either to behave more aggressively or to report greater feelings of hostility than their normotensive counterparts.[53-55] Results of three recent investigations suggest also that an elevated blood pressure may be associated in some individuals with inappropriate submissiveness and in others with inappropriate assertiveness.[35,56,57] Hence, while it is tempting to conclude on the basis of this literature that problems of anger and assertive expression characterize some hypertensive patients, the nature of these difficulties and the reliability of the association remain to be determined.

Although an analogue of the Type A behavior pattern has not been established for hypertension, unlike CHD, there is considerable evidence that the autonomic nervous system is implicated in at least a portion of hypertensive cases. This is particularly true in relation to borderline hypertension, which is defined ordinarily by blood pressures in the range of 140–160/90–100 mmHg.[58] One of the interesting aspects of borderline hypertension, from a behavioral perspective, is the observation that in perhaps 30 percent of such patients there is a significant elevation in the cardiac output, accompanied by only a slight increase in the total peripheral resistance.[59] That this increased cardiac output is attributable to autonomic mechanisms is indicated by the normalization of stroke volume and heart rate under blockade of the sympathetic and parasympathetic innervations[59] and by the presence of elevated concentrations of circulating catecholamines.[60,61] Still, these characteristics apply only to some borderline patients, suggesting that this category of hypertension is itself heterogeneous.

The fact that a variety of mechanisms may contribute to hypertension, moreover, has led some investigators to attempt to identify markers for hypertensive cases in which autonomic influences play a significant role. Often noted in this regard is the work of Esler, Julius, et al.,[62] who report that among a sample of young, mild hypertensives, individuals classified as having high plasma renin activity showed a higher resting concentration of plasma norepinephrine, as well as larger reductions in the cardiac output and peripheral resistance following autonomic blockade, when compared to normal plasma renin hypertensive subjects. Interestingly, the high renin group also responded on a variety of psychometric instruments in a manner indicative of "suppressed hostility." Hence, it appears that in at least one subset of hypertensive patients, an elevated arterial pressure is achieved through actions of the autonomic nervous system and may be associated, in part, with the behavioral attributes of the individual.

In contrast to borderline hypertension, established essential hypertension is typically defined as a blood pressure elevation in excess of 160/100 mmHg.[58] In established hypertension, the total peripheral resistance is usually elevated and the cardiac output is within normal limits.[63] Consequently, if the borderline condition in patients who show an increased cardiac output presages a later established hypertension, a shift in the hemodynamic profile must occur between earlier and later phases of hypertension. Concerning the prognostic significance of borderline hypertension generally, it must be noted that not all persons carrying this diagnosis do show a continued increase in blood pressure over time; in fact, in most cases the blood pressure ultimately returns to normotensive values. Still, there is reasonable evidence that borderline hypertensives as a group are at substantially increased risk for subsequent, sustained hypertension (as well as for the development of clinical CHD) in comparison to normotensive samples.[5,64] In regard to the hemodynamic question, longitudinal studies show also that in many patients with borderline essential hypertension, a gradual decline in the cardiac output occurs over years, accompanied by a progressive rise in the peripheral resistance.[65–68] Hypotheses addressing the mechanism by which "hyperkinetic" borderline hypertensive states may evolve into high-resistance, established hypertension are discussed briefly in a later section of this chapter and are considered in some detail in the chapter by Julius, Weder, and Hinderliter.

Psychophysiologic Reactivity in Essential Hypertension

Evidence that the autonomic nervous system contributes to the elevated blood pressures of some hypertensive individuals has encouraged speculation that exaggerated sympathetic reactivity to stress may represent a marker for later neurogenic hypertension. As in the corresponding literature relating to CHD and atherosclerosis (discussed previously), several types of data bear on associations between acute psychophysiologic reactivity and essential hypertension. These include retrospective and prospective clinical investigations and studies of normotensive individuals who are known to vary in their risk for subsequent hypertension. Unfortunately, there are yet no investigations employing animal models in which physiologic reactions to behavioral stimuli are examined as predictors of either naturally-occurring or psychosocially-induced hypertension. Rats bred specifically for their susceptibility to hypertension (spontaneously hypertensive rats, SHR), however, have been found to react to laboratory stressors with greater rises in blood pressure, heart rate, and plasma catecholamines, relative to normotensive rats of the Wistar-Kyoto (WKY) strain;[69–71] moreover, this psychophysiologic hyperresponsivity among SHRs is detectable even prior to the acquisition of hypertension. Although similar results have not been reported in studies of other selectively bred strains (e.g., New Zealand "genetically hypertensive" versus "normotensive" rats),[72] the SHR findings indicate that in this one model, at least, heightened sympathetic responses to stress accompany a genetic vulnerability to hypertension. In addition, the recent development of both canine and rodent models that are particularly sensitive to psychosocial manipulations[73,74] should provide further opportunity to explore relationships between the development of arterial hypertension and individual differences in behaviorally included physiologic reactivity.

Among prospective investigations involving human subjects, one recent study has found blood pressure reactions to the cold pressor test to be predictive of eventual hypertension.[75] Specifically, subjects classified as cold pressor "hyperreactors"—defined by a blood pressure elevation of at least 25 mmHg systolic or 20 mmHg diastolic, as recorded either on initial measurement (in 1934) or at a second assessment (in 1961)—were found on follow-up in 1979 to be at five-fold greater risk for exhibiting a blood pressure in excess of 160/100 mmHg; follow-up blood pressures in the borderline hypertensive range were also more frequent among "hyperreactors" when compared to individuals who had shown cold pressor responses of lesser magnitude. However, other studies have failed to demonstrate a prospective association between cold pressor reactions and subsequent hypertension.[76,77] Wood, Sheps, et al.[75] suggest that negative results may be attributable, in part, to use of shorter periods of follow-up (e.g., 10 and 18 years), more homogeneous samples, and subjects of younger age at the time of follow-up.

It is unfortunate that only the cold pressor test has yet been employed in longitudinal investigations since, even among the retrospective studies, this stimulus has often failed to discriminate hypertensive and normotensive samples.[78,79] Other investigators have also faulted the cold pressor test because, in most individuals, it does not elicit the pattern of sympathetically mediated myocardial responses thought to be relevant to the hemodynamics of early, neurogenic hypertension.[80] Finally, it has been shown that the cold pressor response varies greatly in magnitude, depending on the manner in which the task is presented to subjects;[81] this finding suggests that the "effective" stimulus attributes of the cold pressor test may differ considerably when this task is administered in different laboratory or clinical settings.

Case-control studies employing a variety of other behavioral stressors, however, have shown significant, and possibly more consistent, differences in the cardiovascular responses of hypertensive and normotensive individuals. These stimuli have included frustrating cognitive tasks, such as mental arithmetic and the Stroop color-word interference test,[82–84] stressful interviews,[85] and laboratory procedures designed to evoke emotions of fear and anger.[55] Although, as noted, hypertensives generally show greater heart rate and/or pressor responses to such challenges, relative to normotensive controls, the nature of the experimental stimulus, and possibly the behavioral attributes of the subject, are important factors in eliciting this increased reactivity. For example, Steptoe et al.[86] report that hypertensive subjects exhibited greater blood pressure responses than normotensive subjects when performing tasks demanding some form of active coping (e.g., video games), but not when exposed to the more passive (but aversive) experience of viewing a distressing film. Other investigators have also found that hypertensive subjects show larger pressor responses than normotensive controls during tasks involving "sensory rejection" (mental arithmetic), but not when performing a "sensory intake" task (word identification)[87] or, as noted earlier, during the cold pressor test.[78,79] Finally, Sullivan, Procci, et al.[42] report that in their sample of patients with primary hypertension, heightened systolic reactions during serial subtraction were observed only among subjects who also scored highest on psychometric indices of anxiety and anger.

A related literature examines the psychophysiologic response characteristics of normotensive individuals who differ by the presence or absence of a family history of essential hypertension. Interest in family history as a possible correlate of reactivity is due to the considerable increase in risk for hypertension that is seen among offspring of hypertensive parents and in the siblings of hypertensives.[28,58,88,89] Matthews and Rakaczky[90] recently published a comprehensive review of studies contrasting the cardiovascular and neuroendocrine reactions of persons with and without a family history of hypertension to a variety of behavioral and physical stimuli. Among the 26 studies reviewed in which "psychological" stressors were employed (e.g., mental arithmetic, shock avoidance), 19 found familial risk for hypertension to be associated with significantly increased blood pressure and/or heart rate reactivity. Also, most failures to demonstrate differences in the cardiovascular responsivity of offspring of hypertensive and normotensive parents either involve early studies (pre-1943) of unclear methodology, sole use of the cold pressor test, or an absence of data confirming parental hypertensive/normotensive status.

As in studies of hypertensive patients, in studies of persons at familial risk for hypertension situational variables and subjects' emotional reactions appear to play an important role in eliciting the heightened reactivity. For example, Hastrup et al.[91] compared the physiologic responses of sons of hypertensive and normotensive parents to both shock avoidance and cold pressor tests (i.e., so-called active and passive coping tasks). This study revealed appreciable group differences in heart rate and systolic pressor responses during the "active" task—avoidance—but only minimal differences in reactions to cold immersion. In addition, Manuck, Proietti, et al.[92] report that while heart rate elevations during mental arithmetic were significantly larger in persons having hypertensive parents, this relationship emerged only among subjects experiencing the greatest anxiety and/or anger while performing the experimental task. Together, these findings suggest that hypertensive persons and persons with a family history of hypertension possess a heightened cardiovascular response potential, but may "express" this underlying hyperreactivity only in relation to situational demands or concomitant affective responses.

Finally, an area of inconsistency in the literature on psychophysiologic reactivity in hypertension concerns the great variety of response measures that discriminate relevant subject groups. Although most published investigations report some significant findings, not all studies show exactly the same relationships. In the familial risk studies, for example, some investigators have reported that the offspring of hypertensive and normotensive parents differ in task-related systolic blood pressure responses, whereas others have noted significant differences primarily in heart rate reactivity (sometimes in conjunction with increased elevations in either systolic *or* diastolic blood pressure). This variability is evidenced even across studies in which investigators have used common experimental procedures, such as mental arithmetic.[93,94] Obviously, cardiovascular reactions at the level of heart rate and blood pressure can reflect varying patterns of hemodynamic adjustment. Blood pressure elevations can stem from either myocardial or vascular changes, or some combination of these. Heart rate acceleration can be due to increased sympathetic drive or parasympathetic withdrawal. It is therefore unclear whether a hyperreactivity among hypertensive patients or in persons at risk for hypertension is associated with one or several underlying response dimensions. The fact that common laboratory tasks also yield differing results when administered by different investigators highlights further the difficulties of specifying salient stimulus attributes and in predicting precise stimulus–response relationships.

Implications for Hypertension

As in CHD, it is yet unclear what relevance transient episodes of acute psychophysiologic arousal, such as those observed in the laboratory, have for an understanding of essential hypertension. However, two possibilities include: (1) consequences of an excessive cardiovascular responsivity for persons who are already hypertensive; and (2) the role of reactivity in the pathogenesis of hypertension itself. Each of these possibilities is considered briefly below.

Psychophysiologic Reactivity in the Hypertensive Individual.   It may be hypothesized that large, behaviorally elicited pressor responses have prognostic significance for hypertensive patients, since in these individuals such reactions are superimposed upon an elevated basal blood pressure. The frequent occurrence of responses of this type might accelerate the development of vascular and end-organ complications of hypertension and, in persons with significant coronary or cerebral artery atherosclerosis, lead to heightened risk for acute clinical events, such as angina pectoris, myocardial infarction, and stroke.[95,96] Particularly relevant in this respect are the observations of Sokolow, Werdegar, and colleagues,[97] who have made extensive use of ambulatory blood pressure recordings in hypertensive patients. These investigators report that ambulatory blood pressure levels (but not blood pressure variability) are more closely associated with cardiovascular complications (e.g., left ventricular hypertrophy) than are resting, or casual, blood pressure determinations. In a recent follow-up of more than 1000 hypertensive individuals, moreover, Perloff et al.[98] found that patients in whom ambulatory blood pressure measurements exceeded values predicted from routine office recordings had a significantly higher cumulative mortality and morbidity over an estimated ten-year period than did hypertensives whose ambulatory recordings fell near or below expected pressures. That the association between ambulatory blood pressure measurements and clinical outcomes obtained irrespective of sex, entry blood pressure, severity of hypertension, and presence or absence of prior cardiovascular events led the authors to conclude that ambulatory recordings provide "…an independent prognostic indicator in the overall risk profile of the individual patient." [98, p. 2797]

Unfortunately, it cannot be determined whether ambulatory blood pressure measurements recorded in the preceding studies reflect reactions to psychologically salient attributes at the times when the readings were taken. Recent observations by Devereux, Pickering, et al.[99] are relevant to this question, however. These investigators report that ambulatory blood pressure assessments during work stress correlated more highly with left ventricular hypertrophy in hypertensive patients than did blood pressure measurements obtained in the clinic or during more quiescent hours of the day.

A remaining question concerns the relationship between ambulatory blood pressure measurements and laboratory assessments of acute psychophysiologic reactivity. As noted at the beginning of this chapter, very little is known regarding the generalization of individual differences in cardiovascular and neuroendocrine reactivity from laboratory to field settings. A few sets of findings, though, are consistent with such generalization. First, Manuck et al.[100] have reported that among working professionals, those who showed the greatest systolic pressor responses to a frustrating cognitive task also exhibited higher peak systolic blood pressures and heightened systolic blood pressure variability in casual measurements recorded over a six-week interval during ordinary occupational activities. Similarly, Matthews et al.[101] have found cardiovascular responses to a variety of laboratory stressors to be correlated significantly with blood pressure measurements obtained during periods of public speaking. As these findings reflect only initial attempts to address the issue of generalization, it is as yet premature to conclude that laboratory measurements of reactivity are valid reflections of physiologic responses to naturally occurring events in patient populations. If such generalization can be established, however, the assessment of physiologic reactions to standardized behavioral stressors might ultimately prove a useful prognostic indicator.

Psychophysiologic Reactivity in the Etiology of Essential Hypertension.   The hypothesis that hypertension itself may arise from the repeated elicitation of large cardiovascular responses to psychological stressors has long provoked both interest and controversy. As noted earlier, any proposal that behaviorally elicited reactivity contributes to the pathogenesis of hypertension must also account for the transition from early hypertension, in which the cardiac output may be elevated significantly, to a later, established hypertensive state, in which the primary hemodynamic characteristic is an increased peripheral resistance. In this regard, one proponent of the reactivity "hypothesis," Obrist,[80] suggests that the markedly increased cardiac output exhibited under "stress" by highly reactive individuals may, with sufficient time, lead to increased resistance in the peripheral vasculature through either of two mechanisms. These include structural changes in the arterioles (e.g., smooth muscle hypertrophy), as proposed by Folkow,[102] and intrinsic autoregulatory processes acting to prevent an overperfusion of body tissues.[e.g., 103] Obrist appears to favor the autoregulatory mechanism since many behavioral challenges elicit elevations in cardiac output which supply oxygen levels beyond concurrent metabolic demands.[104,105]

However, much controversy surrounds autoregulation as a "transitional" mechanism between borderline and established hypertension. For instance, it has been suggested that because cardiac output *and* oxygen consumption are often elevated among borderline hypertensives, the increased output cannot be considered disproportionate to metabolic demand.[e.g.,106] Obrist, Light, and colleagues[107] argue, on the other hand, that such findings are not entirely germane to the "reactivity" hypothesis, since they derive from clinical investigations of resting state hemodynamics; in such studies there exists no meaningful psychological challenge to elicit significant sympathetic myocardial responses. Obrist et al. suggest, instead, that studies of cardiopulmonary relationships *in the actively coping organism* are more relevant to their interpretation of the role of autoregulation.

Recently, Julius and colleagues[5] proposed a second model of psychophysiologic influences in hypertension. Julius suggests that certain well-established behavioral characteristics—such as sociability, sensitivity, and submissiveness—generate "...a near permanent state of enhanced alertness."[108] This heightened vigilance is accompanied by disruption, or alteration, of centrally integrated cardiovascular autonomic tone. The initial consequence of this autonomic alteration is, in part, an increased sympathetic drive on the heart, with concomitantly elevated cardiac output. Julius hypothesizes further that continued sympathetic stimulation in these individuals leads ultimately to down-regulation of adrenergic receptors in the heart, and possibly myocardial structural changes, which then result in decreased cardiac responsiveness and lowered (or normalized) cardiac output. At the same time, development of hypertrophic resistance vessels, with altered wall-to-lumen ratios, may lead to an increased vascular responsivity (and hence, increased resistance).

Aside from the fact that Julius's model does not invoke autoregulation in accounting for the transition from borderline to established phases of hypertension, this hypothesis differs from that of Obrist in two important respects. First, the altered cardiovascular autonomic regulation suggested by Julius requires a relatively persistent sympathetic discharge. This proposal is compatible with a "reactivity" hypothesis only to the extent that "lab-to-life" generalization of reactivity resembles what we termed earlier a "prevailing state model"—that is, where a heightened cardiovascular reactivity observed in the laboratory is most predictive, in daily life, of physiologic states prevailing during the preponderance of waking and active hours. In contrast, Obrist's model is consistent with both the "prevailing state" notion and the hypothesis that a cardiovascular hyperreactivity is exhibited in daily life as repeated episodes of acute and transient sympathetic arousal (i.e., "recurrent activation"). The second distinction involves Julius's proposal that the autonomic characteristics of borderline hypertensives are a reflection of specific behavioral attributes of these individuals. In this regard Obrist's model presumes that behavioral events act as stimuli for the expression of an increased sympathetic reactivity, but does not assume that this "hyperreactivity" is also behavioral in origin.

In both of the foregoing models, autonomic influences (with or without a behavioral correlate) are seen as a "triggering" mechanism in the pathogenesis of hypertension. Another possibility is that the apparent hyperresponsivity of hypertensives and of persons at risk for hypertension is not a primary participant in the sequence of events leading to essential hypertension. As we have suggested elsewhere,[109] a common central nervous system disruption of autonomic control over the heart and vasculature might account for both the greater cardiovascular reactivity of hypertensive patients and their elevated blood pressures. If so, hyperreactivity to psychosocial stimuli in normotensive individuals might predict later hypertension but have no direct or causal role in its development.

Finally, a last avenue of speculation pertaining to psychophysiologic factors in hypertension is suggested by Light, Koepke, et al.[110]. They propose that autonomic mechanisms may contribute to hypertension through disruption of the regulation of blood volume and the control of blood pressure by the kidneys. This hypothesis is consonant with Guyton's notions concerning the importance of the kidneys in any long-term regulation of arterial pressure.[103] Moreover, recent evidence suggests that behavioral stressors can exert substantial influences on renal functioning. For instance, Grignolo et al.[111] reported that shock avoidance induces significant sodium and fluid retention in dogs, especially among those animals exhibiting the greatest heart rate elevations during avoidance procedures. Sodium retention in this animal model is apparently a result of increased reabsorption of sodium in the renal tubules and reflects sympathetic influences on renal nerve activity. That these observations may have specific relevance for human studies is indicated by findings of Light et al., [110] who report that laboratory tasks involving competitive challenge resulted similarly in decreased sodium and fluid excretion among many normotensive, young adult males. In addition, these effects persisted well after termination of the experimental stressor. Yet, interestingly, the effects occurred only in individuals who (1) showed the greatest heart rate reactivity to the experimental task, *and* (2) had either borderline systolic hypertension or a familial predisposition to hypertension. Thus, heart rate reactivity—as an individual differences variable—appears to be associated with a decreased excretion of sodium and fluid, which occurs, specifically, under stress, and then only in persons who are at heightened risk for hypertension.

SUMMARY

It has been hypothesized that physiologic reactivity to behavioral stressors may be implicated in the pathogenesis of CHD and essential hypertension. At present, many aspects of the construct of individual differences in reactivity remain incompletely understood, such as the manner in which laboratory-assessed reactivity may generalize to nonlaboratory settings. Nevertheless, speculation that such reactivity reflects a pathogenic process—or is a marker for correlated pathogenic processes—receives some support from epidemiologic evidence that behavioral factors play a significant role in cardiovascular disease. Several sources of data relevant to hypotheses invoking reactivity in the development of CHD and hypertension have also been reported, although such hypothesis-testing research is still in its early stages. To review briefly, in relation to coronary disease there are currently two studies based on an animal model associating behaviorally elicited heart rate reactivity with severity of coronary artery atherosclerosis, and one prospective study employing human subjects in which diastolic responsivity to the cold pressor test was found predictive of subsequent CHD. Available case-control investigations provide positive but mixed results and vary widely in methodologic rigor. Finally, the majority of studies examining psychophysiologic correlates of the Type A pattern have found a moderate relationship between Type A behavior and physiologic responses to a variety of laboratory stressors. However, Type A-reactivity associations seem partially dependent on the particular Type A assessment technique employed and may vary significantly with differences in situational parameters and sample characteristics.

With respect to essential hypertension, one study has found the cold pressor test to be predictive of later hypertension, and in numerous investigations, hypertensive patients have shown larger cardiovascular reactions to common laboratory stressors than normotensive control subjects. Similar differences have emerged in comparisons of normotensive individuals with and without family histories of hypertension. In addition, persons at risk for hypertension who also exhibit the greatest cardiac responses to stress appear to show an anomolous retention of sodium and fluid when exposed to significant behavioral challenges.

Still, there is little evidence that a physiologic hyperresponsivity to behavioral stimuli contributes appreciably to the *etiology* of CHD or essential hypertension, nor have many attempts been made to establish such direct reactivity-disease links by either experimental or epidemiologic investigation. As a result, the types of evidence that would most clearly implicate autonomic and neuroendocrine reactivity as risk variables remain to be collected. Hence, we believe it is premature to regard reactivity as a "proven" or established risk factor. We would also caution against extrapolation from early research studies to the clinical use of psychophysiologic assessment techniques in relation to cardiovascular disease. On the other hand, the preponderance of available evidence, while largely indirect, is consistent with such relationships, and testable hypotheses have been proposed. Moreover, current data in this area provide ample justification for continued, if not more vigorous, exploration of psychophysiologic factors and of their possible role in mediating behavioral influences in CHD and hypertension.

REFERENCES

1. Herd JA: Physiological basis for behavioral influences in atherosclerosis. In Dembroski TM, Schmidt TH, Blumchen G (eds): *Biobehavioral bases of coronary heart disease*. Basel, Karger, 1983, pp. 248–256.
2. Krantz DS, Manuck SB: Acute psychophysiologic reactivity and risk of cardiovascular disease: A review and methodologic critique. *Psychol Bull* **96**:435–464, 1984.

3. Schneiderman N: Behavior, autonomic function and animal models of cardiovascular pathology. In Dembroski TM, Schmidt TH, Blumchen G (eds): *Biobehavioral bases of coronary disease*. Basel, Karger, 1983, pp. 304–364.

4. Williams RB: Neuroendocrine response patterns and stress: Biobehavioral mechanisms of disease. In Williams RB (ed): *Perspectives on behavioral medicine: (Vol. 2): Neuroendocrine control and behavior*. New York, Academic Press, 1985, pp. 71–101.

5. Julius S, Weder AB, Egan BM: Pathophysiology of early hypertension: Implication for epidemiologic research. In Gross F, Strasser T (eds): *Mild hypertension*. New York, Raven Press, 1983, pp. 219–236.

6. Matthews KA, Jamison W, Cottington EM: Assessment of Type A, anger and hostility: A review of measures through 1982. Proceedings of the NHLBI workshop, *Measuring psychosocial variables in epidemiological studies of cardiovascular disease*. Bethesda, NIH Pub. No. 85-2270, 1985, pp. 207–310.

7. Review Panel: Coronary-prone behavior and coronary heart disease: A critical review. *Circulation* **63**:1199–1215, 1981.

8. Rosenman RH, Brand RJ, et al: Coronary heart disease in the Western Collaborative Group Study: Final follow-up experience of 8½ years. *JAMA* **233**:872–877, 1975.

9. Matthews KA, Glass DC, et al: Competitive drive, pattern A, and coronary heart disease: A further analysis of some data from the Western Collaborative Group Study. *J Chron Dis* **30**:489–498, 1977.

10. Dembroski TM, MacDougall JM, et al: Components of Type A, hostility and anger-in: Relationship to angiographic findings. *Psychosom Med* **47**:219–233, 1985.

11. Williams RB, Haney T, et al: Type A behavior, hostility and coronary atherosclerosis. *Psychosom Med* **42**:539–549, 1980.

12. Dimsdale JE, Jackett TP, et al: The risk of Type A mediated coronary artery disease in different populations. *Psychosom Med* **42**:55–62, 1980.

13. Zyzanski SJ, Jenkins CD, et al: Psychological correlates of coronary angiographic findings. *Arch Intern Med* **136**:1234–1237, 1976.

14. Kahn JP, Kornfeld DS, et al: Type A behavior and the thallium stress test. *Psychosom Med* **44**:431–436, 1982.

15. Stevens JH, Turner CW, et al: The Type A behavior pattern and carotid artery atherosclerosis. *Psychosom Med* **46**:105–113, 1984.

16. Manuck SB, Kaplan JR, Clarkson TB: Behaviorally-induced heart rate reactivity and atherosclerosis in cynomolgus monkeys. *Psychosom Med* **45**:95–108, 1983.

17. Haft JI: Cardiovascular injury induced by sympathetic catecholamines. *Prog Cardiovas Dis* **17**:73–86, 1974.

18. Manuck SB, Kaplan JR, Clarkson TB: Stress-induced heart rate reactivity and atherosclerosis in female macaques. *Psychosom Med* **47**:90, 1985. (Abstract)

19. Keys A, Taylor HL, et al: Mortality and coronary heart disease among men studied for 23 years. *Arch Intern Med* **128**:201–214, 1971.

20. Corse CD, Manuck SB, et al: Coronary-prone behavior pattern and cardiovascular response in persons with and without coronary heart disease. *Psychosom Med* **44**:449–459, 1982.

21. Dembroski TM, MacDougall JM, Lushene R: Interpersonal interaction and cardiovascular response in Type A subjects and coronary patients. *J Human Stress* **5**:28–36, 1979.

22. Krantz DS, Schaeffer MA, et al: Extent of coronary atherosclerosis, Type A behavior, and cardiovascular response to social interaction. *Psychophysiology* **18**:654–664, 1981.

23. Nestel PJ, Verghese A, Lovell RR: Catecholamine secretion and sympathetic nervous responses to emotion in men with and without urthox angina pectoris. *Am Heart J* **73**:227–234, 1967.

24. Sime WE, Buell JC, Eliot RS: Cardiovascular responses to emotional stress (Quiz interview) in post-infarct cardiac patients and matched control subjects. *J Human Stress* 6:39–46, 1980.

25. Shiffer F, Hartler LH, et al: The quiz electrocardiogram: A new diagnostic and research technique for evaluating the relation between emotional stress and ischemic heart disease. *Am J Cardiol* 37:41–47, 1976.

26. Williams RB, Lane JD: Physiological and neuroendocrine response during different behavioral challenges: Differential hyperresponsivity of Type A men. *Science* 218:483–485, 1982.

27. MacDougall JM, Dembroski TM, Krantz DS: Effects of types of challenge on pressor and heart rate responses in Type A and B women. *Psychophysiology* 18:1–9, 1981.

28. Stamler J, Stamler B, et al: Hypertension screening of 1 million Americans. *JAMA* 235:2299–2306, 1976.

29. Weiner H: *Psychobiology and Human Disease*. New York, Elsevier, 1977.

30. Alexander F: Emotional factors in essential hypertension: Presentation of a tentative hypothesis. *Psychosom Med* 1:173–179, 1939.

31. Esler M, Julius S, et al: Mild high-renin essential hypertension: Neurogenic human hypertension? *N Engl J Med* 296:405–411, 1977.

32. Gentry WD, Chesney MA, et al: Habitual anger-coping styles: I. Effect on mean blood pressure and risk for hypertension. *Psychosom Med* 44:195–202, 1982.

33. Hamilton JA: Psychophysiology of blood pressure. *Psychosom Med* 4:125–133, 1942.

34. Haynes SG, Levine S, et al: The relationship of psychosocial factors to coronary heart disease in the Framingham study. *Am J Epidemiology* 107:362–381, 1978.

35. Harburg E, Blakelock EH, Roeper PJ: Resentful and reflective coping with arbitrary authority and blood pressure: Detroit. *Psychosom Med* 41:189–202, 1979.

36. Harburg E, Erfurt JC, et al: Socio-ecological stress, suppressed hostility, skin color, and black-white male blood pressure: Detroit. *Psychosom Med* 35:276–296, 1973.

37. Harburg E, Julius S, et al: Personality traits and behavioral patterns associated with systolic blood pressure levels in college males. *J Chron Dis* 17:405–414, 1964.

38. Kahn HA, Medalie JH, et al: The incidence of hypertension and associated factors: The Israel ischemic heart disease study. *Am Heart J* 84:171–182, 1972.

39. Light KC, Obrist PA: Task difficulty, heart rate reactivity, and cardiovascular responses to an appetitive reactive time task. *Psychophysiology* 20:301–312, 1983.

40. McClelland DC: Inhibited power motivation and high blood pressure in men. *J Abnorm Psychol* 88:182–190, 1979.

41. Miller C, Grim C: Personality and emotional stress measurement on hypertensive patients with essential and secondary hypertension. *Int J Nursing* 16:85–93, 1979.

42. Sullivan PA, Procci WR, et al: Anger, anxiety, guilt and increased basal and stress-induced neurogenic tone: Causes or effects in primary hypertension? *Clin Sci* 61:389S–392S, 1981.

43. Harris RE, Sokolow M, et al: Response to psychologic stress in persons who are potentially hypertensive. *Circulation* 7:572–578, 1953.

44. Gressel GE, Shobe FO, et al: Personality factors in essential hypertension. *JAMA* 140:265–272, 1949.

45. Matarazzo JD: An experimental study of aggression in the hypertensive patient. *J Pers* 22:423–447, 1954.

46. Sapira JD, Scheib ET, et al: Differences in perception between hypertensive and normotensive populations. *Psychosom Med* 33:239–250, 1971.

47. Keane TM, Martin JE, et al: Are hypertensives less assertive? A controlled evaluation. *J Consult Clin Psychol* 50:499–508, 1982.

48. Cochrane R: Hostility and neuroticism among unselected essential hypertensives. *J Psychosom Res* **17**:215–218, 1973.

49. Neiberg NA: The effects of induced stress on the management of hostility in essential hypertension. *Dissertation Abstracts* **17**:1597–1598, 1957.

50. Ostfeld AM, Lebovitz BZ: Personality factors and pressor mechanisms in renal and essential hypertension. *Arch Intern Med* **104**:497–502, 1959.

51. Robinson JD: A study of neuroticism and casual arterial blood pressure. *Br J Soc Clin Psychol* **2**:56–64, 1962.

52. Wheatley D, Balter M, et al: Psychiatric aspects of hypertension. *Br J Psychiatry* **127**:327–336, 1975.

53. Baer PE, Collins FH, et al: Assessing personality factors in essential hypertension with a brief self-report instrument. *Psychosom Med* **7**:653–659, 1979.

54. Mann AH: Psychiatric morbidity and hostility in hypertension. *Psychol Med* **7**:653–659, 1977.

55. Schachter J: Pain, fear, and anger in hypertensives and normotensives. *Psychosom Med* **19**:17–29, 1957.

56. Morrison RL, Bellack AS, Manuck SB: The role of social competence in essential hypertension. *J Consult Clin Psychol* **53**:248–255, 1985.

57. Perini C, Amann FW, et al: Personality and adrenergic factors in essential hypertension. *Contrib Nephrol* **30**:64–69, 1982.

58. Kaplan NM: *Clinical Hypertension.* Baltimore, Williams & Wilkins, 1982.

59. Julius S, Esler M: Autonomic nervous cardiovascular regulation in borderline hypertension. *Am J Cardiol* **36**:685–696, 1975.

60. Kuchel O: Autonomic nervous system in hypertension: Clinical aspects. In Genest J, Koiw E, Kuchel O (eds): *Hypertension.* New York, McGraw-Hill, 1977, pp. 93–113.

61. Goldstein D: Plasma catecholamines and essential hypertension. *Hypertension* **5**:86–99, 1983.

62. Esler MS, Julius S, et al: Mild high-renin hypertension: Neurogenic human hypertension? *N Engl J Med* **296**:405–411, 1977.

63. Dustan HP, Frohlich ED, Tarazi RC: Pressor mechanisms. In Frohlich EC (ed): *Pathophysiology: Altered regulatory mechanisms in disease.* Philadelphia, Lippincott, 1972, pp. 41–66.

64. Julius S: Borderline hypertension: Epidemiologic and clinical implications. In Genest J, Koiw E, Kuchel O (eds): *Hypertension.* New York, McGraw-Hill, 1977, pp. 630–639.

65. Eich RH, Cuddy RP, et al: Hemodynamics in labile hypertension: A follow-up study. *Circulation* **34**:299–307, 1966.

66. Lund-Johansen P: Central hemodynamics in essential hypertension. *Acta Med Scan* **606**:35–42. (Suppl.)

67. Lund-Johansen P: Spontaneous changes in central hemodynamics in essential hypertension—A 10-year follow-up study. In Onesti G, Klimt CR (eds): *Hypertension: Determinants, complications and intervention.* New York, Grune & Stratton, 1979, pp. 201–210.

68. Safar ME, Kamiencka HA, et al: Hemodynamic factors and Rorschach testing in borderline and sustained hypertensives. *Psychosom Med* **40**:620–631, 1978.

69. Hallback M: Interaction between central neurogenic mechanisms and changes in cardiovascular design in primary hypertension. Experimental studies in spontaneously hypertensive rats. *Acta Physiol Scand* **424**:3–59, 1975. (Suppl)

70. Hallback M, Folkow B: Cardiovascular responses to acute mental "stress" in spontaneously hypertensive rats. *Acta Physiol Scand* **90**:684–698, 1974.

71. Hallback-Nordlander M, Lundin S: Cardiovascular reactions in young spontaneously hypertensive rats. In Onesti G, Kim KE, (eds): *Hypertension in the young and old.* New York, Grune & Stratton, 1981, pp. 102–119.

72. McCarty R: Physiological and behavioral responses of New Zealand hypertensive and normotensive rats to stress. *Physiol Behav* **28**:103–108, 1982.

73. Anderson DE: Interactions of stress, salt and blood pressure. *Ann Rev Physiol* **46**:143–153, 1984.

74. Lawler JE, Barber GF, et al: The effects of conflict on toxic levels of blood pressure in the genetically borderline hypertensive rat. *Psychophysiology* **4**:363–370, 1980.

75. Wood DL, Sheps SG, et al: Cold pressor test as a predictor of hypertension. *Hypertension* **6**:301–306, 1984.

76. Eich RH, Jacobsen EC: Vascular reactivity in medical students followed for 10 years. *J Chronic Dis* **20**:583–592, 1967.

77. Harlan WR, Osborne RK, Graybiel A: Prognostic value of the cold pressor test. *Am J Cardiol* **13**:832–837, 1964.

78. Drummond PD: Cardiovascular reactivity in mild hypertension. *J Psychosom Res* **27**:291–297, 1983.

79. Eliasson K, Hjenadahl P, Kahan T: Circulatory and sympatho-adrenal responses to stress in borderline and established hypertension. *J Hypert* **1**:131–139, 1983.

80. Obrist PA: *Cardiovascular Psychophysiology*. New York, Plenum Press, 1981.

81. Dembroski TM, MacDougall JM, et al: Effect of level of challenge on pressor and heart rate responses in Type A and B subjects. *J Appl Soc Psychol* **9**:209–228, 1979.

82. Baumann R, Ziprian H, et al: The influence of acute psychic stress situations on biochemical and vegetative parameters of essential hypertensives at the early stage of the disease. *Psychother Psychosom* **22**:131–140, 1973.

83. Nestel PJ: Blood pressure and catecholamine excretion after mental stress in labile hypertension. *Lancet* **1**:692–694, 1969.

84. Shapiro AP: An experimental study of comparative responses of blood pressure to different noxious stimuli. *J Chronic Dis* **13**:293–311, 1961.

85. McKegney FP, Williams RB: Psychological aspects of hypertension: II. The differential influence of interview variables on blood pressure. *Am J Psychiatry* **123**:1539–1545, 1967.

86. Steptoe A, Melville D, Ross A: Behavioral response demands, cardiovascular reactivity and essential hypertension. *Psychosom Med* **46**:33–48, 1984.

87. Fredrikson M, Dimberg U, et al: Haemodynamic and electrodermal correlates of psychogenic stimuli in normotensive and hypertensive subjects. *Biol Psychol* **15**:63–73, 1982.

88. Paffenbarger PS, Throne MC, Wing AL: Chronic disease in former college students. VIII. Characteristics of youth predisposing to hypertension in later years. *Am J Epidemiol* **88**:25–32, 1968.

89. Paul O: Epidemiology of hypertension. In Genest J, Koiw E, Kutchel O (eds): *Hypertension: Physiopathology and Treatment*. New York, McGraw-Hill, 1977, pp. 613–629.

90. Matthews KA, Rakaczky CJ: Familial aspects of Type A behavior pattern and physiologic reactivity to stress. In Dembroski T, Schmidt T (eds): *Biobehavioral Factors in Coronary Heart Disease*. Heidelberg, Springer-Verlag (in press).

91. Hastrup JL, Light KC, Obrist PA: Parental hypertension and cardiovascular response to stress in healthy young adults. *Psychophysiology* **19**:615–622, 1982.

92. Manuck SB, Proietti JM, et al: Parental hypertension, affect and cardiovascular response to cognitive challenge. *Psychosom Med* **47**:189–200, 1985.

93. Falkner E, Onesti G, et al: Cardiovascular response to mental stress in normal adolescents with hypertensive parents. *Hypertension* **1**:23–30, 1979.

94. Manuck SB, Proietti J: Parental hypertension and cardiovascular response to cognitive and isometric challenge. *Psychophysiology* **19**:481–489, 1982.

95. Sime WE, Buell JC, Eliot R: Psychophysiological (emotional) stress testing: A potential means of detecting early reinfarction victim. *Circulation* **59 and 60**:11–56, 1979. (Abstract)

96. Sokolow M, McIlroy MB: *Clinical Cardiology*. Los Altos, CA, Lange Medical Publications, 1977.

97. Sokolow M, Werdegar D, et al: Relationships between level of blood pressure measured casually and by portable recorder and severity of complications in essential hypertension. *Circulation* **34**:279–298, 1966.

98. Perloff D, Sokolow M, Cowan R: The prognostic value of ambulatory blood pressures. *JAMA* **249**:2792–2798, 1983.

99. Devereux RB, Pickering TG, et al: Left ventricular hypertrophy in patients with hypertension: Importance of blood pressure response to regularly occurring stress. *Circulation* **68**:470–476, 1983.

100. Manuck SB, Corse CD, Winkelman PA: Behavioral correlates of individual differences in blood pressure reactivity. *J Psychosom Res* **23**:281–288, 1979.

101. Matthews KA, Manuck SB, Saab PG: Cardiovascular responses of adolescents during a naturally occurring stressor and their behavioral and psychophysiological correlates. *Psychophysiology*, in press.

102. Folkow B, Grimby G, Thulesius O: Adaptive structural changes of the vascular walls in hypertension and their relation to the control of the peripheral resistance. *Acta Physiol Scand* **44**:255–272, 1958.

103. Guyton AC, Coleman TG: Quantitative analysis of the pathophysiology of hypertension. *Circulation Res* **24**:I1–I19, 1969.

104. Gliner JA, Bedi JF, Horvath SM: Somatic and non-somatic influences on the heart: Hemodynamic changes. *Psychophysiology* **16**:358–363, 1979.

105. Langer AW, Obrist PA, McCubbin JA: Hemodynamic and metabolic adjustments during exercise and shock avoidance in dogs. *Am J Physiol* **5**:H225–H230, 1979.

106. Julius S, Conway J: Hemodynamic studies in patients with borderline blood pressure elevation. *Circulation* **38**:282–288, 1968.

107. Obrist PA, Light KC, et al: Behavioral influences on blood pressure control: Implications for the hypertensive process. In Birkenhager WH, Reid JL (eds): *Handbook on Hypertension*. Amsterdam: Elsevier/North Holland, in press.

108. Julius S: The psychophysiology of borderline hypertension. In Weiner H, Hofer MA, Stunkard AJ (eds): *Brain, Behavior and Bodily Disease*. New York, Raven Press, 1981, pp. 293–305.

109. Manuck SB, Morrison RL, et al: Behavioral factors in hypertension: Cardiovascular responsivity, anger and social competence. In Chesney MA, Rosenman RH (eds): *Anger and Hostility in Cardiovascular and Behavioral Disorders*. Washington, DC, Hemisphere Publishing Co., 1985, pp. 149–172.

110. Light KC, Koepke JP, et al: Psychological stress induces sodium and fluid retention in men at high risk for hypertension. *Science* **220**:429–431, 1983.

111. Grignolo A, Koepke JP, Obrist PA: Renal function, heart rate and blood pressure during exercise and shock avoidance in dogs. *Am J Physiol* **242**:R482–R490, 1982.

3

Potential Role of Cardiovascular Reactivity in Atherogenesis

Thomas B. Clarkson, Stephen B. Manuck, Jay R. Kaplan

The purpose of this chapter is to discuss ways in which behaviorally elicited hemodynamic reactions may participate in the pathogenesis of atherosclerosis. The first section of this chapter describes briefly the natural history of atherosclerosis and emphasizes some important considerations in the study of atherogenesis. This discussion is followed by a summary of the results of our initial studies of the relationship of atherosclerosis to individual differences in cardiac responsivity to stress, as derived from an animal model. The final section of the chapter deals more generally with hemodynamic influences on atherogenesis and with the possibility that such factors promote injury to the arterial endothelium, an early stage in the development of atherosclerotic lesions.

Research described here was supported, in part, by HL14164, HL29028, HL26562 and a grant from the R.J. Reynolds Industries, Inc.

NATURAL HISTORY OF ATHEROSCLEROSIS

Atherosclerosis is a pathologic process affecting the large muscular and elastic arteries, in which the intima, or inner layer of the artery wall, is thickened through an accumulation of lipids, the proliferation of smooth muscle cells, and to some extent, migration of macrophages into the intima.[1] As part of this process, the single layer of endothelial cells that cover and protect the intima is also altered in both morphologic characteristics and function.

Atherosclerosis of the coronary arteries is a usual cause of coronary heart disease, the symptoms of which include myocardial infarction, angina pectoris, and disturbances in the rhythm, performance, and electrical activity of the heart. Atherosclerosis of the cerebral arteries is also of considerable consequence, as it is associated with the occurrence of transient ischemic attacks and stroke. When affecting the abdominal portion of the aorta and its major branches, atherosclerosis may produce, as sequelae, aneurysms and renal and intestinal ischemia. Stenosis of the renal arteries per se may be responsible for both renal ischemia and hypertension. Finally, atherosclerosis of the iliac and femoral arteries can reduce circulation to the legs, resulting in severe cramps and pain in the buttocks and thighs (intermittent claudication) and, occasionally, gangrene in the extremities.

While some degree of atherosclerosis develops in almost all human beings, clinical complications vary greatly in incidence across differing ethnic and geographic groups. The most severely affected populations are the highly industrialized societies of North America and Europe.[2,3] Epidemiologic investigations of the past several decades have succeeded in identifying a number of contributing variables in atherosclerosis and clinical CHD. Among these variables, elevated serum lipid concentrations, arterial hypertension, and cigarette smoking emerge most prominently as determinants of the geographic distribution of clinically significant atherosclerosis, and within geographic areas, these variables act as risk factors for extent and severity of disease.[2,3]

Regarding the natural history of atherosclerosis, it is thought that arterial "injury" is a major factor in the initial development of lesions.[4] Based on the research of many investigators, it now appears that lesion development begins when some form of damage is sustained by the arterial endothelium. Cells die as a consequence and are replaced by a process known as nondenuding desquamation. Specifically, endothelial cells die without leaving a denuded, or endothelium-free, surface; instead, they are squeezed out into the circulation by the replication of cells immediately adjacent to them. Replicating endothelial cells, in turn, exhibit an increased permeability to low-density lipoproteins, allowing the entrance of plasma lipids into the intima. The newly regenerated cells are also thought to liberate mitogenic substances capable of causing smooth muscle cells lying beneath the endothelium to replicate in large numbers and to further promote in these cells a disturbed lipid metabolism and accumulation of lipid.[4,5] Interestingly, while rapid formation of new endothelial cells is apparently the marker for arterial injury and subsequent intimal alterations, normal replication of endothelial cells (which typically have a half-life of six to eight years) does not result in the foregoing changes.

The first type of atherosclerotic lesion observed in the intima of the arteries is the fatty streak; such lesions occur in nearly all children very early in life (beginning within the first six months). Fatty streaks are raised little or not at all and have no known pathologic consequences. They appear first in the aorta, then in the coronary and cerebral arteries. Within high-risk populations, fatty streaks are replaced by fibrous plaques, which develop during young adulthood. These lesions are filled with a gruel of lipid and necrotic material and are covered by a fibromuscular cap. The continued growth of fibrous plaques can lead to arterial stenosis, occlusion, and the clinical manifestations of atherosclerotic disease.[3,6] While direct observation of the evolution of fatty streaks into raised lesions (plaques) is not possible, it is generally accepted that lesion development conforms to the progression described above.[7]

The atherosclerotic plaque represents a clear threat to health and longevity. This threat becomes acute when plaques enlarge to the extent that they prevent an adequate flow of blood to tissues supplied by the affected vessels.[6] Interference with blood supply and occlusion of the artery is not simply a matter of continued plaque growth, however, but may involve a variety of complicating events affecting both the plaque and the underlying vessel.[4] For example, plaques may ulcerate, provoking thrombus formation, and such thrombi may then be incorporated into the ulcerated plaque. Further, platelets involved in thrombus formation may liberate substances, such as thromboxane A_2, which can cause vessel spasm and, quite possibly, death of the distal tissue.[8] The sequence of lesion progression, together with a depiction of resulting clinical manifestations and the hypothesized actions of major risk factors, are presented in Figure 3.1.

At this point we should emphasize that while much is known about the geographic distribution, natural history, and clinical sequelae of atherosclerosis, there is considerable controversy regarding the relative importance of even well-known risk factors. This is not surprising in view of the large differences in arterial lesions that are often observed among individuals having the same "dose" of a given risk variable. Perhaps nowhere is such variability more apparent than in studies of the influence of cholesterol concentrations on coronary artery atherosclerosis. Shown in Figure 3.2, for

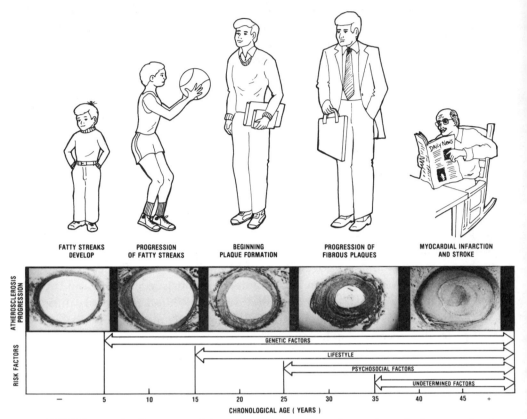

FIGURE 3.1.   An illustration of the progression of atherosclerosis from the fatty streaks of childhood to the fibrous plaques of adulthood and final clinical sequelae. In the figure the natural history is related to the usual chronologic age and stage of life for each step of pathogenesis. Genetic factors are depicted as having an influence at all stages of the disease process. Although psychosocial and life-style factors are indicated at a stage when it is probable that their influences on atherogenesis are most appreciable, it is possible that these variables contribute to lesion development earlier in life as well. The authors greatly acknowledge Sharon Heydrick's contribution to this illustration.

example, are results of the Oslo Heart Study.[9] It is clear from the figure that a significant association exists in this sample between serum cholesterol concentrations and the extensiveness of coronary artery atherosclerosis. The plotted data points illustrate, however, that although many persons with moderately elevated cholesterol concentrations are affected quite markedly, others at the same level of cholesterol have little or no evidence of coronary atherosclerosis. This variability is particularly evident at cholesterol concentrations between 260 and 300 mg/dl, but extends even to concentrations exceeding 350 mg/dl.

The problem of individual variability has led, in turn, to many of the important advances in lipid biology.[10] In their attempts to better understand the role of elevated cholesterol in atherogenesis, for instance, researchers have sought to identify the ways in which various cholesterol fractions are transported and metabolized. A result of this work is the discovery that the various lipoprotein fractions involved in cholesterol transport are of differing atherogenicity. In particular, it has been found that many of the low-density lipoproteins (LDLs) are highly atherogenic, whereas high-density lipoproteins (HDLs) are protective against atherosclerosis. Also significant is the observation that effects of cholesterol on atherogenesis can be influenced by the noncholesterol components of the diet (e.g., the degree of saturation of fatty acids) and by the presence of other physiologic factors, such as arterial hypertension,[11] certain types of immune complexes,[12,13] and cortisol.[14]

We believe the lessons gained from investigation of "established" risk factors, such as lipids, may be germane also to the study of psychosocial effects on atherogenesis. First, we think it is improbable that any single risk variable can account for more than a portion of the total variance in athero-sclerosis. While it is true that perhaps half of such variance remains unexplained by the traditional risk variables, it seems unlikely that this 50 percent will be captured entirely by either single or multiple behavioral phenomena. On the other hand, researchers might well be cautioned against dismissing suspected behavioral influences on atherosclerosis when observing only modest associations in the early stages of investigation. Recall that the gross relationship between serum cholesterol concentrations and coronary artery atherosclerosis—for instance, as depicted in Figure 3.2—is also relatively small. Yet its pursuit has led to important discoveries in lipid biology and, with such advances, to enhanced prediction of atherosclerosis. Much the same history may ultimately characterize the study of psychosocial variables, be it Type A behavior pattern or psychophysiologic reactivity.

With these considerations in mind, we describe in the following section of this chapter our own first attempts to examine the relationship of atherosclerosis to individual differences in cardiac reactivity to stress. This research was conducted at the Arteriosclerosis Research Center of Bowman Gray School of Medicine and, unlike most work in this area (see Chapter 2, this volume by Manuck and Krantz), is based on a nonhuman primate model of atherogenesis.

CARDIAC REACTIVITY AND ATHEROSCLEROSIS

In examining behavioral influences on atherogenesis, we have relied extensively on the cynomolgus macaque (*Macaca fascicularis*) as a suitable animal model. Among the advantages of the cynomolgus monkey is its high susceptibility, given a moderate hyperlipoproteinemia, to development of

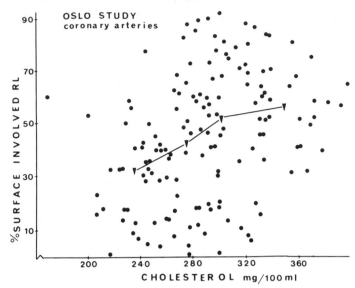

FIGURE 3.2.   Raised atherosclerotic lesions in the coronary arteries of individual cases and the mean of raised lesions (RL), by increasing values of serum cholesterol (quartiles). $N = 150$. (Reprinted with permission from Springer-Verlag Publishers, New York. From "Risk factors for coronary and cerebral atherosclerosis in the Oslo study," by L.A. Solberg, S.C. Enger, et al. In Gotto AM, Smith LC, Allen B, eds, *Atherosclerosis V*.) Reprinted with permission of authors and publisher.

fatty streaks and the rapid progression of such lesions to formation of fibrous plaques.[15–18] In addition, diet-induced atherosclerotic lesions in these animals often exhibit necrosis, mineralization, and the pooling of fat droplets or crystalline lipid.[19,20] Cynomolgus monkeys also experience myocardial infarction more frequently than do other nonhuman primates,[21] and as in human beings, coronary artery atherosclerosis in male cynomolgus monkeys is more extensive than that observed among females.[22,23]

Over the past few years our work has focused on the relationship of atherosclerosis to: (1) psychosocial variables (e.g., environmental perturbation, social status), and (2) individual differences in cardiac response to stress. Principal findings relating to psychosocial variables are described in detail elsewhere [13,24–26] and will not be reviewed in the present chapter. Rather, here we will summarize results of our initial observations concerning associations between idiosyncratic heart rate response to stress and extent of atherosclerosis in the coronary and cerebral arteries and the aorta.[27,28]

The relevant studies involve two cohorts of experimental animals, one composed of 26 adult male cynomolgus monkeys and the other of 21 adult females of the same species. These animals were drawn from larger investigations in which all monkeys were housed in either stable or unstable social groupings; the animals assigned to unstable (stressed) groups were redistributed on a regular basis, whereas "stable" (unstressed) monkeys lived in groups of fixed memberships throughout the investigations. Since our findings regarding associations between cardiac reactivity and atherosclerosis do not vary with the nature of the animals' social groupings (i.e., stable or unstable), data described below are collapsed across conditions of housing. In both studies animals were fed a moderately atherogenic diet and maintained under the experimental conditions for either 22 (males) or 28 (females) months.

Our interest in psychophysiologic reactivity actually arose only towards the end of the period in which these investigations were being conducted and was due to growing speculation that autonomic and neuroendocrine responsivity to behavioral stimuli might be implicated in a broad spectrum of cardiovascular disease, including essential hypertension and coronary heart disease (see Chapter 2 by Manuck and Krantz). Although there is little precedent in the experimental literature for pursuing this phenomenon in an animal model, we nonetheless sought to determine whether monkeys (like human beings) vary in their reactivity to a behavioral stressor and, if so, whether such variability might be related, on necropsy of the animals, to extent of atherosclerosis. Because of the exploratory nature of this research (i.e., as an adjunct to ongoing work), we examined only one cardiovascular response parameter, heart rate. Our selection of heart rate was dictated largely by pragmatic considerations, and, more specifically, by the availability of commercial ECG radiotelemetry devices, which allowed physiologic monitoring in a social environment and without undue disturbance of the animals. Additionally, it should be noted that because heart rate assessments were made on only a single occasion and shortly prior to termination of the animals, the findings described below are essentially retrospective.

Heart rate measurements were obtained on each animal under both resting and stressed conditions. The baseline recordings were obtained during a period of relative quiet, when no laboratory personnel were visible to the monkeys. In contrast, stress-period heart rate measurements were recorded during the presentation of a standard challenge, in which the experimenter displayed a large "monkey glove" in a prominent and threatening manner before the target animals. This maneuver was carried out in a stylized fashion, but similarly to encounters typically preceding the capture and physical handling of monkeys.

Across all animals this stimulus elicited a very pronounced cardiac acceleration. In fact, heart rates in the range of 220–250 beats per minute were not uncommon, and in such monkeys heart rate responses typically exceeded baseline values by greater than 100 percent. Yet, in many other animals heart rates rose less than 50 percent above baseline measurements, suggesting that, as in humans, there exist great individual differences in the behaviorally elicited heart rate reactions of cynomolgus macaques. Data we have collected subsequently on several other groups of cynomolgus monkeys demonstrate that these differences also reflect stable individual characteristics (i.e., are reproducible on repeat testing) and generalize to other conditions of measurement.

At necropsy the coronary arteries of each animal were perfused at 100 mmHg and sections taken from the main branch coronary arteries. These sections were stained by the Verhoeff van Geison method, then projected, and the areas occupied by intima and/or intimal lesions (i.e., the area between the internal elastic lamina and lumen of the artery) measured with the aid of a computer-assisted digitizer. The mean intimal area of all arterial sections, expressed in mm^2, was calculated for each animal. In addition to the coronary arteries, atherosclerosis at the carotid bifurcation was also assessed (again expressed in mm^2) and plaque volume (in mm^3) was measured in 10-cm sections taken from thoracic and abdominal portions of the aorta. Methods used in measurement of atherosclerosis at the latter sites are described in detail in other publications.[25,27,29]

For purposes of analysis the distributions of individual differences in heart rate response to our laboratory stressor were partitioned into clearly differentiated groups of "high" and "low" heart rate reactive animals (viz., upper and lower 30 to 35 percent). Among both male and female monkeys, baseline heart rates did not differ between the "high" and "low" heart rate reactors. Stress-period heart rates of "high" reactors, on the other hand, exceeded those of "low" heart rate reactive animals by approximately 35 bpm.

To examine the relationship of heart rate reactivity to atherosclerosis, intimal area measurements from both the coronary and carotid arteries, as well as measures of aortic plaque volume, were contrasted between the "high" and "low" heart rate reactive groups. These analyses revealed that "high" heart rate reactors had roughly twice the coronary artery atherosclerosis of "low" reactors ($p < 0.05$ for both males and females). A similar relationship was observed between heart rate reactivity and atherosclerosis at the carotid bifurcation and, in males only, in the thoracic portion of the aorta. Atherosclerosis in the abdominal aorta did not differ between "high" and "low" heart rate reactive groups of either male or female monkeys.

We are impressed that much the same associations were obtained in both sexes, especially given the relatively small number of animals examined and the fact that lesion size differed overall between males and females. There are other similarities as well. Among both males and females, for example, heart weight (calculated in proportion to body weight) was significantly greater in "high," compared to "low," heart rate reactors. Also, in both studies "high" reactive animals showed a slight (marginally significant) elevation in the ratio of total-to-HDL cholesterol concentrations. Total serum cholesterol and HDL cholesterol concentrations alone, though, did not differ between "high" and "low" heart rate reactors of either sex, nor did groups differ in systolic or diastolic blood pressure. Interestingly, animals' rates of aggressive behavior—measured over the course of the investigations—correlated positively with heart rate reactivity in male monkeys and negatively in females. This reciprocal association between aggression and heart rate reactivity also paralleled relationships between behavior and coronary artery atherosclerosis in the experiments from which the male and female cohorts were drawn.

We believe the foregoing data provide initial support for the hypothesis that acute psychophysiologic reactivity is related to the development of atherosclerotic lesions and may thereby mediate associations between behavioral attributes of the individual and atherogenesis. Of course, interpretation of these findings is limited by the retrospective nature of the heart rate observations themselves. Yet, it does not appear that differences in the stress-related heart rates of "high" and "low" reactive monkeys were a consequence of their corresponding differences in atherosclerosis. In recordings made on other groups of cynomolgus monkeys, for instance, we have found no differences in the stressed heart rates of animals fed atherogenic and "prudent" diets; these are groups that also differed greatly in extent of atherosclerosis, but due only to dietary manipulation. In addition, we have noted recently that distributions of individual differences in heart rate response to our laboratory challenge are also remarkably stable over time, even though the animals observed are fed an atherogenic diet and are therefore developing progressively more atherosclerosis across successive testing intervals. Still, we view these data as preliminary and look forward to the completion of ongoing investigations that address more directly the prospective association between individual differences in heart rate reactivity (as well as in other hemodynamic and neuroendocrine response parameters) and the development of atherosclerosis.

POTENTIAL MECHANISM

Specific mechanisms by which acute psychophysiologic reactivity may promote lesion development remain unclear, although hypotheses invoking a variety of hemodynamic and neuroendocrine factors have been proposed. Many of these hypotheses are discussed extensively elsewhere in this volume, as in the chapter by Herd on possible neuroendocrine mediation, and by Dembroski on influences of dietary and other injested substances on autonomic response characteristics. Hence, in the remainder of the present chapter we will limit our discussion to only one of the organism's many integrated responses to stress—namely, the hemodynamic disruptions that accompany sympathetic nervous system reactions to behavioral stimuli. We focus on hemodynamic factors, in particular, as we believe that the abrupt changes in arterial pressure and pulse rate characteristic of sympathetically hyperreactive individuals may play a significant role in the early stages of atherogenesis involving injury to the arterial endothelium.

Although, as noted earlier in this chapter, there is now much agreement that arterial injury figures importantly in the initiation of atherosclerotic lesions, it is still unclear how such injury arises *in vivo*. The potential significance of hemodynamic forces (e.g., turbulence, sheer stress) has long been argued, yet it is difficult to isolate hemodynamic states from the many neurohumoral events that contribute to cardiovascular regulation. However, one recent study, reported by Beere and colleagues,[30] bears directly on this issue. These investigators have proposed that a significant elevation in heart rate predisposes to atherosclerosis at points in the arterial tree that are exposed to rapid alterations in the direction and strength of pulsatile blood flow, such as the carotid bifurcation and proximal portions of the coronary arteries. In testing this hypothesis, Beere et al.[30] lowered the heart rates of a group of cynomolgus macaques by surgically ablating the sinoatrial node. These monkeys were then administered an atherogenic diet, as were sham-operated controls. When necropsied six months later, animals having lower postoperative heart rates were found to have developed less than half the coronary artery atherosclerosis of monkeys with more elevated heart rates. Importantly, the "high" and "low" heart rate groups did not differ in serum cholesterol, triglycerides, body weight, or systolic or diastolic blood pressure. Extrapolating from these findings, the authors suggest that protracted elevations in heart rate due to psychosocial challenge, or stress, may similarly account for influences of behavioral factors on atherosclerosis.

Whether the hemodynamic disruptions induced by stress promote atherosclerosis specifically by injuring arterial endothelium is more difficult to determine. There are now techniques for measuring endothelial injury, however. One of the most useful was developed by Schwartz et al.[5] In using this technique, radioactive thymidine is administered prior to necropsy of the animal. This radioactive preparation is taken up preferentially by actively replicating cells. If the artery is fixed properly and coated with a photographic emulsion, the radioactive nuclei can be observed under a scanning electron microscope. This permits the proportion of endothelial cells on the surface of an artery to be calculated, resulting in determination of the endothelial cell turnover rate. This measurement, in turn, is equivalent to the rate of endothelial cell death and replacement.

That behavioral factors can cause significant endothelial injury is indicated in results of recent investigations by Gordon et al.[31] and Hirsch et al.[32] The latter study is of particular interest since it also implicates hemodynamic forces in the initiation of such injury. Hirsch et al. exposed laboratory rats to physical restraint, a procedure that elicited marked rises in heart rate and blood pressure. These animals and unstressed controls were also infused with radioactive thymidine, as described above. Subsequent autoradiographic examination of the animals' aortic intimas showed endothelial cell replication rates to be 500 percent higher in stressed rats relative to controls. Moreover, other groups of stressed animals were administered propranolol during the period of restraint. The "blocked" animals exhibited no significant heart rate or blood pressure elevation under stress, nor did their endothelial cell replication rates differ from those of autonomically intact, unstressed controls. Hence, beta-adrenergic blockade attenuated the hemodynamic response to physical restraint and served to protect the artery against endothelial injury.

These findings suggest that a sufficiently potent behavioral challenge can cause endothelial cells to turn over in a matter of days and that this effect may be attributable to the cardiovascular adjustments associated with sympathetic nervous system responses to stress. What may follow from such injury has been described earlier—namely, the infiltration of plasma lipids into the intima (due to an increased permeability of the replicating endothelium to low-density lipoproteins) and the promotion of intimal smooth muscle cell proliferation, with accompanying disruption of the lipid metabolism of these cells. If behavioral stimuli can promote atherogenesis in this manner, then it is reasonable to hypothesize that persons who exhibit a cardiovascular *hyperresponsivity* under stress will be at greater risk than hemodynamically less reactive individuals. Our studies of behaviorally elicited heart rate reactivity and atherosclerosis in cynomolgus macaques provide initial support for this hypothesis. However, further investigation is now needed to demonstrate a truly prospective relationship between individual differences in cardiovascular reactivity and the development of atherosclerosis, both in animal models and in human beings.

CONCLUSIONS

We believe that individual differences in cardiovascular responsivity to environmental perturbations may be implicated in the sequence of events leading to atherosclerosis, especially those events that figure most prominently at an early stage in lesion development. We should again point out, however, that hemodynamic factors represent only one of several possible variables mediating behavioral effects on atherosclerosis and that the matrix of associated neuroendocrine responses to stress may contribute as well. Recall, too, that we observed small differences in the ratio of total-to-HDL cholesterol concentrations between "high" and "low" heart rate reactive monkeys; this finding suggests that alterations in lipid metabolism may also account, in part, for the relationship between idiosyncratic cardiovascular reactivity and atherosclerosis. Whatever relative importance may be associated with each of these potential mechanisms, though, we are confident that future investigations—particularly those that exploit techniques for examining cellular events in the arteries of animals subjected to well-defined psychological stressors—will add substantially to our understanding of the extensiveness and nature of behavioral influences on atherogenesis.

REFERENCES

1. McGill Jr. HC: Persistent problems in the pathogenesis of atherosclerosis. *Arteriosclerosis* **4**:443–451, 1984.

2. Keys A: Coronary heart disease in seven countries. *Circulation* **41**:1970. (Suppl)

3. Strong JP, Eggen DA, Oaldmann NC: The natural history, geographic pathogenesis and epidemiology of atherosclerosis. In Wissler RW, Geer JC (eds): *The Pathogenesis of Atherosclerosis*. Baltimore, Williams & Wilkins, 1972, pp. 20–40.

4. Ross R: Atherosclerosis: A problem of the biology of arterial wall cells and their interactions with blood components. Arteriosclerosis **1**:293–311, 1981.

5. Schwartz S, Gajdusek C, Shelden S: Vascular wall growth control: The role of endothelium. Arteriosclerosis **1**:107–126, 1981.

6. McGill Jr. HC: *The Geographic Pathology of Atherosclerosis*. Baltimore, Williams & Wilkins, 1968.

7. NHLBI Working Group on Arteriosclerosis: Arteriosclerosis 1981: Report of the Working Group on Arteriosclerosis. (Vol 2). DHEW Publication NIH82 2035, 1982.

8. Neri-Senero GG, Masotti G, et al: Prostacycline thromboxane, and ischemic heart disease. *Atherosclerosis Rev* **8**:139–157, 1981.

9. Solberg LA, Enger SC, et al: Risk factors for coronary and cerebral atherosclerosis in the Oslo Study. In Gotto AM, Smith LC, Allen B (eds): *Atherosclerosis V*. New York, Springer-Verlag, 1980, pp. 67–72.

10. Ahrens EH: After 40 years of cholesterol-watching. *J Lipid Res* **25**:1442–1449, 1984.

11. McGill H, Frank M, Geer J: Aortic lesions in hypertensive monkeys. *Arch Pathol* **71**:96–102, 1961.

12. Clarkson TB, Alexander NJ: Long-term vasectomy. Effects on the occurrence and extent of atherosclerosis in rhesus monkeys. *J Clin Invest* **65**:15–25, 1980.

13. Minick C, Murphy G, Campbell W: Experimental induction of athero-arteriosclerosis by the synergy of allergic injury to arteries and lipid-rich diet: II. Effect of repeated injections of horse serum in rabbits fed a diet cholesterol supplement. *J Exp Med* **124**:635–652, 1966.

14. Troxler RG, Sprague EA, et al: The association of elevated plasma cortisol and early atherosclerosis as demonstrated by coronary angiography. *Atherosclerosis* **26**:151–162, 1977.

15. Armstrong ML, Megan MB: Arterial fibrous proteins in cynomolgus monkeys after atherogenic and regression diets. *Circ Res* **36**:256–261, 1975.

16. Kramsch DM, Hollander W: Occlusive atherosclerotic disease of the coronary arteries in monkeys (*Macaca irus*) induced by diet. *Exp Mol Path* **9**:1–22, 1968.

17. Malinow MR, McLaughlin P, et al: A model for therapeutic interventions on established coronary atherosclerosis in a nonhuman primate. *Adv Exp Bio Med* **67**:3–31, 1976.

18. Wagner WD, St. Clair RW, Clarkson TB: Angiochemical and tissue changes in *Macaca fascicularis* fed an atherogenic diet for three years. *Exp Mol Pathol* **28**:140–153, 1978.

19. Armstrong ML, Trillo A, Prichard RW: Naturally occurring and experimentally induced atherosclerosis in nonhuman primates. In Kalter SS (ed): *The Use of Nonhuman Primates in Cardiovascular Diseases.* Austin, University of Texas Press, 1980, pp. 58–101.

20. Clarkson TB: Symposium summary. In Kalter SS (ed): *The Use of Nonhuman Primates in Cardiovascular Diseases.* Austin, University of Texas Press, 1980, pp. 452–473.

21. Bond MD, Bullock BC, et al: Myocardial infarction in a large colony of nonhuman primates with coronary artery atherosclerosis. *Am J Pathol* **101**:675–692, 1980.

22. Hamm TE, Kaplan JR, et al: Effects of gender and social behavior in the development of coronary atherosclerosis on cynomolgus macaques. *Atherosclerosis* **48**:221–233, 1983.

23. Rudel LL, Pitts LL: Male-female variability in the dietary cholesterol-induced hyperlipoproteinemia of cynomolgus monkeys (*Macaca fascicularis*). *J Lipid Res* **19**:992–998, 1978.

24. Kaplan JR, Adams MR, et al: Psychosocial influences on female 'protection' among cynomolgus macaques. *Atherosclerosis* **53**:283–295, 1984.

25. Kaplan JR, Manuck SB, et al: Social status, environment, and atherosclerosis in cynomolgus monkeys. *Arteriosclerosis* **2**:359–368, 1982.

26. Kaplan JR, Manuck SB, et al: Social stress and atherosclerosis in normocholesterolemic monkeys. *Science* **220**:733–735, 1983.

27. Manuck SB, Kaplan JR, Clarkson TB: Behaviorally induced heart rate reactivity and atherosclerosis in cynomolgus monkeys. *Psychosom Med* **45**:95–108, 1983.

28. Manuck SB, Kaplan JR, Clarkson TB: Stress-induced heart rate reactivity and atherosclerosis in female macaques. *Psychosom Med* **47**:90, 1985. (Abstract)

29. Kaplan JR, Clarkson TB, Manuck SB: Pathogenesis of carotid bifurcation atherosclerosis in cynomolgus monkeys. *Stroke* **15**:994–1000, 1984.

30. Beere PA, Glagov S, Zarins CK: Retarding effect of lowered heart rate on coronary atherosclerosis. *Science* **226**:180–182, 1984.

31. Gordon D, Guyton J, Karnovsky N: Intimal alterations in rat aorta induced by stressful stimuli. *Lab Invest* **45**:14–27, 1983.

32. Hirsch EZ, Maksem JA, Gagen D: Effects of stress and propranolol on aortic intima of rats. *Arteriosclerosis* **4**:526, 1984. (Abstract)

4

Neuroendocrine Mechanisms in Coronary Heart Disease

J. Alan Herd

INTRODUCTION

The first detailed physiological studies during behavioral procedures were studies of cardiovascular and renal function. It is commonly observed that arterial blood pressure rises as part of the behavioral response to environmental stimuli, and it has been suggested that such behavioral responses might contribute to cardiovascular disease through elevations of heart rate and blood pressure. However, the hypothesis that such behavioral factors contribute to atherosclerosis is difficult to support. Indeed, it seems likely that elevations in heart rate and blood pressure merely indicate that psychological factors have relevance to cardiovascular physiology. It seems more likely that atherosclerosis would result from sustained elevations in neuroendocrine factors that are elicited by the same behavioral factors causing increases in heart rate and blood pressure (see chapter by Clarkson, Manuck, and Kaplan). It is also possible that reactivity of neuroendocrine mechanisms might occur without changes in heart rate and blood pressure. Since reactivity to environmental stimuli might involve many different physiological mechanisms, it is worthwhile to examine the potential influence of neuroendocrine reactivity on atherosclerosis and ischemic heart disease. At our present state of knowledge, the effects of neuroendocrines such as cortisol, epinephrine, and norepinephrine on insulin sensitivity might provide a link between environmental events and atherosclerosis.

NATURAL HISTORY OF CORONARY ARTERY DISEASE

Coronary heart disease is caused by inadequate blood flow through arteries supplying the muscle of the heart. Although many different mechanisms may increase myocardial requirements for blood or reduce the flow of blood through coronary arteries, the basic lesion in coronary heart disease usually is coronary atherosclerosis. Consequently, the most important pathophysiological mechanisms in coronary heart disease are those affecting atherogenesis.

Atherosclerosis is a process in which lipids are deposited in the arterial wall. Through some process not well understood, endothelial cells are lifted from the lining of the intima, and lipids gain access to the intima. In response to the altered intimal composition, vascular smooth muscle cells move into the arterial intima and proliferate.

Lipids accumulate in the smooth muscle cells and produce lipid streaks. Later, lipids, fibrous tissue, and other proteoglycan materials are deposited in the extracellular space. Chronic inflammatory cell proliferation, hemorrhage, necrosis, and calcification occur at later stages. Although lipid infiltration into the arterial wall is an important part of atherogenesis, the formation of the atheromatous plaque is initiated by the proliferation of vascular smooth muscle cells. Thus, the pathophysiological mechanisms promoting the primary proliferative process of vascular smooth muscle may be critical for the development of coronary artery disease.

There are many additional stages between the initial fatty streak in the intima and clinical manifestations of coronary heart disease. Additional mechanisms apparently involve aggregation of platelets on the surface of atheromatous plaques. These fibrous plaques also become invaded by vascular smooth muscle cells and surrounded by fibrous connective tissue covering an accumulation of lipids between cells and within cells. Any pathophysiological mechanisms that increase tendency toward platelet aggregation also contribute to the ultimate development of coronary artery disease.

As the atherosclerotic process proceeds, there are no clinical manifestations until a major coronary artery becomes obstructed by more than 50 percent. This is the amount of obstruction necessary to impair the flow of blood to myocardium under maximal demands for coronary blood flow. As the amount of obstruction increases, the possibility for platelet aggregation and thrombosis increases. In addition, aggregation of platelets formed transiently can significantly increase resistance to flow through a coronary artery in a region of obstruction. Consequently, pathophysiological mechanisms that enhance platelet aggregation may cause symptoms from myocardial ischemia. Eventually, some combination of coronary arterial spasm, atherosclerotic obstructive lesions, and platelet aggregation may precipitate complete occlusion of a major coronary artery, causing myocardial infarction or sudden cardiac death.

Since proliferation of vascular smooth muscle appears to be an important process in initiating atherosclerosis, techniques have been developed to study mechanisms stimulating proliferation of these cells. A variety of techniques have been used to obtain arterial smooth muscle cells from the aorta of human fetuses,[1] nonhuman primates,[2] and explants from the aorta of nonhuman primates maintained continuously in tissue culture.[3] These techniques provide the opportunity to study the growth and metabolism of vascular smooth muscle cells in detail.

Studies by several investigators have demonstrated that smooth muscle cells do not proliferate in culture except in the presence of blood serum.[3] Ross and Glomset[4] reported that serum lipoproteins were necessary for optimal cell growth in culture. In addition, Ross, Glomset, et al.[3] demonstrated that addition of platelets and calcium to platelet-poor plasma increased the activity of plasma serum in promoting the proliferation of arterial smooth muscle cells in culture. As shown in Figure 4.1, 5 percent dialyzed plasma serum had little or no effect on proliferation of arterial smooth muscle cells unless the serum was allowed to clot in the presence of platelets. In these experiments, equal numbers of smooth muscle cells were added to culture dishes and incubated in medium containing 1 percent serum. After seven days the dishes were separated into four groups. One group was incubated in serum-free medium. The remaining groups were incubated in medium containing 5 percent dialyzed serum from whole blood containing platelets, 5 percent dialyzed plasma serum exposed during the process to platelets, and 5 percent dialyzed plasma serum in which no platelets were present. Results demonstrated that much of the growth-promoting activity of dialyzed serum was directly or indirectly derived from platelets. These

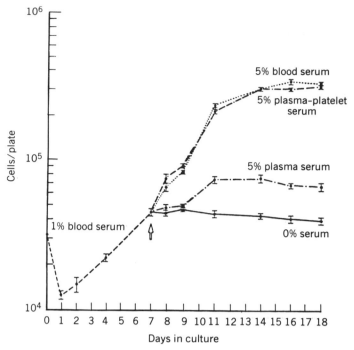

FIGURE 4.1.   Response of arterial smooth muscle in cell culture to blood serum and plasma serum. Abscissa is time in days during which cells were incubated. Ordinate is number of smooth muscle cells in each culture dish.

experiments further illustrate the importance of humoral factors in promoting proliferation of vascular smooth muscle cells.

Neurohumoral risk factors also should be considered. One factor with both clinical and epidemiologic evidence linking it to atherosclerosis is elevated levels of insulin in blood. Patients with atherosclerosis frequently have abnormalities in glucose tolerance,[5] and many have elevated insulin responses to oral glucose compared to control subjects without evidence of vascular disease.[6] In addition, elevated levels of plasma insulin increase the risk of myocardial infarction and coronary heart disease mortality in middle-aged men without overt signs of diabetes or atherosclerosis.[6] These observations suggest that insulin influences development of atherosclerosis and elevated plasma levels increase risk for coronary heart disease.

Neurohumoral risk factors provide a lead for exploring behavioral influences on coronary heart disease. Neuroendocrines, including epinephrine, norepinephrine, and cortisol, influence the interaction of insulin with several metabolic processes. Clinical and epidemiologic evidence relates plasma levels of cortisol to lipid metabolism and severity of coronary heart disease. These effects may be mediated by effects on insulin sensitivity, both through aggravating hyperlipoproteinemia and promoting the basic process of atherogenesis.[5] Thus, the behavioral and physiological influences on neuroendocrine factors that affect insulin sensitivity warrant further discussion.

Cortisol and Atherosclerosis

Corticosteroids have been reported to induce hypercholesterolemia that is related to dosage and duration of therapy. Corticosteroids administered in treatment of rheumatic diseases[7] or elevated in Cushing's syndrome[8] caused hypertriglyceridemia and hypertension. To these clinical observations can be added the evidence that elevated plasma levels of cortisol were associated with early atherosclerosis as demonstrated by coronary angiography.[9]

Troxler et al.[9] had the opportunity to study the association of plasma cortisol and coronary atherosclerosis in young male air crews of the United States Air Force. Coronary angiography was part of the clinical evaluation carried out because of medical conditions or electrocardiographic findings that could preclude flying duty. Plasma cortisol, serum cholesterol, triglycerides, percent body fat, blood pressure, age, smoking habits, and coronary angiograms were measured on 71 men. As part of this evaluation, a standard two-hour oral glucose tolerance test was administered between 8:00 A.M. and 10:00 A.M. A portion of each glucose tolerance test plasma specimen was analyzed for cortisol concentration. Coronary angiograms were scored on a scale of 0 to 6 according to amount of obstruction observed in the right and left coronary arteries. Of the subjects, 48 percent showed no evidence of coronary artery disease, 20 percent showed mild diseases, and 32 percent showed moderate to severe obstruction of the coronary arteries. Significant correlations between elevated serial morning plasma cortisol and moderate to severe coronary atherosclerosis were found. In relation to other risk factors, plasma cortisol was second only to serum cholesterol as a discriminator in that population. In addition, a high degree of correlation was found between levels of cortisol and levels of both cholesterol and triglycerides. Cortisol may have had a direct effect on cholesterol metabolism and an indirect effect on triglycerides through its influence on the interaction of insulin in lipid metabolic processes.

A relationship between cortisol and Type A behavior pattern in air crews has also been reported.[10] Physiological data were those collected as part of the study by Troxler et al.[9] and behavior pattern was assessed by the Friedman and Rosenman Structured Interview.[11] A statistically significant association was found between cortisol and cholesterol for individuals who had either minimal coronary artery disease or significant coronary artery disease but not for subjects without coronary artery disease. An association between cortisol and cholesterol was also found to be significant for the subgroup of individuals with Type A–1 behavior pattern but not for those with Type A–2, Type X, or Type B behavior patterns. The authors interpret these results as suggesting that cortisol secretion that is enhanced in Type A individuals may predispose those individuals to coronary artery disease through effects on lipid metabolism. It also is possible that cortisol influences insulin effects on metabolic processes such as lipid metabolism and promotes atherogenesis through stimulation of vascular smooth muscle.

A further evaluation of mechanisms relating cortisol and atherosclerosis was carried out in nonhuman primates.[12] Cynomolgus monkeys were divided into treatment groups consisting of (1) controlled diet, (2) hydrocortisone cypionate administered orally, (3) 0.25 percent cholesterol diet, and (4) cortisol plus cholesterol diet. Although all animals fed a high cholesterol diet developed hypercholesterolemia, cortisol had no significant effect on serum cholesterol levels in the presence of either diet. After 52 weeks the monkeys were sacrificed and the aortas examined for involvement with atherosclerotic lesions. A significant increase in the percent of aortic intimal surface involved with atherosclerosis was observed in monkeys receiving both cortisol and high cholesterol diet compared to animals receiving only the high cholesterol diet. Cortisol alone did not significantly increase lesion development compared to the control diet. The authors interpret these results as indicating cortisol enhanced the deposition of lipid in the aortas of hypercholesterolemic monkeys. Thus, these studies in an animal model indicate a possible link between behaviorally induced neurohumoral factors and atherosclerosis.

The influence of cortisol on proliferation and protein synthesis of human aortic vascular smooth muscle in cell culture also has been studied.[1] The effect of cortisol on the proliferation of cells and the synthesis of collagen was measured in cultured human aortic smooth muscle cells in the presence of various concentrations of cortisol. Although cortisol increased the synthesis of collagen and other proteins, it actually retarded vascular smooth muscle cell growth. Although abnormalities of these connective tissue macromolecules might be regarded as atherogenic, the smooth muscle cell proliferation and endothelial injury did not occur in vascular cells exposed to cortisol. Apparently, some other pathophysiological mechanism must link cortisol to atherogenesis if vascular smooth muscle cell proliferation is an important component.

Insulin and Atherosclerosis

Epidemiologic studies have demonstrated a relation between plasma insulin levels and the incidence of myocardial infarction and coronary heart disease mortality in middle-aged men.[13] Ducimetier, Eschwege, et al. mea-

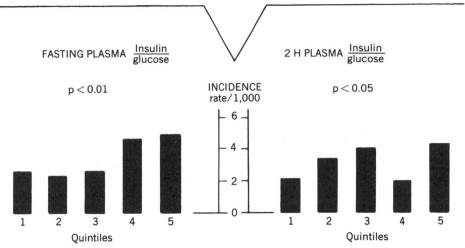

FIGURE 4.2.   Mean annual incidence of coronary heart disease complications according to quintiles of ratios for insulin concentration to glucose concentration in plasma during fasting and two hours after an oral glucose load. From "Relationship of plasma insulin levels to the incidence of myocardial infarction and coronary heart disease mortality in a middle-aged population," by P. Ducimeter, E. Papoz, et al. in *Diabetologia 19*:205–210, 1980. Used with permission.

sured serum cholesterol, serum triglycerides, systolic blood pressure, body weight, and height and also recorded history of cigarette smoking. In addition, they measured plasma glucose and plasma insulin levels before and two hours after a 75 g oral glucose load. The population was 7246 nondiabetic working men aged 43–54 years who were initially free from heart disease and were followed 63 months on the average. As shown in Figure 4.2, they demonstrated that the fasting plasma insulin level and the fasting insulin–glucose ratio were positively associated with risk for myocardial infarction and coronary heart disease mortality, independent of all the other factors. They concluded that high insulin levels constitute an independent risk factor for coronary heart disease complications in middle-aged nondiabetic men.

Stout has reviewed the scientific literature concerning relationship of abnormal circulating insulin levels and atherosclerosis.[14,15] He reviewed the evidence that hyperinsulinemia occurs in patients with arteriosclerosis and is a risk factor for those without clinical manifestations. The high insulin levels associated with obesity, hypertriglyceridemia, and diabetes mellitus of adult onset may be a cause for atherosclerosis in some of those individuals. In addition, he reviewed the evidence that insulin results in proliferation of vascular smooth muscle cells, inhibition of lipolysis, and synthesis of cholesterol, phospholipids, and triglycerides. These effects of insulin might promote atherogenesis. Consequently, the combination of clinical and experimental evidence suggests that high levels of circulating insulin may have a role in the development of atherosclerosis.

A combination of elevated cortisol secretion, hyperinsulinemia, and hypertriglyceridemia may create a vicious cycle with atherogenic potential. Steiner and Vranic[16] reviewed the evidence that hypertriglyceridemia can interfere with metabolic processes involving insulin even without concomitant obesity or diabetes mellitus of adult-onset type. They concluded that hyperinsulinemia can stimulate triglyceride-containing lipids with atherogenic potential, and the combination constitutes a vicious cycle. Insulin apparently has direct effects on vascular smooth muscle proliferation, and triglyceride-containing lipids with atherogenic potential would hasten the process of atherosclerosis. Elevated secretion of cortisol may influence the metabolic response to insulin.

Vascular smooth muscle cells have been studied for effects of insulin on proliferation in cell cultures.[2] Stout et al. compared the growth of cells in culture medium to which insulin had been added in combination with serum. There was a significant linear relationship between the logarithm of the insulin dose and cell growth. In addition, vascular smooth muscle cells showed a diminished response to serum when insulin was extracted from it. However, the highest concentration of insulin produced only 50 percent of the effect observed following incubation in 5 percent serum. Results of these experiments suggest that insulin had growth-promoting properties but that it was not the only growth-promoting factor in serum. Both lipoproteins[4] and platelets[3] also may have the potential of stimulating proliferation of vascular smooth muscle cells.

Metabolic Effects of Cortisol and Epinephrine

It has been known for some time that glucocorticoid excess prolongs the removal of glucose during a glucose tolerance test in normal humans.[17] Also, hypersecretion of adrenal cortical hormones in Cushing's disease has a diabetogenic effect. However, the mechanism whereby glucocorticoids may influence removal of glucose from blood is poorly understood. Shamoon et al.[18] examined the influence of cortisol on glucose metabolism during continuous infusion of cortisol during a period of five hours. Normal adult men and women were studied after consuming a standard carbohydrate diet and fasting overnight before observations were made. The effect of cortisol infusion on plasma glucose and glucose kinetics in the normal human subjects is illustrated in Figure 4.3. Infusion of cortisol increased levels of glucose in plasma without influencing rates of glucose production. Removal of glucose from blood was reduced, which resulted in cortisol-induced

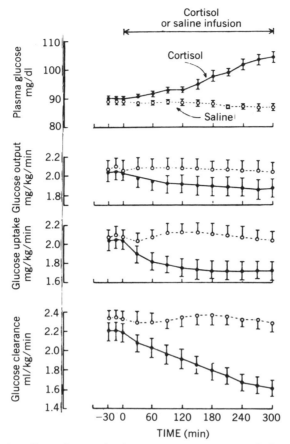

FIGURE 4.3. The effect of cortisol infusion on concentrations of glucose in plasma and glucose kinetics in normal human subjects. Abscissa is time in minutes before and during intravenous infusion of cortisol or saline solution. Ordinate of the upper panel is glucose concentration in plasma (mg/dl), of the second panel is glucose output (mg/kg/min), of the third panel is glucose uptake (mg/kg/min), and in the bottom panel, the ordinate is glucose clearance (ml/kg/min). From "The influence of acute physiological increments of cortisol on fuel metabolism and insulin binding to monocytes in normal humans," by H. Shamoon, V. Soman, and R. Sherwin. *Journal of Clinical Endocrinology and Metabolism* 50:294–297. Copyright © 1980. Reprinted with permission of the Endocrine Society.

hyperglycemia. These effects of cortisol on glucose metabolism occurred in the absence of significant changes in plasma insulin or glucagon concentrations. Concomitant effects on fatty acid and amino acid metabolism suggested that cortisol interfered with the cellular action of insulin.

Similar studies of epinephrine also have been performed in human subjects. Soman et al.[19] studied effects of epinephrine infused intravenously into normal young men and women during a period of four hours. They reported a prompt 45 percent rise in glucose output and a 120 percent rise in free fatty acid levels, both of which declined to basal levels within 90 minutes. No significant effect on plasma insulin or glucagon levels was observed. Rate of removal for glucose from plasma decreased by 25 percent and remained suppressed throughout the four-hour experiment. The authors concluded that epinephrine had a persistent effect in decreasing removal of glucose but only transiently increased the output of glucose and free fatty acids. No effect of epinephrine infusion on beta-adrenergic binding to lymphocytes was observed. Although no direct measurements of insulin activity were made, results of these experiments are compatible with an interference by epinephrine in the influence of insulin on metabolic processes associated with glucose and lipid metabolism.

Further studies of the effects of epinephrine on lipid metabolism were reported by Dimsdale et al.[20] These investigators produced physiological elevations of plasma epinephrine levels in cynomolgus monkeys. A suspension of epinephrine was injected subcutaneously twice each day, producing increases in epinephrine levels for approximately six hours each day. During the two-week period of study, the diets remained constant, and no change in animal weight was observed. After two weeks, the cholesterol levels in plasma increased on the average of 15 mg/dl. Four animals also studied during treatment with saline injections showed no increase in plasma cholesterol levels. Although no studies of the mechanism for increase in cholesterol were performed, results are consistent with a stimulation of lipid metabolism caused by reduced influence of insulin on glucose and lipid metabolism.

Behavioral Influences on Cortisol and Epinephrines

Many investigators have studied behavioral influences on neuroendocrine processes. In general, behavioral factors have been shown to influence secretion of cortisol, epinephrine, and norepinephrine. Although the psychological characteristics of experimental conditions used to test behavioral influences are not well defined, some general characteristics of situations influencing secretion of cortisol and epinephrine can be stated. (See also chapter by Krantz, Manuck, and Wing.)

One characteristic of situations provoking increased secretion of cortisol is novelty of an experimental situation. Davis et al.[21] tested normal young men under a graded exercise tolerance test procedure. One group of subjects was experienced with exercise testing, and the other group had no previous experience with the procedure. The subjects in both groups had similar capacities for physical work. No significant relationship could be demonstrated between maximal oxygen uptake, venous lactate concentrations, Borg ratings of perceived exertion, or serum cortisol responses during exercise. However, the postexercise increase in serum cortisol levels was greater in the naive subjects. Serum cortisol increased 59 percent in the experienced subjects and 138 percent in the naive subjects. The authors concluded that novelty was the major determinant in the increased cortisol response in naive subjects compared to experienced subjects. Furthermore, this cortisol response bore little relationship to maximal oxygen uptake, heart rate, or venous lactate concentrations. Apparently, the magnitude of response observed in cortisol concentrations was influenced more by psychological factors than by the physiological effects of exercise.

The adaptation of response to physiological factors such as novelty or fear of failure also has been studied. Ursin et al. edited a monograph concerning the process of coping in young men under training in the Norwegian Army Parachute School.[22] The authors postulated that adaptation would be a crucial dimension for coping with fear and amelioration of physiological responses. All men were asked to fill a self-rating of fear before and after each jump from a mock tower used in the early stages of training for parachute jumping. Figure 4.4 shows the self-rating of fear reported by men who went through tower training. As can be seen in this figure, there was a gradual reduction in fear levels reported. At the time of

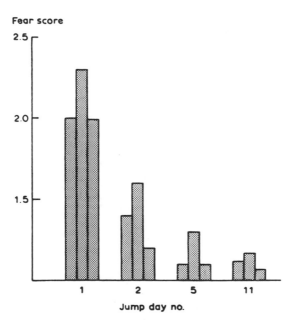

FIGURE 4.4. Self-rating of fear reported by men who went through tower training for parachute jumping. Data are presented for four different jump days. On each day, average scores were determined at the bottom of the tower, just before jumping, and just after the jump. From *Psychobiology of Stress: A Study of Coping Men*, by H. Ursin, E. Baade, and S. Levine (eds.), Orlando FL, Academic. Copyright © 1978. Reprinted with permission.

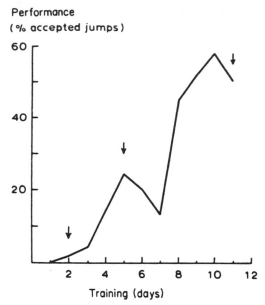

FIGURE 4.5. Performance in the training tower for each day with percentage of accepted jumps for the whole group (criteria for acceptable jumps were changed on day 5 and day 11). Abscissa is time of training in days. Ordinate is percentage of accepted jumps. Arrows indicate sampling days. From *Psychobiology of Stress: A Study of Coping Men*, by H. Ursin, E. Baade, and S. Levine (eds.), Orlando, FL, Academic. Copyright © 1978. Reprinted with permission.

each jump from the mock tower, instructors kept records of the jumps and rated each jump as accepted or not accepted. Figure 4.5 indicates the percentage of jumps that were accepted in the whole group on each training day. As training proceeded, a few more criteria were added in the evaluation of each jump; the irregularities in the curve reflect these changes in criteria for accepted jumps.

Plasma levels of cortisol also were obtained during repeated experiences with parachute training. For each jump day, two samples of blood were obtained, one immediately after the jump and one 20 minutes later. Figure 4.6 shows plasma levels of cortisol for several successive jump days. Values obtained immediately after the jumps showed a highly significant change on successive days, and there was a significant fall from day to day until the third sample day when the levels seemed to plateau. Similar results were reported for blood levels of glucose and free fatty acids. Measurements of epinephrine and norepinephrine in urine demonstrated increased levels during the first jump day with a return to basal levels at the time of the third sample day, that is, jump day five. The authors interpreted these results as demonstrating that improved performances and reduction of fear reduced the magnitude of physiological responses during parachute training.

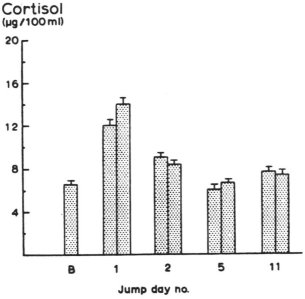

Cortisol
(μg/100ml)

FIGURE 4.6.   Plasma levels of cortisol. The abscissa indicates the number of each jump day and B represents data obtained before training began. Ordinate represents cortisol concentrations in plasma (μg/100ml). On each jump day, two samples of blood were obtained, one immediately after the jump and one 20 minutes later. From *Psychobiology of Stress: A Study of Coping Men*, by H. Ursin, E. Baade, and S. Levine, (eds.), Orlando, FL, Academic. Copyright © 1978. Reprinted with permission.

Another psychological characteristic of test situations is mental task demand and efforts to cope with those demands. Brandenberger, Follenius, et al.[23] measured plasma levels of catecholamines and pituitary adrenal hormones in normal healthy male college students while they performed a short-term memory task under quiet or noise conditions. As shown in Figure 4.7, performing the task led to significant increases in the plasma levels of cortisol. Similarly, there were significant increases in plasma levels of epinephrine and norepinephrine. Cortisol responses in all subjects were greater during the first experimental session than during the second session. Exposure to noise did slightly amplify the cortisol response to the task but had little effect on the plasma levels of epinephrine and norepinephrine. In addition, a significant correlation was found between individual plasma cortisol increments and error rates assessed from an accuracy-of-recall variable. As shown in Figure 4.8, the relation between individual errors and plasma cortisol increases was demonstrated. Although a relation between errors and plasma cortisol persisted in the second session, the increments in plasma cortisol were greatest during the first experimental session. The authors interpreted these results as demonstrating a relationship between sympathoadrenomedullary activity and intentional demand with an addi-

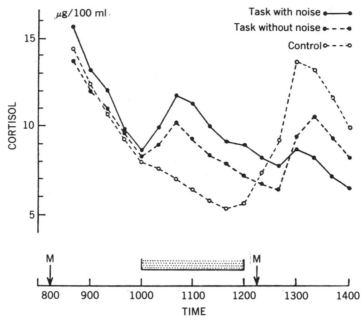

FIGURE 4.7.   Mean plasma cortisol response to task performed either in noise or in quiet conditions, in eight subjects. *M* represents meal intake. From "Plasma catecholamines and pituitary adrenal hormones related to mental task demand under quiet and noise conditions," by G. Brandenberger, M. Follenius, et al. in *Biological Psychology 10*:239–252. Copyright © 1980. Reprinted with permission of North-Holland Publishing.

tional relationship between adrenocortical activity and success in coping with the mental task.

Behavioral influence on catecholamine responses to test situations can be further defined according to differential responses of epinephrine and norepinephrine. Psychological factors have a greater effect on epinephrine responses than in norepinephrine responses, whereas physical factors have a greater effect on norepinephrine responses. LeBlanc, Cote, et al.[24] measured plasma epinephrine and norepinephrine levels as well as blood pressure and heart rate in 12 normal young men. They were studied before, during, and after a cold hand test, a mental arithmetic test, and a combination of both of these tests. Results of these experiments are shown in Figures 4.9, 4.10 and 4.11. As shown in Figure 4.9, systolic blood pressure increased during immersion of one hand in cold water, during the mental arithmetic test, and when both tests were given simultaneously. No significant difference in systolic blood pressure response was seen during any of these trials. In contrast, the response of plasma epinephrine was substantially greater during the mental arithmetic test than during the cold hand test. As shown in Figure 4.10, plasma epinephrine increased during the mental arithmetic

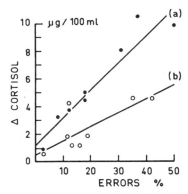

FIGURE 4.8.   Relation between errors and omissions during task performance and increases in concentration of cortisol in plasma. Abscissa is number of errors and omissions committed by each individual expressed as a percentage of all responses. Ordinate is change in concentration of cortisol during each subject's first experimental session and the open circles (o) represent results obtained during each subject's second experimental session. A significant reduction in the slope of data pertaining to the second session was found whether the task was performed in noise or in quiet. From "Plasma catecholamines and pituitary adrenal hormones related to mental task demand under quiet and noise conditions," by G. Brandenberger, M. Folenius, et al. in *Biological Psychology* 10:234–252. Copyright © 1980. Reprinted with permission of North-Holland Publishing.

test and when both tests were given simultaneously but showed little increase during immersion of one hand in cold water. A third pattern of response was observed in levels of plasma norepinephrine. As shown in Figure 4.11, plasma norepinephrine increased during immersion of one hand in cold water, during the mental arithmetic test, and when both tests were given simultaneously. In contrast to the pattern observed with systolic blood pressure and plasma epinephrine levels, plasma levels of norepinephrine remained elevated for at least 10 minutes after beginning each trial, whereas levels of systolic blood pressure and plasma epinephrine had returned to basal levels within the same period of time. Thus, responses of systolic blood pressure and plasma levels of norepinephrine were similar during trials involving either psychological or physical factors. In contrast, response of plasma epinephrine was greater during mental arithmetic than during immersion of one hand in cold water. Apparently, elevations in plasma levels of epinephrine reflect physiological response to psychological factors.

Additional influences of psychological factors on neuroendocrine secretion have been demonstrated in studies of plasma renin activity. Januszewicz, Szanjderman, et al.[25] studied normal men and men with essential hypertension who were hospitalized and maintained on a standard hospital diet with normal sodium intake. Both groups were studied during a mental arithmetic

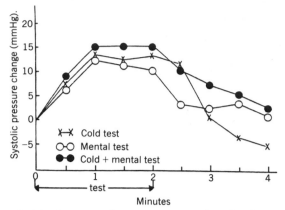

FIGURE 4.9.   Systolic blood pressure during immersion of one hand in cold water (5 °C for two minutes), during a mental arithmetic test (lasting two minutes), and when both tests were given simultaneously. Abscissa is time in minutes with the test administered during the first two minutes. Ordinate is systolic blood pressure change (mmHg). From "Plasma catecholamines and cardiovascular responses to cold and mental activity" by J. LeBlanc, J. Cote, et al. in *Journal of Applied Physiology 47*:1207–1211. Copyright © 1979. Reprinted with permission of the American Physiological Society.

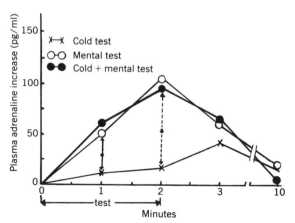

FIGURE 4.10.   Concentration of epinephrine in plasma during immersion of one hand in cold water (5 °C for two minutes), during a mental arithmetic test (lasting two minutes), and when both tests were given simultaneously. Abscissa is the same as described in Figure 4.9. Ordinate is change in plasma epinephrine (adrenaline) (pg/ml). From "Plasma catecholamines and cardiovascular responses to cold and mental activity," by J. LeBlanc, J. Cote, et al. In *Journal of Applied Physiology 47*:1207–1211. Copyright © 1979. Reprinted with permission of the American Physiological Society.

test combined with noise. Concentrations of plasma and urine catecholamines and their metabolites as well as plasma renin activity before and after the test were measured. Measurements of plasma demonstrated significant

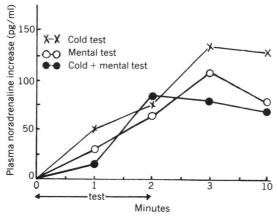

FIGURE 4.11.   Concentrations of norepinephrine in plasma during immersion of one hand in cold water (5 °C for two minutes), during a mental arithmetic test (lasting two minutes), and when both tests were given simultaneously. Abscissa is the same as described in Figure 4.9. Ordinate is increase in concentration of norephinephrine (noradrenaline) (pg/ml). From "Plasma catecholamines and cardiovascular responses to cold and mental activity," by J. LeBlanc, J. Cote, et al. in *Journal of Applied Physiology* 47:1207–1211. Copyright © 1979. Reprinted with permission of The American Physiological Society.

increases in epinephrine, norepinephrine, and plasma renin activity after mental arithmetic. These investigators did not find any substantial differences in the response of catecholamines between hypertensive and normotensive subjects. Elevations in plasma renin activity after mental arithmetic actually was greater in normal subjects than in those with hypertension. Thus, although the authors were not able to detect substantial differences between responses of normal subjects and patients with essential hypertension, they were able to demonstrate a substantial effect of psychological factors on plasma renin activity as well as plasma levels of epinephrine and norepinephrine.

The effects of psychological factors on healthy individuals over longer periods of time than those in the investigations cited above also have been studied. Although many experiments conducted under laboratory conditions suggest a rapid adaptation of physiological responses to psychological factors, observations of normal subjects in natural situations indicate that chronic exposure to psychological factors may have enduring effects on neuroendocrine processes. Timio and Gentili[26] and Timio et al.[27] have studied the neuroendocrine responses in industrial workers under different working conditions. In one set of experiments,[26] serial measurements of urinary epinephrine, norepinephrine, and 11-hydroxycorticosteroid excretion were performed on men during four days of work under a payment-by-results schedule of compensation and during four days of similar work compensated under a fixed-salary schedule. Compared to working under a fixed-salary schedule, subjects showed an increase in mean daily urinary excretion of epinephrine, norepinephrine, and 11-hydroxycorticosteroids when working on a payments-by-results schedule. Similar experiments with another group of workers showed that men had higher levels of urinary epinephrine, norepinephrine, and 11-hydroxycorticosteroids while working on an assembly line than when working outside of the assembly line. The authors interpreted these results as indicating that psychosocial factors common to normal activities have significant effects on neuroendocrine function.

Persistence of behavioral influences on neuroendocrine processes was demonstrated by Timio et al.[27] in studies of similar groups of workers under payment-by-results, fixed daily wage, assembly-line conditions, and ordinary work conditions off the assembly line. Working under alternating schedules consisting of four-day periods in each work condition did not ameliorate the pattern of greater neuroendocrine responses observed during payment-by-results and assembly-line conditions. The authors interpreted results of their experiments as indicating that industrial workers experienced enhanced neuroendocrine responses to psychosocial factors during normal working conditions that also persisted for long periods of time.

Improving Insulin Action on Metabolic Processes

Conditions that reduce the effectiveness of insulin on metabolic processes increase insulin resistance. When insulin resistance was first defined, it was measured by determining the rate of insulin-glucose uptake in patients with non-insulin-dependent diabetes mellitus or patients with severe obesity. The inference that insulin action was reduced was obtained by measuring the effects of insulin injected intravenously on levels of glucose in plasma or by combining administration of glucose and insulin intravenously and measuring plasma glucose concentrations during the next 60 minutes.[28] More recently, the mechanism and significance of insulin resistance has been studied from the perspective of receptor physiology.[29] Insulin, like many other hormones, binds to specific receptors located on the surfaces of cells. Consequently, the number of receptors on target cells as well as the affinity of receptors for insulin determine the influence of insulin on metabolic processes. Direct measurements of insulin receptors on target tissues in several disease states indicate that decreased receptor concentration and affinity are responsible for insulin resistance.[30,31] Also, the number of insulin receptors on tissues removed from patients with several diseases correlated inversely with the concentration of insulin present in plasma of those patients.[32] Many modulators of receptor concentration or affinity have been reported; these include diet, exercise, hormones, and metabolic factors.[33-35]

Ultimately, an important manifestation of insulin resistance is elevated levels of glucose in plasma, higher levels than would be expected in proportion to concentrations of insulin in plasma. A useful indicator of the average blood sugar concentration in an individual over a period of several weeks is the concentration of hemoglobin A1c. This form of hemoglobin is present in red blood cells of normal subjects in a proportion of up to five percent of the total concentration of hemoglobin. In patients with diabetes mellitus and elevated plasma levels of glucose, concentrations of hemoglobin A1c may rise to 15 percent. Because hemoglobin synthesis is a slow and nearly irreversible reaction in red blood cells, the level of hemoglobin A1c reflects concentrations of glucose at the time the red blood cell was formed. Because red blood cells remain in the circulation for approximately 120 days, it takes several weeks for the concentration of hemoglobin A1c to reflect abrupt changes in levels of glucose in blood. Thus, measurement of hemoglobin A1c gives an objective assessment of the average concentration of glucose over long periods of time.[36]

A relationship between hemoglobin A1c, concentration of lipoproteins in plasma, and administration of insulin in patients with adult-onset diabetes has demonstrated a relationship between diabetic control and lipoprotein profile. Schmitt, Poole, et al.[37] found that levels of cholesterol in serum of diabetic patients under poor control were substantially reduced when these patients were treated with insulin. The reduction of cholesterol paralleled the reduction in hemoglobin A1c concentrations. Levels of triglycerides in serum also were markedly reduced following treatment with insulin. Results of these experiments indicate not only the influence of insulin on lipid metabolism but also the value of measuring hemoglobin A1c in assessing average levels of glucose in plasma over long periods of time.

Another approach to studies of insulin resistance has been shown by Bar, Gorden, et al.[38] who measured the concentration of insulin receptors on monocytes. A deficiency of receptors was observed that was inversely related to the basal insulin level, and diet was effective in restoring insulin binding towards normal values. Similar studies in obese subjects[39] demonstrated that insulin receptor deficiency contributed to insulin resistance in obese subjects. Apparently, measurements of receptor concentration and affinity provide an index of average concentrations of insulin in blood. However, studies of receptor physiology indicate they have a half-life that can be measured in hours. Apparently, measurements of receptor concentration and affinity would not provide information about average concentrations of insulin over durations of several days or weeks.

Improving insulin sensitivity can be achieved through several therapeutic measures. The effect of physical training on insulin production in obesity has been demonstrated by Bjorntorp, DeJounge, et al.[40] These investigators studied obese patients during a physical training program that increased maximal oxygen uptake and increased muscle strength. Body weight actually increased during the training program. A normal glucose tolerance test performed before and after the training program showed no change in blood glucose values. However, there was a substantial reduction in the concentrations of insulin in plasma following administration of glucose. The authors interpreted results of these studies as indicating an increased insulin sensitivity of tissues. Since body fat mass was not decreased, the effect of physical training on insulin sensitivity apparently occurred independently of any change of adipose tissue function.

The observation that nondiabetic obese individuals had high circulating levels of insulin[41,42] suggests a resistance to action of insulin. Studies of animal models of obesity indicate that reduction in fat mass through diet corrects the insulin resistance.[43]

SUMMARY AND CONCLUSIONS

Plasma levels of cortisol are related to lipid metabolism and their effects on lipid metabolism may be mediated by effects on insulin sensitivity, causing hyperinsulinemia. High circulating levels of insulin would be expected to promote atherogenesis by direct effects on vascular smooth muscle proliferation and by elevating circulating levels of triglycerides and low-density lipoproteins. Evaluation of this link between behavioral factors and atherogenesis might be aided by measurements of hemoglobin A1c, measurements of insulin receptor concentration and affinity in red blood cells and monocytes, and the measurement of insulin-to-glucose ratios in plasma.

The behavioral influences on neuroendocrine factors apparently involve specific psychological factors. In particular, new situations and tasks that exceed perception of self-competence or elicit intense, sustained efforts to cope enhance neuroendocrine responses. However, further research is necessary to determine the psychological characteristics of situations eliciting exaggerated neuroendocrine responses.

Corrective measures include physiological and behavioral approaches. The physiological influences of physical inactivity and obesity can be overcome by the appropriate corrective measures. The behavioral influences of Type A behavior pattern, psychosocial factors, and conditioning might best be corrected by cognitive restructuring, relaxation training, and, where necessary, isolation of individuals from provocative situations.

REFERENCES

1. Jarvelainen H, Halme T, Ronnemaa T: Effect of cortisol on the proliferation and protein synthesis of human aortic smooth muscle cells in culture. *Acta Med Scand* **660**:114–122, 1982. (Suppl)

2. Stout R, Bierman E, Russell R: Effect of insulin on the proliferation of cultured primate arterial smooth muscle cells. *Circ Res* **36**:319–327, 1975.

3. Ross R, Glomset J, et al: A platelet-dependent serum factor that stimulates the proliferation of arterial smooth muscle cells *in vitro*. *Proc Natl Acad Sci USA* **71**:1207–1210, 1974.

4. Ross R, Glomset J: Atherosclerosis and the arterial smooth muscle cell. *Science* **180**:1332–1339, 1973.

5. Stout R, Bierman E, Brunzell J: Atherosclerosis and disorders of lipid metabolism in diabetes. In Vallance-Owen J (ed): *Diabetes: Its Physiological and Biochemical Basis*. Lancaster, MTP Press, 1975, pp. 125–169.

6. Stout R: The role of insulin in atherosclerosis in diabetics and nondiabetics. A review. *Diabetes* **30**:54–57, 1981. (Suppl 2)

7. Stern M, Kolterman O, et al: Adrenocortical steroid treatment of rheumatic diseases— Effects on lipid metabolism. *Arch Intern Med* **132**:97–101, 1973.

8. Krakoff L, Nicholis G, Amsel B: Pathogenesis of hypertension in Cushing's syndrome. *Am J Med* **58**:216–220, 1975.

9. Troxler R, Sprague E, et al: The association of elevated plasma cortisol and early atherosclerosis as demonstrated by coronary angiography. *Atherosclerosis* **26**:151–162, 1977.

10. Schwertner H, Troxler R, et al: Relationship between cortisol and cholesterol in men with coronary artery disease and Type A behavior. *Atherosclerosis* **4**:59–64, 1984.

11. Rosenman R: The interview method of assessment of the coronary-prone behavior pattern. In Dembroski T, Weiss S, Shields J, Haynes S, Feinleib M (eds): *Coronary-Prone Behavior*. New York, Springer-Verlag, 1978, pp. 55–70.

12. Sprague E, Troxler R, et al: Effect of cortisol on the development of atherosclerosis in cynomolgus monkeys. In Kalter S (ed): *The Use of Nonhuman Primates in Cardiovascular Diseases*. Austin, University of Texas Press, 1980, pp. 261–264.

13. Ducimetiere P, Eschwege E, et al: Relationship of plasma insulin levels to the incidence of myocardial infarction and coronary heart disease mortality in a middle-aged population. *Diabetologia* **19**:205–210, 1980.

14. Stout R: The relationship of abnormal circulating insulin levels to atherosclerosis. *Atherosclerosis* **27**:1–13, 1977.

15. Stout R: Hyperinsulinaemia as an independent risk factor for atherosclerosis. *Int J Obes* **6**:111–115, 1982. (Suppl 1)

16. Steiner G, Vranic M: Hyperinsulinemia and hypertriglyceridemia, a vicious cycle with atherogenic potential. *Int J Obes* **6**:117–124, 1982. (Suppl 1)

17. Fajans S, Conn J: An approach to the prediction of diabetes mellitus by modification of the glucose tolerance test with cortisone. *Diabetes* **3**:296–304, 1954.

18. Shamoon H, Soman V, Sherwin R: The influence of acute physiological increments of cortisol on fuel metabolism and insulin binding to monocytes in normal humans. *J Clin Endocrinol Metab* **50**:495–501, 1980.

19. Soman V, Shamoon H, Sherwin R: Effects of physiological infusion of epinephrine in normal humans: Relationship between the metabolic response and B-adrenergic binding. *J Clin Endocrinol Metab* **50**:294–297, 1980.

20. Dimsdale J, Herd J, Hartley L: Epinephrine mediated increases in plasma cholesterol. *Psychosom Med* **45**:227–232, 1983.

21. Davis H, Gass G, Bassett J: Serum cortisol response to incremental work in experienced and naive subjects. *Psychosom Med* **43**:127–132, 1981.

22. Ursin H, Baade E, Levine S (eds): *Psychobiology of Stress. A Study of Coping Men*. New York. Academic Press, 1978.

23. Brandenberger G, Follenius M, et al: Plasma catecholamines and pituitary adrenal hormones related to mental task demand under quiet and noise conditions. *Biol Psychol* **10**:239–252, 1980.

24. LeBlanc J, Cote J, et al: Plasma catecholamines and cardiovascular responses to cold and mental activity. *J Appl Physiol* **42**:1207–1211, 1979.

25. Januszewicz W, Sznajderman M, et al: The effect of mental stress on catecholamines, their metabolites and plasma renin activity in patients with essential hypertension and in healthy subjects. *Clin Sci* **57**:229s–231s, 1979.

26. Timio M, Gentili S: Adrenosympathetic overactivity under conditions of work stress. *Br J Prev Soc Med* **30**:262–265, 1976.

27. Timio M, Gentili S, Pede S: Free adrenaline and noradrenaline excretion related to occupational stress. *Br Heart J* **42**:471–474, 1979.

28. Reaven GM: Insulin resistance in noninsulin-dependent diabetes mellitus. Does it exist and can it be measured? *Am J Med* 3–17, January 17, 1983. (Suppl)

29. Flier JS: Insulin receptors and insulin resistance. *Ann Rev Med* **34**:145–160, 1983.

30. Roth J, Kahn C, et al: Receptors for insulin, NSILAS, and growth hormone: Applications to disease states in man. *Recent Prog Horm Res* **31**:95–139, 1975.

31. Flier J, Kahn C, Roth J: Receptors, antireceptor antibodies, and mechanisms of insulin resistance. *N Engl J Med* **300**:413–419, 1979.

32. Bar R, Harrison L, Muggeo M: Regulation of insulin receptors in normal and abnormal physiology in humans. *Adv Intern Med* **24**:23–52, 1979.

33. Muggeo M, Bar R, Roth J: Change in affinity of insulin receptors following oral glucose in normal subjects. *J Clin Endocrinol Metab* **44**:1206–1209, 1977.

34. Thomopoulos P, Kosmakos F, et al: Cyclic AMP increases the concentration of insulin receptors in cultured fibroblasts and lymphocytes. *Biochem Biophys Res Comm* **75**:246–252, 1977.

35. Merimee T, Pulkkinen A, Loften S: Increased insulin binding by lymphocyte receptors induced by BOH butyrate. *J Clin Endocrinol Metab* **43**:1190–1192, 1976.

36. Koenig R, Cerami A: Hemoglobin A_{Ic} and diabetes mellitus. *Ann Rev Med* **31**:29–34, 1980.

37. Schmitt J, Poole J, et al: Hemoglobin A_1 correlates with the ratio of low-to-high-density-lipoprotein cholesterol in normal weight Type II diabetes. *Metabolism* **31**:1084–1089, 1982.

38. Bar R, Gorden P, et al: Fluctuations in the affinity and concentration of insulin receptors on circulating monocytes of obese patients. *J Clin Invest* **58**:1123–1135, 1976.

39. Kolterman O, Insel J, et al: Mechanism of insulin resistance in human obesity: Evidence for receptor and postreceptor defects. *J Clin Invest* **65**:1273–1284, 1980.

40. Bjorntorp P, DeJounge K, et al: The effect of physical training on insulin production in obesity. *Metabolism* **19**:631–638, 1970.

41. Karam J, Grodsky G, Forsham P: Excessive insulin response to glucose in obese subjects as measured by immunochemical assay. *Diabetes* **12**:197–204, 1963.

42. Bagdade J, Bierman E, Porte D: The significances of basal insulin levels in the evaluation of the insulin response to glucose in the diabetic and nondiabetic subjects. *J Clin Invest* **46**:1549–1557, 1967.

43. Kahn C, Neville D, Roth J: Insulin receptor interaction in the obese-hyperglycemic mouse. *J Biol Chem* **248**:244–250, 1973.

5

Does Behaviorally Induced Blood Pressure Variability Lead to Hypertension?

STEVO JULIUS, ALAN B. WEDER,
ALAN L. HINDERLITER

Multiple lines of evidence indicate that in a subset of patients with juvenile borderline hypertension, the hypertension may be behaviorally induced; that is, it may result from an abnormal central processing of environmental stimuli. The hemodynamic hallmark of these patients, the hyperkinetic state, is fully neurogenic[1] since all its manifestations can be abolished by pharmacologic blockade of the autonomic nervous system. The hyperkinetic state emanates from a disorder of the central rather than the peripheral nervous system: sympathetic and parasympathetic activities are reciprocally altered; that is, more sympathetic drive is associated with less vagal inhibition.[2] Such reciprocal change suggests a disordering of the function of higher cardiovascular integrative centers, and it is therefore likely that neurogenic borderline hypertension is a state of abnormal central integration of autonomic cardiovascular control.

A number of mechanisms could lead to changes in central integration. In theory, abnormal arterial baroreceptors could decrease afferent inhibition of the medullary cardiovascular centers. However, we were unable to find such an abnormality in our material.[3] Others[4] have reported altered baroreceptor function in borderline hypertension, but their patients had higher blood pressures than ours, and it is accepted that even within the range of borderline hypertension, those with lower blood pressures have normal baroreceptor function.[5] Thus, altered baroreceptor function is likely to be the consequence rather than the cause of hypertension.

A second possible mechanism capable of altering central integration is modulation of medullary function by pathways descending from the cortex and paleocortex. Direct stimulation of rostral sites, such as Hilton has shown for the defense area, can profoundly alter the discharge from the medulla.[6] Evidence that abnormal behavior or abnormal behavioral responses may be involved in the pathogenesis of the abnormal cardiovascular control of borderline hypertension is on the whole convincing. Patients with borderline hypertension repeatedly describe themselves as submissive[7–9] and prone to suppress anger.[7] Furthermore, such patients show excessive blood pressure responses to behavioral stimuli administered in the laboratory, such as mental arithmetic[10,11] or color–word interference testing.[12]

However, a number of questions must be resolved before such observations can explain the pathophysiology of established hypertension, which, based on our present understanding of the natural history of the disease[13] and on accepted clinical practice,[14] is defined in this chapter as a progressive, self-accelerating disease; if established hypertension is untreated, blood pressure increases inexorably and cardiovascular damage results. Borderline hypertension is generally held to antedate established hypertension, but as will be shown, individuals with borderline elevations—that is, those whose blood pressure fluctuates above and below the arbitrary limits used to define the upper boundary of normotension, have heterogeneous clinical outcomes. This chapter explicates some of the problems inherent in attempts to link altered behavior to the progression of some borderline hypertensives to sustained (established) hypertension.

Does Neurogenic Borderline Hypertension Lead to Established Hypertension?

Borderline hypertension is not a uniformly progressive disease. Although the risk for future established hypertension among borderlines is increased,[15,16] that risk is not overwhelming; the majority of such patients *will not* develop hypertension. Recently it was shown that even many patients who on clinical screening have mild to moderate hypertension later regress into the normotensive range.[17] The question, therefore, is whether or not a subset of borderline hypertensives, in particular those with "neurogenic" characteristics as evidenced by a hyperkinetic circulation, high catecholamines, and elevated renin values,[8] are particularly prone to develop future hypertension.

An analysis of the literature on catecholamines in hypertension does not support the importance of neurogenic borderline hypertension as a risk for future established hypertension. An elevation of plasma catecholamines can be found in young hyperkinetic hypertensive subjects, but the inability to find middle-aged or older patients with established hypertension[18] whose plasma catecholamines are similarly elevated is puzzling. Possible explanations include: (1) that the neurogenic juvenile hypertensives are a small group of the total population of patients who ultimately develop established hypertension, so that later, as "true" essential hypertension becomes more prevalent, it is difficult to detect the "neurogenic" subset; (2) that an age-related increase of plasma norepinephrine in normotensive individuals[19] obscures the differences, or (3) that as sensitivity to pressor effects of catecholamines increases in the course of hypertension,[19] less central tone is needed to maintain the same blood pressure elevation. In the last case, it is, however, difficult to visualize a mechanism responsible for such a resetting of the sympathetic tone in the course of hypertension.

Whereas the catecholamine data demand further explanation, certain epidemiologic findings suggest that neurogenic hypertension may indeed evolve into established hypertension. Tachycardia, a hallmark of neurogenic hypertension, is an independent risk factor for the development of future hypertension.[20-22] Thus, when transient hypertension and transient tachycardia are combined, the probability of developing established hypertension substantially increases.[20]

Another line of evidence supporting the predictive importance of neurogenic hypertension stems from the few longitudinal follow-up studies available, all of which suggest a transition from a high cardiac output to a high resistance (therefore established hypertension-like) state. While results in some of these studies may represent only regression towards the mean,[23,24] a recent report by Lund-Johansen is an exception.[25] He found that after 20 years almost all previously borderline and predominantly hyperkinetic subjects developed established hypertension requiring pharmacologic treatment. Although the study lacked a control group, the findings are so robust that they can hardly be disputed.[26]

A high incidence of tachycardia found in children of hypertensive parents also supports the pathophysiologic importance of the hyperkinetic state.[11] Finally, our studies on home blood pressure monitoring show that patients with a tachycardia in the physician's office are equally as likely to have "hypertension" at home as those who did not have a fast heart rate when examined by the physician.[27] Home blood pressure elevation is considered to be more predictive of future hypertension than casual clinic readings. Thus tachycardia, a sign of hyperkinetic circulation, cannot be viewed as an innocuous condition.

In summary, there is epidemiologic and clinical evidence that the hyperkinetic-neurogenic state precedes established hypertension in some patients. However, plasma catecholamine data suggest that either neurogenic hypertensives represent a rather small group within the large pool of patients with established hypertension or, alternatively, that sympathetic activity is enhanced only in the beginning of the disease and that other mechanisms prevail in later phases.

In the past we have speculated what such mechanisms might be.[28] In short, two processes are involved. First is the physiologic decrease of organ responsiveness, which occurs in the chronic environment of increased sympathetic tone. Second are structural changes in cardiovascular organs in response to exposure to elevated blood pressure. In the heart both of these combine to decrease the cardiac output (decreased beta-adrenergic responsiveness and limitation of stroke volume due to decreased cardiac compliance). In resistance vessels the increased wall:lumen ratio due to medial hypertrophy becomes the major factor. It overcomes the possible "down-regulation" of receptors and becomes the basis of positive feedback that amplifies all pressor responses. These different effects of pressure and sympathetic drive on the heart and blood vessels eventually cause a shift from a high-output to a high-resistance state.

Is Increased Blood Pressure Variability a Generalized Phenomenon in Borderline Hypertension?

As indicated earlier, patients with borderline hypertension tend to be hyperreactive to various mental stresses administered in the laboratory.[10–12,29] This raises an important question: Is such hyperreactivity specific to behavioral challenge or are patients with borderline hypertension suffering from a generalized blood pressure dysregulation—that is, a state of exaggerated responsiveness to all stimuli? Such a dysregulation could, for example, occur if the gain of arterial baroreceptors was decreased or if there was an abnormality in processing of inputs into the cardiovascular regulatory center.

There is little support for the existence of generalized dysregulation. Patients with established hypertension have normal blood pressure responses to exercise,[30] tilt,[31] and blood volume expansion.[32] Similarly, patients with borderline hypertension show normal responses to many stimuli such as dynamic exercise,[33-35] isometric exercise,[36] and cold pressor testing.[12,37,38] There is some controversy over blood pressure response to upright posture in borderline hypertension: Some investigators find the response to be normal,[12,31] whereas others report an excessive increase of the blood pressure.[39,40] However, by and large, blood pressure hyperreactivity is limited to behavioral tasks.

The specificity of hyperresponsiveness to mental stresses, as opposed to physical stresses, has been elegantly demonstrated by Eliasson,[12] who directly compared the responsiveness to mental and physical stresses in the same group of borderline hypertensive patients. Responses to color–word interference tests were exaggerated, but the reactions to cold pressor and to orthostatic testing were normal.

The normalcy of blood pressure responses to physical stresses in established and borderline hypertension undermines the rationale for the use of "provocative" physical stresses to predict hypertension. If blood pressure dysregulation is not commonly present in hypertension, how could one expect to predict hypertension by uncovering "first signs" of such dysregulation? Nevertheless, provocative tests have been used to predict hypertension on the theory that hypertension develops through a summation of repeated pressor episodes. Initial enthusiasm for cold pressor testing[41] soon gave way to doubts that the cold pressor test is characteristically abnormal in borderline hypertension[37] and later to doubts that responses to the cold pressor test could reliably predict future hypertension.[38,42] A recent resurrection of the test as a predictor of future hypertension[43] therefore requires careful scrutiny. The work from the Mayo Clinic is provocative; in a retrospective analysis, responses to cold pressor testing predicted future hypertension. However, the paper lacks a proper description of the value of baseline blood pressure values as a predictor of future hypertension. Many blood pressure responses tend to be proportional to the baseline; that is, the absolute increase may be larger, but the percentage increase is the same. Unfortunately, hyperresponsiveness to cold pressor in the Mayo study was arbitrarily defined as being an increment greater than a 20 mmHg, a criterion that could have been influenced by the initial level of blood pressure. The real question is whether the cold pressor test better predicts future hypertension than baseline blood pressure at youth, which in all studies known to us, is the strongest predictor of future hypertension.[16] The Mayo Clinic study does not address this issue.

A recent report by Dlin, Hanne, et al.[44] suggests that blood pressure response to exercise may be a useful predictor of future hypertension. The authors retrospectively examined the records of 5098 males subjected to bicycle ergometry between 1966 and 1977. Criteria for "exaggerated" blood pressure response (ER) to exercise were established: systolic pressure $\geq$ to 200 mmHg and/or diastolic pressure of 10 mmHg or more if the value then

exceeded 90 mmHg. After excluding subjects with resting blood pressure >
140/90 mmHg and those with a "past history of hypertension or renal
disease," the authors identified 102 subjects with ER. A control group with
normal responsiveness (NR)—that is, any response less than the stated ER
criteria—was matched for age, weight/height², skinfold thickness, resting
blood pressure≤140/90 mmHg, heart rate, predicted maximal oxygen uptake,
physical activity, smoking, and family history of hypertension. Follow-up
was accomplished in 75 matched pairs at an average interval of 5.8 years.
Eight subjects in the ER group proved to be hypertensive at follow-up while
none of the NR subjects had developed hypertension. The authors concluded
that exercise systolic blood pressure was a useful predictor of future hypertension. This study, while intriguing, is flawed by a systematic error introduced during matching. Although, as stated, the authors matched for the
absence of hypertension, regarding hypertension as a categorical variable,
their data demonstrate significantly higher mean systolic and diastolic blood
pressures for the ER group at baseline. The magnitude of the differences is
small (2.8 and 4.2 mmHg for systolic and diastolic, respectively), but because
of their higher initial blood pressures, the ER group would be expected to be
at higher risk for future hypertension. Although the authors argue, using
stepwise multiple regression, that exercise systolic blood pressure is the
best predictor of future systolic hypertension, the data as presented are
inadequate to assess the independent predictive value of initial resting
systolic blood pressure. Additional concerns regarding the nonstandardized
exercise work load and the unusual composition of the group studied (trained,
competitive athletes) further weaken the authors' contention that blood
pressure responses to exercise add meaningfully to the predictive value of
resting blood pressures.

As shown earlier in this chapter, patients with borderline hypertension
respond normally to physical stresses but harbor excessive blood pressure
responsiveness to mental stresses in laboratories. This raises the issue of
the generalizability of these laboratory findings. Do those with borderline
hypertension hyperrespond only to certain structured behavioral challenges,
or are they hyperresponsive to a host of other mental stimuli such as those
occurring during their daily activities? Some of these issues are addressed in
other chapters in this book. Our interpretation of the evidence is that the
question requires further investigation and that at present there are no
definitive answers.

Even if the hyperreactivity to laboratory mental stresses is generalizable
and representative of responses to all mental stresses, its effect on overall
blood pressure variability would depend on the balance between the frequency of exposure to mental stresses and the exposure to other physical
factors affecting blood pressure variability. Fourteen years ago[15] we pointed
out that blood pressure variability appears to be normal in borderline

hypertension and that the term "labile hypertension" is erroneously used to describe these patients. Nothing in the newer literature suggests a need to change this assessment.

Studies from several centers utilizing continuous blood pressure monitoring demonstrate that substantial spontaneous fluctuations occur in both normotensive and hypertensive individuals and that relative variability is not increased in those with mildly elevated baseline pressures.[45,46] Mancia, Ferrari, et al.[45] analyzed 24-hour intraarterial recordings in 89 ambulatory subjects. Measures of both short- and long-term variability were lowest in "normotensive" patients (mean blood pressure ≤ 100 mmHg), intermediate in subjects defined as "mildly hypertensive" (mean blood pressure 101–115 mmHg), and highest in those characterized as "severely hypertensive" (mean blood pressure > 115 mmHg). When variability was expressed as a percent of the mean pressure, however, there was no significant difference between the three groups. Horan et al.[47] compared noninvasive 24-hour blood pressure recordings from "borderline hypertensives"—defined as patients with office pressures fluctuating below and above 140/90 mmHg after at least three visits—to those from an equal number of normotensives (blood pressure consistently < 140/90 mmHg) and fixed hypertensives (blood pressure consistently > 140/90 mmHg). When expressed as a standard deviation above the mean, average variabilities in diastolic and systolic pressures were essentially equivalent in all three groups.

Data from the Framingham Study lend additional support to the tenet that patients with borderline hypertension do not have increased blood pressure lability.[48] In a cohort of 5209 men and women followed for 20 years, three blood pressure measurements were obtained at each of 10 biennial examinations. Variability was not consistent in subjects from one evaluation to the next; that is, there were no identifiable patients with consistently labile pressures. Moreover, variability increased as systolic pressure increased and was most pronounced in those with established hypertension. Although during ambulatory or clinical settings, the precise nature of behavioral and physical stimuli cannot be defined, all current evidence suggests that the structured mental stresses capable of provoking exaggerated blood pressure responses in borderline hypertensives either have analogues that occur only infrequently in daily life or that responses to behavioral tasks are uniquely dependent on some aspect of the laboratory setting.

Does Hypertension Develop as a Summation of Pressor Episodes?

Inherent to all of the work on laboratory-induced blood pressure variability is the assumption that recurring stresses cause repeated blood pressure increases, which later result in established hypertension. The conceptual framework for such thinking has been provided by Folkow,[49] who argues that repeated pressor episodes, by causing hypertrophy of the media in arterioles, cause the wall of such hypertrophic resistance vessels to encroach upon the lumen. The consequence of such anatomic change in the resistance vessels is a higher resting resistance to flow and, more importantly, a generalized increase in the responsiveness of blood vessels to all pressor stimuli. A positive feedback system is thus set in motion. More constriction (higher resistance) requires higher pressure to maintain a normal flow, and higher pressure causes more hypertrophy, which in turn further aggravates the condition. This mechanism has been established in experimental hypertension and is considered to be one of the major contributing factors in the acceleration of established human hypertension. The question is whether repeated pressor episodes provoked neurogenically can lead to such medial hypertrophy and to self-sustaining, accelerating hypertension.

The answer can be approached only indirectly. First, if blood pressure variability is a major factor causing hypertension by this mechanism, then variability should be related to hypertensive morbidity. Epidemiologic and clinical data indicate that blood pressure variability is not a predictor of hypertensive cardiovascular damage.[50] Recent work by Devereux et al.[51] provides the first indication that behaviorally induced blood pressure may have a pathogenic significance. These authors found that blood pressures taken at work correlate better with cardiovascular hypertrophy than measurements recorded during any other period of day. However, it is not clear whether elevation of blood pressure during work was continuous or whether indeed there were discrete pressor episodes that contributed to the work-induced cardiovascular damage. Conceptually this is very important. We take no issue with the possibility that behaviorally induced blood pressure elevation, if sustained, may lead to cardiovascular damage. The issue at hand is whether the blood pressure variability is the *mechanism* by which such damage is conferred.

It is very difficult to find experimental support for the role of blood pressure variability or repeated pressor episodes in the development of hypertension. Studies of peripheral[52] or central deafferentation of baroreceptors show that animals can tolerate long periods of labile blood pressure without developing sustained high blood pressure or cardiovascular damage. Particularly dramatic is the work by Talman et al.,[53] who by central nervous system lesions produced chronic, extremely labile blood pressure in rats. The animals did not develop hypertension or cardiovascular damage. Other attempts to induce hypertension by repeated central[54] or peripheral nervous system electrical stimulation[55] raised blood pressure but failed to induce irreversible hypertension. Similarly, attempts to elicit sustained blood pressure elevation by operant conditioning have failed to produce sustained hypertension. Recent demonstrations by Anderson et al.[56] that operant conditioning elicits more robust blood pressure responses when combined with saline infusions are exciting. If such treatment, when applied for extended periods, succeeds in inducing permanent hypertension, a new foundation will be established to understand the factors that facilitate the transition from repeated pressor episodes to established hypertension.

Research Agenda

There is no doubt that behavioral challenges elicit abnormal blood pressure responses in some patients with borderline hypertension. It is equally well proven that patients with neurogenic borderline hypertension consistently show a different personality pattern than normotensive controls. Reasonable support can be found in the literature for the assumption that neurogenic borderline hypertension evolves into sustained hypertension.

The real problem lies in the tendency to interpret this evidence as meaning that behaviorally induced blood pressure variability is *the mechanism* by which hypertension develops. At present, there is very little evidence to support the assumption that hypertension is a simple summation of repeated pressor episodes and that by studying blood pressure responsiveness, one may elucidate a mechanism for the development of hypertension. Blood pressure variability remains an important area of inquiry into human physiology, but it is more likely a corollary of hypertension than an important pathophysiologic factor. Further research to identify new mechanisms is needed. Responses of the renal vasculature to stress,[57] alterations of renal sodium handling during stress,[58] and the interaction between operant conditioning and sodium loading[56] are recent examples of imaginative approaches.

In order to understand the role of behavior in the development of hypertension, further progress is needed in the following areas:

Longitudinal epidemiologic studies to determine the proportion of neurogenic borderline hypertensives that progress to sustained hypertension

Longitudinal studies of high-risk cohorts to determine the prevalence of "neurogenic" versus other types of prehypertensives ("salt sensitive," "low renin," etc.) and to assess the relative propensity of each these subgroups to develop hypertension

Studies of behavioral factors as predictors of future hypertension

Descriptions of the natural history of behavioral factors in the course of the development of hypertension: Do patients with characteristic behavioral styles maintain them throughout their life? What factors ameliorate or accelerate the development of behaviorally induced hypertension?

Studies on the generalizability of laboratory stressor responses

Studies of the independent contribution of blood pressure variability (vs. mean blood pressure level) to cardiovascular morbidity

Animal models to investigate whether repeated pressor episodes lead to hypertension and/or cardiovascular damage

Studies of mechanisms whereby behavior induces hypertension

This research agenda is by no means exhaustive. It does, however, suggest the magnitude of the undertaking that will be necessary to answer the question raised in the title.

REFERENCES

1. Julius S, Esler M: Autonomic nervous cardiovascular regulation in borderline hypertension. *Am J Cardiol* **36**:685–696, 1975.

2. Julius S, Pascual AV, London R: Role of parasympathetic inhibition in the hyperkinetic type of borderline hypertension. *Circulation* **44**:413–418, 1971.

3. Julius S, Hansson L: Hemodynamics of prehypertension and hypertension. *Verh Dtsch Ges Inn Med* **80**:49–58, 1974.

4. Takeshita A, Tanaka S, et al: Reduced baroreceptor sensitivity in borderline hypertension. *Circulation* **51**:738–742, 1975.

5. Eckberg DL: Carotid baroreflex function in young men with borderline blood pressure elevation. *Circulation* **59**:632–636, 1979.

6. Hilton SM: Inhibition of baroreceptor reflexes on hypothalamic stimulation. *J Physiol* **165**:56–57, 1963.

7. Harburg E, Julius S, et al: Personality traits and behavioral patterns associated with systolic blood pressure levels in college males. *J Chronic Dis* **17**:405–414, 1964.

8. Esler M, Julius S, et al: Mild high-renin essential hypertension. Neurogenic human hypertension? *N Engl J Med* **296**:405–411, 1977.

9. Julius S: The psychophysiology of borderline hypertension. In Weiner H, Hofer MA, Stunkard AJ (eds): *Behavior, and Bodily Disease*. New York, Raven Press, 1981, pp. 293–303.

10. Nestel PJ: Blood pressure and catecholamine excretion after mental stress in labile hypertension. *Lancet* **1**:692–694, 1969.

11. Falkner B, Kushner H, et al: Cardiovascular characteristics in adolescents who develop essential hypertension. *Hypertension* **3**:521–527, 1981.

12. Eliasson K, Hjemdahl P, Kahan T: Circulatory and sympatho-adrenal responses to stress in borderline and established hypertension. *J Hypertension* **1**:131–139, 1983.

13. Page LB: Epidemiology of hypertension. In Genest J, Kuchel O, et al (eds): *Hypertension: Physiopathology and Treatment* (2nd ed). New York, McGraw-Hill, 1983, pp. 683–699.

14. Joint National Committee on Detection, Evaluation, and Treatment of High Blood Pressure: The 1984 Report. U.S. Department of Health and Human Services, National Institutes of Health, NIH Publication No. 84–1088, June 1984.

15. Julius S, Schork MA: Borderline hypertension—A critical review. *J Chron Dis* **23**:723–754, 1971.

16. Julius S, Schork MA: Predictors in hypertension. *Ann New York Acad Sci* **304**:38–52, 1978.

17. Australian National Blood Pressure Study: The Australian therapeutic trial in mild hypertension. *Lancet* **1**:1261–1267, 1980.

18. Goldstein DS: Plasma norepinephrine in essential hypertension. A study of the studies. *Hypertension* **3**:48–52, 1981.

19. Lake CR, Ziegler MG, et al: Age-adjusted plasma norepinephrine levels are similar in normotensive and hypertensive subjects. *N Engl J Med* **296**:208, 1977.

20. Levy RL, White PD, et al: Transient tachycardia: Prognostic significance alone and in association with transient hypertension. *JAMA* **129**:585–588, 1945.

21. Paffenbarger Jr RS, Thorne MC, Wing AL: Chronic disease in former college students— VIII. Characteristics in youth predisposing to hypertension in later years. *Am J Epidemiol* **88**:25–32, 1968.

22. Stamler J, Berkson DM, et al: Relationship of multiple variables to blood pressure—Findings from four Chicago epidemiologic studies. In Paul O (ed): *Epidemiology and Control of Hypertension.* Miami, Symposia Specialists, 1975, pp. 307–352.

23. Eich RH, Cuddy RP, et al: Hemodynamics in labile hypertension. A follow-up study. *Circulation* **34**:299–307, 1966.

24. Weiss YA, Safar ME, et al: Repeat hemodynamic determinations in borderline hypertension. *Am J Med* **64**:382, 1978.

25. Lund-Johansen P: Hemodynamic concepts in essential hypertension. *Triangle* **23**:13–23, 1984.

26. Lund-Johansen P: Hemodynamic alterations in early essential hypertension: Recent advances. In Gross F, Strasser T (eds): *Mild Hypertension: Recent Advances.* New York, Raven Press, 1983, pp. 237–252.

27. Julius S, Ellis CN, et al: Home blood pressure determinations: Value in borderline ("labile") hypertension. *JAMA* **229**:663–666, 1974.

28. Julius S: Psychophysiologic evidence for the role of the nervous system in hypertension. In Amery A, Fagard R, et al (eds): *Hypertensive Cardiovascular Disease: Pathophysiology and Treatment.* Boston, Martinus Nijhoff Publishers, 1982, pp. 217–230.

29. Light KC, Obrist PA: Cardiovascular reactivity to behavioral stress in young males with and without marginally elevated casual systolic pressures. Comparison of clinic, home, and laboratory measures. *Hypertension* **2**:802–808, 1980.

30. Conway J, Julius S, Amery A: Effect of blood pressure level on the hemodynamic response to exercise. *Hypertension* **16**:79–85, 1968.

31. Sannerstedt R, Julius S, Conway J: Hemodynamic response to tilt with beta-adrenergic blockade in young patients with borderline hypertension. *Circulation* **42**:1057–1064, 1970.

32. Julius S, Pascual AV, et al: Relationship between cardiac output and peripheral resistance in borderline hypertension. *Circulation* **43**:382–390, 1971.

33. Lund-Johansen P: Hemodynamics in early essential hypertension. *Acta Med Scand* **482**:1–105, 1967.

34. Sannerstedt R: Hemodynamic response to exercise in patients with arterial hypertension. *Acta Med Scand* **458**:1–83, 1966. (Suppl)

35. Julius S, Conway J: Hemodynamic studies in patients with borderline blood pressure elevation. *Circulation* **38**:282–288, 1968.

36. Sannerstedt R, Julius S: Systemic haemodynamics in borderline arterial hypertension: Response to static exercise before and under the influence of propranolol. *Cardiovasc Res* **6**:398–403, 1972.

37. Thomas CB, Duszynski KR: Blood pressure levels in young adulthood as predictors of hypertension and the fate of the cold pressor test. *Johns Hopkins Med J* **151**:93–100, 1982.

38. Eich RH, Jacobsen ED: Vascular reactivity in medical students followed for 10 years. *J Chron Dis* **20**:583–592, 1967.

39. Frohlich ED, Tarazi RC, et al: Tilt test for investigating a neural component in hypertension: Its correlation with clinical characteristics. *Circulation* **36**:387–393, 1967.

40. Hull DH, Wolthuis RA, et al: Borderline hypertension versus normotension: differential response to orthostatic stress. *Am Heart J* **94**:414–420, 1977.

41. Hines Jr EA, Brown GE: The cold pressor test for measuring the reactibility of the blood pressure: Data concerning 571 normal and hypertensive subjects. *Am Heart J* **11**:1–9, 1936.

42. Harlan Jr WR, Osborne RK, Graybiel A: Prognostic value of the cold pressor test and the basal blood pressure: Based on an 18 year follow-up study. *Am J Cardiol* **13**:683–687, 1964.

43. Wood DK, Sheps SG, et al: Cold pressor test as a predictor of hypertension. *Hypertension* **6**:301–306, 1984.

44. Dlin RA, Hanne N, et al: Follow-up of normotensive men with exaggerated blood pressure response to exercise. *Am Heart J* **106**:316–320, 1983.

45. Mancia G, Ferrari A, et al: Blood pressure and heart rate variabilities in normotensive and hypertensive human beings. *Circ Res* **53**:96–104, 1983.

46. Messerli F, Glade L, et al: Diurnal variations of cardiac rhythm, arterial pressure, and urinary catecholamines in borderline and established essential hypertension. *Am Heart J* **104**:109–114, 1982.

47. Horan M, Kennedy H, Padget N: Do borderline hypertensive patients have labile blood pressure? *Ann Intern Med* **94**:466–468, 1981.

48. Kannel W, Sorlie P, Gordon T: Labile hypertension: A faulty concept? The Framingham Study. *Circulation* **61**:1183–1187, 1980.

49. Folkow B: Physiological aspects of primary hypertension. *Physiol Rev* **62**:347–503, 1982.

50. Sokolow M, Wedegar D, et al: Relationship between level of blood pressure measured casually and by portable recorder, and severity of complications in essential hypertension. *Circulation* **34**:279–298, 1966.

51. Devereux RB, Pickering TG, et al: Left ventricular hypertrophy in patients with hypertension: Importance of blood pressure response to regularly recurring stress. *Circulation* **68**:470–476, 1983.

52. Cowley Jr AW, Liard JF, Guyton AC: Role of the baroreceptor reflex in daily control of arterial blood pressure and other variables in dogs. *Circ Res* **32**:564–576, 1973.

53. Talman WT, Alonso DR, Reis DJ: Impairment of baroreceptor function and chronic lability of arterial pressure produced by lesions of A2 catecholamine neurons of rat brain: Failure to evolve into hypertension. In Sleight P (ed): *Arterial Baroreceptors in Hypertension*. Oxford, Oxford Press, 1980, pp. 448–454.

54. Folkow B, Rubinstein EH: Cardiovascular effects of acute and chronic stimulation of the hypothalamic defense area in the rat. *Acta Physiol Scand* **68**:48–57, 1966.

55. Liard JF, Tarazi RC, et al: Hemodynamic and humoral characteristics of hypertension induced by prolonged stellate ganglion stimulation in conscious dogs. *Circ Res* **36**:455, 1975.

56. Anderson D, Kerns W, Better W: Progressive hypertension in dogs by avoidance conditioning and saline infusion. *Hypertension* **5**:286–291, 1983.

57. Hollenberg NK, Williams GH, Adams DF: Essential hypertension: Abnormal renal vascular and endocrine responses to a mild psychological stimulus. *Hypertension* **3**:11–17, 1981.

58. Light KC, Kopeke JP, et al: Psychological stress induced sodium and fluid retention in men at high risk for hypertension. *Science* **220**:429–431, 1983.

DEFINING AND IDENTIFYING INDIVIDUAL DIFFERENCES IN REACTIVITY

6

Psychological Stressors and Task Variables as Elicitors of Reactivity

DAVID S. KRANTZ, STEPHEN B. MANUCK, RENA R. WING

INTRODUCTION AND BACKGROUND

Early work by Walter Cannon[1] demonstrated that there was a massive sympathetic nervous system discharge ("the fight-flight response")

Portions of this chapter were adapted from papers by Krantz and Manuck in *Psychological Bulletin* **96**:435–464, 1984, and from a chapter by Manuck, Krantz, and Polefrone in Steptoe A, Ruddel H, Neus H (eds): *Clinical and Methodological Issues in Cardiovascular Psychophysiology*. Berlin: Springer-Verlag, 1985. We thank the remaining members of the working group on psychological stressors at the NHLBI Stress and Reactivity Conference (Drs. T. M. Dembroski, R. Hughes, S. Julius, J. Kaplan, K. Light, N. E. Miller, H. Meyers, L. Van Egeren, and R. B. Williams) for their helpful input in developing the ideas presented here.

Preparation of this chapter was assisted by NIH grants HL31514 and HL29028, and USUHS grant RO7233.

accompanying behavioral states such as fear and anger. About the same time, based on animal research with a variety of noxious stimuli, Selye[2] popularized the notion of a generalized, or "nonspecific," stress response— that is, that all stressors produce the same three-stage, predominantly adrenal-cortical response pattern called the general adaptation syndrome. Together, the pioneering work of these investigators served to launch an extensive body of research on stress and its physiologic consequences. However, this work emphasized the similarity of responses to different stressors and downplayed the possibility that the meaning of a potentially stressful stimulus and the context in which it is presented exert important influences on resultant physiologic responses.

More recently, considerable data have challenged the early emphasis on a "generalized" stress response. Mason,[3] Lazarus,[4] Frankenhaeuser,[5] and others have suggested that the physiologic (as well as psychologic and behavioral) effects of most physical stressors depend strongly on psychological factors. That is, if physical stressors are not viewed or interpreted as harmful, threatening, or noxious, they can produce smaller and even opposite physiologic responses. Studies that simultaneously measured a number of hormones and cardiovascular responses also indicated that specific stressors can produce rather specific patterns of responses.[3,6–8] Furthermore, operating from another research tradition, psychophysiologists have long noted that attributes of stimuli and the behavioral demands required by these stimuli influence the pattern of cardiovascular reactions that result.[9,10] For example, stressful or arousing tasks that require active efforts to cope produce a different pattern of physiologic responses than tasks that require quiet attentiveness to the environment.[8,10,11]

There are numerous ways of describing and dimensionalizing the various stimulus situations that reliably produce different patterns of bodily responses. However, implicit in a description of a stimulus as *psychological* in nature is the notion that the individual's response to a challenging or stressful stimulus depends on the way that stimulus is interpreted or appraised, the context in which the stimulus occurs, and the personal resources available for coping.[4,12,13] Therefore, psychological "stress" is defined as an internal state of the individual who perceives threats to his or her physical and/or psychic well-being. Stressors are distinguished from psychological "challenges," which are those situations that induce the subject to respond behaviorally by providing positive incentives.

It is not the intention of this chapter to pursue further the distinction between a stress and a challenge. It is quite possible that both types of events may be relevant to health outcomes, even though they are experienced quite differently. Instead, *psychological* eliciting stimuli, whether they be stressors or challenges, will be defined here as those situations that implicitly involve some element of information processing by the subject. This is not to imply that physical stressors such as pain, noise, electric shock, thermal stimuli, or even postural changes do not contain psychological components. Indeed, it is difficult to imagine a stimulus situation that would not involve some interpretation or information processing on the part of the subject. For example, there is evidence that physiologic responses to the anticipation of shock and to the shock itself can be altered by manipulating the instructions given to subjects.[14,15] However, in this chapter we will concern ourselves with situations in which the psychological features of the task are the primary elicitors of reactivity.

We will begin this chapter with a description of tasks utilized as psychological stressors in laboratory studies of reactivity, and will identify and classify stimulus parameters or response requirements thought to be important in producing different patterns of physiologic responses (also see the chapter by Williams). We will then consider whether laboratory indices of reactivity generalize to naturalistic settings. We will close with a consideration of issues in designing appropriate measures for various populations and with a discussion of future research needs.

TASKS USED AS PSYCHOLOGICAL STRESSORS AND CHALLENGES

A variety of experimental tasks and procedures are utilized in laboratory studies of reactivity. Before categorizing these tasks along their qualitative or conceptual dimensions, it makes sense to describe their procedural aspects.

One set of tasks typically involves a moderate to high level of mental challenge. With some exceptions, these tasks tend to evoke fairly sizable responses and can be administered to subjects in a standardized, repeatable manner. Such tasks include (1) mental arithmetic (e.g., counting backward by serial sevens);[16–18] (2) reaction time tasks (e.g., shock avoidance, competitive reaction times);[19,20] (3) cognitive problems (e.g., Stroop color-word test, I.Q. tests or perceptual tests);[21,22] (4) vigilance tasks, which vary on a scale from very-low-demand, monotonous tasks (underload)[21] to tasks that involve moderate demands for the subject to direct attention outward to the environment (sensory-intake tasks),[18,24] to high-demand tasks that overload the subject.[21]

Another group of eliciting tasks are more difficult to administer in a standardized manner. These include situations such as the structured interview (SI) used to measure Type A behavior;[25,26] more stressful face-to-face interviews; public speaking situations; interpersonal games involving cooperation or competition; and role-playing or imagery tasks.[27] Though often difficult to standardize, such tasks may yield important information because they mirror responses to real-life situations and interpersonal interactions.

Last is a category of eliciting tasks involving passive participation (e.g., viewing stressful or pornographic films),[20] or being exposed to physical stimuli, such as the cold pressor test or bursts of noise,[20,28] where the psychological dimensions of the task, such as predictability or controllability, are varied.

DIMENSIONS OF TASKS THAT PRODUCE REACTIVITY

In an attempt to categorize and identify the crucial dimensions of tasks that elicit different patterns of reactivity, several classification schemes have been proposed to explain the intensity and patterning of varying hemodynamic and neuroendocrine responses that can be produced by different stressors.

Quantitative Determinants of Response Intensity

On a purely quantitative basis, the intensity of a subject's responses to the tasks described in the previous section can be increased or decreased by varying the task instructions or task characteristics according to a number of criteria. For example, increasing the positive or negative incentives for task performance, increasing the level of challenge in task instructions, and increasing the subjects' level of engagement/involvement in the experimental situation can heighten physiologic responses. Often these motivational dimensions overlap one another and covary in manipulations of experimental situations. Thus, one study[29] manipulated the level of challenge conveyed in instructions given to subjects prior to a cold pressor test. "High-challenge" instructions, delivered in a crisp tone of voice, informed subjects of the difficulty of the cold pressor task and the need for willpower, whereas "low-challenge" instructions described the task as routine. Results indicated only minimal differences between Type B and Type A coronary-prone subjects in the low-challenge condition and considerably larger and reliable differences in the high-challenge condition (see chapter by Houston). In retrospect, it appears that this manipulation involved not only a heightened challenge but also concomitant increases in subjects' level of engagement-involvement, positive incentive, perceptions of task difficulty, and so on. Explicit and even subtle variations in such aspects of experimental instructions can therefore act to heighten or obscure the detection of individual differences in cardiovascular reactivity. Thus, inclusion of performance-contingent incentives can affect cardiovascular responses to a stressor.

Whether the subjects' cardiovascular reactions vary in direct proportion to the value or amount of incentive applied, however, has not been examined directly.[see 34]

Another set of response-intensity modulators involves the predictability of the stressor and subjects' perceptions about whether they are able to control the stressor (e.g., modify or modulate its outcome). Thus, there is considerable evidence that unpredictable and uncontrollable stressors usually result in heightened physiologic responses.[15] Factors such as task novelty and task difficulty also appear to influence the magnitude of subjects' cardiovascular responses. With respect to novelty, tonic heart rate elevations observed during shock-avoidance tasks[31] and in anticipation of shock[32] appear to be greatest when subjects are provided no prior exposure to the aversive stimulus. Also, cardiovascular reactions recorded on the first pre-sentation of an experimental task (a novel experience) are generally greater than those seen when the same task is administered again on subsequent occasions.[33,58]

Effects of differences in task difficulty on cardiovascular responsivity are somewhat more complicated. For example, Manuck, Harvey, et al.[34] report that increasing the difficulty of an experimental task involving tests of subjects' concept-forming abilities resulted in heightened systolic pressor responses, but only in subjects who believed that performing well at the task would prevent their exposure to a painful auditory stimulus. When subjects believed that exposure to the aversive stimulus was random and independent of performance, their blood pressure responses did not differ from those seen in subjects who were allowed to perform a much easier version of the task.

In another investigation, Obrist, Gaebelein, et al.[20] assigned three subject groups to an experimental procedure in which avoidance of electric shocks was contingent on level of performance in a common reaction-time task; importantly, the criterion for successful avoidance varied in increments across the three groups, which were labeled "easy," "difficult," and "impos-sible." Heart rate and systolic blood pressure elevations during the avoidance task were most pronounced among subjects required to perform the difficult reaction-time task. Responses in this condition were also significantly greater than those among subjects in the "easy" condition and in the "impossible" condition, where subjects were effectively helpless to avoid shock. That similar effects are found when "difficulty" is manipulated during appetitive rather than avoidance tasks also suggests that this relationship is not restricted to situations involving threat of aversive stimulation.[35] Hence, while increased task difficulty potentiates cardiovascular responses to laboratory challenges, eliciting such effects may require the presence of extrinsic incentives for good performance and the use of levels of difficulty that do not exceed individuals' actual abilities.

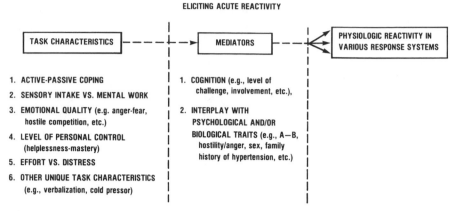

FIGURE 6.1.   Psychological task characteristics and mediators in measuring physiologic reactivity.

To summarize this section, it is possible to manipulate the settings and instructions of experimental tasks so that the physiologic responses produced by these tasks vary in intensity. It cannot yet be determined whether dimensions such as challenge, novelty, and task involvement represent distinct dimensions, or whether they are all ways of varying the subjects' level of involvement in the task.

Qualitative Task Dimensions and Patterns of Physiologic Responding

As we noted earlier, psychophysiologists have long observed that, across groups of individuals, tasks with different behavioral demands produce stereotypically different patterns of physiologic responses. Specifically, several formal task dimension have been observed to elicit qualitatively different patterns of cardiovascular responding. These dimensions and their relationships to reactivity are outlined in Figure 6.1. The schematic presented in the figure also is consistent with the principle that the stressfulness of a stimulus depends on its interpretation or appraisal by the subject.

Active Versus Passive Coping

Recently, Obrist and colleagues[11,20] noted that certain kinds of stressful tasks are more likely than others to produce a pattern of cardiovascular responses indicative of strong beta-adrenergic influences on the heart—that is, increased systolic blood pressure (SBP) and heart rate (HR) but not necessarily increased diastolic blood pressure (DBP). Specifically, it is hypothesized by Obrist and colleagues [11,20] and Light[36] that an important qualitative feature of stressful tasks is whether they require subjects to cope actively or passively with stress. Sympathetic influences on the myocardium are most pronounced when subjects are exposed to task stimuli—such as shock avoidance or competitive reaction times—that require them to exercise active instrumental control over aversive events or over rewards achieved. The notion of active and passive coping denotes a relatively broad construct encompassing many of the nonaversive activities in which one is motivated to exhibit competent and effective performance. Thus, a task such as a challenging reaction-time test where subjects actively respond to avoid shock or to earn a monetary bonus produces this kind of beta-adrenergic response pattern. In contrast, task situations such as the cold pressor or a pornographic film, which subjects tolerate passively, result in lesser SBP and HR changes and greater increases in DBP,[20] since subjects have little opportunity to escape stimulation, short of discontinuing participation in the task.

In addition to demonstrating different response patterns to different types of tasks, evidence linking the "active coping" task variable to beta-adrenergic activation derives from several studies that manipulated the ability to cope within the same task.[31] In a related experiment[34] it was observed that even the *perception* of active behavioral coping over an anticipated event (i.e., without actual control) was accompanied by increased SBP responses. In a subsequent study, a similar response pattern was seen while individuals performed an appetitive reaction-time task in which reward—rather than avoidance of aversiveness—was contingent on subjects' performance. Additional evidence that the pattern of responding associated with active coping was beta-adrenergic in nature derives from a study that observed cardiovascular changes to the tasks when beta-adrenergic responses were pharmacologically blocked.[20]

Sensory Intake Versus Mental Work

Another task dimension thought to elicit a specific qualitative pattern of physiologic responses places emphasis on physiological correlates of information processing and attention. Over 20 years ago, Lacey et al.[37] reported that both acceleratory and deceleratory heart rate responses could be elicited by laboratory experimental tasks, depending on the types of attentional demands placed on subjects. They noticed that heart rate decreased by several beats per minute while subjects performed tasks requiring vigilance (sensory intake) but increased during cognitive problem-solving tasks which require concentration and, hence, rejection of extraneous sensory information from the environment. Subsequent research[38] demonstrated that these directionally opposed cardiac responses often reflect concomitant changes in somatomotor activity—stillness and general somatic inhibition occurring in conjunction with sensory intake and heart rate deceleration, and bodily activation accompanying sensory rejection and heart rate acceleration. Williams, and colleagues[39] have further examined the influence of sensory intake versus sensory rejection on responses of the skeletal muscle vasculature. They proposed that with rejection tasks such as mental arithmetic or cognitive problems requiring "mental work," the defense reaction is activated. This is characterized by emotional arousal, increased motor activity, and a cardiovascular response pattern of increased cardiac output, with a shunting of blood away from the skin and viscera to the skeletal musculature. Thus, forearm blood flow increases and forearm vascular resistance decreases during sensory rejection. However, when sensory intake is required, there is decreased emotional expression and motor activity, decreased heart rate and cardiac output, and vasoconstriction in skeletal muscle, skin, and viscera. Thus, there is reported to be active vasoconstriction during sensory intake[8]. In one study[18] it was further shown that patterns of neuroendocrine (e.g., catecholamine, cortisol, testosterone) also differ between mental work and intake tasks. While these two response patterns described by Williams and colleagues clearly differ from one another, it is rather difficult to define intake tasks that do not involve components of mental work or challenge; therefore, most intake-related tasks fall into a category of producing a mixed pattern of cardiac and vascular reactions. In addition, it is difficult to differentiate, either conceptually or empirically, between tasks that involve mental work and those that involve active coping.

Emotional Quality and Affective States

The particular emotional reaction elicited by an experimental task may also determine the nature of the observed cardiovascular and endocrine response. In fact, early studies in experimental psychophysiology sought to demonstrate differentiation of heart rate, blood pressure reactions, and selected sympathetic nervous system responses during laboratory procedures designed specifically to induce emotions such as fear and anger.[40] In one early study by Ax,[41] anger was associated with larger diastolic pressure responses and with smaller heart rate reactions than those seen during subjects' experiences of fear. More recent investigations have shown that cardiovascular responses differ across a wide range of negative emotions (e.g., fear, anger, sadness, disgust) and differ between positive and negative emotions generally,[42-44] although response differences between different emotions are often subtle and difficult to detect. Though speculative, Ekman et al.[42] hypothesize that such emotion-specific autonomic activity is associated with the patterning of facial muscle contractions characteristic of each emotion, and that these relationships are mediated by feedback from the facial muscles themselves or by "direct connection between the cortex and hypothalamus." It is important to note that despite the findings differentiating fear versus anger in terms of "epinephrine-like" (predominantly beta-adrenergic) and "norepinephrine-like" (predominantly alpha-adrenergic or mixed alpha- and beta-adrenergic responding), there are some inconsistencies and exceptions in this research literature on correlates of emotion.[e.g.,45]

The foregoing studies involve rather dramatic experimental manipulations for the induction of different affective states[41] or precise quantification of the facial expressions indicative of targeted emotions.[42] Studies in which individual differences in emotion or affective response are documented through the use of affect questionnaires and personality inventories yield a less consistent literature. It has been suggested that lack of concordance between self-report indices and physiologic reactions may be due partly to the psychometric deficiencies of "affect" scales typically employed in laboratory studies, especially their insensitivity to defensiveness as a source of nonveridical self-report. Relevant to this point, Weinberger et al.[43] showed that individuals who reported little anxiety, yet scored highly on a measure of defensiveness—so-called repressors—exhibited similar heart rate responsivity to an experimental stressor as persons who acknowledged high levels of anxiety. In addition, highly anxious individuals and repressors both showed larger heart rate reactions than did "true" (i.e., nondefensive)—low-anxiety subjects. These findings suggest that while emotion is related to the magnitude of cardiovascular responses elicited in laboratory studies, this relationship may be obscured when relevant affective experiences of the individual are assessed only via subjective self-report.

The Helplessness-Mastery Dimension: Perceived Control

A large body of psychophysiologic and psychoendocrine research on stress supports the conclusion that the effectiveness of the psychosocial factors in arousing the sympathetic and adrenal-cortical systems depends on the individual's cognitive appraisal of the balance between demands of the situation and personal coping resources.[4,21,46] In particular, the subject's perceived ability to exercise control over environmental stimuli has been demonstrated to be a major determinant of stress reactions resulting from exposure to aversive stimuli.[15,21,47] However, the relationship of perceiving control and of exerting control to physiologic responding is more complex than previously thought and depends on such factors as task difficulty,[34] the nature of the coping response utilized (e.g., active versus passive,[see 11] and the particular physiologic response being measured (heart rate, blood pressure, epinephrine, norepinephrine, galvanic skin response).[21,31] Despite the aforementioned qualifications, it can be generally stated that over the long term, controllability facilitates adjustment to stressors and enhances coping effectiveness, although the effort involved in exerting control may be associated with increases in arousal.[21] The previous discussion of the active-passive coping dimension provides an example of how active controlling efforts can heighten beta-adrenergic responding. Conversely, Seligman's[15] work on the deleterious effects of learned helplessness and research by Glass and Singer[47] on the negative behavioral aftereffects of exposure to uncontrollable stressors document the potentially negative effects of lack of control on health and behavior and provide good reviews of early research on the controllability dimension and its relationship to stress.

In an attempt to explain the circumstances under which catecholamine (sympathetic adrenomedullary) and cortisol (adrenocortical) responses were elevated during stressful tasks, Frankenhaeuser[21] has suggested a mediating role for the subjective experiences of effort and distress. It is proposed that effort and distress can be experienced either singly or in combination: effort without distress is accompanied by elevated catecholamines and suppression of cortisol secretion; effort with distress (the most typical stressful circumstance) is accompanied by an increase in both catecholamines and cortisol; and distress without effort (e.g., giving up, feeling helpless) is associated with a high cortisol output.[21] These conclusions are based on a series of laboratory and field experiments that measured urinary hormones excreted during situations that varied in level of control and predictability. see reviews [5,11] These studies, some of which were conducted in occupational settings, are particularly notable in that they suggest several direct applications for designing work environments and job characteristics so as to optimize effort while minimizing distress. This research program represents one of the few attempts to examine in a naturalistic setting empirical findings derived from laboratory experiments of situational elicitors of reactivity.

Other Task Characteristics

The rather formal approaches for classifying tasks previously described (active vs. passive coping, sensory intake vs. mental work, level of controllability, etc.)[e.g.,48] comprise only several dimensions of potential importance for determining patterns of physiologic responding. For example, another obvious consideration in determining the response elicited by a particular laboratory situation is the physical nature of the task. Specifically, characteristics such as whether dynamic or static exercise is involved, as well as the type of stimulation that is applied (e.g., shock, cold, noise), clearly affect the responses elicited. Certain tasks, such as the cold pressor, produce a time-

related pattern of physiological responding including peripheral vasoconstriction followed by periodic vasodilatation.[49] In addition, Dimsdale and
Moss[50] found preferential release of norepinephrine during physical exercise
and release of epinephrine during the emotional stress of public speaking.

Recent work also shows qualitatively different patterns of endocrine
responses to different situations that do not readily lend themselves to easy
classification into conceptual or descriptive categories. For example, Dimsdale[30] reviewed evidence that naturalistic anxiety situations such as public
speaking or a dental procedure produce large-magnitude increases in epinephrine, laboratory mental arithmetic produced increases of smaller magnitude, and competition either with or without harassment produced yet
smaller increases in epinephrine levels. The magnitude of increases generated
by real-life stressors is, not surprisingly, often larger than those produced
by many laboratory maneuvers. However, it should be noted that qualitative
differences in response often appear as well.[51]

Interactions Between Task and the Person

Another important factor to consider in designing maneuvers to elicit
physiologic reactivity is that there are psychological and biological individual
differences that may produce different patterns of responding to particular
stimuli among various subject groups. Having noted this fact here, we refer
the reader to the chapters in this volume by Houston and by Watkins and
Eaker for a complete discussion of issues relating to individual differences.

GENERALIZATION OF INDIVIDUAL DIFFERENCES IN REACTIVITY

Two important questions relevant to stimuli that elicit reactivity, which
must be addressed in studying reactivity as an enduring individual-difference
variable, concern (1) the intercorrelations between reactivity to a variety of
different tasks and stimuli, and (2) the generalizability from laboratory
assessment to naturalistic field settings. Therefore, we will examine these
issues here in some detail.

Intertask Correlations

Studies have intercorrelated cardiovascular and endocrine responses of
the same subjects to a variety of stressors. Insofar as the specific conceptual
dimensions of tasks (e.g., sensory intake vs. rejection, active vs. passive
coping) predict differential patterning of reactions, one might expect cardiovascular and endocrine reactions to show little reproducibility when assessed

under conceptually different stimulus conditions. It is possible, on the other hand, that consistent individual differences override the influence of stimulus characteristics on physiologic responding.

Cardiovascular Responses

Regarding the sensory intake–mental work dimension, Bunnell[52] recently demonstrated that subjects who differ in the magnitude of their heart rate responses during sensory rejection exhibited parallel, though somewhat smaller, differences when performing sensory intake tasks. In one analysis, two subject groups, labeled reactors and nonreactors, were identified based on their heart rate reactions to mental arithmetic. (Reactors showed a mean heart rate acceleration of +17.5 beats per minute; nonreactors, a mean change of -0.8 beats per minute.) The corresponding heart rates of reactors and nonreactors during an auditory reaction-time task (sensory intake) averaged +2.3 and -4.8 beats per minute, respectively ($p < 0.01$). Hence, subjects who failed to show an increased heart rate during mental arithmetic exhibited the expected cardiac deceleration during sensory intake. On the other hand, those subjects who were most reactive to mental arithmetic showed a slight increase in heart rate while performing the reaction-time task. Interestingly, the Laceys estimate that about 25 percent of individuals do not show deceleration of heart rate when exposed to intake tasks.[53] Bunnell's findings suggest that these anomalous individuals may, in fact, be subjects who exhibit the largest heart rate accelerations when engaged in sensory rejection tasks.

If individual differences in heart rate reactivity observed during a sensory rejection task predict, in part, responses recorded during sensory intake tasks, is the same true of responses to active and passive coping tasks? Table 6.1 lists baseline heart rates and heart rate changes during shock avoidance, the cold pressor test, and a pornographic film, in groups of college-aged males. The four groups ($ns = 14$) represent quartiles of the distribution of heart rate changes observed during shock avoidance and are ranked from most to least reactive. Note that while baseline heart rates of the four groups are comparable, mean heart rate responses during shock avoidance (active coping) vary considerably, from +9 to +57 beats per minute. The rows labeled Cold Pressor and Pornographic Film list corresponding heart rate changes during the two passive coping tasks. While the magnitude of group differences under these conditions is much attenuated, rank order relationships between the four groups are nonetheless retained. In addition, correlations comparing heart rate changes among the three experimental tasks (calculated over all subjects) yield significant Pearson correlation coefficients ranging from +0.53 to +0.58. Correlations of systolic blood pressure changes recorded during the same tasks are also significant and of

TABLE 6.1. MEAN HEART RATE (IN BEATS PER MINUTE) DURING RELAXATION BASELINE, AND MEAN HEART RATE CHANGES (IN BEATS PER MINUTE) DURING THREE LABORATORY TASKS, IN FOUR GROUPS (ns = 14) RANKED BY LEVEL OF HEART RATE REACTIVITY UNDER SHOCK AVOIDANCE.

	Heart Rate Reactivity			
	Most Reactive		Least Reactive	
	I	II	III	IV
Relaxation baseline	63	65	68	67
Change from relaxation baseline during:				
Shock avoidance	+57	+38	+25	+9
Cold pressor	+33	+27	+19	+13
Pornographic film	+23	+15	+12	+5

Source: Adapted from Obrist PA: *Cardiovascular Psychophysiology: A Perspective.* New York, Plenum, 1981.

similar magnitude ($rs = +0.49$ to $+0.75$). Thus, persons who show relatively greater and lesser heart rate and systolic blood pressure reactions during at least one active coping task (shock avoidance) also tend to differ when exposed to painful or arousing stimuli over which they have little or no instrumental control.

It is important to note that heart rate and blood pressure responsivity was assessed by Obrist relative to a "relaxation" baseline recorded under maximally resting conditions and on a day following the administration of experimental stressors. Calculation of intertask correlations based on heart rate changes from a second baseline obtained just prior to the presentation of tasks, reveals *no* significant relationships among subjects' responses to the three task conditions (all $rs < 0.14$). A similar absence of relationship is also noted for systolic blood pressure changes, when these are calculated from pretask baselines. These effects are apparently due to the fact that, unlike relaxation baselines, pretask values were themselves elevated among more reactive subjects, resulting in an underestimation of the heart rate and blood pressure reactions of hyperresponsive individuals. This finding is of potential significance since in most studies of individual differences, "reactivity" is also expressed as a simple change score reflecting the absolute difference between measurements taken during and immediately preceding subjects' performance of experimental tasks.

Other investigators have occasionally reported correlations between measures of heart rate and blood pressure reactivity observed in the same subjects under different conditions (see Krantz and Manuck[55] for a complete review). However, in these studies experimental stimuli were not selected for their relevance to major task dimensions such as sensory intake versus sensory rejection, or active and passive coping. Nevertheless, Dembroski[56] reports that in a sample of undergraduate volunteers, systolic pressor responses during mental arithmetic covaried significantly ($r = 0.57$) with systolic changes seen on administration of the SI for the assessment of Type A behavior pattern. Although a similar relationship characterized subjects' diastolic responses across the two tasks ($r = 0.62$), a more modest correlation was found for heart rate ($r = 0.44$). In contrast, Manuck and Garland[57] report that among young-adult subjects asked to perform two cognitive tasks—mental arithmetic and a concept formation test—the intertask correlation was very high for heart rate responses ($r = 0.86$), moderate for systolic blood pressure reactions ($r = 0.50$), and only marginal for diastolic responses ($r = 0.23$, NS). In a third data set, reported by Hill and Krantz,[58] medical students were presented three tasks: a reaction-time task, a medical quiz, and the Type A SI. Intertask correlations here were significant for all response measures—heart rate, systolic and diastolic blood pressure—and ranged from 0.53 to 0.81. Yet, in a fourth study, Johnston[59] observed very little consistency of heart rate responses across a series of experimental tasks (video games, mental arithmetic, cold pressor test, isometric handgrip), with intertask correlations rarely exceeding 0.30.

The foregoing studies present a mixed picture regarding the influence of task variables on stability of individual differences in cardiovascular reactivity. In some instances the distribution of heart rate or blood pressure reactions to one experimental task appears to be retained when subjects are presented a second or third task to perform—even when these tasks are conceptually quite dissimilar or reflect differences in the major stimulus variables that determine overall patterning of cardiovascular response. However, other investigators find less consistency across tasks or observe consistency on some response parameters and not on others. Among studies in which subjects' cardiovascular reactions *are* reliably correlated across task conditions, the strength of these associations tends to be only moderate.

It is important to note that most of these studies involve administration of multiple tasks in the same setting by the same experimenter, which may tend to inflate the generalization obtained across tasks. More adequate tests of the generalization issue should therefore involve testing in different settings with different experimenters.

Neuroendocrine Responses

Relatively few analyses of intertask correlations in neuroendocrine responses have been published, and these do not allow us to assess specific task dimensions. Glass, Lake, et al.[60] report low but reliable correlations for plasma epinephrine and norepinephrine responses to mental arithmetic and the Stroop color-word test. Forsman and Lundberg[61] report correlations ranging from -.03 to .70 for urinary measures of catecholamines and cortisol responses to reaction-time, vigilance-task, and Stroop tests. In one study, Ward, Mefford, et al.[62] noted that within individuals, different tasks can elicit differing patterns of release of catecholamines. Epinephrine and norepinephrine reactivity to a series of stressful and nonstressful procedures were measured in the same subjects using a continuous blood-drawing procedure. The stress procedures included several that are commonly used in reactivity studies: mental arithmetic, cold pressor, and isometric handgrip, as well as responses to venipuncture, blood pressure measurement, and deep knee bends. Results indicated that all the stressors and physical measures produced increases in epinephrine, but levels of increase differed significantly between stressors. In particular, the mental arithmetic produced greater epinephrine responses than did cold pressor, venipuncture, or either type of exercise. Norepinephrine levels, by contrast, were higher in response to cold pressor and venipuncture procedures than to mental arithmetic and exercise. In addition, regarding the viability of considering reactivity as an organismic individual difference, each subject's levels over time were significantly correlated.

In sum, discrepancies in this literature may reflect a host of methodologic differences among the several studies cited.[55] Still, available data do not support speculation that there exists a general dimension of individual differences in cardiovascular or endocrine reactivity that is entirely independent of eliciting stimulus characteristics. From an assessment standpoint, then, it is unlikely that use of any one experimental challenge will allow an adequate evaluation of the psychophysiologic response characteristics of individuals. Such evaluation may require, instead, construction of a battery of test stimuli that sample across the variety of task variables known to affect cardiovascular responses. In fact, the most interesting individual-difference dimension may not be the distribution of heart rate or blood pressure responses to a single behavioral challenge, but the extent to which intertask consistency is exhibited by individual subjects. Some persons, for example, may show exaggerated pressor reactions under all task conditions, while others may reveal a more variable pattern of responses; in turn, it may be the stereotypically hyperresponsive individual who is at greatest risk for any clinical sequelae that may follow from heightened cardiovascular reactivity to stress.

GENERALIZATION OF LABORATORY MEASURES TO NONLABORATORY SETTINGS

Since the technology for reliably reassuring cardiovascular and endocrine responses in naturalistic settings has been developed only during the past decade, only limited data can be cited regarding lab-to-field generalization of reactivity to stress. In addition, with the exception of the work of Franken-haeuser and colleagues[see 5,21], there have been few attempts to examine the applicability of laboratory-derived conceptual task dimensions to real-life settings.

With new capabilities for ambulatory monitoring of cardiovascular function—especially heart rate and blood pressure—there are opportunities for observing reactivity during naturalistic conditions, which are inevitably less controlled than experimental conditions. Measures of urinary hormone excretion (e.g., as used by Frankenhaeuser's group in Sweden[5,21]) provide another important means of physiologic measurement in naturalistic settings.

Recent data, involving field blood pressure measurements, have been reviewed by Dembroski and MacDougall.[63] Available results generally show positive associations between laboratory and naturalistic measures. In an unpublished study, differences among college students in heart rate responsivity during mental arithmetic have been found to be predictive of heart rate and blood pressure measurements recorded just prior to a midterm examination.[64] Similar findings are reported as well in pilot studies described recently by Dembroski and MacDougall[63] as well as among adolescents.[66] In addition, Manuck, Giordani, et al.[64] noted that among working professionals, those who showed the greatest systolic responses to a frustrating cognitive task also exhibited heightened systolic blood pressure variability in casual measurements recorded over a six-week interval during ordinary occupational activities.

In a similar investigation, Rüddel, Gogolin, et al.[67] reported small but significant correlations between systolic blood pressure changes, measured during mental arithmetic and a structured interview, and mean systolic blood pressures recorded casually for six weeks (significant r range = 0.26 to 0.43). In contrast to the study by Manuck, Giordani, et al.,[64] no comparable association was found between task-related changes and systolic variability during the six-week observation period. An important difference between these two studies is the fact that casual measurements recorded by Rüddel et al. were well within the normal range, and there was no evidence that subjects experienced stress at the time of blood pressure measurement. On the other hand, peak systolic pressures obtained during the workday by Manuck, Giordani, et al. far exceeded subjects' resting baselines. Hence, naturalistic variability of blood pressure may be related more appreciably to reactivity in a laboratory setting when casual measurements are somewhat elevated and, presumably, reactive to events in the individual's own environment.

A recent study by Pickering, Harshfield, and colleagues,[68] using ambulatory blood pressure determinations, revealed good correlations between clinic and ambulatory blood pressure readings in normotensives and patients with essential hypertension but rather poor correlations in borderline hypertensives. Based on these data, they suggested that ambulatory monitoring may be an important method for determining which borderline patients require treatment.

Since naturalistic environments are by their nature less controlled than laboratory situations, it is necessary to impose some organizing structure on what otherwise would be merely a temporal sequence of readings over a 24-hour period. Since blood pressure responses presumably are affected by individual confrontations with stressors varying in intensity and quality, it is helpful for the subject to keep a brief diary that describes the general circumstances at the time of each recording. In addition, in analyzing pressor responses recorded automatically via ambulatory monitoring instruments, it would be useful to know whether the subject was smoking, ingesting caffeine or alcohol, physically active, or interacting with other persons during measurements.

Translating Laboratory Task Dimensions to Field Settings

The many variables operating on individuals in naturalistic settings makes it difficult to generalize to these settings from laboratory-based situations where variables are highly controlled. At least in the occupational stress literature, several broad types of working conditions have been associated with cardiovascular disease risk. These are job demands, job autonomy (decision latitude), and job satisfaction. As described in a recent review by Wells,[69] job demands refer to job conditions that tax or interfere with the worker's performance abilities (e.g., workload, role conflict, and responsibilities). Level of job autonomy refers to the ability of the worker to control the speed, nature, and conditions of work. Job satisfactions include gratifications of the worker's motivations (needs or aspirations) for working.

Of particular relevance to laboratory dimensions are level of control over one's job and job underload or overload. Karasek, Theorell, and colleagues[70] have developed a model suggesting the additive and possibly interactive effects of high job demands and low job autonomy (discretion latitude). Several occupational studies were presented to demonstrate this point. In one sample, it was shown that higher coronary heart disease rates for workers were exhibited by occupations with simultaneously high demands and low autonomy. In the other studies, only main effects for high job demands and low autonomy were found. Given the research of Frankenhaeuser and coworkers[5] demonstrating the effects of level of control over work pace and work overload on urinary endocrine excretion, job settings differing in autonomy and work load would seem to be suitable ways to determine the applicability of laboratory-derived dimensions to naturalistic work settings.

SUMMARY AND CONCLUDING COMMENTS

An ideal psychological stressor for studying reactivity (and its relation to behavior and disease) would be one that previously showed an ability to elicit a stable magnitude and patterning of responses when applied comparably in different laboratories and when presented to different subject groups or to the same individuals on repeated occasions. This ideal presumes, of course, that population differences do not reflect legitimate population differences in reactivity-related *risk*. Where such risk differences might be hypothesized, it is not desirable to attenuate population differences in responses by manipulation of task variables.

However, our review of the literature suggests that few, if any, tasks presently meet all of the aforementioned criteria. Rather, as noted earlier, diverse experimental challenges, including stressful interviews, various psychomotor tasks, cognitive problems, cold water immersion (with different instructionals sets), video games (with and without competition), and anticipation of electric shock have been used by different investigators. These experimental tasks differ along stimulus dimensions involving active versus passive coping, sensory intake versus rejection, and so on, as well as in the tendency to evoke different affective states such as anxiety and anger.

A lack of standardization in the reactivity literature also results from insufficient attempts to replicate the exact procedures and instructional sets used in previous research. Although this diversity is often desirable to establish convergent validity concerning findings in this area, the result of such diversity is an absence of common test protocols that can be applied to different populations (such as in epidemiologic studies) or used reliably by varying groups of investigators.[55,71]

Because there are gaps in current knowledge, and since only moderate correlations have been observed between subjects' physiologic responses to various experimental tasks, it is probable that an adequate test protocol for population-based research will require not one but a variety of laboratory challenges. If current hypotheses about reactivity and disease are to be confirmed or refuted, the challenges used and the patterns of physiologic responses elicited should be consistent with a set of pathogenetic hypotheses. For example, if sympathetic influences on the heart are of primary concern (as in Obrist's model of behavioral effects on hypertension), tasks should be selected that: (1) tend to evoke such responses reliably, (2) yield a significant range of individual differences in reactivity, and (3) elicit much the same responses among individuals retested using the same stimulus. Similar considerations apply where other aspects of autonomic and neuroendocrine reactivity are of interest, as in the hypothesized relation of catecholamines to the development of coronary artery disease.[72] In contrast, it can also be argued that research in this area is at an early exploratory stage, and that the range or types of tasks utilized should not be prematurely limited by existing theory.

In addition, protocols composed of several tasks may represent another way of assessing how individuals may differ in consistency of their physiologic response characteristics. Although it is clear that there is variability among subjects' responses to any single task or stimulus, the extent to which people exhibit comparable reactivity across a variety of challenges may reflect a meaningful dimension of individual differences. Some persons, for instance, may be hyperreactive under all stimulus conditions, whereas others may show a variable, and hence less predictable, level of reactivity.

Task Duration

Although experimental tasks ranged in length from a few minutes to over one hour, investigators have generally used test procedures requiring less than 15 minutes to administer. Special circumstances occasionally call for tasks of greater duration, as in studying shifting hemodynamic adjustments to protracted periods of stress.[73] Longer test intervals allow examination of the persistence of physiologic responses over time (e.g., some individuals may exhibit habituation to task stimuli more quickly than others). However, a major disadvantage of lengthy test procedures is that they restrict the number of different tasks that can be presented within any experimental session. In the absence of any clear indication that longer challenges permit greater discrimination between relevant subject groups (e.g., hypertensives vs. normotensives, Type As vs. Type Bs), it seems that experimental tasks of relatively brief duration—perhaps 5 to 15 minutes each—should prove sufficient for most research applications.

Conclusion

In this chapter, we have described research on task dimensions such as active versus passive coping, sensory intake versus sensory rejection, and level of challenge. However, there appears to be considerable overlap among tasks fitting one or another of these dimensions (for a contrasting view, see Williams' chapter). For example, active coping tasks (e.g., mental arithmetic, reaction time to avoid shocks) are also highly challenging tasks. Sensory-intake tasks (e.g., reaction-time tasks with long intertrial intervals) are often low-challenge tasks eliciting little physiologic responding. Especially regarding catecholamine and cortisol responses, we are presently hard pressed to select a task that will reliably elicit a predominantly epinephrine response, norepinephrine response, or some known combination of these. For use in theory-testing research, a cataloging of specific tasks (e.g., mental arithmetic, reaction time, Stroop test, video game) with respect to the patterns of responses they elicit in different groups (e.g., men, women, old, young) is necessary. There is a clear need for further research to characterize particular tasks according to the types and patterns of physiological responses they elicit. It is difficult to test a pathogenetic theory if the physiologic responses elicited among the aggregate population by a specific laboratory maneuver cannot be predicted in advance.

Finally, there has been very little field research that allows us to characterize naturalistic situations and settings (such as work or family situation) along dimensions that parallel those utilized on short-term laboratory studies of reactivity. Along these lines, it would be useful for further research to examine reactivity in conjunction with occupational and ecological variables (level of control, overload, etc.) thought to be relevant to cardiovascular disease.

REFERENCES

1. Cannon W: *Bodily Changes in Pain, Hunger, Fear, and Rage* (2nd ed). New York, Appleton-Century-Crofts, 1936.
2. Selye H: *The Stress of Life* (2nd ed). New York, McGraw-Hill, 1976.
3. Mason JW: A re-evaluation of the concept of "non-specificity" in stress theory. *J Psychiatr Res* 8:323–333, 1971.
4. Lazarus RS: *Psychological Stress and the Coping Process.* New York, McGraw-Hill, 1966.
5. Frankenhaeuser M: Psychoneuroendocrine approaches to the study of emotion as related to stress and coping. In Howe HE, Dienstbier RA (eds): *Nebraska Symposium on Motivation 1978.* Lincoln, University of Nebraska Press, 1979, pp. 123–161.
6. Elliott GR, Eisdorfer C: *Stress and Human Health: Analysis and Implications of Research.* New York, Springer, 1982.
7. Baum A, Grunberg NE, Singer JE: The use of psychological and neuroendocrinological measurements in the study of stress. *Health Psychol* 1:217–236, 1982.
8. Williams RB: Neuroendocrine response patterns and stress: Biobehavioral mechanisms of disease. In Williams RB (ed): *Perspectives on Behavioral Medicine:* (Vol 2): *Neuroendocrine Control and Behavior.* New York, Academic Press, 1985, pp. 71–101.
9. Engel BT: Response specificity. In Greenfield NS, Sternbach RA (eds): *Handbook of Psychophysiology.* New York, Holt, Rinehart, & Winston, 1972, pp. 571–576.
10. Lacey JI: Somatic response patterning and stress: Some revisions of activation theory. In Appley MH, Trumble R (eds): *Psychological Stress.* New York, Appleton-Century-Crofts, 1967, pp. 14–37.
11. Obrist PA: *Cardiovascular Psychophysiology: A Perspective.* New York, Plenum, 1981.

12. Cohen F, Horowitz MJ, et al: Panel report on psychosocial assets and modifiers of stress. In Elliott GR, Eisdorfer C (eds): *Stress and Human Health: Analysis and Implications of Research*. New York, Springer, 1982, pp. 147–188.

13. Kasl SV: Stress and health. *Ann Rev Public Health* 5:319–341, 1984.

14. Geer JH, Davison GC, Gatchel RI: Reduction of stress in humans through nonveridical perceived control of aversive stimulation. *J Pers Soc Psychol* 16:731–738, 1970.

15. Seligman ME: *Helplessness: On Depression, Development and Death*. San Francisco, Freeman, 1975.

16. Brod J, Fencl V, et al: Circulatory changes underlying blood pressure elevation during acute emotional stress in normotensive and hypertensive subjects. *Clin Sci* 18:269–279, 1959.

17. Falkner B, Onesti G, et al: Cardiovascular response to mental stress in normal adolescents with hypertensive parents. *Hypertension* 1:23–30, 1979.

18. Williams RB, Lane JD, et al: Physiological and neuroendocrine response patterns during different behavioral challenges: Differential hyperresponsivity of Type A men. *Science* 218:483–485, 1982.

19. Dembroski TM, MacDougall JM, et al: Components of the Type A coronary-prone behavior pattern and cardiovascular responses to psychomotor performance challenge. *J Behav Med* 1:159–176, 1973.

20. Obrist PA, Gaebelein CJ, et al: The relationship among heart rate, carotid dP/dt and blood pressure in humans as a function of the type of stress. *Psychophysiology* 15:102–115, 1978.

21. Frankenhaeuser M: The sympathetic-adrenal and pituitary-adrenal response to challenge: Comparison between the sexes. In Dembroski TM, Schmidt TH, Blumchen G (eds): *Biobehavioral Bases of Coronary Heart Disease*. Basel, Karger, 1983, pp. 91–105.

22. Manuck SB, Proietti J: Parental hypertension and cardiovascular response to cognitive and isometric challenge. *Psychophysiology* 19:481–489, 1982.

23. Glass DC, Krakoff LR, et al: Effect of harassment and competition upon cardiovascular and catecholaminic responses in Type A and B individuals. *Psychophysiology* 17:453–463, 1980.

24. Fredrikson M, Dimberg U, et al: Haemodynamic and electrodermal correlates of psychogenic stimuli in normotensive and hypertensive subjects. *Biol Psychol* 15:63–73, 1982.

25. MacDougall JM, Dembroski TM, Krantz DS: Effects of types of challenge on pressor and heart rate responses in Type A and B women. *Psychophysiology* 18:1–9, 1981.

26. Rosenman RH: The interview method of assessment of the coronary-prone behavior pattern. In Dembroski TM, Weiss SM, et al (eds): *Coronary-Prone Behavior*. New York, Springer, 1978, pp. 55–70.

27. Lang PJ: A bio-informational theory of emotional imagery. *Psychophysiology* 16:495–512, 1979.

28. Lovallo WR, Pishkin V: A psychophysiological comparison of Type A and B men exposed to failure and uncontrollable noise. *Psychophysiology* 17:29–36, 1980.

29. Dembroski TM, MacDougall JM, et al: Effect of level of challenge on pressor and heart rate responses in Type A and B subjects. *J Appl Soc Psychol* 9:209–228, 1979.

30. Dimsdale J: Wet holter monitoring: Techniques for studying plasma responses to stress in ambulatory subjects. In Dembroski TM, Schmidt TH, Blumchen G (eds): *Biobehavioral Bases of Coronary Heart Disease*. Basel, Karger, 1983, pp. 175–184.

31. Light KC, Obrist PA: Cardiovascular response to stress: Effects of opportunity to avoid, shock experience and performance feedback. *Psychophysiology* 17:243–252, 1980.

32. Elliott R: Effects of uncertainty about the nature and advent of a noxious stimulus (shock) upon heart rate. *J Pers Soc Psychol* 3:353–356, 1966.

33. Manuck SB, Schaeffer DC: Stability of individual differences in cardiovascular reactivity. *Physiol Behav* **21**:675–678, 1978.

34. Manuck SB, Harvey AE, et al: Effects of coping on blood pressure responses to threat of aversive stimulation. *Psychophysiology* **16**:136–142, 1979.

35. Light KC, Obrist PA: Task difficulty, heart rate reactivity, and cardiovascular responses to an appetitive reaction time task. *Psychophysiology* **20**:301–312, 1983.

36. Light KC: Cardiovascular responses to effortful active coping: Implications for the role of stress in hypertension development. *Psychophysiology* **18**:216–225, 1981.

37. Lacey JI, Kagan J, Lacey BC: The visceral level: Situational determinants and behavioral correlates of autonomic response patterns. In Knapp PH (ed): *Expression of the Emotions in Man*. New York, International University Press, 1963, pp. 161–196.

38. Obrist PA, Webb RA, et al: The cardiac-somatic relationship: Some reformulations. *Psychophysiology* **6**:569–587, 1970.

39. Williams RB, Bittker TE, et al: Cardiovascular and neurophysiologic correlates of sensory intake and rejection: I. Effect of cognitive tasks. *Psychophysiology* **12**:427–433, 1975.

40. Sternbach RA: *Principles of Psychophysiology*. New York, Academic Press, 1966.

41. Ax AF: The physiological differentiation between fear and anger in humans. *Psychosom Med* **15**:433–442, 1953.

42. Ekman P, Levenson RW, Friesen WV: Autonomic nervous system activity distinguishes among emotions. *Science* **221**:1208–1210, 1983.

43. Weinberger DA, Schwartz GE, Davidson RJ: Low-anxious, high-anxious and repressive coping styles: Psychometric patterns and behavioral and physiological responses to stress. *J Abnorm Psychol* **88**:369–380, 1979.

44. Schwartz GE, Weinberger DA, Singer JE: Cardiovascular differentiation of happiness, sadness, anger, and fear following imagery and exercise. *Psychosom Med* **43**:343–364, 1981.

45. Glass DC, Contrada RJ: Type A behavior and catecholamines: A critical review. In Ziegler MG, Lake CR (eds): *Norepinephrine*. Baltimore, Williams & Wilkins, 1984, pp. 346–367.

46. Mason JW: A historical view of the stress field: Part II. *J Human Stress* **1**:22–36, 1975.

47. Glass DC, Singer JE: *Urban Stress: Experiments on Noise and Social Stressors*. New York, Academic Press, 1972.

48. Contrada RJ, Glass DC, et al: Effects of control over aversive stimulation and Type A behavior on cardiovascular and plasma catecholamine responses. *Psychophysiology* **19**:408–419, 1982.

49. Lovallo W: The cold pressor test and autonomic function: A review and integration. *Psychophysiology* **12**:268–283, 1975.

50. Dimsdale J, Moss J: Short-term catecholamine response to psychological stress. *Psychosom Med* **42**:493–497, 1980.

51. Dimsdale JE: Generalizing from laboratory studies to field studies of human stress physiology. *Psychosom Med* **46**:463–469, 1984.

52. Bunnell DE: Autonomic myocardial influences as a factor determining inter-task consistency of heart rate reactivity. *Psychophysiology* **19**:442–448, 1982.

53. Lacey BC, Lacey JI: Studies of heart rate and other bodily processes in sensorimotor behavior. In Obrist PA, Black AH, et al (eds): *Cardiovascular Psychophysiology*. Chicago, Aldine Publishing Co, 1974, pp. 538–564.

54. Manuck SB, Morrison RL, et al: Behavioral factors in hypertension: Cardiovascular responsivity, anger, and social competence. In Chesney MA, Rosenman RH (eds): *Anger and Hostility in Cardiovascular and Behavioral Disorders*. New York, Hemisphere/McGraw-Hill, 1985, pp. 149–172.

55. Krantz DS, Manuck SB: Acute psychophysiologic reactivity and risk of cardiovascular disease: A review and methodologic critique. *Psychol Bull* **96**:435–464, 1984.

56. Dembroski T: Personal communication. 1984.

57. Manuck SB, Garland FN: Stability in individual differences in cardiovascular reactivity: A thirteen month follow-up. *Physiol Behav* **21**:621–624, 1980.

58. Hill DR, Krantz DS: Type A behavior and cardiovascular response in military medical students as a function of academic stress. Paper presented at meeting of the Eastern Psychological Association, Philadelphia, April 1983.

59. Johnston, D. Personal communication. July 1984.

60. Glass DC, Lake CR, et al: Stability of individual differences in physiologic responses to stress. *Health Psychol* **4**:317–342, 1983.

61. Forsman L, Lundberg U: Consistency in catecholamine and cortisol excretion in males and females. *Pharmacol Biochem Behav* **17**:555–562, 1982.

62. Ward MM, Mefford IN, et al: Epinephrine and norepinephrine responses in continuously collected human plasma to a series of stressors. *Psychosom Med* **45**:471–487, 1983.

63. Dembroski TM, MacDougall JM: Validation of the vita-stat automated non-invasive blood pressure recording device. In Herd JA, Gotto AM, et al (eds): *Cardiovascular Instrumentation: Applicability of New Technology to Biobehavioral Research*. Bethesda, MD: National Institutes of Health (Pub. No. 84-1654), 1984, pp. 55–78.

64. Manuck SB, Giordani B, et al: Generalizability of individual differences in heart rate reactivity. Unpublished manuscript, University of Virginia, 1980.

65. Dembroski TM, MacDougall JM: Behavioral and psychophysiological perspectives on coronary-prone behavior. In Dembroski TM, Schmidt TH, Blumchen G (eds): *Biobehavioral Bases of Coronary Heart Disease*. Basel, Karger, 1983, pp. 106–129.

66. Matthews KA, Manuck SB, Saab P: Cardiovascular responses of adolescents during a naturally occurring stressor and their behavioral and psychophysiological predictors. *Psychophysiology*, in press.

67. Ru³ddel H, Gogolin E, et al: Coronary-prone behavior and blood pressure reactivity in laboratory and life stress. In Dembroski TM, Schmidt TH, Blumchen G (eds): *Biobehavioral Bases of Coronary Heart Disease*. Basel, Karger, 1983, pp. 185–196.

68. Pickering TJ, Harshfield GA, et al: Blood pressure during normal daily activities, sleep, and exercise. *JAMA* **247**:992–996, 1982.

69. Wells JA: Chronic life situations and life events. In Ostfeld A, Eaker E (eds). *Measuring Psychosocial Variables in Epidemiological Studies of Cardiovascular Disease*. Bethesda, MD: National Institutes of Health (Publication No. 85-2270), 1985, pp. 105–128.

70. Karasek RA, Theorell TG, et al: Job, psychological factors and coronary heart disease: Swedish prospective findings and U.S. prevalence findings using a new occupational inference method. *Adv Cardiol* **29**:62–67, 1982.

71. Watkins L, Rose R: Demographic variables related to reactivity. In Weiss SM, Matthews KA, et al (eds): *Proceedings of the NHLBI Conference on Stress, Reactivity, and Cardiovascular Disease*. Bethesda, MD: National Institutes of Health (Publication No. 84-2698), 1984, pp. 119–132.

72. Glass DC: Stress, behavior patterns, and coronary disease. *Am Sci* **65**:177–187, 1977.

73. DeGood DE: Cognitive control factors and vascular stress responses. *Psychophysiology* **12**:399–401, 1975.

7

Patterns of Reactivity and Stress

REDFORD B. WILLIAMS, JR.

INTRODUCTION

We are interested in the question of stress and reactivity because certain psychological characteristics, such as Type A behavior[1] and hostility,[2] have been shown to predispose persons to increased risk of cardiovascular disease. An implicit assumption (the "reactivity hypothesis") fueling our concern with stress and reactivity is that persons with such characteristics as Type A behavior and hostility experience degrees of cardiovascular and neuroendocrine reactivity to everyday environmental events (stressors) that are at least partly responsible for the increased disease incidence observed when they are followed in prospective longitudinal studies.

Before we can even begin to speculate regarding the pathogenic role of reactivity, however, it is first necessary to provide a theoretical framework

Preparation of this chapter was supported by a Research Scientist Award from the NIMH, and by grants from the NHLBI and the John D. and Catherine T. MacArthur Foundation.

on which to base our speculations. What is meant by "reactivity"? Do all environmental "stressors" cause the same kind of reactivity? Do all individuals respond to the same environmental stressors with the same reactivity? If we can draw upon empirical research in the stress field to pose acceptable answers to questions such as these, then it will be possible to proceed in a more systematic, informed, and reasoned fashion to design the studies necessary to elucidate pathogenic mechanisms underlying the relationships between certain psychological characteristics and cardiovascular disease.

This chapter will not be a detailed review of research on the range of psychological stressors/challenges that cause different patterns of cardiovascular and neuroendocrine response (see the chapter by Krantz, Manuck, and Wing). Instead, it will present a more interpretive view in which I attempt to integrate diverse lines of evidence from different disciplines into a conceptual framework that may prove useful in moving toward a general understanding of "stress and reactivity."

I shall begin by presenting a model outlining the critical classes of variables we must study to gain an understanding of how environmental events are translated into *patterns* of cardiovascular and neuroendocrine responses that could play a role in pathogenesis. I shall review the experimental evidence supporting the existence of two qualitatively distinct response patterns (which, for descriptive purposes, I shall designate Pattern 1 and Pattern 2) in humans and animals, along with observations about the kinds of environmental stimuli that appear specifically to elicit those patterns. A consideration of brain mechanisms responsible for mediating these response patterns will next serve to buttress the argument for their existence, as well as add to our understanding of classes of environmental stimuli critical for their elicitation.

The organization of this chapter was not chosen without some thought. When it comes to defining those types of environmental stimuli that elicit specific patterns of physiological response, there is room for much controversy. The process of naming psychosocial phenomena often leads scientists to engage in what may be termed "label narcissism": we all love our own labels for things far more than the labels others might choose. Thus, researchers who argue whether "active coping" or "mental work" (see Krantz, Manuck, and Wing, this volume) is the critical determinant of one pattern of physiological response may actually be talking about the same thing but arguing about what name to give it. This possibility comes into sharper focus when one realizes that researchers often use the same task— that is, mental arithmetic—to engender *both* active coping and mental work behaviors in their experimental subjects. To circumvent this particular argument about labels, I shall first present evidence supporting the objectively evident existence of two patterns of physiological response under conditions that might be described as "stressful." If we can agree on at least the broad

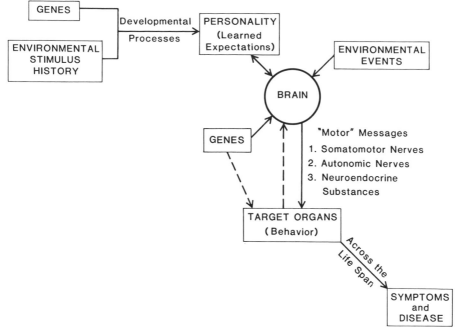

FIGURE 7.1.   Theoretical model illustrating how personality factors, environmental events, and genes interact via the brain's transduction to produce integrated patterns of physiologic response.

outlines of those patterns, then perhaps we can enter a dialogue in which, together, we attempt to characterize the circumstances that elicit either pattern. If we can avoid the "name debate," perhaps it will be easier to get on with the work of understanding the role of reactivity in the pathogenesis of cardiovascular disease.

A THEORETICAL MODEL

Figure 7.1 illustrates my version of the "biopsychosocial" model. This model may be no better than others' attempts at graphic representation of how environmental events are transduced into physiological responses ("reactivity") that could play a role in causing cardiovascular disease. It does illustrate, however, several principles that should be taken into account if we are ever to understand the role of reactivity in cardiovascular disease.

First, and most relevant to the focus of this chapter, the model shows that the "motor messages" sent by the brain to the body's organs following the perception of some environmental event occur in organized *patterns*, rather than as isolated responses, and that these patterns involve all three of the motor effector systems available for the brain's communication with the body—the somatomotor nerves, the autonomic nerves, and the neuroendocrine system. This principle has been most cogently enunciated by the English physiologist S.M. Hilton, who suggests:

> that a new approach may be made by starting from the view that the central nervous system is organized to produce not single, isolated variables, but integrated patterns of response. Any variable which can be described or measured independently is actually a component of several such patterns. . . . In this system, the repertoire of patterned responses [may be] very small.[3, p. 214]

Based on this reasoning, then, I suggest that broad classes of environmental events may produce a relatively small number of integrated patterns of response involving the three motor effector systems. This means that rather than studying only one or two physiologic parameters, we should study as many parameters as possible, so as to more reliably identify consistent patterns of response. If we can identify and agree on the nature of some of these patterns, it might then be possible to characterize the critical types of environmental stimulation that elicit them.

As the model also indicates, the brain's interpretation and transduction of environmental events into patterns of motor messages can be modulated by the personality of the individual as well as his or her genetic makeup. Thus, the model reminds us that different personalities—for example, those producing Type A and Type B behavior—can result in differences in the patterned response to the same environmental stimulus situation. It also calls our attention to the fact that certain genetic characteristics—for example, those also responsible for increased predisposition to essential hypertension—can also influence what happens in the motor outflow tracts following any stimulus.

The above sequence of events—environmental event, interpretation by the brain and transduction into patterns of motor messages, modulation by the personality and genes, and effects of motor messages on target organs—occurs on a more or less acute basis within a limited time span, although such acute effects can be sustained as long as the organism is involved with the given environmental stimulus. The model also suggests, however, that we be mindful of certain other processes that occur over longer, more chronic time periods. First, personality is the result of developmental processes, beginning at birth and extending into adulthood, that involve the interaction between the individual's genetic predispositions and his or her environment. A second chronic process involves the cumulative effect of repeated elicitations of the various patterns of response across the life span. If extensive and intensive enough, these repeated responses could over time lead to pathophysiological changes resulting in the development of cardio-vascular disease.

In the remainder of this chapter I shall review some experimental data that suggests the existence of two qualitatively distinct patterns of response. This will be followed by a consideration of the means by which the brain produces these patterns and by some observations regarding the types of environmental stimuli that elicit them.

TWO PATTERNS OF PHYSIOLOGIC RESPONSE

Obrist has called our attention to the importance of motor activity and the skeletal musculature in determining patterns of response.[4] It follows from this observation that responses of the skeletal muscle vasculature might furnish important clues regarding basic response patterns. The skeletal muscle circulation is one of the most interesting in the body, receiving anywhere from 15 to 20 percent of the cardiac output at rest up to 85 percent under conditions of heavy work or stress. It is the only vascular bed that has neural and neuroendocrine mechanisms that permit it to exhibit both active vasodilatation and active vasoconstriction. For these reasons and because it supports the functions of motor activity so important for life itself, the skeletal muscle vascular bed deserves our attention as we try to identify the basic physiologic response patterns.

In studies with humans a number of investigators have used the relatively simple but reliable method of venous occlusion plethysmography[5] to study skeletal muscle hemodynamics under various experimental conditions. Representative of one group of these studies was the demonstration by Brod, Fencl, and colleagues[6] of an active vasodilatation in the forearm skeletal musculature during performance of mental arithmetic with harrassment. The similarity of this skeletal muscle hemodynamic response in humans to that seen with stimulation of the hypothalamic "defense" area in animals[7] has led to the conclusion that under conditions where "fight or flight" behavior is an appropriate response, active skeletal muscle vasodilatation is a key aspect of the integrated response.[3]

Thus, it seems reasonable to suggest that skeletal muscle vasodilatation may be a valid "marker" of one important response pattern with relevance for the role of reactivity in cardiovascular disease. For the time being, let us refer to this pattern as Pattern 1. Of course, the model presented earlier leads us to recognize that the skeletal muscle vasodilatation is only one ingredient of Pattern 1. Indeed, Brod and coworkers in their pioneering study[6] were able to demonstrate that at the same time the muscle vasodilatation was occurring, vasoconstriction in the skin, kidney, and gastrointestinal tract of their subjects was also occurring. It follows as well that the neuroendocrine system also participates in Pattern 1.

With regard to the other pattern, Pattern 2, based on observations of diastolic blood pressure increases during personal interviews,[8] my colleagues and I studied the muscle hemodynamic response to mental arithmetic, a sensory intake task, and a personal interview.[9,10] During mental arithmetic performance we found, as had many others, an increase in forearm blood flow and a decrease in forearm vascular resistance, indicating active skeletal muscle vasodilatation. In contrast, during the sensory intake task we found that forearm vascular resistance showed a significant *increase*, indicating an active skeletal muscle vasoconstriction. The muscle hemodynamic response to the personal interview provided further clues regarding motoric behaviors associated with muscle vasoconstriction: among those subjects who avoided attending to the interviewer, forearm vascular resistance fell; among those who attended closely to the interviewer, an increase in forearm vascular resistance was observed.

Thus, it appears that, in addition to the skeletal muscle vasodilatation observed during "defense" behavioral activations, there is a second, qualitatively distinct pattern of muscle hemodynamic response that can be elicited, one characterized by active vasoconstriction. As with Pattern 1, for the time being let us refer to this second pattern, characterized by active skeletal muscle vasoconstriction as "Pattern 2." Similarly, if it is truly a marker of one of the "integrated patterns of response" to which Hilton referred, it should also be possible to demonstrate characteristic neuroendocrine responses accompanying the muscle vasoconstriction.

The suggestion that we need to be concerned with two basic response patterns, Pattern 1 with muscle vasodilatation as a marker, and Pattern 2 with muscle vasoconstriction as a marker, is also based on an extensive body of animal research. Anderson and Brady[11] cite research with dogs that leads them to conclude that behavioral states (e.g., shock avoidance) associated with *activation* of the skeletal-motor system lead to pressor responses mediated by increased cardiac output in the face of decreased peripheral resistance, while behavioral *inhibition* (e.g., during preavoidance) of the skeletal-motor system leads to increased blood pressure, which is mediated solely by increases in total peripheral resistance. Based on observations of skeletal muscle vasoconstriction of a cat during alert observation of another cat and vasodilatation during attack, Zanchetti also suggested the existence of a dual cardiovascular response pattern subserving emotional behavior:

> ...one type [skeletal muscle vasoconstriction] being the usual companion of immobile confrontation of the preparatory stage, the other type [skeletal muscle vasodilatation] being characteristic of emotional movement (the classical "defense pattern").[12,p.144]

Given that the existence of the qualitatively distinct skeletal muscle hemodynamic response patterns of vasodilatation and vasoconstriction which appear to characterize two general response patterns—Pattern 1 and Pattern 2—has been demonstrated in numerous experimental studies employing a diverse array of environmental stimuli in both humans and animals, our research group recently undertook a study[13] to characterize the neuroendocrine components of Pattern 1 and Pattern 2. Another purpose was to evaluate the effect of personality-related characteristics (Type A behavior pattern) and genetic factors (family history of cardiovascular disease) on the expression of the two response patterns.

To elicit Pattern 1, we had 31 undergraduate males perform a mental arithmetic task with a prize to the best performer; to elicit Pattern 2, we had these same subjects perform a choice reaction-time task. The tasks were presented in counterbalanced order on two separate occasions, at the same time of day, with a one-week interval between the two experimental sessions. Hemodynamic measures taken during a 20-minute baseline period followed by a 20-minute task period included heart rate (HR), systolic blood pressure (SBP), diastolic blood pressure (DBP), and forearm blood flow (FBF); forearm vascular resistance (FVR) was calculated as the mean blood pressure divided by the FBF. In addition, a Cormed continuous exfusion pump was used to obtain integrated venous blood samples throughout the baseline and task periods. The plasma was spun down and frozen to be subsequently assayed for norepinephrine, epinephrine, cortisol, prolactin, growth hormone, and testosterone.

The main results of interest are shown in Figure 7.2. During mental arithmetic performance, a significant increase in FBF and a significant decrease in FVR were observed, indicating the expected skeletal muscle vasodilatation. With respect to neuroendocrine responses, there were highly significant increases in prolactin (not shown), norepinephrine, epinephrine, and cortisol, while testosterone changed not at all. With the exception of prolactin, all three hormones that showed a significant increase showed significantly larger increases in Type A than in Type B subjects.

During reaction time performance, the pattern of responses was quite different. Overall, there was no change in FVR, a result largely accounted for by the failure of the Type A subjects to show the expected increase, which was observed in the Type B subjects. While norepinephrine showed a significant increase overall, it did not differ between Type A and B subjects. In contrast to the mental arithmetic task, where epinephrine and cortisol were quite responsive, during the reaction-time task these two hormones showed no change. Also in contrast to the mental arithmetic task, in which testosterone was unresponsive, during reaction time performance, a significant overall increase in testosterone was observed, and the increase in Type A subjects was significantly greater than that in the Type B subjects.

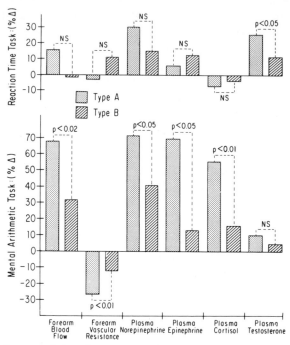

FIGURE 7.2.   Patterns of physiologic response observed during reaction-time task performance and mental arithmetic performance. (Adapted from R.B. Williams, et al. "Type A behavior and elevated physiological and neuroendocrine responses to cognitive tasks," in *Science 218:483–485*, Fig. 29 October 1982. Copyright 1982 by the American Association for the Advancement of Science.)

It was not surprising that epinephrine and cortisol increases were observed as components of Pattern 1. Henry[14] has concluded on the basis of an extensive review of the stress literature that cortisol and epinephrine are released under conditions where the classical "fight or flight" response is activated, and at least one widely accepted situation where the muscle vasodilatation that is the critical marker for Pattern 1 is observed is the defense reaction, or "fight or flight" response. Thus, our findings suggest that, along with the muscle vasodilatation, increased secretion of epinephrine and cortisol are also components of the Pattern 1 response.

The increased testosterone response during the reaction-time task is less easy to interpret at the present time, although there are some intriguing clues as to why this hormone should be secreted under conditions requiring males to attend closely to environmental stimuli. In general, the stress literature suggests that with the exceptions of male sexual behavior and male-male dominance confrontations, the usual effect of "stress" on testosterone levels is to decrease them.[15] There are animal studies, however, which suggest that administration of exogenous testosterone has the effect of increasing persistence in a task, as well as focusing and narrowing attention.[16] Whatever else two males engaged in a dominance confrontation may be doing, they are certainly paying very close attention to one another. Thus, our finding of increased testosterone secretion during an experimental condition requiring close observation of environmental stimuli may be reflecting this hormone's function as a "vigilance hormone." Though it will be important to replicate this finding in further studies, our confidence that the testosterone response we observed is real is bolstered by the observation of Zumoff, Rosenfeld, and coworkers[17] that, in comparison to Type B men, Type A men excrete more testosterone glucuronide in urine during the working but not the nocturnal hours.

If our findings are replicated, it would suggest that, in addition to the association of epinephrine and cortisol with Pattern 1, a reliable neuroendo-crine component of Pattern 2 is increased testosterone secretion. Indeed, preliminary results from a study just completed suggest that the increased testosterone response of Type A males also is exhibited during another sensory intake task, the word identification task. Thus, it appears that the principle of integrated patterns of autonomic and neuroendocrine response that is part of the model shown in Figure 7.1 has been supported by the study described above. Not only are there qualitatively distinct skeletal muscle hemodynamic components of two patterns that have been widely observed, there are also qualitatively distinct patterns of neuroendocrine response observed in association with experimental conditions that are known to elicit the muscle hemodynamic components.

In addition, there is evidence for the participation, also as suggested in the model, of personality factors in modulating the expression of Patterns 1 and 2: Type A males showed greater secretion of cortisol and epinephrine during the condition known to elicit Pattern 1, and greater secretion of testosterone during the condition used to elicit Pattern 2. Finally, the role of the genes in modulating expression of Patterns 1 and 2 also finds some support in the findings of the study cited. Among those subjects with a positive family history of hypertension, the Type A subjects showed a larger cortisol and DBP response to the reaction-time task; among those with a negative family history, the Type A subjects' cortisol and DBP responses were either smaller or not different from those of the Type B subjects.

It would be unwise, of course, to accept as final truth the interpretations I offer above for the findings of a single study involving such a small number of subjects. Replications are clearly needed. I have described these findings in detail, however, because they illustrate the principles advanced at the beginning of this chapter. First, physiologic responses to environmental stimuli occur in patterns; and we found discrete patterns of cardiovascular and neuroendocrine response to two different types of experimental condition, as shown in Figure 7.2. Second, whatever the ultimate number of such patterns that are found, there is much evidence for two patterns, Pattern 1, characterized by muscle vasodilatation, and Pattern 2, characterized by muscle vasoconstriction; we found that when we used conditions shown in prior studies to elicit Pattern 1 and Pattern 2, not only the muscle hemodynamic but also the neuroendocrine responses were qualitatively different. The model also suggests that personality and genetic factors may modulate the brain's transduction of environmental situations into patterns of motor messages, and both Type A behavior pattern and family history of hypertension were found to affect and interact in affecting the responses observed. Thus, although more work will be required to be sure the specific details are correct, the evidence from the study I have described is in strong accord with the principles that underlie the model presented at the beginning of this chapter.

Further support for the importance of what I have chosen to call Pattern 1 and Pattern 2 is to be gleaned from neurophysiological studies in animals relating to brain areas where stimulation leads to increased or decreased peripheral resistance due to muscle vasoconstriction or vasodilatation.

HOW (AND WHEN) DOES THE BRAIN PRODUCE PATTERN 1 AND PATTERN 2?

Electrical stimulation of points in the premotor cortex, the amygdala, the mesencephalic tegmentum, and the central gray matter of the anesthetized cat have long been known to result in a pattern of cardiovascular adjustment characterized by increased cardiac output, vasodilatation in skeletal muscle, and vasoconstriction in skin and viscera; moreover, stimulation of these same points in the awake animal results in motoric behavior indistinguishable from that seen during naturally occurring "defense" reactions.[18] Stimulation of the hypothalamic defense areas in the monkey has also been shown to result in increased plasma corticosteroid levels.[19] Thus, there is ample evidence that mammalian brains contain sites capable of producing the integrated pattern of cardiovascular and neuroendocrine response that our study[13] suggests is characteristic of Pattern 1 in humans.

With respect to brain mechanisms responsible for the production of Pattern 2, the evidence is much less extensive. In awake cats, stimulation of the basal amygdala resulted in a motoric behavior typical of the defense reaction, which was associated with tachycardia and increased aortic blood flow measured distal to the renal arteries (and thus probably due to muscle vasodilatation in areas fed by the iliac arteries).[20] This behavioral and cardiovascular response pattern, of course, is identical to that described in the preceding paragraph relating to brain areas mediating Pattern 1.

When the central amygdala is stimulated, however, a quite different pattern of responses is observed. Motorically, the animal is alert and activated, but the ears are not flattened and the head is not retracted, as with stimulation of the basal amygdala. This pattern was described as more similar to *attack* behavior. The cardiovascular response also differed from that seen with stimulation of the basal amygdala: instead of the decreased peripheral resistance secondary to muscle vasodilatation seen with stimulation of the basal amygdala, stimulation of the central amygdala led to a pressor response associated with increased peripheral resistance probably mediated by vaso-constriction in the iliac vascular bed.

While the basal amygdala appears associated with behavioral and cardio-vascular adjustments characteristic of Pattern 1, the central amygdala appears to be at least one brain area capable of producing behavioral and cardiovas-cular responses more characteristic of what I have been calling Pattern 2. The case for the role of these two amygdaloid complexes in mediating the full-blown expression of Pattern 1 and Pattern 2 as described in the preceding section will be greatly strengthened if further study shows stimulation of the basal amygdala to result in increased plasma epinephrine and cortisol, and stimulation of the central amygdala to result in increased plasma testosterone.

Recent theorizing by Foote and coworkers[21] about the functions of the locus ceruleus (LC) may provide additional insights regarding brain systems responsible for mediating the elicitation by environmental stimuli of the Pattern 2 response. The LC is a collection of adrenergic cell bodies located near the wall of the fourth ventricle at the level of the pons. It is known to supply most of the noradrenergic (NE) innervation to the entire cerebral cortex and cerebellum and much of the noradrenergic innervation of the hypothalamus.

Based on their exhaustive review of the literature pertaining to the anatomic projections, physiology, and function of the LC-NE system, Foote and colleagues conclude that this system "acts at many target sites to somehow enhance the reliability and efficiency of feature extraction from sensory input."[21,p.899] Among the lines of evidence cited in drawing this conclusion: (1) in the monkey, LC-NE discharge increases with orientation toward a syringe filled with a flavored drinking solution; (2) in the rat, behaviors associated with decreased vigilance (e.g., grooming) result in reduced LC-NE discharge; and (3) in both the rat and monkey the most intense activity in LC-NE neurons was observed at times when "surveillance of the external environment (i.e., vigilance) is suddenly and dramatically increased."[21,p.873] The interpretation given these findings is worth quoting:

> Thus it would appear that LC-NE neurons vary their spontaneous activity in relation to vigilance levels. Increased vigilance, as during spontaneous or

sensory-evoked arousal or during orientation to an unexpected or preferred stimulus, is associated with tonically enhanced LC-NE discharge, whereas decreased levels of vigilance, as during sleep, grooming or consumption behaviors, correspond to periods of diminished activity in the LC.[21,p.873]

Given the apparent involvement of the LC in vigilance behaviors and the association of stimulation of the central amygdala with increased vigilance and increased peripheral resistance, it is noteworthy that an LC projection to the central amygdala has been described.[22] These observations suggest that the LC-NE system may play an important role in mediating the motoric and physiological manifestations of Pattern 2, when that pattern is elicited by environmental stimulation. Supportive of such a hypothesis is the observation that NE neurons originating in the LC are responsible for peripheral sympathetic nerve response of two rats to shock-induced fighting, but not for the adrenal medullary response to footshocks administered to one rat.[23]

While much of the evidence cited above is circumstantial, it does make the rather strong case that plausible brain mechanisms do exist whereby the behavioral and physiologic manifestations of Pattern 1 and Pattern 2, as described in preceding sections of this chapter, can be produced. In addition, this evidence contains some clues as to the specific types of environmental situations that elicit these two response patterns. For example, the possible involvement of a major adrenergic system in the brain (the LC) in mediating "surveillance of the external environment (i.e., vigilance)"[21,p.873] suggests the importance of those behaviors associated with such surveillance as a possible determinant of patterned physiological responses.

Finally, this evidence highlights the important principle, suggested by the model in Figure 7.1, that motoric behaviors (such as "fight or flight" or tonic immobility) do not themselves "cause" autonomic and neuroendocrine responses. Rather, it appears that along with autonomic and neuroendocrine responses, the motoric behaviors are but a third component of the integrated patterns of response that result from the brain's interpretation and transduction of environmental events.

WHAT ARE THE ADEQUATE STIMULI FOR PATTERNS 1 AND 2?

To draw firm conclusions regarding the nature of effective stimuli for eliciting Patterns 1 and 2 is difficult because so much of the research upon which we must base answers to this question is fragmented and incomplete. This is because a single study to answer this question would have to sample many physiologic parameters in many types of subjects under many types of conditions. And that is just the easy part; the hard part is that they must be the *right* parameters in the *right* types of subjects under the *right* conditions.

The sheer logistic task of finding enough body surface for the electrodes, strain gauges, transducers, and intravenous and, possibly, intraarterial needles that would be required makes it unlikely that the ideal study in this area will ever be done.

Nevertheless, the extensive research that has been done contains many clues, and it may be possible to begin to answer this question by recalling the experimental conditions, in both human and animal studies, that have been found to elicit one or another response component of Pattern 1 and Pattern 2. (See also the chapter by Krantz, Manuck, and Wing.)

With respect to Pattern 1, the following have been reported to elicit muscle vasodilatation, epinephrine and cortisol responses, or both: (1) situations that elicit fight or flight or defense behavior, such as mental arithmetic with harrassment;[6] (2) mental work, such as mental arithmetic without harrassment[9] or word association testing[24]; (3) active, effortful coping, such as shock avoidance in humans[4] and animals;[11] and (4) uncontrollable aversive stimulus situations.[25]

I am sure I have inadvertently left out other, potentially important examples of experimental behavioral challenges that have been reported to elicit one or more components of what I have called Pattern 1. Nevertheless, the cited examples do contain some common elements. Certainly, situations that induce fear or anxiety appear capable of eliciting Pattern 1, and the muscle vasodilatation, increased cardiac output, and associated neuroendocrine components would appear adaptive—that is, they might confer some survival advantage—when the effectiveness of fight or flight behavior might determine whether the organism lives or dies.

But why would simple mental work also elicit Pattern 1? I have no ready answer but would like to speculate that perhaps mental work—"thinking," if you will—evolved from the motor functions of the brain. If so, then it is possible that intense "mental" effort activates the same motor systems in the brain that subserve intense "motor" effort. If so, this linkage, possibly a vestigial one, would explain why and how hard mental work produces the same physiologic response pattern as hard physical work. This linkage may not be entirely vestigal, however, in that the neuroendocrine components of Pattern 1—that is, epinephrine and ACTH—may actually facilitate such aspects of "thinking" as cortical activation and memory consolidation.

What are the conditions that have been reported to elicit Pattern 2? Again, while surely incomplete, the following list contains some representative examples of studies in which muscle vasoconstriction (either directly measured or inferred from other measures), testosterone secretion, or both have been observed: (1) passive coping, as in watching a pornographic movie;[4] (2) sensory intake, as in reading words projected upside down and out of focus;[9] (3) alert immobility, as during a preavoidance period in the dog;[11] (4) vigilant observation of another animal who appears about to attack;[12] (5) male-male dominance confrontations;[15] and (6) under some conditions, shock-induced fighting in the rat.[23]

As with those conditions that have been reported to elicit elements of the Pattern 1 response, there are also common threads that seem to tie together those conditions cited above as eliciting the Pattern 2 response. Whether under emotionally arousing conditions (e.g., male-male confrontation and shock-induced fighting) or under relatively nonarousing conditions (e.g., simple sensory-intake tasks), those conditions that appear to elicit Pattern 2 responding have in common the element of attentive observation of some aspect of the environment.

So much in science is rediscovery. Beginning well over two decades ago, the Laceys[26] were calling our attention to the importance of mental work and sensory intake as two classes of behavior that are associated with different patterns of somatic and physiologic responses. To the extent that Pattern 1 and Pattern 2, as described in this chapter, are ultimately recognized as valid ways of conceptualizing "reactivity," and to the extent that mental work and sensory intake are at least among the key behaviors eliciting Pattern 1 and Pattern 2, respectively, the Laceys deserve much credit for calling our attention to these phenomena.

HOW DO PATTERN 1 AND PATTERN 2 LEAD TO CARDIOVASCULAR DISEASE?

By now I suspect the reader feels there is more than enough to think about in this chapter, without having to ponder how it all relates to the etiology and pathogenesis of cardiovascular disease (see Manuck and Krantz; Clarkson, Manuck, and Kaplan; Herd; Julius, Weder, and Hinderliter). Therefore, I shall leave it to other chapters in this volume to confront this thorny question. My own thoughts on this issue are presented elsewhere.[27] Beyond that, I can only leave it as an exercise for the reader to draw his or her own conclusions as to implications of what I have said for causal mechanisms.

SUMMARY AND CONCLUSIONS

"Reactivity" might best be understood as a *process* whereby the brain interprets environmental events and, based on the outcome of that interpretation, sends a pattern of somatomotor, autonomic, and neuroendocrine "motor messages" to target organs in the body. This transduction process is modulated by the past history (as reflected in the personality) and genetic makeup of the individual. There may be only a limited number of patterns of response associated with "psychosocial" stimuli (as opposed to "physical" stimuli, such as exercise, diving, or digesting a meal). Two such patterns have been described in this chapter, along with possible mechanisms whereby they are produced by the brain.

I have tried in this chapter to summarize what to some may be a bewildering array of complex data. No doubt I have made inferential leaps with which some may justly quarrel. I hope that I have brought some order to the complexity, and that where I may have erred, the reader will at least be stimulated to ponder what I have said and collect the data necessary to set it right.

For those who might like a summary of the key points made herein regarding Patterns 1 and 2, I offer for your perusal Table 7.1. I welcome efforts to correct the errors and, especially, efforts to fill in the gaps.

TABLE 7.1. VARIOUS DISTINGUISHING CHARACTERISTICS OF PATTERN 1 AND PATTERN 2.

Characteristic	Pattern 1	Pattern 2
Motor activity	Increased ("fight/flight")	Decreased (but alert)
Cardiovascular	Muscle vasodilatation Increased cardiac output	Muscle vasoconstriction
Neuroendocrine	Increased epinephrine, cortisol, and prolactin	Increased testosterone
Effective eliciting stimuli	Defense/emergency situations Fear/anxiety Active, effortful coping Mental work (?sensory rejection) Uncontrollable aversive stimuli	Vigilance (stalking) Sensory intake Passive coping ?Controllable aversive stimuli
Brain areas that mediate	Hypothalamic defense area Basal amygdala	Central amygdala Locus coeruleus ?Lateral hypothalamus

REFERENCES

1. Review Panel on Coronary-Prone Behavior and Coronary Heart Disease: Coronary-prone behavior and coronary heart disease: A critical review. *Circulation* **63**:1119–1215, 1981.

2. Williams RB, Barefoot JC, Shekelle RB: The health consequences of hostility. In Chesney MA, Goldston SE, Rosenman RH (eds): *Anger, Hostility and Behavioral Medicine*. New York, Hemisphere/McGraw Hill, 1985, pp. 173–186.

3. Hilton SM: Ways of viewing the central nervous control of the circulation—old and new. *Brain Res* **87**:213–219, 1975.

4. Obrist PA: The cardiovascular-behavioral interaction—as it appears today. *Psychophysiology* **13**:95–107, 1976.

5. Whitney RJ: The measurement of volume changes in human limbs. *J Physiol* **121**:1–27, 1953.

6. Brod J, Fencl VS, et al: Circulatory changes underlying blood pressure elevation during acute emotional stress (mental arithmetic) in normotensive and hypertensive subjects. *Clin Sci* **18**:269–279, 1959.

7. Abrahams VC, Hilton SM, Zbrozyna A: Active muscle vasodilatation produced by stimulation of the brain stem: Its significance in the defense reaction. *J Physiol* **154**:491–513, 1960.

8. Williams RB, Kimball CP, Willard HN: The influence of interpersonal interaction upon diastolic blood pressure. *Psychosom Med* **34**:194–198, 1973.

9. Williams RB, Bittker TE, et al: Cardiovascular and neurophysiologic correlates of sensory intake and rejection: I. Effects of cognitive tasks. *Psychophysiology* **12**:427–432, 1975.

10. Bittker TE, Buchsbaum MS, et al: Cardiovascular and neurophysiologic correlates of sensory intake and rejection: II. Interview behavior. *Psychophysiology* **12**:434–438, 1975.

11. Anderson DE, Brady JV: Experimental analysis of psychosomatic interactions: Behavioral influences upon physiological regulation. In Davidson RS (ed): *Modification of pathological behavior*. New York, Gardner Press, 1979, pp. 189–231.

12. Zanchetti A: Hypothalamic control of circulation. In Julius S, Esler MD (eds): *The nervous system in arterial hypertension*. Springfield, IL, Thomas, 1976, pp. 136–148.

13. Williams RB, Lane JD, et al: Type A behavior and elevated physiological and neuroendocrine responses to cognitive tasks. *Science* **218**:483–485, 1982.

14. Henry JP: Coronary heart disease and arousal of the adrenal cortical axis. In Dembroski TM, Schmidt TH, Blumchen G (eds): *Biobehavioral Bases of Coronary Heart Disease*. Basel, Karger, 1983, pp. 1–29.

15. Rose RM: Endocrine responses to stressful psychological events. In Sachar EJ (ed): *Advances in Psychoneuroendocrinology*. Philadelphia, Saunders, 1980, pp. 252–276.

16. Thompson WR, Wright JS: "Persistence" in rats: Effects of testosterone. *Physiol Psychol* **7**:291–294, 1979.

17. Zumoff B, Rosenfeld RS, et al: Elevated daytime urinary excretion of testosterone glucuronide in men with the Type A behavior pattern. *Psychosom Med* **46**:223–226, 1984.

18. Abrahams VC, Hilton SM, Zbrozyna A: Active muscle vasodilatation produced by stimulation of the brain stem: Its significance in the defense reaction. *J Physiol* **154**:491–513, 1960.

19. Natelson BH, Smith GP, et al: Plasma 17-hydroxycorticosteroids and growth hormone during defense reactions. *Am J Physiol* **226**:560–568, 1974.

20. Stock G, Schlor KH, et al: Psychomotor behaviour and cardiovascular patterns during stimulation of the amygdala. *Phlugers Archiv* **376**:177–184, 1978.

21. Foote SL, Bloom FE, Aston-Jones G: Nucleus locus coeruleus: New evidence of anatomical and physiological specificity. *Physiol Rev* **63**:844–914, 1983.

22. Bowden DM, German DC, Poynter WD: An autoradiographic, semistereotaxic mapping of major projections from locus coeruleus and adjacent nuclei in *Macca mulatta*. *Brain Res* **145**:257–276, 1978.

23. Williams RB, Richardson JS, Eichelman BS: Location of central nervous system neurons mediating blood pressure response of rats to shock-induced fighting. *J Behav Med* **1**:177–185, 1978.

24. Williams RB, Frankel BL, et al: Cardiovascular response during a word association test and interview. *Psychophysiology* **10**:571–577, 1973.

25. Lundberg U, Frankenhaeuser M: Pituitary-adrenal and sympathetic adrenal correlates of distress and effort. *J Psychosom Res* **24**:125–130, 1980.

26. Lacey JI, Lacey BC: On heart rate responses and behavior: A reply to Elliott. *J Pers Soc Psychol* **30**:1–18, 1974.

27. Williams, RB: Neuroendocrine response patterns and stress: Biobehavioral mechanisms of disease. In Williams, RB (ed): *Perspectives on Behavioral Medicine: Neuroendocrine Control and Behavior*. New York, Academic Press, 1985, pp. 71–101.

8

Physical Stressors as Elicitors of Cardiovascular Reactivity

JAMES C. BUELL, BRUCE S. ALPERT, WALLACE W. McCRORY

The dividing line between physical and psychological stress represents imperfect attempts at separating environment from perception. Nevertheless, certain environmental circumstances will predictably elicit physiologic responses even in the unconscious subject. It is the purpose of this chapter to describe a series of physical maneuvers that elicit consistent physiologic responses in most subjects, even in the presence of unconsciousness or what is characterized as "sleep." As such, responses to these physical stressors are more likely to represent genetic and/or end organ responsivity to environmental provocation than are cognitive tasks, which may be more reflective of learned and habitual processing of environmental events. These physical manipulations do not deny the potent coloring effects of cognitive perception and personalization of the event but represent the best experimental physical maneuvers not regulated by law and therefore available to most scientific investigators.

A precise and uniformly acceptable definition of *cardiovascular reactivity* remains debatable and probably will for some time. This controversy is in part due to the fact that "reactivity" is being discussed by investigators from different disciplines, each with its own bias, perspective, and nomenclature. Nevertheless, there is general agreement that the term involves a specific stimulus and physiologic response and that *reactivity* refers to the physiologic cardiovascular measurable or measurables under investigation in response to a specified stimulus. The psychophysiological perspective has greatly influenced the literature on reactivity to date. Most would agree, however, that the credibility of the fledgling field of psychophysiology occurs in relation to the firmness of its underpinnings in a thorough understanding of cardiovascular physiology. An understanding of cardiovascular physiology precedes an understanding of cardiovascular psychophysiology.

To that extent, physical manipulations were largely responsible for producing the majority of laboratory and clinical observations on which much of our understanding of cardiovascular physiology is based. Understanding pathways and alterations in mechanisms through which changes in cardiovascular physiology occur is necessary if progress is to be made, and certainly those mechanisms are largely regulated by the autonomic nervous system. Administration of autonomic drugs such as agonists or antagonists is a well-known pharmacological strategy for elucidating the mechanisms by which clinical reactivity is expressed. Because independent clinical experimentation with these pharmaceutical agents requires state licensing and medical training, these techniques are not available to all researchers. Admittedly, most physical stressors have psychological components that color the magnitude of response; however, there are a number of physical maneuvers that predictably result in a robust cardiovascular response and in which criteria are well established for normal and abnormal responses. The maneuvers to be discussed have been well studied by physiologists in terms of normal and abnormal response patterns and have a uniform and consistently predictable response. Thus, these physical maneuvers serve as an important screening tool for excluding physiologically abnormal subjects from the psychophysiological studies of supposedly healthy populations. These physical maneuvers should have the following qualities:

1. The stressor is truly physical. The physical sciences demand absence of subjective or qualitative dimensions. The maneuvers must be entirely characterized in physical dimensions and units (i.e., decibels, ergs, degrees, seconds, etc.).

2. There is a characteristic physiologic response pattern that is known to occur in healthy subjects.

3. The technique is reproducible in that it can be applied the same way in individual labs across the country.

4. In the absence of intervention or illness, the response is stable.

5. The stressor can be time-defined.

6. The stressor is plausible; that is, it is similar to stressors encountered in the natural environment.

7. The maneuver is ethical and acceptable both to subjects and investigators.

8. The physical stressor is relatively inexpensive and therefore usable by most investigators.

9. The maneuver is distinctive, that is, a singular maneuver rather than an admixture of maneuvers such as heat plus noise pollution, humidity, or others.

10. There is a dose response capability; that is, the intensity of the stressor can be graded so that a stimulus–response curve can be generated.

The physical stress maneuvers to be discussed fulfill at least some of these criteria. In many cases, because of an enormous literature concerning a topic, the reviews have been relatively cursory, with citations to larger general texts on the subject. An example is exercise physiology, which constitutes an enormous scientific discipline unto itself.

EXERCISE

The circulatory adjustments to exercise differ somewhat depending on the type of exercise performed. In general, hemodynamic responses to exercise may be divided into those characterized as responses to dynamic large muscle work and those characterized as either distinctive for small muscle dynamic or static exercise. In either category, however, circulatory and metabolic adjustments are ultimately directed toward providing optimal flow and oxygen transport to the working muscle.

Dynamic Large-Muscle Work

There have been literally libraries of textbooks written concerning the various physiologic adjustments that take place during dynamic large-muscle exercise. Only the more fundamental aspects of this topic will be addressed in this discussion. The reader is referred to more exhaustive reviews for a better understanding.[1-10] In general, exercise tests are performed in the clinical arena via a step test,[11] bicycle ergometer,[12,13] or treadmill.[1-10,14,15] The rate-limiting factor in achieving and sustaining a given intensity of rhythmic large muscle or leg work is the ability of the oxygen transport system to meet the metabolic demands of the working muscle. When demand exceeds supply of oxygen as the primary rate-limiting factor in the equation, the work is said to shift from aerobic toward anaerobic, which, by virtue of its attendant lactate accumulation and acidosis, can be sustained for only brief periods of time. At rest, skeletal muscle receives only about 15 percent of total cardiac output, few capillaries are open, and there is a steady parasympathetic neural traffic governing and maintaining the heart rate at basal levels. In anticipation of effort and even before exercise begins, there is inhibition of parasympathetic activity with an acceleration of heart rate. Sympathetic traffic over cholinergic vasodilator fibers dilates arterioles in muscles, thereby increasing blood flow. Concomitant adrenergic vasoconstrictor effects on the splanchnic vessels and skin and venoconstriction enhance the opportunity for increased cardiac output. As intensity of workload increases, sympathetic traffic augments vasoconstriction generally; but autoregulation and the accumulation of metabolites in the working muscle, together with heat and acidosis, result in arteriolar dilatation in the working muscle bed. As effort intensifies, a generalized metabolic acidosis shifts the oxyhemoglobin dissociation curve to the right and enhances the extraction of oxygen by the working muscle. This enhanced oxygen extraction yields a widened arterial–venous oxygen difference, with oxygen content of venous blood from the working extremity falling from approximately 15 ml of oxygen per 100 ml of blood to something in the order of 1–2 ml of oxygen per 100 ml of blood. Conversely, the intense sympathetic traffic and profound vasoconstriction in nonworking muscles results in stagnation of flow and an equally avid oxygen extraction such that venous effluent from nonworking limbs has approximately the same oxygen content as that from the working limb. The Fick equation states: cardiac output = oxygen consumption $(V_{O_2})/(A-V)_{O_2}$ difference. Because at maximum effort in large muscle dynamic work, the $(A-V)_{O_2}$ differences are relatively constant in everyone, maximum V_{O_2} becomes an expression of peak cardiac output. In the absence of significant pulmonary disease, cardiac output is the rate-limiting determinant of maximum V_{O_2} and thus peak cardiac output. Oxygen consumption is frequently expressed in terms of mets, or multiples of the resting oxygen consumption, which is approximately 3.5 ml/kg/minute. For example, 10 mets would be 35 ml/kg/minute. During progressive increases in intensity of dynamic large muscle work, there will be a progressive increase in systolic pressure and widening of pulse pressure where blood pressure is measured by the indirect method of cuffed auscultation in the arm. Mean arterial pressure measured from the central aorta shows little or no change. Part of the peripheral blood pressure reading represents artifact by including the kinetic energy factor into the blood pressure reading. Diastolic blood pressure does not normally rise in treadmill exercise, and a collapse of the pulse pressure usually signals impending cardiovascular collapse. At maximum exercise, cardiac output will increase approximately fivefold with little or no change in mean arterial pressure, thus indicating a profound drop in total systemic resistance. While emotion may markedly influence heart rate and blood pressure during submaximal work, the circulatory parameters are usually not affected by psychological factors when the work becomes heavy and approaches maximal effort or exhaustion.

A variety of treadmill and bicycle ergometer protocols exist and may be found in standard references. In general, an exercise tolerance test should have a warm-up phase with its initial stages well below maximum V_{o_2} capacity. It should progressively increase metabolic requirements until the intensity of work can no longer be endured as manifested by exhaustion, marked lactic acidosis, and/or collapse of the pulse pressure. Popular treadmill protocols include those of Bruce, Balke, and Ellestad.[2,11] Bicycle ergometry protocols are less frequently used on American adults but include those of Astrand and Balke. A progressive multistage maximum step test as developed by Balke[11] may also be utilized. Monitoring guidelines and normal standards for health and disease have been published for these protocols.[5-8]

Blood Pressure Reactivity Under Exercise as a Predictor of Hypertension

The blood pressure response to treadmill testing or bicycle ergometry has yielded conflicting results in discriminating between hypertensives and normotensives[16] (see also the chapter by Julius, Weder, and Hinderliter in this volume). Most studies do not show a difference in the reactivity pattern. Normotensive, borderline hypertensive, and hypertensive outpatients may show similar increases in blood pressure, particularly at high work levels. However, several German studies have shown differences.[16] Franz[17] found that the majority of borderline hypertensives generating more than 200 mmHg pressure during supine ergometry manifest established hypertension less than four years later. Others have corroborated the hypothesis that exercise blood pressures may be predictive of future hypertension. Dlin, Hanne, et al.[18] studied a group of normotensive men with exaggerated blood pressure response to exercise versus a similar sample without exaggerated blood pressure response. The exaggerated reactors demonstrated a 10 percent incidence of hypertension within six years, whereas none of the normal reactive group developed hypertension. Our own findings[16,19] suggest that the effects of psychological stressors will be best seen at lower levels of exercise (three mets). These responses may be distinctively reflective of the exaggerated responses manifested during psychophysiologic stress testing of the individual.

Exercise Testing in Children

Exercise, both dynamic and isometric, has been used in adults to elicit measures of reactivity. In children, special precautions and protocol differences must be used in order to obtain useful data. Children should be made familiar with the imposing-looking apparatus and be given time to become accustomed to it. Many groups who perform exercise testing in children prefer to use cycle ergometers because of their similarity to the children's bicycles at home. There are several sizes of ergometers, to ensure that the child can reach the pedals and can crank them at a reasonably constant rate. Children under the age of five may not possess the coordination to pedal consistently, and a treadmill may be necessary. The newer models of treadmills are much smaller and quieter than the older pieces of apparatus and thus are not as imposing.

If maximal oxygen consumption (V_{o_2}) must be obtained, one should realize that the treadmill produces higher maximal oxygen consumption than does the cycle ergometer. This relates to the amount of arm work performed on the treadmill and the support that the ergometer seat gives to the upper half of the body. For reactivity-type testing, however, it is doubtful that truly maximal V_{o_2} tests are needed. The measurement of variables such as blood pressure and cardiac output (index) during exercise are more easily performed on a cycle ergometer.

Normal values for heart rate, systolic and diastolic blood pressure, electrocardiographic variables, and workload have been published for healthy children by several groups.[20-25] Maximal values for heart rate in response to maximal exercise vary from 185 to 210 min^{-1}, somewhat higher than adult values. The use of submaximal target heart rates must be age-adjusted. In general, when you are speaking of adults or children, 225 minus the age in years will approximate peak age-related maximum heart rate, and percentages of that value may then be calculated for submaximal target heart rates.

The standard cycle ergometer protocol uses a progressive, continuous sequence of workloads with three-minute stages. It takes approximately one minute for the child to reach steady state, followed by two minutes for measurement of variables. The workloads are predetermined by weight.[24,25] Healthy children should complete at least three stages of exercise, depending on the protocol used. Blood pressure may be performed at the end of each stage. The investigators at the Medical College of Georgia, including the second author, have utilized a cradle atop an IV pole into which the subject places his or her arm (at chest height) each time blood pressure is measured. This eliminates a great deal of motion artifact. The cycle also is usually quieter than a treadmill, allowing better determination of the fourth phase of the Korotkov sound (K_4) for diastolic pressure. It is imperative to use K_4 (muffling), since, in a large proportion of healthy children, K_5 (disappearance) has not occurred when the pressure manometer has reached zero.

In healthy children two channels of electrocardiogram (ECG) should be monitored during exercise. If this is extremely impractical, then one would be sufficient. It is customary to use V_5 as the sole lead, and lead II as the second lead. No myocardial ischemia would be expected; the prime reasons for ECG monitoring are heart rate and arrhythmia detection.

Measures such as cardiac output may be performed noninvasively by a CO_2 or inert gas (acetylene) rebreathing method. These techniques require extremely expensive pieces of equipment and a dedicated exercise physiologist to provide intense quality control.

It is extremely important for the technical staff exercising children to provide almost constant encouragement and prodding to allow the subject to reach a reasonably maximal effort. The short attention span of a child and his or her unfamiliarity with voluntarily exercising with a good deal of leg discomfort and shortness of breath require that the staff cheer the child through the final stages. An experienced research assistant can judge when a child has achieved a maximal voluntary effort. It is generally accepted that invasive measurements, such as lactate measurements postexercise, are unethical in healthy children and should only be performed on patients in whom a measure of functional reserve capacity is critical.

In a recent study Alpert et al.[26] reviewed 1730 exercise studies performed over a nine-year period. Of these tests, 489 were performed by healthy children. In these subjects no complications of maximal exercise testing were observed. The authors stated that a physician need *not* be present during the testing of healthy children. However, it is recommended that technicians be certified in cardiopulmonary resuscitation.

In general, if the technicians approach the children in a concerned and friendly fashion and encourage them to perform to their maximal capacities, exercise can be a valuable stimulus for measurement of various indices of cardiovascular reactivity. We would encourage investigators to hide all materials that resemble needles and white coats and prominently display bright posters, smiles, and lollipops.

Isometric Exercise

There have been several recent reviews concerning isometric exercise.[27-29] Static, or isometric, exercise always produces a pressor response characterized by an increase in mean arterial pressure in an attempt to overcome the reduced effective perfusion pressures occurring in the region of intense muscle contraction. The ratio of mean arterial pressure to oxygen consumption is much higher with static than with dynamic exercise,[27] and recent studies have shown that the pressor response increases in proportion to both intensity and amount of muscle mass recruited in the maximum voluntary contraction. The mechanisms involved include both central and peripheral mediation, including the intensity of volition, intensity and amount of muscle mass involved, relative proportion of fast- and slow-twitch fibers in the contracting muscles, and increases in metabolites. The abrupt and immediate increase in heart rate is due to withdrawal of vagal tone rather than metabolic adrenoreceptor traffic. The normal response is that of increased sympathetic tone producing an increase in cardiac output accompanied by little or no change in stroke volume,[30] increased left ventricular contractility,[31-33] and no change or only slight elevation of total systemic resistance.[34] Normally, there is no change or only a slight deviation in left ventricular end diastolic and systolic volume.[35] Responses are not dramatically influenced by posture.[36] The maneuver has been used to study effects of several drugs.[37,38]

In the patient with heart disease and severe left ventricular dysfunction,[35,39,40-46] the pressor response is achieved primarily through vasoconstriction because of inability, even under sympathetic drive, for the heart to increase its cardiac output sufficiently. Thus, during isometric exercise the body seems determined, by whatever means available, to increase the blood pressure.[47] This is manifested in normal subjects pretreated with propranolol and atropine and in cardiac transplant subjects wherein the blood pressure increases during isometric exercise despite the absence of cardiac innervation. Isometric exercise is usually performed by having the subject execute a maximum voluntary contraction using a hand dynamometer and then having the subject sustain a force at 30 to 50 percent of maximum voluntary contraction to the point of subjective fatigue, usually on the order of 1.5 to 3 minutes.

PHYSIOLOGICAL RESPONSES TO POSITIONAL OR POSTURAL STRESS

The circulatory adjustments that take place when one goes from the supine to erect position represent a complex orchestration of volume shifts and neurocirculatory adaptive mechanisms.[48–52] When one shifts to an erect position, the force of gravity results in the pooling of a considerable fraction of blood volume in the legs. Normal people, however, engage powerful compensatory mechanisms that permit blood pressure to be maintained. The baroreceptors respond immediately to the fall in pressure and trigger hemodynamic responses that begin within a second or two. Sympathetically mediated arteriolar and venous vasoconstriction occur, vagal restraint on the heart is inhibited, and the sympathetic cardiac nerves exert both positive chronotropic and inotropic effects.[53] When normal people assume an upright position, there is an increase in the mean heart rate of about 35 percent, a rise in diastolic blood pressure of about 15 mmHg, and a 40 percent increase in total peripheral resistance associated with a decrease of approximately 40 percent in stroke volume and an 18 percent drop in cardiac output.[50,54,55] When the healthy, youthful person assumes the erect position, there is an intense peripheral vasoconstriction, both arterial and venous, which is unable to totally restore adequate venous return; therefore, a slight decrease in pulse pressure and more marked decrease in output is observed. Ejection fraction diminishes from 2 to 10 percent.[56] In addition, changing to the upright position results in increases in preejection period, isovolumic contraction time, and the ratio of preejection period to ejection time. There is a decrease in left ventricular ejection time, pulse transmission time, and the ejection time index, reflecting stroke volume changes. No significant changes occur in electromechanical interval, preisovolumic relaxation period, or rapid filling period.[57,58] In addition, the arteriovenous oxygen difference is larger in the sitting than in the supine position, both at rest and during work. During heavy leg work, the oxygen transport per heart beat is the same in supine and sitting positions and the physical working capacity is also of the same order.[55]

Factors in Orthostatic Hypotension

In normal subjects there is a wide variation in the tolerance and capacity to adapt to upright tilting with the incidence of syncope varying from 10 to 20 percent. A fall in systolic and pulse pressure correlates with subsequent development of syncope and the degree of heart rate increase. Nonfainters have a mean fall in cardiac output of 20 percent; fainters, at the time of symptoms, have a mean decrease of 40 percent. Data indicate that acute cardiovascular changes tend to stabilize in nonfainters soon after tilting, and indeed, appropriate hemodynamic responses all tend to occur in less than a minute after change in position. If presyncopal symptoms develop, there is a rapid deterioration of all measurements, manifested by a sudden fall in blood pressure, cardiac output, heart rate, and peripheral vascular resistance, strongly favoring simultaneous activation of vasodepressor and cardioinhibitory reflexes. Sympathetic vasodilator nerves to skeletal muscles can be activated in human beings subjected to postural stress.[59] Furthermore, the normal response is a decrease in forearm blood flow and an increase in venous tone and forearm vascular resistance following upright tilt. These observations suggest that reflex vasodilatation may play a role in fainting, may represent an incomplete adaptation to stress, and may be centrally mediated. In addition, Scheinberg and Stead[60] have demonstrated a 20 percent decrease in cerebral blood flow and a 30 percent decrease in effective cerebral arterial pressure following upright tilting in normal nonfainters. In fainters, Stevens demonstrated a decrease of 64 percent at the time of onset of symptoms in effective cerebral arterial pressure.[59] After three minutes of orthostasis, both late fainters and nonfainters had only a 17 percent and 15 percent decrease respectively in effective cerebral arterial pressure. Whereas there are frequently abrupt and dramatic changes in cardiac output and systemic arterial pressure in young healthy individuals, responses become considerably blunted in patients with heart failure and the elderly.[57,61-64]

Sympathetic Adrenal Medullary Response to Tilt

Normal individuals typically double their plasma norepinephrine (NE) levels after standing for five or ten minutes and triple their levels after moderate exercise. Thus, care must be taken during psychophysiological experiments in which catecholamines are monitored to insure that postural effects are not confounded with other behavioral variables under study. It should also be noted that patients with idiopathic orthostatic hypotension, who have isolated autonomic impairment, show a pronounced depletion of NE in blood vessels innervated by sympathetic nerves.[65] In diabetes, orthostatic hypotension can develop due to autonomic neuropathy and/or volume depletion caused by renal salt and albumin wasting and protein leakage through diseased capillaries.[53] Occasionally, diabetic neuropathy and secondary orthostatic hypotension will develop considerably before the appearance of abnormalities in glucose metabolism.

The change in plasma catecholamine levels in response to standing provides an index of sympathetic adrenergic system activity in response to orthostatic stress.[66] This maneuver is now widely used for comparative studies of adrenergic reactivity under stress conditions in normotensive and hypertensive adult subjects[67] and children. Excessive rise in NE levels with respect to changes in blood pressure after head-up tilt and posture change has been documented in some subjects with essential hypertension.[68] Four out of five hypertensives who were such initial "hyperresponders" were still hyperresponsive when retested one-to-two years later. Eide, Campese, et al.[67] found that hypertensive patients with orthostatic increase of systolic and pulse pressure were more likely to have elevated basal sympathetic tone than unresponsive patients.

Elevated plasma catecholamine concentrations exist in a proportion of patients with borderline hypertension. Similarly, sympathetic overrespon-siveness to some adrenergic stimuli probably occurs in a borderline hyper-tension. The significance of the blood pressure and catecholamine over-responsiveness is uncertain, but it has often been presumed that repeated pressor responses could possibly lead to the subsequent development of permanent hypertension. Further study will be needed to answer this question.[69]

THE COLD PRESSOR TEST

In the 1930s, Hines and Brown[70–72] introduced the cold pressor test as a screening procedure for the detection of vascular hyperreactivity. While it was originally thought that the response to the cold pressor test would predict hypertension, this did not prove to be the case. Subsequently, Keys, Taylor, and colleagues[73] found reactivity to the cold pressor test to be a predictor of coronary heart disease. This, again, was disputed in the studies of Thomas and Duszynski.[74] More recently, cold exposure has been used as a provocateur of coronary spasm and has once again been introduced to the literature as a "standardized" test with a wide range of applications. Cold pressor stress appears in the medical literature as a hemodynamic test useful in studying the effects of some kinds of pharmacologic interven-tion[75–81] and is recently in vogue as a method of producing coronary artery spasm in the cardiac catheterization laboratory.[82,83] The assumption that the physiologic reactions to cold are fairly constant over time is subject to debate, and reactivity to the cold pressor test is probably highly colored by perception of the level of challenge, previous experience, likelihood of discomfort, and so on. Nevertheless, a general trend toward a specific hemodynamic pattern of response emerges.

In healthy, normotensive subjects undergoing a cold pressor test, systolic and diastolic blood pressure increase approximately 15 mm of mercury, mean arterial pressure approximately 17 mm of mercury, left ventricular end diastolic pressure approximately 8 mm of mercury and heart rate about 10 beats per minute.[70–73,78,84–93] Cardiac output remains constant[92–94] whereas ejection fraction decreases[91] somewhat and total systemic resistance increases about 15 percent.[93–94] Changes in coronary blood flow also occur.[95,96] Epinephrine and norepinephrine in plasma increase[97–99] while renin and dopamine beta hydroxylase remain fairly constant.[100,101] In general, the cold pressor test is predominantly an alpha-adrenergic maneuver with vasoconstriction dominating. Nevertheless, high challenge such as "everybody can hold a hand in ice water for two minutes" or "try as hard as you can" can introduce strong beta-adrenergic components and interfere with the reproducibility.[102]

Duration of exposure to cold varies throughout the medical literature, but the general range is from one to five minutes. Because the perception of pain adds beta-adrenergic components to the task, cold exposure on the order of one minute is probably preferable and is the duration that was used in the studies by Keys et al.[73] As a precautionary note, at least one case has been described in which acute myocardial infarction was precipitated by the cold pressor test in a patient with complaints of chest pain.[103]

In summary, emersion of the hand (or foot) in ice water (0–3°C) for approximately one minute generally elicits a vasoconstrictive response mediated predominantly by neurosympathetic pathways rather than circulating epinephrine.[104] Whereas the physiological pattern of hemodynamic response to cold pressor testing is relatively consistent, a review of the epidemiological literature on the cold pressor test and reactivity suggests that it has no consistent value as a predictor of either hypertension or coronary heart disease as a single maneuver (see chapters by Julius, Weder, and Hinderliter, and Krantz, Manuck, and Wing for more detailed discussion).

CARDIOVASCULAR RESPONSE TO NOISE

Retrospective epidemiologic studies have found an increased prevalence of hypertension in those exposed to high levels of noise, such as aircraft traffic patterns and noisy streets. Additional undesirable effects of noise exposure include hearing impairment and possibly cardiovascular disease as well as sleep disturbances.[105] Sustained hypertension has been induced in some animal models with chronic noise exposure,[106] and in some animal models, sodium loading appears to accentuate the response. The topic of the cardiovascular effects of noise have been recently reviewed[105,107–109] and may be summarized as follows:[109]

When loud broadband noise on the order of 95 to 100 decibels is applied, there is an increase in blood pressure in both normotensive and hypertensive subjects. The hemodynamic response is one of vasoconstriction in both patients with hypertension and normotensive subjects with a positive family history for hypertension.[108] The most significant changes occur in diastolic blood pressure and mean arterial pressure, with an increase in total systemic resistance and a trend toward stroke volume suppression.[108] Conversely, hemodynamic responses in normotensive subjects with a negative family history is one of an increase of blood pressure predominantly through enhanced cardiac output. In normotensive subjects plasma catecholamines, prolactin, cortisol, and growth hormone remain relatively unchanged,[108] whereas in hypertensives, plasma norepinephrine is increased with no change in plasma epinephrine and renin.[108] In mild essential hypertension the pressor response appears to be alpha 1 mediated. However, when alpha blockade is instituted, the blood pressure response remains and is then mediated by an increase in cardiac output due to beta activation. According to Ising,[110] chronic noise exposure apparently causes depletion of erythrocyte magnesium. The significance of this observation remains to be determined.

In summary, exposure to loud noise characteristically elicits an increase in blood pressure that is activated by the sympathetic nervous system and probably mediated from the hypothalamus through resetting baroreceptors since if one pathway is blocked (i.e., alpha blockade), elevated blood pressure will be maintained through beta-adrenergic mechanisms via enhanced cardiac output.

SUMMARY

In this chapter we have reviewed the normal cardiovascular adaptive mechanisms to a variety of physical stressors including dynamic large muscle work, isometrics, postural maneuvers, cold exposure, and noise. The expressed purpose of this volume is to examine the relationship among stress, reactivity, and cardiovascular disease. Although there may be much conjecture about that relationship throughout this volume, we should realize that cardiovascular reactivity to treadmill exercise test is an accepted risk factor for cardiovascular disease. Indeed, the development of ischemic ST segment depression and/or chronotropic inadequacy during treadmill exercise is a more powerful predictor of coronary heart disease than most of the traditionally discussed risk factors. Viewed in this way, it is clear that the mere statistical association among a set of phenomena provide little understanding regarding whether reactivity represents the result of a disease, a mechanism for its creation, or a marker for a common process. The fact remains that virtually all cardiovascular disease has a long subclinical incubation period and, particularly in the case of atherosclerotic cardiovascular disease, manifests itself very late in the evolutionary process. Given the existence of well-established normative values for response to graded physical stressors, the proven predictive value of reactivity to physical stress in coronary heart disease, and the well-worked-out physiologic pathways and homeostatic factors that come into play with physical maneuvers, physical stress testing must remain the gold standard against which reactivity to more complex cognitive maneuvers is compared (see also chapters by Krantz, Manuck, and Wing; and by Manuck and Krantz).

REFERENCES

1. Pollack ML, Foster C, et al: Comparative analysis of physiologic responses to three different maximal graded exercise testing protocols in healthy women. *Am Heart J* **103**:363–372, 1982.

2. Committee on Exercise: *Exercise Testing and Training of Apparently Healthy Individuals: A Handbook for Physicians*. Dallas, American Heart Association, 1972.

3. Pollock ML, Bohannon RL, et al: A comparative analysis of four protocols for maximal treadmill stress testing. *Am Heart J* **92**:39–46, 1976.

4. Astrand PO: Quantification of exercise capability and evaluation of physical capacity in man. *Prog Cardiovas Dis* **109**:51–67, 1976.

5. Sheffield LT, Roitman D: Stress testing methodology. *Prog Cardiovas Dis* **109**:33–49, 1976.

6. Fortuin NJ, Weiss JL: Exercise stress testing. *Circulation* **56**:699–712, 1977.

7. Nagle FJ: Physiological assessment of maximal performance. *Exerc Sport Sci Rev* **1**:313–338, 1973.

8. Cooper KH: Guidelines in the management of the exercising patient. *JAMA* **211**:1663–1667, 1970.

9. Wolthuis RA, Froelicher VF, et al: The response of healthy men to treadmill exercise. *Circulation* **55**:153–157, 1977.

10. Astrand PO, Rodahl D: *Textbook of Work Physiology*. New York, McGraw-Hill, 1970.

11. *Physician's Handbook for Evaluation of Cardiovascular and Physical Fitness*. Tennessee Heart Association Physical Exercise Committee, 1970.

12. Thadani U, Parker JO: Hemodynamics at rest and during supine and sitting bicycle exercise in normal subjects. *Am J Cardiol* **41**:52–59, 1978.

13. Cumming GR: Hemodynamics of supine bicycle exercise in "normal" children. *Am Heart J* **93**:617–622, 1977.

14. Patterson JA, Naughton J, et al: Treadmill exercise in assessment of the functional capacity of patients with cardiac disease. *Am J Cardiol* **30**:757–762, 1972.

15. Hossack KF, Kasumi F, Bruce RA: Approximate normal standards of maximal cardiac output during upright exercise in women. *Am J Cardiol* **45**:1080–1086, 1981.

16. Ru³ddel H, McKinney ME, et al: Low workload during physical stress is mental stress testing. In Lollgen H, Mellerowicz H (eds): *Progress in Ergometry: Quality and Test Criteria,* Berlin, Springer Verlag, 1984, pp. 222–228.

17. Franz IW: Ergometrische Untersuchungen zur Beurteilung der Grenzwerthypertonie. *Therapiewoch* **30**:7857, 1980.

18. Dlin RAF, Hanne N, et al: Follow-up of normotensive men with exaggerated blood pressure response to exercise. *Am Heart J* **106**:316–320, 1983.

19. Ru³ddel H, Berg K, et al: Cardiovascular reactivity and blood chemical changes during exercise. *J Sports Med Phy Fitness*, in press.

20. Cumming GR, Everatt D, Hastmen L: Bruce treadmill test in children: Normal values in a clinic population. *Am J Cardiol* **41**:69, 1978.

21. Godfrey S: Methods of measuring the response to exercise in children. In Godfrey S, (ed): *Exercise Testing in Children*. London, WB Saunders Company, 1974, pp 12–41.

22. Riopel DA, Taylor AB, Hohn AR: Blood pressure, heart rate, pressure-rate product and electrocardiographic changes in healthy children during treadmill exercise. *Am J Cardiol* **44**:697–704, 1979.

23. James FW, Kaplan S, et al: Responses of normal children and young adults to controlled bicycle exercise. *Circulation* **61**:902–912, 1980.

24. Alpert BS, Dover EV, et al: Blood pressure response to dynamic exercise testing in healthy children—black vs. white. *J Pediatr* **99**:556–560, 1981.

25. Alpert BS, Flood NL, et al: Responses to ergometer exercise in a healthy biracial population of children. *J Pediatr* **101**:538–545, 1982.

26. Alpert BS, Verrill DE, et al: Complications of ergometer exercise in children. *Pediatr Cardiol* **4**:91–96, 1983.

27. Asmussen E: Similarities and dissimilarities between static and dynamic exercise. *Circ Res* **48**:3–11, 1982.

28. Mitchell JH, Blomquist CB, et al: Static (isometric) exercise: Cardiovascular responses and normal central mechanisms. *Circ Res* **48**:I3–I188, 1981.

29. Painter P, Hanson P: Isometric exercise: Implications for the cardiac patient. *Card Rev Reports* **5**:261–279, 1984.

30. Crawford MH, White DH, Amon KW: Echocardiographic evaluation of left ventricular size and performance during handgrip and supine and upright bicycle exercises. *Circulation* **59**:1188–1196, 1979.

31. Flessas AP, Connelly GP, et al: Effects of isometric exercise on the end-diastolic pressure, volumes, and function of the left ventricle in man. *Circulation* **53**:839–846, 1976.

32. Ehsani AA, Heath GW, et al: Noninvasive assessment of changes in left ventricular function induced by graded isometric exercise in healthy subjects. *Chest* **80**:51–55, 1981.

33. Kino M, Lance VQ, et al: Effects of age on responses to isometric exercise. *Am Heart J* **90**:575–581, 1975.

34. Chrysant SG: The value of grip test as an index of autonomic function in hypertension. *Clin Cardiol* **5**:139–143, 1982.

35. Stefadouros MA, Grossman W, et al: The effect of isometric exercise on left ventricular volume in normal man. *Circulation* **49**:1185–1189, 1974.

36. Quarry VM, Spodick KH: Cardiac responses to isometric exercise. Comparative effects with different postures and levels of exertion. *Circulation* **49**:905–920, 1974.

37. Flessas AP, Ryan TJ: Effects of nitroglycerine on isometric exercise. *Am Heart J* **106**:239–242, 1983.

38. Niarchos AP, Pickering TG, Laragh JH: Cardiovascular responses to isometric exercise and standing in normotensive subjects during converting enzyme inhibition with tepro- tide. *Hypertension* **4**:538–544, 1982.

39. Perez JE, Cintron G, et al: Hemodynamic response to isometric handgrip in acute myocardial infarction. *Chest* **77**:194–196, 1980.

40. Ludbrook PA, Bryne JD, et al: Modification of left ventricular diastolic behavior by isometric handgrip exercise. *Circulation* **62**:357–370, 1980.

41. Matthews OA, Blomquist CG, et al: Left ventricular function during isometric exercise (handgrip); significance of an atrial gallop (S_4). *Am Heart J* **88**:686–693, 1974.

42. Ludbrook P, Karliner JS, O'Rourke RA: Effects of submaximal isometric handgrip on left ventricular size and wall motion. *Am J Cardiol* **33**:30–36, 1974.

43. Siegel W, Gilbert CA, et al: Use of isometric handgrip for the indirect assessment of left ventricular function in patients with coronary atherosclerotic heart disease. *Am J Cardiol* **30**:48–54, 1972.

44. Payne RM, Horwitz LD, Mullins CB: Comparison of isometric exercise and angiotensin infusion as stress test for evaluation of left ventricular function. *Am J Cardiol* **31**:428–433, 1973.

45. Helson RR, Gobel FL, et al: Hemodynamic predictors of myocardial oxygen consumption during static and dynamic exercise. *Circulation* **50**:1179–1189, 1974.

46. Quinones MA, Gaasch WH, et al: An analysis of the left ventricular response to isometric exercise. *Am Heart J* **88**:29–36, 1974.

47. McGraw DB, Siegel W, et al: Response of heart murmur intensity to isometric (handgrip) exercise. *Br Heart J* **34**:605–610, 1972.

48. McCrory WW, Klein AA, Rosenthal RA: Blood pressure, heart rate, and plasma catecholamines in normal and hypertensive children and their siblings at rest and after standing. *Hypertension* **4**:507–513, 1982.

49. Morganti A, Lopez-Ovejero JA, et al: Role of the sympathetic nervous system in mediating the renin response to head-up tilt. *Am J Cardiol* **43**:600–604, 1979.

50. Parker JO, Case RB: Normal left ventricular function. *Circulation* **60**:4–11, 1979.

51. Rankin LS, Moos S, Grossman W: Alterations in preload and ejection phase indices of left ventricular performance. *Circulation* **51**:910–915, 1975.

52. Sanghvi VR, Khaja F, et al: Effects of blood volume expansion on left ventricular hemodynamics in man. *Circulation* **46**:780–787, 1972.

53. Ziegler MG: Postural hypotension. *Annu Rev Med* **31**:239, 1983.

54. Smith JJ, Bush JE, et al: Application of impedance cardiography to study of postural stress. *J Appl Physiol* **29**:133–137, 1970.

55. Bevegard S, Holmgren A, Jonsson B: The effect of body position on the circulation at rest and during exercise, with special reference to the influence on the stroke volume. *Acta Physiol Scand* **49**:279–298, 1960.

56. Poliner LR, Dehmer GJ, et al: Left ventricular performance in normal subjects: A comparison of the responses to exercise in the upright and supine position. *Circulation* **62**:528–534, 1980.

57. Zambrano SS, Spodick DH: Comparative responses to orthostatic stress in normal and abnormal subjects. *Chest* **65**:394–396, 1974.

58. Spodick DH, Meyer M, St Pierre JR: Effect of upright tilt on the phases of the cardiac cycle in normal subjects. *Cardiovasc Res* **5**:210–214, 1971.

59. Stevens PM: Cardiovascular dynamics during orthostasis and the influence of intravascular instrumentation. *Am J Cardiol* **17**:211–218, 1966.

60. Scheinberg P, Stead E: The cerebral blood flow in male subjects as measured by the nitrous oxide technique. Normal values for blood flow, oxygen utilization and peripheral resistance with observations on the effects of tilting and anxiety. *J Clin Invest* **28**:1163–1171, 1949.

61. Levine TB, Francis GS, et al: The neurohumoral and hemodynamic response to orthostatic tilt in patients with congestive heart failure. *Circulation* **67**:1070–1075, 1983.

62. Murata K, Yamane O, et al: Alterations of circulatory responses to upright tilt in cardiac patients. *Jap Heart J* **22**:551–560, 1981.

63. Stefadouros MA, Shahawy ME, et al: The effect of upright tilt on the volume of the failing human left ventricle. *Am Heart J* **90**:735–743, 1975.

64. Thangarajah N, Hames T, et al: The use of impedance cardiography in the young and elderly during postural stress. *Age Aging* **9**:235–240, 1980.

65. Kontos HA, Richardson DW, Norvell JE: Mechanisms of circulation dysfunctions in orthostatic hypotension. *Trans Am Clin Climatol Assoc* **87**:26–35, 1979.

66. Lake CR, Ziegler MC, Kopin IJ: Use of plasma norepinephrine for evaluation of sympathetic neuronal function in man. *Life Sci* **18**:1315, 1976.

67. Eide I, Campese J, et al: Clinical arrangements of sympathetic tone: Orthostatic blood pressure response in borderline primary hypertension. *Clin Exp Hypert* **1**:51–65, 1978.

68. Esler MD, Nestel PJ: Sympathetic responsiveness to head-up tilt in essential hypertension. *Clin Sci* **44**:213–226, 1973.

69. Payen DM, Safar M, et al: Prospective study of predictive factors determining borderline hypertensive individuals who develop sustained hypertension: Prognostic value of increased diastolic orthostatic blood pressure tilt-test response and subsequent weight gain. *Am Heart J* **103**:379–383, 1982.

70. Hines EA, Brown GE: The cold pressor test for measuring the reactibility of the blood pressure: Data concerning 571 normal and hypertensive subjects. *Am Heart J* 11:1–9, 1936.

71. Hines EA: Reaction of the blood pressure of 400 school children to a standard stimulus. *JAMA* **108**:1249–1250, 1937.

72. Hines EA: The significance of vascular hyperreaction as measured by the cold pressor test. *Am Heart J* **19**:408–416, 1940.

73. Keys A, Taylor HL, et al: Mortality and coronary heart disease among men studied for 23 years. *Arch Intern Med* **128**:201–214, 1978.

74. Thomas CB, Duszynski KR: Blood pressure levels in young adulthood as predictors of hypertension and the fate of the cold pressor test. *Johns Hopkins Med J* **151**:93–100, 1982.

75. Velasco M, Romero E, et al: Effects on propranolol on sympathetic nervous activity in hydrallazine treated hypertensive patients. *Br J Clin Pharmacol* **6**:217–220, 1978.

76. Abate G, Polimeni RM, et al: Effects of indomethacin on postural hypotension in Parkinsonism. *Br Med J* **2**:1466–1468, 1979.

77. Anlauf M: Hemodynamic reactions under various stimuli before and during chronic beta blockade. *Arch Intern Pharmacodyn Ther* **244**:76–82, 1980. (Suppl)

78. Gunther S, Green L, et al: Prevention of nifedipine of abnormal coronary vasoconstriction in patients with coronary heart disease. *Circulation* **63**:849–855, 1981.

79. Gunther S, Muller JE, et al: Therapy of coronary vasoconstriction in patients with coronary artery disease. *Am J Cardiol* **47**:157–162, 1981.

80. Cohen IM, O'Connor DT, et al: Long-term clonidine effects on autonomic function in essential hypertensive man. *Eur J Clin Pharmacol* **19**:25–32, 1981.

81. Morrison SC, Chir B, et al: Selective and nonselective beta-adrenoceptor blockade in hypertension: Responses to changes in posture, cold and exercise. *Circulation* **65**:1171–1177, 1982.

82. Raizner AE, Chahine RA, et al: Provocation of coronary artery spasm by the cold pressor test: Hemodynamic, arteriographic and quantitative angiographic observations. *Circulation* **62**:925–932, 1980.

83. Mudge GH, Grossman W, et al: Reflex increase in coronary vascular resistance in patients with ischemic heart disease. *N Engl J Med* **295**:1333–1336, 1976.

84. Pickering GW, Kissin M: The effects of adrenaline and of cold on the blood pressure in human hypertension. *Clin Sci* **2**:201–207, 1936.

85. Thacker EA: A comparative study of normal and abnormal blood pressure among university students, including the cold pressor test. *Am Heart J* **20**:89–97, 1940.

86. Feldt RH, Wenstrand DEW: The cold pressor test in subjects with normal blood pressure. *Am Heart J* **23**:766–771, 1942.

87. Boyer JT, Fraser JRE, Doyle AE: The hemodynamic effects of cold immersion. *Clin Sci* **19**:539–550, 1960.

88. Lacey JI, Lacey BC: The law of initial value in the longitudinal study of autonomic constitution: Reproducibility of autonomic responses and response patterns over a four year interval. *Ann NY Acad Sci* **98**:1257–1290, 1962.

89. Voudoukis KJ: Cold pressor test: A new application as a screening test for arteriosclerosis. *Angiology* **24**:472–479, 1973.

90. McIlhany ML, Schaffer JW, Hines EA: The heritability of blood pressure: An investigation of 200 pairs of twins using the cold pressor test. *Johns Hopkins Med J* **136**:57–64, 1975.

91. Manyari DE, Nolewajk AJ, et al: Comparative value of the cold pressor test and supine bicycle exercise to detect subjects with coronary artery disease using radionuclide ventriculography. *Circulation* **65**:571–579, 1982.

92. Atterhog JH, Eliasson K, Hjemdahl P: Sympathoadrenal and cardiovascular responses to mental stress, isometric handgrip and cold pressor test in asymptomatic young men with primary T wave abnormalities in the electrocardiogram. *Br Heart J* **46**:311–319, 1931.

93. Andren L, Hansson L: Circulatory effects of stress in essential hypertension. *Acta Med Scand* **646**:69–72, 1981. (Suppl)

94. Herrman JM, Schonecke OW, et al: Different endocrinal and hemodynamic response patterns to various noxious stimuli. *Psychother Psychosom* **33**:160–166, 1980.

95. Feldman RL, Whittle JL, et al: Regional coronary hemodynamic responses to cold stimulation in patient without variant angina. *Am J Cardiol* **49**:665–673, 1982.

96. Bassan MM, Marcus HS, Ganz W: The effect of mild-to-moderate mental stress on coronary hemodynamics in patients with coronary artery disease. *Circulation* **62**:933–935, 1980.

97. LeBlanc J, Cote J, et al: Plasma catecholamines and cardiovascular responses to cold and mental activity. *J Appl Physiol* **47**:1207–1211, 1979.

98. Engel RR, Muller F, et al: Plasma catecholamineresponse and autonomic functions during short-time psychological stress. In Usdin E, Kvetnansky R, Kopin IJ, (eds): *Catecholamines and Stress: Recent Advances*. New York, Elsevier North Holland, 1980, pp. 461–466.

99. Wooten CF, Gardon PV: Plasma dopamine beta hydroxylase activity: Elevation in man during cold pressor test and exercise. *Arch Neurol* **28**:103–106, 1973.

100. Winer N, Carter C: Effect of cold pressor stimulation on plasma norepinephrine, dopamine-beta hydroxylase, and renin activity. *Life Sci* **20**:887–894, 1977.

101. Wieland BA, Mefferd RB: Systemic changes in levels of physiological activity during a four month period. *Psychophysiology* **6**:669–689, 1970.

102. Rüddel H, McKinney M, et al: Reliabilität S—Cold pressor test. Herz Medizine **7**:39–43, 1984.

103. Shea DJ, Ockene IS, Green HL: Acute myocardial infarction provoked by a cold pressor test. *Chest* **80**:649–651, 1981.

104. Frey MA, Selm AB, Walther JW: Reflex cardiovascular responses to cold exposure of the face or foot. *Jpn H J* **21**:666–679, 1980.

105. Cohen S, Krantz D, et al: Cardiovascular and behavioral effects of community noise. *Am Sci* **69**:528–535, 1981.

106. Peterson EA, Augenstein JS, et al: Noise raises blood pressure without impairing auditory sensitivity. *Science* **211**:1450–1452, 1981.

107. Andren L: Cardiovascular effects of noise. *Acta Med Scand* **675**:7–45, 1982. (Suppl)

108. Andren L, Hansson L, et al: Noise as a contributory factor in the development of elevated arterial pressure. *Acta Med Scand* **207**:493–498, 1980.

109. Andren L, Hansson L, et al: Circulatory effects of noise. *Acta Med Scand* **213**:31–35, 1983.

110. Ising H: Interaction of noise-induced stress and Mg decrease. *Artery* **3**:205–211, 1981.

9

Cardiovascular Measures of Physiologic Reactivity

NEIL SCHNEIDERMAN, THOMAS G. PICKERING

The purpose of this chapter is to describe hemodynamic and cardiac electrophysiological measures that are likely to be useful in the study of relationships between behavior and cardiovascular regulation. To be maximally useful these measures should be applicable to studies of basic psychophysiology as well as to investigations of possible relationships between biobehavioral factors and medical problems including hypertension, coronary heart disease (CHD), and sudden cardiac death. In setting about this task a number of issues need to be considered.

One matter that deserves attention involves the selection of response measures. Since the physiologic adjustments of an organism consist of an integrated pattern of responses, it is important to select judiciously a sufficient number of response measures to allow for the response pattern and its variation to be identified. Thus, under ideal conditions it is desirable to assess blood pressure, the electrocardiogram, cardiac output and its determinants, peripheral resistance, and blood flow in different vascular beds as well as the status of the heart and coronary arteries. Usually, it is not possible to assess all of these variables, and compromises are necessary. Alternative methods for examining cardiovascular functioning, and the basis for choosing among these methods, are discussed in the present chapter, as are current technological limitations of the available procedures.

A second issue that needs to be considered in relating behavior to cardiovascular regulation involves the specification and implications of using alternative control levels in assessing cardiovascular responses to particular stimulus conditions. It is well known, of course, that cardiovascular activity varies as a function of stimulus conditions and organismic variables. Factors that may influence the pattern, magnitude, and/or duration of cardiovascular functioning include the individual's perception of current stimulus conditions, behavioral response style (e.g., personality), emotional state, genetic background, physical status, and past history. Thus, the blood pressure (BP) and other cardiovascular measures in a seated individual may be influenced by anticipatory set, task instructions, familiarity with the situation, or even whether the measurements are being made by a physician, nurse, or student investigator. The sensitivity of the cardiovascular system to a large number of potentially confounding variables makes the selection of appropriate baseline measures and/or the specification of control levels important concerns in cardiovascular psychophysiological studies. Some of the important considerations involved are discussed in the present chapter.

A third matter that deserves consideration deals with the methods required to evaluate the central nervous system (CNS), autonomic nervous system, and hormonal regulation of relevant hemodynamic and electrophysiologic measures used in cardiovascular psychophysiologic assessment. A number of procedures are described that can be used to evaluate cardiovascular function in terms of (1) primary versus secondary adjustment; (2) parasympathetic versus sympathetic nervous system activity; (3) alpha- versus beta-adrenergic activity; and (4) CNS versus afferent versus efferent functioning.

The present chapter begins with a discussion of the vascular system, including measurement of BP, assessment of the venous circulation, and the evaluation of regional blood flow. This is followed by a discussion of the cardiac output and its measurement, and the determinants of cardiac output and BP. The cardiac cycle is then discussed, including a description of electrocardiographic (ECG) measurement, the assessment of contractility, and the use of systolic time intervals. This is followed by a discussion of circulatory control, including neural and hormonal influences, and a description of methods used to assess the neural and hormonal variables involved in the control of cardiovascular activity.

BLOOD PRESSURE

Systemic arterial BP is a potentially important measure of cardiovascular reactivity for both hypertension and coronary artery disease, although evidence linking acute changes in BP with long-term consequences for either disease is very limited. Although it might be argued that cardiovascular reactivity would be assessed more appropriately by measuring the underlying physiological changes of cardiac output and peripheral resistance, there is some evidence that pressure itself may be the variable that is regulated, at any rate in the acute situation. Thus, noise increases BP by causing a vasoconstriction; if this is prevented by an alpha blocker such as prazosin, the vasoconstriction is prevented, but BP still rises, in this case as a result of an increased cardiac output.[1]

Techniques for Measuring Blood Pressure

Direct Intraarterial Recording.   This method remains the "gold standard" of BP measurement techniques, and any noninvasive method must be validated against it. In addition, it is at the present time the only method that can assess beat-to-beat changes in BP, which may be necessary in studies of BP reactivity. The most commonly used recording sites are the brachial and radial arteries. The exact pressure that is recorded will vary slightly according to the recording site, because the pressure waveform changes as it traverses the circulation, with slightly higher systolic and slightly lower diastolic pressures at more distal sites. Thus, a subject with an aortic pressure of 122/81 mmHg may have a brachial artery pressure of 131/79 and a radial artery pressure of 136/77. The corresponding mean pressures would be 100, 99, and 97.[2]

While intraarterial BP recording is the most accurate method, its accuracy may be limited according to the frequency response of the recording system. Significant errors can occur from either underdamping or overdamping. In practice, its use is greatly limited by its invasiveness, so that it has been used very little in psychophysiological testing of healthy human subjects.

Korotkov Sound Techniques.   Despite persistent efforts to find a superior method, the method first developed by Riva-Rocci in 1896 and Korotkov in 1905 is still the most widely used indirect method of measuring BP. Several studies have compared intraarterial and sphygmomanometric cuff pressures; in general, the correlation between the two has been good, with certain exceptions described below. Correlations of 0.95 have been obtained for systolic, 0.93 for the fifth phase of diastolic, and 0.83 for the fourth phase, with most of the readings being within 5 or 10 mmHg of each other.[3]

1.   Which phase of the Korotkov sounds should be used for diastolic pressure?   It is extraordinary that after 75 years of using the Korotkov sound method for measuring blood pressure, there is still no universal agreement as to whether phase four (muffling) or phase five (disappearance) should be used to express the diastolic pressure. Comparisons with intraarterial pressures have shown that the fifth phase is closer to the true diastolic, being on average 2 mmHg higher, whereas the fourth phase is about 8 mmHg higher.[4] Thus, the difference between the two readings is about 6 mmHg, but this varies greatly from one individual to another, and also according to the circumstances, such as the period following exercise, when the fifth phase may give readings that are much too low.

The official recommendation of the American Heart Association is to use the fourth phase.[5] The reasons given for this recommendation are that: (1) the fourth phase is theoretically more closely related to the true diastolic pressure than the fifth; (2) a change of quality in the sound (as in the fourth phase) is less dependent on the acuity of the observer's hearing than the disappearance of the sound; and (3) the fifth phase may grossly underestimate the true diastolic pressure after exercise. The Framingham survey, which has provided the most important epidemiological data about the risks of high blood pressure and hence the need for treatment, used the fourth phase, but the two most important trials demonstrating the effectiveness of treatment, the Veterans Administration (VA) and Hypertension Detection and Followup Program (HDFP) trials, both used the fifth phase. The situation is a mess. Most people nowadays favor the fifth phase.

2.   Factors leading to errors in indirect measurement of blood pressure.   The cuff method may give erroneous values for several reasons other than merely faulty technique, the most important of which are listed below.

Arm size.   If the cuff is too small relative to the diameter of the patient's arm, the pressure in the cuff will not be adequately transmitted to the artery, so that a higher cuff pressure will be needed to occlude the artery, and falsely high readings will be obtained. It is difficult to give precise correction factors, but in an obese patient with an arm diameter of 40 cm, the standard size cuff (12 × 24 cm) may give both systolic and diastolic readings that are about 15 mmHg too high.[6] It is important, however, that the wide cuff not be used for nonobese patients, where it may lead to an underestimate of the patient's true pressure.[7]

Three adult cuff sizes are currently available: regular (12 × 24 cm), large (15 × 33 cm), and thigh (18 × 36 cm). For nonobese patients (arm circumference below 33 cm), it is best to use the regular cuff; for moderately obese patients (arm circumference 34–42 cm), the large cuff should be used, and for the very obese (arm circumference more than 42 cm), the thigh cuff is recommended.

Age.   Measurement of blood pressure with the cuff method in the very young and the old may present other problems. Thus the Doppler method (Arteriosonde) may be more reliable in infants. In subjects over 60 years old the cuff method may give diastolic readings that are 30 mmHg too high in some cases, although errors in systolic pressure are less marked.[8] The explanation for this finding may be that the stiffer vessels of old people vibrate less well than in the young, so that the Korotkov sound disappears at a higher pressure.

Silent period.   In older people with a wide pulse pressure the Korotkov sounds may disappear midway between the systolic and diastolic pressures (silent period) and reappear again just above diastolic. Failure to recognize this phenomenon can lead to errors.

Unsupported arm.   If the subject is holding his or her arm up during the measurement, this may raise diastolic pressure by as much as 10 percent as a result of the isometric exercise involved.

Observer error and observer bias.   Numerous studies have shown that the recording of blood pressure with a conventional sphygmomanometer is often subjective. In one study, a movie showing the fall of mercury in a sphygmomanometer column with the Korotkov sounds on the sound track was played to a group of trained nurses, and resulted in widely varying estimates of the blood pressure.[9] Many observers show digit preference, with a tendency to record even numbers more than odd ones.

Automatic Noninvasive Recorders

For studies of psychophysiologic reactivity, where repeated measurements of BP are required, it is generally most convenient to use some form of automated recorder. Apart from their convenience, such recorders have the advantage of eliminating observer bias, and many of them can have their output fed into a computer for on-line monitoring.

A large number of recorders are now available, but many of them have not been satisfactorily validated. It is essential that, when automatic recorders are used, they be calibrated for every subject, either with a stethoscope or display of the Korotkov sounds. Ideally, such recorders should be calibrated for detecting change of pressure as well as the basal value.

A novel technique has been used in the Infrasonde recorder. This device differs form a Korotkov sound recorder in that it detects inaudible low-frequency arterial oscillations that commence during gradual cuff deflation at systolic pressure and cease at diastolic pressure.[10] It has the advantage that most of the artifactual sounds that occur during movement are of high frequency, so that this recorder can give reliable readings during exercise.

Oscillometric Techniques.   The oscillometric technique, first described in 1904, is based on the vibrations that are set up in a sphygmomanometer cuff during gradual deflation of the cuff. The onset of the vibrations corresponds to systolic pressure, and maximum vibration occurs at approximately mean arterial pressure. Diastolic pressure can only be detected indirectly. The advantage of the method is that no Korotkov sound detector is needed, so the placement of the cuff is not critical. As originally described, the method was unreliable, but it has recently been revived in two forms, the Dinamap and Medtek blood pressure monitors. Both involve the use of microprocessors for the detection of systolic and mean pressure and the calculation of diastolic pressure. Neither instrument has been extensively validated, but in our experience both give reasonable agreement with the measurements made by a mercury sphygmomanometer in most patients but may seriously be in error in some patients.

Ultrasound Techniques.   The ultrasound technique has been used in the Arteriosonde recorder, which works on the Doppler principle. Instead of a Korotkov sound microphone, and ultrasound transmitter and detector is used. The vibration of the arterial wall that starts as the sphygmomanometer cuff is deflated past systolic pressure causes a phase shift of the reflected ultrasound beam by the Doppler effect, and this point is read as the systolic pressure. Diastolic pressure is recorded as the point at which pronounced diminution of arterial wall motion occurs. The Arteriosonde, which is a fully automatic device, has been found to compare favorably with mercury sphygmomanometers.[11] Its chief disadvantages are its cost and its sensitivity to movement artifact.

Pulse Transit Time

Another noninvasive technique that has been advocated is the measurement of pulse transit time, using either the interval from the R wave to the radial pulse, or the interval between the brachial and radial pulses. While this technique has the advantage of not requiring a cuff and therefore offers the theoretical possibility of continual beat-to-beat measurement, correlations between changes of pressure and transit time have been disappointing, and it is unlikely that the technique will find widespread application.[12,13]

Issues in Using BP as a Measure of Psychophysiologic Reactivity

Continuous versus Intermittent Readings.   A method for detecting beat-to-beat changes of BP is obviously desirable for reactivity studies. The practical limitations of intraarterial BP recording mean that cuff measures must be relied on for the present time. These cannot take readings more than once every 30 seconds, although there have been several attempts to develop servo-controlled cuff tracking methods, which can monitor changes for up to two minutes or so. These measurements have limited applicability, however, because they are likely to show oscillations around the true level of BP and to underestimate the extent of acute changes.

The need to rely on intermittent measures of BP and the errors inherent in single readings means that stimuli for evaluating reactivity should be chosen only if there is a rise of BP that is sustained over several minutes, so that the average of several readings can be taken. Thus, for example, exposure to prolonged noise would be an appropriate paradigm; whereas the startle response to a brief noise would not.

Laboratory versus Ambulatory Readings.   The ultimate aim of the majority of studies of cardiovascular reactivity is to relate the reactivity to the development or progression of cardiovascular disease. In the past, this has been done by using laboratory tests to evaluate reactivity, but the availability of ambulatory recorders now makes it also possible to assess reactivity in a more naturalistic setting. Both methods have their advantages. The laboratory setting permits much greater control of the experimental situation and enables more valid comparisons to be made between different groups of subjects. On the other hand, it might be argued that many of the tasks commonly used in the laboratory setting (e.g., the cold pressor test and video games) do not represent stresses encountered in real life and that the reproducibility and validity of these tests are low. Our own experience is that, while the level of BP measured during psychophysiological stressors correlates reasonably well with the BP measures during ambulatory monitoring, the changes of BP seen during laboratory testing and ambulatory monitoring are very weakly correlated. There are relatively little published data concerning the predictive value of BP changes measured during laboratory testing. In one study the BP response to a cold pressor test was found to predict future coronary heart disease.[14] The evidence relating the cold pressor response to future hypertension is conflicting: one long-term follow-up study found no correlations,[15] whereas another did find a correlation.[16] The BP response to mental arithmetic has been found to predict future hypertension in adolescents.[17] The predictive value of ambulatory monitoring is also beginning to be established.[18]

From the currently available evidence it appears that both types of testing have their place. They should be regarded as complementary rather than as one being superior to the other.

What Should Be Taken as the Baseline Level of BP?   In any study of psychophysiological reactivity, the change of BP that occurs during the stressor must be measured relative to a baseline value. It is customary to take the BP averaged for several minutes before the onset of the task, after the subject has been seated for 15 to 30 minutes. It should be recognized, however, that the anticipation of the task may itself cause some elevation of BP. Thus, in patients with borderline hypertension, we have found that the BP taken while at rest before an exercise test is consistently higher than BPs taken at rest in the clinic or at home.[19]

ASSESSMENT OF THE VENOUS CIRCULATION

Investigations of the role of the veins in modulating cardiovascular reactivity have been very few, despite the fact that veins are richly innervated and are very responsive to adrenergic stimulation. Apart from their function as a conduit, their main physiologic role is as a capacitance reservoir, since approximately 70 percent of the total blood volume normally resides in the veins. During a stressful task such as mental arithmetic, both blood pressure and cardiac output increase, the latter occurring partly because of an intense venoconstriction.

Any method for assessing venous tone in humans has to rely on measurement of pressure-volume relationships in the veins.[20] An increase of venous tone is defined as an increase of pressure relative to volume. In practice, such measurements are usually made in veins of the forearm. Volume changes are measured by plethysmography, using either a water-filled plethysmograph or a mercury-in-rubber strain gauge; pressure is measured directly from a catheter inserted into a large vein. Venous pressure is changed by stepwise inflation of a proximal cuff to about 40 mmHg, and the corresponding changes in volume are noted. In this way, a pressure-volume curve can be constructed.

Transient changes of venous tone may be assessed by maintaining the pressure in the occluding cuff at about 30 mmHg. Once the volume has reached equilibrium, a sudden change in venous tone will be reflected by a change in the pressure and/or volume. A variation of this method is to occlude the circulation to the limb completely, so that the blood volume in the occluded segment is constantly maintained. In this situation, any changes of pressure in the vein must be due to changes in venomotor tone mediated by the sympathetic nerves.[21]

REGIONAL BLOOD FLOW

A major function of the cardiovascular system is to meet the metabolic needs of body tissues. This involves the delivery of oxygen, nutrients, and other substances as well as the removal of waste products. Local blood flow in some tissues performs additional functions. In the skin, for example, it includes the transfer of heat to the surrounding air; in the brain, the regulation of carbon dioxide and hydrogen ion concentration of brain fluids.

The overall blood flow in the circulation of an adult human at rest is approximately five liters per minute. This is referred to as the *cardiac output* and is expressed as the amount of blood pumped by the heart per unit of time. The distribution of the cardiac output, or blood flow, in a resting person is about 28 percent in the liver, 22 percent in the kidneys, and 15 percent in the brain,[22] despite the fact that these organs represent only a small fraction of the body's total mass. Even though skeletal muscle represents 35 to 40 percent of total body mass, blood flow in this tissue at rest is only about 15 percent of the cardiac output. In contrast, during vigorous physical exercise nearly 80 percent of the blood flow goes to skeletal muscle, while the distribution of the blood flow to the liver and kidneys decreases to about 10 percent.[22] Changes in the distribution of the blood flow from that observed in the resting state have also been seen during the defense reaction[23] as well as during behavioral tasks not usually associated with physical exertion, such as mental arithmetic.[24]

Numerous techniques are available for measuring blood flow in various tissues during different experimental conditions. These range from the use of flowmeters through the utilization of radioisotope techniques to the use of other indicator dilution techniques and plethysmography.

Flowmeters

Electromagnetic Flowmeter.   One method of assessing changes in blood flow in different organs involves the use of *electromagnetic flowmeters*. The electromagnetic flowmeter works on the principle that hemoglobin in blood passing through the magnetic field imposed by a flowmeter produces a potential between two electrodes placed across a vessel. When blood flows through the vessel, an electrical voltage proportional to the rate of flow is generated between the two electrodes.

Although electromagnetic flow systems can be highly accurate and reliable, they are somewhat inconvenient. First, because they are subject to drift, each transducer must be accompanied by an occluder to provide a zero flow calibration. Second, the probes to be placed on the blood vessels are bulky because they must contain an electromagnet as well as electrodes. For this reason, use of electromagnetic flowmeters in psychophysiologic research has largely been restricted to large animals such as primates[25,26] and dogs,[27] in which measurements from only a very few vascular beds are desired.

Ultrasonic Flowmeter.   The development of techniques for the continuous measurement of regional blood flow in intact small animals has been facilitated by the use of ultrasonic pulsed Doppler flowmeter systems.[28,29] A piezoelectric crystal as small as 1.0 mm in diameter is used to emit a 20-mHz signal and receive the reflected sound wave from blood cells passing through the cuffed blood vessel. Zero flow is determined without an occluding cuff by simply turning the ultrasound off.

Comparisons of changes in blood flow between electromagnetic and pulsed Doppler flowmeters have shown correlation coefficients of approximately $r = 0.97$. Thus, the pulsed Doppler flowmeter technique appears to be useful for obtaining relative changes of flow concomitantly in a number of blood vessels within conscious, moving animals. The technique may be less useful for determining absolute volume flows quantitatively, since the Doppler shift obtained between animals or between probe sites may vary as a function of the orientation of the probe to the vessel, the coupling medium between the probe and the vessel, or the intrinsic characteristics of the probe.[29]

Radioisotope Techniques

Electromagnetic and ultrasonic flowmeters have proven useful in animal experiments, but their applications are limited. Although it should be feasible to assess some regional flows noninvasively using ultrasonic techniques, this goal has not yet been satisfactorily realized. One reason for using radioactive tracer techniques is therefore to assess regional blood flow in as minimally invasive a manner as possible. Another reason is to permit detailed regional assessments to be made in deeply placed organs or tissues that are not readily accessible to flow probes. The tracer techniques involve the use of a radioactive substance whose direct introduction into the tissue itself or into the main arterial supply can be used to calculate either total organ blood flow or the perfusion rate per unit weight of tissue.

The infusion of radionuclide-coated microspheres into the left side of the heart in experimental animals via a catheter permits the subsequent analysis of blood flow to be made within as well as between organs. Since a variety of nuclides are available, differentially labeled microspheres can be injected during several conditions. Measurements can be made only during a few points in time, however, and the procedure is invasive and requires subsequent sacrifice of the animal for purposes of data analysis.[30]

Briefly, separately labeled 15 μm carbonized plastic microspheres are infused during each experimental condition. The 15 μm spheres are large enough to be trapped by small vessels, but not so small that they circulate more than once. Because separate radionuclide-labeled microspheres can be used for each condition, the technique permits analysis of the flow distribution in as many conditions as there are different nuclides available for labeling the microspheres. Once the experiment is ended, the animal is sacrificed, organs are dissected, tissue samples are placed in scintillation vials, and radioactivity is counted using a gamma scintillation spectrometer.

Although the radioactive microsphere technique provides information about the relative distribution of blood flow in different tissues, it does not by itself provide absolute measures of flow. In order to accomplish this, it is necessary to measure the cardiac output ($\dot{Q}$) concomitant with each injection of radionuclide-labeled microspheres.[31] The amount of blood flow in each organ can then be calculated as:

$$\text{Organ flow (ml/min)} = \frac{\dot{Q} \times \text{number of microspheres in an organ}}{\text{number of microspheres infused}}$$

The number of infused microspheres is determined by the differences in the number of radioactive counts in the injection syringe before and after the infusion. Number of labeled microspheres per injection range from about 50,000 in the rat to approximately 5 million in the dog.

Because the radioactive microsphere method requires scintillation well-counting of tissues, it is restricted to animal studies. Recently, however, regional blood flow has been studied *in vivo* using ^{11}C-labeled albumin microspheres in conjunction with positron emission tomography (PET) in dogs.[32] Briefly, biodegradable human albumin microspheres, 10 to 20 μm in diameter, were labeled with cyclotron-produced ^{11}C and injected into the left atrium. Values of regional blood flow were made from tomograms recorded *in vivo* two to three minutes after injection. These correlated well ($r = 0.96$) with reference values of regional flow, *in vitro*, that were obtained using gamma-emitting microspheres. Since PET permits quantitative, three-dimensional reconstruction of the distribution of tracers in different regions of the body, it may soon be possible to combine the use of biodegradable microspheres with PET to study regional blood flow in conscious humans.

Although PET technology promises to be useful in human research, it is also very expensive and available only in relatively few medical centers. Other, less expensive, more available radioisotope techniques have been developed that allow blood flow in various organs to be studied by examining the clearance of diffusible gases from the blood or by the use of external detectors. Thus, for example, [133]Xenon has been used to determine coronary flow.[33,34] Briefly, the [133]Xenon is dissolved in sterile saline and then injected into a coronary artery. The [133]Xenon diffuses rapidly into the myocardium, but 95 percent of this gas is excreted on its first passage through the pulmonary bed. Coronary blood flow is then calculated by analyzing the [133]Xenon washout curve (i.e., counts per milliliter vs. time) from the myocardium, using either coronary sinus blood or a scintillation camera. Radioisotope techniques have also proven useful in investigations of cerebral, hepatic, pulmonary, renal, skeletal muscle, and skin blood flows.[35]

Application of the Fick Technique to Studies of Regional Flow

Blood flow through a bodily organ can be determined by means of the Fick principle. According to this principle, the total blood flow through an organ during a particular period of measurement can be determined by dividing the total quantity of a blood constituent removed by the amount of the constituent removed from each milliliter of blood. Let us examine the application of the Fick principle to the study of coronary blood flow (CBF) using nitrous oxide (N_2O) as the blood constituent.[36] The method depends on determining the N_2O uptake by the myocardium and the arteriovenous (AV) difference of N_2O across the heart. The Fick equation can then be expressed:

$$CBF = \frac{\text{amount } N_2O \text{ extracted by myocardium}}{\text{AV difference of } N_2O \text{ in blood}}$$

$$= \frac{\text{ml } N_2O/100 \text{ mg myocardium}}{\text{ml } N_2O/\text{ml blood}}$$

In order to get an appropriate measure of venous blood, a catheter is positioned in the coronary sinus. Arterial blood is drawn from a peripheral artery. The subject breathes a gas mixture composed of 15 percent nitrous oxide, 21 percent oxygen, and 64 percent nitrogen over a 10-minute period.

During this time, 10 paired blood samples are drawn from the coronary sinus and a systemic artery. The AV differences are plotted across time to insure that a steady state is reached.[34]

Although using an inert gas to measure regional blood flow eliminates the radioactivity hazards associated with radionuclide methods, employment of the Fick procedure with N_2O as the blood constituent has several disadvantages of its own. First, because the measurement takes at least 10 minutes to perform, acute changes cannot be studied. Second, the need to breathe the N_2O continually during the measurement period may interfere with the experimental protocol (e.g., verbal responses). Third, the N_2O itself may adversely affect behavioral processes. Fourth, the procedure is invasive and not without risk. For these reasons, it appears unlikely that the Fick procedure will find much application for studying regional blood flow in psychophysiological experiments.

Plethysmography

Several methods are available that can indirectly and noninvasively estimate blood flow to a particular segment of the body. These methods are venous-occlusion plethysmography, impedance plethysmography, and photoplethysmography. The term *plethysmography* comes from the Greek, and means the measurement of enlargement. In plethysmography a change in volume of a particular segment of the body is used to provide an indirect estimate of the amount of blood contained in that segment. Plethysmography has been used to study flow changes during static exercise,[37] cold pressor tests,[38] the stress of mental arithmetic,[24] and orienting and defensive reflexes.[39]

Venous-Occlusion Plethysmography.   This method has proven useful for measuring arterial inflow to a limb. The transducer is a mercury-in-rubber or silastic strain gauge[40] that is placed around the largest circumference of the limb (e.g., forearm). At this placement the ratio of muscle to skin and bone is greatest. Two blood pressure cuffs are used in conjunction with the strain gauge. The distal cuff, which is located around the hand or ankle, is inflated to a pressure greater than systolic (e.g., 200 mmHg) to exclude the hand circulation from measurement. This is because blood flow to the hand is largely determined by skin rather than muscle blood flow. The proximal cuff is quickly inflated to a pressure that is above venous pressure but below diastolic arterial pressure (e.g., 40–50 mmHg). This allows for the easy inflow of arterial blood but prevents blood from leaving the segment. As the limb becomes engorged with blood, the mercury-in-rubber strain gauge, which fits around the circumference of the limb between the two cuffs, detects an increase in electrical resistance that is proportional to the circumference change.

The mercury strain gauge can be calibrated by using it in conjunction with an artificial arm and a perfusion pump to assure that the absolute flow is the same as the recorded flow. Voltage changes, as given by microvolt of output per millimeter of change of volume change, can then be recorded. By timing the volumetric changes, blood flow (F) can be derived by constructing a Cartesian plot of volume change (dV) against time after venous occlusion (dt).

$$F = \frac{dV}{dt}$$

This can be expressed as cc/100 cc of limb/min. When mean arterial blood pressure (MAP) is concomitantly measured, vascular resistance in the limb (R) can be calculated as:

$$R = \frac{MAP}{\text{limb flow}}$$

Although venous occlusion plethysmography provides a noninvasive measure of absolute flow, it is subject to artifacts. Many factors, including ischemic pain caused by the distal cuff, ambient temperature, limb position above or below the heart, sympathetic tone, and circulating vasoactive substances, can influence the results obtained and need to be controlled.

Impedance Plethysmography.   Electrical-impedance plethysmography is based on the principle that when electrodes are placed across living tissues such as a limb, the tissues will exhibit a characteristic impedance to a high-frequency AC signal. In a limb, the impedance is determined by the muscle, bone, and volume of blood. Because the amount of muscle and bone remain invariant, changes in impedance (dZ) necessarily reflect changes in blood volume.

In impedance plethysmography four metal-ribbon electrodes are placed around the body segment. The two outer electrodes provide a constant, low-level (100–400 μA) alternating current (25–100 kHz); whereas the two inner electrodes detect the voltage that is dependent on the impedance of the intervening tissue. This impedance is inversely related to the volume of the tissues between the two inner electrodes. A major drawback of the method as just described is the difficulty of obtaining absolute measures of blood volume changes. Impedance plethysmography, however, has been successfully combined with the volume-displacement procedure of venous occlusion.[41] Briefly, a blood pressure cuff was placed proximal to the four impedance electrodes. The cuff was then inflated suddenly to about 40 mmHg to provide venous occlusion. Use of this method provides a reasonable alternative to the mercury-in-rubber strain-gauge procedure and permits the measurement of blood flow to be expressed in absolute terms.

Photoplethysmography.   This method has been widely used by psychophysiologists to study *relative* changes in blood flow.[39,42] It can be applied easily, inexpensively, and noninvasively at many body sites. One variant of the procedure uses a light-emitting diode-transistor plethysmograph.[43] This photoplethysmograph uses a reflective transducer in which an infrared light-emitting diode (LED) and the phototransducer are applied adjacent to one another. The phototransducer provides a linear voltage output with respect to the intensity of the light striking it. Aside from its inability to provide an absolute measure of flow, the major deficiency of the photoplethysmographic method appears to be its extreme sensitivity to movement artifacts.[44] Nevertheless, when appropriately used it has proven to have some use in psychophysiological research.

CARDIAC OUTPUT

Our heart is a two-sided stroke pump. The right side supplies the pulmonary circulation; the left supplies the systemic circulation. Output of the right side is equal to the output of the left. The *cardiac output* is defined as the output of either the left or the right side of the heart per unit of time. Humans at rest have a cardiac output of approximately five liters per minute.

Because cardiac output varies in proportion to the surface area of the body, it is useful in some instances to express cardiac output in terms of a *cardiac index*. The cardiac index may be defined as the cardiac output per square meter of body surface area. Since an average human adult has a body surface area of about 1.7 square meters, the average cardiac index for human adults in about 3.0 liters per minute per square meter.

Cardiac output generally remains fairly proportional to the overall metabolism of the body. Thus, cardiac output tends to vary with increased activity. Highly trained long-distance runners can increase their cardiac ouput from a resting value of 5 liters per minute to a value of 25 or 30 liters per minute during maximal exercise.

Cardiac output can be calculated in various ways. One way is to apply the Fick principle using either oxygen or carbon dioxide as a gas constituent of the blood. Another way is to use an indicator-dilution method. The indicator-dilution method is based on the principle that if a known concentration of indicator is introduced into a flowing stream and the concentration of the indicator is measured at a downstream point as a function of time, it is possible to measure volume flow.[45] A third way of calculating cardiac output ($\dot{Q}$) is to multiply the stroke volume (SV) or blood ejected per heart beat by the heart rate (HR). Thus,

$$\dot{Q} = SV \times HR$$

Heart rate is easily measurable. There are several ways of measuring stroke volume. These include the use of electromagnetic and bidirectional Doppler flowmeters, left ventricular angiography, M-mode echocardiography, and impedance cardiography.

Dilution Methods

Fick Technique.   Previously, we encountered the Fick principle in the study of regional blood flow. In that instance, nitrous oxide was introduced as a gas constituent of blood. The Fick principle can also be applied to the study of the cardiac output in terms of whole body blood flow using either oxygen (O_2) or carbon dioxide (CO_2) as an endogenous gas constituent of the blood. In this case, cardiac output can be calculated as either the amount of O_2 consumed or CO_2 released divided by the arteriovenous (AV) differences in the gas. Thus,

$$\dot{Q} \text{ (liters/min)} = \frac{O_2 \text{ consumed (ml/min)}}{AV \; O_2 \text{ difference (ml } O_2/\text{liter of blood)}}$$

$$\dot{Q} \text{ (liters/min)} = \frac{CO_2 \text{ released (ml/min)}}{AV \; CO_2 \text{ difference (ml } CO_2/\text{liter of blood)}}$$

When oxygen is used as the indicator, oxygen uptake is determined by the gas volume change after 15 minutes of rebreathing from a closed spirometer circuit in which carbon dioxide is removed by passing the expired air through soda lime. The arterial and venous oxygen contents are measured by volumetric techniques on three samples of blood obtained from the pulmonary artery (i.e., mixed venous sample) and systemic arterial catheters over the same time span. Measurement of oxygen concentration in the venous and arterial blood is accomplished using either a Van Slyke manometric or the LexOcon analyzer.[46] When carefully performed, the Fick method just described is the standard against which other indicator-dilution techniques of cardiac output measurement are judged.

Because pulmonary and systemic arterial blood samples are required for the use of the direct Fick method, the technique is limited in its application. This has led to the development of the indirect carbon dioxide Fick method. The approach is noninvasive and requires neither a pulmonary artery catheter nor blood sample.

In the indirect carbon dioxide Fick method, ventilation and mixed expired CO_2 are measured for the calculation of carbon dioxide output (V_{CO_2}) using a spirometer and carbon dioxide gas analyzer. In subjects with normal lung function the arterial carbon dioxide content may be estimated from the end tidal P_{CO_2}.[47] Measurement of venous carbon dioxide content is based on having the subject rebreathe a mixture of carbon dioxide in oxygen from a 5-liter bag.[48] The carbon dioxide concentration is 2–3 percent higher than the anticipated mixed venous carbon dioxide. Carbon dioxide is continuously sampled at the mouthpiece and examined for equilibrium. If equilibrium is not reached in three to four breaths, a bag of different carbon dioxide concentration is substituted. Once the V_{CO_2}, estimated arterial P_{CO_2} ($PaCO_2$), and estimated venous P_{CO_2} ($PvCO_2$) have been determined, the cardiac output can be calculated as:

$$\dot{Q} = \frac{VCO_2}{PaCO_2 - PvCO_2}$$

Commercial systems such as the Beckman Horizon system permit all of the above measurements to be made with computer assistance.

Although the Fick procedures are useful in many situations, their applications in psychophysiologic studies are somewhat limited. First, the direct Fick method is highly invasive. Second, the need to obtain steady states of equilibrium using either the indirect or direct Fick method precludes the use of these procedures for tracking rapid, dynamic responses. Third, the need to breathe through a mask limits the subject's ability to engage in interpersonal communication.

Dye-dilution method.   Calculation of cardiac output by the dye dilution method, like the Fick procedure, assumes that in a steady state the amount of indicator leaving an organ is the same as the amount entering it. Also like the mixed venous oxygen in the Fick method, the dye in an indicator-dilution procedure must be mixed with the venous return before reaching the sampling site. In practice the dye, most often cardiogreen, is injected into the right side of the heart or pulmonary artery, and the arterial blood samples are taken from an aortic catheter previously inserted via the femoral artery.

The dye dilution method may be carried out either rapidly by the single bolus method or by continuous infusion. In either case the arterial samples of blood-dye concentration must be continuously measured. The resultant arterial indicator concentration-time curve is used to calculate cardiac output.

In the commonly used single-bolus method:

$$\dot{Q} = \frac{\text{amount of indicator injected}}{\text{area under concentration-time curve}}$$

The determination of cardiac output using this procedure is valid only if flow remains constant and there is stationarity of flow. Thus, any sudden changes in cardiac output would invalidate the determination.

In the continuous infusion procedure:

$$\dot{Q} = \frac{\text{infusion rate of dye}}{\text{concentration of dye at equilibrium}}$$

To the extent that a steady state flow does not exist or the area under the dye dilution curve is not appropriately corrected for recirculation of the indicator, the results will be invalid.

There are many commercially available, microprocessor-based units for automatic calculation of cardiac output from dye-dilution curves. Although the ear densitometer has been used for the recording of dye concentration, the curves are often too prolonged and gradual to correct accurately for recirculation.

Thermal-Dilution Method.   In this variant of the indicator-dilution method, a cold liquid is used as the indicator. Briefly, a thermistor is used to record the downstream decrease in temperature that provides the thermal-dilution curve. Usually a solution of 5 percent dextrose in water at O°C is used as the indicator. The technique involves using a balloon-tipped catheter incorporating a thermistor at the tip.[49] A second lumen in the catheter permits pressure to be recorded from the catheter tip, and a third lumen serves as an injection port.

The catheter is introduced into an arm vein and advanced into the right atrium. Here the balloon is inflated, keeping the third lumen in position. Blood flow meanwhile guides the tip of the catheter into the right ventricle, and its presence there is confirmed by recording pressure. The catheter is then advanced into the pulmonary artery, where its presence is also confirmed by pressure recording. Then, the balloon is deflated and thermodilution curves are obtained by injection of the cold solution into the atrium via the third lumen.

Although the passage of the Swan-Ganz catheter through a peripheral vein makes the thermal-dilution method the safest of the invasive methods for measuring cardiac output, the equation for calculating cardiac output with the thermal-dilution procedure is the most complex. The specific gravity of the indicator and of the blood, the specific heat of the indicator and of the blood, and an empirical factor used to correct for heat transfer through the injection catheter make up the term K in the equation.

$$\dot{Q} = \frac{V(60 \text{ sec}) \; (T_B \times T_I) \; K}{\text{area under the dilution curve in (sec) (°C)}}$$

where:

V = volume of the indicator
T_B = temperature of pulmonary artery before injection
T_I = temperature of the indicator

The thermal-dilution method is commonly used to determine cardiac output. Many commercially available microprocessor-based instruments are available for automatic calculation of cardiac output from thermodilution data.

Stroke Volume Methods

As previously mentioned, cardiac output can be assessed as the product of stroke volume and heart rate. In animal studies the electromagnetic flowmeter offers a straightforward method for determining stroke volume. In humans blood flow can be measured transcutaneously using a Doppler flowmeter. Whereas the flowmeter approaches to calculating stroke volume depend on a knowledge of blood velocity and the cross-sectional area of the vessel through which the blood is flowing, various imaging methods exist for determining stroke volume, which depend upon a knowledge of end-diastolic volume (EDV) and end-systolic volume (ESV). When using flow-meter procedures, stroke volume is calculated as the integral of flow and:

flow = blood velocity × cross sectional area of vessel

When using imaging procedures stroke volume (SV) is calculated as

SV = EDV − ESV

The imaging procedures include left ventricular angiography, nuclide imaging, and echocardiography. Still another method for estimating stroke volume is by the use of impedance cardiography.

Electromagnetic Flowmeter. Flowmeters are often used to calculate cardiac ouput in animal research, because the flowmeters are highly accurate and permit stroke volume to be assessed during each cardiac cycle. When using an electromagnetic flow probe, it is placed on the pulmonary artery or ascending aorta. Actually, the pulmonary artery is the only place in the circulation where the total cardiac output can be measured using measurements based on a single vessel. However, it is technically difficult to place and maintain a flow probe on the pulmonary artery; therefore, electromagnetic flow probes are most often placed on the ascending aorta. This results in the loss of the contribution to the coronary arteries, which amounts to about 5 percent of the cardiac output. Using either the pulmonary artery or aorta, cardiac output is computed from the equation:

$$\dot{Q} = \left(\begin{array}{c} \text{integral of} \\ \text{systolic velocity} \end{array}\right) \times \left(\begin{array}{c} \text{cross sectional} \\ \text{area of vessel} \end{array}\right) \times \left(\begin{array}{c} \text{heart} \\ \text{rate} \end{array}\right)$$

Ultrasonic Flowmeters. Several groups of investigators have now demonstrated noninvasive Doppler determinations of cardiac output in humans.[50,51] In one study the instrument was equipped with two transducers.[50] The first was an echocardiographic transducer that measured aortic root diameter using A-mode echocardiography; the second was a continuous-wave Doppler probe, which measured the velocity of aortic blood flow.

Aortic root diameter was measured by echocardiography, and the cross-sectional area was calculated by an on-board computer.[50] The continuous-wave Doppler transducer was placed on the suprasternal notch, directed towards the ascending aorta and angled until the maximum velocity signal was obtained. Integral of the systolic velocity signal was calculated by the computer using fast Fourier transform analysis. The computed cardiac output was based on the average of 12 consecutive cardiac cycles. Comparisons between cardiac output calculated by thermodilution and cardiac output computed by the transcutaneous continuous-wave ultrasonic Doppler device correlated 0.97. Interobserver reliability using the Doppler method was reported as 0.98, and interobserver reliability as 0.97. Recorders using the continuous-wave Doppler technique are now available commercially.

Angiocardiography. In left ventricular angiocardiography the geometry of the ventricular contraction is demonstrated by rapid, serial X-ray filming of the radiopaque-dye-filled chamber.[52] In calculating the volumes of the ventricle during end-systole and end-diastole, the ventricular cavity is assumed to be shaped like a football (prolate ellipsoid) with volumes (*V*) calculated as:

$$V = \left(\frac{4\pi}{3}\right)\left(\frac{L}{2}\right)\left(\frac{D_1}{2}\right)\left(\frac{D_2}{2}\right)$$

Where L in the maximal length from mitral valve to apex, and D_1 and D_2 are based on anterior-posterior and lateral projections. Although high resolution quantitative research requires separate determinations of D_1 and D_2, single pulse determinations, with D_1 assumed to equal D_2, are usually adequate for most purposes. Thus,

$$V = \frac{\pi}{6}\left(LD^2\right)$$

Immediately following opacification of the ventricle, the largest and smallest consecutive V silhouettes in each cardiac cycle are taken as end-diastolic volume (EDV) and end-systolic volume (ESV), respectively. Stroke volume (SV) is then calculated as:

$$SV = EDV - ESV$$

Cardiac output derived from angiocardiography correlates highly with cardiac output obtained using the Fick and indicator-dilution techniques. However, in angiocardiography, considerable technical skill is required of the operator and equipment expense is high. The radiation exposure and risk of catheterization to the subject preclude investigative use of this technique except as a by-product of clinically indicated studies.

Radionuclide Tracer Techniques.   Based on the same geometric methods used in angiography, end-diastolic and end-systolic volumes can be determined using radionuclide components of blood for imaging.[53] These geometric techniques are based on films of the first passage of the radionuclide through the heart. Only a short period of time can be sampled, and the risks of radiation preclude the repetition of the radionuclide venous injections more than a very few times.

Measurements of ventricular function can also be obtained after equilibration of a radionuclide. By synchronizing imaging with the cardiac cycle (gating) and by summing over multiple cycles, high spatial resolution can be obtained for assessing end-diastolic and end-systolic volumes.[54] The time used for recording the data may cover one hundred to several thousand cardiac cycles. In view of the long time period during which studies can be performed following a single venous injection, gated imaging would seem to provide a reasonable opportunity for psychophysiologic research collaboration using patients injected for clinical reasons.

Impedance Cardiography.   As indicated in our discussion of regional blood flow, electrical impedance plethysmography is based on the principle that when electrodes are placed across living tissue, the tissue will exhibit impedance to high-frequency alternating current. The same principle applies to impedance cardiography, where four circumferential thoracic electrodes are used to measure pulsatile changes in impedance in order to obtain a signal related to stroke volume.

Briefly, low-intensity, high-frequency alternating current is applied to metal-ribbon electrodes placed around the neck and abdomen. The flow of current through the thoracic tissues produces a potential difference that is detected by two metal ribbon electrodes that are placed around the thorax so that the heart is between them.

Inspiration increases and ejection of the stroke volume from the ventricles decreases the impedance between the potential-measuring electrodes. Because the respiratory-induced change is much larger than the cardiac-induced change, it has been suggested that the subjects should breathe slowly or hold their breaths for a few heart beats during recording.[46] This, of course, could interfere with psychophysiological experiments, prompting the suggestion that either samples should be taken during the same phase of respiration each time or that all samples taken during a 60-second period should be measured and averaged.[55] Since changes in respiration may occur as a function of psychophysiologic manipulations, validation studies are needed to assess the extent to which these manipulations may distort stroke volume changes.

The stroke volume (SV) in impedance cardiography may be calculated as:

$$SV = P\left(\frac{L_2}{Z_0^2}\right)T\left(\frac{dZ}{dt_{max}}\right)$$

where P is the resistivity of blood in ohm-cm at body temperature, L is the distance between the voltage-measuring electrodes in cm, Z_0 is the basal impedance of the thorax in ohms, (dZ/dt_{max}) is the maximum rate of impedance change during T, which is the ejection period.

The stroke volume could actually be calculated as $P(L_2/Z_0^2)$ except that this would include outflow of blood from the thorax as well as outflow from the heart. Therefore, in order to estimate the true volume change that would occur in the absence of thoracic outflow, the maximum rate of impedance change during the early ejection period is determined, because outflow from the thoracic vessels is minimal at the beginning of cardiac ejection.[46]

The value for P, which is the resistivity of blood, should be corrected for measured hematocrit during exercise in view of the known resistivity changes due to hemoconcentration.[56] Other differences in hematocrit between subjects could contaminate the results. Therefore, a correction factor (F) has been introduced to account for differences in packed-cell volume.[57] Thus, the stroke volume equation is now expressed:

$$SV = \frac{PL^2TF}{Z_0^2}\left(\frac{dZ}{dt_{max}}\right)$$

A large number of studies have shown that impedance cardiography tracks *changes* in cardiac output with good accuracy. More controversial is the extent to which the method can be used to obtain absolute measures of cardiac output in psychophysiologic studies. Control over respiratory fluctuations may be a problem as previously noted. Assumptions regarding thoracic cross-sectional area and resistivity may not be entirely valid, and and the model that projects dZ/dt_{max} throughout systole is open to question. The ejection curve that is assumed does not correspond to empirical form. Wave form is apparently sensitive to electrode placement, which in turn can alter greatly dZ/dt_{max}.

These criticisms notwithstanding, if the sources of error are recognized and the technique is validated within a particular laboratory, investigators within that laboratory may find impedance cardiography to be extremely useful for making within-subject comparisons of responses to psychophysiologic challenges. Moreover, since the method permits stroke volume to be assessed noninvasively on a beat-by-beat basis, further validation studies could be very useful in making the procedure an important tool in the arsenal of the psychophysiologist.

Echocardiography.   This method uses the reflection of pulsed ultrasound to provide information about the movement of cardiac structures. In M-mode echocardiography, sound is reflected from interfaces between substances of different acoustic impedance (e.g., myocardium and blood). The time for the emitted sound to be reflected back to the transducer is proportional to the distance from the target. Because temporal resolution is high, both the distance and structure moves and the time required for the movement may be measured. One problem with assessing stroke volume using echocardiography, however, is that the long axis (L) of the left ventricle cannot be directly evaluated because the lung overlying the apex of the heart does not transmit the ultrasound. Consequently, the assumption is made that L = twice the diameter(D) of the ventricle, and volume (V) can thus be calculated as:

$$V = \frac{\pi D^3}{3}$$

The validity of SV being calculated based on the above equation has been a source of controversy.[58,59] When compared with angiocardiographic studies, the use of echocardiographic measurement of stroke volume appears to be in error in the range of 10–15 percent. Although biplane echocardiography might improve the accuracy of stroke volume determinations, this has not yet been adequately tested.[60] Advantages of using M-mode echocardiography for estimating stroke volume are its reasonable cost and noninvasiveness.

DETERMINANTS OF CARDIAC OUTPUT AND BLOOD PRESSURE

Thus far we have described the measurement of cardiac output and BP in some detail. Before turning to a discussion of the cardiac cycle, let us consider briefly the determinants of cardiac output and BP, since an understanding of them will be helpful in our subsequent discussion.

Determinants of Cardiac Output

The determinants of cardiac output are *preload, afterload, myocardial contractility,* and *heart rate.* Each of these affects the events of the cardiac cycle differently. In the case of preload, afterload, and contractility, the effects are on stroke volume and the time required for blood to be ejected from the heart.

One of the major factors determining the amount of blood pumped by the heart during each cardiac cycle is *preload.* This refers to the load placed on the heart due to the amount of blood entering from the vena cava. The intrinsic ability of the heart to adapt itself to changing loads of incoming blood is called the *Frank-Starling law of the heart.* When cardiac muscle becomes stretched due to a greater amount of blood entering the heart, the stretched muscle contracts with increased force, which automatically pumps the increased load into the circulation. This ability of the heart to contract with increased force as its chambers are stretched is not dependent on neuronal or hormonal activity. Instead, it appears to be due to the actin and myosin filaments' being brought to a more nearly optimal degree of interdigitation for achieving contraction. The ability of the heart to contract with increased force to increased stretch is referred to as *heterometric autoregulation.* Preload, or heterometric autoregulation, can be evaluated either in terms of end-diastolic pressure or end-diastolic volume in the left ventricle.

Afterload can be defined as total hindrance to flow; it refers to the load placed on the heart by variables acting downstream. The determinants of afterload are systemic vascular resistance (associated with relative vasoconstriction), blood viscosity and volume, and vascular compliance. To the extent that the heart has to work against an increased afterload, cardiac output is decreased. Mean systolic pressure (MSP) is the best index of afterload, although mean arterial pressure (MAP) also provides a reasonable estimate.

Although systemic arterial BP is usually reported as maximum (systolic) and minimum (diastolic) values, neither is of basic physiologic importance. Instead MSP and MAP are the salient values to be assessed. MSP is the integral of the aortic root pressure tracing during the ejection phase of the cardiac cycle divided by the ejection time. MAP is the integral of the pressure curve of the entire cardiac cycle divided by the interbeat interval. MAP can adequately be approximated as:

$$MAP = \text{diastolic BP} + \frac{\text{systolic BP} - \text{diastolic BP}}{3}$$

providing a reasonable estimate of afterload.

Contractility is by far the most difficult determinant of cardiac output to define and quantify adequately. It is also of considerable interest to psychophysiologists because it is sensitive to autonomic influences associated with behavior. Contractility, which is also referred to as the *inotropic* activity of the heart, has been defined in terms of the heart as a pump or as a muscle. When the heart is considered as a pump, a change in contractility is said to occur when there is an alteration in the amount of work performed by each contraction without a corresponding change in preload. (Note that contractility refers to the tension generated in myocardial muscle although muscle fiber length is not increased; whereas the Frank-Starling mechanism involves a lengthening of the muscle fibers.) When the heart is considered in terms of muscle properties, contractility is said to be altered when velocity of fiber shortening changes. In either the heart-as-pump or heart-as-muscle models, the ideal measure of contractility would be one that is totally unaffected by changes in preload or afterload. For a more detailed discussion of these models, see Larson et al.[61]

Examination of contractility in terms of the heart as a pump has focused on end-systolic pressure, end-systolic volume relationships, which are independent of afterload. The definition of contractility here is in terms of strength rather than velocity of contraction. Assessments of contractility in terms of the heart as a muscle have focused on the velocity of fiber shortening. One of these latter methods involves examining the rate of pressure development in the left ventricle during the isovolumic period of contraction (dP/dt) of the cardiac cycle. An alternative approach has been to measure the velocity of circumferential fiber shortening by echocardiography.

Let us briefly consider the velocity of pressure development during the isovolumic period as a measure of contractility. The isovolumic period occurs when the mitral valve closes and the aortic valve has not yet opened. During this brief instant, the ventricle is contracting and pressure builds within it as the cavity decreases in volume. If one extrapolates the load-velocity curve back to zero load ($P = 0$), the obtained value, V_{max}, is used as a measure of contractility. Various formulas have been proposed to use dP/dt_{max} as an index of contractility, but these formulas have not been able to avoid sensitivity to preload and afterload. The accurate measurement of dP/dt during the isovolumic period of contraction also requires the kind of frequency response that is normally present only in micromanometer-tip catheters.[62]

Given the exquisite sensitivity of dP/dt to preload and afterload, psycho-physiologists needs to assess these variables before making inference about dP/dt_{max} as an index of contractility. In addition, the frequency-response characteristics needed to assess dP/dt_{max} accurately preclude the use of externally recorded carotid pulse tracings measuring aortic dP/dt as an index of contractility.

A more promising approach to the assessment of contractility is the measurement of mean velocity of circumferential fiber shortening by angi-ocardiography[63] and echocardiography.[64] The echocardiographic measure has also been shown to be independent of preload changes.[65]

There is a growing body of evidence suggesting that the duration of mechanical events occurring during the cardiac cycle (i.e., systolic time intervals: STIs) contain important, reliable information about the contractile state of the heart. It appears, for example, that the relationship between electrical and mechanical systole may be one of the simplest and best indices of adrenergic influence on the heart.[66,67]

The three basic STIs, which can be measured noninvasively, are the preejection period (PEP), the left ventricular ejection time (LVET), and total electromechanical systole (Q-S$_2$) as shown in Figure 9.1. These measurements are obtained from simultaneous high-speed recordings of the ECG, a noninvasively monitored carotid pulse tracing, and a phonocardiogram. Apparatus with high-frequency response and high paper speed are required since critical changes must be measured in msec.

The first major STI is mechanical systole (Q-S$_2$). This is measured as the time between the occurrence of the Q wave in the ECG and the occurrence of the second heart sound (S$_2$) in the phonocardiogram. The Q wave marks the onset of ventricular systole and the S$_2$ sound marks the closure of the aortic valve.

The second major STI, LVET, is measured from the upstroke of the carotid pulse tracing to its dicrotic notch. Because LVET is highly sensitive to both preload and afterload, however, it is not useful as an index of contractility. The third major STI, PEP, is derived by subtracting LVET

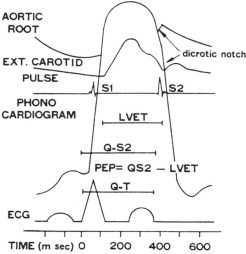

FIGURE 9.1.   Systolic time intervals. Schematic tracing of blood pressure taken internally from the aorta (aortic root); carotid pulse tracing (ext. carotid pulse), phonocardiogram, and electrocardiogram (ECG) taken externally. Note that the upstroke and the dicrotic notch of the carotid pulse tracing are both delayed about 30 to 35 msec after the corresponding events in the ascending aorta so that time from upstroke to dicrotic notch remains a good index of left ventricular ejection time (LVET). Electrical systole (Q-T), mechanical systole (Q-S_2), LVET, and the preejection period (PEP) are assessed noninvasively. (From Schneiderman N, McCabe PM, Hausman KA. Neurogenic influences upon the heart. In Herd JA, Gotto AM, et al: Cardiovascular Instrumentation. Bethesda, MD, NIH Pub. No. 84-1654, 1984, pp. 139–150.

from Q-S_2. PEP is a composite of the electromechanical delay and the isovolumic period of contraction.[61]

All of the intervals require correction for heart rate if comparison is to be made between different subjects or within the same subject at different heart rates. The correction factors are those determined by the regression of STI at different heart rates.[68] However, the PEP/LVET ratio, which has been advocated as a good index of contractility[69], does not require rate correction. Moreover, the PEP/LVET ratio appears to correct for the pre-load and afterload through their reciprocal effects on LVET. Good correlations have been shown between PEP/LVET and left ventricular ejection fraction and between PEP/LVET and dP/dt normalized for afterload.[69]

Heart Rate.   Cardiac output is the product of heart rate and stroke volume. Simply increasing heart rate, however, may not increase cardiac output unless the stroke volume stays the same or increases. Since an increase in heart rate shortens diastole more than systole and since passive filling occurs during diastole, situations exist in which heart rate increases do not lead to an increase in cardiac output because of decreased stroke volume.

Determinants of Blood Pressure

Mean arterial pressure is the product of the cardiac output ($\dot{Q}$) and total peripheral resistance (TPR):

$$MAP = \dot{Q} \times TPR$$

Once MAP and $\dot{Q}$ are known, TPR may be calculated as:

$$TPR = \frac{MAP}{\dot{Q}}$$

Total peripheral resistance has two components. The first of these is the hindrance offered by the tone of the blood vessels—most importantly the arterioles and to a lesser extent the arteries. The second component influencing total peripheral resistance is the viscosity of the blood. Since the latter component does not usually vary appreciably, the major changes in total peripheral (systemic vascular) resistance produced by physiological or pathological processes are due to variations in vessel radius.

A brief example can be used to illustrate how the level of mean arterial pressure is dependent solely on cardiac output and total peripheral resistance. Consider a situation in which the cardiac output is 5 liters/min and mean arterial pressure is 100 mmHg. Then:

$$TPR = \frac{100 \text{ mmHg}}{5 \text{ liters/min}} = 20 \text{ mmHg/liter/min}$$

If cardiac output remains constant at 5 liters/min, but total peripheral resistance increases to 30 mmHg/liter/min due to a reduction in the radius of the arterioles, then:

$$
\begin{aligned}
MAP &= \dot{Q} \times TPR \\
&= 5 \text{ liters/min} \times 30 \text{ mmHg/liter/min} \\
&= 150 \text{ mmHg}
\end{aligned}
$$

Thus, an increase in total peripheral resistance in the absence of a change in cardiac output will increase mean arterial pressure, and hence the afterload on the heart.

HEART RATE AND ELECTROCARDIOGRAM

Measurement of heart rate, usually derived from the ECG, continues to be the most popular measure for assessing cardiovascular reactivity. Technical guidelines have been published for optimal recording, in clinical electrocardiography,[70] which should be followed if aspects of the ECG other than heart rate (e.g., ST segment changes) are being evaluated.

Heart Rate

Because of its ease of measurement, heart rate should be recorded in any study of cardiovascular reactivity. It can be measured either tonically, by counting beats over relatively long periods of a minute or more, or phasically, by measuring the interbeat (RR) interval. As with BP, there is normally a cyclical variation in RR interval, or sinus arrhythmia, which is partly modulated by the pattern of breathing, as described below. The choice of tonic or phasic measurement of heart rate should depend on whether the effect under study is suspected of causing persistent or transient changes of heart rate.

Physiologically, heart rate is the end result of the opposing influences of the sympathetic and parasympathetic influences on the sinus node. At rest, parasympathetic activity predominates, because the intrinsic heart rate, which is the rate occurring when both limbs of the autonomic nervous system are blocked, is around 105 beats per minute.[71] Furthermore, animal studies of the heart rate response to parasympathetic and sympathetic stimulation have shown that the former can produce much more abrupt changes than the latter.[72] Thus, any sudden changes of heart rate occurring during psychophysiological testing are likely to be mediated chiefly by parasympathetic influences. Because of the normally close link between respiration and heart rate, it may be appropriate to monitor respiration as well, if phasic heart rate changes are of interest.[73]

Electrocardiogram

Apart from the heart rate itself, several features of the electrocardiogram may be of interest in psychophysiological testing. These include changes in the ST segment, the T wave, and the Q-T interval.

ST elevation or depression has for many years been used as a method for detecting myocardial ischemia in patients with suspected coronary heart disease, most usually during exercise testing,[74] but also using psychophysiological stressors.[75] Evaluation of ST changes is not without pitfalls, however, for it requires a satisfactory frequency response of the recording system (so that DC shifts can be evaluated), and the changes that are observed may vary according to the position of the recording electrodes. The V_5 position is the one most commonly chosen. During dynamic exercise testing, a depression of the ST segment of more than 0.1 mV occurring 60 msec after the J point is conventionally taken to indicate myocardial ischemia.[74] It is possible that a more reliable index of ischemia may be obtained by relating the ST changes to the changes of heart rate. Even given these criteria, however, ST changes are not wholly specific. During exercise testing, particularly in asymptomatic individuals, there is a significant false positive rate (i.e., individuals who show ST changes in the absence of ischemia), and with sudden changes of heart rate or hyperventilation, transient ST changes may be observed, the meaning of which are unclear.[75]

Amplitude of the T wave has been suggested as a possible index of myocardial sympathetic tone. Under certain circumstances, increases in myocardial sympathetic activity have been associated with the attenuation of T wave amplitude; whereas decreases in myocardial sympathetic activity have been associated with an increase. Thus, electrical stimulation of the cardiac sympathetic nerves has been observed to be accompanied by an attenuation of T wave amplitude,[76,77] and beta-adrenergic blockade has been found to produce an increase.[78,79]

Perhaps the strongest evidence that T wave amplitude may have some use in assessing myocardial sympathetic activity during biobehavioral reactivity experiments was provided in a study examining cardiovascular responses to mental arithmetic and the cold pressor test.[80] Mental arithmetic produced an increase in heart rate, contractility, and cardiac output in conjunction with T wave attenuation. In contrast, the cold pressor test produced a decrease in heart rate, contractility, and cardiac output accompanied by an increase in blood pressure and T wave amplitude. Administration of isoproterenol produced an attenuation of the T wave amplitude, which was blocked by propranolol. Although the results generally support the finding of an inverse relationship between T wave amplitude and myocardial sympathetic activity, enthusiasm for the T wave amplitude measure is tempered by the following considerations. First, the subjects in the study were patients with exaggerated sympathetic responsiveness, so that the generality of results needs to be assessed. Second, T wave amplitude was judged qualitatively, so that the sensitivity of the measure is unknown. Third, the specificity of the measure is unknown with regard to inotropic versus chronotropic effects. Other variables that need to be evaluated before T wave amplitude can be considered useful for assessing myocardial sympathetic activity are the effects of lead placements, differences in heart rate baseline, and the relative sympathetic and parasympathetic drives on the heart against which changes in T wave amplitude are to be judged.

Another aspect of the ECG that is of potential interest to psychophysiologists is the Q-T interval. The Q-T interval is of interest both as a marker of the duration of electrical systole and for determining systolic time intervals (see previous discussion of contractility). It normally varies proportionately to the RR interval, and guidelines have been established for describing such changes. Prolongation of the Q-T interval may be a marker for ventricular arrhythmias and sudden cardiac death.[81] This appears to be primarily the case when Q-T is not only prolonged but is greater than $Q-S_2$ even at rest.[82]

Ambulatory ECG Recording

This technique, which was first described by Holter,[83] is widely used by cardiologists for the evaluation of cardiac arrhythmias, and sophisticated equipment is now available for both making and analyzing the recordings. It has been used relatively little for measuring changes in heart rate, but as with ambulatory BP recording, could be used as a valuable adjunct to laboratory tests of cardiovascular reactivity. Thus in one study it was found that while operating, surgeons may have heart rates of 150 beats per minute or more.[84] ST changes can also be evaluated by this method.

Measurements of Electrical Stability

Electrical instability of the myocardium is thought to be an important feature of sudden cardiac death, and it can be greatly influenced by autonomic effects on the heart. Hence, the study of cardiac arrhythmias occurring during psychophysiological testing provides a potentially important tool for exploring this problem. Nevertheless, it should be appreciated that in human subjects without clinical evidence of heart disease, the observation of minor arrhythmias such as premature contractions does not necessarily have any pathogenic significance.

In animal studies the most valuable technique for investigating the influence of psychophysiologic stressors on electrical stability of the heart involves the induction of repetitive extrasystoles.[85] In dogs that have implanted ventricular electrodes, repeated electrical stimuli can be given at different times in the cardiac cycle and the threshold measured for the production of repetitive extrasystoles. This has been found to be proportional to the threshold for producing ventricular fibrillation. With this technique it has been clearly established that psychophysiologic stressors can elicit decreased electrical stability.

The same repetitive stimulation technique is currently being used by cardiologists in patients thought to be at high risk of developing malignant ventricular arrhythmias. It has two roles: first, the demonstration of sustained ventricular tachycardia by repetitive stimulation has great prognostic significance;[86] second, the effectiveness of antiarrhythmic drugs can be assessed. In principle, such testing could be combined with exposure to psychophysiological stressors.

A related technique, which is in general more applicable to animal studies, is the use of cardiac (usually atrial) pacing to produce controlled changes of heart rate without altering the autonomic influences on the heart.

ASSESSMENT OF AUTONOMIC CONTROL AND METABOLIC REQUIREMENTS

The cardiovascular adjustments that accompany any change in psychophysiological demand occur as a result of alterations of autonomic control of the circulation and of hormonal changes. A commonly expressed hypothesis is that inappropriate elevations of sympathetic nervous system activity, occurring particularly in response to psychophysiologic stressors, may contribute to the development of coronary heart disease and hypertension, although direct supporting evidence is lacking. Some of the techniques that have been used to assess the autonomic control of the circulation are described below.

Parasympathetic (Vagal) Tone

Effector Blockade. The dominant role of the parasympathetic nerves on the beat-to-beat control of heart rate can be clearly shown by blocking vagal influences with atropine. In humans, a dose of 0.04 mg/kg produces complete vagal blockade of the heart. Resting heart rate increases to approximately 110 beats per minute without affecting BP. Beat-to-beat variability is almost completely eliminated.

Respiratory Sinus Arrhythmia. Normally, heart rate accelerates during inspiration and decelerates during expiration. The rhythmic variation in heart rate occurring at the frequency of respiration was first described by Ludwig in 1847[87] and is called respiratory sinus arrhythmia. This sinus arrhythmia can be traced directly to cardioinhibitory motor neurons that project through the vagus nerves and discharge only during expiration.[88] Experiments conducted on anesthetized dogs have shown that the magnitude of sinus arrhythmia correlates 0.97 with parasympathetic control.[89] Thus, the magnitude of respiratory sinus arrhythmia appears to vary directly with the degree of vagal tone.

One procedure that has been used to assess parasympathetic tone in the resting individual involves monitoring the ECG during six respiratory cycles, with each phase of respiration made to last 5 seconds.[90] For each cycle the shortest RR interval during inspiration and the longest RR interval during expiration are measured. These are then averaged across the six cycles. The mean of the longest RR intervals divided by the mean of the shortest RR intervals is then expressed as a "respiratory ratio."

Although the "respiratory ratio" seems to provide a reasonable estimate of parasympathetic tone under highly controlled conditions, this may not be the case in complex reactivity experiments involving speech and/or other movements. In order to get a better estimate of the amplitude of respiratory sinus arrhythmia under these latter conditions, the spectral densities for heart period in relation to respiratory frequencies can be subjected to computer analysis.[91] With this in mind, several animal studies using cross-spectral analysis have been conducted in which vagal activity was manipulated with aortic nerve stimulation and pharmacologic blockades in anesthetized animals,[92] and with pharmacologic interventions in freely moving animals.[93] Results suggest that the amplitude of respiratory sinus arrhythmia assessed by cross-spectral analysis may provide a reasonable estimate of vagal tone in the behaving individual.

Experiments using cross-spectral analysis appear to be quite promising but have not yet fully quantified the relationships between heart rate variability and autonomic control in behaving individuals. The issue appears to be somewhat complicated, because power spectrum analyses of heart rate fluctuation, even in steady state situations, reveal three peaks.[94–96] One peak occurs at high frequency (0.4 Hz), a second at an intermediate frequency (0.12 Hz), and a third at low frequency (0.04 Hz). The high-frequency peak is related to respiratory sinus arrhythmia; whereas the intermediate peak is related to the frequency response of the baroreceptor reflex, and the low-frequency response is related to cyclic variations in peripheral vasomotor tone. Both the high- and intermediate-frequency peaks appear to be under parasympathetic vagal control; whereas the low-frequency peak seems to be influenced by both the discharge of the vagus nerves and sympathetic nervous system activity.

In any event, diminished vagal parasympathetic tone can be inferred from a combination of measures, including elevated basal heart rate, decreased respiratory sinus arrhythmia, and a lack of reflexive bradycardia to increases in systemic arterial BP. Conversely, evidence of substantial vagal tone can be inferred from the combination of a low basal heart rate, marked respiratory sinus arrhythmia, and presence of the cardiac component of the baroreceptor reflex.

Baroreceptor Reflex

An increase in baroreceptor stimulation caused by an increase in systemic arterial pressure leads to reflexive decreases in heart rate and BP unless the reflex is "gated" within the CNS. Conversely, a decrease in baroreceptor stimulation caused by a decrease in BP leads to reflexive increases in heart rate and BP. These reflexive changes help to stabilize BP.

Methods of testing high-pressure baroreceptor integrity and gain include phenylephrine injection, Valsalva maneuver, and brief neck suction. Injection of 50–100 μg of phenylephrine intravenously normally raises arterial BP 20–25 mmHg, which is followed by a reflexive slowing in heart rate.[97,98] By plotting RR interval (msec) from the ECG versus systolic BP (mmHg), a line can be generated that reflects high-pressure baroreceptor sensitivity.

Another method of testing baroreceptor function is by using the Valsalva maneuver, which can be induced by having a subject exhale against a closed valve with sufficient force and duration to support a 40 mmHg column for 10 seconds. The effects of exhaling against a closed valve and then inhaling normally can be divided into four phases.[99] In phase 1, the arterial BP increases transiently as intrathoracic pressure compresses the aorta. A reduction in venous return, which in turn reduces cardiac output, causes a fall in BP during phase 2. This fall plateaus after several seconds owing to reflex vasoconstriction and a slight increase in heart rate. Phase 3 begins one to two seconds after the subject ceases exhaling against the closed valve and consists of a small fall in BP caused by the release of pressure compressing the aorta. In phase 4, which is the phase in which high-pressure baroreceptor function is tested, systolic BP increases within 10 seconds of strain release followed by the reflex slowing of heart rate.

Still another noninvasive method of inducing the high-pressure barore-ceptor reflex involves stimulating the carotid baroreceptors by using pneu-matic suction supplied to an externally imposed neck chamber.[100,101] This procedure involves inducing negative pressure around the neck briefly (i.e., less than 1 sec). Advantages of the method are that it can be used frequently and under a variety of circumstances. Thus, one can evaluate gain as a function of experimental tasks and in relation to heart rate reactivity or control level of heart rate.

Methods of assessing low-pressure barosensory activity include amyl nitrate inhalation,[102] head-up tilt of 60° from a recumbent position,[103] or examining the response to standing. In all three cases an initial fall in arterial BP is normally followed by an increase in heart rate and BP.

Sympathetic Tone

Although quantification of the activity of the sympathetic nervous system has been a subject of great interest for many years, it remains controversial. For the evaluation of the sympathetic contribution to the changes occurring during cardiovascular reactivity testing, the simplest method is to use autonomic blocking drugs. If changes occurring in the heart are of primary interest, the most logical drug to use would be a cardioselective beta-adrenergic blocking agent such as atenolol. Interpretation of the effects of such agents is not without problems, however, because the acute response to beta-adrenergic blockade includes a fall in cardiac output and a reflex increase in alpha-adrenergic activity. Therefore, under certain circumstances it may be difficult to decide whether observed effects are produced directly or as a result of compensatory mechanisms. Blockade of the alpha-adrenergic system may be achieved by the use of drugs such as prazosin, phentolamine, or phenoxybenzamine. The same problems of data interpretation exist with the use of these drugs as with the use of other blocking agents.

Previously, we discussed the use of STI in evaluating contractility. Specifically, the use of PEP/LVET as a noninvasive index of contractility was described. Several intriguing studies using the ECG and phonocardiogram, but omitting the carotid pulse tracing, have provided interesting data concerning increasing beta-adrenergic drives on the heart.[66,67,82] In one experiment[66] changes in electrical systole (Q-T) were compared with changes in mechanical systole (Q-S_2) as a function of isoproterenol (beta-adrenergic agonist) infusion before and after oral propranolol (beta-adrenergic antagonist). During atrial pacing over the physiological range of heart rates (80–140 beats/min), Q-T was shorter but paralleled the duration of Q-S_2. For any given heart rate during isoproterenol infusion, Q-S_2 was shorter than Q-T.

In a more recent study Q-T and Q-S_2 were measured while subjects underwent bicycle ergometer exercise, a tilt test, a 2-minute duration decrease in carotid transmural pressure induced by means of a pneumatic neck chamber, and an injection of phenylephrine.[67] The results obtained were consistent with those described for the previous study. As the heart rate increased with exercise, both Q-S_2 and Q-T shortened, but the shortening was more pronounced for Q-S_2. Similar findings were observed during tilt to the upright position and by increasing and *maintaining* neck tissue pressure. In contrast, intravenous administration of phenylephrine induced a significant increase in BP and a reflexive decrease in heart rate; Q-T and Q-S_2 both increased, but the increase in Q-S_2 was greater. The results of the two experiments just described suggest that the relationship between Q-T and Q-S_2 may provide a reliable index of sympathetic cardiac tone. Quantification of this relationship, its applicability to psychophysiologic research, and its limitations remain to be determined.

Tests for alpha-adrenergic end-organ response involve infusions of phenylephrine or norepinephrine, which normally produce a rise in systolic BP. Patients with end-organ damage reveal blunted BP responses except for cases in which individuals with denervation hypersensitivity reveal an exaggerated pressor response to such infusion.[104] Tests for beta-adrenergic end-organ response involve administration of isoproterenol, which normally increases heart rate and contractility; exaggerated responses may indicate denervation and hypersensitivity.

A test of extraadrenal stores of norepinephrine as opposed to end-organ damage involves the administration of tyramine, which produces its effects through the release of norepinephrine from sympathetic nerve endings.[105] Intravenous doses of 1–3 mg of tyramine usually induce systolic BP increases of about 25 mmHg.

A direct measure of sympathetic nervous system activity with regard to specific projections involves the insertion of metal microelectrodes percutaneously into peripheral nerves, which permits recording from sympathetic efferent fibers.[106] Although the procedure has obvious limitations when applied to human subjects, it does permit the qualitative assessment of changes in sympathetic nervous activity during psychophysiologic testing.

The initial fall in BP after an individual assumes an upright position leads to a decrease in barosensory discharges and a compensatory increase in sympathetic nervous activity leading to the maintenance of normal BP. In orthostatic hypotension associated with CNS damage, a blunted norepinephrine response occurs. In contrast, peripheral neuropathy is associated with the normal release of norepinephrine, which is actually quite large, upon standing, and either a blunted response or an exaggerated response (denervation hypersensitivity) to infusion of norepinephrine.

The cold pressor test is sometimes used as a test of alpha-adrenergic sympathetic activity. A subject placing a limb in ice water (4°C) for 1 minute normally reveals a pronounced increase in BP. A normal increase in plasma norepinephrine with a blunted BP response would indicate normal functioning of the afferent pathway but compromised efferent functioning. Tests using administration of phenylephrine and tyramine could further pinpoint the deficit.

The measurement of plasma catecholamines in conjunction with the kinds of procedures just described is beginning to prove useful in assessments of autonomic function. A potential use for these measures is in helping to distinguish central versus peripheral contributions to sympathetic nervous system activity. Thus, the administration of emotional stressors has been found to increase catecholamines preferentially in subjects with hypertension[107] and Type A behavior pattern.[108]

Assessment of Oxygen Consumption

The most reliable extracardiac index of overall cardiovascular capacity is maximal total body oxygen consumption (Vo_2 max). On a standardized treadmill test, Vo_2 max occurs when measured oxygen uptake reaches a value that does not increase despite further increases in workload. As a measure of functional capacity that differs widely across individuals, it provides a useful way of defining aerobic fitness.

Although VO_2 max is a useful measure of functional capacity, it is limited as a measure of cardiac performance since the relationship between external function and cardiac performance is not necessarily direct. Myocardial oxygen consumption (MVO_2) can be determined directly, however, as the product of myocardial arteriovenous oxygen difference and coronary blood flow. Because these measurements require cardiac catheterization, the direct measurement of MVO_2 has only limited applicability for psychophysiological research.

Since two of the major determinants of MVO_2 can be shown to be heart rate and afterload, several derived indexes based on heart rate and BP have been used to approximate MVO_2. These include the rate-pressure product (i.e., heart rate $\times$ peak systolic BP), the time-tension index (i.e., heart rate $\times$ integral of left ventricular pressure throughout systole), and the triple product of heart rate, systolic BP, and systolic ejection period. Of these indirect measures, the rate-pressure product appears to correlate most highly ($r = 0.90$) with directly measured MVO_2 during upright bicycle exercise.[109] Interestingly, heart rate alone also correlates highly with MVO_2 ($r = 0.88$) under these conditions.

The rate-pressure product has been found to correlate highly with MVO_2 in patients with CHD as well as in normal persons, and after drug-induced alterations in myocardial contractility and systolic ejection time.[109] In patients with angina, symptoms usually appear at a constant rate-pressure product during dynamic exercise,[110] but the relationship does not appear to hold during isometric exercise.[111] At this point, it might be concluded that, within limits and employed with caution, the rate-pressure product may be of some use in indirectly assessing MVO_2 in psychophysiologic experiments. In one study, for example, it was found that when a Stroop color-word test (emotional stressors) was superimposed on steady-state exercise, heart rate, systolic BP, diastolic BP, and rate-pressure product all increased whereas total body oxygen consumption (VO_2) did not. Thus, based on such studies, the hypothesis could be advanced that myocardial oxygen consumption may be increased in the presence of an emotional stressor without the occurrence of a further increase in total body oxygen consumption.

CONCLUSIONS

Until the past few decades, cardiovascular assessment in conscious, behaving humans primarily involved the recording of BP and the ECG, with measures such as cardiac output being monitored far less often. More detailed evaluation of cardiovascular function usually occurred in deeply anesthetized subjects, most often in the animal laboratory. The past two decades have witnessed the increasing use of less invasive procedures such as echocardiography, impedance cardiography, and systolic time intervals, which are highly suitable for examining cardiovascular functioning in behaving humans. This has begun to present opportunities for those interested in studying important relationships between behavior and cardiovascular regulation. The purpose of the present chapter was to discuss some of the methods that are now available for examining the cardiovascular aspects of psychophysiologic reactivity.

REFERENCES

1. Andren L: Cardiovascular effects of noise. *Acta Med Scand* **657**:7–45, 1982. (Suppl)

2. Kroeker EJ, Wood EH: Beat-to-beat alterations in relationship to simultaneously recorded central and peripheral arterial pressure pulses during Valsalva maneuver and prolonged expiration in man. *J Appl Physiol* **8**:483–494, 1956.

3. Holland WW, Humerfelt S: Measurement of blood pressure: Comparison of intra-arterial and cuff values. *Brit Med J* **2**:1241–1243, 1964.

4. Short D: The diastolic dilemma. *Brit Med J* **2**:685–686, 1976.

5. Kirkendall WM, Burton AC, et al: Recommendations for human blood pressure determination by sphygmomanometer. *Circulation* **36**:980–988, 1967.

6. Geddes LA: *The Direct and Indirect Measurement of Blood Pressure.* Chicago, Year Book Medical Publishers, 1970.

7. Maxwell MH, Waks AU, et al: Error in blood pressure measurement due to incorrect cuff size in obese patients. *Lancet* **2**:33–36, 1982.

8. Spence JD, Sibbald WJ, Cape RD: Pseudohypertension in the elderly. *Clin Sci Mol Med* **55**:399s, 1978.

9. Wilcox J: Observer factors in the measurement of blood pressure. *Nursing Res* **10**:4–17, 1961.

10. Van den Berg B: Comparisons of blood pressure measurements by auscultation and Physiometrics Infrasonde recording techniques. *Hypertension* **2**:I8–I17, 1980. (Suppl)

11. George CF, Lewis PJ, Petrie A: Clinical experience with use of an ultrasound sphygmomanometer. *Br Heart J* **37**:804–807, 1975.

12. Pollack MH, Obrist PA: Aortic-radial pulse transit time and ECG Q-wave to radial pulse wave interval as indices of beat-to-beat blood pressure change. *Psychophysiology* **20**:21–28, 1983.

13. Steptoe A, Smulyan H, Gribbin B: Pulse wave velocity and blood pressure change: Calibration and applications. *Psychophysiology* **13**:488–493, 1976.

14. Keys A, Taylor L, et al: Mortality and coronary heart disease among men studied for 23 years. *Arch Intern Med* **128**:201–214, 1971.

15. Harlan WR, Osborne RK, Graybiel A: Prognostic value of the cold pressor test and the basal blood pressure. Based on an eighteen-year follow-up study. *Am J Cardiol* **13**:683–687, 1964.

16. Wood DL, Sheps SG, et al: Cold pressor test as a predictor of hypertension. *Hypertension* **6**:301–306, 1984.

17. Falkner B, Kushner H, et al: Cardiovascular characteristics in adolescents who develop essential hypertension. *Hypertension* **3**:521–527, 1981.

18. Pickering TG, Harshfield GA, et al: What is the role of ambulatory blood pressure monitoring in the management of hypertensive patients? *Hypertension* 7:171–177, 1985.

19. Pickering TG, Harshfield GA, et al: Comparisons of blood pressure during normal daily activities, sleep, and exercise in normal and hypertensive subjects. *JAMA* **247**:992–996, 1982.

20. Shepard JJ, Vanhoutte PM: *Veins and their Control.* Philadelphia, Saunders, 1975.

21. Samueloff SL, Beregard BS, Shepard JT: Temporary arrests of circulation to a limb for the study of venomotor reactions in man. *J Appl Physiol* 21:341–346, 1966.

22. Noodergraaf A: *Circulatory System Dynamics.* New York, Academic Press, 1978.

23. Adams OB, Baccelli G, et al: Cardiovascular changes during naturally elicited fighting behavior in the cat. *Am J Physiol* 216:1226–1235, 1968.

24. Brod J, Fenel V, et al: Circulatory changes underlying blood pressure elevation during acute emotional stress (mental arithmetic) in normotensive and hypertensive subjects. *Clin Sci* **18**:269–179, 1959.

25. Astley CA, Hohimer AR, et al: Effects of implant duration on in vivo sensitivity of electromagnetic flow transducer. *Am J Physiol* 123:H508–H512, 1979.

26. Smith OA, Astley CA, et al: Functional analysis of hypothalmic control of the cardiovascular responses accompanying emotional behavior. *Fed Proc* **39**:2487–2494, 1980.

27. Anderson OE, Yingling JE: Total peripheral resistance changes in dogs during aversive classical conditioning. *Pavlovian J Biol Sci* 13:241–245, 1978.

28. Hartley CJ, Colr JS: An ultrasonic pulsed Doppler system for measuring blood flow in small vessels. *J Appl Physiol* **37**:626–629, 1974.

29. Haywood JR, Shaffer RA, et al: Regional blood flow measurement with pulsed Doppler flowmeter in conscious rat. *Am J Physiol* **241**:H273–H278, 1981.

30. Forsyth RP: Regional blood-flow changes during 72-hour avoidance schedules in the monkey. *Science* **173**:546–548, 1971.

31. Heyman MA, Payne BD, et al: Blood flow measurements with radionuclide-labeled particles. *Prog Cardiovasc Dis* **20**:55–79, 1977.

32. Wilson RA, Shea MJ, et al: Validation of quantification of regional myocardial blood flow in vivo with ^{11}C-labeled human albumin microspheres and positron emission tomography. *Circulation* **70**:717–723, 1984.

33. Bassingthwaighte JB, Strandell T, Donald DE: Estimation of coronary flow by washout of diffusible indicators. *Circulation Res* **23**:259–278, 1968.

34. Saksena FB: *Hemodynamics in Cardiology.* New York, Praeger, 1983.

35. Veall N: Radioisotope techniques for blood flow measurement. In Woodcock J (ed): *Clinical Blood Flow Measurement.* Chicago, Yearbook Medical Publishers, 1976, pp. 61–64.

36. Eckenhoff JE, Hafkenschiel JH, et al: Measurement of coronary blood flow by the nitrous oxide method. *Am J Physiol* **152**:365–364, 1947.

37. Lind AR, Dahms TE, et al: The blood flow through the "resting" arm during hand-grip contractions. *Circulation Res* **48**:I104–I109, 1981. (Suppl)

38. Lovallo W, Zeiner AR: Cutaneous vasomotor responses to cold pressor stimulation. *Psychophysiology* **11**:458–471, 1974.

39. Sokolov EN: *Perception and the Conditioned Reflex.* New York, Pergamon, 1963.

40. Whitney RJ: The measurement of volume changes in human limbs. *J Physiol* **121**:1–27, 1953.

41. Wheeler HB, O'Donnell JA, et al: Occlusive impedance phlebography. *Prog Cardiovasc Dis* **17**:199–203, 1974.

42. Elmore A, Tursky B: A comparison of the psychophysiological and clinical response to biofeedback for temporal pulse amplitude reduction and biofeedback for increases in hand temperature in the treatment of migraine. *Headache* **21**:93–101, 1981.

43. Tahmoush AJ, Jennings JR, et al: Characteristics of a light-emitting diode-transistor photoplethysmograph. *Psychophysiology* **13**:357–362, 1976.

44. Webster JG: Measurement of flow and volume of blood. In JC Webster (ed): *Medical Instrumentation: Application and Design.* Boston, Houghton Mifflin, 1978, pp. 385–433.

45. Stewart GN: The output of the heart in dogs. *Am J Physiol* **57**:27–50, 1921.

46. Geddes LA: *Cardiovascular Devices and their Applications.* New York, Wiley, 1984.

47. Jones NL, Robertson DG, Kane JW: Difference between end-tidal and arterial PCO_2 in exercise. *J Appl Physiol* **47**:954–960, 1979.

48. Collier CR: Determination of mixed venous CO_2 tension by rebreathing. *J Appl Physiol* **91**:25–29, 1956.

49. Forrester JS, Ganz W, et al: Thermodilution cardiac output determination with a single flow-directed catheter. *Am Heart J* **83**:306–311, 1972.

50. Chandraratna PA, Nanna M, et al: Determination of cardiac output by transcutaneous continuous-wave ultrasonic Doppler computer. *Am J Cardiol* **53**:234–237, 1984.

51. Hunstman LL, Stewart DK, et al: Noninvasive Doppler determination of cardiac output in man: Clinical validation. *Circulation* **67**:593–601, 1983.

52. Rackley CS: Quantitative evaluation of left ventricular function by radiographic techniques. In Weissler AM (ed): *Reviews of Contemporary Laboratory Methods.* Dallas, American Heart Association, 1980, pp. 31–72.

53. Mullins CB, Mason DT, et al: Determination of ventricular volume by radioisotope angiography. *Am J Cardiol* **24**:72–78, 1969.

54. Strauss HW, Zaret BL, et al: A scintiphotographic method for measuring left ventricular ejection fraction in man without cardiac catheterization. *Am J Cardiol* **18**:575–581, 1971.

55. Buell J: Impedance cardiography and plethysmography. In Herd JA, Gotto AM, et al (eds): *Cardiovascular Instrumentation.* Bethesda, MD, NIH Publication No. 84-1654, 1984, pp. 227–238.

56. Kobayashi Y, Andoh Y, et al: Impedance cardiography for estimating cardiac output during submaximal and maximal work. *J Appl Physiol* **45**:459–462, 1978.

57. Mohapatra SN, Costeloe KL, Hill DW: Blood resistivity and its implications for calculation of cardiac output by the thoracic electrical impedance technique. *Intensive Care Med* **3**:1–5, 1977.

58. Linhart JW, Mintz GS, et al: Left ventricular volume measurement by echocardiography: Fact or fiction? *Am J Cardiol* **36**:114–118, 1975.

59. Teichholz LE, Kreulen T, et al: Problems in echocardiographic volume determinations: Echocardiographic-angiographic correlations in the presence or absence of asynergy. *Am J Cardiol* **37**:7–11, 1976.

60. Henry WL: Evaluation of ventricular function using two dimensional echocardiography. *Am J Cardiol* **49**:1319–1323, 1982.

61. Larson PB, Schneiderman N, Pasin RD: Physiological bases of cardiovascular psychophysiology. In Coles M, Donchin E, Porges S (eds): *Psychophysiology: Systems, Processes and Applications.* New York, Guilford, in press.

62. Flasetti HL, Mates RE, et al: V_{max} as an index of contractile state in man. *Circulation* **43**:467–479, 1971.

63. Karliner JS, Gault JH, et al: Mean velocity of fiber shortening: A simplified measure of left ventricular myocardial contractility. *Circulation* **44**:323–333, 1971.

64. Cooper RH, O'Rourke RA, et al: Comparison of ultrasound and cineangiographic measurements of the mean rate of circumferential fiber shortening in man. *Circulation* **46**:914–923, 1972.

65. Nixon JV, Murray RG, et al: Effect of large variations in preload on left ventricular performance characteristics in normal subjects. *Circulation* **65**:698–703, 1982.

66. Boudoulas H, Geleris P, et al: Effect of increased adrenergic activity on the relationship between electrical and mechanical systole. *Circulation* **64**:28–33, 1981.

67. DeCaprio L, Ferro G, et al: QT/QS$_2$ ratio as an index of autonomic tone changes. *Am J Cardiol* **53**:818–822, 1984.

68. Weissler AM: *Noninvasive Cardiology*. New York, Grune & Stratton, 1974.

69. Ahmed SS, Levinson GE, et al: Systolic time intervals as measures of the contractile state of the left ventricular myocardium in man. *Circulation* **52**:559–571, 1972.

70. American Heart Association. Recommendations for standardization of leads and of specifications for instruments in electrocardiography and vector cardiography. Report of Committee on Electrocardiography. *Circulation* **35**:583–602, 1967.

71. Jose AD, Collison D: The normal range and determinants of the intrinsic heart rate in man. *Cardiovasc Res* **4**:160–167, 1970.

72. Levy MN, Zieske H: Autonomic control of cardiac pacemaker activity and atrioventricular transmission. *J Appl Physiol* **27**:465–470, 1969.

73. Hirsch JA, Bishop B: Respiratory sinus arrythmia in humans: How breathing pattern modulates heart rate. *Am J Physiol* **241**:H620–H629, 1981.

74. Pollock ML, Wilmore JH, Fox SM: *Exercise in Health and Disease. Evaluation and Prescription for Prevention and Rehabilitation*. Philadelphia, Saunders, 1984.

75. Jacobs WF, Battle WE, Ronan JA: False-positive ST-T-wave changes secondary to hyperventilation and exercise. A cineangiographic correlation. *Ann Intern Med* **81**:479–482, 1974.

76. Rohse WG, Randall WC: Functional analysis of sympathetic innervation of the heart. *Fed Proc* **14**:123–124, 1955.

77. Yanowitz F, Preston JB, Abildskov JA: Functional distribution of right and left stellate innervation of ventricles: Production of neurogenic electrocardiographic changes by unilateral alteration of sympathetic tone. *Circulation Res* **18**:416–428, 1966.

78. Furberg C: Adrenergic beta-blockade and electrocardiographical ST-T changes. *Acta Med Scand* **181**:21–32, 1967.

79. Furberg C: Effects of repeated work tests and adrenergic beta-blockade on electrocardiographic ST and T changes. *Acta Med Scand* **183**:153–161, 1968.

80. Guazzi M, Fiorenti C, et al: Stress-induced and sympathetically-mediated electrocardiographic and circulatory variations in the primary hyperkinetic heart syndrome. *Cardiovasc Res* **9**:342–354, 1975.

81. Schwartz PJ, Periti M, Malliani A: The long Q-T syndrome. *Am Heart J* **89**:378, 1975.

82. Boudoulous H, Sohn YH, et al: The QT>QS syndrome: A new mortality risk indicator in coronary artery disease. *Am J Cardiol* **49**:1229–1235, 1982.

83. Holter HJ: New method for heart studies: Continuous electrocardiography of active subjects over long periods now practical. *Science* **134**:1214–1216, 1961.

84. Foster GE, Evans DF, Hardcastle JD: Heart-rates of surgeons during operations and other clinical activities and their modification by oxprenolol. *Lancet* **1**:1323–1325, 1978.

85. Verrier RL, Lown B: Behavioral stress and cardiac arrythmias. *Ann Rev Physiol* **46**:155, 1984.

86. Hamer A, Vohra J, et al: Prediction of sudden death by electrophysiologic studies in high risk patients surviving acute myocardial infarction. *Am J Cardiol* **50**:223–229, 1982.

87. Anrep GV, Pascual W, Rossler R: Respiratory variations of the heart rate: I. The reflex mechanism of respiratory arrythmia. *Proc R Society* **119**:191–217, 1936.

88. Jordan D, Khalid ME, et al: The location and properties of preganglionic vagal cardiomotor neurons in the rabbit. *Pflugers Arch* **395**:244–250, 1982.

89. Katona PG, Jih F: Respiratory sinus arrythmia: Noninvasive measure of parasympathetic cardiac control. *J Appl Physiol* **39**:801–805, 1975.

90. Hilsted J, Jensen SB: A simple test for autonomic neuropathy in juvenile diabetics. *Acta Med Scand* **205**:385–387, 1979.

91. Porges SW, Bohrer R, et al: New time-series statistic for detecting rhythmic concurrence in the frequency domain: The weighted coherence and its application to psychophysiological research. *Psychol Bull* **88**:580–582, 1980.

92. McCabe PM, Yongue BG, et al: Changes in heart period, heart period variability, and a spectral analysis of respiratory sinus arrythmias during aortic nerve stimulation in rabbits. *Psychophysiology* **21**:1349–1358, 1984.

93. Yongue BG, McCabe PM, et al: The effects of pharmacological manipulations that influence vagal control of the heart on heart period, heart-period variability and respiration in rats. *Psychophysiology* **19**:426–432, 1982.

94. Akselrod SO, Gordon D, et al: Power spectrum analysis of heart rate fluctuations: A quantitative probe of beat-to-beat cardiovascular control. *Science* **213**:220–222, 1981.

95. Kitney RI, Rompelman P: *The Study of Heart Rate Variability.* Oxford, Oxford University Press, 1980.

96. Sayers BM: Analysis of heart rate variability. *Ergonomics* **16**:17–32, 1973.

97. Pickering TG, Gribbin B, Oliver DO: Baroreflex sensitivity in patients on long term hemodialysis. *Clin Sci* **43**:645–657, 1972.

98. Smyth HS, Sleight P, Pickering GW: Reflex regulation of arterial pressure during sleep in man: A quantitative method of assessing baroreflex sensitivity. *Circulation Res* **24**:109–121, 1969.

99. Henrich WL: Autonomic insufficiency. *Arch Intern Med* **142**:339–344, 1982.

100. Eckberg DL: Baroreflex inhibition of the human sinus node: Importance of stimulus intensity, duration and rate of pressure change. *J Physiol (Lond)* **267**:561–577, 1977.

101. Eckberg DL, Cavanaugh MS, et al: A simplified neck suction device for activation of carotid baroreceptors. *J Lab Clin Med* **85**:167–173, 1975.

102. Kersh ES, Kronfield SJ, Unger A: Autonomic insufficiency in uremia as a cause of hemodialysis-induced hypotension. *N Engl J Med* **290**:650–653, 1974.

103. Johnson RH, Lee G de J, Openheimer DR: Autonomic failure with orthostatic hypotension due to intermediolateral column degeneration. *Q J Med* **35**:276–292, 1966.

104. Johnson RH, Spalding JMK: *Disorders of the Autonomic Nervous System.* Philadelphia, F.A. Davis Co., 1974.

105. Ibraham MM: Localization of lesion in patients with idiopathic orthostatic hypotension. *Br Heart J* **37**:868–872, 1975.

106. Wolf S: Microneurography: A technique producing information about factors affecting cardiovascular control. *Psychophysiology* **16**:164–170, 1979.

107. Eliasson K, Kjemdahl P, Kahn T: Circulatory and sympatho-adrenal responses to stress in borderline and established hypertension. *J Hypertension* **1**:131–139, 1983.

108. Glass DC, Krakoff LR, et al: Effect of harassment and competition upon cardiovascular and plasma catecholamine responses in Type A and Type B individuals. *Psychophysiology* **17**:453–463, 1980.

109. Amsterdam EA, Mason DT: Exercise testing and indirect assessment of myocardial oxygen consumption in elevation of angina pectoris. *Cardiology* **62**:174–189, 1977.

110. Scheffield LT, Roitman D: Systolic blood pressure, heart rate and treadmill work at anginal threshold. *Chest* **63**:327–335, 1973.

111. Painter P, Hanson P: Isometric exercise: Implications for the cardiac patient. *Cardiovasc Rev Rpts* **5**:261–279, 1984E.

10

Biochemical Indices of Cardiovascular Reactivity

DAVID S. GOLDSTEIN and ROBERT H. McDONALD

This chapter deals with biochemical measurements that may help in studies of cardiovascular reactivity. A few general principles, which apply to all biochemical indices, are discussed first. Next, specific systems that are likely to participate in cardiovascular responses are described, beginning with the classic sympathetic, renin-angiotensin-aldosterone, and pituitary-adrenocortical systems and ending with other systems or substances with less well-defined relevance to cardiovascular reactivity. The chapter ends with a discussion of future trends in the area.

GENERAL PRINCIPLES

Vertical Organization

Circulatory homeostatic controls are extraordinarily complex and inter-dependent, and so in the intact organism circulating concentrations of vasoactive substances probably never indicate the independent contribution of a given system to cardiovascular responsiveness. One must look beyond the individual substance to consider the system controlling that substance, and beyond the system to consider how systems are integrated to serve adaptive functions.

For instance, circulating levels of catecholamines have been used to provide a biochemical index of "stress" responses. Due to the heterogeneity of sympathetic neural responses among the several vascular beds, circulating catecholamine concentrations, especially when sampled in antecubital venous blood, may not validly reflect average sympathetic tone. Even direct neural recordings, however, may not reflect adequately the contribution of sympathetic outflow to a given circulatory response, because the organism integrates sympathetic responses with responses of other systems depending on the perceived environmental circumstances.

Horizontal Organization

Blood levels of a biochemical substance depend not only on rates of release but also on the translation of releasing stimuli into actual secretion and on metabolic disposition, which can be quite complex. The circulatory effects associated with a given concentration of a biochemical substance depend on the extent of binding to carrier proteins, the number and affinity of receptors, the function of receptor-activation coupling mechanisms in the cells, and secondary activation of homeostatic systems.

Experimental Design

The definition of the appropriate baseline value must be considered before using biochemical measures of reactivity. Reference values often vary as a function of the baseline period, the time of day, the day of the week, the stage of sleep, the stage of the menstrual cycle, the inpatient or outpatient status of the subjects, changes in the subject's personal or social circumstances during the study, medications, medical or psychiatric illnesses, diet, and even poorly understood aspects of the relationship between the investigator and the subject. The investigator also needs to decide whether absolute or percent changes in the biochemical index are likely to provide the more valid measure of reactivity, depending on what is known about the physiology of the system under study; how and whether to assign treatments randomly; and which control group or groups to include. A study where negative findings may result should incorporate provisions for positive controls. When control subjects are studied as part of methods development for a given biochemical substance, the results should not be used to compare them with patients studied at a later date. Instead, the clinical study should include concurrent testing of other control subjects. Depending on the hypothesis under consideration and the system under study, the investigator may have to choose among using a large number of biochemical determinations over a long time period, integrated sampling, or sampling at the same time point in the control subjects and the subjects undergoing an experimental treatment.

Technical Factors

Liquid chromatography, radioimmunoassay, and radioenzymatic procedures are commonly used in measuring levels of biochemical substances, and so they are described briefly here. High-pressure liquid chromatography (HPLC) involves injection of a sample—usually already partially purified—onto a chromatographic column containing an ion-exchange resin or a reversed phase (hydrophobic) packing. A liquid mobile phase is pumped at high pressure through the column, and the characteristics of the column and the mobile phase determine reproducible retention times for elution of the substances of interest from the column. Other substances are not retained on the column and are eluted quickly in a large solvent front. HPLC is a versatile separation technique that must be combined with some detection technique to quantify the amount of the substances of interest being eluted from the column. The detection technique may be ultraviolet detection, fluorescence, electrochemical detection, a radioimmunoassay, or radioenzymatic assay.

A radioimmunoassay (RIA) requires an antibody specific for the substance of interest, a standard for the substance, and a radioactive form of the substance (radioligand). Under suitable conditions, the substance being measured competes with the radioligand for antibody binding sites: the more of the substance present in the sample, the fewer radioactive antigen–antibody complexes form. After a separation step to differentiate bound from free radioligand, the concentration of the substance of interest is determined by measuring the amount of bound and free radioactivity and by comparison with a standard curve to determine how much substance would have resulted in the observed competition for the antibody binding sites. In a radioenzymatic assay, the sample is reacted with a mixture containing an enzyme and a source of radioactivity. The substance of interest is enzymatically converted to a radioactive product, and so the amount of the radioactive product indicates the amount of the substance in the sample.

In the measurement of the often extremely low circulating concentrations of vasoactive substances, the timing, site, and method of sample collection, handling, and storage—as well as the assay technique itself—can influence the results in ways which often can seem mysterious. For instance, when sympathomimetic amines are injected, the neurotransmitter, norepinephrine, almost immediately reaches postsynaptic adrenoceptors to elicit a pressor response, but a much longer time elapses before peak concentrations are achieved in the bloodstream. Circulating levels of peptides may be over-estimated or underestimated if appropriate protease inhibitors and antioxidants are not added to the plasma—overestimation if circulating precursors are cleaved (cut off) enzymatically to yield the peptide of interest, underestimation if the peptide itself is destroyed.

SPECIFIC SYSTEMS OR SUBSTANCES

Sympathetic Nervous System

The sympathetic nervous system plays a major role in determining responses of cardiac output, vascular resistance, and venous capacity during rapid adjustments to environmental stimuli.

The sympathetic outflow to the circulatory system derives from neurons in the brain stem. The axons descend in the spinal cord to synapse with cells in the intermediolateral cell column. Myelinated axons from the intermediolateral column exit the spinal cord to synapse in ganglia of the sympathetic chain or in the adrenal medulla. In the case of sympathetic nerve endings, the postganglionic cells release norepinephrine (NE) in the walls of blood vessels and in the heart; the adrenal medulla releases mainly epinephrine (E).

Networks of sympathetic nerves enmesh arterioles—the average caliber of which determines overall resistance to blood flow—venules, and atrial and ventricular myocardium. Stimulation of the vascular sympathetic innervation releases NE, which binds to postsynaptic alpha-adrenoceptors to cause vasoconstriction; stimulation of the cardiac sympathetics causes enhanced cardiac contractility and increases in cardiac rate and electrical automaticity.

Specific receptors for catecholamines (adrenoceptors) exist in various tissues, including the heart and blood vessels. These receptors for NE and E currently are classified as alpha-1, alpha-2, beta-1, and beta-2. NE binds to alpha-1, alpha-2, and beta-1 receptors, whereas E binds to all of them. Beta-1 receptors appear to predominate in the heart, beta-2 in blood vessel walls, alpha-1 in postsynaptic areas near sympathetic nerve endings, and alpha-2 in the presynaptic and extrasynaptic areas. The number and affinity of these receptors for NE and E can be manipulated and may influence in complex ways the relationship between circulating levels of NE or E and cardiovascular responses to these substances.

Since NE is the neurotransmitter of the sympathetic nervous system, investigators have used circulating concentrations of NE to indicate sympathetic activity.[1] Circulating NE appears to emanate mainly from the myriad sympathetic nerve endings in the walls of blood vessels throughout the body.[2] This multiplicity of origins for circulating NE complicates the interpretation of plasma NE in terms of sympathetic outflow, because in response to several environmental stimuli, disparate directly recorded sympathetic neural responses can occur. One glaring example of this nonhomogeneity is the "defense reaction," in which inhibition of skeletal muscle sympathetic activity contrasts with simultaneous renal vasoconstriction.[3] On the other hand, stimulation of arterial baroreflex afferents causes diffuse sympathetic inhibition.[4]

Even more complicating, several removal processes for NE intervene between the synapse and the plasma. The most important of these is reuptake of NE into the presynaptic axon. These processes determine the concentration gradient between the synapse and the plasma.[5] As a result, in a given patient, a high level of NE may reflect poor NE removal rather than increased sympathetic neural activity, especially in cardiac, pulmonary, renal, or hepatic failure.

Any model relating circulating NE to sympathetic activity must therefore take into account the possible heterogeneity of sympathetic neural responses and the several processes that determine the amount of "spillover" from the neuroeffector junctions to the general circulation.

Environmental stimuli can differentially affect circulating levels of NE and E. Orthostasis (e.g., standing upright), isometric exercise, the cold pressor test, vasodilators, and sympathomimetic amines appear to stimulate increases mainly of circulating NE, whereas psychological stress, hemorrhage, hypoglycemia, central cholinergic stimulation,[6] and caffeine[7] stimulate increases mainly of E. These findings affirm the importance of the first general principle discussed above, relating to vertical organization of "stress" responses. Circulating levels of NE vary as a function of many common factors such as sodium intake, medicines, the perceived stress of the experimental situation, and preclinical as well as overt medical illnesses.

Circulating levels of free dopamine (DA), the precursor of NE and E, appear to be little affected by any of these stimuli. Urinary dopamine excretion in humans increases during sodium loading.[8] Since DA receptors exist in the kidney, it is possible that DA may act locally to increase renal blood flow and sodium excretion. Blockade of DA receptors using metoclopramide increases aldosterone levels,[9] suggesting that aldosterone secretion by the adrenal cortex is under tonic dopaminergic inhibition.

Correlating catecholamine levels with effects of sympathetic stimulation or blockade enhances the utility of these biochemical indices. The finding that some patients with essential hypertension have both high circulating levels of NE and excessive depressor responses to the central sympatholytic, clonidine, supports a pathophysiologic role of increased sympathetic outflow in determining the high blood pressure of those patients.[10] Similarly, the finding that levels of NE are related to peripheral vascular responsiveness to alpha-1 blockade[11] or to pressor responses to injected NE[12] lends pathophysiologic meaning to NE levels in hypertension.

Many studies have used plasma NE to indicate sympathetic tone in a variety of cardiovascular pathologic conditions,[13] and only a few are enumerated here. Several recent reports have considered the possibility that coronary ischemia causes release of myocardial catecholamines which may then lower thresholds for ventricular ectopy.[14] Patients with the coronary-prone (Type A) behavior pattern may have excessive catecholamine responses to a challenge.[15] In baboons, correlated increases in plasma NE and blood pressure have been observed during operant conditioning of increases in diastolic pressure,[16] and similar results recently have been reported in humans.[17] Plasma levels of NE appear to be correlated with vascular hypertrophy in patients with borderline hypertension[18] as well as cardiac hypertrophy in patients with established essential hypertension.[19] Elevated plasma NE is particularly common in young patients with hypertension.[20]

Measuring plasma catecholamines validly and reliably has presented a perennial challenge. Currently, the two most commonly used assay techniques are the catechol-0-methyltransferase radioenzymatic assay (COMT-RE) and liquid chromatography with electrochemical detection (LCED).

In the COMT-RE technique, plasma is reacted with COMT, which is a partially purified liver extract, and radioactive S-adenosyl methionine (SAM), a methyl donor. This catalyzes the transfer of the radioactive methyl group to NE and E, producing the radioactive metabolites, normetanephrine and metanephrine. The metabolites are then separated by thin-layer chromatography, and reaction products of the scraped chromatographic bands undergo liquid scintillation spectroscopy.

In the LCED procedure, plasma is prepared using an alumina extraction, where the catecholamines are adsorbed to the alumina at alkaline pH and desorbed (eluted) at acid pH, and the plasma-derived eluate is injected onto a liquid chromatographic column. The separated catecholamines are quantified by the amount of current produced on exposure of the column effluent to a weak oxidizing potential.

Both techniques offer adequate sensitivity and specificity for measuring plasma catecholamines, but both have limitations. Since the COMT enzyme is only partially purified, endogenous inhibitors of the enzyme can produce bizarre standard curves; SAM decomposes fairly quickly; interfering endogenous or exogenous catechols can also react with COMT to yield artifactually high catecholamine levels; and the technique is difficult, time-consuming, expensive, and requires the use of radionuclides. In the LCED method, co-eluting peaks (i.e., peaks with similar retention times on the column, such as those related to coffee ingestion) can interfere with the peaks for the endogenous catecholamines or the internal standard;[21] the NE peak may be difficult to resolve from the solvent front, which contains all the substances that the column did not retain well; and the sensitivity of the assay may be inadequate for plasma E in venous blood of resting subjects. Both assay techniques require careful supervision and frequent trouble-shooting.

Many investigators have used urinary catecholamine excretion as a simple "integrated" index of overall release of catecholamines. Several points cast doubt on the validity of this application. First, by far the predominant catecholamine in human urine is dopamine, which may derive from renal dopaminergic nerves or circulating dopa, the amino acid precursor of dopamine, and which may not reflect in any direct way sympathetically mediated NE release. Second, a large and probably variable proportion of NE released from sympathetic nerve endings is metabolized before it appears in the urine. To quantify total NE turnover in the body would require measurements not only of urinary NE excretion but also of excretion of the several NE metabolites. Third, the kidney probably does not act as a passive filter for NE; instead, it is likely that urinary NE excretion is determined importantly by local release in the kidney. Even if urinary catecholamine excretion did provide a valid measure of overall sympathetic tone, the long time periods required for collecting urine obviate using urinary catecholamine excretion in situations involving rapid cardiovascular and sympathetic responses to environmental stimuli.

Renin-Angiotensin-Aldosterone System

The renin-angiotensin-aldosterone system (RAS) is another classic system involved with both acute and long-term circulatory homeostasis.

Circulating levels of the proteolytic enzyme renin derive mainly from modified smooth muscle cells in the walls of the afferent arterioles to glomeruli of the kidney. The released renin cleaves a decapeptide from the amino terminal end of an alpha-2 macroglobulin, angiotensinogen, to form angiotensin I (AI). Renin has no other known physiological role. In capillary beds, especially in the lung, angiotensin converting enzyme (ACE) cleaves two amino acids from the carboxy terminus of AI to yield the extremely potent octapeptide, angiotensin II (AII). Medications such as captopril inhibit

ACE and are being used successfully to treat hypertension and heart failure. Another enzyme besides renin, called tonin, can directly cleave AII from angiotensinogen. AII can be converted to AIII, another physiologically active form, by cleaving a terminal aspartic acid residue. Further cleavage of the angiotensin peptide to the hexapeptide inactivates it.

Many stimuli affect renin release and can be classified in terms of activation of receptors in the kidney, renal sympathetic activity, and substances in the bloodstream.

Intrarenal vascular receptors respond to stretch by inhibiting renin release, and so decreases in renal perfusion pressure cause increases in circulating renin. The macula dense area of distal tubular cells which, together with the afferent and efferent arterioles, constitute the juxtaglomerular apparatus (JGA), appears to sense changes in the chemical composition of tubular fluid and to influence renin release from the specialized afferent arteriolar cells in the JGA. Increases in sodium and chloride delivery to the macula densa inhibit renin secretion. Since calcium gluconate and calcium chloride infused into the renal artery both inhibit renin secretion, it is possible that JGA cells also sense and respond to the calcium ion.[22]

The renal nerves exert tonic excitatory stimulation of renin release. Since the beta-adrenoceptor blocker propranolol can abolish renin release during renal nerve stimulation, it appears that renin release results in this case from beta adrenergic stimulation in the kidney. The renal efferents participate in reflexes involving systemic baroreceptors and the brain. Stimulation of "low-pressure" atrial baroreceptors by inflating a balloon in the right atrium stimulates vagal afferents that cause reflexive inhibition of renin release.[23] Stimulation of "high-pressure" baroreceptors, stretch receptors in the walls of major arteries including the carotids, also inhibits RAS activity.

A large number of substances injected at pharmacologic doses into the renal artery affect renin release. These include the catecholamines; sodium, potassium and calcium ions; angiotensin; vasopressin; and the prostaglandins.

AII is one of the most powerful vasoconstrictors known. In addition to its direct effect on receptors on arteriolar smooth-muscle cells, it enhances release of NE from sympathetic nerve endings and E release from the adrenal medulla. It may also reach specific central neural sites involved with pressor responses.

A second major action of AII is to stimulate secretion of the mineralocorticoid hormone, aldosterone, from the adrenal cortex. Aldosterone, in turn, stimulates sodium reabsorption by renal tubules. The RAS therefore influences vasoconstrictor tone, extracellular fluid (including blood) volume homeostasis, and possibly central nervous system mechanisms subserving cardiovascular control. Adrenocorticotropin (ACTH), secreted by the pituitary gland, angiotensin, and the potassium ion are the major known stimuli of aldosterone secretion. Other possible influences include dopamine and serotonin.

RAS activity affects cardiovascular responsivity. AII enhances blood pressure responses to sympathetic stimulation. Baseline levels of plasma renin activity (PRA) can predict the magnitude of the decrease in blood pressure after ACE inhibition.[24] Patients with low levels of PRA tend to have enhanced adrenocortical responsiveness to angiotensin,[25] and this may explain both their low PRA levels and their high blood pressure. Hypertensives with low PRA and plasma NE are especially responsive to diuretics.[26]

Measurement of activity of the RAS has depended mainly on a radio-immunoassay for PRA, the rate of AI production when test plasma is exposed to angiotensinogen. Recently, a method for direct RIA of renin has been introduced.[27] Since AII concentrations are very small (about 5–100 pg/ml), and since AIII and the inactive hexapeptide virtually invariably cross-react with AII (i.e., the RIA antibody does not distinguish AII, AIII, and the hexapeptide), a successful RIA for AII has proven quite elusive. The combination of liquid chromatography with RIA may help to quantify these species separately.[28]

Several components of the RAS exist in the brain. The functional significance of the putative central neural RAS is unknown.

Orthostasis, sodium restriction, and depletion of extracellular volume substantially increase levels of PRA. Adequate classification of patients into high-, normal-, and low-renin subgroups requires control or monitoring of body position at the time of blood sampling, of medications, and of urinary sodium excretion.

Pituitary-Adrenocortical Axis

The pituitary-adrenocortical axis (PAA) contributes importantly to the organism's integrated response to several types of environmental stress. Probably the best clinical evidence for the functional role of the PAA is that patients with Addison's disease, who have adrenocortical failure, tolerate any surgery poorly. Stresses such as surgery are associated with increased serum levels of cortisol, which is released from adrenal cortical cells. The clinical status of patients in septic shock can improve dramatically upon intravenous administration of corticosteroids. Exactly how corticosteroids help the organism to tolerate stress is unknown.

Glucocorticoids such as cortisol interact with sympathetic function at several levels. They stimulate the enzyme in the adrenal medulla that converts NE to E, and they inhibit extraneuronal uptake of NE. The adrenal cortex and medulla share an arterial blood supply that flows in a cortico-medullary direction. Circulating catecholamines may augment ACTH release (see below).

The release of cortisol depends on ACTH, a hormone secreted by the anterior pituitary gland. ACTH release is subject to negative feedback control by circulating cortisol. Recently, a hypothalamic releasing factor, corticotropin releasing factor (CRF), has been isolated and synthesized. CRF stimulates ACTH release, and cortisol can inhibit this action.[29] Since beta-adrenoceptor agonists such as isoproterenol stimulate *in vitro* ACTH release and ganglionic blockade with chlorisondamine inhibits stress-induced ACTH release,[30] the pituitary may be a central neural site for an interaction between the sympathetic nervous system and the PAA. Incubation of adrenomedullary cells with CRF stimulates intracellular adenylate cyclase and catecholamine release (personal observations). When injected into human subjects, however, CRF has had no acute cardiovascular effect.[31]

The pituitary-adrenocortical axis has been viewed as a classic stress system. However, during the mainly psychological stress of wisdom tooth extractions, serum cortisol levels do not increase, whereas plasma levels of the catecholamines—particularly epinephrine—do.[32] It is possible that PAA activity is increased specifically in stressful situations involving novelty.[33]

Most clinical pathology laboratories routinely perform serum cortisol measurements. Urinary 17-hydroxycorticosteroid or cortisol excretion can be used for testing of responses occurring over several hours or days but not for acute responses. Measurement of ACTH and CRF, however, requires RIAs. Beta-lipotropin, melanocyte stimulating hormone, beta-endorphin, and pro-opiomelanocortin can cross-react with ACTH. As with all RIAs, the validity of the measurement technique for ACTH depends on the specificity of the antibody, and so the investigator should exercise caution in drawing inferences from levels of total ACTH immunoreactivity.

Other Vasoactive Peptides

A large and rapidly growing number of peptides have been identified that, when injected into the bloodstream or central nervous areas, have hemodynamic effects. These include vasopressin, atrial natriuretic factor, neuropeptide Y, substance P, neurotensin, bombesin, and endogenous opioids. Their functional roles in circulatory homeostasis are being vigorously explored. All exist at low concentrations requiring RIAs for detection, and, to a variable degree, cross reactivity with other peptide fragments presents a major challenge to the assay techniques.

Release of vasopressin from the posterior pituitary is determined by hypothalamic "osmoreceptors," cardiopulmonary and arterial baroreflex afferent stimulation, and angiotensin II. Vasopressin at pharmacologic doses causes vasoconstriction and antidiuresis. Since Brattleboro rats, a strain lacking vasopressin, can develop some forms of experimental hypertension, the pathophysiologic role of vasopressin in hypertension is uncertain.[34] Brattleboro rats do not develop DOCA-salt hypertension. Chronic vasopressin infusions to levels several-fold higher than normally circulate only produce mild increases in blood pressure.

Kallikrein-Kinin System and Prostaglandins

There are no convincing studies to date demonstrating an abnormality of the kallikrein-kinin system or of prostaglandins in any cardiovascular disease, and so the utility of biochemical measurements of these substances in studies of cardiovascular reactivity is open to question. Nevertheless, the kinin and prostaglandin systems are involved in complex ways with vascular responsiveness and with renal sodium handling and so merit consideration.[35]

Kallikrein is a serine protease found in blood, sweat, saliva, urine, the kidney, the exocrine pancreas, and the gastrointestinal tract. Renal and urinary kallikrein release lysyl-braydkinin from kininogen, and plasma kallikrein results in formation of bradykinin, an extremely potent vasodilator. Decreased urinary kallikrein excretion has been described in clinical hypertension, but kallikrein excretion depends on race and renal status. ACE blockers increase urinary kinin excretion, kinins stimulate prostaglandin secretion, and elevated kallikrein excretion occurs in most patients with primary hyperaldosteronism. These findings suggest links among the kinin, prostaglandin, and renin-angiotensin systems, but these relationships have not yet been clearly defined.

Prostaglandins are products of arachidonic acid metabolism. The nomenclature for the various prostaglandin species is complex. The prostaglandins (PGs) relevant to the cardiovascular system include those of the PGE and PGF series. Both norepinephrine and angiotensin stimulate PGE_2 release in the kidney, and PGE_2 opposes the vasoconstrictor and antidiuretic effects of these agents. Prostaglandins modify NE release during sympathetic stimulation; conversely, sympathetic stimulation leads to PGE_2 release. When RAS activity is stimulated, such as by renal arterial constriction, prostaglandin release tends to normalize renal flow; when renal prostaglandin synthesis is inhibited by indomethacin, renal arterial constriction can result in malignant hypertension. The zonal distribution of blood flow in the kidney influences sodium and water excretion, and prostaglandins redistribute flow toward the inner cortex and medulla. Prostaglandins also appear to affect JGA mechanisms for renin release.

One would expect that because, in general, prostaglandins decrease renal vascular resistance, a defect in prostaglandin synthesis or release may participate in hypertension. Most attempts to induce hypertension by administering cyclooxygenase inhibitors, which block synthesis of prostaglandins from arachidonic acid, have failed.

Some products of arachidonic acid metabolism exert vasoconstrictor effects—for example, thromboxane and PGF_2-alpha. The mechanisms by which the arachidonic acid metabolic cascade can be channelized away from these substances are unknown.

Measuring circulating levels of bradykinin and prostaglandins requires RIAs that, because of low concentrations, instability of the biochemicals, and cross-reactivity, are difficult.[36] Gas chromatography with mass spectrometry (GC-MS) has been used successively to measure prostaglandins, but the methodology is cumbersome and the equipment expensive. Currently, these methodological problems obviate the routine use of circulating bradykinin or prostaglandin levels in studies about cardiovascular reactivity.

Ion Fluxes and Intracellular Biochemistry

The measurement of transmembrane ion fluxes, intracellular ion concentrations, and intracellular "second messenger" substances provides a different form of biochemical index which may be related to cardiovascular reactivity. The ions most likely to be important are sodium and calcium; the second messengers of note are cytoplasmic ionized calcium, cyclic adenosine triphosphate (AMP), and cyclic guanosine monophosphate (GMP).

The transmembrane movement of sodium is controlled by several pumps, Na-K ATPase being most prominent. Inhibition of this pump, which causes increases in intracellular sodium, augments vasoconstrictor responses. The mechanism of action of the cardiotonic digoxin includes inhibition of Na-K ATPase. In red blood cells, other systems regulating transmembrane sodium movement include Na-Na exchange, Na-K cotransport (which is blocked by furosemide), and passive diffusion down an electrochemical gradient. Initial studies have indicated abnormalities in one or more of these systems in blood cells of patients with essential hypertension, but no single abnormality has been proven to play a pathophysiologic role. Age, sex, body weight, and race appear to be important interacting factors.

The recently introduced Quin 2 technique has allowed measurement of intracellular free calcium.[37] In this technique Quin 2, a fluorescent dye, enters cells and irreversibly binds ionized calcium. As cytoplasmic calcium increases, the amount of Quin 2 fluorescence increases. Erne, Bolli, et al.[38] have reported remarkably strong agreement between platelet intracellular calcium measured using the Quin 2 technique and blood pressure in patients with essential hypertension. In spontaneously hypertensive rats, however, intracellular free calcium is not increased, either in platelets (personal observations) or vascular smooth muscle cells.[39] This is probably because the concentration of intracellular calcium is controlled by several mechanisms, and a perturbation that stimulates transmembrane Na-Ca exchange only transiently affects intracellular calcium.

The role of cyclic AMP as an intracellular second messenger is by now well established. The chain of intracellular events linking membrane receptors occupied by hormones or neurotransmitters (first messengers) and cellular activation often includes cyclic AMP generation in the cell. Activated receptors stimulate adenyl cyclase in the cell membrane. The cyclase converts adenosine triphosphate (ATP) in the cytoplasm to cyclic 3′, 5′-adenosine monophosphate (cyclic AMP); cyclic AMP then activates protein kinases. A well-known example of such cellular activation is the positive inotropic effect of catecholamines in cardiac muscle cells. The intracellular cascade of events subsequent to cyclic AMP generation that leads to liberation of cytoplasmic calcium, the interaction between actin and myosin molecules, and muscular contraction is the subject of active research.

Much less is known about cyclic GMP. Vasorelaxants such as nitroprusside, acetylcholine, and histamine produce accumulation of cyclic GMP in vascular cells, the latter two by an endothelium-dependent mechanism.[40] Very recent studies have indicated that the atrial natriuretic factor also stimulates cyclic GMP.[41] Cyclic GMP stimulation is associated with protein kinase activity and incorporation of phosphorus into several smooth muscle proteins. The factor in endothelium required for stimulation of cyclic GMP accumulation in response to acetylcholine and histamine appears to be a metabolite of arachidonic acid.[42]

Techniques for measuring transmembrane ion fluxes vary among laboratories, and these differences, as well as differences in the subject populations, appear to have caused discrepancies in the obtained results. Intracellular calcium is currently best measured by the Quin 2 technique. Adjustments must be made for autofluorescence by reagants or fluids involved in the measurement and the sample preparation procedures must not artifactually activate mechanisms controlling intracellular calcium. An example where this may happen is decapitation of small animals to obtain blood samples to quantify platelet intracellular calcium. Decapitation profoundly and almost instantly increased circulating epinephrine, which activates platelets. The techniques involving intracellular dyes to measure calcium are limited mainly to *in vitro* use. Cyclic AMP and cyclic GMP can be measured using commercially available RIA kits.

FUTURE TRENDS

Many vasoactive biochemicals exist at such low concentrations in the bloodstream that an RIA is required to detect them. Although RIAs offer specificity and sensitivity, cross-reactivity with other structurally similar substances has led to somewhat tortuous searches for more potent, more specific antibodies. Combining a separation technique such as liquid chromatography with RIA has the potential for alleviating the cross-reactivity problem. Chromatographic separations based simply on molecular weight, for instance, can improve the specificity of RIAs where the cross-reacting substance is a large precursor or a metabolic fragment. The combination of a chromatographic separation with RIA should enable better measurement of angiotensin II, atrial natriuretic factor, neuropeptide Y, and other peptides of interest.

When one considers the hierarchical organization discussed at the beginning of this chapter, it becomes clear that biochemical indices of cardiovascular reactivity must be dealt with as they exist in the organism: as parts of systems that are integrated to serve homeostatic needs.[43] The central nervous system is the logical site for studying this integration. Correlating cardiovascular responses and circulating levels of biochemicals during stimulation or after ablation of specific brain nuclei is likely to expand our knowledge about central neural integration of cardiovascular reactivity. For instance, circulating levels of vasopressin increase in association with hypertension caused by lesions of the nucleus tractus solitarius of the brainstem, and combined ganglionic and vasopressin blockade abolishes hypertension.[44] Recently introduced techniques—nuclear magnetic resonance and positron emission tomography—provide functional as well as anatomic information, and one may expect that these techniques will be used to measure brain biochemical indices of cardiovascular reactivity.

Cardiovascular function is influenced importantly by the parasympathetic nervous system. To date it has been thought that the parasympathetic neurotransmitter acetylcholine does not circulate at all because of the rapidity and completeness of degradation by acetylcholinesterase. This assumption is being reconsidered. If acetylcholine does circulate, then blood levels of acetylcholine may provide an important biochemical index of parasympathetic activity and increase our understanding about reflexive circulatory controls.

The atrial natriuretic factor (ANF) is a peptide released from cardiac atria in response to atrial stretch or intravascular volume loading. The substance circulates in the bloodstream. Injected ANF inhibits vasoconstrictor responses to several agonists and stimulates urinary sodium excretion. The location of the sensor and the pharmacology of the agent suggest that ANF may serve a physiological role in volume homeostasis. One may expect many future studies about this substance. A receptor blocker for ANF also would be a major advance in understanding the function of this possible natriuretic hormone.

Finally, our understanding of adrenergic receptors has expanded greatly with recent developments in molecular genetics, and one may anticipate direct measurement of the number and activity of adrenergic and other receptors relevant to cardiovascular reactivity.

REFERENCES

1. Lake CR, Ziegler MG, Kopin IJ: Use of plasma norepinephrine for evaluation of sympathetic neuronal function in man. *Life Sci* **18**:1315–1326, 1976.

2. Hume WR, Bevan JA: The structure of the peripheral adrenergic synapse and its functional implications. In Ziegler MG, Lake CR (eds), *Norepinephrine*. Baltimore: Williams & Wilkins, 1984, pp. 47–54.

3. Folkow B: Physiological aspects of primary hypertension. *Physiol Rev* **62**:347–504, 1982.

4. Ninomiya I, Nisimaru N, Irisawa H: Sympathetic nerve activity to the spleen, kidney, and heart in response to baroceptor input. *Am J Physiol* **221**:1346–1351, 1971.

5. Goldstein DS, McCarty R, et al: Relationship between plasma norepinephrine and sympathetic neural activity. *Hypertension* **5**:552–559, 1983.

6. Kennedy B, Janowsky DS, et al: Central cholinergic stimulation causes adrenal epinephrine release. *J Clin Invest* **74**:972–975, 1984.

7. Robertson D, Frolich JC, et al: Effects of caffeine on plasma renin activity, catecholamines and blood pressure. *New Engl J Med* **298**:181–186, 1978.

8. Alexander RW, Gill JR, et al: Effects of dietary sodium and of acute saline infusion on the interrelationship between dopamine excretion and adrenergic activity in man. *J Clin Invest* **54**:194–200, 1974.

9. North RH, McCallum RW, et al: Tonic dopaminergic suppression of plasma aldosterone. *J Clin Endocrinol Metab* **51**:64–69, 1980.

10. Goldstein DS, Levinson PD, et al: Clonidine suppression testing in essential hypertension. *Ann In Med* **102**:42–48, 1985.

11. Kiowski W, van Brummelen P, Buhler FR: Plasma noradrenaline correlates with alpha-adrenoceptor-mediated vasoconstriction and blood pressure in patients with essential hypertension. *Clin Sci* **57**:177s–180s, 1979.

12. Philipp T, Distler A, Cordes A: Sympathetic nervous system and blood-pressure control in essential hypertension. *Lancet* **2**:959–963, 1978.

13. Goldstein DS: Plasma catecholamines in clinical studies of cardiovascular diseases. *Acta Physiol Scand* **527**:39–41, 1984. (Suppl)

14. Abrahamsson T, Almgren O, Carlsson L: Ischemia-induced local release of myocardial noradrenaline. *J Cardiovasc Pharmacol* **7**:S19–S23, 1985. (Suppl 5)

15. Friedman M, Byers SO, et al: Plasma catecholamine response of coronary-prone subjects (Type A) to a specific challenge. *Metabolism* **24**:205–210, 1975.

16. Goldstein DS, Harris AH, et al: Plasma catecholamines and renin during operant blood pressure conditioning in baboons. *Physiol Behav* **26**:33–37, 1981.

17. Cohn JN, Yellin AM: Learned precise cardiovascular control through graded central sympathetic stimulation. *J Hypertension* **2**:77–79, 1984. (Suppl 3)

18. Egan B, Julius S: Vascular hypertrophy in borderline hypertension: Relationship to blood pressure and sympathetic drive. *Clin Exp Hyper* **A7**:243–255, 1985.

19. Corea L, Bentivoglio M, et al: Plasma norepinephrine and left ventricular hypertrophy in systemic hypertension. *Am J Cardiol* **53**:1299–1303, 1984.

20. Goldstein DS: Plasma catecholamines in essential hypertension: An analytical review. *Hypertension* **5**:86–99, 1983.

21. Goldstein DS, Stull R, et al: Dihydrocaffeic acid: A common contaminant in the liquid chromatographic-electrochemical measurement of plasma catecholamines in man. *J Chromatog* **311**:148–153, 1984.

22. Watkins BE, Davis JO, et al: Intrarenal site of action of calcium on renin secretion in dogs. *Circ Res* **39**:847–853, 1976.

23. Zehr JE, Hasbargen JA, Kurz KD: Reflex suppression of renin secretion during distention of cardiopulmonary receptors in dogs. *Circulation Res* **38**:232–239, 1976.

24. Case DB, Atlas SA, et al: Clinical experience with blockade of the renin-angiotensin-aldosterone system by an oral converting-enzyme inhibitor (SQ 14,225, captopril) in hypertensive patients. *Prog Cardiovasc Dis* **21**:195–206, 1978.

25. Kisch ES, Dluhy RG, Williams GH: Enhanced aldosterone response to angiotensin II in human hypertension. *Circ Res* **38**:502–506, 1976.

26. Masuyama Y: Responses to antihypertensive agents in relation to the pathogenic factors in essential hypertension. *Jap J Med* **21**:158–160, 1982.

27. Hofbauer KG, Wood JM, et al: Increased plasma renin during renin inhibition. Studies of a novel immunoassay. *Hypertension* **7**:I61–I65, 1985. (Suppl I)

28. Nussberger J, Brunner DB, et al: True versus immunoreactive angiotensin II in human plasma. *Hypertension* **7**:I1–I7, 1985. (Suppl I)

29. Widmaier EP, Dallman MF: The effects of corticotropin-releasing factor on adrenocorticotropin secretion from perfused pituitaries *in vitro*: Rapid inhibition by glucocorticoids. *Endocrinology* **115**:2368–2374, 1984.

30. Rivier C, Vale W: Modulation of stress-induced ACTH release by corticotropin-releasing factor, catecholamines and vasopressin. *Nature* **305**:325–327, 1983.

31. Donald RA, Espiner EA, et al: The effect of corticotropin-releasing factor on catecholamine, vasopressin, and aldosterone secretion in normal man. *J Clin Endocrinol Metab* **58**:463–466, 1984.

32. Goldstein DS, Dionne R, et al: Circulatory, plasma catecholamine, cortisol, lipid, and psychological responses to a real-life stress (third molar extractions): Effects of diazepam sedation and of inclusion of epinephrine with the local anesthetic. *Psychosom Med* **44**:259–272, 1982.

33. Natelson BH, Tapp WN, et al: Humoral indices of stress in rats. *Physiol Behav* **26**:1049–1054, 1981.

34. Krakoff LR, Elijovich F, Barry C: The role of vasopressin in experimental and clinical hypertension. *Am J Kidney Dis* **5**:A40–A47, 1985.

35. Margolius HS. Kallikrein and kinins in hypertension. In Genest J, Kuchel O, et al: *Hypertension: Physiopathology and Treatment.* New York: McGraw-Hill, 1983, pp 360–373.

36. van Leeuwen BH, Millar JA, et al: Radioimmunoassay of blood bradykinin: Purification of blood extracts to prevent cross-reaction with endogenous kininogen. *Clin Chim Acta* **127**:343–351, 1983.

37. Tsien RY: New calcium indicators and buffers with high selectivity against magnesium and protons: Design, synthesis, and properties of prototype structures. *Biochem* **19**:2396–2404, 1980.

38. Erne P, Bolli P, et al: Correlation of platelet calcium with blood pressure. Effect of antihypertensive therapy. *New Engl J Med* **310**:1084–1088, 1984.

39. Nabika T, Velletri PA, et al: Increase in cytosolic calcium and phosphoinositide metabolism induced by angiotensin II and [arg]vasopressin in vascular smooth muscle cells. *J Biol Chem* **260**:4661–4670, 1985.

40. Furchgott RF, Zawadzki JV: The obligatory role of endothelial cells in the relaxation of arterial smooth muscle by acetylcholine. *Nature* **288**:373–376, 1980.

41. Ohlstein EH, Berkowitz BA: Cyclic guanosine monophosphate mediates vascular relaxation induced by atrial natriuretic factor. *Hypertension* **7**:306–310, 1985.

42. Furchgott RF: Role of endothelium in responses of vascular smooth muscle. *Circ Res* **53**:557–573, 1983.

43. Esler MD, Hasking GJ, et al: Noradrenaline release and sympathetic nervous system activity. *J Hypertension* **3**:117–129, 1985.

44. Sved AF, Imaizumi T, et al: Vasopressin contributes to hypertension caused by nucleus tractus solitarius lesions. *Hypertension* **7**:262–267, 1985.

PART III

ATTRIBUTES ASSOCIATED WITH REACTIVITY

11

Psychological Variables and Cardiovascular and Neuroendocrine Reactivity

B. KENT HOUSTON

Individual differences in cardiovascular and neuroendocrine responsivity have intrigued scientists for some time. Moreover, both psychological and biological factors have been considered as contributors to such individual differences.[1]

The author wishes to thank the members of the task group on "Psychological Markers and Correlates of Reactivity," namely, Craig Ewart, Margaret Chesney, Katrina Johnson, Viktor Khramelashvili, James Lane, Stephen Manuck, Patrice Saab, Gary Schwartz, and Alvin Shapiro, whose participation contributed to the present chapter. Thanks also go to David S. Holmes, Lynn Pace, and Karen Kelly for their comments on an earlier draft of the manuscript. Preparation of this chapter was supported, in part, by a Biomedical Science Support Grant (#4169-X711-8).

207

The purpose of the present chapter is to examine the research in which relationships between psychological variables and neuroendocrine and cardiovascular reactivity have been investigated. General issues and recommendations for future research will also be discussed.

The research reviewed here is intended to be representative of the area rather than comprehensive. Further, it is confined to that in which reactivity was elicited by identifiable circumstances. In addition, the focus will be on those studies that deal with ostensibly enduring psychological characteristics rather than with transient or situationally specific characteristics such as state anxiety[2] or state anger.[3] The rationale for this is that since the development or progression of a cardiovascular disorder takes time, it would seem that psychological characteristics, if they contribute to this process, should endure for a period of time as well. However, that does not mean that particular psychological characteristics need to endure indefinitely and/or up to the point at which cardiovascular disease is clinically identified.

Few studies on relationships between enduring psychological characteristics and neuroendocrine reactivity have been done apart from those on the Type A behavior pattern. Research involving neuroendocrine responsivity will thus be limited to the following section.

TYPE A BEHAVIOR PATTERN

Foremost among the psychological variables that have been assessed for their relationship to reactivity is the Type A behavior pattern. Individuals exhibiting the Type A behavior pattern are characterized by vigorous speech, impatience, a chronic sense of time urgency, enhanced competitiveness, aggressive drive, and often some hostility.[4] The relative absence of Type A characteristics defines the contrasting Type B behavior pattern. The Type A behavior pattern is most commonly measured by means of a structured interview (SI),[4] the Jenkins Activity Survey (JAS),[5] and the Framingham Type A Scale (FTAS).[6]

Numerous studies have been conducted in which the relationship between Type A behavior and subjects' neuroendocrine and/or cardiovascular responses to various situations have been examined. Studies that vary in use of tasks, experimental manipulations, gender of subjects, and measures of Type A behavior are reviewed here to typify this area of research.

In a study by Friedman and associates[7] of SI-defined Type A and Type B employed males, a pair of subjects (one Type A and one Type B) was presented with a complex puzzle and told that the first member of the pair to solve the puzzle would receive a bottle of French wine. Compared to Type B subjects, Type A subjects were found to respond to the task with a significantly greater increase in plasma norepinephrine (NE) but not in plasma epinephrine (E).

In a study by Glass and associates (Study II),[8] SI-defined Type A and Type B employed males performed an electronic pong game under instructions that it was a test of hand-eye coordination. In addition, subjects received fairly frequent failure feedback on their performance. Relative to Type Bs, Type As were found to respond to the task with significantly greater systolic blood pressure (SBP) and diastolic blood pressure (DBP) and marginally significantly greater heart rate (HR) ($p = 0.08$) and plasma E ($p = 0.06$).

In another study by Glass and associates of SI-defined Type A and B employed males (Study I),[8] a confederate made a series of harassing remarks to the subject (harass condition) or was silent (no harass condition) while he competed on an electronic pong game. Further, in both conditions, the subject failed to win on two-thirds of the games and consequently lost a prize. Type A subjects in the harass condition responded with significantly greater increases in SBP, HR, and plasma E than Type B subjects in the harass condition or than either Type A or Type B subjects in the no harass condition. Thus, it appears that Type A subjects were differentially aroused specifically by the harassing comments made by the confederate. There were no significant differences in SBP, DBP, HR, E, or NE between Type A and Type B subjects in response to the task in the no harass condition. This may have been due to Type A subjects' perceiving that it was too difficult to be successful in the situation because the task was too hard and/or the confederate was too good.

SI-defined Type A and Type B males (a combination of college students and working adults) in another study by Glass and associates[9] performed a vigilance task and a subsidiary memory task under instructions that emphasized the need for good performance. Relative to Type B subjects, Type A subjects were found to respond to the tasks with greater increases in SBP ($p < 0.01$), DBP ($p < 0.06$), plasma E ($p < 0.05$), and plasma NE ($p < 0.07$).

In a study by Contrada and associates of SI-defined Type A and Type B adult employed males,[10] subjects performed a reaction-time task while they were exposed either to high-intensity noise that increased over trials plus occasional shocks that decreased over trials or to low-intensity noise plus occasional shocks, both of which decreased over trials. Half of the subjects within each aversive stimulation condition were led to believe that avoidance of the aversive stimulation was contingent on their performance on the reaction-time task; the other half of the subjects were led to believe that avoidance of the aversive stimulation was not contingent on their performance. Across conditions, Type As exhibited significantly greater HR responses than Type Bs. However, the analyses revealed complicated higher-order interactions for SBP, DBP, and both plasma E and NE levels.

These complex interactions may have been due to the complexity of the design of the study. To the dispassionate reader, they are very difficult to interpret.

In a study by Manuck and Garland,[11] JAS-defined Type A and Type B college males performed a difficult concept-formation task either in a high-incentive condition with monetary inducements for correct responses or a low-incentive condition without monetary inducements. Across incentive conditions, Type As exhibited significantly greater SBP responses to the task than Type Bs.

In a study by Gastorf,[12] JAS-defined Type A and Type B male and female college students were given either solvable or unsolvable anagrams on which to work. Half of the subjects in both the solvable and unsolvable conditions were told that the anagrams were easy to solve; the other half were told that the anagrams were difficult to solve. Relative to Type B subjects, Type A subjects did not differ significantly in SBP or DBP responses to the solvable anagrams that had been described as easy, but did manifest significantly greater SBP responses to the anagrams in the other three conditions. Because of the brevity of the tasks and the ambiguity of the anagrams, it is unlikely that subjects accurately perceived the true difficulty of the unsolvable anagrams.

In a study by Jorgensen and Houston,[13] JAS-defined Type A and Type B college males and females performed three tasks: the Stroop Color-Word Interference Test, a mental arithmetic task (serial subtraction of sevens), and a difficult shock avoidance task. Relative to Type Bs, Type As exhibited significantly greater DBP responses to the Stroop task and marginally significantly ($p < 0.06$) greater DBP responses to the shock avoidance task. Type As and Type Bs did not differ significantly in cardiovascular responses to the mental arithmetic task.

In a study by Lane et al.,[14] JAS-defined Type A and Type B college females performed a mental arithmetic task (serial subtraction of 13s). Similar to the results of the Jorgensen and Houston study,[13] there were no significant differences between Type As and Type Bs in their cardiovascular responses to the mental arithmetic task. Perhaps serial subtraction tasks are too difficult to elicit differences in reactivity between Type A and Type B college students.

In a study by Dembroski, MacDougall, et al.,[15] Type A behavior was measured by both the SI and JAS. College male subjects performed three tasks: (1) a reaction-time task that was described as a test of the subject's speed of reaction; (2) an electronic pong game that was described as a test of subject's hand-eye coordination; and (3) a series of difficult anagrams under a time limit. SI-defined Type A subjects manifested significantly greater SBP and HR responses across the three tasks than Type B subjects. JAS-defined Type A subjects manifested significantly greater SBP and DBP responses across the three tasks than Type B subjects. Overall, there was no appreciable difference between the SI and JAS in prediction of cardiovascular reactivity during the experimental tasks.

Type A was also measured by the SI and JAS in a study by Corse, Manuck, et al.[16] Adult males who either did or did not have coronary heart disease (CHD) performed a difficult concept task, a mental arithmetic task (serial subtraction of 17s), and the picture completion subtest of the Wechsler Adult Intelligence Scale. Across CHD categories, SI-defined Type As responded to the tasks with significantly greater SBP and DBP than did Type Bs. There were no significant differences in cardiovascular responses to the tasks between JAS-defined Type A and Type B subjects. Thus, the SI predicted cardiovascular responses to the tasks better than did the JAS.

In a study of college males by Dembroski, MacDougall, et al.,[17] three measures of Type A behavior were employed: the SI, JAS, and FTAS. Subjects performed a cold pressor test and a reaction-time task under high- and low-challenge conditions. The difficulty of the respective tasks was emphasized in the high-challenge but not low-challenge conditions. In both high- and low-challenge conditions, SI-defined Type As exhibited significantly greater SBP responses to both tasks than Type Bs. SI-defined Type As also exhibited significantly greater HR responses to the reaction-time task across challenge conditions but significantly greater HR responses to the cold pressor task only in the high-challenge condition. JAS-defined Type As relative to Type Bs responded only to the reaction-time task in the low-challenge condition with significantly greater SBP and greater peripheral vasoconstriction (less finger pulse volume), FPV) but not greater DBP or HR. FTAS-defined Type As relative to Type Bs responded only to the reaction-time task in the low-challenge condition with significantly less FPV but not greater SBP, DBP, or HR. In general, then, the SI predicted cardiovascular reactivity to the tasks better than did either the JAS or FTAS.

Type A behavior was measured by the SI, JAS, and FTAS in two studies of college females reported by MacDougall et al.[18] Subjects in the first study were exposed to two tasks: the cold pressor test and a reaction-time task. Instructions for both tasks emphasized the tasks' difficulty. No differences between Type As and Type Bs as defined by any of the three measures were found for cardiovascular responses to the two tasks. Subjects in the second study had cardiovascular responses measured while they underwent the SI (which is mildly annoying), during a brief though difficult American history quiz, and during a reaction-time task with monetary incentive for good performance. SI-defined Type As relative to Type Bs responded with greater SBP to the SI and quiz but did not differ significantly in cardiovascular responses to the reaction-time task. Neither JAS-defined Type As and Type Bs nor FTAS-defined Type As and Type Bs differed significantly in cardiovascular responses to either task. Thus neither the SI nor JAS nor FTAS predicted these women's cardiovascular responses to the reaction time or cold pressor tasks.

In another study of college females by Lawler, Schmied, et al.,[19] subjects were presented with three tasks: a mental arithmetic task (addition and multiplication) and two sets of Raven's problems. There were no significant differences between SI-defined Type As and Type Bs or JAS-defined Type As and Type Bs in their cardiovascular responses to the experimental tasks. Thus, neither the SI nor the JAS was predictive of these women's cardiovascular responses to the experimental tasks.

The available research suggests (see also general reviews)[20-25] that Type A behavior is most likely to be related to reactivity in situations in which the individual is annoyed or harrassed or is motivated to accomplish something that is viewed as somewhat difficult but not exceedingly so. Moreover, differences between Type A and Type B individuals are most frequently found in SBP and plasma E. Studies in which psychophysiological measure Type A—Type B differences are found also may differ in task requirements and/or affects generated (e.g., anxiety versus anger). Further, it should be noted that the SI measure of Type A behavior predicts reactivity more strongly than does either the JAS or FTAS. This point is most clearly seen in the results of investigations in which both SI and questionnaire measures of Type A behavior are contained in the same study. Finally, Type A—Type B differences in cardiovascular reactivity are less likely to be found for female than male subjects. This may be explained by women's sex-role expectations concerning their performance in the experimental situation.[13,18,22] Specifically, it has been suggested that Type A—Type B differences in cardiovascular responses are less likely to be found for women when the situation with which they are confronted is not congruent with traditional sex-role expectations for good performance (e.g., working on difficult manual, cognitive, or physically stressful tasks) than when the situation is congruent with sex-role expectations for good performance (e.g., engaging in verbal tasks or interaction).

HOSTILITY, ANGER, AND AGGRESSION

Anger, hostility, and aggression are three interrelated concepts that have been implicated in the development of cardiovascular disease.[26-28] However, there is a fair amount of ambiguity and heterogeneity in the conceptual definitions of these constructs. Anger is generally regarded as an emotional state that involves displeasure, ranging in intensity from mild irritation to rage, and that frequently is accompanied by the impulse to inflict harm.[see references 28-30] Aggression, on the other hand, has been defined as behavior that results in harm to people or objects, and hostility has been defined as an enduring attitude of ill will and a negative view of others.[see 27] The distinction between these latter two concepts is often blurred: aggressive behavior is frequently described as being motivated by anger or hostility, and hostility has been described as leading to angry feelings and motivating aggressive behavior.[28] Probably because of the lack of clear and/or consistent differences in the meanings of the two terms, *aggression* and *hostility* have frequently been used interchangeably.

Several studies have been conducted in which individual difference measures of anger, hostility, or aggression have been related to reactivity. In a study of college males by Holroyd and Gorkin,[31] the relation between the Novaco scale (a measure of self-reported anger to a variety of potentially provoking situations) and cardiovascular reactivity was examined in role-played social interactions. Subjects who obtained *low* scores on the Novaco scale manifested greater SBP and HR responses to the role-play tasks than subjects who obtained high scores on the Novaco scale. Low Novacao scores were viewed by the authors as reflecting inhibition of anger expression, which served to exacerbate cardiovascular reactions to the role-played social situations.

In another study of college males by Harburg,[32] the relationship between self-reported hostility and cardiovascular reactivity to the cold pressor test was examined. In contrast to the Holroyd and Gorkin findings, subjects who reported greater hostility in minor interpersonal conflicts were found to manifest greater DBP responses to the cold pressor test. Hokanson[33] studied blood pressure responses of male college students to mental arithmetic (serial subtraction of 3s) with and without harassment from the experimenter. A measure of "test hostility" was derived from a combination of scores from the Manifest Hostility Scale, three TAT protocols scored for hostile content, and rated unfriendliness toward two individuals in pictures. Subjects high in test hostility responded with greater SBP to the task with harassment than did subjects low in test hostility; no differences were found in the no harassment condition.

Several studies have been conducted in which ratings of hostility derived from the SI assessment of Type A individuals have been related to cardiovascular reactivity. One rating procedure, that for hostile content, focuses exclusively on the content of the interviewee's answers. Another rating procedure for hostility (sometimes referred to as "clinical rating" of hostility or "potential for hostility") focuses on voice stylistics (e.g., surliness, condescension) as well as content.[34]

Dembroski, MacDougall, and associates have conducted several studies in which one or both hostility ratings were related to cardiovascular reactivity. In a study of college males by Dembroski, MacDougall, et al.,[15] subjects' cardiovascular responses to a reaction-time task, an electronic game, and difficult anagrams were assessed. Subjects' SBP and HR responses across the three tasks were found to be significantly correlated with the clinical ratings of hostility. Somewhat similar results were obtained in a study of college women by MacDougall et al. (Study I).[18] Subjects' SBP and HR responses to a reaction-time task were found to be significantly correlated with clinical ratings of hostility. Contrasting results, however, were obtained in another study (Study II) of college women.[18] Subjects' HR responses to a reaction-time task were found to be significantly negatively correlated with the clinical rating of hostility. However, in neither of these studies were significant relationships obtained between ratings of hostile content and measures of cardiovascular reactivity. In another study by Dembroski, MacDougall, et al.,[17] college males performed two tasks, a cold pressor task and a reaction-time task, under high-and low-challenge conditions. The rating of hostile content was found to correlate with DBP responses to the cold pressor task in the low-challenge condition and with SBP responses to the reaction-time task in both the high- and low-challenge conditions.

Cardiovascular responses of adult male coronary and noncoronary patients to the SI itself and during an oral American history quiz were studied by Dembroski et al.[35] Across patient categories, the rating of hostility content was found to be significantly related to SBP responses to the quiz but apparently not to the SI itself. A combined clinical rating for hostility and competition was also examined in this study as well as in the study by Dembroski et al.[17] mentioned above. However, because the contribution of the two constructs, hostility and competition, cannot be disentangled in the results, they will not be considered here. In a study of college women (Study II), MacDougall et al.[18] found the clinical rating of hostility to be significantly related to SBP responses to both the SI and the oral American history quiz.

In a study involving hostility ratings by Glass et al.,[3] the cardiovascular responses of working adult males to a mental arithmetic task (serial subtraction) and a modified Stroop task were examined. Both the clinical rating of hostility and the rating of hostility content were found to be negatively related to DBP responses to the tasks; the clinical rating of hostility was also found to be negatively related to SBP responses to the tasks.

In a study of *cynomolgus* monkeys by Manuck, Kaplan, and Clarkson,[36] relationships among HR responses to threatened capture and physical handling, aggressive behavior, and coronary atherosclerosis were investigated. Monkeys who were high in HR reactivity were rated as more behaviorally aggressive and were found, at autopsy, to have more extensive coronary atherosclerosis.

The studies reviewed above are fairly, though not entirely, consistent in reporting relationships between cardiovascular reactivity and variables that are associated with anger, hostility, and/or aggression. The direction of these relationships, however, is surprisingly inconsistent. Some studies suggest that individuals with *high* scores on the variable exhibit greater cardiovascular reactivity,[15,32,33] while other studies suggest that it is individuals with *low* scores on the variable who exhibit greater cardiovascular reactivity.[3,18] (Study II)

There are at least two possible explanations for the findings of negative relationships between aggression-related variables and cardiovascular reactivity. One is that individuals who obtain high scores on such variables may feel threatened by unforeseen aspects of the experimental situation, withdraw from involvement in it, and thus be relatively less reactive. The second potential explanation is that such negative relationships may be due to oppositional behavior toward the experiment or experimenter by some individuals who obtain high scores on such variables. In other words, such individuals may cooperate less, become less involved, and so on to "hurt" the experiment and/or the experimenter, and thus appear less reactive. If in the sample the proportion of oppositional individuals is large among those who obtain high scores on the measure, or if some unforeseen aspects of the situation elicit oppositional behavior on the part of subjects with high scores, then a negative association may be found between scores on the measure and cardiovascular reactivity.

An explanation that would reconcile findings of both positive and negative relationships between aggression-related variables and reactivity is the following. In the population, there may be a U-shaped relationship between scores on aggression-related variables and cardiovascular reactivity. Individuals who obtain high scores on such variables and a certain proportion of individuals who obtain low scores on such variables may be the more reactive. Some of the individuals who obtain low scores on measures of such variables may deny or suppress aggressive feelings and/or behavior[31] and in fact may be very emotionally volatile, physiologically reactive individuals. In different studies, then, different parts of this U-shaped relationship may be sampled, and/or different studies may contain different proportions of the defensive, low-score individuals. Hence, some studies find negative relationships, and others find positive relationships; still others find no relationships, but they rarely are published because of the bias against publication of nonsignificant results.

DOMINANCE

Dominance is of interest as a potential correlate of cardiovascular reactivity in part because of the association of aggression with dominance/submission, and also because both variables have been implicated in cardiovascular disease.[37] Working within an animal model framework, Kaplan, Manuck, et al.[38] found that dominant monkeys in unstable social environments exhibited more atherosclerosis than submissive monkeys in the same environments or dominant monkeys in stable social environments. However, a significant relationship was not found between dominance/submission and HR responses to threatened capture.[36] It is possible that the stressor employed, that is, threatened capture, was not sufficiently relevant to the construct of dominance/submission to bring out such a relationship.

COMPETITIVENESS

Interest in competitiveness and cardiovascular disease has stemmed largely from research on components of Type A behavior. In a reanalysis of some data from the Western Collaborative Group Study, competitiveness (in particular with peers) was prospectively associated with the incidence of CHD.[39]

Several studies have been conducted in which ratings of competitiveness derived from the SI have been related to cardiovascular reactivity. One such rating is derived from the verbal behavior of the subjects (e.g., verbal duets, interrupting the interviewer),see [34] hence the construct measured by this procedure is probably best construed as verbal competitiveness. Another rating of competitiveness is based on the content of subjects' responses.

In a study of college males by Dembroski, MacDougall, et al.,[15] subjects' SBP responses across a reaction-time task, an electronic game, and a difficult anagrams task were found to be significantly correlated with ratings of verbal competitiveness. However, contrasting results have also been found. In studies of college women by MacDougall, Dembroski, et al.,[18] ratings of verbal competitiveness were not reported to be significantly correlated with cardiovascular responses to a reaction time task in either of two studies, or with cardiovascular responses to the SI itself, or to an oral American history quiz (Study II). Moreover, in a study of working adult males by Glass, Lake, et al.,[3] subjects' cardiovascular responses to a mental arithmetic task and a modified Stroop task were not found to be significantly related to ratings of verbal competitiveness. Additionally, a negative correlation that approached significance ($p < 0.078$) was observed between ratings of verbal competitiveness and DBP responses across the two tasks. In a study of college males by Dembroski, MacDougall, et al.[17] a content rating of competitiveness was found to be significantly related to SBP responses to a reaction-time task in a low- but not high-challenge condition. No significant relationship between cardiovascular responses and the content rating of competition was found for a cold pressor task.

Other scores that have been derived from the SI that contain the term *competition* in their labels have been examined for their possible relationships with cardiovascular reactivity in various studies. However, these results will not be reviewed here because of problems in interpreting the measures.

To illustrate, in some instances, ratings of verbal competitiveness have been combined with ratings of hostility,[17,35] which, as mentioned above, renders interpretation difficult. The conceptual meaning and operationalization of other ratings is unclear; for example, the content rating of competitive drive used by Glass et al.,[3] the content rating of hard-driving competitiveness used by Dembroski, et al.[35]

In sum, the evidence is equivocal concerning a relationship between competitiveness as assessed via the SI and cardiovascular reactivity in men, and the evidence is consistent in showing the lack of such a relationship for women. However, because there is little construct validity for the measure of verbal competitiveness or any other ostensible measure of competitiveness that is derived from the SI, the implications of these findings for the relationship between the concept of competitiveness and reactivity is currently uncertain.

INHIBITED POWER MOTIVATION

Inhibited power motivation is a psychological variable that, akin to Type A behavior, combines elements of aggression and competition and has been found to predict hypertension.[40] Individuals who are characterized by inhibited power motivation are described as being motivated to control others but to inhibit overt expression of aggression. In one of the few prospective studies relating a psychological variable with subsequent elevated blood pressure, McClelland[40] found that a measure of inhibited power motivation significantly predicted elevated SBP and DBP and signs of hypertensive pathology in a group of men 20 years later. However, in a study of working adult males, Glass et al.[3] did not find that a measure of inhibited power motivation was related to subjects' cardiovascular responses to a mental arithmetic task or modified Stroop task. There is reason to believe, however, the experimental arrangement in the Glass et al. study did not engage the power motives of subjects.

ANXIETY

Anxiety has been associated with the development of cardiovascular disease, and in particular, CHD.[41] Further, the relationship between various measures of anxiety and cardiovascular response have been investigated in several studies.

In a study of college males, Hodges[42] did not find a relationship between general anxiety as measured by the Manifest Anxiety Scale and HR responses during a difficult task following threat to self-esteem or during a difficult task in which subjects expected unavoidable shocks. Similarly, in a study of college males Houston[43] did not find a relationship between general anxiety as measured by the trait portion of the State-Trait Anxiety Inventory and HR responses during a memory task that included the threat of shock for mistakes. Male and female college students verbally responded to videotaped questions under either evaluative threat or nonthreat conditions in a study by Smith et al.[44] No relationship was found between general anxiety as measured by the trait portion of the State-Trait Anxiety Inventory and cardiovascular responses to the interview. In a study of working adult males by Glass et al.,[3] general anxiety as measured by the 16 Personality Factor Questionnaire was not found to be related to cardiovascular responses across a mental arithmetic task and a modified Stroop task. However, test anxiety as measured by the Test Anxiety Questionnaire was found to be significantly correlated with SBP, DBP, and HR responses across the two tasks. In contrast to the latter findings, Holroyd, Westbrook, et al.[45] in a study of college women did not find a relation between test anxiety as measured by the Test Anxiety Scale and HR responses during a difficult anagrams task. Knight and Borden[46] studied reactions of college males and females to a verbal task that involved social evaluation. Social anxiety, as measured by the social anxiety subscale of the Activity Preference Questionnaire, was not found to be related to either HR or FPV responses during the evaluative task, though subjects with high social anxiety were found to exhibit lower FPV in anticipation of the task.

In sum, there appears to be little consistent evidence for a direct relationship between measures of anxiety and cardiovascular reactivity. However, research in which defensive underreporting of anxiety has been taken into consideration suggests a different conclusion. In a study of college males by Weinberger et al.,[47] a measure of general anxiety (the Manifest Anxiety Scale) and a measure of defensiveness (the Marlowe-Crowne Social Desirability Scale) were used to identify a nondefensive low-anxious group of subjects, a defensive group who were ostensibly underreporting anxiety (termed "repressors"), and a high-anxious group composed of both defensive and nondefensive high-anxiety subjects. Subjects' HR was monitored while they gave associations to phrases of neutral, sexual, or aggressive content. High-anxious and repressor subjects were found to manifest greater HR responses to the task than low-anxious subjects. In a similar study Asendorpf and Scherer[48] monitored male college students' HR responses during a phrase association task like that of Weinberger et al.[47] and during an amusing film and two neutral films. High-anxious and repressor subjects, defined as in the Weinberger et al. study,[47] were found to exhibit greater HR responses during the phrases association task and the first neutral film than did low-anxious subjects. The findings from these two studies suggest that there is a relationship between general anxiety and cardiovascular reactivity when defensive underreporting of anxiety is taken into account.

COPING MANEUVERS: DENIAL

The term *defensiveness* has been used in two different ways in regard to stress emotions. It has been used to refer to the tendency for some people to report less stress than they experience—in other words, to engage in "verbal denial."see [49] The Social Desirability Scale employed in the studies by Weinberger et al.[47] and by Asendorpf and Scherer[48] is used as a measure of such defensiveness (verbal denial). The term *defensiveness* has also been used to refer to attempts to actually reduce the affective, physiological, and/or behavioral concomitants of stressful emotions—in other words, to engage in maneuvers to reduce stress.

In a study of anxiety-reducing maneuvers in college males, Houston[50] investigated the relationship between scores on the Little-Fisher Denial Scale and cardiovascular reactivity during a memory task under conditions of both avoidable and unavoidable shock. Subjects with low trait denial scores evidenced significantly greater HR reactivity across both shock conditions than did subjects with high trait denial scores. The latter subjects were interpreted as having more effective responses for coping with the stress encountered in the experimental situation.

More research needs to be done on the relation between how people characteristically cope with stress and their cardiovascular responses to stressful situations. Consideration should also be given to the possibility that characteristic ways of coping with stress may moderate the relationship between other psychological variables and cardiovascular reactivity. For example, Type A individuals who have more effective responses for coping with stress may exhibit less cardiovascular reactivity to situations that pose a threat to their sense of mastery than do Type A individuals who have less effective coping responses.

LOCUS OF CONTROL

Locus of control[51] refers to differences in people's beliefs that what happens to them is the result of their own behavior and attitudes (internal control) versus the result of luck, fate, chance, or powerful others (external control). A measure of locus of control has been related to cardiovascular reactivity in several studies. In a study of college males, Houston[52] found that subjects with internal locus of control exhibited greater HR responses during a memory task under conditions of both avoidable and unavoidable shock than did those with external locus of control. In a study of college males, Manuck et al.[53] found that, compared to those with external locus of control, subjects with internal locus of control responded to a difficult concept-formation task with significantly greater SBP responses in one study (Study I); these same differences approached significance in the second study (Study II). In a study of college males by DeGood,[54] subjects were exposed to an aversive shock-avoidance procedure in which the subjects' control over rest periods was varied. Subjects either had control and could temporarily escape the situation by taking a rest period or did not have control and had rest periods imposed on them. The greatest DBP reactivity was observed among subjects with internal locus of control who did not have control over rest periods, and among subjects with external locus of control who did have control over rest periods. Thus, DBP reactivity was greatest when the actual controllability of the aversive situation was incongruent with the individual's general beliefs about locus of control. It should be noted, however, that in the Houston study,[52] HR reactivity was not influenced by incongruity between an individual's locus of control and the actual controllability of shock. Instead, subjects with internal locus of control exhibited greater HR responses independent of the controllability of shock. In sum, then, it appears that individuals with internal locus of control exhibit greater cardiovascular reactivity in various situations though those with external locus of control may exhibit greater DBP reactivity under certain limited circumstances.

INTROVERSION/EXTROVERSION

Briefly, introversion/extroversion[55] reflects the extent to which people are oriented toward their own private experiences (introversion) or toward the external environment and the people and objects around them (extroversion). Eysenck[55] hypothesized that introversion/extroversion is related to differences in the ascending reticular activating system and in cortical arousal. In particular, introverts are hypothesized to be more cortically aroused and to have lower thresholds for responses to sensory stimulation. Thus, one might expect that introverts would exhibit greater reactivity. Indeed, there is some evidence that introverts exhibit greater electrodermal reactivity in various situations,[56] but relatively little evidence exists concerning a possible relation between introversion/extroversion and cardiovascular reactivity.[57] In a study of college males (Study II), Geen[58] investigated the relation between introversion/extroversion as measured by Eysenck's Personality Inventory and HR responses to differing levels of noise. Introverts were found to exhibit greater HR responses than extroverts to noise of intermediate levels, but introverts and extroverts did not differ in HR responses to the most and least intense levels of noise. In contrast, in a study of working adult male subjects, Glass et al.[3] found no relationship between introversion/extroversion as measured by the 16 PF and measures of cardiovascular reactivity to a mental arithmetic task and a modified Stroop task.

RELEVANT BUT UNEXPLORED PSYCHOLOGICAL VARIABLES

There are some psychological variables that have been found to be related to either cardiovascular disease or to risk factors for cardiovascular disease, but which have seldom been investigated for their relationship to reactivity. Jenkins[41] reviewed the research that indicates an association between neuroticism and cardiovascular disease. Theoretically, neuroticism is a promising variable to investigate in relation to reactivity. Eysenck[55] hypothesized that individuals high in neuroticism are characterized by overactive autonomic nervous systems, which one might anticipate would lead them to be more reactive in situations that engaged this psychological dimension. Thus, for both empirical and theoretical reasons, research on the relationship between neuroticism and reactivity seems warranted.

Field dependence/independence is another variable of interest in this regard. Field dependence/independence refers to the kinds of orientations or frameworks people employ in making perceptual judgments. People at one extreme (field independent) rely more on internal frames of reference, while people at the other extreme (field dependent) rely more on external frames of reference in making perceptual judgments.[59] In relation to risk for cardiovascular disease, field-dependent individuals have been found to have higher levels of serum cholesterol than field-independent individuals.[60,61]

In an investigation of male and female medical students, McCranie et al.[62] studied the interaction of field dependence/independence and Type A in predicting subjects' levels of serum lipids. It was found that JAS-defined Type A individuals who are field dependent had the highest levels of cholesterol and low-density lipoprotein. One interpretation of these findings was that field dependent Type A individuals were more autonomically aroused. However, whether field dependence/independence interacts with Type A behavior in predicting reactivity awaits further investigation.

CONCLUSIONS, GENERAL CONSIDERATIONS, AND RECOMMENDATIONS

The available evidence suggests that under appropriate eliciting conditions the Type A behavior pattern is related to neuroendocrine and cardiovascular reactivity. Furthermore, the following psychological variables are related to cardiovascular reactivity: (1) aggression-related variables (viz., angerability, hostility, and aggressiveness), but as noted, the nature of the relationships, whether positive or negative, is at present unclear; (2) anxiety, if defensive underreporting of anxiety is taken into consideration; and (3) locus of control. The available evidence does not indicate that verbal competitiveness as assessed from the SI is related to reactivity. Based on research and/or theory several psychological variables appear promising as potential correlates of reactivity (viz., denial, dominance, inhibited power motivation, introversion/extroversion, and neuroticism) and/or as potential moderators of the relationships between reactivity and other variables (denial, field dependence/independence, etc.). However, there is at present insufficient evidence concerning these variables to draw any conclusions, and further investigation is definitely warranted.

Several issues and recommendations need to be considered in conducting future research on psychological correlates of reactivity, particularly in the context of predicting cardiovascular disease. An essential consideration for experimental research is the conceptual or theoretical relevance of the experimental situation for the psychological variable in question. As described earlier, a possible reason why no relationship was found between dominance and HR reactivity in the study by Manuck et al.[36] and no relationship was found between inhibited power motivation and reactivity in the study by Glass et al.[3] is that the experimental manipulations were not conceptually relevant to the constructs in question. It is very unlikely that a psychological variable will be related to reactivity in every situation. Rather, psychological variables can be expected to interact with situational demands in influencing reactivity. Most of the studies mentioned above did not include more than one experimental situation; thus, the importance of possible interaction effects has not been made as salient as it should be. Because a good deal of research has been conducted on the relation between Type A behavior and reactivity, Type A–Type B by situation interactions have received more attention. For example, studies in which more than one experimental condition was employed have found that differences in reactivity between Type A and Type B individuals varied as a function of harassment during competition[8] and perceived task difficulty.[12]

Naturalistic, nonexperimental studies of the relationships between psychological variables and reactivity call for a similar consideration of situational features. For example, Type A–Type B differences in psychophysiological arousal during working hours are most likely influenced by the degree of challenge or competition involved. Further, hostile individuals would be expected to have more frequent and/or intense psychophysiological responses to work and/or domestic situations that included more potential for frustration, interpersonal conflict, and the like. Prospective studies of cardiovascular disease that include measures of psychological variables should increase in their power for predicting incidence of cardiovascular disease by including measures of the life situations that people face and by including interactions between psychological and situational variables in their prediction equations.

Mention of naturalistic studies underscores the desirability of extending investigations of relationships between psychological variables and reactivity beyond laboratory paradigms. The generalizability of relationships obtained in the laboratory needs to be empirically demonstrated. Relevant to this issue, there is preliminary evidence indicating that measures of reactivity obtained in the laboratory correlate with measures of reactivity obtained in natural settings.[63,64] Despite the value of such research, it alone does not establish the generalizability of relationships between psychological variables and reactivity obtained in the laboratory (see chapter by Krantz, Manuck, and Wing).

It would be advantageous to the experimental rigor of naturalistic studies to use settings in which the eliciting circumstance can be fairly well specified, for example, anticipating, during, or following experiences such as medical procedures, public presentations or performances, and evaluative situations such as examinations or standardized job interviews. Additionally, much can be learned from the use of ambulatory monitoring of cardiovascular variables, which, when accompanied by journals of daily activities, allow a rough study of the correlation of subjects' daily experiences with cardiovascular reactions. Although somewhat lacking in experimental rigor, such a procedure allows the investigator to examine various expected relations. For example, the relationship between hostility and cardiovascular arousal can be studied in situations of varying levels of interpersonal conflict.

Most of the research in which psychological variables have been related to measures of reactivity have employed white males who are predominantly college-aged and from the middle class. As a result, little is known about the psychological correlates of reactivity in individuals who are female, nonwhite, and/or from other ages and socioeconomic classes (see chapter by Watkins and Eaker). Thus, future studies of relationships between psychological variables and reactivity should take into consideration and preferably investigate systematically the possible effects of such demographic variables as gender, age, socioeconomic status, and ethnicity on such relationships.

Demographic variables may have artifactual as well as genuine effects on relationships between psychological variables and reactivity. For instance, demographic variables may influence subjects' perceptions of the experimental situation. For example, the perceived sex-role appropriateness of an experimental task may influence how involved men or women become with the task and hence influence their potential reactivity.[see 22] Moreover, demographic variables may influence subjects' cooperation and motivation. For example, it is unlikely that the motivation of an 18-year-old college student when asked to perform a difficult mental arithmetic task (e.g., serial subtraction of 7s) will be the same as that of an 18-year-old, educationally disadvantaged, inner-city youth. These problems point to the potential need for adjusting the experimental situation to match the characteristics of individuals from different subject populations. Moreover, these problems indicate that it may not be possible to employ psychologically standard or uniform tasks in an epidemiological study whose subjects are heterogeneous with regard to demographic variables.

Demographic variables may influence cardiovascular reactivity. Take, for example, gender. There is evidence that womens' cardiovascular responsivity varies with phases of the menstrual cycle.[see 65,66] These findings suggest that, to the extent possible, cardiovascular reactivity in women should be assessed with knowledge of the phase of each subject's menstrual cycle at the time of testing or, ideally, at a common point in the cycles of all participating women.

Demographic variables may also influence measurement of the psychological variables. For example, age, gender, socioeconomic class, or ethnicity may influence how self-report items are interpreted and therefore answered. Thus, special care needs to be taken to insure that psychological measures are valid for different subject populations.

Three other issues concerning measurement need to be considered in future studies of psychological variables and reactivity. One is that within a given study, multiple methods of measuring a psychological variable should be employed. For example, some studies of Type A individuals and reactivity have benefited from employing both observational (the SI) and questionnaire methods of measuring A/B Type.[15-18] Furthermore, it would be desirable to include measures of multiple psychological variables in each study. For example, measures of Type A behavior, anxiety, introversion/extroversion, and inhibited power motivation were obtained by Glass et al.[3] Most of the studies reviewed above investigated a single psychological variable—just Type A behavior, just anxiety, and so on. Since studies that obtain significant relationships are more likely to be published than studies that do not obtain significant relationships, some of the relationships reported in the literature may be spurious, hence the strength and breadth of the relationships between psychological variables and reactivity may be exaggerated by a review of the published research. If studies were to include measures of multiple psychological variables that are relevant to the experimental situation—and assuming that such studies will be published because one or more of the relationships would be found to be significant—then the aggregate literature would provide a better perspective on the strength and breadth of relationships between psychological variables and reactivity. (However, this is not a foolproof suggestion since otherwise well-done studies that find no or few significant relationships are at a competitive disadvantage for being published and hence will not have the corrective effect on the aggregate literature that they should have.) Lastly, it would be desirable to include measures of neuroendocrine reactivity. As mentioned earlier, apart from research on Type A and Type B individuals, investigations of enduring psychological characteristics have rarely included measures of neuroendocrine activity.

A final issue for research concerns how a psychological variable and its relationship with reactivity fit into the etiological model of a cardiovascular disease. There are at least two possibilities. One is that neither the psychological variable nor reactivity is causally linked with cardiovascular disease, but either or both may be correlated with (a marker for) a factor or process that is causally linked with cardiovascular disease. For example, reactivity or a psychological variable or both may be correlated with a pathogenic behavior (e.g., smoking) or a pathogenic biological factor (e.g., family history of hypertension). A second possibility is that reactivity and/or a given psychological variable may play a role in a causal chain leading to a cardiovascular disease. It should be noted that if a psychological variable, but not the reactivity associated with it, plays a role in a causal chain (e.g., in leading individuals to engage in high-risk health behaviors), then the reactivity associated with that psychological variable would become a marker variable. The converse is true as well.

In designing epidemiological research, it is important to develop a priori conceptualizations of how psychological variables and reactivity fit into an etiological model for cardiovascular disease. Such conceptualizations will determine what variables to include in the study. Although measurement of many potentially important variables may fairly frequently be included in epidemiological studies, others may not (sodium retention under stress, response stereotypy, etc.).[see 67] Thus, the way one conceptualizes how the relationship between a psychological variable and reactivity fits into the etiological model of a cardiovascular disease may lead to the inclusion of measures of variables that might not otherwise be included.

Moreover, one's conceptualization of the etiological model would influence the nature of the statistical analyses that would be applied to the data. Most epidemiological studies of CHD have assessed the predictive power of psychological variables singly, after controlling for other variables. As Meehl[68] has argued eloquently, decisions as to whether one does or does not control for a variable should depend on the explicit conceptualization of how the variable fits into an etiological model. Moreover, statistical procedures exist, namely, path analysis and structural models,[see 69] for evaluating different etiological models. The state of epidemiological research will be advanced by a more careful consideration of epidemiological models, particularly when psychological variables are included. This will allow science to more properly evaluate the role(s) that psychological variables, as well as reactivity, play or do not play in the development of cardiovascular disease.

REFERENCES

1. Krantz DS, Manuck SB: Measures of acute physiologic reactivity to behavioral stimuli: Assessment and critique. In *Proceedings of the NHLBI Workshop on Measuring Psychosocial Variables in Epidemiologic Studies of Cardiovascular Diseases*. Bethesda, MD, NHLBI Pub. No. 85-2270, 1985, pp. 407–451.

2. Bloom LJ, Houston BK, Burish TG: An evaluation of finger pulse volume as a psychophysiological measure of anxiety. *Psychophysiology* 13:40–42, 1976.

3. Glass CD, Lake CR, et al: Stability of individual differences in physiological responses to stress. *Health Psychol* 2:317–341, 1983.

4. Rosenman RH: The interview method of assessment of the coronary-prone behavior pattern. In Dembroski TM, Weiss S, et al (eds): *Coronary-Prone Behavior*. New York, Springer-Verlag, 1978, pp. 55–69.

5. Jenkins CD: A comparative review of the interview and questionnaire methods in the assessment of the coronary-prone behavior pattern. In Dembroski TM, Weiss S, et al (eds): *Coronary-Prone Behavior*. New York, Springer-Verlag, 1978, pp. 71–88.

6. Haynes SG, Levine S, et al: The relationship of psychosocial factors to coronary heart disease in the Framingham study: I. Methods and risk factors. *Am J Epidemiol* 107:362–383, 1978.

7. Friedman M, Byers SO, et al: Plasma catecholamine response of coronary-prone subjects (Type A) to a specific challenge. *Metabolism* 24:205–210, 1975.

8. Glass DC, Krakoff LR, et al: Effect of harassment and competition upon cardiovascular and plasma catecholamine responses in Type A and Type B individuals. *Psychophysiology* 17:453–463, 1980.

9. Glass DC, Krakoff LR, et al: Effect of task overload upon cardiovascular and plasma catecholamine responses in Type A and B individuals. *Basic Appl Soc Psychol* 1:199–218, 1980.

10. Contrada RJ, Glass DC, et al: Effects of control over aversive stimulation and Type A behavior on cardiovascular and plasma catecholamine response. *Psychophysiology* 19:408–419, 1982.

11. Manuck SB, Garland FN: Coronary-prone behavior pattern, task incentive and cardiovascular response. *Psychophysiology* 16:136–147, 1979.

12. Gastrof JW: Physiologic reaction of Type A's to objective and subjective challenge. *J Human Stress* 7:16–20, 1982.

13. Jorgensen RS, Houston BK: The Type A behavior pattern, sex differences, and cardiovascular response to and recovery from stress. *Motiv Emot* 5:201–214, 1982.

14. Lane JD, White AD, Williams Jr. RB: Cardiovascular effects of mental arithmetic in Type A and Type B females. *Psychophysiology* 21:39–46, 1984.

15. Dembroski TM, MacDougall JM, et al: Components of the Type A coronary-prone behavior pattern and cardiovascular responses to psychomotor performance challenge. *J Behav Med* 1:159–176, 1978.

16. Corse CD, Manuck SB, et al: Coronary-prone behavior pattern and cardiovascular response in persons with and without coronary heart disease. *Psychosom Med* **44**:449–459, 1982.

17. Dembroski TM, MacDougall JM, et al: Effects of level of challenge on pressor and heart rate responses in Type A and B subjects. *J Appl Soc Psychol* **9**:209–228, 1979.

18. MacDougall JM, Dembroski TM, Krantz DS: Effects of type of challenge on pressor and heart rate responses in Type A and B women. *Psychophysiology* **18**:1–9, 1981.

19. Lawler KA, Schmied L, et al: Type A behavior and physiological responsivity in young women. *J Psychosom Res* **28**:197–204, 1984.

20. Dembroski TM, MacDougall JM, et al: Perspectives on coronary-prone behavior patterns. In Krantz DS, Baum A, Singer JE (eds): *Handbook of Psychology and Health.* Hillsdale, NJ, Erlbaum, 1983, pp. 57–83.

21. Holmes DS: An alternative perspective concerning the differential psychophysiological responsivity of persons with the Type A and Type B behavior patterns. *J Res Pers* **17**:40–47, 1983.

22. Houston BK: Psychophysiological responsivity and the Type A behavior pattern. *J Res Pers* **17**:22–39, 1983.

23. Krantz DS, Glass DC, et al: Behavior patterns and coronary disease: A critical evaluation. In Cacioppo JT, Petty RE (eds): *Perspectives on Cardiovascular Psychophysiology.* New York, Guilford, 1983, pp. 315–346.

24. Matthews KA: Psychological perspectives on the Type A behavior pattern. *Psychol Bull* **91**:293–323, 1982.

25. Wright RA, Contrada RJ, Glass DC: Psychophysiologic correlates of Type A behavior. In Katkin ES, Manuck SB (eds): *Advances in Behavioral Medicine.* Greenwich, CT, JAI, 1984, pp. 39–88.

26. Appel MA, Holroyd KA, Gorkin L: Anger and the etiology and progression of physical illness. In Temoshok L, Van Dyke C, Zegans LS (eds): *Emotions in Health and Illness: Theoretical and Research Foundations.* New York, Grune & Stratton, 1983, pp. 73–87.

27. Matthews KA: Assessment of Type A, anger, and hostility in epidemiological studies of cardiovascular disease. Paper presented at the NIH workshop, "Measuring Psychosocial Variables in Epidemiological Studies of Cardiovascular Disease." Galveston, TX, December, 1983.

28. Spielberger CD, Jacobs G, et al: Assessment of anger: The State-Trait Anger Scale. In Butcher JN, Spielberger CD (eds): *Advances in Personality Assessment* (Vol. 2). Hillsdale, NJ. Erlbaum, 1983, pp. 159–187.

29. Izard CE: *Human Emotions.* New York, Plenum, 1977.

30. Kaufmann H: *Aggression and Altruism.* New York, Holt, Rinehart & Winston, 1970.

31. Holroyd KA, Gorkin L: Young adults at risk for hypertension: Effects of family history and anger management in determining responses to interpersonal conflict. *J Psychosom Res* **27**:131–138, 1983.

32. Harburg E: Covert Hostility: Its Social Origins and Relationship to Overt Compliance. Unpublished doctoral dissertation, University of Michigan, 1962.

33. Hokanson JE: Vascular and psychogalvanic effects of experimentally aroused anger. *J Pers* **29**:30–39, 1961.

34. Dembroski TM: Reliability and validity of methods used to assess coronary-prone behavior. In Dembroski TM, Weiss SM, et al (eds):*Coronary-Prone Behavior.* New York, Springer-Verlag, 1978, pp. 95–106.

35. Dembroski TM, MacDougall JM, Lushene R: Interpersonal interaction and cardiovascular responses in Type A subjects and coronary patients. *J Human Stress* **5**:28–36, 1979.

36. Manuck SB, Kaplan JR, Clarkson TB: Behaviorally induced heart rate reactivity and atherosclerosis in cynomolgus monkeys. *Psychosom Med* **45**:95–108, 1983.

37. Weiner H: *Psychobiology of Essential Hypertension.* New York, Elsevier, 1979.

38. Kaplan JR, Manuck SB, et al: Social status, environment, and atherosclerosis in cynomolgus monkeys. *Arteriosclerosis* **2**:359–368, 1982.

39. Matthews KA, Glass DC: Competitive drive, Pattern A, and coronary heart disease: A further analysis of some data from the Western Collaborative Group Study. *J Chronic Dis* **30**:489–498, 1977.

40. McClelland DC: Inhibited power motivation and high blood pressure in men. *J Abnorm Psychol* **88**:182–190, 1979.

41. Jenkins CD: Recent evidence supporting psychologic and social risk factors for coronary disease. *N Engl J Med* **294**:987–994; 1033–1038, 1976.

42. Hodges WF: Effects of ego threat and threat of pain on state anxiety. *J Pers Soc Psychol* **8**:364–372, 1968.

43. Houston BK: Dispositional anxiety and the effectiveness of cognitive coping strategies in stressful laboratory and classroom situations. In Spielberger CD, Sarason IG (eds): *Stress and Anxiety* (Vol 4). Washington, DC, Hemisphere, 1977, pp. 205–226.

44. Smith, TW, Houston BK, Zurawski RM: Irrational beliefs and the arousal of emotional distress. *J Counsel Psychol* **31**:190–201, 1984.

45. Holroyd KA, Westbrook T, et al: Performance, cognition, and physiological responding in test anxiety. *J Abnorm Psychol* **87**:442–451, 1978.

46. Knight ML, Borden RJ: Autonomic and affective reactions of high and low socially-anxious individuals awaiting public performance. *Psychophysiology* **16**:209–213, 1979.

47. Weinberger DA, Schwartz GE, Davidson RJ: Low-anxious, high-anxious, and repressive coping styles: Psychometric patterns and behavioral and physiological responses to stress. *J Abnorm Psychol* **88**:369–380, 1979.

48. Asendorpf JB, Scherer KR: The discrepant repressor: Differentiation between low anxiety, high anxiety, and repression of anxiety by autonomic-facial-verbal patterns of behavior. *J Pers Soc Psychol* **45**:1334–1346, 1983.

49. Houston BK: Anxiety, defensiveness, and differential prediction of performance in stress and nonstress conditions. *J Pers Soc Psychol* **17**:66–68, 1971.

50. Houston BK: Viability of coping strategies, denial, and response to stress. *J Pers* **41**:50–58, 1973.

51. Rotter J: Generalized expectancies for internal versus external control of reinforcement. *Psychol Monog* **80**(1, Whole No. 609), 1966.

52. Houston BK: Control over stress, locus of control, and response to stress. *J Pers Soc Psychol* **21**:249–255, 1972.

53. Manuck SB, Craft S, Gold KJ: Coronary-prone behavior pattern and cardiovascular response. *Psychophysiology* **15**:403–411, 1978.

54. DeGood DE: Cognitive control factors in vascular stress responses. *Psychophysiology* **12**:399–401, 1975.

55. Eysenck HJ: *The Biological Bases of Personality.* Springfield, IL, Thomas, 1967.

56. Stelmack RM: The psychophysiology of extraversion and neuroticism. In Eysenck HJ (ed): *A Model of Personality.* New York, Springer-Verlag, 1981, pp. 38–64.

57. Geen RG: The psychophysiology of extraversion-introversion. In Cacioppo JT, Petty RE (eds): *Social Psychophysiology.* New York, Guilford, 1983, pp. 391–416.

58. Geen RG: Preferred stimulation levels in introverts and extraverts: Effects on arousal and performance. *J Pers Soc Psychol* **46**:1303–1312, 1984.

59. Goodenough DR: Field dependence. In London H, Exner Jr. JE (eds): *Dimensions of Personality.* New York: Wiley, 1978, pp. 165–216.

60. Flemenbaum A, Anderson RP: Field dependence and blood cholesterol: An expansion. *Percept Mot Skills* **46**:867–874, 1978.

61. Flemenbaum A, Flemenbaum E: Field dependence, blood uric acid and cholesterol. *Percept Mot Skills* **41**:135–141, 1975.

62. McCranie EW, Simpson ME, Stevens JS: Type A behavior, field dependence, and serum lipids. *Psychosom Med* **43**:107–116, 1981.

63. Dembroski TM, MacDougall JM: Behavioral and psychophysiological perspectives on coronary-prone behavior. In Dembroski TM, Schmidt TH, Blumchen G (eds): *Biobehavioral Bases of Coronary Heart Disease.* Basel, Karger, 1983, pp. 106–129.

64. Manuck SB, Giordani B, et al: Generalizability of individual differences in heart rate reactivity. Unpublished manuscript, Bowman Gray School of Medicine, 1980.

65. Light KC: Cardiovascular responses to effortful active coping: Implications for the role of stress in hypertension development. *Psychophysiology* **18**:216–225, 1981.

66. Little BC, Zahn TP: Changes in mood and autonomic functioning during the menstrual cycle. *Psychophysiology* **11**:579–590, 1974.

67. Light KC, Koepke JP, et al: Psychological stress induces sodium and fluid retention in men at high risk for hypertension. *Science* **110**:429–431, 1983.

68. Meehl PE: High school yearbooks: A reply to Schwarz. *J Abnorm Psychol* **77**:143–144, 1971.

69. Bentler PM: Multivariate analysis with latent variables: Causal modeling. *Ann Rev Psychol* **31**:419–456, 1980.

12

Population and Demographic Influences on Reactivity

LAURENCE O. WATKINS and ELAINE EAKER

Epidemiologic studies have revealed variations in the prevalence and incidence of the major cardiovascular diseases, coronary heart disease and hypertension, in different population groups and in groups of individuals defined on the basis of certain demographic characteristics. Variables that have been important in this regard include age, gender, racial or ethnic origin, marital status, and socioeconomic factors such as level of education, income, occupation, place of residence, and social mobility. Investigations of

The authors gained valuable insights from extensive groups discussion with Richard Rose, Alexander Aleksandrov, Katherine Detre, Clarence Grim, George Kaplan, Robert Levenson, Barbara McCann, and Richard Surwit. Sherman James offered valuable criticisms of an earlier draft of this chapter. The expert editorial assistance of Teresa Williams is gratefully acknowledged.

231

the relationships among stress, reactivity, and cardiovascular disease should take account of population-demographic variables because such an approach might delineate important aspects of the reactivity-disease relationship. This approach is justified for the following reasons:

1. Demographic characteristics and population group membership may serve as markers for common processes that determine reactivity.
2. Differences in reactivity among population groups or groups of individuals with different demographic characteristics may help to explain differences in the cardiovascular disease experiences of these groups.
3. Population-demographic group membership may modify the putative impact of reactivity on cardiovascular disease; *or* group membership, reactivity, and exposure to other risk factors may act in a synergistic manner to influence the development or progression of cardiovascular disease.

The relationship between reactivity and cardiovascular disease is currently unclear. Therefore, it is important initially to clarify the relationship of population-demographic characteristics to reactivity. To facilitate this, reactivity must be defined and the different ways in which it can be measured should be recognized. Reactivity results from a complex interaction among central nervous system activation and control, neuroendocrine responsiveness, renal function, and cardiovascular end-organ receptor sensitivity. Responses of different organs or organ systems should be assessed independently. Thus, measures of reactivity might include hormone levels and clearance rates, electrolyte or solute excretion rates, heart rate and blood pressure changes, as well as measures of nervous system function such as the galvanic skin response and sudomotor responsiveness. Because cultural influences specific to certain population-demographic groups may influence responses to standardized psychological stressors, reactivity should also be tested with "physiologic" challenges as far as is possible. In certain gender subgroups or in certain ethnic groups in specific sociocultural settings, the use of standardized psychological stressors may also yield valuable insights. However, it may be impossible to devise culturally neutral cognitive challenges.

This chapter takes the following approach to population-demographic variables: First, the relationship between the variable and cardiovascular disease is reviewed briefly. Next, the available evidence on the relationship between the variable and reactivity is examined. The problem of defining or operationalizing the variable is addressed, then specific additional descriptors that might be important in the study of reactivity are considered and problem areas for such studies are identified.

AGE

Relationship to Cardiovascular Disease

An individual's age is a well-known determinant of cardiovascular disease risk. In industrialized societies [1] and in many nonindustrialized societies, [2,3], mean blood pressures rise with age. Similarly, the prevalence of hypertension (pressures greater than an arbitrarily defined limit) [4] rises with age in the adult population. The observed cross-sectional rise in blood pressure with age is so well known that it is commonly accepted as normal. [5] However, cross-sectional evaluations in many nonindustrialized societies have revealed blood pressures at low normal levels in subjects of all ages. [6] In addition, blood pressure remains unchanged over relatively long periods in a large proportion of adults in industrialized societies. [7] For example, in the Thousand Aviator study, [8] in over half of the group followed for over 24 years in middle adulthood, there was no systemic rise in systolic blood pressure. In contrast to the findings among adults, blood pressure has been shown to increase with age in infants and children in both industrialized and nonindustrialized societies. This suggests that it is a universal phenomenon and is a natural consequence of growth or biological maturation. [9]

The prevalence and incidence of coronary heart disease increase with age in industrialized societies, and though the incidence is lower in nonindustrialized societies, a similar age-related phenomenon appears to be present. [10] Autopsy studies in a variety of locations have revealed that the atherosclerotic process appears to begin in childhood and adolescence, and severe atherosclerotic lesions may be present in young adults. [11,12]

Investigations of the pathogenesis of essential hypertension suggest that it is a heterogeneous group of diseases characterized by varying disorders of blood pressure regulation. Neuroendocrine, renal, and vascular factors all appear to contribute to the development and maintenance of elevated blood pressure. [13] Cardiovascular regulation changes during the different developmental phases of hypertension. Lund-Johansen [14] observed that in hypertensive young adults in the age range of 17–29 years, cardiac output was high and peripheral resistance was not significantly different from that in control subjects, while in hypertensives over 30 years of age, the total peripheral resistance was significantly higher than in the controls, while the cardiac output was similar to that of controls. An evolution from a "high flow–normal resistance" to a "high flow–high resistance" and a "normal flow–high resistance" pattern to a "low flow–high resistance pattern" was postulated. However, similar invasive studies in young subjects (mean age 14.5 years) have revealed that elevated total peripheral resistance may account for elevated blood pressure levels, though it is unclear whether this study is truly the initial state of the disease. [15]

Age and Reactivity

There is abundant evidence from comparisons of young and old subjects under similar conditions to support the assertion that there are age-related changes in neuroendocrine activity with aging.[16] For example, there are age-related declines in plasma renin activity and aldosterone excretion.[17,18] In addition, interest has recently focused on changes in sympathetic nervous system activity and cardiovascular responsiveness with increasing age. The review by Rowe and Troen[16] includes important methodological observations concerning assessment of sympathetic nervous system activity under basal conditions and in response to hemodynamic stimuli. Circulating plasma norepinephrine probably is derived largely from sympathetic nerves innervating vascular walls, and venous plasma norepinephrine levels appear to provide a useful estimate of average sympathetic outflow.[19] However, this is an area of controversy, and Folkow, Di Bona, and coworkers suggest that because of variation of norepinephrine levels in different vascular beds, sampling from a variety of sites may be necessary to clarify the relationships between norepinephrine levels and sympathetic activity.[20] The available data indicate that among normotensive subjects, plasma norepinephrine levels increase significantly with age.[21,22] However, Goldstein, Lake, and coworkers[22] have shown that young hypertensive subjects tend to have relatively high plasma norepinephrine levels, and when hypertensive subjects are examined, no age-related increase is observed. There are many theoretical reasons to believe that the sympathetic nervous system is implicated in the development and maintenance of elevated blood pressures,[23] and Goldstein, Lake, and coworkers[22] have suggested that "further studies are required in relatively young subjects with essential hypertension and age-matched controls to determine how—or whether—enhanced sympathetic nervous system activity in this age group *causes* high blood pressure." In such studies, account must be taken of the caveats concerning variation in norepinephrine levels in different vascular beds.[20]

In older normotensive subjects, despite higher norepinephrine levels there is less exercise-induced tachycardia and greater blood pressure response to exercise than in younger subjects, differences that are magnified in hypertensive subjects.[21] In addition, there is an age-related decrease in cardiovascular response to isoproterenol stimulation,[21,24,25] which implies a decrease in beta-adrenoreceptor function. Studies of blood vessels[26] and the myocardium[27,28] of animals and of lymphocytes in man[29] suggest that this is at least partially the consequence of decreased vascular sensitivity to intracellular levels of cyclic nucleotides and/or altered intracellular mechanisms of calcium ion transport, factors affected by isoproterenol stimulation. In addition, it has been suggested that while the vasodilator response to beta-adrenergic stimuli decreases, alpha-1 adrenoreceptor-mediated vaso-constriction may increase with age. The animal data are conflicting in this regard,[26] though there are age-related increases in alpha-adrenoreceptor-mediated human platelet aggregation.[30] However, Scott has reported no variation with age in the response of isolated human arteries to norepinephrine.[31]

Activity of the parasympathetic arm of the autonomic nervous system, which can be measured only indirectly in humans, probably also declines with age. This may be inferred from the decline in variability of resting heart rate with age.[32]

Though measurement of reactivity reveals differences between subjects in different age groups, these measurements may not have prognostic or predictive significance. For example, vascular reactivity to the cold pressor test was not a predictor of subsequent blood pressure change in either a three-to-seven-year follow-up of a sample of children and adolescents aged 5–19[33], or a group of 385 men followed for 18 years in the Thousand Aviator study.[34] Vascular reactivity to the cold pressor test has been shown to be less in young subjects than in old ones.[35] Palmer and coworkers observed a progressively larger response of blood pressure and pulse to cold stress with increasing age and a parallel increase in plasma norepinephrine levels.

On the basis of studies on infants followed from birth to 16 months of age, Schachter and coworkers[36,37] have suggested that because of an inverse association between the child's heart rate and the parent's blood pressure, a low heart rate in the child might be a good index of risk of adult hypertension. Heart rate reactivity was not assessed in this study. However, the work of Campos and coworkers[38] and Schwartz and coworkers[39] on heart rate responses of prelocomotor (5 months) and locomotor (9 months) infants placed on the visual cliff demonstrates a developmental shift. The younger infants manifest heart rate deceleration to this visual stress, and the older infants heart rate acceleration. The latter authors[39] postulated that the cardiac acceleration observed in the older infants was indicative of defen-siveness, fear, or the "fight or flight" response. The significance of this manifestation of cardiovascular reactivity is unclear.

Definition and Additional Descriptors

While a simple biological or chronological definition of age may appear adequate for studies of adults, it may not be adequate for studies of children and adolescents. There is evidence from a variety of studies that in evalua-tions of the relationship between age and blood pressure during adolescent development, account should be taken of such factors as pubertal development,[40] height, weight, skeletal age, and other indices of body maturation.[41,42] It is plausible that reactivity might also be affected by such factors, and they should be included in the design of studies of adolescents. In addition, cross-sectional studies of adults may be confounded by cohort effects. Prospective evaluation would help to minimize these effects.

GENDER

Relationship to Cardiovascular Disease

Epidemiologic studies reveal that myocardial infarction and sudden death occur 10–20 years later in women than in men.[43] In older women the incidence of coronary heart disease appears not to have a simple relationship to age but to be related also to the cessation of menstruation.[44]

Longitudinal Framingham data show a steady increase of systolic and diastolic blood pressure with age among men and women.[45] Cross-sectional U.S. studies have demonstrated that blood pressure levels are higher in men than in women, except that the levels in postmenopausal women surpass those of men of the same age.[46] The difference between the longitudinal and the cross-sectional data may be due to differential mortality of men with elevated blood pressures.

When the risk factors for coronary heart disease among women and men are compared, there is a large amount of overlap. Some studies have shown glucose intolerance to be a significant risk factor for coronary heart disease among women but not among men,[47] but this is not a uniform finding.[48] Even when account is taken of the recognized risk factors—systolic blood pressure, cigarette smoking, serum cholesterol, relative weight, and glucose intolerance—men have two to three times greater risk of developing coronary disease than women.[49]

Because of the large gender differential in coronary heart disease, one might speculate that if reactivity were a risk factor, there might be a gender differential for physiological reactivity to various stressors.

Gender and Reactivity

Only a few studies have examined gender differences and similarities in cardiac and neuroendocrine responsiveness to various stressors. In addition, there is a paucity of information on variation of women's physiological reactivity with the menstrual cycle, menopausal status, hormonal therapy, and oral contraceptive use. However, in the studies that have examined both females and males, a certain consistency is apparent and further systematic study is warranted.

Von Eiff, Wilhelm, and coworkers[50] have detected effects of exogenous and endogenous estrogens and progestins on blood pressure responses to stress in normotensive women. In a group of ovariectomized women, they observed significantly greater changes in systolic blood pressure response during mental arithmetic in those treated with long-acting estrogens or a combination of estrogens and progestins than in a placebo-treated group. In normally menstruating women, a significant inverse relationship between the degree of estrogenic activity in the preovulatory phase of the cycle and the systolic blood pressure response to mental arithmetic was observed only among 31-to-40-year-old women.

The research of Frankenhaeuser and coworkers demonstrates that important gender differences exist in neuroendocrine responses in male and female university students.[51] During rest and relaxation, sex differences in catecholamine excretion are slight, but in challenging performance situations consistent differences appear. For stress induced by intelligence testing, a color-word conflict task, and venipuncture, females show a lack of adrenaline increase, while males show a significant rise. These researchers also looked at a "real-life" stress situation (a six-hour examination for matriculating from high school). They found that females increased their adrenaline secretion, but the rise was significantly higher for males. It is important to note that females did not perform less efficiently than males on any of the above tests; however, self-reports showed males had increased feelings of success and confidence, while females reported feelings of discomfort and failure.

Elevated blood pressure levels appear to have different effects on cognitive function in men and women. Shapiro, Miller, and coworkers[52] have found that among mild hypertensives, women perform mental tasks with lower speed and accuracy than men at the same level of blood pressure. These effects are diminished after administration of antihypertensive medications.

Similarities in adrenaline secretion have been found in males and females who fill similar social roles.[53] For example, women in "nontraditional" roles tend to respond to achievement demands by an increase in adrenaline secretion that is similar in degree to that of males. Women engineering students, bus drivers, and lawyers who perform the same tasks as males show adrenaline excretion similar to males in response to a cognitive-conflict task.

Frankenhaeuser maintains that the physiological response to stress is based on learned coping responses.[53] She examined the reactivity of females challenged in the so-called female areas of competence (home, family, children). When mothers and fathers took their 3-year-old child to the hospital, women secreted at least as much adrenaline, noradrenaline, and cortisol as men. Frankenhaeuser speculates that girls are trained to be more flexible in responding to situational challenges and to discriminate more closely among various cues than boys. Boys tend to be more consistently achievement-oriented in a variety of situations and invariably respond by increasing catecholamine secretion.

Although it has been shown that plasma cortisol is constant throughout the menstrual cycle,[54] there is evidence that there is fluctuation in cortisol levels in relation to stress over the menstrual cycle. Marinari and coworkers studied the effect of psychological stress on adrenocortical reactivity during the premenstrual and midcycle phases of women who were either using or not using oral contraceptives.[55] They found that women tested in the premenstrual phase exhibited greater adrenocortical reactivity to psychological stress than those tested at midcycle. The women who were taking oral contraceptives (all were "combination" pills) did not exhibit this premenstrual increase in physiological reactivity to psychological stress. All subjects reported equivalent affective responses to the stress situation, regardless of cycle status or use of oral contraceptives. As a check for constancy in plasma cortisol levels, the researchers measured the baseline cortisol levels in two additional groups, at midcycle and in the premenstrual phase. There was no difference in plasma cortisol between premenstrual and midcycle status.

To address the question of whether catecholamine output is related to estrogen level, Collins, Hanson, and coworkers examined the psychophysiological stress responses in postmenopausal women before and after hormonal replacement therapy.[56] Because younger women show a consistently smaller increase of adrenaline output than males when exposed to achievement stress, it was hypothesized that estrogen might have an inhibitory effect on catecholamine secretion. This suggestion would be consistent with the inverse relationship between blood pressure response to mental arithmetic and degree of estrogenic activity observed by von Eiff and coworkers.[50] The results indicated that use of an estrogen-progestin combination did not influence catecholamine excretion. However, the effects of exogenous and endogenous hormones were assumed to be the same in this study, which may not be the case. The authors speculate that androgens may regulate the enhanced secretion of adrenaline in the male stress response.

The majority of studies concerning psychophysiological responses of Type A and Type B persons have used male subjects. Those studies that have utilized women have reported mixed results; some have shown Type A females to be more physiologically reactive to various stimuli than their Type B counterparts.[57-59] Others have failed to show such differences in reactivity in women.[60-62] MacDougall and coworkers[63] have found that women who exhibit Type A behavior show larger hemodynamic responses than women with Type B behavior, but the situations that evoke such responses may be very different for females and males.

Additional Descriptors

Although research on gender differences and reactivity has examined and controlled for some physiological characteristics that may be related both to reactivity and to gender differences (e.g., relative weight), it would also be important to examine cigarette smoking, alcohol intake, education, and physical activity, as well as those factors discussed above that are specific to women such as menstrual cycle phase, and use of oral contraceptives and exogenous hormones.

Problems

Overall, it appears that women are less physiologically reactive than men. The gender differences are more consistent with neuroendocrine than with cardiovascular indicators of reactivity. In addition, women may be more responsive to stressors during the premenstrual phase of their cycle, and oral contraceptives may suppress this physiological reaction. More research is needed to examine variations in reactivity over the menstrual cycle and over the female life cycle. Differences in physiological reactivity between prepubescent and pubertal adolescents, both male and female, should be examined. In both young and old women, the effect of endogenous and exogenous hormones should be explored. In particular, the effect of estrogen replacement therapy and reactivity in postmenopausal women should be examined, and account should be taken of whether menstruation ceased naturally or as a result of surgery.[64]

The data suggest profound sociocultural influences on reactivity in women. As women move into more male-dominated occupations and assume traditional male responsibilities, their degree of reactivity may increase. In this regard, a number of questions should be addressed. For example, are girls socialized in a manner that protects them from "hyperreactive" responses shown by boys, or are the differences entirely biological? Do women who enter the more "nontraditional" roles lose a "learned coping response," or are the differences biologically determined? Do women with reactivity similar to men have higher androgen levels than other women, and are they at increased risk of coronary disease? More research is needed on differential gender responses to similar stimuli, and special attention should be paid to determining the meaning of the stimuli, degree of involvement in the task, interpretation of threat, and expectation of success or failure.

Gender differences in reactivity may also be affected by other variables discussed in this chapter, including age, education, occupation, marital status, and socioeconomic status, as well as a number of other behavioral characteristics.

RACE/ETHNICITY

Race/Ethnicity and Cardiovascular Disease

Race and ethnic origin may be important variables for studies of reactivity and its relationship to cardiovascular disease. In many settings there are significant racial and ethnic differences in the prevalence and incidence of hypertension, stroke, and coronary heart disease. Differences in reactivity may account for some of these differences.

In the United States, differences in the cardiovascular disease experience of different racial and ethnic groups have been described. The prevalence of hypertension in black adults is about twice that observed in white adults,[65,66] though it is significant that mean blood pressures in national samples are no different in blacks and whites until about age 25.[46] There is regional variation in blood pressure levels within racial groups. Black women in the South have mean systolic blood pressures 8 to 9 mmHg higher than in the Midwest and Northeast.[46] No such variation has been observed among black or white men. White women in the South have mean systolic blood pressures 4 to 5 mmHg higher than white women in the West. Regional variation has also been observed among children and adolescents.[67]

A recent California statewide survey[68] revealed similar prevalences of hypertension (blood pressures greater than 140/90 mmHg) in blacks and Filipinos, while the prevalence of hypertension among adults of Japanese origin was substantially lower than that among whites. In an earlier study, Japanese males aged 45 to 64 in northern California had been found to have systolic and diastolic pressures 6 mmHg higher than those of their counterparts in Japan.[69] It should be noted that there is wide variation in hypertension prevalence rates in different areas of Japan.[70]

The predisposition to develop hypertension does not appear to be a characteristic common to black people everywhere.[71,72] Epidemiologic studies in rural areas of Tanzania[73] and the Gambia[74] have detected a prevalence of hypertension by the World Health Organization criteria as low as two percent in some populations. In West Africa blood pressures of urban residents are generally higher than those of rural residents,[2] though there are exceptions to this trend.[75] In particular, systolic blood pressures of rural Ghanaians at most ages are 20 to 25 mmHg lower than those of both urban Ghanaians and U.S. blacks, while the differences for diastolic blood pressure are in the range of 10 to 15 mmHg.[76] It is also noteworthy that the age-adjusted prevalences of hypertension among Zulu men and white men in urban South Africa are approximately equal, 23 percent and 22 percent respectively, though there is an excess of hypertension among Zulu women.[77] In the Caribbean, despite similarities of racial origin and cultural background among the black populations, there are marked variations in the prevalence of hypertension, as low as 14 percent in a St. Lucian village[78] and as high as 33 percent in an urban area of Trinidad.[79]

In the United States, coronary disease mortality in black men is slightly less than that observed in white men, while coronary mortality in black women exceeds that observed in white women.[80] Mortality data from a small number of prospective studies appear to be in general accord with the national statistics.[81] Incidence data from studies that included inadequate numbers of blacks suggest a substantially lower incidence of coronary disease in blacks compared to whites.[80] Studies among men of Japanese ancestry have revealed a gradient in the occurrence of coronary disease.[82,83] It is lowest in Japan (which has the lowest mortality from coronary disease of any industrialized country), intermediate in Hawaii, and highest in California. Japanese-Americans who had adhered most strongly to the traditional Japanese culture had a coronary disease prevalence as low as that observed in Japan, whereas the group most acculturated to Western culture had a much higher CHD prevalence.[83] Somewhat similar relationships have been detected in the Honolulu Heart Program with respect to coronary heart disease prevalence, but not incidence.[84,85]

Race/Ethnicity and Reactivity

Relatively few studies have compared reactivity to psychological stimuli in members of different racial or ethnic groups. Lazarus, Tomita, and coworkers[86] detected greater skin conductance in Japanese than in American subjects exposed to a stressful film. They speculated that the Japanese subjects might be "unusually sensitive to the disturbing aspects of the experimental situation." One study of autonomic responses to a startle tone revealed similar heart rate responsivity when black men and women were compared to their respective white gender groups.[87] Basal skin resistance was significantly higher in blacks than in whites, but the galvanic skin response was similar in white males, black males, and black females. Some investigators suggest that differences in autonomic reactivity among white ethnic groups may result from culturally determined differences in the significance ascribed to the experimental stimulus.[88]

It has been hypothesized that styles of coping with racism employed by American blacks might be related to blood pressure responses to stress. Clark and Harrell[89] tested the hypothesis that an apathetic (passive) cognitive coping style would be associated with less blood pressure reactivity than other styles, and that the Type A behavior pattern would be associated with greater blood pressure reactivity. A significant correlation in the expected direction was detected only between Type A behavior and diastolic blood pressure.

Some data are available on responsiveness to physical stress in black and white subjects. Alpert, Dover, and coworkers[90] examined blood pressure responsiveness in black and white adolescents to the stress of treadmill exercise. They observed that peak exercise blood pressures were higher in black females aged 6 to 15 years than in white females, even when account was taken of body surface area. Similar differences were observed among males when account was taken of both age and body surface area. These investigators suggested that systemic vascular resistance might differ in these populations during exercise. The Bogalusa Heart Study investigators[91,92] have examined responses to isometric arm exercise and the cold pressor test in black and white children. They reported no overall black-white differences, but black boys in the highest of three blood pressure strata had significantly higher systolic blood pressures during the isometric exercise and cold pressor tests than the other race-sex groups in the same stratum.

Sever, Peart, and coworkers[93,94] in their studies of black (West Indian or African) and white factory workers in London detected no significant racial difference in plasma norepinephrine, but mean plasma renin activity was 55 percent lower in blacks than in whites. The latter difference was not related to differences in sodium intake, and there was no association between plasma renin activity and blood pressure. Subsequent studies from this group of investigators[95] have revealed that white men have higher levels of plasma renin activity than white women, but among blacks, women tend to have higher levels. The reactivity of the renin-aldosterone system appears to be lower in black than in white normotensive subjects. However, the data are somewhat conflicting. Luft, Grim, and coworkers[96] examined furosemide-stimulated plasma renin activity in age-matched groups of black and white subjects. They detected a significantly greater response in white men than in black men, but there were no differences between the groups of women, or overall between white and black subjects. In contrast, Kaplan, Kem, and coworkers[97] detected significantly higher plasma renin activity following furosemide administration in normotensive white subjects than in black subjects in a non-age-matched sample. Luft and coworkers[98-100] have also reported significantly lower sodium excretion in response to similar sodium loads in black than in white normotensive subjects. Considered in the light of observations by Fujita, Henry, and coworkers,[101] these data suggest that in the United States a larger *proportion* of blacks than whites may be salt-sensitive. However, it should be noted that the higher prevalence of hypertension in blacks compared to whites in Evans County, Georgia, could not be accounted for by a greater dietary intake of sodium.[102] Reviews of possible pathophysiologic bases for racial blood pressure differences by Gillum[103] and Langford[104] indicate that the issue remains unresolved.

Definition

Studies of the relationships between disease and race have typically employed self-reports of racial identification. In some studies comparisons of individuals of African and Indian ancestry have required that three or four grandparents be identified by subjects as being of common ancestry in order for the subject to be regarded as either African or Indian.[105]

Ethnicity or ethnic origin is not coterminous with racial heritage.[106] There is disagreement among sociologists concerning the definition of ethnicity. Current controversy exists as to whether or not ethnicity should be identified with culture-specific behavior or cultural awareness. In the epidemiologic studies of Japanese in Hawaii and California, interviews have been used to ascertain individuals' perceptions of their cultural heritage, cultural identification, and cultural practices.[82] The latter included consideration of such factors as food consumption, language, membership in organizations, and social networks. Researchers in this area may find useful the discussion and ensuing recommendations by Moy concerning problems experienced in the U.S. Health Interview Survey.[107]

Problem Areas

Race has profound limitations as a category for epidemiologic research.[108] In studies of cardiovascular disease and reactivity, race should not be regarded as a proxy for genetic constitution. Lewontin[109] estimates, from studies of protein variation among populations, that 84.5 percent of human genetic diversity can be attributed to variation between individuals within populations; differences between populations within racial groups account for 8.3 percent of total species variation, while variation among races accounts for only 6.3 percent. Thus, the ability of interracial comparisons to detect genetic differences is restricted. In addition, special problems attend the study of black-white differences in the United States. In the United States, "black" is a sociological category and does not describe a group with genetic characteristics that are unequivocally identifiable.[110] U.S. and Caribbean black populations are derived from varying degrees of admixture between Caucasions and Negroes and, regarded from this point of view, are racially heterogeneous. Reed's examination of this issue indicates that these populations also exhibit genetic heterogeneity.[110] This heterogeneity is neglected in most epidemiologic studies involving black-white comparisons, though investigators frequently speculate concerning genetic forces. Moreover, investigators often make naive statistical assumptions concerning the ability of analytic techniques to dissect the genetic and environmental contributions to *quantitative* individual or group characteristics. The insights of Feldman and Lewontin[111] and of Kempthorne[112] in this regard deserve wider currency among investigators who wish to advance the state of knowledge in this area. Because of confounding of presumed genetic relationships by "environmental" associations, genetic causation cannot be inferred from population-based (as distinct from familial) studies.

These considerations should not be taken to imply that racial comparisons should be avoided. In fact, because of differences in disease risk and experience, black-white comparisons in the United States may be particularly useful. Several are currently being pursued under the sponsorship of the National Heart, Lung and Blood Institute. The observed black-white differences in hypertension prevalence and incidence in the United States are diminished when statistical correction is made for education[65,113] or social class.[114] However, even this apparently simple statistical manipulation does not take adequate account of "environmental" differences in black-white comparisons, since institutional racism in the United States has resulted in a *nonrandom* distribution of educational attainment and social class with respect to race. On average, blacks of equivalent educational achievement have lower occupational attainment than whites, and even in comparable occupations, have lower incomes.[115] Thus, racial identification is probably more important as a measure of exposure to certain common experiences.[116] In this regard it may eventually prove more valuable to identify characteristics of an individual's educational opportunities, social experiences, socioeconomic attainment, psychological resources, and styles of coping with behavioral stressors. The work of James and coworkers examining the influence on blood pressure of both educational resources and an active coping style (labeled "John Henryism") in black men is an important step in this direction.[117]

Evidence is accumulating that recent life-stress experience has striking effects on physiological reactivity.[118] In general, investigators who would elucidate the links between reactivity and race or ethnic origin should take explicit account of the sociohistorical context and the cultural characteristics of cohorts of individuals whose life experience is being examined. The research design and analytic techniques employed by Ward[119] in studies of migrants suggest appropriate approaches to examining genetic and socio-cultural influences in populations undergoing change.

Other Demographic Variables and Reactivity

The remaining demographic variables, marital status and the "socioeco-nomic" variables, have been shown to be related to cardiovascular disease, but few data are available on their relationship to reactivity. The evidence concerning their relationship to cardiovascular disease will be reviewed briefly, and comments will be made on their relevance to studies of reactivity.

Marital Status.   Since the beginning of the century, national statistics have shown that among both men and women, at all ages and in both white and nonwhite racial groups, married persons live longer on average than those who are single, widowed, or divorced.[120] Among American men younger than age 65, the mortality rate from coronary disease among the unmarried is about twice that of the married.[121] Similarly, numerous studies have examined the impact of bereavement on morbidity and mortality among widows and widowers. Chandra and coworkers[122] have demonstrated that among survivors of hospital admission for acute myocardial infarction, the subsequent mortality rate over 10 years of follow-up was significantly greater among the unmarried (single, divorced, separated, and widowed) than among the married. It has been suggested that the advantage expe-rienced by the married is related to the diminution of the effects of stress by social support.[121] It is unknown whether the married actually exhibit lesser degrees of reactivity in response to stress. This issue should be examined in groups matched on age, sex, and other relevant variables.

Social Class/Socioeconomic Status.   In general, recent studies have indi-cated an inverse relationship between social class and the incidence of coronary disease.[124–126;c.f.127] Data have been adduced to suggest that the socioeconomic strata at greatest risk may have changed in particular societies as these societies evolved from agrarian to urban, industrialized cul-tures.[128–130] In many of these studies, the social class difference in coronary disease experience has been only partly explained by differences in the distribution of the major risk factors.[125,131] Data on the prevalence and incidence of hypertension in different educational strata have already been cited.[65] Social class or socioeconomic status and variables customarily employed to define it, including occupation, education, income, and place of residence, have been shown to be related to the prevalence and incidence of cardiovascular disease.

Occupation.   The studies of Cobb and Rose indicated that air traffic controllers had a higher risk of developing hypertension than did airmen who underwent regular physical examinations during the same time period.[132] The annual incidence was higher in air traffic controllers, and the mean age at onset of hypertension was significantly lower. Moreover, hypertension was diagnosed earlier in those air traffic controllers working in high-stress situations (as measured by traffic density) than in those working in low-stress areas. However, in a prospective evaluation, air traffic controllers who reported being under greater tension were not more likely to develop hypertension than those who reported lower levels of tension.[133]

Kasl and Cobb[134] detected no significant effect of job loss caused by a permanent plant closing on men whom they followed for two years. Some urban-rural differences were found, but the authors concluded that the blood pressure data provided little support for the general hypothesis that unemployment increases cardiovascular risk.

James and coworkers[135] examined the notion of a strategy of active coping, called John Henryism, among black male workers in rural North Carolina. They found that among men who had high scores on the John Henryism scale and who had achieved some degree of job success, those who felt that being black had reduced their chances for success had significantly higher diastolic blood pressures than those who felt that being black had helped them. In addition, among the employed, concern with job security was associated with elevated systolic pressures. These data suggest that work-related stressors may be associated with increased risk of hypertension in rural, unskilled blacks.

The prevalence and incidence of coronary disease have been found to be associated with "type of occupation" within some cultures.[136] Some data indicate that occupational or habitual physical activity may provide a partial explanation for the observed differences.[137] Perhaps more important from the point of view of stress, reactivity, and disease, are studies that relate occupational stress to cardiovascular disease. Useful reviews of these data, which contain some theoretical insights, have been provided by House[138] and Kasl.[139]

Recent studies have sought to relate occupational overload, perceived job stress, pace of work, and lack of autonomy to the risk of coronary disease. Swedish investigators[140–142] have demonstrated that occupations characterized by high demand and few opportunities for control or growth are associated with elevated risk of myocardial infarction. In addition, the pace of work has some influence on measures of reactivity. For example, workers who do machine-paced work excrete larger amounts of catecholamines than those who do not.[143,144] A recent Dutch study[145] detected a much higher risk of first myocardial infarction among self-employed men compared to those employed by others and an even more striking risk differential for self-employed women compared to housewives. Among men, this heightened risk appeared to be associated not with working excessive hours but rather with feeling driven to work with great intensity and against the clock. Thus, there is ample evidence that occupational exposures may be an important class of variables in studies of cardiovascular disease risk.

The diversity of the findings suggests that a particular occupation should be regarded as a marker for an amalgam of physical and emotional stressors. Thus, classification of individuals according to their occupations provides no more than a convenient shorthand for a certain life experience or exposure. However, it may be inappropriate to assume that the occupational stress implied by a particular job title is unique, or for that matter, quantifiable. In addition, limited data[146] suggest that there may be important differences among individuals in their tendencies to change their consumption of tobacco, alcohol, or caffeine (substances that influence reactivity), in response to variations in perceived occupational stress. These potential changes should be addressed in studies of occupational variation in reactivity. Personality factors (such as the Type A behavior pattern) and situational factors (such as social support) may also affect perception of and responses to occupational stressors[147] and may have implications for cardiovascular disease. For example, in the Framingham Study, Type A men in white-collar occupations were at higher risk of heart disease regardless of social and psychological characteristics of their wives, whereas the effect of behavior type among men in blue-collar occupations was modified by their wives' characteristics.[148]

The implications of occupation for reactivity should be assessed by means of simple descriptive studies. If warranted, prospective designs can be employed among members of occupations that appear to confer the highest risk of subsequent cardiovascular disease.

Education. The inverse association between blood pressure (or the prevalence of hypertension) and years of education has already been noted.[66] Educational attainment generally parallels social class, and both are inversely related to the prevalence and incidence of coronary disease. Weinblatt, Ruberman, and coworkers[149] have observed that among survivors of acute myocardial infarction who had complex ventricular arrhythmias, men with eight years of schooling or less had a three-fold higher risk of sudden death than men with more education. Jenkins[150] proposed a hypothesis to account for this difference based on the inadequate preparation of men with low education to deal with the complexities of modern life and the consequences of this for autonomic nervous system function. Subsequent analyses suggested that psychosocial stress does not account for the differences in observed sudden death rates.[151] However, the evaluation was retrospective, and the results of a prospective trial now in progress should provide further information.

Similar hypotheses on the influence of education on blood pressure levels, particularly among black males, have been proposed by Tyroler and James.[152] James and coworkers have provided partial confirmatory data concerning the interaction between an active coping style ("John Henryism") and low education as joint contributors to resting diastolic blood pressure.[117] Tyroler[153] has examined five-year mortality of men in the Referred Care group in the Hypertension Detection and Follow-up Program: the death rate was highest in the group with lowest educational attainment, and blacks were at higher risk of death than whites.

Because the influence of education on reactivity may be age-cohort specific and may vary within racial or ethnic groups, it may be necessary in studies of the influence of education on reactivity and cardiovascular diseases to assemble groups that are relatively homogeneous with regard to age, race/ethnicity, and sex, and within which there is appreciable diversity in education. The degree of diversity that is necessary for the detection of significant effects is suggested by the observations in the Hypertension Detection and Follow-up Program.[65]

CONCLUSIONS

There are striking deficiencies in the data on population-demographic influences on reactivity. These suggest that descriptive studies are required. This applies particularly to race, occupational status, social class or socioeconomic status, and education. If socioeconomic status itself is to be used as a demographic variable, the methods proposed by Green[154] for its assessment in research on health behavior may be adequate.

In the absence of data on the relationship of the variables listed above to reactivity, it is difficult to make firm recommendations concerning the variables that should be included in prospective studies of stress, reactivity, and cardiovascular disease. However, the available data suggest that the influence of age and sex should be examined explicitly. Studies of reactivity that take into account the presence or absence of a family history of disease are most likely to yield information on genetic variation in reactivity. The same cannot be said of studies comparing individuals from different racial or ethnic groups. Studies that employ racial comparisons should take account of sociocultural variables. The sociocultural variables that are important for racial and ethnic comparisons are for the most part similar to those that should be included in comparisons of men and women.

In assessment of the importance of population-demographic variables in any relationship between reactivity and disease, certain analytical considerations must be borne in mind. Reactivity can be regarded as a dependent variable partly determined by one or more population-demographic variables. Alternatively, reactivity may be regarded as an independent variable, along with population-demographic variables, in studies that assess the relationships between risk factors (including reactivity and population-demographic characteristics) and disease. In this case, explicit consideration of the population-demographic variables allows for testing of the hypothesis that there is a causal relationship between reactivity and disease under a variety of conditions. For example, in a study population there may be an association between population-demographic group membership and cardiovascular disease. If appropriate statistical adjustment for the influence of variations in reactivity has little or no influence on the strength of this association, while adjustment for population-demographic group membership diminishes or enhances markedly the association between reactivity variables and the disease outcome, it might then be argued that the relationship between population-demographic group membership and disease is not mediated through reactivity, but that a relationship between reactivity and disease is evident only because of the association of reactivity with population-demographic group membership. On the other hand, if the strength of reactivity-disease association does not vary dramatically from one population-demographic group to another, the reactivity-disease relationship would be regarded as a direct one. Moreover, the relationship between population-demographic group membership and disease would not be mediated by variations in reactivity. In practice, such simple, causal relationships and hypothesis testing are implausible, because other risk factors may also be associated with both reactivity and the population-demographic characteristics, and account would also have to be taken of their impact.

The problems raised by demographic and population variables for elucidating the stress-reactivity cardiovascular disease relationship are well summarized in a statement by Marmot:

> A vital part of studying disease in humans is to study the occurrence of disease in populations. This kind of epidemiological research program is restricted by the lack of suitable psychosocial measures of predisposition or precipitants that may be used cross-culturally and in different social groups. Until such

measures are developed and applied systematically, a step in the demonstration of causation will be missing. We have a dilemma. We can study stress intensively, psychologically and biochemically, in individuals, but large numbers are needed to study the development of disease. For the most part, the need for large numbers has precluded the application of intensive measures to where disease occurs—in the population at large.[155, p.383]

This dilemma still defies resolution. One solution may be to focus on high-risk population-demographic groups in order to identify variations in reactivity and to delineate their relationship to cardiovascular disease. Similar relationships may not hold in lower-risk groups, but this would be an efficient, inexpensive approach and might yield useful information for disease prevention programs. The alternative approach is to pursue the stress-reactivity relationship at a physiological and biochemical level in the hope of identifying mechanisms by which reactivity might influence cardiovascular disease. This would be similar in principle to laboratory research that seeks to link the major risk factors to the atherosclerotic process. Neither approach will provide all the required information, but there appears to be no dearth of testable hypotheses.

REFERENCES

1. Epstein FH, Eckoff RD: The epidemiology of high blood pressure-geographic distributions and etiological factors. In Stamler J, Stamler R, Pullman TN (eds): *The Epidemiology of Hypertension.* New York, Grune & Stratton, 1967, pp. 155–166.

2. Pobee JOM: Epidemiological report from West Africa. In Gross F, Strasser T (eds): *Mild Hypertension: Recent Advances.* New York, Raven, 1983, pp. 33–54.

3. Mugambi M: Epidemiological report from East Africa. In Gross F, Strasser T (eds): *Mild Hypertension: Recent Advances.* New York, Raven, 1983, pp. 55–61.

4. Pickering G: Normotension and hypertension: The mysterious viability of the false. *Am J Med* **65**:561–563, 1978.

5. Why does blood-pressure rise with age? *Lancet* **2**:289–290, 1981. (Editorial)

6. Fries ED: Salt, volume and the prevalence of hypertension. *Circulation* **53**:589–595, 1976.

7. Jenkins CD, Somervell PD, Hames CG: Does blood pressure usually rise with age?...or with stress? *J Human Stress* **9**:4–12, 1983.

8. Oberman A, Lane NE, et al: Trends in systolic blood pressure in the Thousand Aviator cohort over a twenty-four year period. *Circulation* **36**:812–822, 1967.

9. Szklo M: Epidemiologic patterns of blood pressure in children. *Epidemiol Rev* **1**:143–169, 1979.

10. McGlashan ND: Causes of death in ten English-speaking Caribbean countries and territories. *Bull Pan Am Health Organ* **16**:212–223, 1982.

11. Strong JP: Atherosclerosis in human populations. *Atherosclerosis* **16**:193–200, 1972.

12. McGill Jr HC, Geer JC, Strong JP: Natural history of human atherosclerotic lesions. In Sandler M, Bourne GH (eds): *Atherosclerosis and Its Origin.* New York, Academic Press, 1983.

13. Tarazi RC: Pathophysiology of essential hypertension: Role of the autonomic nervous system. *Am J Med* **75** (October 17):2–8, 1983.

14. Lund-Johansen P: Hemodynamics in early essential hypertension. *Acta Med Scand* **482**:3–105, 1967. (Suppl)

15. Uhari M, Paavilainen T: Haemodynamic changes in essential hypertension in young subjects. *Cardiology* **69**:219–223, 1982.

16. Rowe JW, Troen BR: Sympathetic nervous system and aging in man. *Endocrinol Rev* **1**:167–179, 1980.

17. Crane MG, Harris JJ: Effects of aging on renin activity and aldosterone excretion. *J Lab Clin Med* **87**:947–959, 1976.

18. Finch CE: Neuroendocrine and autonomic aspects of aging. In Finch CE, Hayflick L, (eds): *Handbook of the Biology of Aging.* New York, Van Nostrand Reinhold, 1977, p. 262.

19. Goldstein DS, McCarty, R, et al: Relationship between plasma norepinephrine and sympathetic neural activity. *Hypertension* **5**:552–559, 1983.

20. Folkow B, DiBona GF, et al: Measurements of plasma norepinephrine concentrations in human primary hypertension, *Hypertension* **5**:399–403, 1983.

21. Bertel O, Buhler FR, et al: Decreased beta-adrenoreceptor responsiveness as related to age, blood pressure, and plasma catecholamines in patients with essential hypertension. *Hypertension* **2**:130–138, 1980.

22. Goldstein DS, Lake CR, et al: Age-dependence of hypertensive-normotensive differences in plasma norepinephrine. *Hypertension* **5**:100–104, 1983.

23. Abboud FM: The sympathetic system in hypertension. *Hypertension* **4**:208–225, 1982. (Suppl II)

24. Van Brummelen P, Buhler FR, et al: Age-related decrease in cardiac and peripheral vascular responsiveness to isoprenalin: Studies in normal subjects. *Clin Sci* **60**: 571–577, 1981.

25. Vestal RE, Wood AJJ, Shand DG: Reduced B-adrenoceptor sensitivity in the elderly. *Clin Pharmacol Ther* **26**:181–186, 1979.

26. Fleisch JH: Age-related changes in the sensitivity of blood vessels to drugs. *Pharmacol Ther* **8**:477–487, 1980.

27. Lakatta EG: Age-related alteration in the cardiovascular response to adrenergic mediated stress. *Fed Proc* **39**:3173–3177, 1980.

28. Lakatta EG, Yin FCP: Myocardial aging: Functional alterations and related cellular mechanisms. *Am J Physiol* **242**:H927–H941, 1982.

29. Dillon N, Chung S, et al: Age and beta adrenoceptor-mediated function. *Clin Pharmacol Ther* **27**:769–772, 1980.

30. Johnson M, Ramey E, Ramwell PW: Sex and age differences in human platelet aggregation. *Nature* **253**:355–357, 1975.

31. Scott PJW: The effect of age on the response of human isolated arteries to noradrenaline. *Br J Clin Pharmacol* **13**:237–239, 1982.

32. Waddington JL, MacCulloch MJ, Sambrooks JE: Resting heart rate variability in man declines with age. *Experientia* **35**:1197–1198, 1979.

33. Hofman A, Valkenburg HA: Determinants of change in blood pressure during childhood. *Am J Epidemiol* **117**:735–743, 1982.

34. Harlan WR, Osborne RK, Graybiel A: Clinical studies: Prognostic value of the cold pressor test and the basal blood pressure: Based on an eighteen-year follow-up study. *Am J Cardiol* **13**:683–687, 1964.

35. Palmer GJ, Ziegler MG, Lake CR: Response of norepinephrine and blood pressure to stress increases with age. *J Gerontol* **33**:482–487, 1978.

36. Schachter J, Kuller LH, Perfetti C: Blood pressure during the first five years of life: Relation to ethnic group (black or white) and to parental hypertension. *Am J Epidemiol* **119**:541–553, 1984.

37. Schachter J, Kuller LH, Perfetti C: Heart rate during the first five years of life: Relation to ethnic group (black or white) and to parental hypertension. *Am J Epidemiol* **119**:554–563, 1984.

38. Campos JJ, Langer A, Krowitz A: Cardiac responses on the visual cliff in prelocomotor human infants. *Science* **70**:196–197, 1970.

39. Schwartz AN, Campos JJ, Baisel EJ: The visual cliff: Cardiac and behavioral responses on the deep and shallow sides at five and nine months of age. *J Exp Child Psychol* **15**:86–99, 1973.

40. Katz SH, Hediger ML, et al: Blood pressure, growth and maturation from childhood through adolescence: Mixed longitudinal analyses of the Philadelphia Blood Pressure Project. *Hypertension* **2**:55–69, 1980. (Suppl I)

41. Prineas RJ, Gillum RF, et al: The Minneapolis Children's Blood Pressure Study: Part 2: Multiple determinants of children's blood pressure. *Hypertension* **2**:24–28, 1980. (Suppl I)

42. Voors AW, Harsha DW, et al: Relation of blood pressure to stature in healthy young adults. *Am J Epidemiol* **115**:833–840, 1982.

43. Dawber TR: Incidence of coronary heart disease, stroke and peripheral arterial disease. In Dawber TR (ed), *The Framingham Study. The Epidemiology of Atherosclerotic Disease.* Cambridge, Harvard University Press, 1980, pp. 59–75.

44. Kannel WB, Hjortland MC, et al: Menopause and risk of cardiovascular disease: The Framingham Study. *Ann Intern Med* **85**:447–452, 1976.

45. Dawber TR: Observations on blood-pressure measurement. In Dawber TR (ed): *The Framingham Study: The Epidemiology of Atherosclerotic Disease.* Cambridge, Harvard University Press, 1980, pp. 76–90.

46. Department of Health, Education and Welfare: *Blood Pressure Levels of Persons 6–74 Years. U.S. 1971–1974.* Bethesda, MD, DHEW Publication No. (HRA) 78–1648, 1978.

47. Kannel WB, McGee DL: Diabetes and glucose tolerance as risk factors for cardiovascular disease: The Framingham Study. *Diabetes Care* **2**:120–126, 1979.

48. Barrett-Connor E, Wingard DL: Sex differential in ischemic heart disease mortality in diabetes: A prospective population-based study. *Am J Epidemiol* **118**:489–496, 1983.

49. Truett J, Cornfield J, Kannel W: A multivariate analysis of the risk of coronary heart disease in Framingham. *J Chronic Dis* **20**:511–524, 1967.

50. von Eiff AW, Wilhelm A, et al: The effect of estrogens and progestins on blood pressure regulation of normotensive women. *Am J Obstet Gynecol* **109**:887–892, 1971.

51. Frankenhaeuser M, von Wright M, et al: Sex differences in psychoneuroendocrine reactions to examination stress. *Psychosom Med* **40**:334–343, 1978.

52. Shapiro AP, Miller RE, et al: Behavioral consequences of mild hypertension. *Hypertension* **4**:355–360, 1982.

53. Frankenhaeuser M: The sympathetic-adrenal and pituitary-adrenal response to challenge: Comparison between the sexes. In Dembroski TM, Schmidt TH, Blumchen G (eds): *Biobehavioral Bases of Coronary Heart Disease.* Basel, Karger, 1983, pp. 91–105.

54. Aubert M, Lemarchand-Beraud T, et al: Cortisol secretion during the normal menstrual cycle. *Acta Endocrinol Congress* Abstract #78, 1971. (Suppl 155)

55. Marinari KT, Leshner A, Doyle M: Menstrual cycle status and adrenocortical reactivity to psychological stress. *Psychoneuroendocrinology* **1**:213–218, 1976.

56. Collins A, Hanson U, et al: Psychophysiological stress responses in postmenopausal women before and after hormonal replacement therapy. *Human Neurobiol* **1**:153–159, 1982.

57. Weidner G, Matthews KA: Reported physical symptoms elicited by unpredictable events and the Type A coronary-prone behavior pattern. *J Pers Soc Psychol* **36**:213–220, 1978.

58. Lundberg U, Forsman L: Adrenal-medullary and adrenal-cortical responses to under-stimulation and overstimulation: Comparison between Type A and Type B persons. *Biol Psychol* **9**:79–89, 1979.

59. Lawler KA, Rixse A, Allen MT: Type A behavior and psychophysiological responses in adult women. *Psychophysiology* **20**:343–350, 1983.

60. Manuck SB, Craft SA, Gold KJ: Coronary-prone behavior pattern and cardiovascular response. *Psychophysiology* **15**:403–411, 1978.

61. Waldron I, Hickey A, et al: Type A behavior pattern: Relationship to variation in blood pressure, paternal characteristics and academic and social activities of students. *J Human Stress* **6**:16–27, 1980.

62. Lane JD, White AD, Williams Jr RB: Cardiovascular effects of mental arithmetic in Type A and Type B females. *Psychophysiology* **21**:39–46, 1984.

63. MacDougall JM, Dembroski TM, Krantz DS: Effects of types of challenge on pressor and heart rate responses in Type A and Type B women. *Psychophysiology* **18**:1–9, 1981.

64. Sullivan JL: The sex difference in ischemic heart disease. *Perspect Biol Med* **26**:657–671, 1983.

65. Hypertension Detection and Follow-up Program Cooperative Group: Race, education and prevalence of hypertension. *Am J Epidemiol* **106**:351–361, 1977.

66. Department of Health and Human Services: *Hypertension in Adults 25–74 Years of Age, US, 1971–1975.* Bethesda MD, US DHHS Publication (PHS) 81–1671, 1981.

67. Department of Health, Education, and Welfare: *Blood Pressure Levels of Youths 12–17 Years.* Bethesda, MD, US DHEW Publication No. (HRA) 77–1645, 1977.

68. Stavig GR, Igra A, Leonard AR: Hypertension among Asians and Pacific Islanders in California. *Am J Epidemiol* **119**:677–692, 1984.

69. Kagan A, Harris BR, et al: Epidemiologic studies of coronary heart disease and stroke in Japanese men living in Japan, Hawaii, and California: Demographic, physical, dietary and biochemical characteristics. *J Chronic Dis* **27**:345–364, 1974.

70. Kimura T, Ota M: Epidemiologic study of hypertension: Comparative results of hyper-tensive surveys in two areas of Japan. *Am J Clin Nutr* **17**:381–390, 1965.

71. Cruickshank JK, Beevers DG: Epidemiology of hypertension: Blood pressure in blacks and whites. *Clin Sci* **62**:1–6, 1982.

72. Watkins LO: Worldwide experience: Coronary artery disease and hypertension in black populations. *Urban Health* **13**:30–35, 1984.

73. Vaughan JP: Blood pressure and heart murmurs in a rural population in the United Republic of Tanzania. *Bull WHO* **52**:89–97, 1979.

74. Ree GH: Arterial pressures in a West African (Gambian) rural population. *J Trop Med Hyg* **76**:65–70, 1973.

75. Beiser M, Collomb H, et al: Systemic blood pressure studies among the Serer of Senegal. *J Chronic Dis* **29**:371–380, 1976.

76. Pobee JOM, Larbi EB, et al: Blood pressure distribution in a rural Ghanaian population. *Trans R Soc Trop Med Hyg* **71**:66–72, 1977.

77. Seedat YK, Seedat MA: An interracial study of the prevalence of hypertension in an urban South African population. *Trans R Soc Trop Med Hyg* **76**:62–71, 1982.

78. Khaw KT, Rose G: Population study of blood pressure and associated factors in St. Lucia, West Indies. *Int J Epidemiol* **11**:372–377, 1982.

79. Watkins LO: Coronary heart disease and coronary heart disease risk factors in black populations in developing countries: The case for primordial prevention. *Am Heart J* **108**:850–862, 1984. (Suppl)

80. Gillum RF: Coronary heart disease in black populations. I. Mortality and morbidity. *Am Heart J* **104**:839–851, 1982.

81. Watkins LO: Epidemiology of coronary heart disease in black populations: Methodologic proposals. *Am Heart J*, **108**:635–640, 1984. (Suppl)

82. Marmot MG, Syme SL: Acculturation and coronary heart disease in Japanese-Americans. *Am J Epidemiol* **104**:225–247, 1976.

83. Yano K, Reed DM, McGee DL: Ten-year incidence of coronary heart disease in the Honolulu Heart Program. *Am J Epidemiol* **119**:653–666, 1984.

84. Reed D, McGee D, et al: Acculturation and coronary heart disease among Japanese men in Hawaii. *Am J Epidemiol* **115**:894–905, 1982.

85. Reed D, McGee D, et al: Social networks and coronary heart disease among Japanese men in Hawaii. *Am J Epidemiol* **117**:384–396, 1983.

86. Lazarus RS, Tomita M, et al: A cross cultural study of stress-reaction patterns in Japan. *J Pers Soc Psychol* **4**:622–633, 1966.

87. Korol B, Bergfeld GR, McLaughlin LJ: Skin color and autonomic nervous system measures. *Physiol Behav* **14**:575–578, 1975.

88. Sternback RA, Tursky B: Ethnic differences among housewives in psychophysical and skin potential responses under electric shock. *Psychophysiology* **1**:241–246, 1965.

89. Clark VR, Harrell JP: The relationship among Type A behavior, styles used in coping with racism, and blood pressure. *J Black Psychol* **8**:89–99, 1982.

90. Alpert BS, Dover EV, et al: Blood pressure response to dynamic exercise in healthy children—black vs white. *J Pediatr* **99**:556–560, 1981.

91. Berenson GS, Voors AW, et al: Racial differences of parameters associated with blood pressure levels in children—The Bogalusa Heart Study. *Metabolism* **28**:1218–1228, 1979.

92. Voors AW, Webber LS, Berenson GS: Racial contrasts in cardiovascular response tests for children from a total community. *Hypertension* **2**:686–694, 1980.

93. Sever PS, Peart WS, et al: Are racial differences in essential hypertension due to different pathogenetic mechanisms? *Clin Sci Mol Med* **55**:383–386, 1978.

94. Sever PS, Peart WS, et al: Ethnic differences in blood pressure with observations on noradrenaline and renin. *Clin Exp Hypert* **1**:733–744, 1979.

95. Meade TW, Imeson JD, et al: The epidemiology of plasma renin. *Clin Sci* **64**:273–280, 1983.

96. Luft FC, Grim CE, et al: Differences in response to sodium administration in normotensive white and black subjects. *J Lab Clin Med* **90**:555–562, 1977.

97. Kaplan NM, Kem DC, et al: The intravenous purosemide test: A simple way to evaluate renin responsiveness. *Ann Intern Med* **84**:639–645, 1976.

98. Luft FC, Rankin LI, et al: Cardiovascular and humoral responses to extremes of sodium intake in normal black and white men. *Circulation* **60**:697–706, 1979.

99. Luft FC, Grim CE, et al: Effects of volume expansion and contraction in normotensive whites, blacks, and subjects of different ages. *Circulation* **59**:643–650, 1979.

100. Luft FC, Weinberger MH, et al: Sodium sensitivity in normotensive human subjects. *Ann Intern Med* **98**:758–762, 1983.

101. Fujita T, Henry WL, et al: Factors influencing blood pressure in salt-sensitive patients with hypertension. *Am J Med* **69**:334–344, 1980.

102. Grim CE, Luft FC, et al: Racial differences in blood pressure in Evans County, Georgia: Relationship to sodium and potassium intake and plasma renin activity. *J Chronic Dis* **33**:87–94, 1979.

103. Gillum RF: Pathophysiology of hypertension in blacks and whites: A review of the basis of racial blood pressure differences. *Hypertension* **1**:468–475, 1979.

104. Langford HG: Is blood pressure different in black people? *Postgrad Med J* **57**:749–754, 1981.

105. Miller GJ, Beckles GLA, et al: Serum lipoproteins and susceptibility of men of Indian descent to coronary heart disease. The St. James Survey, Trinidad. *Lancet* **2**:200–203, 1982.

106. Patterson O: The nature, causes, and implications of ethnic identification. In Fried C (ed): *Minorities: Community and Identity*. New York, Springer-Verlag, 1983, pp. 25–50.

107. Moy CS: Determining ethnic origin in an interview survey: Problems and recommendations. *Public Health Rep* **92**:414–420, 1977.

108. Cooper R: A note on the biological concept of race and its application in epidemiologic research. *Am Heart J* **108**:715–723, 1984. (Suppl)

109. Lewontin RC: The apportionment of human diversity. *Evolutionary Biol* **6**:381–398, 1973.

110. Reed TE: Caucasian genes in American Negroes. *Science* **165**:762–768, 1969.

111. Feldman MW, Lewontin RC: The heritability hang-up. *Science* **190**:1163–1168, 1975.

112. Kempthorne O: Logical, epistemological and statistical aspects of nature–nurture data interpretation. *Biometrics* **34**:1–23, 1978.

113. Keil JE, Sandifer SH, et al: Skin color and education effects on blood pressure. *Am J Public Health* **71**:532–534, 1981.

114. Keil JE, Tyroler HA, et al: Hypertension: Effects of social class and racial admixture: The results of a cohort study in the black population of Charleston, South Carolina. *Am J Public Health* **67**:634–639, 1977.

115. Hogan DP, Pazul M: The occupational and earnings returns to education among black men in the North. *Am J Sociol* **87**:905–920, 1982.

116. Washington ED, McLoyd VC: The external validity of research involving American minorities. *Human Dev* **5**:34–339, 1982.

117. James SA, Hartnett SA, Kalsbeek WD: John Henryism and blood pressure differences among black men. *J Behav Med* **6**:259–278, 1983.

118. Pardine P, Napoli A: Physiological reactivity and recent life-stress experience. *J Consult Clin Psychol* **51**:467–469, 1983.

119. Ward RH: Genetic and sociocultural components of high blood pressure. *Am J Phys Anthropol* **62**:91–105, 1983.

120. Somers AR: Marital status, health, and use of health services: An old relationship revisited. *JAMA* **241**:1818–1822, 1979.

121. Lynch JJ: *The Broken Heart: The Medical Consequences of Loneliness*. New York, Basic, 1977.

122. Chandra V, Szklo M, et al: The impact of marital status on survival after an acute myocardial infarction: A population-based study. *Am J Epidemiol* **117**:320–325, 1983.

123. Rose G, Marmot MG: Social class and coronary heart disease. *Br Heart J* **45**:13–19, 1981.

124. Koskenvuo M, Kaprio J, et al: Incidence and prognosis of ischaemic heart disease with respect to marital status and social class: A national record linkage study. *J Epidemiol Community Health* **35**:192–196, 1981.

125. Holme I, Helgeland A, et al: Four-year mortality by some socioeconomic indicators: The Oslo Study. *J Epidemiol Community Health* **34**:48–52, 1980.

126. Salonen JT: Socioeconomic status and risk of cancer, cerebral stroke, and death due to coronary heart disease and any disease: A longitudinal study in Eastern Finland. *J Epidemiol Community Health* **36**:294–297, 1982.

127. Antonovsky A: Social class and the major cardiovascular diseases. *J Chronic Dis* **21**:65–106, 1968.

128. Cassel J, Heyden S, et al: Incidence of coronary heart disease by ethnic group, social class, and sex. *Arch Intern Med* **128**:901–906, 1971.

129. Marmot MG, Adelstein AM, et al: Changing social-class distributions of heart disease. *Br Med J* **2**:1109–1112, 1978.

130. Morgenstern H: The changing association between social status and coronary heart disease in a rural population. *Soc Sci Med* **14A**:191–201, 1980.

131. Leren P, Helgeland A, et al: The Oslo Study: CHD risk factors, socioeconomic influences, and intervention. *Am Heart J* **106**:1200–1206, 1983.

132. Cobb S, Rose RM: Hypertension, peptic ulcer, and diabetes in air traffic controllers. *JAMA* **224**:489–492, 1973.

133. Jenkins CD, Hurst MW, et al: Biomedical and psychosocial predictors of hypertension in air traffic controllers. In Defares PB (ed): *Stress and Anxiety* (Vol 9). Washington, DC, Hemisphere, 1985.

134. Kasl SV, Cobb S: The experience of losing a job: Some effects on cardiovascular functioning. *Psychother Psychosom* **34**:88–109, 1980.

135. James SA, LaCroix AZ, et al: John Henryism and blood pressure differences among black men II. The role of occupational stressors. *J Behav Med* **6**:257–273, 1984.

136. Morris JN, Kagan A, et al: Incidence and prediction of ischaemic heart disease among London busmen. *Lancet* **2**:553–559, 1966.

137. Brand RJ, Paffenbarger Jr RS, et al: Work activity and fatal heart attack studied by multiple logistic risk analysis. *Am J Epidemiol* **110**:52–62, 1979.

138. House JS: Occupational stress and coronary heart disease: A review and theoretical integration. *J Health Soc Behav* **15**:12–27, 1974.

139. Kasl SV: Epidemiologic contributions to the study of work stress. In Cooper CL, Payne R (eds): *Stress at Work*. New York, Wiley, 1978, pp. 3–48.

140. Alfredsson L, Theorell T: Job characteristics of occupations and myocardial infarction risk: Effect of possible confounding factors. *Soc Sci Med* **17**:1497–1503, 1983.

141. Karasek RA, Baker D, et al: Job decision latitude, job demands and cardiovascular disease: A prospective study of Swedish men. *Am J Public Health* **71**:694–705, 1981.

142. Karasek RA, Theorell T, et al: Job, psychological factors and coronary heart disease. *Adv Cardiol* **29**:62–67, 1982.

143. Frankenhaeuser M, Cardell B: Underload and overload in working life. *J Human Stress* **2**:35–46, 1976.

144. Froberg J, Karlsson CG, et al: Conditions of work: Psychological and endocrine stress reactions. *Arch Environ Health* **21**:789–797, 1970.

145. Magnus K, Matroos AW, Strackee J: The self-employed and the self-driven: Two coronary-prone subpopulations from the Zeist Study. *Am J Epidemiol* **118**:799–805, 1983.

146. Conway TL, Vickers Jr RR, et al: Occupational stress and variation in cigarette, coffee, and alcohol consumption. *J Health Soc Behav* **22**:155–165, 1981.

147. McMichael AJ: Personality, behavioral and situational modifiers of work stressors. In Cooper CL, Payne R (eds): *Stress at Work*. New York, Wiley, 1978, pp. 127–147.

148. Eaker ED, Haynes SG, Feinleib M: Spouse behavior and coronary heart disease in men: Prospective results from the Framingham Heart Study II. Modification of risk in Type A husbands according to the social and psychological status of their wives. *Am J Epidemiol* **118**:23–41, 1983.

149. Weinblatt E, Ruberman W, et al: Relation of education to sudden death after myocardial infarction. *N Engl J Med* **299**:60–65, 1978.

150. Jenkins CD: Low education: A risk factor for death. *N Engl J Med* **299**:95–96, 1978.

151. Ruberman W, Weinblatt E, et al: Education, psychosocial stress and sudden cardiac death. *J Chronic Dis* **36**:151–160, 1983.

152. Tyroler HA, James SA: Blood pressure and skin color. *Am J Public Health* **68**:1170–1172, 1978.

153. Tyroler HA: Race, education, and 5-year mortality in HDFP stratum I referred care males. In Gross F, Strasser T (eds): *Mild Hypertension: Recent Advances.* New York, Raven, 1983, pp. 163–176.

154. Green LW: Manual for scoring socioeconomic status for research on health behavior. *Public Health Rep* **85**:815–827, 1970.

155. Marmot MG: Stress, social and cultural variations in heart disease. *J Psychosom Res* **27**:377–384, 1983.

13

Familial Influences on Cardiovascular Reactivity to Stress

RICHARD J. ROSE

INTRODUCTION

Familial risk for essential hypertension (EH) was documented in 1934 by Ayman[1] in a study of 1524 members of 277 families; the prevalence of hypertension, defined as pressure exceeding 140/80 mmHg, increased from a 3 percent base rate observed in offspring of normotensive parents to 28 percent in children of one hypertensive parent and 48 percent in children of two hypertensive parents. In the half-century since Ayman's early report, familial risk has received increasing attention in efforts to understand the developmental precursors of cardiovascular disease. In coronary heart disease (CHD), as in most other multifactorial disorders, the study of the normal, at-risk offspring of affected parents has assumed strategic importance in etiological research.

259

This chapter briefly reviews evidence of heritable variation in the level of casual blood pressure (BP) and in cardiovascular reactivity to imposed stress. Heritability of BP level is convincingly established in the consistent results from large, representative twin studies and extended family data sets. Twin studies of cardiovascular stress reactions, by contrast, are of recent origin, few in number, and limited in sampling and design. Nonetheless, these studies suggest significant genetic variance in cardiovascular reactivity and thereby underscore the importance of assessing stress responses in normotensive offspring of hypertensive parents (see also chapter by Falkner and Light). The chapter concludes with a selective review of those studies and suggests the promise of future research based on more powerful research designs.

FAMILIAL AGGREGATION OF CASUAL BLOOD PRESSURE

Twin-family and adoption studies of casual blood pressure have a long history with results that convincingly document the influence of additive genes. A study by Stocks,[2] reported more than 50 years ago, is illustrative. Twin and non-twin siblings of school age were evaluated at the Galton Laboratories. Blood pressures were measured in 218 like-sex twin pairs, and the observed correlations led Stocks to conclude that heritability of blood pressure was demonstrable "to almost the same extent" as was true for height or weight.

A contemporary investigation of twin schoolchildren [3] replicates Stock's early observation. Like-sex twins who were studied in the Collaborative Perinatal Project were assessed at age 7 in 12 university-affiliated U. S. hospitals from 1966 to 1973. Blood pressures were recorded from 197 twin pairs, and the intraclass correlations for diastolic pressure (DBP) were 0.54 for 115 monozygotic (MZ) pairs and 0.27 for 82 dizygotic (DZ) pairs. The correlations reliably differ ($p < 0.01$) and, under conventional assumptions, yield a heritability estimate, h^2, of 0.53.

Virtually identical results have been obtained in several large samples of adults. Male twins, ascertained through the NAS-NRC twin registry of U.S. Armed Forces veterans, provided data for the National Heart, Lung and Blood Institute (NHLBI) collaborative study of CHD risk factors.[4] A sample of 248 MZ and 264 DZ twin pairs, born between 1917 and 1927, were examined during 1969–1973. Intraclass correlations for DBP were 0.58 for MZs and 0.27 for DZs. These results were replicated with a sample of adult Norwegian twins,[5] most of whom were identified through a population-based twin registry and seen at either age 35 or 59, with approximately equal representation of sex and zygosity within each age group. For the total sample of 236 twin pairs, the rs were $r_{MZ} = 0.59$ and $r_{DZ} = 0.24$ for DBP. The remarkable consistency of the correlations at two ages and in two cultures quite different in life style led the Norwegian investigators to underscore the contribution of genetic variance to observed levels of casual BP.

Familial aggregation of casual pressures has been demonstrated in large family studies as well. BP data from a study of adopted French-Canadian schoolchildren[6] and data from an evaluation of the multiple genetic and environmental relationships found in kinships of MZ twin parents[7] have been subjected to sophisticated model-fitting analyses with results that replicate one another and complement conventional twin analyses. In both data sets an adequate fit to observed data required a parameter of additive genetic variance, and h^2 estimates were virtually identical (0.61 and 0.63).

Such studies, however, may be a gross oversimplification, because they implicitly assume a static effect of genetic variance on BP throughout development. In reality, gene effects must be expected to vary with age, and the effect of age may depend on gender and familial history of EH and CHD. To demonstrate the point, longitudinal twin studies are required, and to our knowledge, none has been reported. But an approximation can be made from hierarchical multiple regression (HMR) analysis of cross-sectional twin data, and an HMR analysis[8] of twins, ages 16 to 33, reveals significant gene $\times$ age interactions in the prediction of cotwin resemblance for casual BP. Thus, gene effects on blood pressure are developmentally modulated— that is, larger at some ages than at others. In separate analyses of twin brothers and twin sisters, an age $\times$ gene $\times$ risk interaction is evident, revealing that the developmental modulation of genetic influence on BP differs according to parental history of EH.

Finally, it was apparent years ago that casual BP may not be the most relevant trait for etiological research. Exaggerated lability, as well as elevated level, may characterize the cardiovascular responses of prehypertensive individuals. Osborne et al.[9] cogently framed the rationale for genetic studies of lability/reactivity. Interpreting their data on basal and casual BP mea- surements in adult twins, they noted significant differences in intrapair variance in the two sets of readings and suggested that twin studies of diurnal variation in BP would be of interest. They concluded that "the lability of the blood pressure (and) its reactivity to specific stimuli... may be the most promising avenues for further genetic investigations."

TWIN STUDIES OF CARDIOVASCULAR RESPONSE TO STRESS

In perhaps the earliest twin study of cardiovascular reactivity, McIlhany and colleagues evaluated basal blood pressures and response to the cold pressor test in 200 pairs of normotensive twins of mean age 14.0 years. The preliminary analysis of these data, published in 1957,[10] reported that for both systolic and diastolic pressures, mean intrapair differences were significantly larger in DZ pairs at basal measurement and during maximum response to cold pressor challenge. Some 17 years later, more detailed analyses of these important data appeared.[11] The incremental change (delta) in pressure from minimum observed during 20 minutes rest to the higher of two pressures made during a 1-minute cold pressor was analyzed as a measure of reactivity. For diastolic readings the average delta exceeded 22 mmHg. Intraclass correlations for the delta in diastolic response were 0.74 for 83 MZ pairs and 0.42 for 67 like-sex DZ pairs. Both correlations and their difference are highly significant, and a heritability estimate based on them [2($r_{MZ} = r_{DZ}$] is 0.64. Comparison of the within-pair mean squares yields an F value of 2.70, $p < 0.01$. Results for systolic pressure were very similar, and separate analyses by gender were quite consistent. The authors concluded that "genetic factors play an important role in the control of blood pressure over the normal range of vascular reactivity."

In 1967 Shapiro and colleagues[12] reported results of a carefully designed study of cardiovascular reactivity in which 12 MZ and 12 like-sex DZ twin pairs were exposed to two stressors, ischemic pain and the Stroop Color-Word Interference Test. The sample was self-selected and too small to yield much statistical power to the analysis. (Simulation studies[13] of the power of the classic twin study document the sobering fact that a minimum of 100 pairs, equally split by zygosity, may be required for genetic analyses of traits that exhibit moderate heritabilities.) Further, the raw data were neither age- nor gender-adjusted, and the small sample prohibits separate analyses by sex (15 of the 24 pairs were female; age range was not specified). In such small samples, failure to adjust raw data for age and gender differences can markedly inflate pair-wise resemblance.[14] Despite these serious limitations, however, the work of Shapiro, Nigotero, and colleagues remains valuable. The twin study effectively complements earlier work by the same investigators with hypertensive individuals and matched controls. The study was carefully designed and attentive to procedural detail and measurement precision. All subjects were tested in a standardized protocol begun at 8:00 A.M. following an overnight fast. For these reasons, results of the study are of heuristic interest, despite the constraints imposed by limited sampling.

To permit a comparison of their data to results reported by McIlhany and colleagues,[11] delta values were computed from the pre- and post-stimulus data listed in Tables 1 and 2 of Shapiro et al.,[12] and these delta values were submitted to modern twin analyses, employing routines developed at Indiana University.[15] The mean blood pressure (MBP) data reported by Shapiro and colleagues approximate the DBP results of McIlhany et al. For MBP response to the Stroop test, the DZ/MZ ratio of within-pair mean squares, the conventional test of genetic variance, yields an F value of 1.75 and intraclass correlations were $r_{MZ} = 0.72$ and $r_{DZ} = 0.24$. Although neither contrasts of mean squares nor correlations are significant, these results suggest that evidence of genetic variance would emerge with larger twin samples. For the ischemic pain stimulus (based on 11 MZ and 12 DZ pairs with complete data), the relevant statistics were $F = 2.74$ ($p < 0.052$), and $r_{MZ} = 0.43$, $r_{DZ} = 0.33$. In short, these data effectively complement those of McIlhany and permit the inference that genetic modulation of cardiovascular response to stress is demonstrable in adulthood as well as in adolescence.

Several twin studies using small samples are consistent with this inference. Vandenberg et al.[16] monitored heart rate (HR) responses to startling auditory and visual stimuli in 22 MZ and 16 DZ pairs of adolescent twins. Ratios of DZ/MZ within-pair variances were 2.38 ($p < 0.05$) in response to a light flash and 2.93 ($p < 0.01$) in response to a hammer dropping about three feet from the subject when a solenoid was activated. Block[17] studied 21 pairs of MZ twins, ages 16–28 years, in a conditioned discrimination procedure in which one of two tones was reinforced with electric shock. The intraclass correlation for HR measured before stress was 0.73, that for the delta in HR during conditioning was 0.67. Kryshova and colleagues[18] report that BP responses to metered cold and hot stimuli were very similar in a sample of 11 MZs representing a wide age range; only two DZ pairs were observed, and no statistical analyses were presented.

As part of a larger study, W.I. Hume[19] has reported genetic influences on level and reactivity of two cardiovascular measures, heart rate and finger pulse volume (FPV). The twin sample consisted of 95 like-sex pairs, ages 16 to 55, but nearly 60 percent were 16 to 25 with very few pairs over age 40. The twins volunteered in response to advertising appeals and, not surprisingly,[20] the sample includes many more twin sisters than twin brothers. Extensive genotyping identified 44 pairs as MZ, 51 as DZ. The twins underwent a standardized protocol designed to assess levels of physiological arousal; a 60-second cold pressor test was included. The physiological measures were sampled during three rest periods and at intervals throughout the protocol. Two measures are of particular interest here: twin comparison for resting HR and FPV (the mean amplitude of six FPV samples taken at 10-second intervals during the last minute of the rest periods) and the magnitude of HR and FPV in response to the cold pressor, expressed as the delta observed between initial level and maximum change observed during immersion of the hand. For resting HR, the intraclass correlations were 0.67 for 37 MZ pairs and 0.33 for 46 DZ pairs. Both correlations are highly significant, as is their difference, and the intrapair comparison of mean squares yielded $F = 3.91$ ($p < 0.01$). HR response to the cold pressor exhibited significant familiality, but no heritability ($r_{MZ} = 0.41$; $r_{DZ} = 0.39$). By contrast, the change in FPV during the cold pressor yielded intraclass correlations of $r_{MZ} = 0.54$ and $r_{DZ} = 0.18$ and an F value of 2.09 ($p < 0.05$). A principal component analysis of 21 variables from 128 subjects in the experiment identified a first factor of "autonomic arousal" on which the highest loading variable was FPV response to cold pressor; for this factor of autonomic reactivity, $r_{MZ} = 0.57$ and $r_{DZ} = 0.16$ with $F = 2.23$ ($p < 0.05$).

The most recent twin study of cardiovascular reactivity[21] is of special significance, for it not only establishes genetic variance in HR response, but also generates new evidence that cardiovascular hyperresponsivity may be a risk factor in the development of sustained hypertension. A sample of 80 male twin pairs, equally divided by zygosity and aged 16 to 24, was monitored during a video game previously shown to elicit intense cardiac reactivity in some individuals with a parental history of hypertension. Two eight-minute episodes of "space invaders" were played on a microprocessor each preceded by a four-minute relaxation period. Heart rate was recorded from ECG leads. For each subject, cardiac reactivity was defined as the average increment in beats per minute of HR during the video game from the average level observed during the preceding rest. Two delta values were obtained for each subject to permit an assessment of the test-retest stability of this index of reactivity; correlations were in the mid 0.70s for both MZ and DZ cotwins, suggesting that on immediate retesting, cardiac reactivity is a stable parameter of individual variation. The average delta was about seven beats per minute, and it was not associated with twin type.

The mean level of HR observed during the video game and the increment from preceding rest were highly correlated in MZ twins ($p < 0.01$); correlations from DZ twin brothers were lower and not significant. Several models were then fit to the four mean squares generated by the twin data. The simplest model includes a single parameter and implies that all observed variance in HR is attributable to idiosyncratic experience and/or measurement error. The model predicts the four mean squares are uniform. A second "environmental model" assumes an additional parameter of common experience independent of zygosity—that is, that in addition to individual experience, environmental differences shared by siblings influence HR response to task-induced stress. Goodness-of-fit tests of these models required that both be rejected. A third model, including a parameter of additive genetic effects in addition to one of idiosyncratic experience, was then tested. This model, testing for differences due to genetic variation, predicts that the ratio of mean squares observed within and between twin pairs depends on zygosity. The model adequately fit the data and yielded an h^2 estimate of 0.48 ± 0.11.

In 59 of the 80 families of the twins, the parents were interviewed, medical histories were obtained, and BP levels of parents were measured. In 11 of the 59 families, both parents either showed high casual BPs (SBP≥ 140 or DBP ≥ 90) or were under treatment for essential hypertension. The mean cardiac reactivity of the twin sons from these 11 families with positive parental history of EH was 11.6 beats per minute compared to a mean delta of 6.2 for the rest of the sample ($p < 0.01$).

Finally, Rose and his colleagues have reported[22] initial findings from a laboratory study of cardiovascular reactivity to five stressors in 239 pairs of normotensive adolescents and young adults, including 111 pairs of MZs, 66 pairs of like-sex DZs and 54 pairs of unrelated, age- and gender-matched controls. The stressors, each two minutes in duration, were presented in a fixed order: mental arithmetic, Stroop test, mirror-drawing, hand grip, and cold pressor. Preliminary analyses[23] from repeated measures ANOVAs of the BP data reveal significant pair-wide resemblance for the MZs, reliable but lower similarity in DZs, and, as expected, no resemblance in either average level or profile pattern of unrelated pairs.

TWIN STUDIES OF LABILITY OF BLOOD PRESSURE

Follow-up studies by Rose and colleagues[24] have investigated genetic influences on the level and lability of casual pressures self-monitored in the home environment. A sample of more than 110 like-sex twins, about equally split by sex and zygosity and including many participants in the laboratory study, were taught to monitor their blood pressures 6 times daily for 14 to 28 days. Preliminary analyses of these unique data document that both level (means) and lability (variances) of the home-monitored pressures exhibit significant genetic variance. Levels of DBP are significantly elevated, and labilities of pressures suggestively so, in sons with a confirmed parental history of EH. Both level and lability of BP appear to be stable characteristics of the individual twins: significant correlations were found over time (A.M. vs. P.M. pressures) and across measurement in a subset of twin participants who recorded their pressures over 16 to 24 hours on ambulatory monitors.[25]

An earlier study from Czechoslovakia[26] measured BPs 6 times at four-hour intervals from 8 A.M. to 4 A.M. in 15 twin pairs admitted to the hospital to control diet and exercise. Despite constraints of the small sample, significant h^2 estimates were obtained for BPs measured throughout the circadian cycle, and for four MZ and three DZ pairs in which one or both cotwin had EH, the repeatedly measured DBPs also revealed genetic variance. Because these investigators were unable to document heritable variance for a single measurement of casual BP, their data provide additional evidence that lability of pressure throughout the 24 hours, rather than its level at one point in time, is an important focus of future study.

CARDIOVASCULAR REACTIVITY IN NORMOTENSIVES AT RISK FOR EH

Retrospective studies document hyperresponsivity to stress among hypertensive adults. Does the exaggerated stress-reactivity precede—or follow—development of their sustained hypertension? (See also chapter by Falkner and Light.) If the former, it should characterize their normotensive children as well. Doyle and Fraser[27] were among the first to evaluate this possibility: compared to age-matched controls, for whom both parents had verified BPs<160/100 mmHg, adult sons of a hypertensive parent exhibited significantly greater change in forearm circulation to infused norepinephrine. Because the exaggerated reactivity occurred at an age (21 to 35 years) when casual BPs were normal, the heightened vascular sensitivity was assumed to represent a heritable predisposition to EH.

In the 23 years since that early report, numerous studies have compared cardiovascular reactivity in matched normotensives with and without a familial history of EH. Results permit the inference that normotensives who are at elevated risk for EH are hyperresponsive to stress and that their elevated BP levels reflect increased peripheral resistance rather than elevated cardiac output.

Reliable elevations in BP are produced by brief (10-minute) exposure to loud noise (95 to 100 dbA). Because a relationship has been found between elevated BP and noise-induced changes in the audiograms of automobile workers,[28,29] effects of industrial noise constitute a natural stress of ecological significance. Further, familial history of EH is associated with a specific hemodynamic pattern: normotensives with or without a family history of EH show elevated DBPs to industrial noise, but the increased BPs of those with positive history are due to vasoconstriction, while increments in pressure of normotensives with negative history are largely due to increased cardiac output.[30] These findings have been interpreted[28] as evidence of genetically determined individual differences in cardiovascular response to noise.

Swedish investigators[31,32] have used invasive techniques to compare hemodynamic patterns in relatives of hypertensives with age- and weight-matched controls. Elevated BPs characterize the relatives at rest and at most comparative stages during a standardized protocol that included isometric hand grip, cold pressor, and psychological stress. The elevated BPs of those at familial risk for EH appear to be due to increased peripheral resistance rather than increased cardiac output. Hyperresponsivity to stress in those with a positive familial history was most evident in contrasts of older relatives and controls, a finding that parallels other evidence that catecholamine and BP responses to cold pressor or paced mental arithmetic increase with age.[33,34]

Cardiovascular stress responses may well exhibit age × risk interaction, such that differences between normotensives with and without familial history of EH may be larger beyond age 40. But the influence of familial history can be demonstrated in early childhood. Compared to age-matched offspring of normotensive parents, five- and six-year-old children of a hypertensive father show increased BP responses to a Diptheria-Tetanus booster injection.[35] And Falkner, Onesti, and colleagues[36] found exaggerated BP and HR reactions to paced mental arithmetic among normal adolescents with a confirmed parental history of EH. The at-risk adolescents showed greater reactivity and significantly slower return to baseline following 10 minutes of mental stress.

Evidence of heightened cardiovascular stress reactivity among adolescents and young adults with positive familial history is accumulating rapidly.[37] A tabulation of 27 recent studies,[38] reveals that 19 of the 27 yield clear evidence that familial history of EH or CHD increases BP, HR, and plasma renin activity. Four additional studies showed an interactive effect of familial history and personality characteristics of the participants. Only four studies failed to find a familial risk effect and, of these, three used only the cold pressor as the stress stimulus. Given the heterogeneity of sampling, measurement, and design that characterize these studies, the overall consistency of the results underscores the robust influence of familial history on cardiovascular stress reactivity. Finally, evidence of test-retest stability of individual differences in reactivity is also mounting,[39-42] and it is likely that reactive individuals can be identified early in life and tracked over time.

FUTURE DIRECTIONS

The studies reviewed above permit a number of interim conclusions.

1. Differences in cardiovascular reactivity to laboratory stress are relatively stable characteristics of individuals. Test-retest stability over periods from minutes to months reveal that some individuals are characteristic "reactors," while others are not. This distinction, similar

to the traditional psychophysiological differentiation of "stable" and "labile" individuals, is the starting point for current studies of cardio-vascular stress response.

2. Cardiovascular reactivity is moderately heritable. Indeed, heritability estimates for measures of reactivity are at least comparable to those obtained for casual levels of pressure. They may be higher.

3. Exaggerated patterns of cardiovascular reactivity are associated with a positive familial history of essential hypertension and coronary heart disease. Higher levels of casual pressure, increased responsive-ness to transient stressors, and delayed recovery to baseline are all characteristic of individuals whose parental history for cardiovascular disease is positive.

4. The lability of BP in natural environments is also reliable and heritable. The levels of home-monitored BPs are associated with positive family history for cardiovascular disease. Whether this is true for lability as well as level is not yet established. Finally, the correspondence of laboratory stress to life events is yet to be adequately documented.

The big question remains: does increased cardiovascular reactivity con-stitute a risk factor for the development of cardiovascular disease? Does cardiovascular hyperreactivity to psychological challenge constitute a herit-able predisposition to essential hypertension? The answer to these questions will require not merely more data but new kinds of data.

We require family studies of cardiovascular reactivity rather than the study of singleton or twin offspring of hypertensive and control parents. The rationale for such family studies has been well-articulated by Childs[43] in a recent review of the causes of essential hypertension. Childs correctly argues that family methods have not been fully exploited because most previous research, such as that briefly reviewed above, merely contrasts the cardiovascular responsiveness of normotensive offspring of hypertensive parents with appropriate controls. Invariably, however, the cardiovascular responsiveness of the parents is untested. "Perhaps it is taken for granted that the parents, known to be hypertensive, would, if tested, behave the same way," but it is the comparison of entire families that is essential: "Intrafamily likeness and between-family difference is the incisive test of the genetic origin of the phenotype ... "[43, p. 23]; Childs concludes that if we do *all* the tests and gather *all* the data—demographic, physiological, biochemical, psychological—on *all* members of the families, results can be understood in the joint context of intrafamilial likeness and interfamilial differences.

An initial effort to perform this kind of study on children and their parents is in progress by Matthews and her colleagues.[44] A representative sample of children in grades K, 2, 4, and 6, their parents, and available siblings, ages 8 to 18, are tested in a stress protocol including serial subtraction, mirror drawing, and isometric hand grip. The projected data set, 130 complete family units, will be extremely informative. Research designs employing twin offspring and their parents may provide an even more robust test of genetic and environmental sources of variation on cardiovascular response patterns. The full potential of twin data in elucidating the development of essential hypertension/coronary heart disease employs a path analysis of the covariance matrices of data obtained from MZ and DZ twins and their parents. These balanced pedigrees (mother, father, and their twin siblings) yield an unusually efficient and incisive approach to the estimation of genetic and environmental parameters. This pedigree structure, based on twin children reared by their biological parents in their natural homes, can estimate effects of parental phenotype on offspring traits separately from effects attributable to parents' transmitted genes. That approach may prove particularly useful in efforts to identify the effects of parental modeling of, say, dietary habits or psychosocial life styles on blood pressure independently of the transmissible genetic effects from parent to offspring on cardiovascular response patterns.

We also need longitudinal follow-up studies in order to assess the role of cardiovascular hyperresponsivity as a risk factor in the development of cardiovascular disease. And again, those longitudinal studies will be most efficient and robust if they employ twins rather than singletons as subjects. Analysis of longitudinal twin data may offer new insights into CHD risk factors. Such analyses can be used to explore the stability of genetic and environmental influences on a metric trait measured in MZ and DZ twins at two points in time. The model-fitting approach involves specifying a path analytic model whose parameters are appropriate to the developmental observations and to one's hypothesis concerning the stability and change of genetic and environmental influences over time. The correlations observed in the data set are then expressed in terms of the theoretical parameters of the hypothesized model, the adequacy of which is evaluated with a goodness-of-fit test, comparing the correlations predicted by the model with those empirically observed.

The path analytic model assumes that the observed measures for each twin are the effects of that twin's genetic and environmental influences operating at the time of observation. The resemblance of cotwins is a function of correlated paths that express the effects of shared environments and shared genes, the latter specified as unity for MZs and 1/2 for DZs under typical assumptions. Causal paths from genetic and environmental parameters can then be specified. The observed data yield intraclass correlations of MZ and DZ cotwins at both initial testing and at follow-up. In addition to these four correlations, we now uniquely have the cross correlations for MZs and DZs—for example, of twin A at initial testing with twin B at follow-up. And, finally, the test-retest stability of individual twins yields a seventh correlation. The model parameters are then estimated from these observed correlations using minimization routines. Longitudinal twin data analyzed in this fashion will permit choices between the simplest possible model (one that specifies heritabilities at the two periods of testing to be equal and assumes that the same genetic influences operate at both time periods) to more complex models that allow the correlation between genetic influences at initial and follow-up testing to vary, perhaps with both systematic and idiosyncratic environmental effects in which the stability of such effects over time becomes a major parameter in the model. In short, longitudinal twin data have the efficiency and power to address developmental issues in research on CHD risk factors, importantly including age and gender differences in risk.

SUMMARY

The study of stress-reactivity in normotensive offspring of hypertensive parents has emerged as a central strategy in efforts to delineate developmental precursors of EH and CHD. To fully exploit that strategy, investigators should: (1) verify parental health status of both controls and at-risk samples; (2) employ standardized stress protocols including tasks requiring active, coping responses; (3) measure multiple psychophysiological (and biochemical) parameters; (4) evaluate the stability of individual differences in reactivity over time and their generalizability from laboratory analogues to life events; (5) study entire family units to assess intrafamilial resemblance and interfamilial variation simultaneously; and, finally, (6) commit time, energy, and resources for the longitudinal follow-up studies requisite to the evaluation of reactivity as an antecedent risk factor in cardiovascular disease.

REFERENCES

1. Ayman D: Heredity in arteriolar (essential) hypertension: A clinical study of blood pressure of 1524 members of 277 families. *Arch Intern Med* **53**:792–798, 1934.
2. Stocks P: A biometric investigation of twins and their brothers and sisters. *Ann Eugenics* **4**:49–107, 1930.
3. Havlik RJ, Garrison RJ, et al: Detection of genetic variance in blood pressure of seven-year-old twins. *Am J Epidemiol* **109**:512–576, 1979.
4. Feinleib M, Garrison RJ, et al: The NHLBI twin study of cardiovascular disease risk factors: Methodology and summary of results. *Am J Epidemiol* **106**:284–295, 1977.
5. Heiberg A, Magnus P, et al: Blood pressure in Norwegian twins. In Gedda L, Parisi P, Nance WE (eds): *Twin Research 3, Part C: Epidemiological and Clinical Studies.* New York, A.R. Liss, 1981, pp. 163–168.

6. Annest JL, Sing CF, et al: Familial aggregation of blood pressure and weight in adoptive families, II. Estimation of the relative contributions of genetic and common environmental factors to blood pressure correlation between family members. *Am J Epidemiol* **110**:492–503, 1979.

7. Rose RJ, Fulker DW, et al: Heritability of systolic blood pressure: Analyses of variance in MZ twin parents and their children. *Acta Genet Med Gemellologiae* **29**:143–149, 1980.

8. Rose RJ, Miller JZ, Grim CE: A developmental-genetic analysis of casual blood pressure: Effects of age, gender, genes and familial risk. Unpublished manuscript, 1984.

9. Osborne RH, De George FV, Mathers JAL: The variability of blood pressure: Basal and casual measurements in adult twins. *Am Heart J* **66**:176–183, 1963.

10. Hines Jr EA, McIlhany L, Gage RP: A study of twins with normal blood pressures and with hypertension. *Trans Assoc Physicians* **70**:282, 1957.

11. McIlhany ML, Shaffer JW, Hines Jr EA: Heritability of blood pressure: An investigation of 200 pairs of twins using the cold pressor test. *Johns Hopkins Med J* **136**:57–64, 1975.

12. Shapiro AP, Nigotero J, et al: Analysis of the variability of blood pressure, pulse rate, and catecholamine responsivity in identical and fraternal twins. *Psychosom Med* **30**:506–520, 1968.

13. Martin NG, Eaves LJ, et al: The power of the classical twin study. *Heredity* **40**:97–116, 1978.

14. McGue M, Bouchard Jr TJ: Adjustment of twin data for the effects of age and sex. *Behav Genet* **14**:325–343, 1984.

15. Christian JC, Kang KW, Norton Jr JA: Choice of an estimate of genetic variance from twin data. *Am J Hum Genet* **26**:154–161, 1974.

16. Vandenberg SG, Clark PJ, Samuels I: Psychophysiological reactions of twins: Hereditary factors in galvanic skin resistance, heartbeat, and breathing rates. *Eugenics Q* **12**:7–10, 1965.

17. Block J: Monozygotic twin similarity in multiple psychophysiologic parameters and measures. In Wortis J (ed): *Recent Advances in Biological Psychiatry* (Vol IX). New York, Plenum, 1967, pp. 105–118.

18. Kryshova NA, Beliarva ZV, et al: Investigation of the higher nervous activity and of certain vegetative features in twins. *Sov Psychol Psychiatr* **1**:36–41, 1962.

19. Hume WI: Physiological measures in twins. In Claridge G, Canter S, Hume WI (eds): *Personality Differences and Biological Variations: A Study of Twins.* Oxford, Pergamon, 1973, pp. 87–114.

20. Lykken DL, Tellegen A, Du Rubeis R: Volunteer bias in twin research: The rule of two-thirds. *Soc Biol* **25**:1–9, 1978.

21. Carroll D, Hewitt JK, et al: A twin study of cardiac reactivity and its relationship to parental blood pressure. *Physiol Behav* **34**(34):103–106, 1985.

22. Rose RJ, Miller JZ, Grim CE: Familial factors in blood pressure response to laboratory stress: A twin study. *Psychophysiology* **19**:583, 1982.

23. Rose RJ, Grim CE, Miller JZ: Familial influences on cardiovascular stress reactivity: Studies of normotensive twins. *Behav Med Update* **6**:21–24, 1984.

24. Rose RJ, Tanner CK, Christian JC: Familial influences on lability of blood pressure: Data from normotensive twins. *Circulation* **68**:III-344, 1983.

25. Rose RJ: Familial influences on ambulatory blood pressure: Studies of normotensive twins. In Weber MA, Drayer JIM (eds): *Ambulatory Blood Pressure Monitoring.* Darmstadt, Steinkopff Verlag, 1984, pp. 167–172.

26. Barcal R, Simon J, Sova J: Blood-pressure in twins. *Lancet* **ii**:1321, 1969.

27. Doyle AE, Fraser JRE: Essential hypertension and inheritance of vascular reactivity. *Lancet* **ii**:509–511, 1961.

28. Andren L: Cardiovascular effects of noise. *Acta Med Scand* **657**:1–45, 1982. (Suppl)

29. Johnsson A, Hansson L: Prolonged exposure to a stressful stimulus (noise) as a cause of raised blood pressure in man. *Lancet* i:86, 1977.

30. Andren L, Piros S, et al: Different hemodynamic reaction patterns during noise exposure in normotensive subjects with and without heredity for essential hypertension. *Clin Sci* 63:3715–3745, 1982.

31. Ohlsson O, Henningsen NC: Hemodynamic investigations on relatives of patients with essential hypertension. *Acta Med Scand* 625:7–12, 1978. (Suppl)

32. Ohlsson O, Henningsen NC: Blood pressure, cardiac output, and systemic and vascular resistance during rest, muscle work, cold pressure test and psychological stress. *Acta Med Scand* 212:329–336, 1982.

33. Palmer GJ, Ziegler MG, Lake CR: Response of norepinephrine and blood pressure response to stress increases with age. *J Gerontol* 33:482–487, 1978.

34. Barnes RF, Raskind M, et al: The effects of age of the plasma catecholamine response to mental stress in man. *J Clin Endocrinol Metab* 54:64–69, 1982.

35. Warren P, Fischbein C: Identification of labile hypertension in children of hypertensive parents. *Conn Med* 44:77–79, 1980.

36. Falkner B, Onesti G, et al: Cardiovascular response to mental stress in normal adolescents with hypertensive parents. *Hypertension* 1:23–30, 1979.

37. Krantz DS, Manuck SB: Measures of acute physiologic reactivity to behavioral stimuli: Assessment and critique. In *Proceedings of the NHLBI Workshop Measuring Psychosocial Variables in Epidemiologic Studies of Cardiovascular Disease.* Bethesda, MD, NIH Pub. No. 85-2270, 1985, pp. 407–451.

38. Matthews KA, Rakaczky CJ: Familial aspects of the Type A behavior pattern and physiologic reactivity to stress. In Dembroski TM, Schmidt TM, Blumchen G (eds): *Biobehavioral Bases of Coronary Heart Disease.* Heidelberg, Springer-Verlag, in press.

39. Manuck SB, Schaeffer DC: Stability of individual differences in cardiovascular reactivity. *Physiol Behav* 21:675–678, 1978.

40. Manuck SB, Garland FN: Stability of individual differences in cardiovascular reactivity: A thirteen month follow-up. *Physiol Behav* 21:621–624, 1980.

41. Giordani B, Manuck SB, Farmer JF: Stability of behaviorally-induced heart rate changes in children after one week. *Child Dev* 52:533–537, 1981.

42. Glass DC, Lake CR, et al: Stability of individual differences in physiologic responses to stress. *Health Psychol* 2:317–342, 1983.

43. Childs B: Causes of Essential Hypertension. In Steinberg AG, Bearn AG, et al (eds): *Progress in Medical Genetics (Vol 5), Genetics of Cardiovascular Disease.* Philadelphia, Saunders, 1983, pp. 1–34.

44. Matthews KA: Personal communication, 1984.

PART IV

STIMULATORS
OF STRESS-INDUCED
REACTIVITY

14

Overview of Classic and Stress-Related Risk Factors: Relationship to Substance Effects on Reactivity

THEODORE M. DEMBROSKI

Significant declines in deaths due to all cardiovascular disease have been observed for the past 15 years.[1] But despite the recent reductions in

Preparation of this chapter was supported by a research grant (HL-22809) awarded to the author by the National Heart, Lung and Blood Institute.

mortality rates, cardiovascular diseases still remain the leading causes of morbidity and mortality in the United States and in most industrialized societies. Indeed, heart and vascular diseases typically account for more than one-half of all deaths in any given year in the United States.[1] Even in their nonlethal acute manifestations, these diseases produce an aftermath of immense social and psychological suffering. The economic costs of these diseases by far exceed that of any other diagnostic group and may be approaching $100 billion in 1984. The latter figure is not surprising in light of the fact that National Health Interview Surveys reveal that between 15 and 20 percent of the U.S. population has one or more of the heart or vascular diseases.

Investigation by basic, applied, and clinical research of all aspects of heart and blood vessel disease clearly has uncovered a variety of factors that may be participating in the etiology of these diseases. Included here are environmental, psychosocial, nutritional, biological, and genetic influences involved in the etiology, prevention, and control of cardiovascular diseases. In short, the determinants of cardiovascular diseases are complex and multifaceted. In this connection, for example, many prospective and retrospective epidemiological studies conducted in the United States and in other countries have uncovered two separate categories of factors that are predictive of the incidence and prevalence of clinical coronary heart disease (CHD).

CATEGORY I: THE CLASSIC RISK FACTORS

The first category includes the so-called traditional risk factors such as elevations in serum cholesterol, blood pressure, and cigarette smoking frequency.[2-7] Various dietary and consumatory habits, amount of physical exercise, and failure to maintain hypotensive therapy are all behaviors that have been implicated either theoretically or empirically in one form or another in elevations of the classic risk factors. Consequently, during the past two decades, the traditional risk factors and associated behaviors have received immense attention in both primary and secondary prevention efforts. In fact, enormous amounts of resources derived from both the public and private sectors have been devoted to programs of intervention designed to alter relevant behaviors in order to reduce risk factors in a clinically significant fashion.[8,9]

Although the data linking the classic risk factors to clinical manifestations of CHD morbidity and mortality are persuasive, in many instances the best combination of traditional risk factors is not associated with the majority of new cases of CHD.[10-12] In fact, the dramatic twentieth-century rise and recent decline of cardiovascular-related morbidity cannot easily be explained by changes in diet, physical activity, diagnostic procedures, age structure of the population, genetic factors, or modification of the classic risk factors.[1,12] Additional problems are encountered when attempts are made to uncover invariant and consistent relationships between traditional risk factors and the incidence of CHD within certain cultures dissimilar to the United States.[5,13] Here, Rosenman, in particular, has pointed out a number of relevant examples including these facts: that CHD rates for males in Framingham are much higher than those for their counterparts in Yugoslavia, Hawaii, Puerto Rico, Paris, and Japan, despite both significant similarities and differences in dietary practices; that alterations in diet do not appear related to either levels of serum cholesterol in population studies or to the incidence of CHD within populations; that CHD rates are higher in East than West Finland despite similar diets; that recent declines in CHD rates in Italy occurred despite significant increases in dietary intake of red meat; that the traditional risk factors or dietary factors are not related to the progression of underlying coronary atherosclerosis as determined by repeat cardiac catheterization, and so on.[12] On the intervention side of the coin, these and similar observations have led Kaplan to suggest that many health promotion practitioners make at least four assumptions without careful scrutiny of the validity of the data on which the assumptions rest.[13] To illustrate, applying Kaplan's analysis to the diet would involve assumptions that (1) certain dietary practices (e.g., salt, fat intake) increase the risk of CHD; (2) changes in diet can reduce the probability of CHD; (3) dietary practices can be easily changed; and (4) interventions used to accomplish the changes are cost effective. Reviews of the evidence in support of these assumptions by Rosenman, Kaplan, and others generally do not strongly support any of these assumptions for the diet.

With these cautionary notes in mind, it should also be emphasized that either interventions or primary and secondary prevention efforts may still prove to strongly support the assumptions of health promotion practitioners in such areas as hypertension control and cigarette smoking cessation.[6,7,13] In sum, although the relationship between traditional risk factors and CHD morbidity and mortality remains very important, the variance in clinical CHD manifestations left unexplained by these factors has promoted a broadened search for additional pathways that may participate in atherogenesis, the pathophysiology of CHD, and ultimately, the prevention and control of CHD. Here, the expanded search has resulted in a second separate category of risk factors that generally is related to the concepts of stress and coronary-prone behaviors.

CATEGORY II: THE STRESS-RELATED RISK FACTORS

A variety of stress-related factors have been examined for association with hypertension, CHD, and sudden cardiac death, including such diverse attributes as anxiety, neuroticism, depression, social-occupational mobility, status incongruity, socioeconomic status, job freedom, occupational demand, and the like.[10] Although interesting findings continue to emerge regarding factors in the work place, for example,[14] the most compelling evidence supporting the role of behavioral factors in the pathogenesis of CHD is derived from research focusing on the Type A coronary-prone behavior pattern.[15] The Type A pattern, first characterized by Drs. Rosenman and Friedman, consists of extremes of environmentally induced hard-driving behavior, sense of time urgency, competitiveness, hostility, anger proneness, and vigorous voice and psychomotor mannerisms.[16] Independently of the classic risk factors, the Type A pattern has been prospectively and retrospectively implicated in the incidence and prevalence of clinical CHD morbidity and mortality,[10,14,15,17] and severity of underlying coronary artery disease (CAD).[18,19-20,21] Recently, however, research has failed to replicate the prospective relationship between the global Type A pattern and the incidence of clinical CHD in the Multiple Risk Factor Intervention Trial,[22] and several studies have reported no relationship between Pattern A and severity of coronary atherosclerosis at the time of cardiac catheterization.[23-27]

In sum, there are many inconsistencies in epidemiological findings regarding the relationship between the classic risk factors and clinical CHD, and, as just pointed out, there are many inconsistencies regarding the relationship between the global Type A pattern and CHD morbidity, mortality, and CAD severity. However, exciting progress is being made in attempts to refine both the classic risk factors and the stress-related risk factors. For example, advances have been made by the procedure of fractioning cholesterol into components of low-density lipoproteins (LDL) and high-density lipoproteins (HDL). Results here reveal that the former confers risk and the latter has a protective effect (see Herd[28] for a discussion of the role of behavioral factors in the production of LDL and HDL). Similarly, relationships between behavioral factors and clinical CHD and CAD have been strengthened by the procedure of measuring separately the different components of the multidimensional Type A pattern.[29] Briefly, some components of Type A, particularly hostility, as well as other attributes not ordinarily considered aspects of the Pattern A—for example, anger suppression, may be related to CHD and/or CAD even when global Type A pattern may or may not be significant in its association.[14,21,23,24,30-32] Viewed in this light, coronary-prone behavior is an evolving concept that will take on novel meaning and fresh reconceptualization as research findings emerge to guide the process.

RISK FACTORS AND REACTIVITY

An increasingly promising and productive approach to both the classic and stress-related risk factors is based on the belief that both categories can operate in concert to accelerate the atherosclerotic process and/or participate in precipitating a clinical event. From this perspective, risk factors can operate both in a static manner (e.g., clinic determinations of levels of cholesterol, blood pressure, and self-report of average smoking behavior) and in a dynamic manner (e.g., stress-induced levels of cholesterol, blood pressure, and cigarette smoking). At the outset, it should be made clear that dynamic reactions of classic risk factors in response to behavioral challenge are associated with a host of complex physiologic processes involving the central nervous system (CNS), autonomic nervous system (ANS), and associated mechanical and neuroendocrine activity.[28,33]

CHOLESTEROL AND REACTIVITY

Dimsdale and Herd[34] have recently reviewed a body of research that had remained largely dormant for more than a decade. The review clearly revealed that a majority of 60 studies showed significant increases in cholesterol and especially free fatty acid levels in response to emotional arousal induced by a variety of stressors that ranged from laboratory-based cold immersion and psychological challenges to a variety of stressful real-life events. The effect held, even when dietary intake was strictly controlled. An important task for future research is to determine whether differential stress-induced lipemic response constitutes a legitimate individual difference variable. In other words, test-retest reliability studies are needed to establish whether individuals can be generally classified into challenge-induced hyperlipemic and hypolipemic responders. If such is the case, sophisticated neuroendocrine research will be needed to identify basic physiological mechanisms that are involved in generating the hyperlipemic and hypolipemic reactivity. In this regard it will be very important to determine how dietary factors may operate in a hyperlipemic response to stress. As Dimsdale and Herd[34] point out, another central question for future study is whether individuals who show the hyperlipemic response are more prone to CHD. As will be discussed shortly, a variety of biobehavioral attributes have been associated with challenge-induced hemodynamic activity. If the hyperlipemic response to emotional arousal should prove to be a stable attribute, it will be of great interest to determine whether the same biobehavioral attributes that characterize the high pressor–heart rate responder also relate to the high lipid reactor. A best guess at this point is that such will be the case because of the intimate participation of catecholamine and other hormonal activity in both cardiovascular reactivity and lipid mobilization[28,33] (see Williams, this volume). In this connection it will be important to determine the interrelationship of a variety of challenge-induced cardiovascular, neuroendocrine, and lipid responses.

BLOOD PRESSURE AND REACTIVITY

It has been well known for some time that blood pressure (BP) can be profoundly influenced by a variety of situational and psychological factors.[35,36] In fact, since a growing body of research has demonstrated that BP is typically significantly higher in clinical situations than at home, highest of all at work, and lowest of all during sleep,[37] it is plausible that, in part, clinical determinations of BP may fall on a continuum of reactivity levels. Viewed from this perspective, so-called static or clinical determinations of BP may be a rough index of BP reactivity to challenge. If such a relationship can be demonstrated, the possibility exists that some combination of a range of more specific challenge-induced reactive levels of pressor responses may be a better predictor of future morbidity and mortality than clinic-based BP determinations. Both the research teams of Sokolow, Werdegar, et al.,[38] for instance, and more recently Devereux, Pickering, et al.[39] have demonstrated that BP response during work stress is more closely associated with left ventricular hypertrophy than clinic determinations. Since both studies were retrospective, the cause and effect relationship is unclear. However, recently Perloff et al.[40] showed that high ambulatory BP levels relative to clinic-derived BP values carried a higher risk for future cardiovascular events. Likewise, Keys, Taylor, et al.[11] demonstrated that the diastolic blood pressure (DBP) response to the cold pressor test was the best predictor available of incidence of CHD during the course of a 23-year prospective study. Similarly, prevalence studies have reported that laboratory-based challenge-induced cardiovascular reactivity was more pronounced in coronary patients than matched controls.[41–43] However, it is important to note that the results of all studies addressing this issue have not been consistent. (For a review, see Manuck and Krantz, this volume.)

Additional circumstantial evidence has involved BP reactivity in the CHD process by linking it with a variety of risk factors for CHD. For example, challenge-induced BP responses have also been associated with the Type A coronary-prone behavior pattern, family history of hypertension, borderline hypertension, essential hypertension, the male sex, and the black race[44-46] (see also Manuck and Krantz, and Falkner and Light, this volume). Here, a particularly intriguing line of research involves programmatic efforts to examine the relationship of the Type A pattern to challenge-induced levels of cardiovascular response. As of early 1984 Krantz and Manuck were able to identify at least 37 studies that had investigated challenge-induced physiologic reactivity in Type A and Type B subjects[46] (see also Manuck and Krantz, this volume). The challenges included such diverse maneuvers as "stress" interviews, mental arithmetic and other cognitive problems of varying difficulty, television games (e.g., Atari "Breakout") with and without harassment, isometric hand grip, cold pressor test with either low- or high-level challenge instructions, and the like. Of the 37 studies 26, or about 70 percent, reported greater levels of physiological reactivity in Type A than in Type B subjects (see Houston, this volume). These studies were launched with the rationale that psychophysiologic study of the Type A pattern may offer a methodology whereby certain mechanisms through which the Type A pattern confers risk may be uncovered. However, as mentioned earlier, recent findings have called into question the status of the global Type A pattern as an unequivocal risk factor for CHD and have suggested that certain components of Type A, such as hostility, may carry more of an associative burden with CHD than other components.[29] If such continues to be the case, the same rationale that guided psychophysiologic research of the Type A pattern can be applied to components of Type A and other attributes (such as anger suppression) that have been identified in epidemiological research as significant correlates of CHD.

Challenge-induced BP reactions may be relatively stable over time and thus may qualify as legitimate individual difference variables[46] (see Krantz, Manuck, and Wing, this volume). Thus, person variables, situational and task variables, and other physiologic patterns associated with BP reactivity remain important as a research focus in its own right. For example, a recent twin study revealed a significant heritability estimate for challenge-induced physiologic activity, which implicates constitutional factors in the process (see Rose, this volume). Interestingly, some of the attributes such as hostility that have been predictive of reactivity levels also have shown significant heritability levels.[45] The findings thus raise the possibility of some genetic influence on both physiologic reactivity and psychological attributes (e.g., hostility), which raises the question of whether there is a genetic basis to Type A behavior, hostility, physiologic reactivity, and clinical CHD operating in a complex phenotype-genotype manner.[29,45,46] If such is the case, the interesting possibility exists that such attributes as Type A behavior and hostility may be epiphenomena generated by more fundamental physiologic processes, or alternatively, that they may operate to exacerbate these processes in a cycliclike fashion.

The mosaic becomes even more complicated when dietary factors are considered. Recent evidence suggests that alterations in dietary consumption of sodium and potassium can increase challenge-induced BP reactivity of humans. Rankin, Luft, et al.,[47] for instance, have demonstrated that five to seven day increases in sodium intake significantly enhanced BP responses of normotensive subjects to intravenous infusion of norepinephrine. Whether the sodium intake increase would also augment BP response to psychological challenge was not tested. However, Skrabal, Aubock, et al.[48] showed that two weeks of moderate dietary salt restriction paralleled by increased potassium intake reduced the BP reaction of normotensive humans to both norepinephrine infusion *and* the challenge of mental arithmetic. Similar results have been reported for caffeine-stress interactive effects on BP.[64] The above research, together with animal work by Anderson et al.,[50] suggests that stress-diet interaction research is likely to yield new and useful information regarding both acute and chronic BP regulation (see chapters by Shapiro, Lane, and Henry; and Falkner and Light, this volume).

CIGARETTE SMOKING AND REACTIVITY IN MEN

So far, the discussion has focused on how situational and behavioral factors can interact to affect dynamic reactions of the traditional risk factors of levels of serum cholesterol and blood pressure and how such reactions have been intimately related to a variety of factors that may be important in the pathogenesis of CHD. Recently, our research team has turned its attention to the exploration of how environmental and behavioral factors can affect cardiovascular reactions to another major risk factor, cigarette smoking.

Despite the fact that many smokers increase consumption of cigarettes before, during, and after bouts of acute stress, most research concerned with the effects of smoking on cardiovascular and neuroendocrine responses has investigated smoking in a relaxed state, usually with the subject in a recumbent posture.[51,52] The few studies that have attempted to investigate how cigarette smoking and stress may combine to affect physiologic response either used passive stressors, inadequate designs, or incomplete and inappropriate measures.[53-57] Much smoking occurs during daily activity in which active coping is required by the demands of the environment, such as on the job. Since stress-related active coping alone is associated with increased ANS activity, and since the effects of nicotine alone operate in a generally similar fashion to stimulate sympathetic and parasympathetic ganglia, we reasoned that the combined effects of stress and cigarette smoking would interact to produce larger cardiovascular responses than either stress alone or smoking alone.[58]

To evaluate the latter hypothesis, a 2 × 2 factorial design was used in which the variables were smoking versus sham smoking (unlighted cigarette) and stress (video game) versus no stress (relaxation), respectively. All subjects were young male smokers ($n = 51$) who first were monitored for one hour during which no smoking was permitted. A 10-minute baseline period followed, which established that experimental groups were statistically homogeneous with regard to resting HR and BP values. Afterwards all subjects were challenged (stressed) with a "test of eye-hand coordination" involving a moderately difficult video game (Atari "Breakout"). The initial test game was initiated for three reasons. First, to confirm that the experimental groups were homogeneous with respect to challenge-induced hemodynamic activity; second, to record initial performance skill for playing the game; and third, to assess challenge-induced physiological response in order to test the proposition that hyperreactivity to a psychological challenge might be related to hyperreactivity induced by cigarette smoking. Randomly assigned subjects then either smoked or sham-smoked a cigarette and afterwards either relaxed or again played the video game (stress) under instructions to improve performance.

Results revealed that the condition of sham smoke/relax had virtually no effect on cardiovascular reactions, whereas the conditions of smoking/relaxing and sham smoking/stress produced similar increase (15/9 mmHg) in BP and HR (15 beats per minute, bpm). In sharp contrast, subjects who smoked and then engaged in the video game (stress) evidenced about twice the magnitude of BP and HR increases relative to subjects who only smoked and subjects who engaged only in the video games. In fact, the Rate Pressure Product Index (a rough index of myocardial O_2 consumption) suggested a synergistic effect that reflected levels of increase beyond the additive effects. A second major finding of the study revealed a significant correlation between BP response to the initial game (i.e., before any cigarette smoking) and BP response to simply smoking a cigarette followed by relaxation. In other words, subjects who were "hot" reactors to psychological challenge tended to be "hot" reactors to the effects of cigarette smoking alone. An important task for future research is to determine whether such is the case when the psychological challenge is separated from the bout of cigarette smoking by more than a few minutes.

Since stress alone and smoking alone both have a demonstrable impact on ANS activity, it seems clear that the combination has much more pronounced effects on cardiac function and arteriolar tone with associated increases in

HR, stroke volume, BP, and vascular resistance. These and related hormonal activity can affect thrombotic occlusion, myocardial oxygen depletion (aggravated even more by enhanced carbon monoxide levels), and increased vulnerability to a variety of arrhythmias.[28,33,51] All of these processes are almost certainly more significantly affected in the "hot" relative to the "cold" reactor, which suggests why some smokers may be at higher risk than other smokers. Of course, a prospective study is needed to address the issue, but from a physiological perspective, stress-related smoking is likely to increase risk for a CHD event, especially in those with advanced underlying atherosclerosis and, in this regard, the hyperreactor is likely to be at highest risk of all during and after such activity. Finally, it is conceivable that the stress-smoking interaction may produce transient performance decrements in complex psychomotor activity. The stress/smoking group showed a decrement in performance relative to the initial test game whereas the stress/sham smoking group actually showed performance enhancement.

CIGARETTE SMOKING AND REACTIVITY IN WOMEN

In the above study all participants were young white males. Cigarette smoking is also a potent risk factor for CHD and sudden cardiac death in women.[59,60] Yet, surprisingly little is known about physiologic response to cigarette smoking in women due to the use of primarily male subjects in such research and where women have been included, analysis of sex differences has not been reported.[61] There is ample reason to study stress-smoking effects on women because evidence suggests that women may respond with *less* physiologic response to stress than their male counterparts.[62] Certainly, to our knowledge, there have been no adequately controlled studies of how cigarette smoking and stress combine to affect cardiovascular reactions of women. Consequently, we have very recently conducted a study similar to that described above in which young women subjects were recruited as participants.[63]

Young women who were smokers ($n = 43$) were treated similarly to their male counterparts in the stress-smoking study described above. The exceptions were that after the initial test game, those in the stress condition (video game) were offered the opportunity of winning an additional $10 for superior performance (to enhance challenge) and the women played the game for at least 12 minutes after either smoking or sham smoking one cigarette. All groups were statistically homogeneous both with respect to baseline values and challenge-induced physiologic response to the initial test game prior to any smoking manipulation. Results revealed similar interactive effects of stress-smoking in women to those observed in men.

For example, during 8 to 12 minutes after sham smoke/relax, subjects were slightly below baseline (e.g., Δ SBP -0.7 mmHg). In other words, pretending to smoke had virtually no impact on BP during subsequent relaxation. Subjects in the sham smoke/stress condition were similar in BP response to those in the smoke/relax condition (e.g., Δ SPB 4.7 and 5.8 mmHg, respectively). In sharp contrast, 8 to 12 minutes after smoking a cigarette, subjects in the smoke/stress (video game) condition still showed substantial and sustained increases in cardiovascular response (e.g., Δ SBP 18.7 mmHg). Similar results were obtained for DBP and HR over the same time frame. These results clearly suggest that the stress/smoking combination is at least additive and may very well go beyond to produce synergistic effects.

In order to determine whether the smoking/stress interaction would occur in response to a different kind of challenge, one apparently more relevant to women,[49] the women were subsequently subjected to the Rosenman Type A structured interview (SI). Following a five-minute recovery period, subjects either once again sham smoked or smoked a cigarette. Afterwards, a women experimenter administered the SI in a mildly to moderately challenging manner while cardiovascular reactions were monitored. Again, pronounced and sustained differences between the groups were obtained over the entire course of the 12 to 15 minute interview. For example, HR reactions among those women who had smoked prior to the interview were consistently five to six times higher than in those who had sham smoked. In addition, as was the case with the males, "hot" reactivity to the initial test game was correlated with "hot" reactivity to cigarette smoking alone while relaxing. A new finding in this study was that amount of cigarettes typically smoked in a day, "hot" reactivity to the initial test game, and hostility scores were all significantly intercorrelated. The finding is in accord with results obtained in two previous studies of women,[49] in which high hostility scores were characteristic of women who smoke and women who responded with "hot" physiologic reactions to psychological challenge. The latter findings were based on a comparison of smokers versus non-smokers. The present study went beyond to show that number of cigarettes smoked among smokers was significantly correlated with both hostility scores and "hot" reactivity.

SUMMARY

The findings reviewed here clearly indicate that there are very complex relationships present, involving genetic factors, classic risk factors, stress, personality attributes, consumatory behaviors, and physiologic reactivity. Moreover, the observation that many consumatory behaviors covary (e.g., cigarette smoking, caffeine, alcohol) and that each can affect cardiovascular reactions to challenge[64,65] makes it clear that sorting out individual and interactive effects is a complex challenge for future research. Even more difficult will be identifying CNS, ANS, and related mechanical and neuroendocrine processes operating during interactive effects as well as gaining a precise understanding of how such processes are related to pathophysiological mechanisms in atherogenesis and clinical CHD. At the very least, new findings in this area offer more evidence of the importance of primary and secondary prevention programs. In designing such programs, one might well consider that the two separate categories of risk factors described at the outset of this paper are not so separate after all. The latter recognition should lead to more complex and useful analyses in epidemiological research that may uncover new risk factors reflecting the combination of classic and stress-related risk factor interactions that are much more potent together than the simple additive effects would suggest.

REFERENCES

1. Havlek RJ, Feinleib M (eds): *Proceedings of the Conference on the Decline in Coronary Heart Disease Mortality* Bethesda, MD, National Institutes of Health, 1979, pp. 79–161.

2. Aravanis C: The classic risk factors for coronary heart disease: Experience in Europe. *Prev Med* **12**:16–19.

3. Blackburn H: Diet and atherosclerosis: Epidemiologic evidence and public health implications. *Prev Med* **12**:2–10.

4. Kannel WB, Doyle JT, et al: Precursors of sudden coronary death. *Circulation* **51**:606–613, 1975.

5. Keys A: Coronary heart disease in seven countries: XIII multiple variables. *Circulation* **41**:138–144, 1970.

6. The Pooling Project Research Group: Relationship of blood pressure, serum cholesterol, smoking habits, relative weight, and ECG abnormalities to incidence of major coronary events: Final report of the pooling project. *J Chronic Dis* **31**:201–306, 1978.

7. Surgeon General: *Smoking and Health*. Washington, DC, Office of Smoking and Health, Department of Health, Education and Welfare Publication No. (PHS) 79–50066, U.S. Government Printing Office, 1979.

8. Farquhar JW: The community-based model of life style intervention trials. *Am J Epidemiol* **108**:103–111, 1978.

9. MRFIT Research Group: Risk factor changes and mortality results. *JAMA* **248**:1465–1477, 1982.

10. Jenkins CD: Recent evidence supporting psychologic and social risk factors for coronary disease. *N Engl J Med* **294**:987–994, 1033–1038, 1976.

11. Keys A, Taylor HL, et al: Mortality and coronary heart disease among men studied for 23 years. *Arch Intern Med* **128**:201–214, 1971.

12. Rosenman RH: Current status of risk factors and Type A behavior pattern in the pathogenesis of ischemic heart disease. In Dembroski TM, Schmidt TH, Blumchen G (eds), *Biobehavioral Bases of Coronary Heart Disease*. New York, Karger, 1983, pp. 5–17.

13. Kaplan R: The connection between clinical health promotion and health status. *Am Psychol* **39**:755–765, 1984.

14. Haynes SG, Feinleib M, Kannel W: The relationship of psychosocial factors to coronary heart disease in the Framingham study: III: Eight-year incidence of coronary-heart disease. *Am J Epidemiol* **111**:37–58, 1980.

15. Rosenman RH, Brand RJ, et al: Coronary heart disease in the Western Collaborative Group Study: Final follow-up experience of 8½ years. *JAMA* **233**:872–877, 1975.

16. Rosenman RH, Friedman M: Neurogenic factors in pathogenesis of coronary heart disease. *J Psychosom Res* **21**:323–331, 1974.

17. Brand R: Coronary-prone behavior as an independent risk factor for coronary heart disease. In Dembroski TM, Weiss SM, et al (eds): *Coronary-prone Behavior*. New York, Springer-Verlag, 1978, pp. 11–24.

18. Blumenthal JA, Williams RB, et al: Type A behavior pattern and coronary atherosclerosis. *Circulation* **58**:634–639, 1978.

19. Frank KA, Heller SS, et al: Type A behavior pattern and coronary angiographic findings. *JAMA* **240**:761–763, 1978.

20. Friedman M, Rosenman RH, et al: The relationship of behavior pattern A to the state of the coronary vasculature: A study of 51 autopsied subjects. *Am J Med* **44**:525–538, 1968.

21. Williams RB, Hanes TL, et al: Type A behavior, hostility, and coronary atherosclerosis. *Psychosom Med* **42**:539–549, 1980.

22. Shekelle RB, Hulley S, et al: The MRFIT behavior pattern study. II: Type A behavior pattern and incidence of coronary heart disease. *Am J Epidemiol* **122**:559–570, 1985.

23. Arrowood M, Uhrich K, et al: New markers of coronary-prone behavior in a rural population. *Psychosom Med* **44**:119, 1982.

24. Dembroski TM, MacDougall JM, et al: Components of Type A, hostility and anger-in: Relationship to angiographic findings. *Psychosom Med* **47**:219–233, 1985.

25. Dimsdale JE, Hackett TP, et al: Type A behavior and angiographic findings. *J Psychosom Res* **23**:273–276, 1979.

26. Krantz DS, Sanmarco MI, et al: Psychological correlates of progression of atherosclerosis in men. *Psychosom Med* **41**:467–476, 1979.

27. Scherwitz L, McKelvain R, Laman C: Type A behavior, self-involvement, and coronary atherosclerosis. *Psychosom Med* **45**:47–57, 1983.

28. Herd JA: Physiological basis for behavioral influences in arteriosclerosis. In Dembroski TM, Schmidt TH, Blumchen G (eds): *Biobehavioral Bases of Coronary Heart Disease*. New York, Karger, 1983, pp. 248–256.

29. Dembroski TM, MacDougall JM: Beyond global Type A: Relationships of paralinguistic attributes, hostility, and anger-in to coronary heart disease. In Field T, McCabe P, Schneiderman N (eds): *Stress and Coping*. Hillsdale, NJ, Erlbaum, 1985, pp. 223–242.

30. Barefoot JC, Dahlstrom WG, Williams RB: Hostility, CHD incidence and total mortality: A 25-year follow-up study of 255 physicians. *Psychosom Med* **45**:59–63, 1983.

31. Matthews KA, Glass DC, et al: Competitive drive, pattern A, and coronary heart disease: A further analysis of some data from the Western Collaborative Groups Study. *J Chronic Dis* **30**:489–498, 1977.

32. Shekelle RB, Gale M, et al: Hostility, risk of coronary heart disease, and mortality. *Psychosom Med* **45**:109–114, 1983.

33. Schneiderman N: Behavior, autonomic function and animal models of cardiovascular pathology. In Dembroski TM, Schmidt TH, Blumchen G (eds): *Biobehavioral Bases of Coronary Heart Disease*. New York, Karger, 1983, pp. 304–364.

34. Dimsdale JE, Herd JA: Variability of plasma lipids in response to emotional arousal. *Psychosom Med* **44**:413–430, 1982.

35. Ayman D, Goldshine AD: Blood pressure determinations in patients with essential hypertension. I: The difference between clinic and home readings. *Am J Med Science* **200**:465–474, 1940.

36. Brod J: Haemodynamic basis of acute pressor reactions and hypertension. *Br Heart J* **25**:227, 1963.

37. Pickering TG, Harshfield GA, et al: Blood pressure during normal daily activities, sleep, and exercise. Comparison of values in normal and hypertensive subjects. *JAMA* **247**:992–996, 1982.

38. Sokolow M, Werdegar D, et al: Relationship between level of blood pressure measured casually and by portable records and severity of complications in essential hypertension. *Circulation* **34**:279–298, 1966.

39. Devereux RB, Pickering TG, Harshfield GA: Left ventricular hypertrophy in patients with hypertension: Importance of blood pressure response to regularly occurring stress. *Circulation* **68**:470–476, 1983.

40. Perloff D, Sokolow M, Cowan R: The prognostic value of ambulatory blood pressures. *JAMA* **249**:2792, 1983.

41. Corse CD, Manuck SB, et al: Coronary-prone behavior pattern and cardiovascular response in persons with and without coronary heart disease. *Psychosom Med* **44**:449–459, 1982.

42. Dembroski TM, MacDougall JM, Lushene R: Interpersonal interaction and cardiovascular response in Type A subjects and coronary patients. *J Human Stress* **5**:28–36, 1979.

43. Sime WE, Buell JC, Eliot RS: Cardiovascular responses to emotional stress (quiz #3) interview in post-myocardial infarction patients and matched control subjects. *J Human Stress* **6**:39–46, 1980.

44. Dembroski TM, MacDougall JM, et al: Perspectives on coronary-prone behavior. In Krantz DS, Baum A, Singer JE (eds): *Handbook of Psychology and Health*. Hillsdale, NJ, Erlbaum, 1983, pp. 57–83.

45. Matthews KA: Psychological perspectives on the Type A behavior pattern. *Psychol Bull* **91**:293–323, 1982.

46. Krantz DS, Manuck SB: Acute psychophysiologic reactivity and risk of cardiovascular disease: A review and methodologic critique. *Psychol Bull* **96**:135–464, 1984.

47. Rankin LT, Luft FC, et al: Sodium intake alters the effects of norepinephrine on blood pressure. *Hypertension* **3**:650–656, 1981.

48. Skrabal F, Aubock J, et al: Effect of moderate salt restriction and high potassium intake on pressor hormones, response to noradrenaline and baroreceptor function in man. *Clin Sci* **59**:157–160, 1980.

49. MacDougall JM, Dembroski TM, Krantz DS: Effects of types of challenge on pressor and heart rate responses in Type A and B women. *Psychophysiology* **18**:1–9, 1981.

50. Anderson DE, Kearns WD, Better WE: Progressive hypertension in dogs via avoidance conditioning and saline infusion. *Hypertension* **5**:286–291, 1983.

51. Cryer PE, Haymond MW, et al: Smoking, catecholamines, and coronary heart disease. *Cardiovas Med* **2**:471–474, 1977.

52. Koch A, Hoffman K, et al: Acute cardiovascular reactions after cigarette smoking. *Atherosclerosis* **35**:67–75, 1980.

53. Fuller RGD, Forrest DW: Cigarette smoking under relaxation and stress. *Irish J Psychol* **3**:165–180, 1977.

54. Gilbert DG, Hagan RL: The effects of nicotine and extraversion on self-report, skin conductance, electromyographic, and heart responses to emotional stimuli. *Addict Behav* **5**:247–257, 1980.

55. Hatch JP, Bierner SM, Fisher JG: The effects of smoking and cigarette nicotine content on smokers' perception and performance on a psychosocially stressful task. *J Behav Med* **6**:207–217, 1983.

56. Golding J, Mangan GL: Arousing and dearousing effects of cigarette smoking under conditions of stress and mild sensory isolation. *Psychophysiology* **19**:449–456, 1982.

57. Nesbitt PD: Smoking, physiological arousal, and emotional response. *J Pers Soc Psychol* **25**:137–144, 1963.

58. MacDougall JM, Dembroski TM, et al: Selective cardiovascular effects of stress and cigarette smoking. *J Human Stress* **9**:13–21, 1983.

59. Talbott E, Kuller LH, et al: Sudden unexpected death in women. *Am J Epidemiol* **114**:671–682, 1981.

60. Willett WC, Hennekens CH, Bain C: Cigarette smoking and nonfatal myocardial infarction in women. *Am J Epidemiol* **113**:575–582, 1981.

61. Freestone S, Ramsay LE: Effect of coffee and cigarette smoking on the blood pressure of untreated and diuretic-treated hypertensive patients. *Am J Med* **71**:348–353, 1982.

62. Frankenhaeuser M: The sympathetic-adrenal and pituitary-adrenal response to challenge: Comparison between the sexes. In Dembroski TM, Schmidt TH, Blumchen G (eds): *Biobehavioral Bases of Coronary Heart Disease*. New York, Karger, 1983, pp. 91–105.

63. Dembroski TM, MacDougall JM, et al: Selective cardiovascular effects of stress and cigarette smoking in young women. *Health Psychol* **4**:153–167, 1985.

64. Lane JD: Caffeine and cardiovascular responses to stress. *Psychosom Med* **45**:447–451, 1983.

65. Levenson RW, Sher KJ, Grossman LM: Alcohol and stress response dampening: Pharmacological effects, expectancy and tension reduction. *J Abnorm Psychol* **89**:528–538, 1980.

15

Smoking, Stress, Cardiovascular Reactivity, and Coronary Heart Disease

LEONARD H. EPSTEIN, J. RICHARD JENNINGS

Smoking is related to coronary heart disease (CHD).[1] Likewise, as reviewed elsewhere in this book (see chapters by Clarkson, Manuck, and Kaplan; Herd; and Manuck and Krantz), stress and cardiovascular reactivity may be related to coronary heart disease. The purpose of this chapter is to suggest the links that may exist among smoking, stress, reactivity, and

The authors thank the other members of the working group on nicotine for their assistance in organizing the research covered in this chapter. The members of the working group were: Drs. J. Alan Herd, Theodore Dembroski, Craig Ewart, Marianne Frankenhaeuser, Jay Kaplan, Donald Leon, and Lawrence Van Egeren. Special appreciation is extended to Alan Herd, who assisted in the coordination of this working group.

291

heart disease. The chapter will be divided into six sections. Two initial sections will provide a background for examining the role of psychological stress and reactivity in heart disease. These sections are on the epidemiology of smoking and CHD and the acute physiological consequences of cigarette smoking. In the next three sections hypotheses about how smoking may be related to CHD will be developed. The first hypothesis is that stress or use of substances related to smoking (coffee, alcohol) may causes smokers to smoke, and the relationship between smoking and heart disease may be indirectly due to the fact that stress causes smokers to smoke more. The second hypothesis is that smoking may alter the perception and subsequent behavior of smokers in stressful situations, thus increasing the dose of stress and amplifying detrimental cardiovascular effects. The third hypothesis is that the effects of smoking on CHD are due to the interactions of smoking and stress to influence CHD risk so that smokers are at greater risk if they smoke and are under stress than if they only smoked. In the final section, techniques in behavioral pharmacology important for experimental research testing these hypotheses will be reviewed.

EPIDEMIOLOGY OF SMOKING AND HEART DISEASE

Investigators have estimated that 25 to 33 percent of heart disease is related to smoking.[1] Smoking has been related to the three main clinical manifestations of coronary heart disease: myocardial infarction (fatal or not), other death from CHD (sudden or not), and angina pectoris. However, smoking is not positively related to hypertension, as blood pressures of smokers are lower than those of nonsmokers.[2]

The Framingham Heart Disease Epidemiology Study provides a good demonstration of the effects of smoking on CHD. The risk of a smoker's developing myocardial infarction (MI) or other death from CHD is 2.2 times that of a nonsmoker.[3] The effects of smoking on CHD are consistent across the National Cooperative Pooling Project centers: Framingham, Albany Cardiovascular Health Center Study, and the Tecumseh Health Study. In the pooled sample the relative risks ranged from 2.6 to 4.0, with a pooled risk of 3.2.[1]

Based on the general findings that smokers are two to four times as likely as nonsmokers to develop CHD, there are at least four factors that influence the impact of smoking on CHD: age of the smoker, dose, age when smoking was initiated, and sex of the smoker.

First, smokers are at greater risk for getting CHD in comparison to nonsmokers when they are younger. The National Cooperative Pooling Project[1] showed relative risks for smokers compared to nonsmokers of 4.1,

4.8, 3.1, and 1.7 for the age groups of 45 to 49, 50 to 54, 55 to 59, and 60 to 64, respectively. Thus, the risk rises from 45 to 54, and then decreases after 60 years of age.

Second, the dose of smoking, measured in terms of number of cigarettes smoked per day or inhalation patterns, is related to increased risk. When smokers in the National Cooperative Pooling Project[1] were expressed as nonsmoker, one-half pack per day, one pack per day, and greater than one pack per day, an increasing relationship was shown for the younger groups, ages 45 to 49 and 50 to 54. No effect of increasing dose was apparent for the older men. Likewise, inhaling also influences the relative risk, with inhalers showing greater risk than noninhalers. Independent of smoking rate, inhalers had 2.2 times the risk of CHD compared to nonsmokers, while noninhalers showed a relative risk of 1.4.[4]

The relationship between dose and CHD is based on the number of cigarettes smoked per day as the estimate of dose. While the use of this rather simple estimate does predict CHD, it could be argued that the number of cigarettes smoked may not reflect the true intake of nicotine or carbon monoxide, since the content of cigarettes is changing, and smoking 40 low-tar, low-nicotine cigarettes may be related to CHD risk in a different way than smoking 40 high-tar, high-nicotine cigarettes. Research attempting to assess the effects of decreasing smoke yield on CHD have not produced convincing evidence that smokers can lower their risk of CHD by switching cigarette brands. For example, Kaufman, Helmrich, et al.[5] compared smoking rate, brand, and estimated nicotine and carbon monoxide yield in men who had suffered a nonfatal MI and in non-MI controls. The expected relationships between smoking and CHD were observed, with younger smokers at greater risk than older smokers, and a dose-response relationship was observed when dose was estimated by the number of cigarettes smoked per day. However, there were no differences in risk for index and control smokers in terms of estimated nicotine and carbon monoxide intake established by multiplying number by rated cigarette yield. Methodological factors that may qualify the use of number of cigarettes as a measure of smoking will be discussed in the final section, on behavioral pharmacology.

The age of initiation of smoking also influences CHD risk. Young (45- to 54-year-old) smokers in the American Cancer Society 25-state study[6] who began smoking before the age of 14 had a relative risk of 3.47, while those beginning to smoke between the ages of 15 and 24 had a relative risk of 3.11, and those beginning after age 25 had a relative risk of only 2.37.

Sex is an important moderator of risk for heart disease. Young women have lower rates of CHD than young men;[3,6] consequently, smoking exerts less of a relative risk on young women than on young men. For example, the American Cancer Society 25-state study showed relative risks for smoking of 2.81 for 45-to 54-year-old men and women from the ages of 55 on. For example, 55- to 64-year-old men and women have relative risks of 1.84 and 1.69. The Swedish study[7] showed the effects of age of initiation on CHD in women. Beginning to smoke at a young age (younger than 16) was associated with a relative risk of 2.00, compared to 1.10 and 1.30 for smokers beginning at ages 17 or 18 and after age 19, respectively. One important risk factor that interacts with smoking is the use of oral contraceptives. Smokers who used oral contraceptives were 5.6 times as likely to have an MI as smokers who did not use oral contraceptives; 9.7 times as likely to have an MI as nonsmoking oral contraceptive users; and 39 times as likely to have an MI as nonsmokers who did not use oral contraceptives.[8]

Smoking interacts synergistically with other cardiovascular risk factors to influence CHD. The increment in risk of CHD for a smoker with elevated blood pressure or elevated serum cholesterol compared to a smoker with normal pressure or normal cholesterol levels was threefold. Smoking, hypertension, and elevated lipids showed similar relative risks of 2.3; however, the relative risk when all three were combined was 8.2.[9]

In summary, the epidemiology data show that smoking is a very strong risk factor for CHD. A number of variables that influence the effect of smoking on CHD have been studied, such as dose, age, and sex. Approximately 30 percent of the variance in CHD is due to smoking. The interactions of stress, cardiovascular reactivity, and CHD may be important in determining how smoking affects coronary heart disease.

CARDIOVASCULAR REACTIONS TO NICOTINE DOSE

Smoking induces clear cardiovascular changes. We must consider how these cardiovascular changes interact with cardiovascular reactivity to other events, for example, stressful events. Cardiovascular reactions to stress while smoking may differ substantially from reactions to stress when not smoking or from reactions seen in nonsmokers. Prior to looking at such relationships, we will examine the dose-response relation between smoking and cardiovascular change in volunteers smoking in neutral or nonstressful laboratory settings.

Cigarette smoking induces rapid changes in cardiovascular function. Heart rate, blood pressure, and cardiac output increase during smoking and remain elevated for as long as two hours.[10] The parametric effects of nicotine and cardiovascular response were examined by reviewing a set of recent articles. The studies varied in the type of placebo dose employed, details of administration of cigarettes, and the smoking history of human volunteers. Typically, habitual smokers were deprived of cigarettes for at

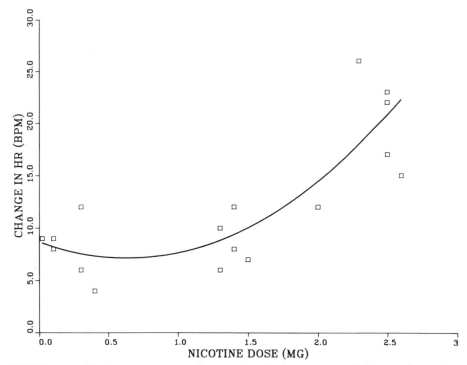

FIGURE 15.1.   Heart rate responses relative to placebo dose response. Values are the results reported in the studies reviewed. The points have been fit with the best least squares fit. The parabolic equation $y = 8.7 - 5.0x + 3.9x^2$ accounted for 68 percent of the variance.

least four hours and then smoked one cigarette of known nicotine content. Most studies compared one or two nicotine doses to a control. Despite variations in design, technique, and smoking history of volunteers, the results to be summarized were reasonably consistent.

The heart rate response to nicotine dose has been well studied. Nine studies[10–18] were used to compile the data used to create Figure 15.1. Mean change in heart rate for each dose examined in a study is plotted. The results showed considerable variations in heart rate for the placebo, which varied between lettuce leaf placebos and imaginary smoking. Responses to nicotine doses are, however, reasonably consistent and have been plotted relative to the heart rate during the placebo dose. The result suggests a positively increasing function with two interesting features. Rather small doses initiate heart rate increases to the same degree as midrange doses, while doses in the highest range initiate a second substantial rise in heart rate.

Figure 15.2 represents a similar tabulation of results from dose response studies of blood pressure.[10–15,18] The studies varied considerably in blood pressure values for the placebo dose, although dose response functions were parallel between studies. Again, the blood pressures for the placebo

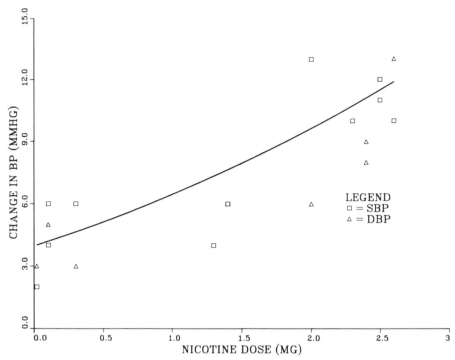

FIGURE 15.2. Blood pressure responses relative to placebo dose response. Systolic and diastolic values are presented separately, but only the systolic values are fit with the curve displayed. The best least squares fit to the systolic points was the linear equation $y = 3.8 + 3.0x$ accounting for 77 percent of the variance. A similar equation ($y = 3.5 + 2.4x$) accounted for 71 percent of the variance in the diastolic blood pressure points.

doses were subtracted from the dose values. As in Figure 15.1, the results suggest that small doses of nicotine lead to substantial increases in both systolic and diastolic pressure. The equality of the systolic and diastolic responses over the dose range is noteworthy.

Less is known about nicotine dose effects on cardiovascular contractility and vascular impedance. Indices of beta-sympathetic effects on the cardiac muscle seem to show little consistent change with nicotine dose; neither preejection period not the ratio preejection period/left ventricular ejection time is consistently altered across studies.[14,15,19] Cardiac output does seem to increase with dose, although only two studies were found.[15,18] Another change that seems reliable but not consistently dose-dependent is vasoconstriction in the fingers and toes.[17]

Further examination of the effects of nicotine on myocardial function and vascular resistance is desirable. In the interim, however, available results suggest that nicotine—even in small doses—results in widespread cardiovascular change. Heart rate, systolic and diastolic blood pressure, and cardiac output increase with dose; the peripheral vasculature constricts, but little, if any, reliable change occurs in myocardial contractility. The pattern of cardiovascular changes suggests a withdrawal or overshadowing of vagal tone, alpha-sympathetic activation, and mild beta-sympathetic activation. The response is similar to that seen with mild exercise, particularly isometric exercise.[14] This analogy is strengthened by biochemical changes that also occur with cigarette smoking: increases in catecholamines, blood lactate, and cortisol.[10,20] Note, however, that the decrease in diastolic pressure indicative of decreased peripheral resistance that occurs with aerobic exercise does not occur with nicotine.[21] From a functional perspective the value of a marked cardiovascular response in the absence of metabolic demand can be questioned, particularly when such a response is combined with an equally marked response to another nonmetabolic demand—psychological stress.

RELATIONSHIPS BETWEEN STRESS, CARDIOVASCULAR REACTIVITY, AND CORONARY HEART DISEASE

In this section three different hypotheses relating smoking, stress, and cardiovascular reactivity will be explored, based on the effects of stress and coffee and alcohol use on smoking dose; the effects of smoking on stress; and the interactive effects of stress and smoking on cardiovascular reactivity.

Indirect Effects of Stress and Substance Use on Smoking

The first hypothesis is that smoking shows a dose-response relationship with CHD, and variables like stress that may increase smoking may be indirectly influencing CHD. Stated differently, if stress increases smoking, then stress may increase the probability of heart disease by increasing smoking. Persons who are under more stress may smoke more, and thus have more CHD. Likewise, smoking may also be influenced by other substance use, as coffee drinking or alcohol use. These substances may also be increasing the probability of CHD by increasing smoking. The empirical relationship between smoking and stress or substance use serves as the basis for this hypothesis.

Stress and Smoking.   One of the major reasons reported for smoking is to relax.[22] As might be expected from these attributions, cessation rates are influenced by reasons for smoking. Smokers who smoke for affect control show lower cessation rates than smokers who smoke from habit.[22] Most relevant to the present hypotheses are the studies showing increased smoking in stress compared to nonstress conditions. For example, subjects smoked more cigarettes and took more puffs per cigarette in shock than in nonshock conditions.[23] Likewise, subjects smoked more during an EEG examination than in less stressful circumstances.[24] Finally, in a very interesting study on the interaction of smoking and level of environmental stimulation on EEG and skin conductance levels, subjects were asked to smoke or sham smoke in either white noise (stress) or sensory isolation conditions while puff frequency, strength, and duration were measured.[25] An increase in puff strength of 38 percent was observed when subjects were smoking or sham smoking under stress. Finally, in a prospective study of 600 medical students over 10 to 24 years of follow-up, subjects who smoked throughout the study period reported more stress at the initial interview than subjects who had stopped smoking or who had never smoked.[26]

Smoking, Coffee, and Alcohol Use.   Smoking may relate to the use of other substances. While these relationships will be discussed in other chapters, it may be useful to summarize the interrelationships among these health behaviors to suggest how they may prompt smoking and thus increase smoking dose. A comprehensive review of the relationships between smoking, coffee, and alcohol use was presented by Istvan and Matarazzo.[27]

Epidemiological studies have shown that people who drink a lot of alcohol are also likely to smoke. For example, in a study of 91,659 persons, 65 percent and 62 percent of male and female heavy drinkers were smokers, while 26 percent and 18 percent of male and female nondrinkers were smokers.[28] Likewise, among 20,056 subjects, 11 percent of the heavy drinkers were nonsmokers, compared to 48 percent smokers.[29]

Laboratory research has shown that drinking can set the occasion for smoking. In an analysis of the relationship between alcohol and smoking, subjects provided with alcohol or a placebo smoked more on days when they were given alcohol than on days when they were given a placebo, indicating that the enhanced smoking was not due to the increased socialization that often occurs during drinking, and that the relationship was dose-dependent.[30]

Smoking is also related to coffee consumption. Thirty-eight percent of men and 37 percent of women who were high coffee consumers also were smokers, while only 12 percent and 6 percent of nonsmoking men and women were high coffee consumers.[31] The Framingham data showed a remarkable rank order correlation of 0.99 between categories of coffee drinking and smoking.[32]

In addition, laboratory studies have shown that providing coffee to smokers will set the occasion for smoking. For example, in our laboratory,[33] we showed that smokers smoked more when given caffeinated or decaffeinated coffee than when given a coffee substitute (Postum), water, or no beverage, but smoking rate did not show a dose-response relationship to cups of coffee consumed. The fact that the amount of smoking in the presence of either caffeinated or decaffeinated coffee was not different but that the amount of smoking with both was higher than with Postum, which was also higher than with water or nothing, suggests that the effects of coffee are not caffeine dependent, but rather are based on conditioning by having coffee paired with smoking numerous times. Kozlowski[34] compared smoking nicotine intake by filter analysis for smokers who were given decaffeinated coffee with 0, 75, 150, and 300 mg of caffeine added. Results showed no differences in intake of nicotine for heavy users of caffeine in any of the caffeine conditions. However, among light caffeine users, greatest intake of nicotine took place when they were given no caffeine.

Thus, in summary, stress, coffee, or alcohol can increase the probability of smoking. Since epidemiological studies have shown a dose-response relationship of smoking with heart disease, behavioral variables that increase smoking may increase the probability of heart disease.

Effects of Smoking on Stress

The second hypothesis relating stress, smoking, and heart disease is that smoking alters the perception of environmental and bodily cues leading to a dissociation between bodily state and environmental demand. This dissociation is likely to increase exposure to nonmetabolic cardiovascular changes due either to smoking or stress, which may increase the risk of CHD. The effect of smoking on the regulation of psychological stress is complex and has been covered in three excellent reviews.[35-37] Salient aspects of the influence of smoking on the perception and evaluation of stressful situations and subsequent behavior are summarized in this section.

Smoking, like stress, involves changes in subjective, behavioral, and physiological state. These changes are perceived and play a role in the initiation and maintenance of behavior. Typically, when stress induces dysphoria and a perception of arousal, we act to decrease stress. If, however, subjective and bodily cues are altered by smoking, we may interpret cues differently and act differently. A first step in this argument is to examine the effects of smoking on subjective, behavioral, and physiological states.

Smokers report smoking for both relaxation and stimulation.[35] Similarly, nicotine has been categorized pharmacologically as a stimulant or a depressant and induces both types of effects.[35] Nicotine generally acts as a stimulant for the autonomic nervous system (see prior section on cardiovascular changes) and might thus be expected to be accompanied by muscle tension and central nervous system activation, that is, fast, low-voltage EEG and amplified evoked potentials. In fact, nicotine is a muscle relaxant and induces complex central nervous system changes. Resting EEG generally appears "more aroused" after smoking; the dominant alpha wave frequency is increased.[35] Evoked potential and contingent negative variation changes have, however, been found to depend on stimulus intensity and individual characteristics; that is, smoking will induce different directions of change in different individuals and in different situations.[35-38] Gilbert[35] suggests that the evoked potential results argue for studies of physiological reactivity in situations other than the usual, resting condition. Such studies may show, for example, that stimulant effects do not occur in all individuals if tested in stressful conditions. In one relevant study,[39] ambulatory recording of heart rate did not show increased heart rate response to smoking, in marked contrast to laboratory studies.

The self-reports of subjective states by smokers have been supported in laboratory trials. Research suggests that most smokers deprived of cigarettes and then asked to perform a task or fill out ratings will report less anxiety and aggressive feelings after smoking a nicotine cigarette than after smoking a placebo.[37] There may be important individual differences in the effects of smoking on subjective state. For example, smokers who smoke for tranquility have been found to perform differently after smoking from smokers who smoke for arousal.[40] The animal literature suggests that smoking reduces negative emotions and aggression and increases tranquility.[35] In sum, smoking alters subjective and physiological states, but the effects are complex. Changes in the autonomic and central nervous systems may differ, and may depend on both the environmental setting and the individual. Smokers can be separated into those who smoke for tranquility and those who smoke for arousal, but these subjective differences may not be due to differences in physiological responses to smoking.

The literature on perceptual changes after smoking may relate to the seemingly conflicting reports of tranquility and arousal. Depending on the nature of the stimulation and focus of attention, smoking seems to attenuate some cues and amplify others. Early studies found that electric shock thresholds were higher after smoking a nicotine cigarette than after smoking a placebo,[41] and Epstein, Dickson, et al.[42] reported decreased sensitivity to kinesthetic information while smoking during mental arithmetic. Both of these influences might lead to a reduced sensitivity to a potentially stressful stimulus. This is consistent with an enhancement of alertness or arousal only if this alertness is focused away from relatively peripheral bodily cues. Smokers report an increase in focused alertness—an increased ability to concentrate on a single task to the exclusion of distractions.[35,36] Such an effect is consistent with an inverted U model of arousal suggesting that smoking increases arousal, thereby narrowing the focus of attention.[43] Thus, while smoking, smokers would be more focused on their primary activities, and less aware of peripheral irritants and subtle cues, such as minor bodily aches and pains, and signs of interpersonal difficulties. A similar hypothesis has been advanced for the effects of Type A behavior.[44,45]

Briefly, the attentional hypothesis suggests that health-relevant information is available from relatively subtle events. One class of events are mild aches and pains that are easy to ignore but that may be signs of disease. While smoking, these signs would be unavailable to the smoker, thus removing a signal to seek appropriate medical evaluation. A second class of health-relevant but subtle cues are social cues for emotional support. Appropriate responses to such cues are likely to be necessary to maintain a supportive social network. If smokers miss such while smoking, their networks may be impoverished, and any health benefits of social support may than be compromised.

A final area to consider in the smoking-stress relationships is the effects of smoking on task performance. We have argued that smoking may selectively alter bodily state and the perception of environmental and bodily cues, but we have not shown that these changes have a functional effect, that is, that they change performance or behavior. Performance can index effects of subjective state and perceptual changes and also act as a stressor itself—with poor performance increasing stress and good performance decreasing it. In habitual smokers, smoking during simple vigilance type tasks leads to consistently better performance than nonsmoking, particularly late in the testing session.[46] The maintained performance occurs despite reports of decreased alertness that are similar in smoking and nonsmoking conditions. Other studies show similar enhancement of performance when smokers are compared to nonsmoker controls, rather than nonsmoking smokers.[37] Such results can again be related to the inverted U model of arousal if smoking leads to small increases in arousal that permit appropriately enhanced attention. The model also predicts that smoking with a high nicotine dose and performing a task requiring flexible attention leads to decreased rather than improved performance. However, at this time such evidence seems unavailable, and the other evidence reviewed suggests that treating smoking as a stimulant inducing general arousal may be too simple an approach to a comprehensive model of smoking and stress.

In conclusion, smoking does influence stress regulation in both positive and negative ways. Smoking probably exacerbates the detrimental effects of stress by inappropriately maintaining performance beyond the time when active coping is adaptive, by decreasing the perception of important but not salient bodily and social cues, and possibly by impairing performance on complex tasks. In contrast, smoking may combat stress by improving performance on simple, continuous tasks, by reducing aggressive and negative feelings, and by inducing tranquility during periods of high subjective arousal. Both benefits and costs of smoking depend on the match between the demands of the situation and the changes induced by smoking. Overall, however, to the smokers, smoking appears to be a positive tool for combating stress. When smoking is acting to reduce perceived stress, the negative aspects of smoking are less apparent to the smoker but may in fact be more significant from the health perspective. Smoking potentiates physiological responses in the absence of metabolic need, and due to the addictive nature of smoking, it does so repeatedly, even when smoking is not being used as a stress-reducing or performance-enhancing tool.

Interaction of Stress and Smoking

The third hypothesis is that stress and smoking interact in an additive or synergistic fashion to promote CHD. This hypothesis is based on the assumption that the magnitude of cardiovascular change in response to laboratory stressors is related to the subsequent development of CHD. In this way, stimuli that amplify cardiovascular change to laboratory stressors may make the effects of stressors more salient and more predictive of CHD However, simple cardiovascular change is not a sufficient definition of reactivity. For example, exercise produces large and sustained cardiovascular response to standardized laboratory stressors, and most people believe that exercise is good for the cardiovascular system.[21] Thus, a response must be mediated by mechanisms similar to those that influence the stress response in order to be considered as evidence for cardiovascular reactivity. Mac-Dougall, Dembroski, et al.[47] have suggested that the mechanisms that influence cardiovascular function for both smoking and stress are similar. Both alter cardiovascular function in part by increasing sympathetic nervous system activity, and both are associated with release of norepinephrine in the heart and smooth muscles, and epinephrine from the adrenal medulla. In addition, smoking may act directly on the central nervous system, potentiating sympathetic nervous system activity. Thus, smoking is similar to the action of stress in many ways and may not only add to the cardiovascular changes produced by stress, but may also potentiate sympathetic nervous system activity.

Two studies have measured cardiovascular change in subjects under stress and smoking situations. In the first study, MacDougall et al.[47] had young male moderate-rate smokers (15.9 cigarettes/day) participate in one of four experimental conditions formed by crossing smoking/sham smoking with stress (playing Atari "Breakout")/nonstress. Smoking involved smoking a 1.0 mg nicotine Marlboro cigarette in a standardized way. The experiment involved two phases. In the first phase, all subjects played the video game to obtain a baseline estimate of reactivity. The next phase involved three trials of smoking or sham smoking followed by game playing or rest. Results for systolic and diastolic blood pressure, heart rate, and rate-pressure product showed a similar pattern. No changes were observed for subjects in the sham smoking/rest condition, while increases of a similar magnitude were observed for both stress and smoking conditions, with additive effects of smoking plus stress. For example, smoking or stress was associated with about a 15 beats per minute (bpm) increase in heart rate, while smoking plus stress produced increases of about 30 bpm. The increases were relatively stable across the three trials.

Epstein, Dickson, et al.[42] were interested in the effects of smoking on perception of muscle tension as a function of concurrent task requirements. The study involved a within-subject design in which each of 12 moderate rate, young subjects (6 male, 6 female) participated in four conditions, with smoking/nonsmoking crossed with mental arithmetic/relaxation. Subjects smoked their regular cigarette in a standardized manner. Each session of the experiment involved a 15-trial electromyography (EMG) magnitude production task,[48] in which subjects produced EMG levels that corresponded to subjective estimates of different intensities. During the one-minute intertrial intervals, the smoking and stress conditions were imposed. Heart rate was measured to document the degree of arousal produced by the experimental manipulations. Analysis across both sexes showed reliable effects of smoking and stress on heart rate change, with an average increase due to smoking of 9.2 bpm, with an average change due to stress of 8.5 bpm. The combination of stress plus smoking resulted in an average increase of 13.0 bpm. Analysis by sex showed significant interaction of smoking and stress only for females. Males showed no differences in heart rate change to stress and smoking conditions, and thus no interaction between stress and smoking.

The results of these two studies suggest that smoking plus stress may enhance cardiovascular responses more than stress alone. The effects have been observed only in moderate-rate young smokers, and research should be extended to older smokers, who are at greater risk for CHD. In addition, there may be effects of the type of stressor and type of cigarette on cardiovascular change that should be systematically explored.

APPLICATIONS OF BEHAVIORAL PHARMACOLOGY TO CARDIOVASCULAR REACTIVITY AND STRESS

Since the primary response in cardiovascular reactivity research involves heart rate or blood pressure changes from baseline, and since these changes may be directly influenced by nicotine and drug administration, it is important to understand how various behavioral pharmacological principles may be relevant in research of this type.

The first methodological point in research of this type is the identification of the pharmacological agent. In smoking, the agent of interest is often nicotine. However, investigators must be aware that the subject is presented with much more than nicotine or carbon monoxide (CO) when smoking. For this reason, research in which the method of nicotine delivery is via smoking may be confounding the pharmacological stimuli. Alternative methods of delivering nicotine, such as intravenously, by gum, or by "liquid snuff,"[49–51] are preferable as they isolate the pharmacological stimulus. However, they are not ideal preparations since the route of administration and mechanism of action of these alternative ways to administer nicotine are different from that of smoking. A method of delivering nicotine that is similar to smoking would be an important methodological contribution to this area of research.

Research on nicotine dose suggests that careful attention must be paid to the standardization of dose across subjects. One method is to deliver the same dose per subject, another is to deliver the same relative dose, based on mg/kg of body weight. If the dose of nicotine is delivered independent of smoking, then the amount of the nicotine dose can be calibrated. However, when nicotine is delivered by smoking, direct measures of nicotine intake are needed to equate the intake across subjects. One method for quantifying nicotine intake is to perform an analysis of nicotine in cigarette butts, as Kozlowski[34] did in his analysis of the interaction of smoking and coffee drinking. Second, direct measures of smoking topography are available, in which the intake of smoke volume, as well as microanalyses of the act of smoking, such as puff, puff duration, and cigarette duration are recorded.[52] The control of nicotine dose across subjects may not equate cardiovascular change across subjects. The smoking history and usual nicotine intake of the subject may be an important consideration. Cardiovascular change is also likely to be related to the tolerance of subjects to nicotine.[53] If subjects who usually smoke high-nicotine cigarettes are given low levels of nicotine for study, their level of cardiovascular change may be much lower than typical. In addition, the time of day is an important determinant of tolerance. If subjects are measured late in the day after they have smoked many cigarettes, then it might be expected that their responses will be less than those of individuals who have not smoked at all that day.

Cardiovascular changes due to smoking may be related to baseline levels of heart rate. Baseline levels of cardiovascular function, as well as the amount of change, may vary as a function of period of withdrawal. Resting heart rate and blood pressure will change after cessation,[54] and these changes may interact with stress or smoking to influence the magnitude of heart rate change.

The importance of understanding the dose and actions of nicotine can be shown by examining the research on high- and low-yield cigarettes and CHD. There is a similarity in risk of CHD for smokers who smoke different yield cigarettes, and this fact is in many ways not surprising. The rated yield of cigarettes based on smoking machines is not an accurate estimate of the actual intake of smokers, as smokers may take different numbers of puffs on low-yield cigarettes compared to high-yield cigarettes;[55] smokers may block the holes of low-yield cigarettes;[56] and smokers may alter their topography in order to extract a usual level of nicotine from lowered-yield cigarettes.[57] In addition, a number of studies have shown similar CO and serum nicotine levels across subjects who have self-selected high- and low-yield cigarettes.[58,59] In our laboratory, 40 smokers of high yield cigarettes were randomly assigned to a group that was faded from their standard brand to lower-yield cigarettes or a group that continued to smoke their standard cigarettes.[60] The number of cigarettes smoked was held constant across the groups. Results showed no differences in expired CO levels across the groups, even though the intake of nicotine and CO were drastically reduced. Thus, even though the levels of nicotine and CO in the cigarettes were known, these levels may not actually reflect the exposure of the subjects.

One way to improve the prediction of risk by dose and to quantify the exposure of subjects may be to directly measure the dose by the use of expired air (COa) or serum (COHb) measures of CO, or serum or salivary thiocyanate (SCN) or nicotine measures. Wald, Howard, et al.[61] showed that COHb was very useful in the prediction of CHD, above and beyond the information on number of cigarettes per day. Male smokers with COHb levels greater than 5 percent were 21 times as likely as someone with a COHb of less than 3 percent to develop CHD. The effect was independent of number of cigarettes; thus if two men smoked the same number of cigarettes but differed in COHb levels, the COHb was predictive of risk.

Serum SCN measures were assessed as predictors of CHD in men living in East and West Finland.[62] The SCN values could be used to discriminate occasional (1–9 cigarettes per day) from more regular users but could not differentiate moderate and heavy smokers. In addition, the SCN values were directly related to CHD risk, with coronary mortality rising from 11.4 percent to 18.9 percent in East Finland, and 6.7 percent to 11.2 percent in West Finland as SCN values increased from below 50 to 51–90, to greater than 90.

SUMMARY

The research reviewed shows that smoking, stress, and cardiovascular reactivity are related. While the research in this area is very new, several points can be made:

1. Smoking is related to CHD, and there are a variety of epidemiological risk factors that may be important to examine when studying smoking, stress, reactivity, and CHD relationships. These include sex, age, duration of smoking, and dose of smoking.

2. Stress, coffee consumption, and alcohol use increase the rate of smoking in smokers. Each of these variables may be contributing to CHD by increasing the dose of smoking.

3. Smoking and stress interact in cardiovascular reactivity, so that the cardiovascular response is larger for someone who smokes under stress than someone who smokes during relaxation.

4. Smoking may serve to increase the dose of stress to which a person is exposed by decreasing the perceptual sensitivity to bodily cues associated with stress, or by improving performance during fatigue or stress, thereby reducing performance cues normally associated with the termination or avoidance of a stressor.

5. Methodology in behavioral pharmacology should be used to determine the smoking dose and to reduce the influence of other factors that may influence cardiovascular reactivity, such as drug tolerance.

RECOMMENDATIONS FOR FUTURE RESEARCH

1. The interactive or synergistic effects of smoking, reactivity, and CHD should be established. Are smokers who are the most reactive the ones who get CHD? Or are there relationships between smoking and sex, age, duration, or smoking dose and reactivity that best predict the development of CHD?

2. The relationships between smoking, reactivity, and stress or substance use should be established. Are the smokers who are the most reactive the ones who are under the most stress, or the ones who use the most coffee or alcohol?

3. The mechanism for the effect of smoking on affect regulation should be better understood. The role of smoking on perception of cues related to components of the stress response that may influence symptoms perception or social support should be investigated.

4. The interactions between smoking and stress response should be studied. Different types of stressors, such as physical stressors, and the characteristics of the pharmacological stimulus should be evaluated.

5. The role of smoking in reactivity should be established in prospective cessation studies, in which the immediate and long-term effects of

cessation on reactivity are understood. Is there a decrease in reactivity to stressors in reactive smokers after smoking cessation?

REFERENCES

1. U.S. Department of Health and Human Services: *The Health Consequences of Smoking: Cardiovascular Disease. A Report of the Surgeon General.* Rockville, MD, Department of Health and Human Services, DHHS Publication No. (PHS) 34–50204, 1983.

2. U.S. Department of Health, Education, and Welfare. *Smoking and Health: A Report of the Surgeon General.* Bethesda, MD, U.S. Department of Health, Education, and Welfare, Public Health Service, Office of the Assistant Secretary for Health, Office on Smoking and Health, DHEW Publication NO. (PHS) 79–50066, 1979.

3. Dawber TR: *The Framingham Study: The Epidemiology of Atherosclerotic Disease.* Cambridge, MA, Harvard University Press, 1980.

4. Doll R, Hill AB: Mortality of British doctors in relation to smoking: Observations in coronary thrombosis. In Haenzel W (ed): *Epidemiological Approaches to the Study of Cancer and other Chronic Diseases.* Bethesda, MD, U.S. Department of Health, Education and Welfare, National Cancer Institute, 1966, pp. 205–268.

5. Kaufman DW, Helmrich SP, et al: Nicotine and carbon monoxide content of cigarette smoke and the risk of myocardial infarction in young men. *N Engl J Med* **308**:409–413, 1983.

6. Hammond EC, Garfinkel L: Coronary heart disease, stroke, and aortic aneurysm. Factors in the etiology. *Arch Environ Health* **19**:167–182, 1969.

7. Wilhelmsen L, Bergtsson C, et al: Multiple risk prediction of myocardial infarction in women compared to men. *Br Heart J* **39**:1179–1185, 1977.

8. Shapiro S, Rosenberg L, et al: Oral contraceptive use in relation to myocardial infarction. *Lancet* **31**:743–747, 1979.

9. Kannel WB: *Habits and Coronary Heart Disease. The Framingham Heart Study.* Bethesda, MD, U.S. Department of Health and Human Services, National Heart Institute, Public Health Service, 1966.

10. Spohr U, Hofmann W, et al: Evaluation of smoking-induced effects on sympathetic, hemodynamic and metabolic variables with respect to plasma nicotine and COHb levels. *Atherosclerosis* **33**:271–283, 1979.

11. Aronow WS, Dendinger J, Rokaw SN: Heart rate and carbon monoxide level after smoking high-, low-, and non-nicotine cigarettes: A study in male patients with angina pectoris. *Ann Intern Med* **74**:697–702, 1971.

12. Frankenhaeuser M, Myrsten AL, et al: Dosage and time effects of cigarette smoking. *Psychopharmacologia* **13**:311–319, 1968.

13. Koch A, Hoffmann K, et al: Acute cardiovascular reactions after cigarette smoking. *Atherosclerosis* **35**:67–75, 1980.

14. Rabinowitz BD, Thorp K, et al: Acute hemodynamic effects of cigarette smoking in man assessed by systolic time interval and echocardiography. *Circulation* **60**:752–760, 1979.

15. Raeder EA, Burckhardt D, et al: Effects of smoking and inhalation of carbon monoxide on systolic time intervals and blood pressure: Differences between two types of cigarettes and a cigar. *Chest* **75**:136–141, 1979.

16. Smith DL, Tong JE, Leigh G: Combined effects of tobacco and caffeine on the components of choice reaction-time, heart rate, and hand steadiness. *Percept Mot Skills* **45**:635–639, 1977.

17. Suter TW, Buzzi R, Battig K: Cardiovascular effects of smoking cigarettes with different nicotine deliveries. *Psychopharmacology* **80**:106–112, 1983.

18. Tachmes L, Fernandez RJ, Sackner MA: Hemodynamic effects of smoking cigarettes of high and low nicotine content. *Chest* **74**:243–246, 1978.

19. Markiewicz K, Cholewa M: Effect of several cigarettes smoked uninterruptedly on left ventricular systolic time intervals in healthy subjects. *Acta Physiol Pol* **33**:91–100, 1982.

20. Cryer PE, Haymond JW, et al: Norepinephrine and epinephrine release and adrenergic mediation of smoking-associated hemodynamic and metabolic events. *N Engl J Med* **295**:573–577, 1976.

21. Robinson S: Physiology of muscular exercise. In Mountcastle VB (ed): *Medical Physiology* (Vol 2). St. Louis, Mosby, 1974, pp. 1273–1304.

22. Pomerleau OF, Adkins DM, Pertschuk M: Predictors of outcome and recidivism in smoking-cessation treatment. *Addict Behav* **3**:65–70, 1978.

23. Schachter S, Silverstein B, et al: Studies of the interaction of psychological and pharmacological determinants of smoking. *J Exp Psychol* (Gen) **106**:3–40, 1977.

24. Comer AK, Creighton DE: The effect of experimental conditions on smoking behavior. In Thornton RE (ed): *Smoking Behaviour: Physiological and Psychological Influences*. Edinburgh, Churchill Livingston, 1978, pp. 76–86.

25. Mangan GL, Golding J: An "enhancement" model of smoking maintenance. In Thornton RE (ed): *Smoking Behaviour: Physiological Influences*. Edinburgh, Churchill Livingston, 1978, pp. 87–114.

26. Thomas CB: The relationship of smoking and habits of nervous tension. In Dunn WL (ed): *Smoking Behavior: Motives and Incentives*. Washington, DC, Winston, 1973.

27. Istvan J, Matarazzo JD: Tobacco, alcohol, and caffeine use: A review of their interrelationships. *Psychol Bull* **95**:301–326, 1984.

28. Klatsky AL, Friedman GD, et al: Alcohol consumption among white, black, or Oriental men and women: Kaiser-Permanente multiphasic health examination data. *Am J Epidemiol* **105**:311–323, 1977.

29. Kaprio J, Hammer N, et al: Cigarette smoking and alcohol use in Finland and Sweden: A cross national twin study. *Int J Epidemiol* **106**:194–202, 1977.

30. Griffiths RR, Bigelow GE, Liebson I: Facilitation of human tobacco self-administration by ethanol: A behavioral analysis. *J Exp Anal Behav* **25**:279–292, 1976.

31. Friedman GD, Siegelaub AB, Seltzer CC: Cigarettes, alcohol, coffee and peptic ulcer. *N Engl J Med* **290**:569–473, 1974.

32. Dawber TR, Kannel WB, Gordon T: Coffee and cardiovascular disease: Observations from the Framingham study. *N Engl J Med* **291**:871–874, 1974.

33. Marshall WR, Epstein LH, Greene SB: Coffee drinking and cigarette smoking: I. Coffee, caffeine and cigarette smoking behavior. *Addict Behav* **5**:389–394, 1980.

34. Kozlowski LT: Effects of caffeine consumption on nicotine consumption. *Psychopharmacology* **47**:165–168, 1976.

35. Gilbert DG: Paradoxical tranquilizing and emotion-reducing effects of nicotine. *Psychol Bull* **86**:643–661, 1979.

36. Leventhal H, Cleary PD: The smoking problem: A review of the research and theory in behavioral risk modification. *Psychol Bull* **88**:370–405, 1980.

37. Stepney R: Smoking behaviour: A psychology of the cigarette habit. *Chest* **74**:325–344, 1980.

38. Knott VJ, Venables PH: Separate and combined effects of alcohol and tobacco on the amplitude of the contingent negative variation. *Psychopharmacology* **70**:167–172, 1980.

39. Cellina GU, Honour AJ, Littler WA: Direct arterial pressure, heart rate, and electrocardiogram during cigarette smoking in unrestricted patients. *Am Heart J* **89**:18–25, 1975.

40. Myrsten A, Anderson K, et al: Immediate effects of cigarette smoking as related to different smoking habits. *Percept Mot Skills* **40**:515–523, 1975.

41. Mendenhall WL: A study of tobacco smoking. *Am J Physiol* **72**:549–557, 1925.

42. Epstein LH, Dickson BE, et al: The effect of smoking on perception of muscle tension. *Psychopharmacology* **83**:107–113, 1984.

43. Easterbrook JA: The effect of emotion on CO utilization and the organization of behavior. *Psychol Rev* **66**:183–201, 1959.

44. Jennings JR: Attention and coronary heart disease: A reconceptualization of behavioral risk factors. In Baum A, Krantz DS, Singer JE (eds): *Handbook of Psychology and Health*. Hillsdale, NJ, Erlbaum, 1983, pp. 85–124.

45. Matthews KA, Brunson B: Allocation of attention and Type A coronary prone behavior. *J Pers Soc Psychol* **38**:525–537, 1979.

46. Waller D, Levander S: Smoking and vigilance: The effects of tobacco smoking on CFF as related to personality and smoking habits. *Psychopharmacology* **70**:1331–1336, 1980.

47. MacDougall JM, Dembroski TM, et al: Cardiovascular effects of stress and cigarette smoking. *J Human Stress* **9**:13–21, 1983.

48. Stevens SS: Problems and methods of psychophysics. *Psychol Bull* **55**:177–196, 1958.

49. Kumar R, Cooke EC, et al: Is nicotine important in tobacco smoking? *Clin Pharmacol Ther* **21**:520–529, 1977.

50. Russell MAH, Jarvis MJ, Feyerabend C: A new age for snuff? *Lancet* **1**:474–475, 1980.

51. Russell MAH, Jarvis MJ, et al: Nasal nicotine solution: A potential aid to giving up smoking? *Br Med J* **286**:683–684, 1983.

52. Creighton DE, Noble MJ, Whewell RT: Instruments to measure, record and duplicate human smoking patterns. In Thornton RE (ed): *Smoking Behaviour: Physiological and Psychological Influences*. Edinburgh, Churchill Livingston, 1978, pp. 277–288.

53. Jarvik ME: Tolerance to the effects of tobacco. In Krasnegor NA (ed): *Cigarette Smoking as a Dependence Process*. Bethesda, MD, Department of Health, Education, and Welfare, NIDA Research Monograph 23, 1979, pp. 150–158.

54. Hughes JR, Hatsukami DK, et al: Effect of nicotine on the tobacco withdrawal syndrome. *Psychopharmacology* **83**:82–87, 1984.

55. Kozlowski LT, Rickert WS, et al: Have tar and nicotine yields of cigarettes changed? *Science* **209**:1550–1551, 1980.

56. Kozlowski LT, Frecker RC, et al: The misuse of "less hazardous" cigarettes and its detection: Hole-blocking of ventilated filters. *Am J Public Health* **70**:1202–1203, 1980.

57. Epstein LH, Ossip DJ, et al: Measurement of smoking topography during withdrawal or deprivation. *Behav Ther* **12**:507–519, 1981.

58. Benowitz NL, Hall SM, et al: Smokers of low-yield cigarettes do not consume less nicotine. *N Engl J Med* **309**:139–142, 1983.

59. Russell MAH, Sutton SR, et al: Long-term switching to low-tar low-nicotine cigarettes. *Br J Addict* **77**:145–158, 1982.

60. Ossip DJ, Epstein LH, et al: Does switching to low tar/nicotine/CO yield cigarettes decrease nicotine dependence and cardiovascular risk? *J Consult Clin Psychol* **51**:234–241, 1983.

61. Wald N, Howard S, et al: Association between atherosclerotic diseases and carboxyhaemoglobin levels in tobacco smokers. *Br Med J* **1**:761–765, 1973.

62. Heliovaara M, Karvonen MJ, et al: Serum thiocyanate concentration and cigarette smoking in relation to overall mortality and to deaths from coronary heart disease and lung cancer. *J Chron Dis* **34**:305–311, 1981.

16

Caffeine, Cardiovascular Reactivity, and Cardiovascular Disease

DAVID SHAPIRO, JAMES D. LANE, JAMES P. HENRY

Caffeine ranks with alcohol and nicotine as one of the most widely used (and abused) psychotropic agents in contemporary society. It occurs naturally in such foods and beverages as coffee, tea, cocoa, and chocolate, and it is commonly added to soft drinks and prescription and nonprescription medications. Caffeine is used in forms, concentrations, and amounts that vary widely from country to country and individual to individual. This greatly complicates the analysis of its significance for behavior and health. Although caffeine has generally been considered benign, evidence concerning

We thank members of the caffeine working group at the conference for their discussion of the issues. Dr. Shirley Mueller contributed the material on phenylpropanolamine.

its acute and chronic effects on behavior, emotional state, and physiological functioning provides good justification for hypothesizing that it is an important stimulator and modulator of stress effects on cardiovascular reactivity. Consequently, caffeine is of significance as a risk factor for cardiovascular disease. Scientific debate continues, especially about the last statement, with different interpretations of the clinical, experimental, and epidemiological data. This is understandable given the complexity of the interactions involved and the relatively meager data available. Nonetheless, public interest in the potential health hazards of caffeine has increased in recent time, as shown by the promotion and increased availability of decaffeinated and caffeine-free beverages. A current revival of scientific research on caffeine is also evident.

This chapter will focus on psychophysiological studies of caffeine, with special attention given to its role as a stimulator of cardiovascular responses and as a modulator or potentiator of environmental and stress influences on cardiovascular reactivity. To place this research into perspective, we will present a brief overview of the behavioral and physiological changes brought about by caffeine and how these changes depend on the circumstances in which it is used. The role of caffeine as a risk factor for cardiovascular disease will be reevaluated in the light of the epidemiological and experimental evidence. The chapter will conclude with specific recommendations on research that needs to be done on caffeine in relation to cardiovascular reactivity and disease.

CAFFEINE AND BEHAVIOR

The effects of caffeine on behavior have been extensively reviewed by Calhoun,[1] Gilbert,[2] and Weiss and Laties.[3] These effects will not be discussed in detail but briefly summarized for the purposes of this chapter. Caffeine is a central nervous system stimulant that has been found to increase activity levels, reduce fatigue, enhance alertness and vigilance, and interfere with sleep.[2] For example, caffeine produced increased vigilance and decreased reaction time in boys (mean age 10.6), and it did not have a calming effect, as in the case of amphetamine, but increased motor activity.[4] However, the energizing properties of caffeine may increase or decrease the efficiency of performance depending on the complexity of the task involved, prevailing arousal level of the individual, various other individual characteristics, and many other factors.[2]

Caffeine has negative as well as positive influences on behavior. Repeated dosage of caffeine, especially in emotionally arousing or threatening situations, may be associated with increased anxiety and other emotional behaviors. For example, students drinking moderate to large amounts of caffeinated beverages had significantly higher scores for anxiety and depression together with impaired academic performance than did abstainers.[5] Twenty to thirty percent of persons consuming an excessive amount of caffeine were reported to develop physiological and psychological reactions indistinguishable from anxiety neurosis.[6] In an experimental demonstration of the effects of caffeine on anxiety, normal subjects were administered the Multiple Affect Adjective Checklist before and one hour after double-blind administration of 0 mg, 150 mg, or 300 mg of caffeine per 45.36 kg of body weight and after controlling for caffeine tolerance. Caffeine was found to increase anxiety, depression, and hostility.[7]

The observation by Gilbert, Marshman, et al.[8] that about 6 to 9 mg/kg/day of caffeine regularly induces dependence implies that more than four to six cups (1000–1500cc) of strong coffee a day is probably excessive for the average person. Physical dependence is characterized by the occurrence of various withdrawal symptoms when chronic use of this substance is interrupted (e.g., irritability, drowsiness, fatigue, headache symptoms, impaired performance in tasks, and depressed mood). These symptoms are eliminated by ingesting caffeine.[2]

There is also a great range of individual sensitivity to caffeine. Greden described addiction to caffeine in psychiatric inpatients who consumed as little as 4 mg/kg/day. Some rare persons even have trouble with free use of decaffeinated coffee with doses of caffeine as low as 0.4 mg/kg/day. Even persons habituated to caffeine may display irritability, anxiety, and a tendency to depression.[6,9] Over a three-week period, De Freitas and Schwartz[10] substituted decaffeinated coffee ad lib for regular coffee used by patients in a closed ward of a psychiatric hospital. Neither the patients nor the ward staff were aware of the substitution. When regular coffee was reinstated, patients showed a statistically significant deterioration of behavior, as reflected by routine measures of increased hostility, suspicion, and tension.

The popularity of caffeinated beverages is mainly due to their promotion of rapid clear thinking and decreased fatigue: "... valued commodities in an achievement-oriented society."[6] These positive behavioral effects of caffeine probably account for the widespread use of the substance, which, in the case of coffee, was estimated in 1972 to range from 13.5 kg of green coffee bean per capita per year in Sweden, to 6.3 kg in the United States, and 0.5 kg in Japan.[2] These can be roughly translated into 5.4, 2.5 and 0.2 cups daily on the average for individuals 9 years of age and older. Coffee consumption increases with age, with estimates in the United States of 2.47 cups per day for the 25 to 29 age group, and 3.51 cups for the 30 to 39 age group, then declines somewhat with further age. Surveys of coffee consumption in the United States (1972) and Canada (1969) indicated that about 75 percent of people drink one or more cups of coffee a day, and about 20 to 25 percent drink more than four cups a day.[2] Aside from coffee, consumption of tea, cola, and other caffeine-containing beverages is quite common and varies widely from country to country, but good estimates of the incidence of their usage in different populations are not readily available. Moreover, the caffeine content of these other beverages also varies widely. Gilbert[2] presents a summary of the caffeine content of these beverages as reported in various studies. The overall concentrations ranged from 352 to 893 μg/ml in ground coffee, 133 to 500 μg/ml in tea, and 40 to 163 μg/ml in colas. Given the physiological and health significance of caffeine (see below), the extent of caffeine use in various populations and the concentrations and substances in which it is used needs to be documented in great detail. Greater attention should also be given to studies on the influences of caffeine on behavior, both positive and negative, as well as on the association between caffeine use and various individual characteristics. For example, we would expect Type A individuals to be moderate to heavy users of caffeine, given the fact that caffeine enhances alertness and suppresses fatigue, behaviors displayed by Type As, thereby further facilitating Type A behavior. Other features of Type A behavior, such as impatience or anger, may be potentiated by use of caffeine.

PHARMACOLOGY AND PHYSIOLOGY OF CAFFEINE

Caffeine is rapidly and completely absorbed into the blood, often reaching peak plasma levels within 15 to 45 minutes after consumption. However, there are wide individual variations.[11] Caffeine readily penetrates into tissues and attains wide distribution throughout the body. It is not eliminated very effectively by the kidney and must be converted by the liver into metabolites that are more easily excreted. On the average, five to six hours are required to eliminate half of the caffeine in plasma (half-life). However, a number of factors will alter the rate of transformation of caffeine. Fetal and newborn humans have a severely limited capacity to metabolize caffeine, which extends the half-life to three to four days. This half-life shortens with maturation into childhood. Although there are no overall sex differences in caffeine metabolism, pregnancy will increase the half-life to 18 hours and oral contraceptives to 10.7 hours. In contrast, cigarette smoking will decrease the plasma half-life to 3 to 4 hours.

The mechanisms of caffeine's physiological effects are not yet well understood. Caffeine was thought to produce its physiological effects through an inhibition of the breakdown of cyclic adenosine monophosphate (cAMP), a compound that appears to mediate the actions of many neurotransmitters and hormones in the nervous system. However, several arguments have evolved against this hypothesis. First, the excitatory or stimulatory effects of caffeine are not produced by all inhibitors of cAMP breakdown, which suggests that such inhibition is insufficient to reproduce the effects of caffeine. More importantly, the results of *in vitro* studies suggest that the concentrations normally present *in vivo* are probably not sufficient to increase cAMP levels. Caffeine concentrations required to do so would be toxic or lethal in an intact animal.

An alternative hypothesis suggests that caffeine may act as an antagonist of the influences of endogenous adenosine, which itself affects neural, cardiovascular, respiratory, renal, and other physiologic processes. Several lines of evidence support this alternative.[11] Administered adenosine tends to have sedative effects, thus caffeine blockade of the effects of adenosine could produce apparent stimulation. Caffeine and adenosine often have opposite effects on other physiological systems as well. In some cases, caffeine and adenosine produce similar physiological effects, a fact which suggests that some effects of caffeine may well be mediated by other mechanisms. Caffeine will compete for occupancy of adenosine receptor sites, and the rank order of binding for a number of caffeinelike compounds parallels the relative strengths of behavioral effects.[12]

The adenosine-receptor blockade hypothesis is also supported by evidence that chronic caffeine consumption will increase both the number of adenosine receptors[13] and their sensitivity to adenosine.[14] Thus, symptoms of caffeine withdrawal (such as headache and fatigue) may reflect increased sensitivity to endogenous adenosine during caffeine withdrawal after blockade is ended. This hypothesis also helps explain the phenomena of tolerance and withdrawal. Although this hypothesis has recently gained support, most scientific reports agree that both the normal physiological function of endogenous adenosine and the effects of caffeine on this function require further study before the hypothesis can be completely accepted. If caffeine acts by inhibiting the normal blockade by adenosine of sympathetic nervous system (SNS) activity, then caffeine would be expected to increase sympathetic arousal even at rest when SNS activity is low. When SNS activity increases, such as during stress, the blockade of adenosine inhibition by caffeine would have even greater influence on the effective SNS arousal, potentially magnifying the effects of stress on the cardiovascular system and other stress response systems by eliminating the inhibitory adenosine effect. The potential exists then for a potentiation of the effects of stress by caffeine, as well as for tonic effects on cardiovascular physiology.

The physiological effects of caffeine are similar in many respects to the effects produced by psychological stress and fit closely the pattern often described as the "fight or flight" response, which is mediated by the sympathetic adrenal medullary system. These effects are reviewed by Rall.[15] Caffeine increases cardiac output and systolic and diastolic blood pressure. Heart rate has been shown to increase and to decrease, with the direction of effect probably related to the effective drug level in the body. Caffeine can increase heart rate through direct stimulation of the heart but can apparently also slow heart rate both directly through stimulation of vagal centers and indirectly through the baroreceptor-mediated responses to the increased blood pressure. Some but not necessarily all of these cardiovascular effects may be mediated at the humoral level. Caffeine is known to increase plasma catecholamines, with greater increases in epinephrine than norepinephrine, to increase plasma renin activity, and to increase levels of free fatty acids.

Robertson and colleagues carried out two major studies on the physiological effects of caffeine. In the first study, Robertson, Frolich, et al.[16] examined the effects of a single 250 mg dose of caffeine in non–coffee drinkers. Plasma caffeine reached a maximum level after 60 minutes. By this time, caffeine had increased blood pressure by 14/10 mmHg, plasma norepinephrine by 75 percent, epinephrine by 207 percent and plasma renin activity by 57 percent. Heart rate fell after ingestion of caffeine, reaching a low of about 4 beats per minute (bpm) below baseline after 45 minutes, and it subsequently rose slightly above baseline for the remainder of the session (total three hours). There was also a 20 percent increase in respiration rate, which appears to be another characteristic response to caffeine.

The second study, by Robertson, Wade, et al.,[17] suggested that tolerance develops to caffeine. Cardiovascular and hormonal responses to caffeine were eliminated almost completely after one to four days of consumption of large doses (250 mg at each meal). The study was carried out in coffee drinkers who abstained from methylxanthines for three weeks prior to the study. An additional group of coffee drinkers was studied after only 24 hours of abstinence. The pressor response in these latter subjects was about half as great as the pressor response in the three-week abstainers. The greatest pressor response occurred in subjects with the lowest caffeine levels.

Tolerance has also been reported for other physiological and behavioral effects of caffeine, for example, bradycardia, sleep disturbance, and mood.[17,2] However, such findings are open to other interpretations, inasmuch as individual differences may be confounded with the tolerance differences. If tolerance does develop, that is, if the cardiovascular and humoral effects diminish with repeated use of caffeine, then its potential as a risk factor for cardiovascular disease may be questioned.

Other interpretations of the Robertson, Wade, et al. study [17] should be considered as well. First, the data were obtained under resting nonstimulus conditions. Subjects may readily habituate their responses to caffeine and to the test situation as a whole under such nonchallenging conditions. Less tolerance or no tolerance might be observed if the same subjects were exposed to more demanding stimuli or tasks. This conclusion is supported by research reviewed below on the hormonal and pathophysiologic effects of regular caffeine consumption in mice studied under long-term conditions of psychosocial stress (about five months). Second, rather large doses were used, 250 mg three times a day, in the successive daily sessions. The degree of tolerance might be less apparent or reduced with more typical doses of caffeine (about 100–150 mg per administration).

Given that smoking and drinking coffee often go together, it is important to consider their combined effects on cardiovascular and other responses. As a stimulant, caffeine has many physiological effects comparable to those of nicotine.[18] One recent study[19] compared the effects of an inert control substance (orange squash), coffee (200 mg caffeine), smoking (two cigarettes each containing 1.7 mg nicotine), and coffee and smoking combined in hypertensive subjects who were habitual smokers and who used coffee and tea regularly, after overnight abstinence. Neither subjects nor experimenters were blind as to the substances used. Smoking by itself elevated blood pressure by 10/8 mmHg for 15 minutes, followed by a decline toward baseline. Coffee by itself elevated blood pressure by about the same amount (10/7 mmHg), with the major changes occurring between one and two hours after ingestion. Coffee and smoking combined produced a more sustained increase in blood pressure of comparable magnitude, starting at five minutes after drinking the coffee and beginning smoking and continuing for two hours. The combination of smoking and coffee had larger effects on blood pressure than either stimulus by itself. It cannot be determined from these data whether the interaction is multiplicative or simply additive. Untreated and diuretic-treated patients showed similar pressure responses. The interaction of drinking coffee and smoking cigarettes on heart rate was not significant. The increase in heart rate to smoking by itself and to smoking and coffee combined was about the same; the placebo and coffee alone conditions produced comparable heart rate changes—a slight increase at first and then a decrease below baseline. Thus, it could be concluded that coffee and cigarette smoking combined contribute significantly to elevated pressure levels in hypertensives. This conclusion is also supported by the observation that pressure levels did not reach clinic-measured hypertensive levels after overnight abstention of both substances and that recordings made during the placebo period showed continued reduced pressure levels. Comparable comparisons are needed to examine the interaction of these two substances under circumstances of challenge, such as mental arithmetic stress or aversive stimulation.

A note should be added here about phenylpropanolamine, which is a sympathomimetic widely marketed in diet pills. It is estimated that 20 million people in the United States ingest phenylpropanolamine-containing diet pills every year (80 percent women). Therefore, 10 percent of our population intermittently but commonly take phenylpropanolamine. In spite of its prevalent use, often in combination with caffeine, the effect of phenylpropanolamine on the cardiovascular system is not well known. Caffeine can increase blood pressure and enhance stress reactions. Phenylpropanolamine can increase blood pressure, but its effect on stress reactions has not been studied. Phenylpropanolamine may act additively or synergistically with caffeine, thus their combination has the potential for damaging effects. This area needs further examination.

A final area of research relevant here concerns individual differences in response to caffeine. The physiological effects of caffeine have been related to extraversion-introversion.[20] Increasing caffeine doses produced a linear increment in tonic skin conductance levels in extraverts but had little effect on this response in introverts. Higher doses of caffeine also increased phasic skin conductance response amplitudes in extraverts but decreased such responses in introverts. However, there is little systematic research relating this or other personality variables to caffeine-induced cardiovascular reactivity. Nor is there much research on differential physiological reactivity to caffeine itself related to anger coping style, anxiety level, or other such individual differences relevant to hypertension or heart disease.

CAFFEINE AND CARDIOVASCULAR REACTIVITY

Caffeine is an extraordinarily effective but nontoxic psychotropic substance whose influence on the sympathetic adrenal medullary system depends on the circumstances in which it is used. Cobb[21] studied unemployed factory workers who consumed caffeinated beverages while experiencing anxiety and distress at home awaiting reemployment. They excreted significantly more norepinephrine in urine than noncaffeine users. Later when they had regular jobs, the caffeine lost its effect. Conway, Vickers, et al.[22] reported that intake of caffeine and nicotine, but not alcohol, increased significantly during the most arduous two-week period of a 10-week recruit training program for promotion. This fits in with the common observation that caffeine is consumed under stressful conditions in which heightened physiological reactivity is more likely. This fact also suggests a rationale for examining the combined effects of caffeine and stressful stimuli.

The first experimental study by Lane[23] of the interactive effects of caffeine and stress on physiological responses in humans demonstrated that the cardiovascular effects produced by the administration of caffeine could add to those produced by concurrent psychological stress. The study used a placebo-controlled within-subject design to examine the effects of a moderate dose of caffeine (250 mg, equivalent to two cups of strong coffee) on the cardiovascular responses of 10 young males who did not regularly consume caffeine. Measures of heart rate and systolic and diastolic blood pressure were recorded during the four phases of each session, which began with resting baselines both before and 45 minutes after drug administration. Subjects then performed a difficult, competitive mental arithmetic task with instructions for speed and accuracy. The session ended with a poststress recovery period. Compared to placebo, this acute dose of caffeine raised both systolic and diastolic blood pressure during all three postdrug phases. The elevation was consistent across rest, task, and recovery periods and ranged from 7 to 10 mmHg for systolic and 6 to 8 mmHg for diastolic pressure. In this study there was no evidence for any potentiation or magnification of stress responses after caffeine nor were there any effects of caffeine on the magnitude of heart rate response. However, the level of blood pressure during the stressful task was significantly higher after caffeine than after placebo. The nature of the effect suggested that the combination of caffeine and stress represents a potential for increased risk of cardiovascular disease.

A second study employed essentially the same experimental procedures with caffeine users who did and did not have a family history of hypertension, 18 healthy normotensive males in each group.[24] The study was conducted double-blind, and each subject was administered different doses of caffeine on different days (3 mg, 125 mg, 250 mg) with the order counterbalanced among subjects. The effects of caffeine were observed under resting conditions, during the stress of mental arithmetic, and during recovery. The overall effects of caffeine were remarkably similar to those obtained by Lane.[23] Caffeine and mental stress combined additively to increase blood pressure. In addition, significantly larger blood pressure increases were shown to stress, to caffeine, and to the combination of both by the subjects with a family history of hypertension.

A subsequent study by Lane[25] explored the possible interactions of caffeine and stress using a wider range of cardiovascular measures. Thirty-three young males who did not regularly use caffeine participated in the study. Several possible individual difference predictors of cardiovascular response were assessed, including Type A behavior measured by the Jenkins Activity Survey and family history of hypertension. The same within-subject, placebo-controlled design was used as previously, with predrug and postdrug resting baselines, a competitive mental arithmetic task, and recovery period. Forearm blood flow (FBF) and forearm vascular resistance (FVR) were assessed in addition to heart rate and blood pressure. Once again, caffeine elevated systolic and diastolic blood pressures at rest, during the stress, and during the recovery period, replicating the earlier results. The effect on forearm blood flow was not the simple elevation seen for blood pressure. Although caffeine did not affect resting levels of FBF, the drug magnified the FBF responses to the stressful task. The increase in FBF elicited by the competitive, mental arithmetic task was 47 percent greater after consumption of caffeine than after placebo. None of these differences was found to be related to Type A behavior. Although differences in cardiovascular reactivity between subjects with and without family history of hypertension have been reported in other studies, such differences did not emerge in the present study. The effects of caffeine on the forearm blood flow response to psychological stress seen in this study provide evidence that caffeine and stress may indeed interact; that is, the cardiovascular responses to stress may be exaggerated or amplified if caffeine has been consumed.

The best evidence for such an interaction comes from animal research involving long-term prospective studies of the effects of caffeine. Henry and Stephens[26] studied mice living either peacefully as siblings in boxes or interacting under conditions of chronic psychosocial stress in population cages. These cages feature multiple entries to discourage the formation of territory and to encourage confrontations through the physical arrangements of various one-way connecting passages. In addition, centrally located food and water force proximity in rival males. The mice were exposed to various degrees of social stress and caffeinated water or beverages for three to nine months. Inasmuch as mice live only 2 to 2.5 years, six months is their equivalent of the 20 years or so before progressive arteriosclerotic heart disease develops in humans. Caffeine increased the severity of myocardial fibrosis in even mildly stressed mice living as siblings in boxes. Sibling mice in boxes drinking coffee for six or more months developed more cardiomyopathy, expressed as myocardial fibrosis, than controls drinking water. Coffee had increased the animals' excitability and hence the intensity of their social interactions.

Bovet-Nitti and Messeri[27] came to similar conclusions from their study of population growth curves of randomly bred mice confined to large cages. They showed that the chronic ingestion of caffeine or amphetamine prevented an increase in population. This effect was not observed with nicotine, but 100 μg/ml of caffeine was sufficient to produce this effect. This is an amount between the 20 μg/ml remaining in decaffeinated coffee and the 560 μg/ml found in strong brewed coffee. Even at the low caffeine concentration of 100 μg/ml, the authors report increased aggression, which was responsible for infant deaths and some delay in giving birth. Caffeine at half the strength of brewed coffee (250 μg/ml) led to a more serious delay in live births and population growth.

In more recent research, Henry and Stephens[28] studied the effects of caffeine in water and of tea and coffee on mice living as peaceful siblings in boxes and as agitated members of a competitive social system in population cages. Their previous work had established that male mice psychosocially stressed in the presence of females develop hypertension, cardiovascular damage, and chronic interstitial nephritis. In these conditions, plasma renin, corticosterone, and adrenal-catecholamine synthetic enzymes were increased, and their lifespan was halved.[29] Even the addition of 3.3 mg caffeine/day/kg of mouse body weight (the equivalent of drinking 20 μg/ml decaffeinated coffee) intensified these effects. The caffeine-induced enhancement of the competitive social stimulation of their neuroendocrine system resulted in a further increase of plasma renin and corticosterone levels as well as increased blood pressure and adrenal weight. These changes together with accelerated mortality, cardiac fibrosis, and interstitial nephritis indicate that the chronic consumption of caffeinated beverages adds to the risk of psychosocial stress.

It may be concluded that attempts to isolate the physiological effects of caffeine under resting conditions only are insufficient and that its true potency needs to be assessed in the presence of other appropriate biobehavioral circumstances (e.g., different conditions of psychosocial stress, smoking and other physical risk factors, and various critical individual differences).

CAFFEINE AS A RISK FACTOR FOR CARDIOVASCULAR DISEASE

The role of caffeine as a risk factor for hypertension and heart disease has not been extensively investigated and the main published reports do not arrive at a consistent conclusion. The research in this field varies greatly in its quality, and a major problem turns on the difficulties of objectifying and quantifying caffeine use on the basis of current and retrospective individual reports of the type, quantity, and concentration of caffeine-containing foods and beverages used. In several instances, the critical data involved were only incidentally and incompletely collected or were analyzed as an afterthought. The choice of appropriate control groups has also been argued extensively.[30]

The first major study reported that patients ($N = 276$) with acute myocardial infarction were found to drink appreciably more coffee than chronically ill control patients ($N = 1104$).[31] The difference could not be explained by associated cigarette smoking. Results from the Kaiser-Permanente Epidemiologic Study of Myocardial Infarction showed no independent association between coffee drinking (more than six cups a day) and a subsequent myocardial infarction ($N = 464$).[32] A further evaluation of the link between caffeine and myocardial infarction was made by Jick, Miettinen, et al.[33] based on survey data of 12,759 hospitalized patients, including 440 with the diagnosis of myocardial infarction. The risks of infarction among those drinking one to five and six or more cups of coffee a day were estimated to be increased by 60 and 120 percent, respectively, controlling for age, sex, post-coronary heart disease, hypertension, congestive heart failure, obesity, diabetes, smoking, occupation, or the use of sugar with coffee. Interestingly, tea drinking was not found to be a risk factor for infarction. Extensive data from the Framingham Study did not confirm an independent association between caffeine use and cardiovascular disease (1992 men, 2500 women).[34] A statistically significant increase in risk with increasing coffee consumption was observed for "death from all causes," which could be accounted for statistically by the association between coffee drinking and cigarette smoking. A negative result was also reported by Hennekens, Drolette, et al.[35] The subjects were 649 patients who died within 24 hours of onset of symptoms of coronary heart disease. Coffee drinking and myocardial infarction were found to be only weakly and nonsignificantly associated in a study of 487 women, 30 to 49 years of age.[36]

Two other major studies have attacked the problem in a different way by relating coffee consumption (and smoking and other variables) to cholesterol. Drinking coffee had been shown to increase free fatty acids and triglycerides, effects comparable to those produced by smoking.[16] These effects are related to increases in catecholamines. Thus, there is a good basis for finding a link between caffeine and cholesterol. In the first study,[37] the investigators sampled 361 people from the Evans County cohort. Low-density lipoprotein cholesterol levels were significantly higher for those who smoked cigarettes and drank five or more cups of coffee a day than among abstainers of either substance. The latter showed higher levels of high-density lipoproteins. Smoking and coffee drinking interacted in affecting low-density lipoproteins and total cholesterol, but coffee drinking by itself did not offset lipid levels. The second study,[38] carried out in Tromso, Norway, included data from 7213 women and 7368 men, ages 20 to 54. Coffee consumption was found to be positively associated with total cholesterol and triglycerides in both sexes, a relation that withstood statistical corrections for age, body-mass index, leisure-time activity level, cigarette smoking, and alcohol use.

Aside from the numerous statistical and methodological complications of epidemiological studies noted earlier, it seems clear that the particular interactions of coffee drinking and cigarette smoking and convictions about their relative significance have also contributed to the scientific confusion. The two habits go together, making it difficult for epidemiologists to disentangle their effects as risk factors for heart disease and sudden cardiac death. In an evaluation of coffee drinking and sudden death due to coronary disease, Hennekens, Drolette, et al.[35] confirmed the well-known but controversial findings of Jick, Miettinen, et al.[33] that the risk ratio is approximately doubled in those who drink six or more cups of coffee a day. Jick et al. claimed that the risk ratio for coffee could not be attributed to confounding by smoking. Their experimental design was criticized in the debate following publication, and their results were not generally accepted. Hennekens et al.

recorded their confirmation of the findings of Jick's group as a "restricted analysis" and went on to use stepwise multiple regression analysis. After correcting for the effect to be expected from cigarette smoking, the risk for coffee vanished. They recognized the difficulty in attribution but commented that controlling for variables associated with exposure to caffeine depends on whether or not these variables are considered to be a link in the same causal pathway. They agreed that if the variable—in this case, smoking—is involved in the same pathway, then is should not be controlled for. Classically, carbon monoxide has been considered responsible for much of the effect of smoking. Such a mechanism could not result from drinking coffee. Therefore, they corrected their data by the known factor for smoking. However, as discussed above, smoking and drinking caffeinated beverages stimulate the sympathetic adrenal medullary system in much the same way. Carruthers[39] argued that norepinephrine release in the hypothalamus is the final common pathway in many situations, including smoking. It is not surprising that the two habits are so closely enmeshed. If the catecholamines are involved, it means that smoking should not incur the entire blame for the effects of caffeine any more than caffeine should be blamed for the nicotine-based effects of smoking. A synergistic relation was suggested above by Heyden, Heiss, et al.[37] who found that caffeine alone did not affect blood lipids but that the nicotine-based effects of smoking and caffeine interact to raise low-density lipoproteins and total cholesterol.

In a recent study of ventricular premature beats and coronary risk factors, Hennekens teamed up with Lown and others to investigate the relationship between premature beats and certain risk factors, including smoking.[40] Like Orth-Gomer, Edwards, et al.,[41] they found a strong correlation between these irregularities and age in their sample of 10,000 men, 35 to 57 years old. There was no relationship between premature beats and cholesterol or blood pressure, but there was a statistically significant association with smoking. In the discussion the authors commented that since smokers do not have increased incidence of cardiac ischemia compared with nonsmokers, it may have actually been the coffee drinking that accompanies the smoking habit that was related to the ventricular beats.

Needless to say, the controversy is not over, and further research, both experimental and epidemiological, will be needed to answer the question on the relative significance of caffeine and nicotine as risk factors for cardio-vascular disease. Our hypothesis is that they are both implicated, and that nicotine should not be considered to account for the effects of caffeine. Moreover, although no firm conclusions can be drawn from the existing epidemiological data, our overview of research on the cardiovascular and other physiological effects of caffeine, especially in interaction with acute and chronic stress and with other risk factors (smoking, family history of hypertension) suggests that chronic caffeine consumption may be a highly significant risk factor for cardiovascular disease. Given its widespread use, it deserves much more attention than it has been given. In 1976 Gilbert[2] arrived at a conclusion that still holds today:

> The only reasonable way to conclude this section is to be somewhat inconclusive regarding the role of caffeine on cardiopathology. The evidence remains as Paul[42] characterized it in 1968, too suggestive and intriguing for dismissal but inadequate to permit firm and positive statements as to etiological significance.... the balance of evidence appears to me to be moving towards implication of caffeine in heart disease, probably at intake levels higher than those considered in most studies so far (i.e., probably at the equivalent of about eight cups of coffee and upwards), but at levels consumed by an appreciable proportion of the middle-aged population of many countries.[2,p.142]

SUMMARY AND RECOMMENDATIONS

Caffeine is a potent stimulator of cardiovascular and hormonal changes. When combined with acute and chronic stress, it modulates cardiovascular reactions to stress and probably intensifies such effects. Human research examining such interactions has been primarily limited to short-term stimulation, mainly to mental arithmetic stress. The experimental procedures employed by Lane[23] and Greenberg[24] provide a good experimental model for examining the synergistic effects of combining caffeine with psychological stress. Aside from mental arithmetic, other challenges should be studied, for example, video games, competitive social interactions, and situations provoking anger, anxiety, irritability, impatience, and depression. Any task or situation of relevance to cardiovascular functioning and disease would be of special significance. For purposes of contrast with active coping tasks, simple tests of motor performance, vigilance, or passive stress (cold pressor test) should be employed. The experimental procedures should also be extended by examining the interaction of stress of a longer duration in combination with repeated dosage of caffeine. In this context, the question of tolerance effects of chronic caffeine use requires thorough investigation, as it is fundamental to the analysis of the role of caffeine as a risk factor for cardiovascular disease. Tolerance under conditions of various environmental demands and challenges should be studied.

Individual characteristics should also be examined. For example, the inconsistent findings concerning family history of hypertension and response to caffeine need to be followed up in further study. Age and sex differences are also of probable significance. There are certain other candidates for further research along these lines, for example, Type A behavior pattern, neuroticism, anger coping style, and extraversion/introversion. We need to know more about sensitivity to caffeine; for example, who do some people drink lots of coffee and others avoid it completely? What else accounts for tolerance and dependence? Sleep electrophysiological studies of tolerance/withdrawal may aid in this exploration.

At the very least, we recommend that research on cardiovascular reactivity take account of whether or not subjects are caffeine users and whether or not they have used or abstained from caffeine and for how long prior to participation in experimental studies. No doubt caffeine may account for a significant portion of the variance of cardiovascular responses under various resting or stress conditions and does require control.

From a methodological standpoint, double-blind studies of the acute effects of caffeine should attend to the method of administration and appropriate placebo. Because of individual differences in absorption and possible adverse effects, the caffeine should be dissolved in liquid rather than given in a capsule. Because of the somewhat bitter taste of caffeine and the typical nonbitter taste of a placebo, both tastes should be made equivalent or masked by some other substance. If it is desirable to include the influence of stimulus characteristics of coffee, then decaffeinated coffee should be used as the vehicle. Whenever possible, the dose should be determined on the basis of body weight or body surface area.

As to epidemiological or prospective studies, the methodological issues are extremely complex and beyond the scope of this overview. We cannot help but agree with Gilbert: "To the outsider, there seems to be no field as subject to contrary statistical interpretation as epidemiology, save perhaps economics."[2, p. 140] In any case, current opinions that caffeine is unimportant as a risk factor for disease are certainly not warranted by the experimental, clinical, and epidemiological data that have been discussed in this chapter. Unlike the case of tobacco use, which is more easily quantified, greater care should be taken to document the various caffeine-containing substances used. Detailed diaries may be needed. Comprehensive assessments of caffeine use should be made part of long-term prospective studies of cardiovascular disease, and the effects of caffeine considered in interaction with concurrent psychosocial and environmental stress.

REFERENCES

1. Calhoun WH: Central nervous system stimulants. In Furchtgott E (ed): *Pharmacological and Biophysical Agents and Behavior*. New York, Academic Press, 1971, pp. 181–268.
2. Gilbert RM: Caffeine as a drug of abuse. In Gibbings RJ, Israel Y, et al (eds): *Research Advances in Alcohol and Drug Problems* (Vol. III). New York, Wiley, 1974, pp. 49–176.

3. Weiss B, Laties VG: Enhancement of human performance by caffeine and the amphetamines. *Pharmacol Rev* **14**:1–36, 1962.

4. Elkins RN, Rapoport JL, et al: Acute effects of caffeine in normal prepubertal boys. *Am J Psychiatry* **138**:178–183, 1981.

5. Gilliland K, Andress D: Ad lib caffeine consumption, symptoms of caffeinism, and academic performance. *Am J Psychiatry* **138**:512–514, 1981.

6. Greden JF: Anxiety or caffeinism: A diagnostic dilemma. *Am J Psychiatry* **131**:1089–1092, 1974.

7. Veleber DM, Templer DI: Effects of caffeine on anxiety and depression. *J Abnorm Psychol* **93**:120–122, 1984.

8. Gilbert RM, Marshman JA, et al: Caffeine content of beverages as consumed. *Can Med Assoc J* **114**:205–208, 1976.

9. Greden JF, Fontaine P, et al: Anxiety and depression associated with caffeinism among psychiatric inpatients. *Am J Psychiatry* **135**:963–966, 1978.

10. De Freitas B, Schwartz G: Effects of caffeine in chronic psychiatric patients. *Am J Psychiatry* **136**:1337–1338, 1979.

11. Neims AH, von Borstel RW: Caffeine: Metabolism and biochemical mechanisms of action. In Wurtman RJ, Wurtman JJ (eds): *Nutrition and the Brain* (Vol 6). New York, Raven, 1983, pp. 1–30.

12. Snyder SH, Katims JJ, et al: Adenosine receptors and behavioral actions of methylxanthines. *Proc Nat Acad Sci USA* **78**:3260–3274, 1981.

13. Boulenger JP, Patel J, et al: Chronic caffeine consumption increases the number of brain adenosine receptors. *Life Sci* **32**:1135–1142, 1983.

14. von Borstel RW, Wurtman RJ, Conlay LA: Chronic caffeine consumption potentiates the hypotensive action of circulating adenosine. *Life Sci* **32**:1151–1158, 1983.

15. Rall TW: Central nervous system stimulants: The xanthines. In Gilman AG, Goodman LS, Gilman A (eds): *The Pharmacological Basis of Therapeutics* (6th ed). New York, MacMillan, 1980, pp. 269–274.

16. Robertson D, Frolich JC, et al: Effects of caffeine on plasma renin activity, catecholamines and blood pressure. *N Engl J Med* **298**:181–186, 1978.

17. Robertson D, Wade D, et al: Tolerance to the humoral and hemodynamic effects of caffeine in man. *J Clin Invest* **67**:1111–1117, 1981.

18. Cryer PE, Haymond MW, et al: Norepinephrine and epinephrine release and adrenergic mediation of smoking-associated hemodynamic and metabolic events. *N Engl J Med* **295**:573–577, 1976.

19. Freestone S, Ramsay LE: Effect of coffee and cigarette smoking on the blood pressure of untreated and diuretic-treated hypertensive patients. *Am J Med* **73**:348–354, 1982.

20. Smith BD, Wilson RJ, Jones BE: Extraversion and overhabituation and dishabituation. *Psychophyisology* **20**:29–35, 1983.

21. Cobb J: Physiologic changes in men whose jobs were abolished. *J Psychosom Res* **18**:245–258, 1974.

22. Conway TL, Vickers Jr RR, et al: Occupational stress and variation in cigarette, coffee, and alcohol consumption. *J Health Soc Behav* **22**:155–165, 1981.

23. Lane JD: Caffeine and cardiovascular responses to stress. *Psychosom Med* **45**:447–452, 1983.

24. Greenberg WP: The effects of caffeine and stress on blood pressure in individuals with parental history of hypertension. Doctoral dissertation, University of California, 1983.

25. Lane JD: Caffeine potentiates cardiovascular responses to stress. Paper presented at the Stress, Reactivity, and Cardiovascular Disease Conference, Oglebay Park, WV, April 1984.

26. Henry JP, Stephens PM: High blood pressure and myocardial fibrosis in coffee drinking CBA mice. *Fed Proc* **29**:386, 1970. (Abstract)

27. Bovet-Nitti F, Messeri P: Central stimulating agents and population growth in mice. *Life Sci* **16**:1393–1402, 1975.

28. Henry JP, Stephens PM: Caffeine as an intensifier of stress-induced hormonal and pathophsyiologic changes in mice. *Pharmacol Biochem Behav* **13**:719–727, 1980.

29. Henry JP, Stephens PM: *Stress, Health, and the Social Environment: A Sociobiologic Approach to Medicine.* New York: Springer-Verlag, 1977.

30. Rosenberg L, Slone D, et al: Case-control studies on the acute effects of coffee upon the risk of myocardial infarction: Problems in the selection of a hospital control series. *Am J Epidemiol* **113**:646–653, 1981.

31. Boston Collaborative Drug Surveillance Program: Coffee drinking and acute myocardial infarction. *Lancet* **2**:1278–1281, 1972.

32. Klatsky AL, Friedman GD, Siegelaub AB: Coffee drinking prior to acute myocardial infarction. *JAMA* **226**:540–544, 1973.

33. Jick H, Miettinen OS, et al: Coffee and myocardial infarction. *N Engl J Med* **289**:63–67, 1973.

34. Dawber TR, Kannel WB, Gordon T: Coffee and cardiovascular disease. *N Engl J Med* **291**:871–874, 1974.

35. Hennekens CH, Drolette ME, et al: Coffee drinking and death due to coronary heart disease. *N Engl J Med* **294**:633–637, 1976.

36. Rosenberg L, Slone D, et al: Coffee drinking and myocardial infarction in young women. *Am J Epidemiol* **111**:675–682, 1980.

37. Heyden S, Heiss G, et al: The combined effect of smoking and coffee drinking on LDL and HDL cholesterol. *Circulation* **50**:22–25, 1979.

38. Thelle DS, Arnesen E, Forde OH: Does coffee raise serum cholesterol? *N Engl J Med* **308**:1454–1457, 1983.

39. Carruthers M: Modification of the noradrenaline related effects of smoking by beta-blockade. *Psychol Med* **6**:251–256, 1976.

40. Hennekens CH, Lown B, et al: Ventricular premature beats and coronary risk factors. *Am J Epidemiol* **112**:93–99, 1980.

41. Orth-Gomér K, Edwards ME, et al: Relation between ventricular arrhythmias and psychological profile. *Acta Med Scand* **207**:31–36, 1980.

42. Paul O: Stimulants and coronaries. *Postgrad Med* **44**:196–199, 1968.

17

The Interactive Effects of Stress and Dietary Sodium on Cardiovascular Reactivity

BONITA FALKNER, KATHLEEN C. LIGHT

The value obtained in the measurement of blood pressure reflects the functioning of many physiologic components including the nervous system, cardiovascular system, and renal-endocrine system. It is likely that there is inherited variation in these systems for structure and physiologic activity. Furthermore, there are a variety of environmental factors providing stimuli to which these various systems respond. Thus, blood pressure is a measurable response emerging from a multicomponent physiologic system under genetic direction and responding to a variety of external or environmental inputs (see also chapter by Rose). With this in mind, it is apparent that the problem of determining disease-related variations in blood pressure regulation that ultimately result in hypertension with vascular injury is an issue of extraordinary complexity. As more data have accumulated about the specific stimulus-system responses, such as stress-induced change in cardiac output or salt-induced change in blood pressure, it is clear that it is necessary to consider the interaction of systems and environmental stimuli to understand regulatory variations that impose significant risk for cardio-vascular injury and disease. The focus of this chapter will be to discuss the interactive effects of environmental stress and dietary sodium and potassium on blood pressure and cardiovascular reactivity.

The epidemiological literature is abundant in studies that suggest that variations in the prevalence of hypertension among different societies and cultures may be due in part to differences in salt ingestion. As described in a number of excellent review articles,[1-5] societies where salt consumption averages less than one gram per day have little or no hypertension, and blood pressure does not increase with age among adults in these societies as it does among adults in the United States and other nations where salt intake typically exceeds 10 grams per day. Furthermore, in societies where salt ingestion often exceeds 20 grams per day, such as those in many regions of Japan, hypertension has been reported among a still higher proportion (30 to 40 percent) of the adult population.[2,6]

These observations cannot be interpreted as unequivocal evidence of a causal relationship between high salt intake and hypertension. As critics have noted,[7,8] these investigations had a number of shortcomings. First, the blood pressure measurements were not always obtained in a standardized way. Second, the societies differed in numerous ways other than salt intake, including many life-style characteristics that may be labeled as environmental stressors.

In addition, studies within the same population attempting to correlate salt intake with blood pressure have not always yielded consistent results. Certain investigations that have failed to obtain a positive relationship between sodium and blood pressure (including the recent report by McCar-ron and associates)[9] have been criticized for using subjects' reports on food items consumed in a given day as their measure of sodium intake. This method may yield inaccurate estimates since subjects may deliberately or accidentally make errors in their reports, discretionary salt used in cooking or at the table is disregarded with this estimation procedure, and a single day's intake may be a poor reflection of usual dietary habits. However, other studies relying on more accurate 24-hour urine collections to estimate daily sodium intake have likewise yielded a mixture of positive[10-12] and negative results[13-15] concerning the postulated association between salt ingestion and blood pressure.

The most definitive evidence concerning the relationship between salt ingestion and blood pressure has been derived from investigations where dietary salt intake was increased and decreased in a systematic, verifiable way. These studies reveal that blood pressure responses to changing salt intake are *not* uniform across all individuals; high salt intake increases blood pressure and salt restriction lowers it in some individuals, while many others show no blood pressure alterations, and a few others may respond with changes in the opposite direction.[16-22] All of the factors that may relate to greater salt sensitivity are not yet determined, but evidence suggests that among normotensive persons, this characteristic is more common among blacks than among whites, among adults older than 45 or 50 than among younger persons, and among those with a family history of hypertension.[22-26] Sodium sensitivity is also more frequent among hypertensive and borderline hypertensive patients than among normotensive individuals, although it is certainly not a universal characteristic of those with hypertension.[16,22,23] Evidence from animal and human studies also suggests that the pressure rise associated with high salt intake in sodium-sensitive persons may be partly attenuated if potassium intake is also increased.[6,24,26-29]

The increased prevalence of salt sensitivity among blacks and among persons with a family history of hypertension both have been interpreted as probable indications of a genetic contribution to this environmentally initiated rise in blood pressure. This interpretation of a significant genetic influence on sodium handling is reinforced by research in animal models, particularly the development of salt-sensitive and salt-resistant rat strains by Dahl and colleagues,[30] and by recent human studies of sodium excretion patterns in monozygotic versus dizygotic twins performed by Grim, Miller, and associates.[31] However, reports are also emerging that provide evidence demonstrating that behavioral stress may interact with sodium intake and genetic susceptibility to result in potentially pathogenic changes in cardio-vascular reactivity and blood pressure regulation. Changes in sodium intake have been shown to result in changes in sympathetic nervous system function, including levels of circulatory catecholamines, and alpha- and beta-receptor activity.[32] Other studies have focused on local vascular responses in the salt-loaded state. Rankin, Luft, et al.[33] have demonstrated an increased blood pressure response to infused norepinephrine in normo-tensive individuals at higher levels of salt intake. Patients with borderline hypertension were studied by Mark, Lawton, et al.[16] who reported that norepinephrine infusion in these individuals resulted in increased forearm vascular resistance and a decrease in forearm blood flow in the salt-loaded state. Therefore, there is clinical evidence in humans that the cardiovascular response to neurogenic stimuli is augmented by greater levels of sodium intake.

The relationship of sodium balance to blood volume and total body fluid is largely mediated by the kidneys through their regulation of salt and water excretion or retention. A classic control theory is that of Coleman, Guyton, and coworkers,[34,35] who propose that the renal excretory system controls blood pressure by regulating blood volume through increasing or decreasing sodium excretion. In their laboratory these researchers have demonstrated that when blood pressure is increased, normal kidneys will respond by increasing the excretion of salt and water, thus producing a pressure diuresis or pressure natriuresis. This rate of excretion, which is increased relative to intake, reduces body fluid, including the blood volume. The lowered blood volume will result in a lower cardiac output and lower blood pressure. The renal-volume control system as described is a regulatory system that is relatively slow in onset but prolonged in duration. The renal excretory output will not revert to normal until arterial blood pressure returns to its original baseline level, a process that may require weeks to accomplish.[34,35]

This simplified description of Guyton's theory assumes normal renal function and stability of other factors affecting renal function, including neurohumoral factors such as catecholamines, angiotension, aldosterone, vasopressin, and renal sympathetic nerve activity. The theoretical extension of this concept into the pathogenesis of hypertension requires the input of some factors that would chronically alter the function of the renal volume control system for regulation at a new set point, that is, a higher baseline blood pressure. Factors to account for this resetting may be those that trigger the initial pressure elevation; another possibility is that the resetting may occur in autoregulatory processes enacted to adapt to the interplay between pressure and tissue perfusion.[36,37]

Whether the renal adjustments in sodium excretion represent an initial step in the process of developing hypertension or whether these changes occur as a secondary effect has been an unsettled issue in humans.[37,38] However, interesting data have emerged from studies of the spontaneously hypertensive rat (SHR). Mature SHRs with established hypertension exhibit normal or somewhat exaggerated excretion rates of sodium and water at their usual high pressures. Reduction of renal arterial pressure in these SHRs to a normotensive level results in reduced sodium excretion.[39] Young SHRs have been shown to retain sodium and water before development of blood pressure elevation. After their blood pressures rose, the excretion rate for sodium returned to normal.[40] Hemodynamic variations have also been observed in the young SHR. There is reported to be a transient phase involving increased cardiac output and normal vascular resistance at age 5 to 6 weeks, followed by a rise in vascular resistance at 11 to 17 weeks.[41] These observations in SHRs indicate that reduced excretion of sodium and water precedes and may trigger a primary phase in development of hypertension. Furthermore, they suggest that renal regulation of body sodium balance may be an important determinant of the eventual level at which blood pressure stabilizes.

The contribution of behavioral stress to hypertension development in animals that have some genetic susceptibility toward increased sodium and water retention is indicated by the work of Lawler, Barker, and associates.[42] These investigators developed a borderline hypertensive rat model by mating an SHR rat with a normotensive rat from the Wistar-Kyoto strain. The offspring developed only marginal blood pressure elevations in the usual laboratory environment, but showed sustained hypertension and associated myocardial pathology after 12 weeks of exposure to a stressful shock-avoidance conflict task. Although the physiological processes inducing this stress-related progression of hypertension are only currently being evaluated, a probable contributing factor is altered renal function, inducing sodium and water retention. Recently, Lundin and Thoren[43] demonstrated that exposure to stress induces exaggerated sodium and water retention in the SHR parent strain, and Koepke and DiBona[44] have verified that stress-induced sodium retention in SHR is further enhanced by increasing dietary sodium intake. Both studies have obtained evidence that the changes in sodium excretion induced by stress are associated with increased activity of the renal sympathetic nerves.[43,44]

As previously mentioned, renal excretory function may be modified by several neural and humoral factors including circulatory catecholamines and the renal sympathetic nerves. Chronic infusion of norepinephrine into the renal artery will induce hypertension in dogs. This effect will increase directly in relation to sodium intake.[45,46] In normotensive humans, Rankin, Luft, et al.[33] have demonstrated an enhanced pressor response to infused norepinephrine at higher levels of sodium intake. Thus, increased sodium intake appears to alter vascular reactivity to sympathetic stimuli. Various hypotheses to explain this response include sodium-induced changes in vessel structure, vascular elasticity, or displacement of other cations, in particular potassium or calcium.[47-49] These effects may not be mutually exclusive and each may contribute to the process.

While the mechanisms have not been delineated with precision as yet, it is apparent that sympathetic nervous system activity and sodium-fluid volume balance are mutual augmenters of blood pressure. To determine the relationship of these interactive elements to the pathogenesis of clinical hypertension involves more long-term exposure to high salt intake plus behaviorally induced stress resulting in stimulated sympathetic nervous system activity. The interaction of behavioral stress and sodium loading has been investigated in a few animal models. Anderson et al. studied this interaction in dogs receiving continuous saline infusion and shock-avoidance stress for two weeks.[50] This combination of high salt intake and daily stress led to progressive elevations in 24-hour levels of blood pressure, although neither the saline infusion alone nor the avoidance stress alone was sufficient to raise blood pressure. These investigators also found that when the dietary potassium intake was increased, there was an attenuation of the blood pressure response.[29]

Additional studies in dogs have been performed to investigate their renal stress responses in a condition of normal salt balance. Koepke et al.[51] studied renal excretory response during behavioral stress in conscious dogs. These investigators found that in most but not all dogs the aversive conditioning resulted in a decrease in urine flow associated with unchanged glomerular filtration rate and reduced sodium excretion. Among all dogs, greater increases in cardiovascular activity during stress were associated with greater decreases in renal excretion. Surgical renal denervation abolished this excretory response to stress in four of five dogs. It was proposed that the excretory changes during stress were due to increased renal tubular reabsorption, that there was central integration with the cardiovascular responses, and that this involved the renal nerves.[51] With pharmacologic manipulation, it appeared that a central nervous system beta-adrenoreceptor mechanism may mediate the renal excretory response to stress.[52] Previous research with another animal model, Doca-salt hypertension in rats, has indicated that destruction of central adrenergic neural pathways can prevent or reverse development of the disorder during its initiation, but cannot effectively modify the mechanisms that sustain the hypertension once it is fully established.[53]

Experimental data, then, indicate that there is a central mediating pathway affecting renal excretory function which may be activated by behavioral stress. Also, variation in sodium balance will alter this stress excretory activity.[44,54] The process by which this raises blood pressure remains to be determined but could operate through an initial stage of sodium and volume retention with increased cardiac output, or inappropriate sodium retention with increased total peripheral resistance due to altered vascular response to adrenergic activity. Further, it is conceivable these two possibilities are not mutually exclusive but may occur in different phases.

The preceding reports have focused on animal models for investigating the renal sodium excretion and centrally mediated stress. The human excretory response to behavioral stress has been studied by Light, Koepke, and associates[55] in young adult males. After establishing a high urine flow rate by oral drinking and voluntary voiding, pairs of young men performed a series of competitive mental tasks. In this study one group of subjects demonstrated stress-induced retention of sodium and water. This group consisted of subjects who showed high heart rate during stress and who were considered at high risk for hypertension, because each had a hypertensive parent or had borderline hypertension. All other subjects showed a trend toward increased rather than decreased excretion of sodium and water during the stress period. These findings then provided evidence that psychological stress can induce sodium retention in some humans as well as in animal models. They also indicate that the retention of sodium is associated with the combination of high sympathetic response to stress and the presence of known risk factors for hypertension.

As previously discussed, an increased sodium intake has been shown to enhance the cardiovascular responses to infusions of sympathetic agonists. More recent studies have also shown that increasing and decreasing sodium and potassium intake can alter blood pressure and heart rate responses to behavioral stressors. In one investigation, Falkner and coworkers[56] studied normotensive adolescents with and without hypertensive parents at rest and during the behavioral stress of difficult mental arithmetic. The studies were repeated in each subject following a two-week period of oral salt loading, which consisted of ingesting 10 grams of sodium chloride per day in addition to their usual diet. Prior to salt loading, the offspring of hypertensive parents had a higher resting systolic blood pressure than the offspring of normotensive parents. After the salt loading, the offspring of hypertensive parents had higher systolic pressure and diastolic pressure with lower heart rate both at pretask rest and during stress. The responses in the offspring of normotensive parents were unchanged following the salt loading. While the salt loading appeared to augment the stress reactivity, the greatest change in those offspring who were sensitive to sodium appeared to be the rise in pretask baseline blood pressure following the salt loading.[56]

In a contrasting study of adult patients with borderline hypertension, lowering the salt intake was found to reduce cardiovascular reactivity to behavior challenge, although baseline values were not changed. Ambrosioni, Costa, et al.[57] studied the cardiovascular responses to mental arithmetic, bicycle exercise, and isometric handgrip exercise of patients on two different diets. One diet consisted of a free intake of salt; the second involved a 50 percent reduction of usual salt intake for six weeks. Although lowering the salt intake did not decrease the baseline pressures, it did reduce the systolic and diastolic pressures during each of the mental and physical challenges. Relevant to the theory that membrane cation transport is involved in hypertension, these subjects also showed a significant reduction in intracellular sodium content of their lymphocytes.

The investigation by Ambrosioni and associates[57] measured the sodium concentration within white blood cells. These values may reflect the sodium content of other body cells. Recently, physiologic studies have investigated the mechanisms of transport of sodium across cell membranes. At least two separate mechanisms have been clearly identified, the sodium-lithium (Na-Li) countertransport system and the sodium-potassium (Na-K) cotransport system. The systems differ biochemically in their sensitivity to inhibitors such as furosemide and p-chloromercuribenzoate, their $K_o.5$ for internal lithium, and their dependence on chloride.[58] The function of both transport systems seems to be the extrusion of sodium from within cells against its electrochemical gradient. Studies of cation transport across red blood cell membranes in patients with essential hypertension have shown that alterations of sodium transport can be identified in these patients. A reduction in the rate of outward Na-K cotransport has been described in hypertensive families.[59,60] Others have demonstrated a marked elevation in the Na-Li countertransport system accompanied by normal or elevated Na-K cotransport in hypertensive Caucasians.[61,62] Recently, Canessa, Spalvins, et al.[63] reported another variation of cation transport in American black hypertensives consisting of low Na-K cotransport and no elevation of the Na-Li countertransport. These studies indicate that there are at least two subsets of cation transport alterations (low Na-K cotransport and elevated Na-Li countertransport), which may differentially affect hypertensives of distinct ethnic origins. Of further interest in the investigation of Canessa, Spalvins, et al.[63] was the detection of the same abnormality in Na-K cotransport in adolescent offspring of hypertensive parents. One of 10 adolescents with normotensive parents had a lower furosemide-sensitive K efflux rate versus 8 of 13 adolescents of hypertensive parents with a markedly reduced K efflux rate. These adolescent offspring of hypertensive parents had been shown in a previous study to have a more pronounced cardiovascular response to stress. When subjected to the mental stress of difficult mental arithmetic, the young offspring of hypertensive parents responded with a greater increase in blood pressure and heart rate than young offspring of normotensive parents.[64]

The variations of cation transport rates across the membranes of red blood cells identified in these studies may be indicative of cation transport in other body cells, such as the renal tubular cells or vascular smooth muscle cells. Such cells, having an alteration in their capacity to extrude intracellular sodium, may also vary in their response to other stimuli, such as the response of vascular smooth muscle cells to sympathetic stimuli. Thus, it is possible that variations in cation transport may provide a biologic link between behavioral stressors and cardiovascular responsivity. Further investigation will be necessary to establish the validity of this relationship.

In another more complex clinical study, Skrabel, Auböck, and coworkers[26] investigated the effects of altering dietary sodium and potassium on cardiovascular reactivity in young normotensive individuals at rest and during stress. This study involved 20 male medical students, 10 with a negative family history of hypertension and 10 with a positive family history of hypertension. All subjects were studied after two weeks on each of four different dietary regimens consisting of (1) normal intake (200 mEq Na, 80 mEq K daily); (2) reduced sodium (50 mEq Na, 80 mEq K); (3) increased potassium (200 mEq Na, 200 mEq K); and (4) reduced sodium with increased potassium (50 mEq Na, 200 mEq K). A reduction of sodium intake did not significantly decrease resting blood pressure in the entire subject group. However, there was a reduction in systolic and/or diastolic pressure of 5 mmHg or more in 12 subjects, including 8 of the 10 individuals with a positive family history of hypertension. Increasing potassium intake without decreasing sodium intake led to a decrease in the resting diastolic blood pressure in 10 persons, 7 of whom had a positive family history of hypertension. All but one of these subjects had also responded to lowering sodium intake. During the mental stress task, which consisted of mental arithmetic, subjects demonstrated a similar blood pressure response on all diets except the combination of low sodium–high potassium, which resulted in a reduction in the blood pressure response but an enhancement of heart rate reactivity. This combination diet also reduced the blood pressure increase to a controlled infusion of norepinephrine. These observations support the concept that a low sodium intake combined with a high potassium intake may reduce the pressor response to sympathetic tone, and vascular sensitivity may be affected by this diet. The investigators[26] attributed these results in part to a decrease in total body fluid volume, which was evaluated in a subsample of subjects using the sodium isotope, Na-24. Additionally, the low sodium–high potassium diet increased baroreceptor sensitivity as indicated by the ratio of the pulse rate decrease to increase in mean arterial pressure observed during norepinephrine infusion. A later study by Skrabel, Herkolz, and associates[65] indicated that individuals who were "salt sensitive" (roughly 40 percent of normotensives in their sample) also showed greater pressor responses to infused norepinephrine than "salt-resistant" persons, on both high- and low-salt diets. Salt-sensitive subjects were identified as those who showed a significant drop in resting casual blood pressure after two weeks of moderate salt restriction (50 mEq/day).

SUMMARY

Available evidence now demonstrates that a high sodium intake augments pressor responses to behavioral stress. Recent studies also indicate that behavioral stress can induce retention of sodium and water, at least over short time periods. These two issues indicate an interactive contribution of sodium and stress factors in the modulation of blood pressure and cardio-vascular reactivity. The emerging evidence that potassium intake may attenuate these responses provides another potential environmental coun-terregulatory factor. Furthermore, the demonstrable variations in pressure and reactivity induced by changes in these environmental factors are more pronounced in subjects with borderline hypertension or a family history of hypertension. Thus, further research into these interactions would appear to be an important initiative for investigations focusing on the pathogenesis of hypertension.

Nonetheless, considerable gaps in understanding this process still exist. To clarify and delineate this process, further investigations of the renal and cardiovascular effects of stress exposure under conditions of sodium loading and sodium depletion are needed. Experimental designs should continue to address differences in response patterns associated with racial group, age, sex, and clinical status. Efforts to examine relationships to personality dimensions like Type A behavior or suppressed hostility are also to be encouraged. Studies focusing on real-life stressors may be difficult but could provide especially convincing evidence relating to the significance of the combination of high sodium and stress. In addition to sodium, further studies that also account for levels of potassium balance will be required. It is also quite likely that the role of other cations such as calcium and magnesium must also be concurrently evaluated before a clear understanding of the stress-sodium interaction can be derived. In addition, the most appropriate methodology will require attention to baseline state of sodium, potassium balance, route and duration of electrolyte loading or depletion, and condition of the neuroendocrine system at the time of study. Although difficult and challenging to execute, the performance of these types of rigorous investigations will add greatly to the delineation of the complex interactive systems involved in blood pressure regulation.

REFERENCES

1. Dahl LK: Salt intake and hypertension. In Genest J, Koiw E, Kuchel O (eds), *Hypertension: Physiopathology and Treatment.* New York, McGraw-Hill, 1977, pp. 548–559.
2. Freis ED: Salt, volume and the prevention of hypertension. *Circulation* 53:589–594, 1976.
3. Meneely GR, Battarbee HD: High sodium-low potassium environment and hypertension. *Am J Cardiol* 38:768–785, 1976.
4. Morgan T, Jyers J, Carney S: The evidence that salt is an important aetiological agent, if not the cause of hypertension. *Clin Sci* 57:4594–4625, 1979. (Suppl 5)
5. Poep LB: Epidemiologic evidence on the etiology of human hypertension and its possible prevention. *Am Heart J* 91:527–534, 1976.
6. Sasaki N: High blood pressure and the salt intake of the Japanese. *Jap Heart J* 3:313–324, 1962.
7. Pickering GW: Salt intake and essential hypertension. *Cardiovasc Rev Reports* 1:13–17, 1980.
8. Simpson FO: Salt and hypertension: A sceptical review of the evidence. *Clin Sci* 57:463–480, 1979. (Suppl 5)
9. McCarron DA, Morris C, Cole C: Blood pressure and nutrient intake in the United States. *Science* 217:267–269, 1982.

10. Morgan T, Carney S, Wilson M: Interrelationship in humans between sodium intake and hypertension. *Clin Exp Pharmacol Physiol* **2**:127–129, 1975. (Suppl 2)

11. Doyle AE, Chua KG, Duffy S: Urinary sodium, potassium and creatinine excretion in hypertensive and normotensive Australians. *Med J Austral* **2**:898–900, 1976.

12. Waern V, Aberg H: Blood pressure in 60-year-old men. *Acta Med Scand* **206**:99–105, 1979.

13. Thulin T, Karlberg BE Schersten B: Plasma renin activity, aldosterone and sodium excretion in women in high and low casual blood pressure levels. *Acta Med Scand* **203**:405–410, 1978.

14. Simpson FO, Waal-Manning HJ, et al: Relationship of blood pressure to sodium excretion in a population survey.*Clin Sci Mol Med* **55**:5373–5375, 1978. (Suppl 4)

15. Ljungman S, Aurell M, et al: Sodium excretion and blood pressure. *Hypertension* **3**:318–326, 1981.

16. Mark AL, Lawton WJ, et al: Effects of high and low sodium intake on arterial pressure and forearm vascular resistance in borderline hypertension. *Circ Res* **36–37**:I194–I198, 1975. (Suppl I)

17. Kirkendall WM, Connor WE, et al: The effect of dietary sodium chloride on blood pressure, body fluids, electrolytes, renal function and serum lipids of normotensive man. *J Lab Clin Med* **87**:418–434, 1976.

18. Kawasaki T, Delea CS, et al: The effect of high-sodium and low-sodium intakes on blood pressure and other related variables in human subjects with idiopathic hypertension. *Am J Med* **64**:193–198, 1978.

19. Sullivan JM, Ratts TE, et al: Hemodynamic effects of dietary sodium in man: A preliminary report. *Hypertension* **2**:506–514, 1980.

20. Takeshita A, Imaizumi T, et al: Characteristic responses to salt loading and deprivation in hypertensive subjects. *Circ Res* **51**:457–464, 1982.

21. Miller JZ, Daugherty SA, et al: Blood pressure response to dietary sodium restriction in normotensive adults. *Hypertension* **5**:790–795, 1983.

22. Myers J, Morgan T: The effect of sodium intake on the blood pressure, related to age and sex. *Clin Exp Hypert* **A5**:99–118, 1983.

23. Lever AF, Beretta-Piccoli C, et al: Sodium and potassium in essential hypertension. *Br Med J* **283**:463–468, 1981.

24. Luft FC, Rankin LI, et al: Cardiovascular and humoral responses to extremes of sodium intake in normal black and white men. *Circulation* **60**:697–706, 1979.

25. Pietinen PI, Wong O, Altschul AM: Electrolyte output, blood pressure and family history of hypertension. *Am J Clin Nutr* **32**:997–1005, 1979.

26. Skrabel F, Auböck J, Hortnägl H: Low sodium-high potassium diet for prevention of hypertension: Probable mechanisms of action. *Lancet* **2**:895–900, 1981.

27. Battarbee HD, Dailey JW, Meneely GR: Dietary sodium and potassium-induced transient changes in blood pressure and catecholamine excretion in the Sprague-Dawley rat. *Hypertension* **5**:336–345, 1983.

28. MacGregor GA, Smith SJ, et al: Moderate potassium supplementation in essential hypertension. *Lancet* **2**:567–570, 1982.

29. Anderson DE, Kearns WD, Warden TJ: Potassium infusion attenuates avoidance-saline hypertension in dogs. *Hypertension* **5**:415–420, 1983.

30. Dahl LK, Heine M, Tassinari L: Effects of chronic excess salt feedings. Induction of self-sustaining hypertension in rats. *J Exp Med* **114**:231–236, 1961.

31. Grim CE, Miller JZ, et al: Genetic influences on renin, aldosterone and the renal excretion of sodium and potassium following volume expansion and contraction in normal man. *Hypertension* **1**:583–590, 1979.

32. Nicholls GM, Kiowski W, et al: Plasma norepinephrine variations with dietary sodium intake. *Hypertension* 2:29–32, 1980.

33. Rankin LI, Luft FC, et al: Sodium intake alters the effects of norepinephrine on blood pressure. *Hypertension* 3:650–656, 1981.

34. Coleman TG, Guyton AC: Hypertension caused by salt loading in the dog: III. Onset of transients of cardiac output and other circulatory variables. *Circ Res* 25:153–160, 1969.

35. Guyton AC, Coleman TG: A systems analysis approach to understanding long range arterial blood pressure control and hypertension. *Circ Res* 35:159–176, 1974.

36. Coleman TG, Smar RE, Murphy WR: Autoregulation versus other vasoconstrictors in hypertension: A critical review. *Hypertension* 1:324–330, 1979.

37. Gavras H: Possible mechanisms of sodium dependent hypertension: Volume expansion or vasoconstriction? *Clin Exp Hypert* A4:737–749, 1982.

38. Lever AF, Beretta-Piccoli C, et al: Sodium and potassium in essential hypertension. *Br Med J* 283:463–468, 1981.

39. Arendshorst WJ, Beierwaltes WH: Renal tubular reabsorption in spontaneously hypertensive rats. *Am J Physiol* 236:F38–F47, 1979.

40. Beierwaltes WH, Arendshorst WJ, Klemmer PJ: Electrolyte and water balance in young spontaneously hypertensive rats. *Hypertension* 4:908–915, 1982.

41. Smith TL, Hutchins PM: Central hemodynamics in the developmental stage of spontaneous hypertension in the unanesthetized rat. *Hypertension* 1:508–517, 1979.

42. Lawler JE, Barker GF, et al: Effects of stress on blood pressure and cardiac pathology in rats with borderline hypertension. *Hypertension* 3:496–505, 1981.

43. Lundin S, Thoren P: Renal function and sympathetic activity during mental stress in normotensive and spontaneously hypertensive rats. *Acta Physiol Scand* 115:115–124, 1982.

44. Koepke JP, DiBona GF: High sodium intake enhances renal nerve and antinatriuretic responses to stress in SHR. *Hypertension* 7:357–363, 1985.

45. Katholi RE, Carey RM, et al: Production of sustained hypertension by chronic intrarenal norepinephrine infusion in conscious dogs. *Circ Res* 40:I118–I126, 1977. (Suppl I)

46. Cowley Jr. AW, Lohmeier TE: Changes in renal vascular sensitivity and arterial pressure associated with sodium intake during long term intrarenal norepinephrine infusion in dogs. *Hypertension* 1:549–558, 1979.

47. Friedman SM, Friedman SL: Cell permeability, sodium transport and the hypertensive process in the rat. *Circ Res* 39:433–441, 1976.

48. Blaustein MP: Sodium ions, calcium ions, blood pressure regulation and hypertension: A reassessment and a hypothesis. *Am J Physiol* 232:C165–C173, 1977.

49. Mulvaney MJ, Hansen PK, Aalkjaer C: Direct evidence that the great contractility of resistance vessels in spontaneously hypertensive rats is associated with a narrowed lumen, a thickened media and an increased number of smooth muscle cell layers. *Circ Res* 43:854–864, 1978.

50. Anderson DE, Kearns WD, Belter WE: Progressive hypertension in dogs by avoidance conditioning and saline infusion. *Hypertension* 5:286–291, 1983.

51. Koepke JP, Light KC, Obrist PA: Neural control of renal excretory function during behavioral stress in conscious dogs. *Am J Physiol* 245:R251–R258, 1983.

52. Koepke JP, Grignolo A, et al: Central beta adrenoceptor mediation of the antinatriuretic response to behavioral stress in conscious dogs. *J Pharmacol Exp Ther* 227:73–77, 1983.

53. Lamprecht F, Richardson JS, et al: 6-Hydroxydopamine destruction of central adrenergic neurons prevents or reverses developing DOCA-salt hypertension in rats. *J Neurol Transm* 40:149–158, 1977.

54. DiBona CF: The functions of the renal nerves. *Rev Physiol Biochem Pharmacol* 94:76–181, 1982.

55. Light KC, Koepke JP, et al: Psychological stress induces sodium and fluid retention in men at high risk for hypertension. *Science* **220**:429–431, 1983.

56. Falkner B, Onesti G, Angelakos ET: Effect of salt loading on the cardiovascular response to stress in adolescents. *Hypertension* **3**:II195–199, 1981. (Suppl II)

57. Ambrosioni E, Costa FV, et al: Effects of moderate salt restriction on intralymphocytic sodium and pressor response to stress in borderline hypertension. *Hypertension* **4**:789–794, 1982.

58. Canessa M, Bie I, Tosteson DC: Li-K cotransport in human red cells. *J Gen Physical* **80**:149–168, 1982.

59. Dagher G, Garay R: A Na-K cotransport assay for essential hypertension. *Can J Biochem* **58**:1069, 1980.

60. Cusi D, Barlassina C, et al: Familial aggregation of cation transport abnormalities and essential hypertension. *Clin Exp Hypert* **3**:871–874, 1981.

61. Canessa M, Adragna N, et al: Increased sodium-lithium countertransport in red cells of patients with essential hypertension. *N Engl J Med* **302**:772–776, 1980.

62. Adragna N, Canessa M, et al: Red cell Li-Na countertransport and Na-K cotransport in patients with essential hypertension. *Hypertension* **4**:798–804, 1982.

63. Canessa M, Spalvins A, et al: Red cell sodium countertransport and cotransport in normotensive and hypertensive blacks. *Hypertension* **6**:344–351, 1984.

64. Falkner B, Onesti G, et al: Cardiovascular response to mental stress in normal adolescents with hypertensive parents. *Hypertension* **1**:23–30, 1979.

65. Skrabel F, Herholz H, et al: Salt sensitivity in humans is linked to enhanced sympathetic responsiveness and to enhanced proximal tubular reabsorption. *Hypertension* **6**:152–158, 1984.

PART V

MODULATORS OF STRESS-INDUCED REACTIVITY

18

Alcohol, Reactivity, and the Heart: Implications for Coronary Health and Disease

ROBERT W. LEVENSON

The relationships between alcohol and cardiovascular function and disease are inherently complex. A full accounting of these relationships would require making at least four critical distinctions: (1) acute effects of alcohol consumption versus effects associated with long-term moderate use versus effects associated with long-term chronic abuse; (2) effects on alcoholics versus effects on nonalcoholics; (3) effects on individuals with healthy cardiovascular systems versus individuals with cardiovascular disease; and

This research has been supported by NIAAA grant AA05004.

(4) effects of alcohol on resting, basal cardiovascular levels versus effects on cardiovascular reactivity. The existing literature on alcohol and the heart has not always taken account of all of these distinctions. Nonetheless, we do know that alcohol has a major impact on the heart and on processes of cardiovascular health and disease. In this chapter I will attempt to describe these effects and explore their bases.

ALCOHOL METABOLISM

At the outset, some basic principles of alcohol metabolism will be reviewed to facilitate an understanding of the cardiovascular effects that will be described later. Alcohol (ethanol) is absorbed rapidly into the blood stream from the stomach and the small intestine. The rate of absorption is slowed by the presence of food in the stomach. Maximally, only about 10 percent of the alcohol that is consumed is excreted or otherwise eliminated. Alcohol cannot be effectively stored in body tissues, thus the remaining 90 percent that is not eliminated directly in urine, breath, or perspiration is metabolized. Ethanol metabolism takes place primarily in the liver. There the ethanol is oxidized by enzymes (mainly alcohol dehydrogenase; ADH) into its first metabolite, acetaldehyde, which is a toxic substance that has its own set of damaging cardiovascular effects. Normally, the acetaldehyde is quickly metabolized to form acetate. However, in the presence of drugs used to treat alcoholism, such as Antabuse (disulfiram), the metabolism of acetaldehyde is inhibited and its levels increase. Acetate can be oxidized to carbon dioxide and water or utilized for lipid synthesis.

Alcohol metabolism proceeds at a fairly steady rate of 100 mg ethanol/kg body weight/hour. This is not an overly efficient system, given typical alcohol doses. For example, a 150-pound individual drinking one-ounce shots of 80 proof vodka would not completely metabolize even one drink in an hour (approximately 4/5 ounce would be metabolized). Extrapolating from this rate, one can see that, following a heavy bout of drinking in which a number of drinks were consumed, the removal of alcohol from the blood stream would take many hours. Experienced drinkers can take advantage of this constant metabolic rate to maintain a fairly constant blood alcohol level by spreading out their consumption of alcohol. Just as the rate of ethanol metabolism cannot be accelerated to accommodate an episode of rapid, high-quantity drinking, it also cannot be accelerated to meet short-term needs for energy. Thus, alcohol is not a particularly good food source to select when extra energy is required in a short period of time. Interestingly, alcohol cannot be metabolized by the heart, as there is no ADH present within the myocardium. However, the presence of acetaldehyde dehydrogenase in the heart enables the metabolism of acetaldehyde.

ALCOHOL: LINKS WITH DISEASE

Chronic alcohol use can have deleterious effects on a strikingly wide range of organ systems. In a recent report to Congress on alcohol and health,[1] evidence was reviewed that indicates alcohol is associated with disease processes in the gastrointestinal system, the liver, the cardiovascular system, the skeletal musculature, and the endocrine system. For present purposes I will focus on the harmful effects of alcohol on the heart.

Coronary Heart Disease

Alcohol can damage the heart both indirectly, through dietary factors associated with alcoholism (e.g., malnutrition), or directly. I will review some of the major disorders that result from each of these paths.

Dietary-Mediated Disorders. In the realm of dietary-mediated disorders, beriberi heart disease and cobalt beer cardiomyopathy are among the most prominent. Beriberi heart disease is caused by a deficiency in thiamine that persists for several months. Implicated in this disorder are diets that emphasize consumption of high-carbohydrate foods such as polished rice and alcohol, both of which are deficient in thiamine. In this disorder there is a marked dysfunction in circulation, primarily related to a reduction in peripheral vascular resistance. In response, both heart rate and cardiac output are increased, with a resultant decrease in circulation time. Symptoms include warm skin, widened pulse pressure, anemia, apical systolic murmur, enlargement of the heart, dilation of the pulmonary arteries, and neuritis of the peripheral nerves. A second dietary-mediated disorder, cobalt beer cardiomyopathy, was responsible for a high mortality rate among beer drinking alcoholics in the 1960s. During that period, cobalt was added to beer to improve its foaming qualities. The disorder that resulted was characterized by right-sided congestive cardiac failure[2] due in part to cobalt toxicity and in part to malnutrition. With the banning of the practice of adding cobalt ions to beer, cobalt beer cardiomyopathy has been virtually eliminated.

Alcoholic Cardiomyopathy. Alcoholic cardiomyopathy is the term applied to primary heart muscle disease in alcoholics that is not related to coronary, hypertensive, valvular, congenital, or pulmonary heart disease, but rather to an intrinsic defect in the heart muscle itself.[3] It should be added that there is increasing evidence from studies that have controlled for malnutrition that this disorder results from a direct toxic effect of acetaldehyde on heart muscle.[4-6] The damage, which consists of noninflammatory lesions of the myocardium, appears to be centered in the mitochondria.[7,8] As these structures are involved in the oxidation of energy sources, the availability of energy to the heart muscle is greatly compromised, and over time this can lead to congestive heart failure. Increased myocardial accumulation of lipids is another feature of the disorder. Symptoms consist of shortness of breath and signs of congestive failure (e.g., edema, chest pain, fatigue, palpitation, blood-stained sputum). Alcoholic cardiomyopathy is slow to develop (10 years of heavy drinking is typical) and recovery is also slow (typically taking up to six years after the cessation of drinking).

Other Harmful Effects of Alcohol on Heart Function.   Alcohol has pernicious effects on the efficiency of the heart's contraction. This has been shown most clearly in terms of an impairment of left ventricular functioning at moderate doses in humans[9,10] and in animals.[11-13] Alcohol has been shown to negatively affect biochemical processes in the heart that are necessary for muscle contraction, including calcium uptake and binding,[14] and sodium/potassium activation of adenosine triphosphatase (ATPase) activity of cardiac plasma membranes.[15] These effects of alcohol on the heart muscle no doubt contribute to findings that alcohol intoxication and alcoholism lead to an increase in cardiac arrhythmias.[16,17] These arrhythmias are thought to be involved in some cases of sudden death, particularly among young alcohol users.[18] Among patients with existing heart disease, the depressant effects of alcohol on myocardial performance are potentially quite dangerous.[19]

ALCOHOL: LINKS WITH CORONARY HEALTH

Thus far I have presented an overwhelmingly negative picture of the long-term effects of alcohol abuse on the heart. Clearly, like all other drugs, there is a dose at which the substance becomes toxic. For alcohol, the toxic effects are particularly insidious for two reasons. First, they seem to be cumulative over time, with a number of alcohol-related cardiac disorders taking years to develop (e.g., 10 years for alcoholic cardiomyopathy). And second, in the short term, moderate alcohol consumption may have a number of beneficial effects on the heart.

Epidemiological Studies

There is now a substantial amount of evidence from a large number of epidemiological studies indicating that moderate consumption of alcohol (approximately two or three drinks per day) is associated with a lowered risk for coronary heart disease. The nature of the relation seems to be J-shaped, with heavy drinkers being at the highest risk, followed by nondrinkers (i.e., abstainers), followed by moderate drinkers. Whether a given study finds this J-shaped relation or more of a U-shaped relation (i.e., heavy drinkers and nondrinkers being at equally elevated risk compared to moderate drinkers) may depend on a number of factors, including the range of consumption levels that are sampled.

In the best of these studies, controls have been included for other risk factors such as smoking, age, race, and gender. A number of different methodologies have been used. Hennekens et al.[20] compared drinking patterns in patients with heart disease and in matched controls. They found more abstainers and heavy drinkers among the patients. Using data from participants in Oakland's Kaiser-Permanente Health Plan, Klatsky et al.[21] found that moderate drinkers were less often found among cardiac patients than among controls, while abstainers were *more* often found among patients than among controls. In the prospective Tecumseh Community Health Study[22] the J- shaped relation was also found, with even higher risk for heart disease among former drinkers who had stopped drinking. In the prospective Honolulu Heart Study,[23] moderate drinkers were found to be at the lowest risk for myocardial infarctions. In a prospective study of Puerto Rican men,[24] the J-shaped relation was found for angina pectoris, nonfatal myocardial infarctions, and nonsudden coronary heart disease death. In both this study and the prospective Yugoslavia Cardiovascular Disease Study,[25] no association was found between alcohol consumption and sudden cardiac death.

As is often the case with these kinds of epidemiological data, there are a number of problems. Relationships between alcohol consumption and cardiac health may well be mediated by other factors, and the direction of causality cannot be determined. Measurement problems also abound. There are a number of ways of determining how much alcohol a person consumes on average, most of which involve retrospective recall. Regardless of how accurate such recall is over the short term, it is unlikely that most people can maintain this kind of accuracy over the long term. If it is the cumulative effects of chronic alcohol use that are thought to be of etiologic significance in some forms of heart disease, then a measure of the pattern of alcohol consumption over a 5 to 10 year period is called for. Of course, such a measure would be very difficult to obtain. There are other problems as well. LaPorte et al.,[26] in a very thorough examination of the implications of the alcohol–heart disease relation, point to the importance of separating life-long nondrinkers from those who have stopped drinking after a history of heavy consumption. It is unlikely that the pathways that mediate the purported higher risk for heart disease among heavy drinkers are the same as those that mediate the risk for abstainers. As indicated earlier, whether a curvilinear relationship appears to be U-shaped or J-shaped may be a function of where the lines between categories of drinking are drawn and how wide a range of consumption levels are included.

What seems to be most consistent in all of these studies is the lowered risk for coronary disease among moderate social drinkers. I will turn now to an examination of some potential mediators of this lowered risk.

Alcohol and High Density Lipoproteins

One potential mediator of the lowered risk for coronary heart disease among moderate drinkers that has received a great deal of attention is the relationship between alcohol consumption and the production of high-density lipoprotein cholesterol. Cholesterol is a lipid that is nonsoluble in water; to be transported in the blood stream it must be attached to a soluble substance. To accomplish this, cholesterol binds with various lipoproteins, which are termed low-density lipoprotein (LDL) or high-density lipoprotein (HDL), depending on their density and molecular structure. At one time it was thought that the overall level of serum cholesterol was correlated positively with risk for coronary heart disease;[27] however, it is now believed that the correlation is positive for LDL, but negative for HDL.[28,29] The role of HDL in coronary health is not fully understood. HDL appears to transport cholesterol from the tissues to the liver for excretion. It is also thought to be less likely to be incorporated in atherogenic plaques than LDL,[30] and may even block the incorporation of LDL in these plaques.

Alcohol consumption has been shown to be associated with elevated serum HDL levels in a number of studies.[31–34] This has led to speculation that the association between moderate alcohol consumption and lowered risk for coronary heart disease may be mediated in part by the increase in HDL associated with alcohol consumption. This speculation is strengthened by the observation that the amount of alcohol associated with significantly elevated HDL levels[35] and the amount of alcohol associated with lowered risk of coronary heart disease are similar (i.e., about three drinks per day). Elevated HDL levels seem to recede quickly once alcohol consumption is reduced; thus, sustaining these levels would require a long-term commitment to maintaining a level of moderate drinking (with the incumbent risks of increased tolerance leading to increasingly higher levels of drinking). Furthermore, the clinical significance of the HDL increase associated with alcohol is uncertain, especially since the subclass of HDL that is increased by alcohol consumption is not the subclass (i.e., HDL_2) that is thought to have anti-atherogenic properties.[36]

Alcohol and Diminished Neuroendocrine Reactivity

Perhaps the most elegant and convincing work are the animal studies carried out by Brick and Pohorecky.[37–39] In a series of studies with rats, they have shown that alcohol diminishes the stress-induced increases in the blood of (1) free fatty acids and (2) corticosterone. There is an intimate intertwining of functions in stress between the autonomically mediated changes in cardiac function, the release of free fatty acids from adipose tissue (mediated by direct sympathetic innervation of these tissues or by action of catecholamines released from the adrenal medulla), and the release of corticosterone from the adrenal cortex. Lowered neuroendocrine activation could have beneficial cardiovascular effects. For example, Carruthers[40] has pointed to the potentially atherogenic effects of the free fatty acids released under the influence of catecholamine action in response to stress. In addition, both the catecholamines and corticosteroids may have direct toxic effects on the coronary arteries.[41] If Brick and Pohorecky's findings in rats hold for humans and, thus, alcohol consumption in humans also reduces the amount of catecholamines, free fatty acids, and corticosterone released in response to stress, then the potential benefits for cardiovascular health would be considerable.

Alcohol and Diminished Cardiovascular Reactivity

In this section I will be presenting data obtained from my own laboratory relevant to understanding the acute effects of alcohol consumption on cardiovascular reactivity. This work has studied only nonalcoholic experienced social drinkers (they drink approximately two drinks per day) and will be used to develop a second potential bridge between moderate alcohol use and cardiovascular health—diminished cardiovascular reactivity. The notion that a reduction in cardiovascular reactivity is health-promoting is based on models of cardiovascular disease that posit a causal role for an overreactive heart and vasculature. This hyperreactivity model is implicit in many psychological theories of the etiology of coronary heart disease. For example, one hypothesized mediational pathway between the Type A personality profile and cardiovascular disease is cardiac hyperreactivity.[e.g.,42,43] It is unknown whether hyperreactivity reflects the presence of an ongoing disease process or whether it is a causative element in disease etiology (or both). Models of the role of cardiac hyperreactivity in the etiology of cardiac disease range from simple heuristic models (e.g., "a heart that is always working harder wears out faster") to the elaborate. An example of the latter can be found in Obrist's model,[44] in which cardiac hyperreactivity is linked with atherosclerotic processes in the etiology of essential hypertension. Clearly, if these models are true, or even partly true, anything that reduces cardiovascular reactivity has the potential for interrupting or slowing these disease processes.

In our work[45–47] subjects have been administered a weight-corrected dose of alcohol, typically utilizing a double-blind balanced placebo design.[48] A wide range of central nervous system, autonomic nervous system, and behavioral variables have been studied, both in terms of how alcohol affects *basal* levels and how it affects *reactivity* when the subject is exposed to laboratory stressors (e.g., loud tones, electric shock, self-disclosure). We have studied approximately 400 subjects in these studies, and the pattern of cardiovascular findings that has emerged has been remarkably consistent.

Subjects start the experimental procedure in a completely sober state (verified by Breathalyzer) and then consume one of three doses of alcohol (either 0 g ethanol/kg, 0.5 g/kg, or 1.0 g/kg body weight) in 45 minutes. For example, a 145-pound subject would consume 7 ounces of vodka in the high dose (1 g/kg) condition, which would produce a blood alcohol concentration of approximately 0.10 percent. This is the legal intoxication limit in most states. We wait another 30 to 45 minutes to allow for absorption and then obtain "basal" physiological measures while subjects wait for the experiment to start. Using these procedures, we have found in three different studies that alcohol causes an increase in resting heart rate and a lengthening of pulse transmission time (i.e., the time interval between the R wave of the electrocardiogram to the arrival of the pulse pressure wave at the finger). Longer pulse transmission times are indicative of decreases in cardiac contractile force, to the extent that part of the lengthening is accounted for by longer preejection periods.[49] Obviously our procedures are not ideal for obtaining estimates of baselines, since subjects know they will be subjected to the stressor later in the experiment. Nonetheless, these cardiovascular findings are quite consistent with those reported by others who have utilized other baseline procedures. This is true both for heart rate[50–53] and for measures of contractile force.[9,10,54,55]

In Figure 18.1 these effects can be seen across three dosage conditions. In all of our studies, we have found heart rate increases of about six beats per minute and pulse transmission time increases of about 11 msec in the 1 g/kg

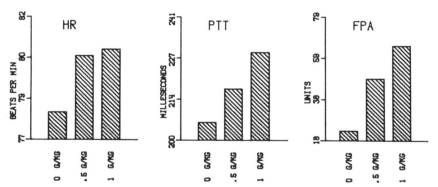

FIGURE 18.1.   Effects of three doses of alcohol on prestressor cardiovascular levels: heart rate (HR), pulse transmission time (PTT) and finger pulse amplitude (FPA).

high dose, compared to the 0 g/kg no-alcohol condition. We also measured finger pulse amplitude in one study, and found alcohol to increase it; this would be consistent with alcohol's known vasodilative properties.

It is likely that changes in heart rate and in contractility are compensatory adjustments that function to maintain a stable cardiac output (probably the heart rate increase compensates for a direct depressant effect on the myocardium produced by alcohol). While these are statistically significant changes, they are not clinically significant. Nonetheless, from the point of view of the experimenter hoping to assess cardiac *reactivity*, they must be taken into account. While these changes are not so large as to run the risk of subjects' reaching cardiac ceiling and floor limits, they are sufficiently large to play havoc with the interpretation of reactivity differences across conditions.

There are many mathematical approaches to the problem of adjusting for differing baselines across conditions (as would occur in a study of cardiovascular reactivity that compared intoxicated and sober subjects). These approaches range from the computation of simple change scores (which we have used in our research), to more complicated techniques based on regression and covariance. Any of the standard correction techniques is better than no correction. Unfortunately, the literature includes many studies that have failed to distinguish the effects of alcohol on cardiovascular *baselines* from the effects on cardiovascular *reactivity*, and also with studies that have found basal effects, but then have failed to correct for them in their analyses of reactivity.

After correcting for basal effects, we have consistently found alcohol to diminish cardiovascular reactivity. This has occurred in multiple studies, using different stressors, and in measures of both heart rate and pulse transmission time. In Figures 18.2 and 18.3, these effects, which we have termed "stress response dampening" effects of alcohol, can be seen for heart rate and pulse transmission times. In contrast to the effects of alcohol on basal levels for these two measures (which were in different "directions"—an arousal effect in speeding heart rate, and a relaxant effect in lengthening pulse transmission time), the effects on reactivity consisted of the same diminished reactivity for both. It is also interesting to note that the stress response dampening effects of alcohol are not global autonomic effects. Skin conductance responding, for example, has not been attenuated by alcohol in any of our studies.

Our confidence in the robustness of these effects on cardiovascular reactivity has been increased by similar findings from other laboratories.[56,57] However, it should be noted that we have found that pronounced dampening of cardiovascular reactivity occurs only with the high dose (1 g/kg). This can be readily seen in Figure 18.4, in which changes in heart rate and pulse

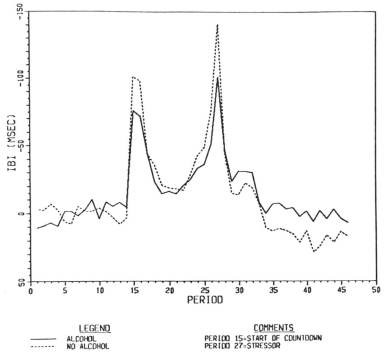

FIGURE 18.2.   Alcohol dampens the heart rate response to stress.

transmission time from prestressor levels are plotted for three different doses during times of maximum cardiovascular reactivity (i.e., while subjects watch a timer count down the last few seconds before the stressor, when they receive a painful electric shock, and while they give a self-disclosing speech).

The overall picture from this research to date is that of diminished cardiac reactivity produced by a fairly high dose of alcohol. Assuming models of cardiovascular disease etiology that posit an etiological role for heightened cardiac reactivity are true, these findings that alcohol reduces cardiovascular reactivity provide another mediational pathway for understanding the relation between moderate alcohol use and lowered incidence of coronary heart disease.

As always there are caveats. All of the results I have described were obtained with nonalcoholic subjects with healthy cardiovascular systems. Alcoholic subjects may well present a different picture, with greater tolerance to the cardiovascular effects of alcohol combined in some fashion with greater vulnerability to the cumulative toxic effects of alcohol. In addition, subjects with existing cardiovascular disease may be much more sensitive to the myocardial depressant effects of alcohol. This could become life threat-

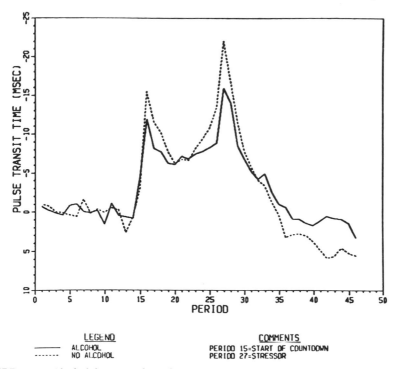

FIGURE 18.3.   Alcohol dampens the pulse transmission time response to stress.

ening at high doses. Finally, the effects of alcohol on cardiovascular reactivity may well be as sensitive to the drinker's position on the slope of the ethanol absorption curve as are the central nervous system effects. Many of these latter effects reverse in direction and rebound at different times over the time course of absorption.

Alcohol and Diminished Emotional Reactivity

The final pathway to be explored is that of alcohol's effects on emotional reactivity. Here what we know is based only on the most preliminary of data. A great deal of study has been done on the effects of alcohol on subjects' self-reports of mood. However, I know of no previous work that has looked at the emotional effects of alcohol using a behavioral measure that affords the same precision of measurement for emotional reactivity that has been obtained for measurement of cardiac reactivity. My interest in this problem derives from dissatisfaction with the self-report measures of emotional state that have typically been used in this context.

In our laboratory, using standard mood inventories, we have consistently found that intoxicated subjects reported feeling more "cheerful" and more

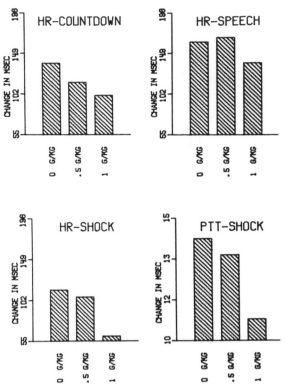

FIGURE 18.4.   Effects of three doses of alcohol on cardiovascular responses to stress: heart rate (HR) and pulse transmission time.

"pleasant" than sober subjects. The generic problems with these kinds of self-report measures are well known and need not be repeated here. In the context of alcohol, however, with its profound effects on the central nervous system, the differences in cognitive and appraisal processes in intoxicated and sober subjects are so profound as to make the use of self-report measures even more suspect. In addition, mood inventories essentially provide only a "basal" or "tonic" retrospective measure.

In studies of reactivity, what is needed is a more continuous and fine-grained measurement. At first we tried to obtain this by having subjects rate their tension levels continuously on a joystick-type device. While the results in the prestressor phase were consistent across studies (i.e., subjects reported feeling less tense at higher doses of alcohol), they were much less consistent during the stressor procedure. Intoxicated subjects often "forget" to adjust the dial. When they did remember, and when differences were found as a function of alcohol dosage, it was uncertain whether it was their "tension" levels or their "appraisal" facilities that had been altered.

For all of these reasons, and because alterations in subjects' emotional reactivity must be considered as potential explanations for alterations in autonomic and in neuroendocrine reactivity, we began to explore the use of measures of momentary changes in facial expression as a method for understanding the changes in emotional reactivity brought about by alcohol. We chose the face for a number of reasons. Of all the nonverbal emotional systems, its response patterning in different emotional states is best established. It is a very fast response system; emotional facial expressions typically come and go from the face in a matter of seconds. The face is integrated with autonomic functioning in emotion in a number of ways. Among these are the autonomically mediated changes in the face such as blushing, blanching, crying, and sweating. The face can be studied unobtrusively from video recordings. And finally, anatomically based methods now exist for decomposing complex facial expressions into their component muscle contractions, and for relating these facial expressions to discrete emotional states (e.g., Ekman and Friesen's Facial Action Coding System, FACS[58]).

Using FACS we have scored the facial responses to electric shock of 21 women, 7 at each of three different doses of alcohol. The process of FACS scoring is very slow, taking about one hour to score one minute of facial behavior from repeated slow-motion viewing of video tape. By year's end we hope to have completed scoring the facial behavior of 100 subjects of both genders and under two different kinds of stressful situations. In the meantime, what we have found to date has been quite interesting.

Based on observing the facial responses of many experimental subjects to shock over the years, we have identified three response "windows" that are differentiable. First, there is the *anticipation* to the shock. This occurs in the last five seconds prior to the shock, while subjects watch the seconds remaining before the shock countdown on a digital display. Second, there is the *shock* itself. Most subjects show an expression that starts about 500 msec after the shock. Third, there is the *secondary reaction*, which occurs three to five seconds after the shock. In each of these windows we have obtained evidence that alcohol reduces the emotional impact of the stressor.

Anticipation. There is great variability in the anticipation response window. Some subjects show expressions that signify fear; others show expressions that signify contempt. Some subjects show attempts at *controlling* emotion that focus around the mouth. These include lip biting, lip tightening (orbicularis oris muscle), pressing the lips together, raising the chin boss (mentalis muscle). Some show "false" smiles, which involve only the mouth and not the eyes and cheeks.[59] The effects of alcohol in this window are seen most clearly in these attempts at emotional control. In Figure 18.5, alcohol is

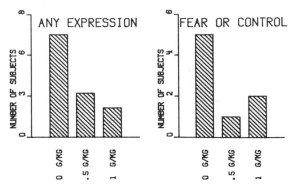

FIGURE 18.5.   Alcohol reduces emotional reactivity in anticipation of electric shock, as indicated by facial response.

shown to reduce the overall amount of expression in anticipation of the shock, and in particular, the occurrence of expressions of fear and emotional control. We have interpreted this as signifying that alcohol has made the stressor seem less stressful, and made subjects feel less of a need to try to control their emotional behavior or to put on a "brave front" (i.e., false smiles) for their own benefit or that of the experimenter. In terms of the implications of these findings for understanding patterns of cardiovascular arousal, it is important to note that heightened cardiovascular reactivity may be associated both with the arousal of certain negative emotions[e.g.,60] and with attempts to reduce or repress emotional expression.[61-62]

Shock.   In the shock window, almost all of our subjects showed some variant of the prototypical facial expression of fear. The most commonly represented element of this expression was the contraction of the risorius

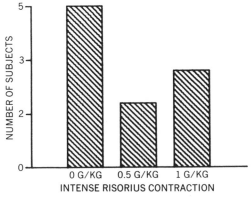

FIGURE 18.6.   Alcohol reduces emotional reactivity to shock, as indicated by intensity of the risorius contraction.

muscle, which pulls the lip corners straight back toward the ears. This is a central feature of the facial expressions that signify both fear and pain. Since it was common to all subjects, the intensity of the risorius contraction provided a convenient index of fear intensity. FACS allows scoring the intensity of muscle contraction on a five-point scale. In Figure 18.6, it can be seen that alcohol reduced the intensity of the risorius contraction, providing some indication that the shock was less impactful.

Reaction.   The reaction window is perhaps the richest in terms of the emergence of individual variation, since the subject often provides a secondary reaction. This is a kind of emotional "comment," which may reflect some appraisal of what has come before. Subjects are often "surprised" at their reactions and even amused by them. It is also a time to release tension, since, in our experimental procedure, there is no further stress or discomfort after the shock has been administered. Again, alcohol reduced the amount of facial expressive behavior. In Figure 18.7, alcohol is shown to reduce the occurrence of genuine or "felt" smiling (this is smiling that includes the eyes and cheeks in addition to the mouth).[59] As was the case in the anticipation and shock windows, alcohol reduced the amount of emotional responsivity. Intoxicated subjects accumulated less tension, and thus, they had less tension to release.

These findings provide preliminary evidence that alcohol reduces the emotional reactivity of subjects and/or the emotional impact of stressful events. In the brief but emotionally charged 10-second period that we have studied, sober subjects rode an emotional "roller coaster" from anticipatory fear and dread, to attempts to control their emotional response, to fear and pain, and to joyful release. Intoxicated subjects traversed a much "flatter"

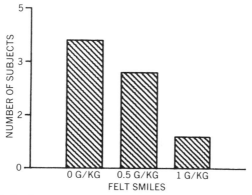

FIGURE 18.7.   Alcohol reduces emotion reactivity in reaction to shock, as indicated by reduced occurrence of genuine smiling.

path with fewer perturbations. As was seen with their cardiovascular systems, alcohol reduced their emotional reactivity. How much of the reduction in cardiovascular reactivity that we and others have associated with alcohol consumption is secondary to this reduction in emotional reactivity is unknown. It is unlikely that the two kinds of reactivity will ever be completely separable, since the evolutionary connections between the autonomic nervous system and emotion are so strong. But with these emotional data, as with the cardiovascular data, the potential mediational link between moderate alcohol consumption and reduced cardiovascular disease is clear. If alcohol makes the world seem less stressful, and if it makes the individual less emotionally labile, then two kinds of health benefits might ensue. First, if emotional arousal (e.g., anger, hostility) plays a role in the etiology of coronary heart disease, then a beneficial aspect of moderate alcohol consumption may derive from a diminution in these emotional/psychological factors. Second, if cardiovascular and/or endocrine hyperreactivity have etiological significance in the development of coronary heart disease, then a reduction in the emotional fuel for these arousal systems could be highly beneficial.

CONCLUDING COMMENTS

Alcohol use is clearly a significant and complex factor in any consideration of coronary disease and coronary health. Alcohol is a dualistic entity with both a harmful and a helpful side. In this chapter I have tried to portray both sides of the alcohol/cardiovascular relation. The injurious effects of alcohol, which contribute to cardiovascular, liver, and a wide range of other diseases, present a very negative case against heavy drinking. If to this evidence are added the other harmful effects of alcohol—the high potential for addiction, the damage to life and property associated with drunken driving, and the damage to mental health, to family functioning, and to society—then there can be little serious consideration given to endorsing the increased use of this drug. However, in looking at the other side of the issue, there is much that is potentially beneficial in terms of cardiovascular health that may be derived from the moderate use of alcohol. Added to this evidence are the other social "benefits" of drinking—the pervasive role that alcohol plays in our ritualized behaviors of courtship and mating, in celebration, in rites of passage, and in professional and business life.

My goal in writing this chapter has been to explore what is known about alcohol and the heart. Still, it is hard to ignore the practical implications of this research. Advocating moderate drinking as a means for increasing cardiovascular health would clearly be premature. We do not know enough about alcohol's effects on the heart, or about the boundaries of time and amount that delineate "health-promoting" drinking. Perhaps even more glaring than our lack of knowledge about drinking is our lack of knowledge about drinkers. Even if we established conclusively that alcohol could promote cardiovascular health, and even if we knew precisely how much alcohol, consumed for how long, would have this desirable effect (without producing injury to other bodily systems), we would still need to know a great deal more before encouraging the use of this addictive substance. In particular, we would need to discover methods for managing drinking that would keep today's moderate drinker from becoming tomorrow's alcoholic. Considering how little success the medical and behavioral sciences have had in developing methods for controlling addictive behaviors, it seems best to consider the use of alcohol as an adjunct to cardiovascular health to be an undeniably alluring Siren, but one best avoided.

REFERENCES

1. National Institute on Alcohol Abuse and Alcoholism: *Fifth Special Report to the U.S. Congress on Alcohol and Health*. Washington, DC, NIAAA, 1983.
2. Alexander CS: Cobalt-beer cardiomyopathy. A clinical and pathological study of twenty-eight cases. *Am J Med* **53**:395–417, 1972.
3. Khetarpal VK, Volicer L: Alcohol and cardiovascular disorders. *Drug Alcohol Depend* **7**:31–37, 1981.
4. Pader E: Clinical heart disease and electrocardiographic abnormalities in alcoholics. *Q J Stud Alcohol* **34**:774–785, 1973.
5. Regan TJ, Levinson GE, et al: Ventricular function in noncardiacs with alcoholic fatty liver: Role of ethanol in the production of cardiomyopathy. *J Clin Invest* **48**:397–407, 1969.
6. Steinberg JD, Hayden MT: Prevalence of clinically occult cardiomyopathy in chronic alcoholism. *Am Heart J* **101**:461–464, 1981.
7. Alexander CS: Electron microscopic observations in alcoholic heart disease. *Br Heart J* **29**:200–206, 1967.
8. Alexander CS, Sekhri KK, Nagasawa HT: Alcoholic cardiomyopathy in mice: Electron microscopic observations. *J Mol Cell Cardiol* **9**:247–254, 1977.
9. Ahmed SS, Levinson GE, Regan TJ: Depression of myocardial contractility with low doses of ethanol in normal man. *Circulation* **48**:378–385, 1973.
10. Child JS, Kovic RB, et al: Cardiac effects of acute ethanol ingestion unmasked by autonomic blockade. *Circulation* **59**:120–125, 1979.
11. Gimeno AL, Gimeno MF, Webb JL: Effects of ethanol on cellular membrane potentials and contractility of isolated rat atrium. *Am J Physiol* **203**:194–196, 1962.
12. Spann JF, Mason DT, et al: Actions of ethanol on the contractile state of the normal and failing cat papillary muscle. *Clin Res* **16**:249, 1968. (Abstract)
13. Nakano J, Moore SE: Effects of different alcohols on the contractile force of the isolated guinea pig myocardium. *Eur J Pharmacol* **20**:266–270, 1972.
14. Swartz MH, Repke DI, et al: Effects of ethanol on calcium binding and calcium uptake by cardiac microsomes. *Biochem Pharmacol* **23**:2369–2376, 1974.

15. Williams JW, Tada M, et al: Effects of ethanol and acetaldehyde on the $(N^+ + K^+)$-activated adenosine triphosphatase activity of cardiac plasma membranes. *Biochem Pharmacol* **24**:27–32, 1975.

16. Ettinger PO, Wu CF, et al: Arrhythmias and the "holiday heart": Alcohol-associated cardiac rhythm disorders. *Am Heart J* **95**:555–562, 1978.

17. Greenspon AJ, Leier CB, Schaal SF: Acute ethanol effects cardiac arrhythmias and conduction in man. *Clin Res* **29**:200, 1981. (Abstract)

18. Gould L, Shariff M, et al: Cardiac hemodynamics in alcoholic patients with chronic liver disease and a presystolic gallop. *J Clin Invest* **48**:860–868, 1969.

19. Conway N: Hemodynamic effects of ethyl alcohol in coronary heart disease. *Am Heart J* **76**:581–582, 1968.

20. Hennekens CH, Rosner B, Cole DS: Daily alcohol consumption and fatal coronary heart disease. *Am J Epidemiol* **107**:196–200, 1978.

21. Klatsky AL, Friedman CD, Siegelaub AB: Alcohol consumption before myocardial infarction. Results from the Kaiser-Permanente epidemiologic study of myocardial infarction. *Ann Intern Med* **81**:294–301, 1974.

22. Chafetz ME (ed): *Alcohol and Health*. Bethesda, MD, Department of Health, Education, and Welfare Publication, 1974, pp. 68–72.

23. Yano K, Rhoads GG, Kagan A: Coffee, alcohol and risk of coronary heart disease among Japanese men living in Hawaii. *N Engl J Med* **297**:405–409, 1977.

24. Kittner SJ, Garcia-Palmieri MR, et al: Alcohol and coronary heart disease in Puerto Rico. *Am J Epidemiol* **117**:538–550, 1983.

25. Kozarevic D, Demirovic J, et al: Drinking habits and coronary disease. *Am J Epidemiol* **116**:748–758, 1982.

26. LaPorte RE, Cresanta JL, Kuller LH: The relation of alcohol to coronary heart disease and mortality: Implication for public health policy. *J Public Health Policy* **1**:198–223, 1980.

27. Kannel WB, Dawber TR: Contributors to coronary risk, implications for prevention and public health: The Framingham study. *Heart Lung* **1**:797–809, 1972.

28. Gordon T, Castelli WP, et al: High density lipoprotein as a protective factor against coronary disease. The Framingham Study. *Am J Med* **62**:707–714, 1977.

29. Kannel WB, Dawber TR: Contributors to coronary risk: Ten years later. *Heart Lung* **11**:60–64, 1982.

30. Miller NE: The evidence for the antiatherogenicity of high-density lipoprotein cholesterol level. *Lipids* **13**:914–919, 1978.

31. Belfrage P, Berg B, et al: Alterations of lipid metabolism in healthy volunteers during long-term ethanol intake. *Eur J Clin Invest* **7**:127–131, 1977.

32. Castelli WP, Doyle JT, et al: Alcohol and blood lipids, the cooperative lipoprotein phenotyping study. *Lancet* **2**:153–155, 1977.

33. Hulley SB, Cohen R, Widdowson G: Plasma high-density lipoprotein cholesterol level. Influence of risk factor intervention. *JAMA* **238**:2269–2271, 1977.

34. Williams P, Robinson D, Baily A: High density lipoprotein and coronary risk factors in normal men. *Lancet* **2**:72–75, 1979.

35. Thornton J, Symes C, Heaton K: Moderate alcohol intake reduces bile cholesterol saturation and raises HDL cholesterol. *Lancet* **2**:819–821, 1983.

36. Johansson BG, Nilsson-Ehle P: Alcohol consumption and high-density lipoprotein. *New Engl J Med* **298**:633–634, 1978.

37. Brick J, Pohorecky LA: Ethanol-stress interaction: Biochemical findings. *Psychopharmacology* **77**:81–84, 1982.

38. Brick J, Pohorecky LA: The neuroendocrine response to stress and the effect of ethanol. In Pohorecky LA, Brick J (eds): *Stress and Alcohol Use*. New York, Elsevier, 1983, pp. 389–402.

39. Brick J, Pohorecky LA: Role of nonadrenergic neurons in ethanol-induced elevation of free fatty acids and corticosterone. *Life Sci* **35**:207–212, 1984.

40. Carruthers ME: Aggression and atheroma. *Lancet* **2**:1170–1171, 1969.

41. Henry JP: Coronary heart disease and arousal of the adrenal cortical axis. In Dembroski TM, Schmidt TH, Blumchen G (eds): *Biobehavioral Bases of Coronary Heart Disease.* Basel, Karger, 1983, pp. 365–381.

42. Houston BK: Psychophysiological responsivity and the Type A behavior pattern. *J Res Pers* **17**:22–39, 1983.

43. Krantz DS, Glass DC, et al: Behavior patterns and coronary disease: A critical evaluation. In Cacioppo JT, Petty RE (eds): *Perspectives on Cardiovascular Psychophysiology.* New York, Guilford Press, 1982, pp. 315–346.

44. Obrist PA: *Cardiovascular Psychophysiology.* New York, Plenum Press, 1981.

45. Levenson RW, Sher KJ, et al: Alcohol and stress response dampening: Pharmacological effects, expectancy, and tension reduction. *J Abnorm Psychol* **89**:528–538, 1980.

46. Levenson RW: Alcohol, affect, and physiology: Positive effects in the early stages of drinking. In Gottheil E (ed): *Stress: Alcohol and Drug Interactions,* in press.

47. Sher KJ, Levenson RW: Risk for alcoholism and individual differences in the stress-response-dampening effect of alcohol. *J Abnorm Psychol* **91**:350–367, 1982.

48. Rosenhow DJ, Marlatt GA: The balanced placebo design: Methodological considerations. *Addict Behav* **6**:107–122, 1981.

49. Newlin DB, Levenson RW: Pre-ejection period: Measuring beta-adrenergic influences upon the heart. *Psychophysiology* **16**:546–553, 1979.

50. Blomquist G, Saltin B, Mitchell JH: Acute effects of ethanol ingestion on the response to submaximal and maximal exercise in man. *Circulation* **42**:463–470, 1970.

51. Dengerink HA, Fagan NJ: Effect of alcohol on emotional responses to stress. *J Stud Alcohol* **39**:525–539, 1978.

52. Naitoh P: The effect of alcohol on the autonomic nervous systems of humans; psychophysiological approach. In Kissin B, Begleiter H (eds): *The Biology of Alcoholism: Vol 2. Physiology and Behavior.* New York, Plenum, 1972, pp. 367–433.

53. Riff DP, Jain AC, Doyle JT: Acute hemodynamic effects of ethanol in normal human volunteers. *Am Heart J* **78**:592–597, 1969.

54. Knott DH, Beard JD: Changes in cardiovascular activity as a function of alcohol intake. In Kissin B, Begleiter H (eds): *The Biology of Alcoholism: Vol 2. Physiology and Behavior.* New York, Plenum, 1972, pp. 345–365.

55. Timmis GC, Ramos RC, et al: The basis for differences in ethanol induced myocardial depression in normal subjects. *Circulation* **51**:1144–1148, 1975.

56. Lehrer PM, Taylor HA: Effects of alcohol on cardiac reactivity in alcoholics and nonalcoholics. *Q J Stud Alcohol* **35**:1044–1052, 1974.

57. Wilson GT, Abrams DB, Lipscomb R: Effects of increasing levels of intoxication and drinking pattern on social anxiety. *J Stud Alcohol* **41**:250–264, 1980.

58. Ekman P, Friesen WV: *Facial Action Coding System.* Palo Alto, CA, Consulting Psychologists Press, 1978.

59. Ekman P, Friesen WV: Felt, false and miserable smiles. *J Nonverbal Behav* **6**:238–252, 1982.

60. Ekman P, Levenson RW, Friesen WV: Autonomic nervous system activity distinguishes among emotions. *Science* **221**:1208–1210, 1983.

61. Notarius CI, Levenson RW: Expressive tendencies and physiological response to stress. *J Pers Soc Psychol* **37**:1204–1210, 1979.

62. Weinberger DA, Davidson RJ, Schwartz GE: Low-anxious, high-anxious, and repressive coping styles: Psychometric patterns and behavioral and physiological responses to stress. *J Abnorm Psychol* **88**:369–380, 1979.

19

Exercise as a Modulator of Cardiovascular Reactivity

JOEL E. DIMSDALE, BRUCE S. ALPERT, NEIL SCHNEIDERMAN

INTRODUCTION

In twentieth-century cardiology, judgments about exercise have ranged from regarding it as a threat for the heart patient to a necessity for his or her rehabilitation. Even for the general population there have been dramatic changes in the valuation of exercise. In the 1850s exercise was considered sufficiently demeaning to be part of the punishment for British felons. In contemporary American culture many regard exercise as a vital ingredient for mental and physical health.

This chapter reviews four broad areas pertinent to the effects of aerobic fitness (AF) on reactivity to stress. Initially, we will review the epidemiological literature about the cardiovascular consequences of fitness or its opposite

365

(sedentary life style). Next, we will review the literature relating fitness to enhanced morale. We will then highlight some physiological changes brought about by AF. Finally, we will examine the evidence tying AF to decreased cardiovascular reactivity to behavioral stressors.

CONSEQUENCES OF SEDENTARY VERSUS ACTIVE LIFE STYLE

Epidemiologic studies indicate that physically inactive individuals have a higher incidence of myocardial infarction (MI) and mortality than do active individuals. The magnitude of the effects and the exact causes are difficult to evaluate, however, because of methodological problems. For instance, many studies fail to delineate the actual "dose" of physical activity.[1] Thus, it is difficult to conclude that the enhanced health is attributable to aerobic fitness per se as opposed to low-level physical activity or something associated with such activity.

Strong evidence for a causal relationship between physical inactivity and coronary heart disease (CHD) would require a randomized intervention trial. Such a trial would need a large number of individuals to be randomized by age and sex into exercise and control conditions. Evidence of long-term adherence to each of the experimental conditions would also be necessary. In order to assess the relationship between physical inactivity and CHD, it would also be necessary to evaluate differences in long-term AF, hormonal and hemodynamic variables, and the presence of other known risk factors (e.g., hypertension, hypercholesterolemia, obesity, smoking frequency, Type A behavior pattern).

Prior to 1970 most evidence supporting a relationship between physical inactivity and CHD came from two kinds of retrospective studies. One consisted of case-control studies.[2,3] The other consisted of cross-sectional investigations comparing the rates of CHD in active versus sedentary people.[4-9] Most of the early studies considered only job activity, which was inferred from job titles. For example, London bus drivers were reported to have higher CHD and mortality rates than conductors,[5,6] mail carriers lower mortality than postal clerks,[4] and railway switchmen lower CHD morbidity rates than railway clerks or executives.[7] These early retrospective studies suggest the existence of a relationship between physical inactivity and CHD, but such studies are limited because they did not consider (1) selection factors that might influence entry into or transfer between job categories; (2) physical fitness; (3) leisure-time activities; and/or (4) differences in activity level by employees in the same job category.

Since 1970 approximately 15 prospective population studies have been reported. Most of these studies have evaluated risk factors, attempted to assess activity levels, and worked to minimize self-selection. The majority, but not all of these studies, have reported a positive relationship between relative physical inactivity and CHD.

The Framingham study found that CHD incidence and mortality were positively related to self-reports of physical activity in men but not women.[10] Among men, the relationship between physical inactivity and CHD was independent of age, blood pressure, smoking, and cholesterol levels; however, the magnitude of the effect was smaller than for the other risk factors. The lack of effect for women and the small size of the effect for men may reflect the fact that the population in Framingham was mainly sedentary, and women had an even smaller gradient of physical activity than men.[11] Support for this view comes from a Finnish study in which low activity assessed by job classification was associated with a 1.5-fold risk of MI in men and a 2.4-fold risk in women over a seven-year period, even after adjustment for other risk factors.[12]

A 22-year prospective study of more than 3000 San Francisco longshoremen strongly supports the view that job-related physical activity reduces CHD mortality.[13–15] The investigators found a significantly lower rate of CHD mortality in men whose work activity required over 8500 kcal of energy expenditure per week, even after adjustment for known risk factors. Direct measurement of oxygen consumption of workers in various job classes, and concerted attempts to reclassify each worker annually when they transferred to new jobs, added precision to the research design. The large differences in work activity level observed between the least and most active groups maximized the opportunity to detect differences. The positive findings obtained in this study provide reasonable evidence that high levels of physical activity may protect against CHD.

Morris, Chave, et al.[16] found that leisure-time activity can reduce CHD risk in men holding sedentary office jobs. They found that the relative risk in men reporting vigorous leisure-time activity was two-thirds that of men who remained sedentary during the first two years of that study. Men who persisted in their vigorous activity through an eight-year follow-up period had half the CHD incidence of sedentary individuals.

In a study that took into account both work and leisure activities, Paffenbarger, Brand, et al.[14] assessed student activity levels of Harvard University alumni. These alumni received a questionnaire inquiring about their current activity levels. Based on the responses obtained, the investigators derived an index of estimated weekly energy expenditures. During the next ten years, the incidence of MI among active alumni (i.e., whose weekly energy expenditure during physical activity was over 2000 kcal) was half that of their sedentary classmates. Of particular interest was the finding that a physically active adulthood was associated with low risk of MI, regardless of previous activity level as a student. Alumni who were varsity athletes were at low risk only if they continued to exercise.

Although inactivity may increase the risk of CHD, the interval during which exercise occurs is itself associated with increased risk. In order to assess the relative risks and benefits of vigorous exercise, Siscovick, Weiss, et al.[17] interviewed the wives of 133 men without a history of heart disease who had suffered cardiac arrest during vigorous exercise. From interviews with the wives of a random sample of healthy men, the investigators estimated the amount of time members of the target community spent in vigorous exercise. The study suggested that while the risk of cardiac arrest is transiently increased during vigorous exercise, habitual vigorous exercise is associated with an overall decreased risk of cardiac arrest.

It is important to emphasize that demurring studies have also appeared, questioning the relationship between activity and CHD.[18] Nonetheless, the epidemiologic literature generally suggests an inverse relationship between CHD and physical activity. The basis of the relationship seems less clear, however, since the studies on which the association is based have had difficulty (1) adequately quantifying levels of activity actually performed; (2) determining the extent to which sedentary life style is self-selected; and (3) monitoring changes in fitness as well as activity level and other life-style variables.

EFFECTS OF EXERCISE ON MORALE

There are strong feelings about the effects of exercise on morale. In Victorian England exercise was used as a punishment. This permitted the English physiologist, Edward Smith, to perform some of the first quantitative studies of exercise physiology in the 1850s. Smith relied on prisoners who had been sentenced to hard labor on prison treadmills, since physical activity was viewed as a tool for human degradation.[19] Interestingly, during the same period in the United States, Oliver Wendell Holmes was one of the leaders of the Muscular Christianity Movement, which advocated vigorous exercise as a means of developing emotional and moral health.[20]

The Holmes view has won out (at least temporarily) in our culture. Within the past decade there has been a tremendous resurgence of enthusiasm for physical fitness, mainly through running or jogging. Books, clubs, and magazines guide millions of enthusiasts. Although some of the enthusiasm stems from the conviction that exercise leads to improved cardiovascular health, much of the enthusiasm appears to be unrelated to exercise's consequences for cardiovascular functioning. Rather, exercisers claim to feel better physically and to have improved morale. These beliefs are widely held and are shared by a large part of the medical community. One poll found that 98 percent of physicians believe that running markedly improves psychological as well as physical health.[21]

Paralleling the popular cultural enthusiasm for exercise, there has been considerable scientific enthusiasm for exercise's effects on morale. Sachs and Buffone[22] recently have compiled a bibliography of over 1000 references pertaining to the psychology of exercise. Many of these studies claim that running ameliorates depression, anxiety states, and phobias.

Despite the large number of papers and abstracts on this topic, there have been few controlled studies that support the claims that exercise is an effective psychological therapy. This is not an easy hypothesis to establish since people exercise for many reasons and presumably experience diverse benefits. Furthermore, exercise programs do not operate in a vacuum. Many aspects of life-style change in conjunction with a regular exercise program.[23-25]

What are the immediate effects of acute exercise on subjective states such as anxiety? Low-level exercise has a slight beneficial effect on anxiety.[23,26] Following intense exercise, regular exercisers, when compared to beginning exercisers, report a significantly greater reduction of anxiety.[27] Using electromyographic activity as a stress index, DeVries and Adams[28] found that following vigorous exercise, the resting action potential was reduced by 58 percent, more of a reduction than was caused by the anxiolytic agent meprobamate.

On the other hand, studies suggesting a specific effect of acute exercise on anxiety have been challenged. For example, Bahrke and Morgan[29] assigned regular exercisers randomly to one session of exercise, to meditation, or to quiet rest with a Reader's Digest. All of these interventions were equivalently effective in reducing anxiety. It is important to emphasize the consequences of this random assignment of subjects.

Far more studies have examined the morale effects of sustained exercise. Unfortunately, with few exceptions,[e.g.,30] and as Folkins and Sime[24] and Goff and Dimsdale[25] have discussed, the overwhelming majority of these studies are retrospective and measured aspects of mood and personality in exercisers versus some other group. Such studies generally conclude that exercisers are more self-confident, less depressed, and less tense. These studies ignore the fact that the comparison groups may differ on criteria other than exercise. Personality characteristics may attract a person to running and possibly help sustain that interest. Such personality characteristics, not exercise, may be more closely related to changes in mood. The more recent prospective studies suggest that exercise training programs have only slight effects on personality measures, with the exception of an improvement in self-concept.

Recently some investigators have examined other aspects of personality or behavior in relation to exercise. Blumenthal, Williams, et al.,[31] for instance, demonstrated that Type A behavior could be significantly modified by a 10-week exercise program. Lobitz, Brammel, et al.[32] not only reconfirmed these findings but also found that exercise was more effective than anxiety management training in reducing Type A behavior. In explaining these findings, some have suggested that Type A individuals in particular may derive a particular sense of benefit from the mastery and self-control afforded by an exercise program.

A number of studies have examined the effects of exercise on depression. A running program was found roughly equivalent to time-limited psycho-therapy in improving depression.[33] When the investigators attempted to replicate these findings with a larger sample size, they encountered an interesting problem that illustrates the difficulties of studying this area without the influence of confounding variables: 75 percent of those in their runners' group dropped out of the study. In the original study each patient was assigned an individual running therapist with whom to jog; in the repeat study, *groups* of patients jogged with a therapist. After the investigators realized the severity of their dropout problem with the runners, they switched back to using an individual running therapist, and the running dropout rate returned to an acceptable level.[34] This experience is noteworthy in that it demonstrates the profound influence of factors other than the AF per se on patients' compliance and response to exercise programs.

Folkins[35] has completed one of the few randomized studies of exercise and morale; he assigned subjects to an exercise or to a control group, paying careful attention in both groups to issues of compliance. Both groups met three times weekly for 12 weeks. The exercise group showed a significant improvement in levels of anxiety and depression. The emphasis on compliance may have been a crucial ingredient in this study's success. One of the problems that has cropped up in many studies is that control subjects frequently "drop in" to exercise centers and exercise even though they were assigned a different activity. This makes measurement of treatment effects all the more difficult.

Some work suggests prominent differences between men and women in terms of their response to an exercise conditioning program.[36] Women, the least fit and the most anxious or depressed, tended to respond best to a conditioning program; however, this response occurred only if the patients were generally compliant with the exercise program.

Exercise programs are now used in many cardiac rehabilitation programs. Kavanaugh, Shepard, et al.[37] found that such programs led to a lessening of depression; however, the improvement in depression did not correlate with improved AF but rather with compliance with the program. This is a crucial issue for the field. If morale improves in exercise programs, it is crucial to understand whether that improvement is a direct function of the changes in AF or a result of some other aspect of the program. McPhearson, Paivio, et al.[27] contrasted men assigned to graduated aerobic exercise or to recreational swimming. After 24 weeks, both groups had increased their sense of well-being dramatically and equivalently, despite the fact that the recreational swimmers had not significantly improved their physical fitness.

Many writers suggest that exercise programs lead to significant short-term benefits in the morale of post-MI patients. However, few have attempted the difficult task of examining the long-term consequences of such programs. One of the few efforts along these lines (The National Exercise and Heart Disease Project) could not demonstrate a sustained improvement in morale in exercisers over a two-year period.[38]

BIOLOGIC EFFECTS OF EXERCISE

The physiologic responses to exercise and coronary disease are complex; a complete discussion of these changes is well beyond the scope of this chapter. Several aspects related to reactivity, however, are pertinent and need introduction. These include exercise's effects on lipids and carbohydrates, receptors, weight, blood pressure, hormones, and the combined effects of emotional stress and exercise.

Lipids and Carbohydrates

It is generally accepted that moderate, sustained, high-intensity exercise will alter the cholesterol profile in healthy individuals.[39-46] The directions and magnitudes of these changes are shown in Table 19.1. A summary derived from many studies[46] suggests that the changes in lipids are more pronounced in males than in females. The explanation for the sex differences in lipid response has not been clarified.

In response to exercise, in males, there is a uniform increase in high-density lipoprotein (HDL) cholesterol, a fairly uniform reduction in low-density lipoprotein (LDL) cholesterol, and a decrease in the plasma triglycerides. Usually, there has been a reduction in total cholesterol, but this has not always been a significant one. After training, the body is in an improved state to eliminate cholesterol from peripheral stores by increasing the HDL fraction, which carries cholesterol away from such sites. Epidemiological studies have traditionally noted a decrease in coronary disease in individuals with a lipid profile similar to that found in the exerciser. Related to these lipid results, studies such as those by Leon, Conrad, et al.[47] have shown that

TABLE 19.1. CHANGES IN LIPIDS AND LIPOPROTEINS IN RESPONSE TO 10 WEEKS OF EXERCISE[a]

	Cholesterol mg/dl	HDL Cholesterol mg/dl	LDL Cholesterol mg/dl	HDL/LDL	Triglycerides mg/dl	Weight kg
MEN						
Control	207 ±9	42 ±2	133 ±8	0.35 ±0.23	176 ±23	85 ±2
Percent change	d4 ±2	i5 ±2	d6 ±3	i12 ±3	d10 ±5	d1 ±0.4
	$p < 0.04$	$p < 0.04$	$p < 0.05$	$p < 0.003$	$p < 0.06$	$p < 0.001$
WOMEN						
Control	187 ±6	59 ±2	112 ±6	0.57 ±0.37	72 ±5	62 ±1
Percent change	d4 ±2	d1 ±2	d4 ±3	i8 ±4	i14 ±7	d1 ±0.4
	$p < 0.06$	NS	NS	NS	$p < 0.06$	$p < 0.06$

[a]Change scores are expressed as mean percent change ±S.E.

Note: d = decrease
i = increase

Source: Abstracted from Brownell KD, Bachorik PS, Ayerle RS: Changes in plasma lipid and lipoprotein levels in men and women after ten weeks of exercise. *Metabolism* 31:1142–1146, 1982. Reprinted by permission of the American Heart Association, Inc.

fitness leads to a reduction in the fasting blood sugar, plasma insulin level, and a similar percentage (35 percent) decrease in the ratio of insulin/glucose concentrations. Thus, it may not be unreasonable to advocate exercise as a primary prevention strategy for all individuals.

Receptors

Beta-adrenergic blockade with medications such as atenolol, propranolol, metoprolol, and oxprenolol is commonly prescribed for coronary patients. The effects of these medications on plasma lipids and lipoproteins have been studied recently.[48,49] The beta blockade leads to changes that would give a less favorable coronary risk profile. In a group of patients with prior MI,[50-51] both men and women had reductions in HDL and increases in triglycerides while on propranolol, when compared to those patients on placebo. Other studies have reached similar conclusions—that the medications produced an increase in triglycerides and very low-density lipoprotein (LDL) cholesterol, with a decrease in HDL and free fatty acids. Some have suggested that subtle catecholamine-mediated changes in plasma lipid concentrations might provide a mechanism for the relation between stress and the development of cardiovascular events.[49] These studies form a basis for the contention that unopposed alpha stimulation produces lipid changes that may be detrimental.

AF lowers plasma catecholamines at rest and at submaximal workloads.[52] If these decreases lead to lower secretion during periods of stress, then fitness will be related to reduced reactivity.

Weight

In a review of the relation between aerobic exercise and weight, Epstein and Wing[53] discussed the reduction in body fat that occurs during the achievement of AF. The loss of weight achieved through exercise was directly related to caloric expenditure in both obese and nonobese subjects; weight control could not be achieved solely on the basis of an exercise program without attending to diet simultaneously. Patients with coronary disease, as well as the population in general, should be encouraged to maintain ideal weight both by caloric restriction and exercise.

Blood Pressure

One of the prime determinants of myocardial oxygen consumption (demand) is the afterload component—blood pressure. Since the physiologic mediator of coronary disease is the myocardial oxygen supply/demand balance, any factor that improves this ratio may be considered highly favorable. Exercise reduces demand by decreasing blood pressure; thus, oxygen supply problems may be mitigated.

When healthy individuals train, their resting systolic and diastolic blood pressure falls, thus improving the demand balance. Studies of adult and adolescent hypertensives[54-58] demonstrate a reduction of blood pressure induced by exercise training. In most cases the blood pressure did not return to the normal range, but a significant reduction was achieved. In some patients, even after the cessation of the exercise training program, the reduced blood pressure levels were maintained. It is thus desirable for healthy individuals to achieve AF as a tool for long-term maintenance of normal blood pressure.

Bove and Squires recently observed that AF was associated with altered circulatory response to a cold pressor test. The investigators studied a small convenience sample of individuals with varying amounts of AF. Marathon runners developed smaller increases in blood pressure in response to a cold pressor test although their blood pressures at rest were not significantly different from those of sedentary subjects.[59] These findings suggest that AF may be associated with altered reactivity, at least to cold and perhaps to stressors as well.

Hormones

The maintenance of homeostasis depends on the interaction of numerous hormones. Bjorntorp, Holm, et al.[60] studied a group of obese subjects and controls before and after a six-week training period. Prior to exercise, the obese individuals had decreased glucose tolerance, hyperinsulinemia, elevated blood glycerol, increased free fatty acids, decreased growth hormone response, and increased noradrenaline output, when compared to the controls. After training, the subjects had decreased insulin levels, with a corresponding increase in plasma glycerol. Glucose levels did not change, implying an increased peripheral sensitivity to insulin. Noradrenaline output remained high and growth hormone remained low in the subjects. Thus, exercise training led to some favorable changes in the obese subjects.

EXERCISE EFFECTS ON PATIENTS WITH CORONARY DISEASE

The benefits of exercise in healthy individuals were highlighted above. There is a similar wealth of literature that addresses the responses to an exercise program for patients with coronary artery disease. Investigators from several countries have shown that there is a distinct advantage in decreased morbidity and mortality for patients who participate on a regular basis in a rehabilitation exercise program.[61-63] These studies show the effects but do not investigate the possible mechanisms by which these effects occur.

Parallel to some of the topics discussed above—that is, lipids, hormones, insulin, weight, carbohydrates, and so on—there are data that demonstrate that the coronary patient can achieve similar benefits from exercise when compared to the control subject. For instance, exercise's effect of lowering the systolic blood pressure has been demonstrated for the coronary patient.[50] In addition, reductions in catecholamines during exercise have been measured.[50] While the mechanism is still under debate, after an aerobic training period, angina patients can usually perform more work before onset of symptoms. In an extensive review of exercise in coronary patients, Fletcher[64] concluded that aerobic training leads to an increased cardiac output of similar proportion to that observed in normal subjects. It remains to be determined whether myocardial oyxgen supply has increased via increased collateral formation, and/or oxygen demand has decreased through a lowering of the tension time index (mean blood pressure × heart rate), and/or tolerance to pain has also changed.

Combined Emotional and Exercise Stress

The physiology of combined emotional stress and aerobic exercise is receiving increasing attention. Both steady-state exercise[65] and sustained emotional stress[66-68] lead to increases in heart rate and blood pressure. Recent studies conducted on healthy women[69] and CHD patients[70] have shown that exercise plus emotional stress lead to augmented hemodynamic effects despite the fact that oxygen uptake is not comparably changed. Siconolfi, Garber, et al. exercised CHD patients on a treadmill at 60 percent of the subject's maximal heart rate.[70] A Stroop color-word test was added one minute after the subject reached steady-state exercise. The result of superimposing the behavioral stressor on the steady-state exercise for 11 minutes was to increase significantly heart rate, systolic and diastolic blood pressure, and pressure-rate product (systolic blood pressure × heart rate). On the other hand, oxygen uptake increased briefly during the first two minutes of the Stroop test but then returned to the steady-state exercise level. The increased hemodynamic activity without a concomitant change in oxygen uptake may have implications for the appropriateness of competitive exercise for patients with CHD. The generalizability of exercise prescriptions based on traditional treadmill tests may be limited when exercise is combined with competitive activities having a substantial emotional component.

AEROBIC FITNESS AND REACTIVITY TO STRESSORS

There are a number of ways in which physical activity may be health-promoting in terms of cardiovascular disease. This chapter has highlighted some aspects of basic exercise physiology and some of the epidemiological data about sedentary life style and coronary or hypertensive risk. This has provided crucial background material to understanding *how aerobic fitness may modulate cardiovascular reactivity to behavioral stressors.* Despite the belief by committed exercisers that AF results in decreased stress and anxiety as well as improved coping resources, data to support these beliefs are limited. This is partially because there are three research questions implicitly embedded in the problem:

1. Does AF lead to improved morale and coping with stressors? As discussed above, there is more conviction than data to support this proposition.
2. Does AF lead to decreased heart rate and blood pressure responses to stressors?
3. What physiological mechanisms could account for such decreased reactivity, if present?

The cardiovascular adaptations to an AF training program include a reduction of heart rate and systolic blood pressure both at rest and during exercise. During exercise, the fit individual can consume more oxygen (VO_2), has a higher cardiac output, and can extract more oxygen from the blood (A-V difference). Do such decreases in exercise-induced reactivity occur in response to psychological stressors as well?

If AF were a modulator of heart rate and/or blood pressure reactions to psychological stressors, then any decrease in reactivity may be related to altered sensitivity of alpha- and/or beta-receptors or to altered neuroendocrine release. To date, studies by Williams and colleagues[71–74] have shown that no change in human or animal cardiac beta-receptors occurs in response to training. However, these investigators were able to demonstrate down-regulation of muscarinic and alpha-receptors in the hearts of trained rats. In contrast, peripheral skeletal muscle and lung beta-receptors were up-regulated with training. These studies highlight the tissue specificity of beta-receptors and may help explain the improvement in glucose/glycogen metabolism that occurs with improved AF. More data are needed to support the hypothesis of AF-induced changes in receptor functioning.

Proponents argue that exercise has a beneficial effect on the ability of the individual to navigate through life stress with some measure of equanimity.

The direct association, however, between AF and decreased psychophysiologic reactivity cannot be easily made because many other variables change simultaneously during the achievement of AF. These include:

1. The AF individual decreases his or her traditional risk profile with respect to variables such as smoking, cholesterol and its subfractions, obesity, blood pressure, and possibly sodium intake and handling.
2. In the process of evolving an exercise program, many individuals change their social behavior. Jogging, for instance, enhances a social network, which in turn may be a more relevant modulator of reactivity than the AF per se.
3. The enthusiasm fostered by AF programs may lead to decreased stress reactivity by the Hawthorne effect (i.e., the phenomenon by which any change leads to an improvement, albeit temporarily).

There are, as yet, surprisingly few studies concerning the effects of AF on the variables of cardiovascular reactivity to behavioral stressors. Sinyor, Schwartz, et al.[75] studied 15 trained and untrained male university students. The subjects performed a number of tasks—mental arithmetic, a quiz, and the Stroop color-word test. Blood samples were obtained for measurement of epinephrine, norepinephrine, cortisol, and prolactin. In response to the stressors listed above, there was no difference between AF subjects and unfit subjects with respect to change in heart rate. There was, however, a significantly faster return to baseline heart rate values following stress in the trained students. Unfortunately, blood pressure values were not obtained in this study. Despite the lack of difference in peak epinephrine and norepinephrine, there was an earlier peak of norepinephrine in the AF subjects in response to mental arithmetic. There were no differences between groups in plasma cortisol response to any of the challenges. The authors' conclusion was that there may be a relationship between AF and cardiovascular reactivity.

A recently completed study performed by Lake and coworkers[76] involved 61 university undergraduates. Five challenges were imposed: (1) the Type A structured interview (SI); (2) exposure to a boa constrictor; (3) mental arithmetic; (4) cold pressor; (5) competitive card game. Neither degree of fitness nor Type A classification affected the heart rate or blood pressure responses (delta values) to challenges 2, 3, and 4. During the SI, however, systolic and diastolic blood pressures were highest for the Type A individuals and for sedentary subjects. There was an interaction between Type A personality and sedentary behavior pattern such that the blood pressure increases were most pronounced for the sedentary Type A individuals. In contrast to the responses elicited by the SI were the responses to the card game. The blood pressure response of fit Type A individuals was greater than either the sedentary A, sedentary Type B, or fit Type B individuals. These findings suggest that a task-specific change in cardiovascular reactivity may exist and needs further evaluation. Since the fit group were varsity athletes, it is possible that factors other than AF per se may be accounting for these findings. The fit group's increased blood pressure reactivity to a competitive card game may reflect their ability to match arousal level to task requirements. What is abundantly clear from this study, however, is that no one clear relationship emerges between AF and stressor reactivity.

Two reports of the effect of training on exercise-induced hormonal responses[77,78] found decreased catecholamine and cortisol responses to physical stress after training. Fit subjects had higher insulin responses to work after achieving AF. While these studies do not directly address the area of reactivity to behavioral stressors, they may be useful in pointing to mechanisms for the association between AF and reactivity.

Hull et al.[79] studied 55 subjects with varying AF and examined their heart rate, blood pressure, and plasma catecholamine response to viewing a stressful movie, performing a Stroop test, and performing a graded maximal exercise test. Systolic blood pressure and heart rate responses to the behavioral stressors were not influenced by AF. For subjects older than 40, diastolic blood pressure responses to the behavioral stressors were significantly lower in the fit than the unfit group. Fitness did not affect the norepinephrine or epinephrine responses to behavioral stressors.

Two additional studies failed to demonstrate exercise-induced reactivity differences between trained and untrained individuals. Hagberg, Hickson, et al.[80] confirmed the observation that heart rate returned to baseline more quickly in athletes following the cessation of exercise. However, there was no difference between fit and unfit subjects after cessation of exercise in the rate of decline of plasma norepinephrine. Thus, these data imply that differences in sympathetic activity might not explain the differences in heart rate recovery. The other report, by Cox et al.,[81] noted that heart rate responses to Weschler Adult Intelligence Scale and Stroop tests did not differ in magnitude between trained and untrained subjects. However, the trained subjects' heart rate values did return to baseline more quickly.

McGowan et al.[82] examined heart rate, electromyographic tone, and self-reported mood in subjects who had just completed 15 minutes of exercise and who were then required to perform a mental arithmetic task. The exercise, performed at various intensities, was unrelated to mood or physiological responses to the math stressor.

The responses to mental stress (Stroop color-word test) were examined in 19 men and women before and after a seven-week aerobic exercise program.[83] A control group was not included. As expected, the heart rate, systolic and diastolic blood pressure, and pressure-rate products all decreased in response to the achievement of AF. However, the change from baseline triggered by the stressor was higher for each of the hemodynamic variables after training than before, despite the fact that the peak values for each variable were lower. While it may be assumed that peak levels of blood pressure are important in vascular damage and sustained hypertension or coronary events, the acute changes induced by stressors may be equally important.

Keller and Seraganian[84] examined fluctuations of electrodermal activity as an indirect index of autonomic reactivity. In a powerful design feature, they randomly assigned subjects to one of three 10-week programs—aerobic exercise, meditation, and music appreciation. There were no significant differences among the groups' responses to psychological stressors at the beginning of the 10-week period. However, by the sixth week the exercise group had achieved much lower electrodermal fluctuation during stressful tasks in the laboratory. This study utilized a strong design but one that could have been much stronger had the authors used more direct measures of physiological reactivity.

SUMMARY AND RECOMMENDATIONS

As is evident in this chapter, definitive conclusions about the interactions of exercise, mood, and reactivity are difficult to come by because of certain design issues.

1. There are profound selection biases in most studies of exercise. It is exceedingly difficult to find a study where subjects have been randomly assigned to the various treatment groups.

2. The contents of the exercise intervention are rarely examined for other beneficial ingredients. Exercise programs affect one's group affiliation and social support networks. Furthermore, exercise programs are usually administered with a great deal of enthusiasm, and one wonders whether it is the enthusiastic optimism or the exercise per se that is the operative factor.

3. Many studies fail to distinguish between exercise and AF. By using AF as our dependent variable, it is possible to draw a dose-response curve of the degree of fitness as it relates to other variables. Unfortunately, AF is rarely used as an index measure in behavioral medicine studies; instead, such studies dichotomize between exercisers and nonexercisers.

The few studies presently available do not demonstrate conclusively that AF modulates stress-induced cardiovascular reactivity. More research is needed to define more clearly whatever relationship may exist. What follows are some considerations as to the past methodology and considerations for future studies.

Simple and inexpensive assessments of AF, such as utilizing the step test or a mechanical cycle ergometer, are available to researchers from varied backgrounds.

Aerobic fitness may be viewed both as an independent variable and as a confounding variable. In the former role, AF may be manipulated with respect to the possible effects on reactivity. In the latter situation, AF may mask the effects of other variables related to cardiovascular reactivity. In prospective studies, subject differences in AF could significantly confound manipulations; thus, AF levels need to be matched on entry. Further, changes in exercise habits should be monitored and covaried during the period of follow-up.

As an independent variable, the influence of AF on reactivity may itself be confounded by the effects of other group differences. The self-selection processes that lead some adults to regularly engage in exercise may be predictive of reactivity. "Convenience samples" characterize much of the literature associating jogging with behavioral measures, and such studies are severely limited as a consequence. Matching on age and gender at a minimum are clearly required in a study that asks whether an exercise program affects reactivity.

In much of the current literature examining the behavioral effects of AF, investigators have employed a simple pre-post design with no controls. Typically, the subjects exhibit significantly less reactivity on follow-up. With this design the investigator has no assessment of the effects of retesting per se. At least some psychological tasks widely used in laboratory investigations of cardiovascular reactivity exhibit significant habituation effects on retesting at short intervals. These potentially serious problems of practice effects and/or regression to the mean mandate control groups, appropriately matched on entry into the study, but from whom the AF training is withheld. Ideally, one would employ a cohort reasonably homogeneous on many personal and demographic characteristics and randomly allocate subjects into control and intervention subgroups. One such possible cohort might be found in a group of army recruits at completion of basic training; all would be in a state of excellent AF and would be reasonably matched on background variables. Following assignment, half of the recruits might continue in a state of AF, while the remaining half, assigned to tasks such as clerk-typist school, would be deconditioned.

Attention to attitudinal life-style differences between aerobically fit and sedentary groups is likewise important in designing a protocol. Risk factors may differ and affect outcome measures.

In designing studies to assess the effects of aerobic fitness on cardiovascular reactivity, protocols might consider reactivity assessments during stressful encounters in more naturalistic settings, such as in the workplace or in the field, in addition to the laboratory. Would differences in reactivity best be observed within subjects, in a longitudinal context where AF level is experimentally manipulated? Would such differences relate to psychological inventories designed to assess coping behavior?

Given the potential importance of the relationship between AF and reactivity to behavioral stressors and, given the present paucity of data, further research appears warranted, both for basic knowledge and for potential use in clinical interventions.

REFERENCES

1. LaPorte R, Adams L, et al: The spectrum of physical activity, cardiovascular disease and health: An epidemiologic perspective. *Am J Epidemiol* 120:507–517, 1984.

2. Frank CW, Weinblatt E, et al: Physical inactivity as a lethal factor in myocardial infarction among men. *Circulation* 34:1022–1032, 1966.

3. Shapiro S, Weinblatt E, et al: Incidence of coronary heart disease in a population insured for medical care (HIP). *Am J Public Health* 59:1–101, 1969.

4. Kahn HA: The relationship of reported coronary heart disease mortality to physical activity of work. *Am J Public Health* 53:1058–1067, 1963.

5. Morris JN, Heady JA, et al: Coronary heart disease and physical activity of work. *Lancet* 2:1053–1057, 1111–1120, 1953.

6. Morris JN, Heady JA, Raffle PAB: Physique of London busmen: Epidemiology of uniforms. *Lancet* 2:569–570, 1956.

7. Taylor HL, Kleptar E, et al: Death rates among physically active and sedentary employees of the railroad industry. *Am J Public Health* 52:1697–1707, 1962.

8. Taylor HL, Blackburn H, et al: Five-year follow-up of employees of selected U.S. railroad companies. *Circulation* 41:20–39, 1970. (Suppl I)

9. Zukel WJ, Lewis RH, et al: A short-term community study of the epidemiology of coronary heart disease: A preliminary report on the North Dakota study. *Am J Public Health* 49:1630–1639, 1959.

10. Kannel WB, Sorlie P: Some health benefits of physical activity: The Framingham Study. *Arch Intern Med* 138:857–861, 1979.

11. Rigotti NA, Thomas GS, Leaf A: Exercise and coronary heart disease. *Ann Rev Med* 34:391–412, 1983.

12. Salonen JT, Puska P, Tuomilehto J: Physical activity and risk of myocardial infarction, cerebral stroke and death. *Am J Epidemiol* 115:526–537, 1982.

13. Brand RJ, Paffenbarger RS, et al: Work activity and fatal heart attack studied by multiple logistic risk analysis. *Am J Epidemiol* 110:52–62, 1979.

14. Paffenbarger RS, Brand RJ, et al: Energy expenditure, cigarette smoking, and blood pressure level as related to death from specific diseases. *Am J Epidemiol* **108**:12–18, 1978.

15. Paffenbarger RS, Hale WE, et al: Work-energy level, personal characteristics, and fatal heart attack: A birth-cohort effect. *Am J Epidemiol* **105**:200–213, 1977.

16. Morris JN, Chave SPW, et al: Vigorous exercise in leisure time and the incidence of coronary heart disease. *Lancet* **1**:333–339, 1973.

17. Siscovick DS, Weiss NA, et al: The incidence of primary cardiac arrest during vigorous exercise. *N Engl J Med* **311**:874–877, 1984.

18. Leren P, Helgeland A, et al: Effect of propranolol and prazosin on blood lipids: The Oslo Study. *Lancet* i:4–6, 1980.

19. Morse RL: *Exercise and the Heart.* Springfield, IL, Charles C Thomas, 1974.

20. Lucas JA, Smith RA: *Saga of American Sport.* Philadelphia, Lea & Febiger, 1978.

21. Byrd OE: The relief of tension by exercise: A survey of medical viewpoints and practices. *J Sch Health* **33**:238–239, 1963.

22. Sachs ML, Buffone GW: Bibliography: Psychological considerations in exercise, including exercise as psychotherapy, exercise dependence (exercise addiction) and the psychology of running. Unpublished manuscript, 1983.

23. Morgan WP, Roberts JA, Feinerman AD: Psychologic effect of acute physical activity. *Arch Phys Med Rehabil* **52**:422–425, 1971.

24. Folkins CH, Sime WE: Physical fitness training and mental health. *Am Psychol* **36**:373–389, 1981.

25. Goff D, Dimsdale J: The psychological effects of exercise. *J Cardiac Rehabil* **5**:234–240, 1985.

26. Sime W: A comparison of exercise and meditation in reducing physiological response to stress. *Med Sci Sports* **9**:55, 1977.

27. McPhearson B, Paivio A, et al: Psychological effects of an exercise program for post infarct and normal adult men. *J Sports Med Phys Fitness* **8**:95–102, 1965.

28. deVries H, Adams G: Electromyographic comparison of single dose of exercise and meprobamate as to effects on muscular relaxation. *Am J Phys Med* **51**:130–141, 1972.

29. Bahrke M, Morgan W: Anxiety reduction following exercise and meditation. *Cognitive Ther Res* **2**:323–334, 1978.

30. Blumenthal J, Williams RS, et al: Psychological changes accompany aerobic exercise in healthy middle-aged adults. *Psychosom Med* **44**:529–536, 1982.

31. Blumenthal J, Williams RB, et al: Effects of exercise on the Type A (coronary-prone) behavior patterns. *Psychosom Med* **42**:289–296, 1980.

32. Lobitz C, Brammel H, et al: Physical exercise and anxiety management training for cardiac stress management in a nonpatient population. *J Cardiac Rehabil* **3**:683–688, 1983.

33. Greist J, Eischens R, et al: Running as a treatment for depression. *Comp Psychiatry* **20**:41–54, 1979.

34. Greist J, Eischens R, Klein M: Addendum to running through your mind. In Sacks MH, Sachs ML (eds): *Psychology of Running.* Champaign, IL, Human Kinetics Publishers, 1981.

35. Folkins C: Effects of physical training on mood. *J Clin Psychol* **32**:385–388, 1976.

36. Folkins C, Lynch S, Gradner M: Psychological fitness as a function of physical fitness. *Arch Phys Med Rehabil* **53**:503–508, 1972.

37. Kavanagh T, Shepard R, et al: Depression following myocardial infarction: The effect of distance running. *Ann NY Acad Sci* **301**:1029–1038, 1977.

38. Stern M, Cleary P: National exercise and heart disease project: Long-term psychosocial outcome. *Arch Intern Med* **142**:1093–1097, 1982.

39. Haskell WL: Exercise-induced changes in plasma lipids and lipoproteins. *Prev Med* **13**:23–36, 1984.

40. Lennon DLF, Stratman FW, et al: Total cholesterol and HDL-cholesterol changes during acute, moderate-intensity exercise in men and women. *Metabolism* **32**:244–249, 1983.

41. Lehtonen A, Viikari J: Serum triglycerides and cholesterol and serum high density lipoprotein cholesterol in highly physically active men. *Acta Med Scand* **204**:111–119, 1978.

42. Lopez SA, Vial R, et al: Effect of exercise and physical fitness on serum lipids and lipoproteins. *Atherosclerosis* **20**:1–9, 1974.

43. Rothis TC, Cote R, et al: Relationship between high density lipoprotein cholesterol and weekly running mileage. *J Cardiac Rehabil* **2**:109–112, 1982.

44. Harting GH, Foreyt JP, et al: Relation of diet to high-density-lipoprotein cholesterol in middle-age marathon runners, joggers, and inactive men. *N Engl J Med* **302**:357–361, 1980.

45. Frey MAB, Doerr BM, et al: Exercise does not change high-density lipoprotein cholesterol in women after ten weeks of training. *Metabolism* **31**:1142–1146, 1982.

46. Brownell KD, Bachorik PS, Ayerle RS: Changes in plasma lipid and lipoprotein levels in men and women after a program of moderate exercise. *Circulation* **65**:477–484, 1982.

47. Leon AS, Conrad J, et al: Effects of a vigorous walking program on body composition, and carbohydrates and lipid metabolism of obese young men. *Am J Clin Nutr* **32**:1776–1787, 1979.

48. Leren P, Helgeland A, et al: Effect of propranolol and prazosin on blood lipids: The Oslo Study. *Lancet* **i**:4–6, 1980.

49. Day JL, Metcalfe J, Stimpson CN: Adrenergic mechanisms in control of plasma lipid concentrations. *Br Med J* **284**:1145–1148, 1982.

50. Barnard RJ: Long-term effects of cardiac function. *Exerc Sport Sci Rev* **3**:113–133, 1975.

51. Shulman RS, Herbert PN, et al: Effects of propranolol on blood lipids and lipoproteins in myocardial infarction. *Circulation* **67**:I19–I21, 1983. (Suppl I)

52. Lehmann M, Kenl J, et al: Plasma catecholamines in trained and untrained volunteers during graduated exercise. *Int J Sports Med* **2**:143–147, 1981.

53. Epstein LH, Wing RR: Aerobic exercise and weight. *Addict Behav* **5**:371–388, 1980.

54. Boyer JL, Kasch FW: Exercise therapy in hypertensive men. *JAMA* **211**:1668–1671, 1970.

55. Hagberg JM, Goldring D, et al: Effect of exercise training on the blood pressure and hemodynamic features of hypertensive adolescents. *Am J Cardiol* **52**:763–768, 1983.

56. Krotkiewski M, Mandroukas K, et al: Effects of long-term physical training on body fat, metabolism, and blood pressure in obesity. *Metabolism* **28**:650–658, 1979.

57. Ressl J, Chrastek J, Jandova R: Hemodynamic effects of physical training in essential hypertension. *Cardiologica* **32**:121–133, 1977.

58. Roman O, Camuzzi AL, et al: Physical training program in arterial hypertension. A long-term prospective follow-up. *Angiology* **32**:230–243, 1981.

59. Bove A, Squires R: Exercise conditioning alters circulatory response to the cold pressor test. *J Am Coll Cardiol* **5**:518, 1985.

60. Bjorntorp P, Holm G, et al: Physical training in human hyperplastic obesity. IV. Effects on the hormonal status. *Metabolism* **76**:319–328, 1977.

61. Shepard RJ: The value of exercise in ischemic heart disease. A cumulative analysis. *J Cardiac Rehabil* **3**:294–298, 1983.

62. Rechnitzer PA, Pickard HA, et al: Long-term follow-up study of survival and recurrence rates following myocardial infarction in exercising and control subjects. *Circulation* **45**:853–857, 1972.

63. Kallio V, Hamalianen H, et al: Reduction in sudden deaths by a multifactorial intervention programme after acute myocardial infarction. *Lancet* **II, Part** 2:1091–1094, 1979.

64. Fletcher GF: Long-term exercise in coronary artery disease and other chronic disease states. *Heart Lung* **13**:28–46, 1984.

65. Astrand PO, Rodahl K: *Textbook of Work Physiology* (2nd ed). New York, McGraw-Hill, 1977.

66. Brod J, Fencl V, et al: Circulatory changes underlying blood pressure elevation during acute emotional stress (mental arithmetic) in normotensive and hypertensive subjects. *Clin Sci* **18**:269–279, 1959.

67. DeBusk RG, Taylor GB, Agras WS: Comparison of treadmill exercise testing and psychological stress testing soon after myocardial infarction. *Am J Cardiol* **43**:907–914, 1979.

68. Schiffer F, Hartley LH, et al: The quiz electrocardiogram: A new diagnostic and research technique for evaluating the relation between emotional stress and ischemic heart disease. *Am J Cardiol* **37**:41–47, 1976.

69. Garber CE, Siconolfi SF, et al: Hemodynamic effects of mental stress during exercise. *Med Sci Sports Exerc* **15**:183, 1983. (Abstract)

70. Siconolfi SF, Garber CE, et al: Circulatory effects of mental stress during exercise in coronary artery disease patients. *Clin Cardiol* **7**:441–444, 1984.

71. Williams RS: Physical conditioning and membrane receptors for cardioregulatory hormones. *Cardiovasc Res* **14**:177–182, 1980.

72. Williams RS, Eden RS, et al: Autonomic mechanisms of training bradycardia: Beta-adrenergic receptors in humans. *J Appl Physiol* **51**:1232–1237, 1981.

73. Williams RS, Schaible TF, et al: Effects of endurance training on cholinergic and adrenergic receptors of rat heart. *J Mol Cell Cardiol* **16**:395–403, 1984.

74. Williams RS, Karon MG, Daniel K: Skeletal muscle beta-adrenergic receptors: Variations due to fiber type and training. *Am J Physiol* **246**:E160–E167, 1984.

75. Sinyor D, Schwartz SG, et al: Aerobic fitness level and reactivity to psychosocial stress: Physiological, biochemical, and subjective measures. *Psychosom Med* **45**:205–217, 1983.

76. Lake B, Schneiderman N, Tocci N: The Type A behavior pattern, physical fitness, and psychophysiological reactivity. *Health Psychol* **4**:169–187, 1985.

77. Hartley LH, Mason JW, et al: Multiple hormonal responses to graded exercise in relation to physical training. *J Appl Physiol* **33**:602–606, 1972.

78. Winder WW, Hickson RC, et al: Training-induced changes in hormonal and metabolic responses to submaximal exercise. *J Appl Physiol* **46**:766–771, 1979.

79. Hull E, Young S, Ziegler M: Aerobic fitness affects cardiovascular and catecholamine responses to stressors. *Psychophysiology* **21**:253–260, 1984.

80. Hagberg JM, Hickson RC, et al: Disappearance of norepinephrine from the circulation following strenuous exercise. *J Appl Physiol* **47**:1311–1314, 1979.

81. Cox J, Evans J, Jamieson J: Aerobic power and tonic heart rate responses to psychosocial stressors. *Pers Soc Psychol Bull* **5**:160–163, 1979.

82. McGowan C, Robertson R, Epstein L: The effect of bicycle ergometric exercise at varying intensities on the heart rate, EMG, and mood status response to a mental arithmetic stressor. *Res Q Exerc Sport* **56**:131–137, 1985.

83. Garber CE: The effects of regular exercise on circulatory reactivity to mental stress. *Med Sci Sports Exerc* **16**:139, 1984. (Abstract)

84. Keller S, Seraganian P: Physical fitness level and autonomic reactivity to psychosocial stress. *J Psychosom Res* **28**:279–287, 1984.

20

Pharmacologic and Behavioral Modulators of Cardiovascular Reactivity: An Overview

RICHARD S. SURWIT

Hyperreactivity of the autonomic nervous system has been assumed to be a primary factor contributing to the development of cardiovascular disease.[1,2] Both behavioral and pharmacologic treatments of cardiovascular disease often work by reducing the effects of autonomic nervous system on cardiovascular end organs.[2] This chapter briefly reviews pharmacologic and behavioral interventions that reduce cardiovascular reactivity by dampening the effects of the autonomic nervous system. Related material is reviewed in greater depth in chapters by Jacob and Chesney and by Shapiro, Krantz, and Grim.

PHARMACOLOGIC AGENTS

Pharmacologic agents used to modify cardiovascular reactivity may be classified into four groups: alpha-adrenergic receptor blockers, beta-adrenergic receptor blockers, centrally acting agents, adrenergic neuron blocking agents, and calcium channel blockers.[3] The generic names of the most common agents in each class are listed in Table 20.1.

Alpha-adrenergic blocking agents such as phenoxybenzamine and prazosin typically decrease peripheral resistance by relaxing smooth muscle in the vascular walls. Beta-adrenergic blocking agents are commonly used to reduce cardiac output by blocking the effects of catecholamines on the myocardium. Centrally acting agents such as methyldopa act by stimulating centers in the central nervous system. Many of these agents have been thought to act on alpha-adrenergic neurons in the tractus solatarius producing an inhibition of peripheral sympathetic activity. A fourth class of agents includes drugs that interfere with chemical mediation at the postganglionic adrenergic nerve endings. These drugs may deplete stores of the neurotransmitter or prevent their release. Reserpine is one such agent. During chronic administration, it impairs the release of norepinephrine from peripheral adrenergic neurons.[3]

TABLE 20.1. PHARMOCOLOGIC MODULATORS OF SNS ACTIVITY

I.	Alpha-Adrenergic Blockers	
	A.	Phenoxybenzamine
	B.	Prazosin
	C.	Phentolamine
	D.	Tolazoline
II.	Beta-Adrenergic Blockers	
	A.	Propranolol
	B.	Nadolol
	C.	Timolol
	D.	Metoprolol
III.	Centrally Acting Agents	
	A.	Clonidine
	B.	Methyldopa
IV.	Adrenergic Neuron Blocking Agents	
	A.	Guanethidine
	B.	Reserpine
V.	Calcium Channel Blockers	
	A.	Nifedipine
	B.	Verapamil

The final class of agents more recently used in the treatment of cardio-vascular hyperreactivity is the calcium channel blockers. Nifedipine is one commonly used calcium channel antagonist. It appears to inhibit the trans-membrane influx of calcium ions into cardiac muscle and other smooth muscle. This suppresses cardiac or smooth muscle response to sympathetic stimulation.[4]

Although all of these agents are to some degree effective in the treatment of various forms of cardiovascular disease, there is a significant incidence of adverse reactions to many of these drugs.[3] For instance, alpha-adrenergic blockers have been reported to produce gastrointestinal distress and headache while beta-adrenergic blockers are sometimes associated with depression, lack of energy, and impotence. Centrally acting agents such as methyldopa have frequently been associated with impotence in males, while adrenergic neuron blocking agents such as reserpine have frequently been cited as causing severe depression. One of the reasons why patients report adverse reactions from pharmacotherapy is that most pharmacologic agents are relatively nonspecific in action. For instance, because of the pervasiveness of alpha- and beta-adrenergic receptors throughout the body, most of the alpha and beta blockers have systemic effects beyond those targeted in the cardiovascular system. Other agents such as reserpine, which have thera-peutic effects peripherally, can have serious debilitating central nervous system effects. These problems become particularly troublesome when therapy must be chronic as in the treatment of hypertension or angina pectoris. Similarly, the cost/benefit ratio of these treatments becomes ques-tionable when disease is mild, such as in borderline hypertension.

BEHAVIORAL TECHNIQUES

The use of behavioral techniques in the treatment of cardiovascular disease came in part as a response to the quest for alternatives to pharmaco-therapy as well as an outgrowth of the development of biofeedback and instrumental conditioning of autonomically mediated responses. Early bio-feedback experiments suggested that autonomically innervated responses could be voluntarily controlled. Furthermore, these experiments suggested that this control could be specific to the target organ being trained. A good example of this early work is a study by Shapiro et al.[5] which demonstrated that palmar skin potential, reflecting sudomotor activity, could be voluntarily controlled. One group of subjects was given a reward each time a skin potential response occurred; a second group was given the same number of rewards but at times when the response was absent. The first group showed increases in the response rate relative to the second group, which showed a response rate decrement. The fact that the same reward, with instructions held constant, could be used either to enhance or diminish the autonomic response argued strongly that the control was voluntary. Lowering variations in the electrodermal response was found not to be associated with such physiologically related functions as skin conductance, heart rate, and respiration, suggesting that this control was relatively specific. An example of the specificity of biofeedback and conditioning techniques in achieving cardiovascular control was provided by Schwartz.[6] He developed an on-line procedure for tracking both phasic and tonic patterns of blood pressure and heart rate in real time and showed that subjects could learn to control patterns of simultaneous changes in both functions. That subjects could learn, to some extent, to differentiate heart rate and blood pressure responses emphasized the plasticity of central control of cardiovascular responses. If these biofeedback techniques could indeed produce specific changes in cardiovascular activity, then they could be seen as behavioral analogues to various forms of pharmacotherapy.[1]

Several experimental investigations of behavioral control of cardiovascular reactivity led to the suggestion that specific biofeedback techniques would produce more potent attenuation of particular cardiovascular responses

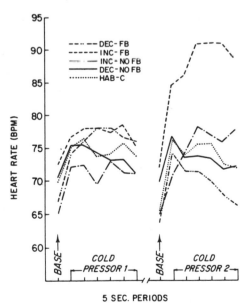

FIGURE 20.1.   Mean heart rate in successive five-second periods during cold pressor test prior to and following exposure of half the subjects to heart rate feedback. Reprinted by permission of Elsevier Science Publishing Co., Inc. from R. Vicotr, J.A. Mainardi, D. Shapiro, "Effect of biofeedback and voluntary control procedures on heart rate and perception of pain during the cold pressure test," by *Psychosomatic Medicine, Vol. 40,* pp. 216–225. Copyright 1978 by the American Psychosomatic Society, Inc.

than less specific relaxation procedures. One study by Victor, Mainardi, and Shapiro[7] demonstrated that subjects given specific heart rate feedback to decrease their heart rate in response to cold pressor test (DEC–FB group) were significantly more successful than subjects who were instructed to decrease their heart rate without being given specific biofeedback (INC-No FB group; Figure 20.1). Similarly, Steptoe[8] demonstrated that pulse transit time feedback was significantly more effective in increasing transit time (a measure that some consider to be related to blood pressure) than relaxation training during which subjects were given a challenging task (see Figure 20.2).

Despite these successful experimental studies demonstrating the specificity of biofeedback techniques in modifying sympathetically mediated responses, clinical trials of biofeedback and relaxation have failed to show that there are any specific advantages for biofeedback techniques over relaxation strategies in treating cardiovascular disease. For example, Surwit et al.[9] reported findings of a controlled group outcome study in which two types of biofeedback training were compared to a form of meditation in the treatment of borderline hypertension. Twenty-four borderline hypertensives served as subjects and were evenly divided into three treatment conditions. All subjects received two one-hour baseline sessions and eight one-hour biweekly treatment sessions. The first treatment group received binary feedback for simultaneous reductions of blood pressure and heart rate. The second group received analogue feedback for combined forearm and frontalis electromyographic (EMG) activity. The third group received a meditation-

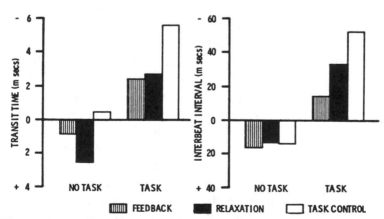

FIGURE 20.2.   Mean pulse transit time (left) and interbeat interval (right) responses during training trials with and without simultaneous task performance. Data plotted changes from average baseline with upward bars representing greater cardiovascular activation. (From A. Steptoe "Control of cardiovascular reactivity and the tretment of Hypertension." In Surwit RS, Williams Jr., RB, et al (eds.), *Behavioral Treatment of Disease*. New York, Plenum, 1982.) Reprinted with permission of the authors and publisher.

relaxation procedure modeled after Benson.[10] Six weeks following the last treatment session, all subjects received a one-hour treatment follow-up session. The three treatment groups all showed significant reductions in pressure over trials during each session, implying that each of the behavioral methods tested was equally effective as a clinical intervention.

Though no clinical advantage could be demonstrated for the "specific" biofeedback techniques, some investigators have reported impressive clinical results in the use of relaxation in a variety of cardiovascular problems. Patel[11] proposed to modify the sympathetic nervous system contribution to hypertension by using skin resistance biofeedback in combination with yoga breathing-relaxation exercises and meditation to treat a group of 20 hypertensive patients. Initial average blood pressure on medication was 160/102 mmHg. Following 36 half-hour sessions over a three-month period, average blood pressure dropped to 134/86 mmHg. Furthermore, total drug requirement was reduced by 42 percent. Only four patients failed to demonstrate improvement. These results were replicated in a later study[12] in which increased medical attention and repeated blood pressure measurements were used as a placebo control. After a 12-month follow-up, the treatment group had an average pressure reduction of 20.4/14.2 mmHg compared to no change for the controls. Smaller but equally consistent improvements in blood pressure following the application of an abbreviated form of meditation training have been reported by Benson, Rosner, et al.[13] and Stone and DeLeo.[14] Progressive relaxation training has also been used as an effective therapy for hypertension.[e.g., 15]

Another approach to the treatment of hypertension that appears promising incorporates the patient's self-monitoring of blood pressure with relaxation strategies. Whereas in many cases certain behavioral techniques such as relaxation can be effectively applied to the treatment of disease without clarification of the relationship of stress to symptom severity, it is always useful to assess the relationship between the symptom and the environment in which the patient lives. As applied to the treatment of hypertension, such an intervention involves frequent monitoring and graphing of blood pressures throughout the day in order to clarify the relationship of environmental stimuli to pressor responses. Relaxation or other behavioral techniques aimed at reducing blood pressure would then be applied to those situations in which blood pressure was most likely to be elevated. The outcome of such an intervention is illustrated in the following case report.[1] As shown in Figure 20.3a, this patient showed wide fluctuations in systolic and diastolic blood pressure throughout the day. During weekly sessions, blood pressure graphs were analyzed and the patient was given instructions as to how to change his behavior, including the practice of relaxation, in order to modify his blood pressure. The results of this therapeutic intervention are illustrated in Figures 20.3b, 20.3c and 20.3d. As can be seen, by the end of 10 weeks the

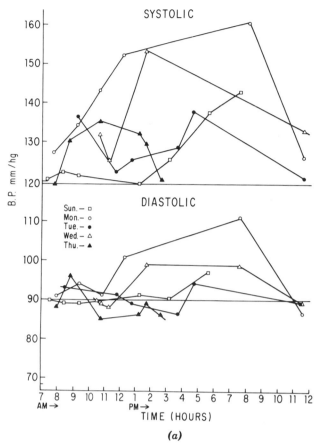

FIGURE 20.3.   Daily systolic and diastolic blood pressures of behavioral treatment with self home blood pressure monitoring. (*a*) Week 1, (*b*) Week 4, (*c*) Week 7, and (*d*) Week 10. (From R.S. Surwit, R.B. Williams, D. Shapiro, *Behavioral Approaches to Cardiovascular Disease*. New York, Academic, 1982.) Reprinted with permission of the authors and publisher.

variability in blood pressure was greatly reduced, yielding an essentially normotensive pattern.

Behavioral methods have also been used successfully in the treatment of Raynaud's disease. Raynaud's disease is a vasospastic disorder involving the digits of the upper and lower extremities. Patients suffering from the disease report experiencing discoloration and sometimes pain in the fingers and toes upon exposure to cold or emotional stress.[16] Although there is some debate as to the mechanism of the vasomotor disorder, it is considered to be an example of excessive peripheral vasomotor reactivity.[16] In one study by Surwit et al.,[17] 30 female patients diagnosed as suffering from idiopathic Raynaud's disease were trained to control their digital skin temperature using either autogenic training or a combination of autogenic training and skin temperature biofeedback. All subjects were exposed to an

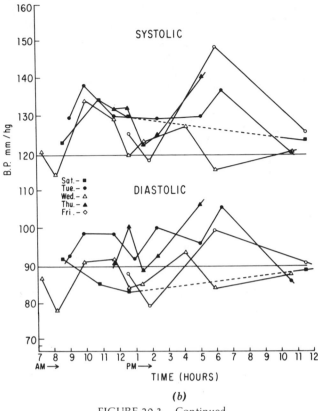

FIGURE 20.3.   Continued

initial cold stress procedure in which they were seated in an experimental chamber while the ambient temperature was slowly dropped from 26°C to 17°C over 72 minutes. Skin temperature and other cardiovascular responses were monitored during the temperature change. This procedure was given to half of the subjects immediately before and immediately following a full month training sequence. The remaining half of the sample was exposed to an additional cold stress challenge prior to treatment as a no treatment control. The study results are illustrated in Figure 20.4. Autogenic training and biofeedback combined with autogenic training were equally effective in producing a significant improvement in subjects' ability to maintain digital skin temperature relative to both their initial cold stress as well as to the second cold stress given with the no-treatment control sample. All treated subjects also reported approximately 50 percent reduction in vasospastic attack frequency. In a subsequent study,[18] subjects were given autogenic training, skin temperature feedback, or EMG feedback, as a treatment for

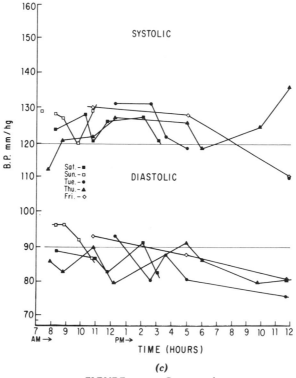

(c)

FIGURE 20.3.   Continued

Raynaud's disease. Again, all three treatments were equally effective in producing a significant attenuation of vasospastic frequency as well as increased resistance to a controlled cold challenge.

Migraine and vascular headache represent another category of cardiovascular disease in which vascular instability has frequently been attributed, in part, to the autonomic nervous system.[19] Interest in the application of behavioral techniques to the treatment of migraine can be traced to the early work of Sargent et al.[20] These investigators reported that spontaneous recovery from a migraine was correlated with a 10°F increase in digital skin temperature over a two-minute period. They reasoned that if spontaneous increases in skin temperature were associated with headache relief, then inducing digital vasodilitation voluntarily may provide a behavioral treatment for migraine. The rationale for this intervention is that increased digital bloodflow is accompanied by decreased adrenergic sympathetic nervous system (SNS) activity.[1,20] Numerous studies and case reports published between 1972 and the present substantiate the utility of digital skin temperature feedback, autogenic training, and teaching patients to warm

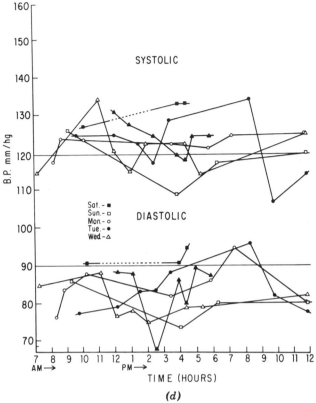

(d)

FIGURE 20.3. Continued

their hands in the alleviation of migraine headaches.[1] However, as with other disorders, nonspecific relaxation techniques have been shown to be as effective as biofeedback procedures in the treatment of migraine.[1] For instance, in one widely cited study, Blanchard, Theobald, et al.[21] applied a controlled group outcome design to test the differential efficacy of temperature biofeedback as compared to progressive muscle relaxation or a waiting-list control. Ten subjects were given temperature feedback with autogenic training and ten subjects were given progressive muscle relaxation training. Both groups were encouraged to practice at home. Ten subjects constituted a waiting-list control. Subjects in both the temperature feedback and relaxation condition showed significantly greater decreases in the frequency and intensity of migraine headaches than did the waiting-list control. Interestingly, subjects receiving progressive relaxation did slightly better than subjects receiving temperature biofeedback and autogenic training. At a one month follow-up the gains were maintained in 9 out of 13 in the group receiving temperature feedback and in all the subjects receiving relaxation training.

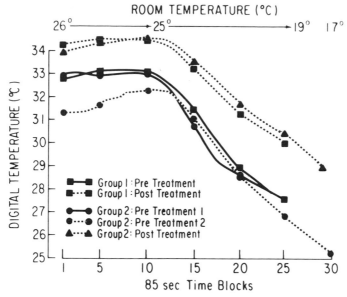

FIGURE 20.4.   Mean digital temperatures during pretreatment and posttreatment cold stress tests. Recording of skin temperature began after a 10-minute stabilization. From R.S. Surwit, R.N. Pilon, C.H. Fenton in "Behavioral treatment of Raynaud's disease," by *Journal of Behavioral Medicine*, 1:329, 1978. Reprinted with permission of authors and Plenum Press.

NEUROENDOCRINE MECHANISMS OF RELAXATION AND BIOFEEDBACK

Despite the ubiquitous application of relaxation and biofeedback procedures to all sorts of cardiovascular disease, little is known about the neuroendocrine mechanism by which such training affects cardiovascular responsivity. Nevertheless, over the past eight years, a number of studies have appeared in the literature in which the neuroendocrine consequences of relaxation were explored. In 1976 Stone and DeLeo[14] reported small but significant blood pressure reductions (15/10 mmHg) in 19 patients who practiced a Buddhist relaxation procedure for six months. These changes were found to be accompanied by significant reductions in plasma dopamine beta-hydroxylase, a catecholamine metabolite. Furthermore, patients practicing relaxation also showed decreases in furosemide-stimulated plasma reactivity, suggesting a decrease of sympathetic tone in the kidney. Davidson, Winchester, et al.[22] trained six patients with surgically implanted tantalum myocardial markers in deep muscle relaxation. Trained subjects demonstrated a decrease in norepinephrine levels as well as indices of myocardial contractility during relaxation as compared to a control state. Mathew, Ho, et al.[23] examined the neuroendocrine effects of progressive relaxation training and EMG biofeedback in 20 outpatients with migraine headache. After eight sessions of EMG biofeedback-assisted relaxation training, trained subjects were seen to show lower levels of epinephrine, norepinephrine, as well as monoamine oxidase activity compared to untrained controls who also underwent two venopunctures. This same group[24] reported similar findings when they compared the effects of relaxation training in a group of 15 anxious patients and 15 nonneurotic controls who were examined twice without any intervention.

Other investigators have reported contradictory results. Hoffman, Benson, et al.[25] studied the neuroendocrine effects of the relaxation response,[10] a variation on the meditation procedure, in 19 normal volunteers. In contrast to previous investigations, the effects of venopuncture were more carefully controlled by admitting patients to a clinical research unit 10 to 12 hours prior to testing and withdrawing all blood samples via an indwelling intravenous catheter which was inserted 30 minutes before the withdrawal of the first blood sample. Plasma norepinephrine levels were determined while the subject was supine, after five minutes of standing, and while the subject was practicing an isometric hand grip. These measurements were repeated before and after half the subjects were trained in the relaxation response. Following training, subjects who practiced relaxation showed significantly higher levels of plasma norepinephrine than subjects who were not trained in relaxation in response to the isometric hand grip. No differences in systolic blood pressure, diastolic blood pressure, or heart rate between the groups were observed. These findings were interpreted as indicating that alpha-adrenergic receptors may have been down-regulated in those subjects who practiced relaxation, but SNS activity itself increased with relaxation. Finally, Surwit and Feinglos[26,27] admitted 12 non-insulin-dependent diabetic patients to a clinical research unit for nine days. All subjects received the glucose tolerance test and an insulin sensitivity test. Half of the subjects were then given five days of progressive relaxation and EMG biofeedback training while the other half of the subjects remained in the hospital without training. Glucose tolerance tests and insulin sensitivity tests were then repeated while subjects who learned relaxation practiced their relaxation strategies. All subjects had low levels of catecholamines and there was no significant difference in catecholamine levels between subjects trained in relaxation and controls. As in the Hoffman et al. study, blood samples were withdrawn by an indwelling catheter that had been inserted well before test samples were withdrawn.

The effects of relaxation on adrenocortical responding have also been studied. Jevning et al.[28] reported that plasma cortisol concentrations decreased in long-term practitioners of "transcendental meditation" (TM) during the practice of relaxation. Similar changes were not found in controls at rest or in controls who were learning meditation for the first time. These results were contradicted in a report by Michaels et al.,[29] in which practiced meditators (TM) and untrained controls were studied while practicing meditation or sitting quietly with their eyes closed. No significant differences in plasma cortisol, plasma renin activity, plasma aldosterone, or plasma lactate were found between the two groups. DeGood and Redgate[30] studied the effects of progressive relaxation and EMG biofeedback on plasma cortisol responding in 24 subjects who were characterized as to trait anxiety using the Spielberger State-Trait Anxiety Scale. The 12 participants who scored above the median on initial trait anxiety showed significant reductions in plasma cortisol over eight sessions of relaxation training. In contrast, subjects who scored low in trait anxiety showed no change. Surwit and Feinglos[26,27] also studied the effects of progressive relaxation and EMG feedback on plasma cortisol levels. In their study, previously described, subjects receiving progressive relaxation and EMG biofeedback showed significant decreases in plasma cortisol after training compared to untreated controls. This change in plasma cortisol was accompanied by a significant improvement in glucose tolerance in treated patients.

The data on the effects of meditation and relaxation procedures on various neuroendocrine parameters appear to be contradictory. The apparent confusion may be due to the considerable methodological difficulties inherent in assessing the neuroendocrine effects of relaxation. At this time it would be most prudent to withhold judgment as to what neuroendocrine mechanisms mediate the apparent effects of relaxation on cardiovascular reactivity. Nevertheless, it is obvious that if relaxation procedures do influence cardiovascular responding, then some neuroendocrine changes must be taking place. There was a suggestion that relaxation may decrease cardiovascular responsivity by decreasing sympathetic activity directly. There is an equal amount of data that suggests that relaxation produces decreased adrenocortical responses as well. Recent evidence suggests that glucocorticoids may play a significant role in cardiovascular reactivity. Several studies have shown that increased levels of glucocorticoids can increase vasomotor responding to catecholamines.[e.g. 31,32] Idiopathic Raynaud's disease has also been associated with high levels of plasma cortisol.[33] In that glucocorticoids are known to prevent the down-regulation of beta-adrenergic receptors[34] as well as prevent the degradation of catecholamines in the synaptic cleft,[32] glucocorticoids apparently play an important role in modulating the reactivity of cardiovascular end organs to SNS stimulation. If relaxation techniques really do influence adrenocortical activity, then they would be predicted to have a modulating effect on cardiovascular reactivity even if they do not directly influence the sympathetic nervous system itself.

SUMMARY

Hyperreactivity of the autonomic nervous system has been assumed to be a primary factor contributing to the development of cardiovascular disease. Pharmacologic treatments of cardiovascular disease usually operate either by inhibiting sympathetic nervous system activity through central stimulation or by interfering with efferent sympathetic activity at the level of the effector organ, the receptor, or the postganglionic nerve ending. A variety of biofeedback and relaxation techniques have also been demonstrated in some cases to reduce cardiovascular responsivity (see chapter by Jacob and Chesney). These techniques have been shown to have some degree of clinical efficacy in the treatment of hypertension, peripheral vasomotor disorders, and migraine headache. However, the neuroendocrine mechanisms by which these procedures exert their effects are not clearly understood. There is suggestive evidence that biofeedback and relaxation procedures work by reducing the activity of both the sympathetic nervous system and the adrenocortical axis.

REFERENCES

1. Surwit RS, Williams Jr RB, Shapiro D: *Behavioral Approaches to Cardiovascular Disease.* New York, Academic Press, 1982.

2. Herd AJ: Behavioral factors in the physiological mechanisms of cardiovascular disease. In Weiss SM, Herd JA, Fox BH (eds): *Prospectives on Behavioral Medicine.* New York, Academic Press, 1981, pp. 55–64.

3. Weiner N: Drugs that inhibit adrenergic nerves and block adrenergic receptors. In Gillman AG, Goodman LS, Gillman A (eds): *Goodman and Gillman's Pharmacological Basis of Therapeutics* (6th Ed.). New York, Macmillan, 1980, pp. 176–210.

4. Stone PH, Turiz G, Muler JE: Efficacy of nifedipine therapy for refractory angina pectoris. *Am Heart J* **104**:672–681, 1982.

5. Shapiro D, Crider AB, Tursky B: Differentiation of an autonomic response to operant reinforcement. *Psychonom Sci* **1**:147–148, 1964.

6. Schwartz GE: Voluntary control of human cardiovascular integration and differentiation through feedback and reward. *Science* **175**:90–93, 1972.

7. Victor R, Mainardi JA, Shapiro D: Effect of biofeedback and voluntary control procedures on heart rate and perception of pain during the cold pressure test. *Psychosom Med* **40**:216–225, 1978.

8. Steptoe A: Control of cardiovascular reactivity and the treatment of hypertension. In Surwit RS, Williams Jr RB, et al (eds): *Behavioral Treatment of Disease*, New York, Plenum, 1982, pp. 159–172.

9. Surwit RS, Shapiro D, Good MI: A comparison of cardiovascular biofeedback, neuromuscular biofeedback, and meditation in the treatment of borderline essential hypertension. *J Consult Clin Psychol* **46**:151–263, 1978.

10. Benson H: *The Relaxation Response*. New York, Morrow, 1975.

11. Patel CH: Yoga and biofeedback in the management of hypertension. *Lancet* **7837**:1053–1055, 1973.

12. Patel CH, North WRS: Randomized control trial of yoga and biofeedback in management of hypertension. *Lancet* **7925**:93–95, 1975.

13. Benson H, Rosner BA, et al: Decrease blood pressure in borderline hypertensive subjects who practice meditation. *J Chron Dis* **27**:163–169, 1974.

14. Stone RA, DeLeo J: Psychotherapeutic control of hypertension. *N Engl J Med* **294**:80–84, 1976.

15. Taylor CB, Farquhr JW, et al: Relaxation therapy and high blood pressure. *Arch Gen Psychiatr* **34**:339–342, 1977.

16. Spittell Jr JA: Raynaud's phenomenon and allied vasospastic conditions. In Farbairn JF, Juergens JC, Spittell A (eds): *Allen-Barker-Hines Peripheral Vascular Disease* (4th Ed). Philadelphia, Saunders, 1972, pp. 387–420.

17. Surwit RS, Pilon RN, Fenton CH: Behavioral treatment of Raynaud's disease. *J Behav Med* **1**:323–335, 1978.

18. Keefe FJ, Surwit RS, Pilon RN: Biofeedback, autogenic training, and progressive relaxation in the treatment of Raynaud's disease. *J Appl Behav Anal* **13**:3–11, 1980.

19. Lance JW: *Mechanism and management of headache* (3rd Ed). Boston, Butterworths, 1978.

20. Sargent JD, Green EE, Walters ED: The use of autogenic feedback training in a pilot study of migraine and tension headaches. *Headache* **12**:120–125, 1972.

21. Blanchard EB, Theobald D, et al: Temperature feedback in the treatment of migraine headaches. *Arch Gen Psychiatr* **35**:581–588, 1978.

22. Davidson DM, Winchester MA, et al: Effects of relaxation therapy on cardiac performance and sympathetic activity in patients with organic heart disease. *Psychosom Med* **41**:303–309, 1979.

23. Mathew RJ, Ho BT, et al: Catecholamines and migraine: Evidence based on biofeedback-induced changes. *Headache* **20**:247–252, 1980.

24. Mathew RJ, Ho BT, et al: Catechol-O-Methythransferase and catecholamines in anxiety and relaxation. *Psychiatr Res* **3**:85–91, 1980.

25. Hoffman JW, Benson H, et al: Reduced sympathetic nervous system responsivity associated with the relaxation response. *Science* **215**:190–192, 1982.

26. Surwit RS, Feinglos MN: The effects of relaxation on glucose tolerance in non-insulin-dependent diabetes mellitus. *Diabetes Care* **6**:176–179, 1983.

27. Surwit RS, Feinglos MN: Relaxation induced improvement in glucose tolerance is associated with decreased plasma cortisol. *Diabetes Care* **7**:203–204, 1984.

28. Jevning R, Wilson AF, Davidson JM: Adrenocortical activity during meditation. *Hormone Behavior* **110**:54–60, 1978.

29. Michaels RR, Parra J, et al: Renin, cortisol, and aldosterone during transcendental meditation. Psychosom Med **41**:50–54, 1979.

30. DeGood DE, Redgate DS: Interrelationship of plasma cortisol and other activation indices during EMG biofeedback training. *J Behav Med* **5**:213–224, 1982.

31. Schmid PG, Eckstein JW, Abboud FM: Comparison of effects of deoxycorticosterone and dexamethasone on cardiovascular responses on norepinephrine. *J Clin Invest* **46**:590–598, 1967.

32. Goldie RG: The effects of hydrocortisone on responses to an extraneural uptake of isoprenaline in cat and guinea pig atria. *Clin Exp Pharmacol Physiol* **3**:225–233, 1976.

33. Surwit RS, Allen LM, et al: Neuroendocrine response to cold in Raynaud's syndrome. *Life Sci* **32**:995–1000, 1983.

34. Davies AE, Lefkowitz RG: Regulation of beta-adrenergic receptors by steroid hormones. *Ann Rev Physiol* **46**:119–130, 1984.

21

Pharmacologic Agents
as Modulators
of Stress

ALVIN P. SHAPIRO, DAVID S. KRANTZ, CLARENCE E. GRIM

INTRODUCTION

The elicitation and expression of stress responses undoubtedly involve a complex series of biological events. Stimuli may arise from the internal milieu of the subject or from the external environment; they are perceived and processed through the several levels of the central nervous system; they are lent cognition, emotional content, specificity, and intensity through the past and present experiences or future expectations of the subject; finally, they are expressed by various voluntary and involuntary

This chapter was prepared with the assistance of Thomas Clarkson, D.V.M.; Katherine Detre, M.D.; Peter Kaufman, Ph.D.; Robert E. Miller, Ph.D.; Kristina Orth-Gomer, M.D.; and Redford Williams, M.D.

behavioral reactions. But whatever the sequence of these events, there is a highly significant set of peripheral manifestations of stress that involve autonomic nervous system (ANS) reactivity and produce signs and symptoms in a variety of organ systems of the individual. The perception of these manifestations of peripheral reactivity by the individual may in turn elicit anxiety and perpetuate the stimulus-reaction sequence. For instance, as Cannon pointed out years ago,[1] the individual suffering from fear about dealing with a personal confrontation may experience cardiovascular concomitants of this anxiety, resulting in tachycardia, flushing, and sweating, symptoms that in turn can be perceived and interpreted in a fashion that will exacerbate the fear. Autonomic reactivity can affect many organ systems, including gastrointestinal function, endocrine and hormonal release, and even immunological responses, but our discussion in this paper will be primarily concerned with cardiovascular manifestations that are mediated by the sympathetic component of the ANS.

The standard approach to ameliorating the peripheral manifestations of stress has been to interfere with the central nervous system (CNS) perception and/or processing of the stimulus by the use of various forms of psychotherapy, including relaxation techniques, or by different types of CNS sedatives or tranquilizers. Psychotherapy thus purports to "teach" the patient not to perceive a given stimulus as threatening, while agents that act on the CNS would serve to inhibit the activation of the sympathetic nervous system (SNS) following central input. The development of pharmacological compounds that block peripheral receptors, notably the adrenergic blocking agents, represents a different approach to this problem, which in effect "permits" the CNS input and output to occur essentially unchanged but prevents the symptomatic activation of cardiovascular receptors mediating such responses as heart rate and blood pressure changes.

Adrenergic receptors include both alpha and beta types. The former mediate primarily vasoconstrictive events and peripheral alpha blockers such as Dibenzyline and phentolamine have been employed therapeutically and diagnostically for many years to inhibit norepinephrine-induced vasoconstriction and to control blood pressure. Recent development of knowledge concerning the existence of alpha 1 and alpha 2 classes of these receptors has led to more specific alpha blockers (e.g. prazosin), which have added to our ability to control hypertension with such drugs. However, alpha blockers have not been employed in the control of anxiety and stress. On the other hand, drugs that block the beta receptors and affect those aspects of stress and cardiovascular response more closely associated with epinephrine-like manifestations and norepinephrine stimulation of the heart are being widely utilized. Hence, our discussion will concern itself primarily with these agents.

The use of beta blocking drugs to control stress responses has a number of *philosophical* as well as *pragmatic* considerations. Philosophically, one might argue that the administration of a pharmacologic compound to prevent a "naturally" occurring biologic event—rather than attempting to prevent the stimulus, perhaps by environmental or social change—amounts to drug manipulation of the individual. Surely, when carried to its extreme, this may be a valid argument. On the other hand, when the stress-eliciting stimulus is not an unusual one but its impact on the individual becomes exaggerated by his or her personal processing of the event, and when the medication is not one that induces drug dependency, the approach of peripheral blockade seems as reasonable as any other therapeutic technique involving medication. Blockade of the end organ response by medication is a clearly accepted therapeutic maneuver in such diverse medical conditions as peptic ulcer (cimetidine), hyperthyroidism (propylthiouracil) and for many years even for angina pectoris (nitrates). Moreover, if repeated acute responses of the cardiovascular system to stress play a role in the development of chronic diseases such as hypertension and coronary artery atherosclerosis, at least in individuals already experiencing a predilection to these ailments, an argument can be made for the use of peripherally blocking drugs as preventive agents, as well as for the symptomatic relief they offer.

Pragmatically, the problems concerned in the use of beta blocking drugs for clinical purposes include the type of beta blockers used, the CNS and peripheral side effects of these compounds, the long-term effects of blocking beta-adrenergic effects, and the projected scope of indications for their use. Their use in otherwise healthy individuals raises particular concerns regarding side effects and long-term outcomes, and we will specifically discuss these contraindications.

BETA BLOCKERS

Actions and Types of Beta Blockers

As mentioned above, the pharmacologic agents that have particular clinical relevance in control of peripheral manifestations of SNS stimulation are the class of drugs known as beta blockers. These are agents that affect the peripherally located beta receptors which are stimulated by adrenergic transmitters, that is, norepinephrine in the heart and epinephrine. The beta receptors are of two types, beta 1, which influence cardiac rate and contractility, and beta 2, which mediate bronchiolar dilation, vasodilation in skeletal muscle, and certain metabolic events such as gluconeogenesis, and renin secretion from the kidney. The beta blockers prevent those actions mediated through the receptors by competitively binding to the receptors and thus inhibiting the effect of the transmitters.

A large number of beta blockers have been developed. It is important to remember when using these drugs clinically and in designing research studies, that although all beta blockers share similar chemistry and biologic actions, they differ among themselves primarily in terms of three character-istics: (1) selectivity for the beta 1 or beta 2 receptor; (2) duration of action; and (3) solubility.

Selectivity defines the relative affinity of the blocker for the beta 1 or the beta 2 receptor. All block both receptors, but as their development has proceeded, they have been designed to preferentially block the beta 1 events (e.g., cardiac) rather than the beta 2; thus certain side effects of beta 2 blockade such as bronchospasm and delayed return of blood sugar after insulin hypoglycemia can be minimized. What should be clearly understood however, is that selectivity for beta 1 receptors is relative to dosage and as dosage is increased, beta 2 blockade becomes increasingly evident as a clinical problem.

Duration of effect is a function of the half-life of the compounds, while solubility defines the major pathways of metabolism as well as their potential for crossing the blood-brain barrier and thus exerting CNS activity. Lipid-soluble compounds are extensively metabolized in the liver and also enter the CNS; hydrophilic compounds are primarily excreted by the kidney and have lesser affinity for the CNS. These considerations as regards CNS activity by beta blockers have been recently reviewed by Turner.[2]

Currently, seven compounds are FDA approved and available in the United States. These are shown with their comparative differences in regard to these three characteristics in Table 21.1. Propranolol is the oldest, and the prototype. It is nonselective, lipophilic, and relatively short-acting. At the other end of the scale is atenolol, which is beta-1 selective, hydrophilic, and relatively long acting. Pindolol has an additional characteristic—namely clinically significant partial agonist or intrinsic sympathomimetic activity (ISA), which accounts for the fact that it causes less bradycardia and is probably responsible for the relative lack of renin suppression by this drug. All the compounds share to some extent one other property, namely mem-brane stabilizing activity (MSA), which seems not to be related to beta blockade. This property is a quinidinelike effect on heart muscle, and is believed by some investigators to have a bearing on the antiarrhythmic properties of the various compounds, but probably has little clinical relevance. A beta blocker which has only recently been approved in the United Stated, but already has been extensively utilized in other countries, is labetalol, which has the property of combining alpha 1 blockade with nonselective beta blockade. The clinical role of this unique compound, particularly in

TABLE 21.1   BETA-BLOCKING DRUGS APPROVED IN UNITED STATES (1984)

Drug	Selectivity	Duration of Action[a]	Solubility
Propranolol	Nonselective	Short	Lipophilic
Metoprolol	Selective	Intermediate	Lipophilic
Nadolol	Nonselective	Long	Hydrophilic
Timolol	Nonselective	Short	Lipophilic and Hydrophilic
Atenolol	Selective	Long	Hydrophilic
Pindolol[b]	Nonselective	Short	Lipophilic
Labetalol[c]	Nonselective	Short	Lipophilic

[a]Short = half-life 4–6 hours;
Intermediate = half-life 6–12 hours;
Long = half-life >12 hours;
[b]Significant intrinsic sympathomimetic activity
[c]Intrinsic alpha 1 blocking activity

regard to the context of use for stress management which we are discussing, remains to be clearly defined.

There are many other beta blocking compounds that have been and will be developed, as pharmacologists attempt to emphasize certain of the three characteristics over the others. Clearly, the degree of selectivity, the duration of action, and the ability to penetrate the CNS are properties that are pertinent to the desirable and undesirable clinical effects. Thus, patients with pulmonary disease, diabetics on insulin, and individuals with peripheral vascular disease need a drug with minimal beta 2 blockade and subjects with renal impairment should preferentially be treated with a lipophilic drug. Those patients with poor compliance may have improved adherence on a drug with longer duration of action, while patients with CNS symptoms such as insomnia and nightmares are said to do better on hydrophilic agents. Similarly, in designing research on effects of beta blockers, investigators must take these differences into account and recognize as well that the presence or absence of certain effects are functions of not only the type but also the dose of the given drug.

Cardiovascular Outcomes Following Beta Blockade

The cardiovascular effect of the beta blockers that is most evident clinically is the reduction in heart rate due to blockade of the SNS effect (e.g., norepinephrine) on beta 1 receptors in the heart. This negative chronotropic effect results in a fall in cardiac output which may be abetted by an additional negative inotropy (e.g., decrease in myocardial contractility). Moreover, the heart will have a dampened response in the form of a lesser increase in its rate and output to physiological and psychological stimuli. Such an effect in a "healthy" heart will not interfere with its function, except perhaps with extreme demand, as in an athlete performing at his or her peak, but in the damaged heart with reduced reserve, it can be responsible for precipitation of heart failure.

The modest reduction of blood pressure by beta blockers alone is probably primarily a function of reduction of cardiac output, with perhaps an additional role played by reduction of renin release from the kidney. However, the fact that the selective beta 1 blockers are effective in lowering blood pressure argues against a major role for beta 2 blockade of plasma renin activity (PRA) in vasodilation. On the other hand, the fact that a beta blocker with ISA such as pindolol can lower blood pressure when heart rate and PRA levels are minimally depressed does suggest that mechanisms other than a drop in cardiac output and/or decrease in PRA are responsible for blood pressure fall. What such a mechanism may be, remains controversial.[3]

As already mentioned, the effect of beta blockers on reactivity are primarily indicated by the dampening of heart rate response to such diverse stimuli as tilting, hypoglycemia, exercise, and mental arithmetic.[3-5] Blockade of pressor responses to stimuli is less evident and in some instances, these responses may in fact be exaggerated. This probably results from the hyperreactivity of the unopposed alpha receptors that develops in the face of beta 2 blockade, a situation that produces the clinical counterpart of the phenomenon of "epinephrine reversal."[5,6] Epinephrine is normally both an alpha and beta 2 stimulant. When the beta 2 effects are blocked, epinephrine then acts like norepinephrine peripherally, as a "pure" alpha agonist.

Effects of Beta Blockers in Controlling Cardiovascular Stress Responses and Anxiety

The use of beta blockers to control cardiovascular responses to stress and the application of this information to control anxiety has grown slowly over the years from several directions. Even before the development of the concept of beta receptors and their blockade, and following the work of Cannon[1] in animals, evidence had accrued on the production of anxiety in humans by injection of adrenaline, and this literature is reviewed briefly by Pitts and Allen.[7] As more specific beta agonists were developed, these investigations focused on the problem of whether "anxiety-prone" individuals were more apt to have symptoms than "normal" individuals, but nevertheless, considerable evidence was accumulated that there was indeed a somatopsychic interplay that occurred when sympathomimetic cardiovascular events were elicited.

Beta blockers became available in the early 1960s, and by 1965 data indicating relief of anxiety correlating with heart rate slowing after propranolol administration were reported. Evidence since then, which has brought beta blockers into further consideration as modulators of stress, has come essentially from three sources: (1) from studies which have looked at control of anxiety states with beta blockers, as contrasted with CNS tranquilizers; (2) from use of the drugs to decrease "nervousness" in stressful situations such as performance anxiety; and (3) from the reports of the prophylactic value of beta blockers after myocardial infarction.

In anxiety states, anecdotal reports followed by controlled and uncontrolled trials, both short- and long-term, along with comparisons with CNS-acting drugs such as benzodiazepines have been appearing in the literature since the mid-1960s. These are reviewed by Pitts and Allen[7] and recently by a concise report in the *Medical Letter*.[8] The results of these studies can be summarized as follows:

1. Beta blockers seem to be most effective when the anxiety state includes somatic symptomatology, such as palpitations, tachycardia, and tremors.

2. Comparisons with benzodiazepines often display equal efficacy, although the benzodiazepines may be superior when psychic symptoms such as fear, panic, and apprehension are predominant.

3. Although side effects of the short-term use of beta blockers are usually minimal and the drugs are not physiologically addictive, care should be observed in their administration in the clinical situations mentioned earlier where various physiologic contraindications are present.

4. Although the evidence that CNS effects such as sedation and insomnia are caused by penetration of drugs into the CNS is not established in a quantitative sense, nevertheless, the drugs that are hydrophilic seem to create somewhat less of a problem in producing such consequences than do those that are lipophilic. In any case, both types seem equally effective in diminishing somatic symptoms of anxiety, which supports their primary peripheral site of action.

Following a variety of anecdotal and word-of-mouth communications on the effect of beta blockers in relieving symptoms in stressful situations, a number of controlled trials have appeared in the literature. Such situations include ski jumping, car racing, lecturing, examinations, musical performances, and surgical performances.[9-15] The studies have generally shown slowing of pulse rate and a lessened feeling of "dis-ease" in such subjects. The recent report by Neftel, Adler, et al.[14] deserves particular comment. These investigators studied a group of 22 performing string players and examined not only somatic criteria (heart rate and urinary norepinephrine and epinephrine) but also devised a self-rating scale for stage fright and measured instrumental technical-motor performance. Atenolol, a hydrophilic and beta 1 selective agent, was used. Their results indicated a significant pulse rate decrease when atenolol was given as compared to placebo, decrease in the discomfort of stage fright, and no impairment of technical-motor performance; in fact, there was slight evidence of improvement in the latter, which was in accord with other studies of this nature using more subjective measures of task performance. Catecholamine levels were higher when the subjects were beta blocked, as was expected from the known pharmacology of these drugs and also has been noted in other studies. One can only speculate, however, as to the significance of such an increase in terms of potential short- or long-term negative effects of the catecholamines. Of particular importance is the fact that atenolol was used successfully in this experiment, whereas other studies with similar results have used nonselective and lipophilic agents; this argues strongly that it is the blockade of peripheral sympathomimetic effects, and not primarily CNS penetration of the drugs, that accounts for their efficacy. Of note is a recent report by James et al.[16] that pindolol was similarly able to attenuate heart rate and at least systolic blood pressure responses, in spite of its partial agonist (ISA) effects, and to alleviate stage fright in a group of professional musicians, without interfering with performance.[10] Thus, clinically the ISA property of pindolol does not block the dampening of the stress response, although "side-by-side" comparisons with other beta blockers would be of interest.

The increasing utilization of beta blockers for control of performance anxiety is illustrated by a recent survey of speakers at an international cardiology meeting, reported by Gossard et al.[17] They queried 489 presentors about their use of drugs to allay stress when presenting. Replies were received from 229, of whom 13 percent reported using beta blocking drugs, virtually all of whom perceived them as significantly decreasing their anxiety.

The clinical utility of beta blockers was first demonstrated in treatment of angina pectoris where they proved quite effective in its management. Since clinically the production of angina is often the consequence of an emotionally stressful situation leading to increased cardiac work and coronary artery ischemia, this example of beta blocker efficacy is itself a powerful demonstration of the peripheral beta-adrenolytic effect of these drugs. In addition, clinicians report anecdotally that patients with angina pectoris who are successfully treated with beta blockers will report less anxiety as a consequence of this peripheral cardiac "protectiveness."

However, it was the successful use of beta blockers to prevent recurrent cardiac events in patients' postmyocardial infarction (MI) that has most impressed clinicians and investigators with their potential value in blocking cardiac responses to stress. In several large placebo-controlled clinical trials,[18,19] beta blockers have been given to patients following MI, and a significant reduction has been shown in the incidence of recurrent infarction and in sudden death. There have been few side effects associated with this impressive outcome, and it has been shown with several of the beta blockers, including compounds with either selective or nonselective characteristics and hydrophilic and lipophilic solubilities.

Although the mechanism of this protective effect is uncertain, from the standpoint of the subject of this chapter, the fact that the difference seems to occur primarily during the first year after infarction, when recurrence has its highest incidence, can be taken as an argument that prevention of tachycardia and potentially lethal arrhythmias, plays a major role.[20] With beta blockers, we may be supplying an "antidote" to the circumstances pointed out by the English surgeon, John Hunter, who is responsible for one of the first clinical descriptions of angina pectoris. Hunter, who suffered from the disease himself, stated, "I am at the mercy of any fool who would enrage me" and indeed is said to have died suddenly while attending a stormy hospital staff meeting!

Beta Blockers as Primary Preventive Agents of MI and Other Cardiovascular Diseases

Is there evidence that the data from "secondary prevention" can be extended to primary prevention of MI with beta blocker therapy in asymptomatic individuals? Although beta blockers are presently administered frequently to individuals who have not had an MI but have such ailments as hypertension, angina pectoris, and certain types of arrhythmias which put them at higher risk for MI, it is unlikely that convincing data of primary prevention in healthy subjects can emerge from such usage.

To mount a study in asymptomatic, healthy people to answer the question is perhaps possible but would require large numbers of patients, long follow-up, and a huge expense, all of which combine to make it a study of rather unlikely feasibility. Accordingly, clinical use of beta blockers on a large scale in healthy subjects to prevent cardiac stress cannot currently be recommended. Moreover, although the side effects noted in the large-scale clinical trials of secondary prevention have generally been mild, patients have been highly selected to omit those with particular potential for adverse reactions. In addition, patients who had had an MI are motivated in a fashion that makes them certainly more tolerant of symptoms such as fatigue, insomnia, and occasional impotence that one might expect healthy subjects to be. There are unanswered questions about long-term use of these drugs ranging from the effects of continued elevation of catecholamines on other organ systems to the potential for changes in blood lipids. Finally, there is the continuing concern that one or more of the beta blockers may yet prove to have harmful systemic and/or vascular effects as did practolol, a highly effective beta 1 selective compound that achieved considerable use outside of the United States until it was shown to produce a form of sclerosing fibrositis.

What can be considered, however, is the use of beta blockers in controlled trials not only in the patients with known cardiovascular disease as mentioned earlier, but also in normal individuals in certain other high-risk groups. These include individuals with specific genetic, metabolic, physiologic, and behavioral characteristics that make their target organs particularly vulnerable to stress or render them especially susceptible to stress from certain environmental or interpersonal situations.

Effects of Beta Blockers on Behavior

Several recent studies have suggested that certain behaviors may be consequences of cardiovascular disease, rather than causal agents. Thus, in mild hypertensives, significant, albeit clinically unobtrusive, changes in cognitive, perceptual, and psychomotor areas have been noted that are alleviated when blood pressure is lowered.[21,22] However, the relationship of such improvement to the type of antihypertensive drug used has not been specifically studied, and in fact, some agents may aggravate behavioral deficits.[23] There is a need to look specifically at the effects of beta blockers on performances of various behavioral tasks in hypertensives as compared to other drugs acting centrally and/or peripherally.

A number of studies have also been reported recently on the effect of beta blockers on Type A and Type B behavior. The argument has been put forth by Krantz and Durel that the Type A behavior pattern may in fact be partially a reflection of sympathetic responsivity, rather than the generally held view that the Type A person has particularly exaggerated sympathetic responses.[24] Were this so, one then might expect to see changes in Type A behavior following administration of sympatholytic drugs such as the beta blockers. In one correlational study, Krantz, Durel, et al. have indeed demonstrated that patients with coronary artery disease who were receiving propranolol, as part of their usual medical program were lower on certain Type A characteristics than those receiving diuretics, nitrates, or benzodiazepines.[25] In another study, Schmieder, Friedrich, et al. have provided evidence that Type A behavior is dampened in hypertensive patients treated with the beta blocker atenolol, as contrasted to a group treated with a thiazide diuretic.[26] These interesting reports require further research with greater attention to the utilization of placebo controls, to the mechanisms of the process, and to the measurement of changes in peripheral reactivity.

Nevertheless, the concept that dampening of peripheral responses, particularly those of cardiovascular importance, may "feed back" to influence CNS-initiated behavior is an exciting one that deserves continued study.

To the extent that the Type A behavioral pattern is indeed a risk factor in coronary artery disease, its diminution by pharmacologic agents could represent a significant contribution to the prophylaxis of this disorder. In a broader sense, this concept has a potentially wide application in the evaluation of behavioral consequences of a large number of disease states. Somatopsychic sequences can be influenced by a conglomerate of variables that range from the age, sex, and general physical state of the subject to his or her demographic and psychosocial status, and these variables need careful analysis in such studies. In turn, drugs used to treat various diseases may change behavior through their own intrinsic effects or through alleviation of the disease per se, and its consequent influences on behavior.

PHARMACOLOGIC VERSUS NONPHARMACOLOGIC TREATMENT

In recent years interest in nonpharmacologic treatment of stress-related disorders such as migraine headaches, hypertension, Raynaud's syndrome, and idiopathic arrhythmias, has centered primarily on the use of biofeedback and relaxation techniques. Theoretically, both of these techniques rely on affecting the SNS, either through autonomic conditioning in the former or diminished CNS-to-ANS activation in the latter. In effect, then, behavioral therapists are trying to accomplish through CNS manipulation what the sympatholytic drugs achieve peripherally.

For instance, although relaxation techniques will achieve significant, albeit small, declines in blood pressure, questions concerning the duration of effects, the persistence of change outside of the laboratory, and the efficacy as compared to drugs remain largely unanswered.[27,28] Compliance for the long term is also a problem; it is often simpler, for instance, for a patient to "take a pill" once a day than to practice daily relaxation in a disciplined way. As with dieting and exercising regularly to control obesity, regular relaxation requires a life-style change that many patients cannot achieve or maintain. Studies to compare drugs with relaxation and/or biofeedback are necessary and have been few to date. Luborsky, Crits-Christoph, et al. showed greater efficacy of drugs, mainly the thiazide diuretics, as compared to relaxation, biofeedback and exercise, in a small group of hypertensive patients and noted the greatest declines in those receiving medication.[29] Shapiro, Jacob, et al.[30] have described a study comparing atenolol to a diuretic, with and without relaxation, and to relaxation alone, and noted the greatest fall in blood pressure with the beta blocker, with no significant increase in the effect, once outside the therapist's office, by the addition of relaxation to either drug. Thus, in hypertension at least, it would appear that a beta blocker can accomplish the same dampening effect on cardiovascular arousal as does relaxation, with probable greater efficacy and perhaps in a fashion that is simpler and less time-consuming than the behavioral technique. On the other hand, in a properly motivated patient who wishes to avoid drugs with their potential side effects and who permits careful monitoring for evidence of disease progression, behavioral techniques can represent at least a temporary alternative or an additive treatment that can possibly decrease dose and number of drugs required and reduce daily variability of blood pressure and heart rate. Certainly, more research is necessary to examine such combined effects, to seek improvement of relaxation and biofeedback methods, and to better define the types of patients most amenable to behavioral approaches.

By contrast, Raynaud's disease, where peripheral vasospasm occurs in response to cold and other less specific stressors, there is evidence for improved control by the combination of vasodilators and relaxation therapy.[31] Similarly, in chronic and acute pain syndromes, behavioral techniques may be helpful in reducing drug requirements. This is a particularly exciting area for further research in view of current interest in endogenous opioid compounds.

ANIMAL STUDIES

As alluded to earlier in this chapter, long-term studies in humans of the prophylactic effects of beta blockers on atherogenesis and heart disease is neither financially nor epidemiologically feasible, let alone ethically justifiable from our present state of knowledge. Nevertheless, there are appropriate animal models, particularly primates, in which properly designed experiments are possible and to some extent are underway. At present, such studies are observational analyses of longitudinal changes in lipids and atherosclerosis and include examination of the influences of stress,[32,33] and are going on in several primate centers. Prospective studies evaluating long-term effects of a variety of atherogenic factors could be readily developed. For instance, in regard to beta blockers, after preliminary evaluation of dosage and pharmokinetics of several different types of beta blockers in monkeys, a combined "clinical trial" across several centers could be established in which behavioral scientists, clinical pharmacologists, nutritionists, lipid biochemists, cardiologists, and others could cooperate to try to answer a variety of questions concerning the possible role of beta blockers, or other sympatholytic agents, in the development and prevention of atherosclerosis and its complications.

CONCLUSIONS AND PROSPECTS

Traditionally, the goal of therapy in reducing stress responses and their potentially detrimental outcomes to health in humans has been to alleviate the conscious and/or unconscious impact of the stimulus on the CNS. This has been accomplished by various forms of psychotherapy and by CNS drugs—sedatives, tranquilizers, and antidepressants—with the drugs hopefully used only as temporary expedients. Another way has been to attempt to change the stimulus by environmental manipulation, either on a personal, interpersonal, or sociological level. What we have discussed in this review is an increasing interest in accomplishing this goal with drugs that are blockers of sympathetic arousal and work peripherally, have little or no direct CNS effect, provide minimal systemic side effects, and are not conducive to drug dependency. Beta-adrenergic blocking agents in particular have these characteristics. However, to assume they that they are benign agents, which have the potential for broad application to the management of stress in a healthy population and will provide a pharmacologic Nirvana, represents an unrealistic and indeed a potentially quite harmful expectation.

First of all, that cardiovascular disease will regularly result from psychological stress is not established. It is considered a minor causal factor by many cardiologists and is understood by physiologists only in broad terms and generally with minimal knowledge of specific mechanisms. Moreover, stress responses in some circumstances may be important to development of a properly conditioned cardiovascular system (e.g., exercise, certainly a stress, albeit primarily a physical challenge, can have quite beneficial cardiac effects). Accordingly, dampening stress responses may not always be in the best interests of the healthy patient.

Second, systemic side effects of beta blockers can be unexpected and/or cumulative in long-term use. Moreover, it has been an oft-repeated consequence in clinical medicine and pharmacology that a drug that does not seem to induce physiologic dependency when introduced nevertheless has psychologically addictive or abuse potential. Accordingly, we cannot recommend these drugs for long-term prophylaxis against cardiovascular disease in healthy individuals, although animal studies to determine their mechanisms of action and potential value should be encouraged.

On the other hand, in individuals in high-risk categories such as patients with hypertension, coronary artery disease, and recurrent arrhythmias, the therapeutic role of beta blockers is clear and philosophically is no different than using a variety of other medications—nitrates, calcium channel blockers, alpha sympatholytic agents—to prevent stress responses in targeted organs. Given otherwise equal indications, beta blockers may offer the additional advantage over other drugs of preventing CNS feedback of cardiovascular events that might engender further anxiety. The potential role for beta blockers as modulators of certain aspects of behavior that are considered as risk factors for disease—for example, the Type A personality—depends both on the further evaluation of the controversial issue of the precise role of Type A behavior and its components in the genesis of coronary atherosclerosis and on controlled studies of the comparative effects on this behavior of the beta blockers and other drugs. We would encourage such studies.

The use of these agents in preventing the symptoms of situational stress is and will continue to be controversial, in terms of their effect on performance, their potential for abuse, and the relative contribution of central to peripheral mechanisms in their actions. In athletic events, studies are needed in which the possible detrimental effects of beta blockers on high-level performance demanding peak cardiovascular efficiency is contrasted with their potential improvement of performance by allaying anticipatory anxiety.[34] However, granted that a favorable balance can be shown for certain sports, their use will then be judged under the same standards and with the same controversies that currently prevail in athletics concerning the use of steroids, stimulants, and other drugs believed to improve performance. On the other hand, their use to allay task anxiety by musicians, actors, lecturers, and exam takers is a broader issue with less clear guidelines; here individual decisions, hopefully under the guidance of knowledgeable health care providers, will be made. Again, research is necessary, with particular attention to the pathopharmacology of these agents.

Beta blockers, and future drugs of similar conceptualization, which affect the peripheral receptors mediating the autonomic functions of the cardiovascular system, represent one of the most significant pharmacologic contributions of the past two decades. This pharmacologic concept has had broad therapeutic application to other organ systems that are beyond the scope of this chapter. Consider, for instance, the almost simultaneous development of the histamine receptor blockers—for example, cimetidine—which have been so successfully used in managing another "stress disease," namely, peptic ulcer. It is worth noting that it was certainly not a coincidence, but more likely a product of a broad concept, that the same brilliant investigator, James Black, was responsible for originating both beta blockers and histamine blockers.

Nevertheless, whereas the therapeutic indications for receptor blockers are increasingly clear, we would again emphasize that the extension of these effects to healthy subjects is treacherous and can undo much of the currently salutary accomplishment. Beta blockers provide useful tools to investigate relationships between peripheral and central manifestations of the stress response in carefully controlled experiments. Hopefully, in addition to their obvious clinical value in a number of specific illnesses, their potential for furthering scientific understanding of the various components of the stress response will be exploited.

REFERENCES

1. Cannon WB: *Bodily Changes in Fear, Hunger and Rage.* New York, D. Appleton & Co., 1923.
2. Turner P: Beta adrenoreceptor blocking drugs and the central nervous system in man. In Turner P, Shand D (eds): *Recent Advances in Clinical Pharmacology* London, Churchill, 1983, pp. 223–234.
3. Frishman WH, Silverman R: Physiologic and metabolic effects of beta blockers. In Frishman WH (ed): *Clinical Pharmacology of Beta Adrenoreceptor Blocking Drugs.* New York, Appleton-Century-Crofts, 1980, pp. 15–34.
4. Lloyd-Mostya RH, Oram S: Modification by propranolol of cardiovascular effects of hypoglycemia. *Lancet* **2**:1213–1215, 1975.
5. Nicotero JA, Beamer VL, et al: Effects of propranolol on the pressor response to noxious stimuli in hypertensive patients. *Am J Cardiol* **22**:657–666, 1968.
6. Obrist PA, Guebelein CJ, et al: The relationship among heart rate, carotid dP/dt, and blood pressure in humans. *Psychophysiology* **15**:102–115, 1978.
7. Pitts Jr FN, Allen RE: Beta adrenergic blockade in the treatment of anxiety. In Matthew RJ (ed): *Biology of Anxiety.* New York, Brunner-Mazel, 1982, pp. 134–161.
8. Beta adrenergic blockers for anxiety. *Med Let* **26**:61–63, 1984.
9. Imhof PR, Blatter K, et al: Beta-blockade and emotional tachycardia; radiotelemetric investigations in ski jumpers. *J Appl Physiol* **27**:366–369, 1969.
10. McMillen WP: Oxyprenolol in the treatment of anxiety due to environmental stress. *Am J Psychiatr* **132**:965–968, 1975.
11. Taggart P, Carruthers M, Somerville W: Electrocardiogram, plasma catecholamines and lipids and their modification by oxyprenolol when speaking before an audience. *Lancet* **2**:341–346, 1973.
12. Krope P, Kohrs A, et al: Evaluating mepindolol in a test model of examination anxiety in students. *Pharmacopsychiatria* **15**:41–47, 1982. (Abstract)
13. Brantigan CP, Brantigan TA, Joseph N: Effect of beta blockade and beta stimulation on stage fright. *Am J Med* **72**:88–94, 1982.
14. Neftel KA, Adler RH, et al: Stage fright in musicians: A model illustrating the effect of beta blockers. *Psychosom Med* **44**:461–469, 1982.
15. James IM, Pearson RM, et al: Effect of oxyprenolol on stage-fright in musicians. *Lancet* **2**:952–956, 1977.
16. James IM, Burgoyne W, Savage IT: Effect of pindolol on stress-related disturbances of musical performance: preliminary communication. *J Royal Soc Med* **76**:194–196, 1983.
17. Gossard D, Dennis C, DeBusk RF: Use of beta-blocking agents to reduce the stress of presentation at an international cardiology meeting: Results of a survey. *Am J Cardiol* **54**:240–241, 1984.
18. Beta Blocker Heart Attack Trial (BHAT) Research Group: Randomized trial of propranolol in patients with myocardial infarction. *JAMA* **247**:1707–1714, 1982.
19. The Norwegian Multicenter Study Group: Timolol-induced reduction in mortality and reinfarction in patients surviving acute myocardial infarction. *N Eng J Med* **304**:801–807, 1981.
20. Lichstein E, Morganroth J, et al: Effect of propranolol on ventricular arrhythmia. The beta blocker heart trial experience. *Circulation* **67**:5–10, 1983.

21. Shapiro AP, Miller RE, et al: Behavioral consequences of mild hypertension. *Hypertension* 4:355–360, 1982.

22. Miller RE, Shapiro AP, et al: Effect of antihypertensive treatment on the behavioral consequences of elevated blood pressure. *Hypertension* 6:202–208, 1984.

23. Solomon S, Hotchkiss E, et al: Impairment of cognitive function by antihypertensive medication. *Psychosom Med* 41:582–586, 1979.

24. Krantz DS, Durel LA: Psychobiological substrates of the Type A behavior pattern. *Health Psychol* 2:393–411, 1983.

25. Krantz DS, Durel LA, et al: Propranolol medication among coronary patients: Relationship to Type A behavior and cardiovascular response. *J Hum Stress* 8:4–12, 1982.

26. Schmieder R, Friedrich G, et al: The influence of beta blockers on cardiovascular reactivity and Type A behavior pattern in hypertensives. *Psychosom Med* 45:417–423, 1983.

27. Shapiro AP, Schwartz GE, et al: Behavioral methods in the treatment of hypertension. *Ann Intern Med* 86:626–636, 1977.

28. Shapiro AP, Jacob RG: Non-pharmacologic approaches to the treatment of hypertension. *Ann Rev Public Health* 4:285–310, 1983.

29. Luborsky L, Crits-Christoph P, et al: Behavioral versus pharmacological treatments for essential hypertension—a needed comparison. *Psychosom Med* 44:203–213, 1982.

30. Shapiro AP, Jacob RG, et al: Comparison of relaxation, pharmacotherapy, and their interaction in the treatment of hypertension. *Proceedings 10th Meeting*, International Society of Hypertension, Interlaken, Switzerland, June 1984, p. 979. (Abstract)

31. Surwit RS, Pilon RN, Fenton CH: Behavioral treatment of Raynaud's Disease. *J Behav Med* 1:323–335, 1978.

32. Manuck SB, Kaplan JR, Clarkson TB: Behaviorally induced heart rate reactivity and atherosclerosis in cynomolgus monkeys. *Psychosom Med* 45:95–108, 1983.

33. Kaplan JR, Manuck SB, et al: Social status, environment and atherosclerosis in cynomolgus monkeys. *Arteriosclerosis* 2:359–368, 1982.

34. Bengtsson C: Impairment of physical performance after treatment with beta blockers and alpha blockers. *Brit Med J* 288:671–672, 1984.

22

Psychological and Behavioral Methods to Reduce Cardiovascular Reactivity

ROLF G. JACOB, MARGARET A. CHESNEY

The increasing attention being given to cardiovascular psychophysiological reactivity as a marker, correlate, and potential risk factor for disease has been accompanied by a renewed interest in behavioral strategies for modifying such reactivity. This chapter will review research relevant to the question of whether or not cardiovascular responses to stressors can be modified by behavioral or psychological means. The behavioral techniques that have been studied with respect to their effects on cardiovascular reactivity include cognitive techniques, techniques based on muscular or mental relaxation, and biofeedback techniques.

The use of psychological or behavioral techniques to modify cardiovascular reactivity rests on certain assumptions regarding the nature of the stress response. For each technique the primary assumptions will be discussed and the outcome of research regarding reactivity modification will be reviewed. The studies to be reviewed will include those that (1) have employed a standard laboratory stressor such as aversive stimulation, challenging tasks, or muscular exercise; (2) have measured the response of a cardiovascular parameter such as heart rate or blood pressure to that stressor; (3) have involved a strategy to modify within volitional control of the subject; and (4) have been published in refereed journals. Cognitive approaches to reactivity modification will be presented first, followed by relaxation therapy and biofeedback. We recognize that, in addition to the treatment strategies to be addressed, one effective avenue for reducing reactivity is to avoid, remove, or modify the stressor or aversive stimulus. However, clinical techniques based on this principle, such as assertive training or counseling for life-style changes, are beyond the scope of this chapter.

COGNITIVE APPROACHES

Cognitive approaches to the modification of reactivity are predicated on the assumption that cognitive factors influence cardiovascular responses to aversive stimuli. Specifically, this perspective asserts that the stress response is affected by cognitive appraisal of whether a stimulus is stressful, as well as related cognitions regarding the anticipated magnitude, probability of occurrence, and timing of an aversive stimulus.[1,2] Therefore, to the extent that such cognitive appraisals can be altered, physiological reactivity to stress should be modifiable.

The influence of cognitive appraisal on stress reactivity was initially demonstrated by a series of experiments utilizing a stressful anthropological film depicting a ritual involving genital mutilation or a film depicting industrial accidents. In these early studies, various attitudes based on Freudian defense mechanisms were induced via preparatory messages or via a narrative accompanying the film.[3-5] It was found that a film with a soundtrack emphasizing "intellectualization," "reaction formation," or "denial" resulted in lower heart rate responses to the stressful events in the film than did the same film played without a soundtrack. A reflection of how influential these studies became is the fact that the industrial accident film, *It Did Not Have to Happen*, was employed as a stressor in virtually all subsequent studies that assessed the effects of various treatment strategies on film-induced stress stimuli.

The intellectualizing, reaction-forming, or denying coping styles in the above studies were induced by the experimenters and were not designed to be within the volitional control of the subject. Important for the focus of this chapter, however, are coping techniques that can be employed by the subject for the purpose of self-control. One way to accomplish self-control is to deliberately self-impose a particular attitude toward the stressor. Although the number of such self-imposed attitudes is potentially unlimited, only five techniques have been subjected to research: detachment, redefinition, attentional diversion, focusing of attention, and modification of self-statements.

Detachment as a volitional coping strategy was contrasted with *involvement* for its effects on autonomic responses to stressful scenes in the film *It Did Not Have to Happen* in an early study by Koriat, Melkman, et al.[6] In the detachment condition, subjects were told to "...maintain as much total detachment from [the stressful scene] as you are capable of..." and to be "...as unemotional as possible while watching the disturbing scenes in the movie..." In the "involvement" condition, subjects were asked to allow themselves to become upset at the moving events in the film. In a third, "natural," condition, subjects were merely told that the experiment involved psychophysiological monitoring. Subjects watched the film four times, twice for the purpose of obtaining baseline measurements and then once with each of the two attitudinal sets in counterbalanced order. The investigators found that detachment resulted in significantly lower heart rates during the movie than involvement, particularly in those subjects whose trial involving detachment was scheduled after they had already completed the involvement trial. However, detachment did not result in heart rate responses that were lower than those obtained in the subjects in the natural condition. Thus, this experiment indicated that the self-imposed attitudinal set of involvement could increase cardiovascular reactivity, supporting the assumption that certain cognitive sets can mediate cardiovascular responses to stimuli. However, this experiment did not convincingly demonstrate that detachment could *reduce* cardiovascular reactivity.

Another coping strategy, *redefinition*, was assessed in a study by Holmes and Houston.[7] The redefinition strategy involved asking the subjects to try not to be afraid of threatened electric shocks by thinking about them as "an interesting new type of physiological sensation." Redefinition was contrasted with *isolation*, a coping strategy that appeared to be similar to the detachment strategy employed by Koriat, Melkman, et al.[6] Sixty-four subjects were assigned to four conditions: threat of shock plus redefinition, threat of shock plus isolation, threat of shock without instructions in coping strategies, and no threat. The threat of electric shock was signaled by a light; however, subjects did not actually receive shock. The results of the experiment indicated that both coping strategies (isolation and redefinition) were associated with lower heart rate compared with the threat-only condition. Thus, this study was one of the first to demonstrate that cardiovascular response to stress could be reduced using a cognitive technique.

In a follow-up experiment, Bloom, Houston, et al.[8] compared two strategies, *attentional diversion* or distraction (reading a book), and *redefinition* (writing out reasons why a subject should not be afraid of shock), with a control (no instructions). In the experiment, which involved 192 subjects, the investigators assessed these strategies in the context of threat of shock versus no threat and of high versus low expectancy that the coping strategies would enable them to be calm and relaxed. They found that attentional diversion resulted in a significantly decreased pulse rate compared with both the control and redefinition strategies, whereas redefinition did not reduce pulse rate compared to control. Thus, Bloom and coworkers were not able to replicate the effect of redefinition found in the early study by Holmes and Houston,[7] a discrepancy that the authors attributed to the fact that the threat had been ambiguous in the earlier but not in the latter study. That is, when shock was not actually delivered, redefinition was successful, but redefinition could not overcome the actual experience of shock. Furthermore, the Bloom study did not replicate an earlier study by Houston and Holmes[9] in which it had been found that avoidant thinking, a technique that appeared similar to distraction, actually resulted in an *increase* of heart rate as well as skin resistance. Nonetheless, in the Bloom experiment, attentional diversion emerged as a promising new strategy.

The attentional-diversion strategy was also assessed in a one-session experiment involving the cold pressor test by Grimm and Kanfer.[10] Fifty-eight normal subjects were assigned to one of four different strategies: attentional diversion (thoughts of scenes involving a trip with a friend and planning a party), relaxation, suggestion of decreased pain, and control. It was found that attentional diversion resulted in significantly greater pain tolerance than the other strategies. Furthermore, both attentional diversion and relaxation resulted in decreased heart rate before the second immersion.

Another method of coping with pain stimuli involves *focusing of attention*. In a recent study, Leventhal, Brown and colleagues[11] found that subjects could reduce their subjective experience of distress during a cold pressor test by focusing their attention exclusively on the sensations in the hand immersed in the water. This strategy was more effective than focusing on both the hand and the entire body or focusing on the emotional reactions to the pain. However, Leventhal and coworkers did not assess whether the differences in distress were accompanied by differences in cardiovascular reactivity. More recently, the effect of focusing attention was assessed on the blood pressure response to cold pressor pain in an experiment by Ahles et al.[12] Three cognitive strategies were compared: attention to the sensation in the immersed hand, attention to emotions, and distraction. The earlier findings by Leventhal and coworkers[11] with respect to reducing subjective distress (i.e., that the attention-to-sensation strategy was the most effective) were replicated. No difference among the strategies with respect to blood pressure reactivity was found.

The fifth cognitive technique of altering stress response is *changing self-statements*. This is the primary intervention of the cognitive behavioral tradition initiated by Ellis[13] and Meichenbaum.[14] In this strategy, subjects are taught to identify their appraisals of stimuli that may arouse stress. Through training, these stress-arousing thoughts, labeled "negative self-statements," are replaced with "positive self-statements." For example, a self-statement in anticipation of an event, such as "This is really going to be a pressure-cooker of a meeting," is replaced with "I'm prepared for the meeting and can handle any questions that come my way."

Girodo and Stein[15] compared the effect of changing self-statement with the denial and intellectualization strategy employed by Lazarus and coworkers, employing the film, *It Did Not Have to Happen*, as a stressor. They assigned 40 normal female subjects to one of four conditions: *arousal self-talk*—subjects were taught to emit "16 coping self-statements that focused on internal events"; *film self-talk*—subjects were taught the intellectualization and denial strategies; *information*—subjects were given a description of the film content but no coping strategies; and *no treatment control*. The investigators found that heart rate *increased* in both self-talk groups during a 10-minute waiting period between the intervention and the actual viewing of the film, a finding attributed to the cognitive rehearsal activities in these groups. While the subjects were actually watching the film, however, there were no differences between the strategies with response to heart rate. Thus, changing self-statements failed to reduce cardiovascular reactivity. However, subjective anxiety levels during the film showed treatment effects favoring the two self-talk groups.

Recently the strategy of modifying self-statements was assessed for its effect on reaction to clinical pain. Kaplan and coworkers[16] provided one of four interventions to patients scheduled to undergo a painful electromyographic (EMG) examination: cognitive reappraisal (or restructuring); relaxation; relaxation plus cognitive reappraisal; and attention control (a 15-minute interview by the experimenter). Cognitive reappraisal involved the use of various "positive" self-statements, such as "This does hurt, but I can handle it . . . one step at a time . . . relax." The authors found that subjects in all of the three treatment groups, including cognitive reappraisal, had significantly lower heart rates during the electromyographic examination than the control group. Furthermore, the two relaxation groups had lower mean heart rates than the two groups not receiving relaxation. However, even though heart rate was the lowest in the combined relaxation–cognitive restructuring group, the difference between relaxation only and the relaxation–cognitive restructuring combination was not significant. Thus, Kaplan and coworkers showed that the use of positive self-statements alone was somewhat effective in reducing cardiovascular response to painful stimulation, but not as effective as relaxation.

In summary, it appears that cognitive strategies have shown promise to be able to modify cardiovascular effects of stress, but the results of specific strategies have been inconsistent across studies. However, studies in which these techniques have been employed involved short-term interventions, typically only one session in which instructions were given to engage in one particular coping strategy. Further research would be needed to test these strategies after more extensive training or in combination with other techniques. In particular, the first four strategies (detachment, redefinition, attentional diversion, and narrowing the focus of attention), which have never been developed as comprehensive treatment programs, are candidates for further study in view of their elegance and simplicity.

RELAXATION THERAPY

Relaxation therapy is a collective term for a number of different techniques aimed at accomplishing a state of both physical and mental deactivation. The main methods practiced in the United States are progressive muscular relaxation, meditation, autogenic relaxation, and biofeedback-assisted relaxation. In progressive muscular relaxation, emphasis is primarily on reducing physical tension. Subjects arrive at a state of deep muscular relaxation by going through a series of systematic exercises in which they learn to relax one muscle group at a time by first tensing it and then letting go. This method was developed by Edmund Jacobson in the early decades of this century.[17] Jacobson's technique was quite elaborate and took considerable time to learn. Later, abbreviated programs were developed. For a detailed description of such a program, the reader is referred to a manual by Bernstein and Borkovec.[18]

In meditation, emphasis is on the mental aspects of relaxation. During meditation, subjects direct their attention to a specific mental stimulus, such as a sound or a thought. By subjects' focusing their attention in this manner, meditation should help them to become less aware of their worries and concerns. Meditation is an important component in Eastern religious practices. A meditation technique stripped of such religious connotations is the "relaxation response" treatment derived from transcendental meditation by Beary and Benson.[19] In this method, subjects mentally repeat the word "one" while sitting in a relaxed position.

In autogenic relaxation, emphasis is on both the mental and physical. The subject is asked to meditate on certain phrases, called autogenic phrases. These phrases reflect the physical or mental sensation states experienced during the state of relaxation. Examples of such phrases are "My right arm is heavy," or "Both feet are warm." Autogenic training was developed by Schulz in Europe at about the same time that progressive muscular relaxation was initiated in the United States.[20]

In biofeedback-assisted relaxation, certain physiological variables are measured that covary with the state of relaxation, such as electromyocardiographic activity, skin conductance, the electroencephalogram, or finger temperature. The readings of the variable are displayed prominently to the subject so that the subjects receive feedback of the depth of their relaxation. Biofeedback and biofeedback-assisted relaxation are described in more detail in the final sections of this chapter.

Hemodynamic and Neuroendocrinological Effects of Relaxation Meditation or Biofeedback-Assisted Relaxation: Opposite of Those Induced by Stress?

An assumption or rationale often given for the use of relaxation techniques is that they produce physiological changes that are the opposite of those produced by "stress." Although it is beyond the scope of this chapter to cover all the physiological effects of relaxation or meditation, this section reviews the effects of relaxation or meditation on certain hemodynamic and neuroendocrinological variables of interest to the stress response for the purpose of providing an extra perspective for understanding the effects of these techniques on cardiovascular reactivity. With two exceptions, the hemodynamic or endocrinologic studies of this section did not employ laboratory stressors. Following this section, the research on the effect of relaxation and meditation on actual cardiovascular stress responses is reviewed.

The hemodynamic effects of autogenic relaxation were assessed via invasive techniques by Lantzsch and Drunkenmolle[21] in 10 hypertensive patients. There was a decrease in cardiac output and stroke volume but an increase in total peripheral resistance. However, in an earlier study with normotensive persons, autogenic training was associated with the opposite pattern: an increase in cardiac output and stroke volume but a decrease in peripheral resistance. Thus, the effects of relaxation differed depending on the hypertensive state of the subject.

Davidson, Winchester, and coworkers[22] fluoroscopically determined various parameters of ventricular function in six cardiac patients with implanted metallic markers before, during, and after a session of progressive muscular relaxation. They found a decrease in cardiac circumferential shortening velocity and ejection fraction and an increase in end-systolic volume. Cardiac output and stroke volume decreased, but not significantly. The investigators also determined catecholamine levels before and during relaxation. Plasma norepinephrine levels decreased during relaxation in five of the six patients; these changes in plasma norepinephrine correlated with changes in both heart rate and systolic pressure.

Messerli, Decarvalho, and coworkers[23] studied hemodynamic parameters in 11 borderline hypertensive patients receiving blood pressure feedback. Subjects were taught either to increase or to decrease diastolic pressure during different periods in the same session. The total treatment lasted from 7 to 10 sessions. It was found that within-session changes of blood pressure were associated primarily with changes in cardiac output, while peripheral resistance and stroke volume remained constant. Across sessions, on the other hand, changes of blood pressure were associated primarily with changes in total peripheral resistance, while cardiac output and stroke volume remained constant. Thus, it appears that the within-session, or acute, effects of blood pressure feedback may be different from its long-term effects across sessions.

In addition to the effects of relaxation on hemodynamic parameters and catecholamines, the adrenocortical hormones have been studied. In an uncontrolled study, DeGood and Redgate[24] assessed the effects of eight weekly EMG feedback training sessions in 24 volunteers who differed in self-report measures of anxiety. They found a significant decline of cortisol levels across sessions, but only in subjects scoring above the median on anxiety. Furthermore, changes in cortisol levels covaried with changes in heart rate and vasoconstriction.

In a controlled outcome study, McGrady, Yonker, and coworkers[25] studied the effect of eight weeks of EMG biofeedback-assisted relaxation in 43 hypertensive patients, 25 of whom had been randomly assigned to relaxation treatment and 18 to control. A battery of biochemical tests, including cortisol, aldosterone, renin, and 24-hour urinary excretion of cortisol, catecholamines, and vanillylmandelic acid (VMA) was obtained before and after treatment. Urinary cortisol excretion and plasma aldosterone significantly differentiated treatment from control subjects; both these substances decreased more in the treatment group than in the control group. Furthermore, plasma cortisol levels decreased somewhat in the treatment group but increased in the control group; the difference between the groups was marginally significant. No differences were found in plasma renin activity and urinary excretion of catecholamines or VMA.

Plasma renin levels and aldosterone were also examined in a large-scale study utilizing biofeedback-assisted relaxation by Patel, Marmot, and Terry.[26]

It was found that both renin and aldosterone levels decreased significantly more in the treatment group than in the control group. Furthermore, changes in aldosterone (but not renin) correlated with changes in blood pressure.

In summary, most studies on progressive muscular relaxation, autogenic training, and biofeedback-assisted relaxation show at least some hemodynamic or hormonal changes that appear to be the opposite of those expected from stress. However, the effects on specific physiological variables seem to vary and may depend on subject characteristics or whether acute or long-term changes are being assessed.

Studies on meditation techniques provide a less consistent picture, with some studies even showing changes that could be considered indicative of *increased* stress. For example, with respect to hemodynamic changes, Jevning, Wilson, and coworkers[27] compared experienced meditators engaging in meditation with controls engaging in rest. They found a small *increase* in cardiac output and an increase in nonrenal, nonhepatic blood flow during meditation. By contrast, hepatic blood flow decreased. The authors speculated that meditation might be conducive to hemodynamic changes aimed at increasing cerebral blood flow or skin blood flow.

Contradictory results have also been obtained with respect to cortisol. Jevning and coworkers[28] assessed cortisol and testosterone levels in experienced meditators, nonmeditators, and the same nonmeditators after they had undergone three or four months of training in transcendental meditation. Blood samples were obtained before, during, and after a subject had engaged in a session of meditation; nonmeditators merely rested. For the experienced meditators there was a decline of cortisol during meditation, whereas for the nonmeditators and for the nonmeditators examined after three months of meditation practice, there was no change. In a similar study, however, Michaels, Parra, and coworkers[29] obtained no significant differences when they compared cortisol levels in meditators and controls before, during, and after meditation.

With respect to plasma renin levels, Stone and DeLeo[30] studied the effect of a six-month course of meditation on supine, standing, and furosemide-stimulated renin levels in hypertensive patients. Although the treatment group did show a decline in furosemide-stimulated renin levels, no changes were obtained in the unstimulated standing or supine levels, a finding that contrasts with those obtained with biofeedback-assisted relaxation in the study by Patel and coworkers[26] described earlier. Furthermore, no changes in renin levels were obtained in two additional meditation studies with hypertensives.[31,32]

Catecholamine changes obtained with meditation appear to contradict the notion that meditation can reduce the effect of stress, at least to a larger degree than could be accomplished by mere rest. Michaels and coworkers[33] studied catecholamine changes while subjects were engaging in transcendental meditations, obtaining blood samples from experienced meditators and resting nonmeditators before, during, and after a session. The investigators found no differences between meditators and controls and therefore concluded that, with respect to catecholamine levels, the meditative state did not differ from ordinary rest.

Lang, Dehof, and coworkers[34] studied catecholamines before and after rest, meditation, and physical exercise in meditators in an experiment comparing 10 advanced meditators with 10 somewhat less experienced meditators who, however, still had several years of meditation experience. The core experiment consisted of a sequence involving 30 minutes of supine rest, followed by an initial 3-minute supine bicycle ergometer test, 30 minutes of meditation versus sitting/reading, and a final 3-minute exercise test. Thus, meditation or sitting was always preceded by an initial exercise test, and the final exercise test was preceded either by 30 minutes of meditation or by 30 minutes of sitting/reading. The results are complex because the advanced and less experienced meditators differed in their responses. After completion of meditation, the advanced meditators *increased* their norepinephrine levels by almost 100 percent, whereas the less experienced meditators showed no significant changes. In the advanced meditators, norepinephrine levels were even higher after meditation than after the postmeditation exercise test. Conversely, the less experienced meditators displayed lower levels of norepinephrine after meditation than after the subsequent exercise test. Exercise heart rate and blood pressure changes paralleled the changes in catecholamines. Advanced meditators displayed higher exercise heart rates after meditation than after reading, whereas the less experienced meditators showed no clear effect due to preexercise activity. These results could imply that in advanced meditators, meditation had arousing effects, that is, effects similar to those of a challenging task. The interpretation that meditation can result in increased arousal would be consistent with findings by Corby, Roth, and coworkers,[35] who found significant degrees of physiological activation in expert meditators of the Ananda Marga school. As an example, they presented a recording of physiological parameters during a "near samadhi" event, or moment of profound religious experience, during which heart rate increased to more than 120 beats per minute.

A final study examining catecholamines during meditation was conducted by Hoffman, Benson, and coworkers.[36] Subjects with no prior experience in meditation were assigned to a treatment and a delayed treatment group. The treatment involved meditation twice daily for 30 days. A graded isometric handgrip test was performed before and after treatment, and during the corresponding time period for the controls. It was found that during the posttreatment test period norepinephrine levels were significantly higher than during the pretreatment test in the meditation group, whereas norepinephrine levels remained essentially stable in the delayed treatment group. Furthermore, after the latter subjects had undergone the meditation program, a similar increase in norepinephrine was observed. Heart rate and blood pressure, however, showed no effect of treatment. Because the increased norepinephrine levels after meditation were not associated with changes in heart rate or blood pressure, the authors concluded that one effect of the meditation program was to alter the receptor sensitivity to catecholamines. The lack of correspondence between norepinephrine levels and cardiovascular parameters may, of course, have other explanations, such as differences in accuracy in the measurement of the hormonal and cardiovascular parameters.

Another interpretation of the results obtained by Hoffman and coworkers and by Lang and coworkers is that some forms of meditation produce activating changes similar to those induced by a challenging task. One explanation for this activation could be that in the testing situation meditators are challenged to "prove" that they have mastered the technique and that they have achieved a unique state of consciousness. Consequently, they are victims of performance anxiety. Another explanation is that some meditative techniques require prolonged postural immobility, which could become painful or require effort to maintain. A third explanation is that different meditation techniques have different objectives. Certain "spiritually" oriented techniques that aim to produce religious experiences[e.g.,35] may require an amount of mental efforts, for example, focusing on a complex "mantra" (specific imaginal word or sound), equivalent to the effort required by mental arithmetic. A final explanation is that meditation results in an increased physiological flexibility, a "fine-tuning" of the system, leading to an increased ability to meet various demands. Therefore, in stressful situation, meditation would facilitate the emergence of the endocrinological or hemodynamic changes that are optimal for effort and coping.

Relaxation, Meditation, and Cardiovascular Reactivity to Stress

After the preliminary discussions of the physiological effects of meditation and relaxation and biofeedback-assisted relaxation of the preceding section, we now review the evidence on whether these procedures can reduce cardiovascular reactivity. We limit the discussion to meditation and relaxation and some biofeedback-assisted relaxation for the biofeedback section concluding this chapter.

Of the basic relaxation or meditation techniques, progressive muscular relaxation and meditation are the two relaxation techniques that have been most studied with respect to their effects on cardiovascular reactivity.

Autogenic training has been assessed primarily for its effect on skin temperature during exposure to cool ambient temperatures.[37,38] Since this stressor is idiosyncratic for patients with Raynaud's disease, we will not discuss these studies here.

The early experiments assessing the effects of relaxation with laboratory stressors involved progressive muscular relaxation.[39–42] These studies were a consequence of general interest in modifying anxiety responses in a "counterconditioning" paradigm, an interest that had been prompted by the clinical successes of systematic desensitization as developed by Wolpe.[43] Most of these studies were interested primarily in galvanic skin responses. e.g.,[40] In some of these studies, heart rate reactivity was also determined.

Perhaps the most influential early studies were conducted by Paul[41] and Paul and Trimble.[42] These studies had subjects imagine scenes that induced anxiety as a "stressor" and assessed the effect of treatment via a composite physiological lability score, calculated as an individually weighted average of heart rate, electromyographic tension levels, and skin conductance. Unfortunately, the use of such lability scores precludes the assessment of heart rate reactivity per se in these studies. Briefly, these studies found that progressive relaxation and hypnotic relaxation both resulted in a reduction of lability scores compared with self-relaxation control. Furthermore, relaxation sessions conducted by a therapist were more effective than tape-recorded relaxation instructions.

A less frequently cited study by Folkins, Lawson, and coworkers[39] that used a portion of the industrial accident film, *It Did Not Have to Happen*, as a stressor obtained negative results. One hundred nine subjects were assigned to one of four groups: control (taped instruction in "how to improve your study habits"); taped relaxation training; cognitive rehearsal (imagining this accident scene in the film); and desensitization (cognitive rehearsal plus relaxation). The treatments extended over three sessions. Analysis of the results was complicated by the fact that differences in baseline (prefilm) autonomic levels developed. Results indicated that the cognitive rehearsal group showed the lowest and the control group showed the highest skin conductance reactivity. The reactivity differences were not significant, however, for scores adjusted for baseline differences. Heart rate showed a rather surprising pattern: relaxation was associated with the highest and control with the lowest heart rates in response to the accident film; however, the differences were not statistically significant. The results were explained by the hypothesis that the film and the relaxation exercise were competing for the subjects' attention, resulting in the type of heart rate acceleration often found in situations calling for "sensory rejection."

Another rather early study on relaxation was conducted by Lehrer,[44] who assessed four treatment conditions: relaxation, increased muscle tension, unchanged muscle tension, and no instructions. He found that, as expected, heart rate increased in the increased-tension group and decreased in the relaxation group. However, heart rate also decreased in the unchanged-tension group. Thus, relaxation failed to produce unique reductions in cardiovascular reactivity compared with unchanged tension. The author speculated that the fact that the relaxation instructions were taped or the brevity of the intervention accounted for the latter null effect.

Therefore, in a subsequent study, Lehrer extended the duration of training to four sessions over a four-week period.[45] Furthermore, he assessed the effects of treatment both in normal subjects and in patients suffering from anxiety neurosis. A second group of normal subjects also received alpha feedback training; the findings concerning this technique will be presented later in the section on biofeedback. The stressors consisted of a reaction-time task and representation of a series of loud noise bursts. The results indicated that in the anxiety-disordered patients relaxation was associated with a reduction of cardiac accelerative responses to both the noise bursts and reaction-time tasks, whereas in the normal subjects relaxation did not result in a decrease in reactivity.

The studies reviewed so far have involved progressive muscular relaxation. The first study to evaluate the effect of meditation on cardiovascular reactivity was conducted by Goleman and Schwartz.[46] These investigators compared experienced meditators and nonmeditators in the following three experimental conditions: meditation, self-relaxation with eyes open, and self-relaxation with eyes closed. The subjects engaged in their assigned activity for a period of 20 minutes. Before and after this period, they watched the stressful film, *It Did Not Have to Happen*. The authors found that, within the meditation condition, experienced meditators had a significantly more rapid postaccident heart rate *recovery* than nonmeditators, although while viewing the accidents, meditators actually had the highest heart rates. Experienced meditators also had a more rapid recovery than those meditators who had been assigned to the self-relaxation conditions. Goleman and Schwartz discussed these results in terms of the "increased physiological flexibility" noted previously. They argued that experienced meditators, by showing the increases in heart rate necessary for effective response to stress and then showing a more rapid recovery following stress, were more optimally suited to cope with stress than the nonmeditators.

Meditation has also been examined for its effect on reactivity to the cold pressor test. Mills and Farrow[47] examined the effects of this test in experienced meditators and controls. Two cold pressor tests were separated by 20 minutes of meditation (meditators) or self-relaxation (controls), self-relaxation involving "relaxation" without specific instructions. The results indicated that although the meditators reported a greater reduction of subjective distress during the second test, there were no objective differences between the groups in heart rate reactivity.

Besides film and cold pressor stress, meditation has also been tested for its effect on dynamic and static muscular exercise. Recall that two studies concerning muscular exercise[34,36] discussed in the preceding section essentially had obtained negative results. In a third study, Benson and coworkers[48] assessed heart rate and oxygen consumption in eight meditators with six months experience during a submaximal bicycle ergometer test in steady-state conditions. After warm-up, a 10-minute nonmeditation period was scheduled followed by a 10-minute meditation period and another 10-minute nonmeditation period. While there was no decrease in heart rate, there was a significant decrease of oxygen consumption during meditation. A fourth study was recently conducted by Gervino and Veazey[49] in which 11 sedentary normal females were first trained in relaxation response meditation for four to five weeks and then tested in one submaximal exercise test session during which they either meditated or did not meditate in eight-minute periods following an *ABAB* design. Results indicated that systolic pressure and oxygen consumption product declined significantly during meditation periods. Heart rate showed no statistically significant changes, although the pattern was similar to that of blood pressure and oxygen consumption.

Meditation and relaxation were compared in a study by Lehrer, Schoickett, and coworkers in which burst of light and noise served as the stressor.[50] Thirty-four subjects, none of whom had had prior experience with meditation or relaxation, were assigned to meditation, progressive muscular relaxation, or a no-treatment control condition. The training involved four sessions over four weeks and daily home practice. It was found that treatment had no effect on cardiac accelerative responses to stress. Given the essentially negative results of the above Lehrer study[50] and the earlier research showing that subject variables such as anxiety proneness might influence the effect of treatment, Lehrer, Woolfolk, and coworkers[51] replicated the above study in subjects with higher-than-average scores on an anxiety inventory. In addition to noise stress, they employed the film, *It Did Not Have to Happen*, as a stressor. The results were very similar to the earlier experiment: there were no differences between relaxation and meditation with respect to cardiac acceleration in response to stress. Furthermore, neither treatment resulted in decreased reactivity. Thus, even with these more "abnormal" subjects, neither meditation nor relaxation resulted in decreased cardiovascular reactivity.

A final study comparing relaxation with meditation was performed by Kirsch and Henry,[52] utilizing speech-anxious subjects. Pulse rate was measured before a four-minute speech test. This study compared two self-administered desensitization programs with meditation only and no treatment. All three treatments included coping skills instructions. One of the two desensitization conditions involved pairing fear imagery with progressive muscular relaxation; the other involved pairing fear imagery with relaxation response meditation. It was found that, although only the desensitization/progressive muscular relaxation condition showed a significant reduction in anticipatory pulse rate, the difference in reactivity reduction between the muscular relaxation and meditation groups was not significant. Furthermore, greater pulse rate reductions occurred in subjects who rated treatment as highly credible; the correlation between credibility ratings and pulse rate change was 0.45, $p < 0.02$.

With the exception of the Kirsch and Henry studies and the studies involving exercise stress, the research reviewed so far essentially involved reactivity to "passive" stressors. Another class of stressors involves challenging tasks that require an active response by the subject, such as mental arithmetic or reaction-time tasks. Wilson and Wilson[53] assessed the effects of 15 minutes of progressive muscular relaxation on inhibiting cardiovascular response to an active task, paired-associate learning. Investigators included two control groups, one in which subjects relaxed without specific relaxation instruction and one in which subjects engaged in handgrip tension. The 63 subjects were characterized by either high, medium, or low anxiety. The investigators found that, for the highly anxious subjects only, heart rate was significantly reduced with muscle relaxation. No differences were found between the three conditions in the medium and low anxiety groups.

Boswell and Murry[54] performed a study involving a mental arithmetic task and a difficult college-level IQ test. They assigned subjects to one of four groups matched for anxiety levels: progressive muscular relaxation, meditation, no-treatment control, and a second control procedure, antimeditation, which involved walking briskly while concentration on problems. The treatments involved daily practice for two weeks. The results of this study were negative: the investigators could not find any evidence for a treatment effect on heart rate response during stress.

Jorgensen and coworkers[55] assessed the effects of anxiety management training in the treatment of hypertension with 18 hypertensive subjects in a study involving an immediate- versus delayed-treatment design in which 10 subjects received treatment immediately and 8 subjects received treatment approximately six weeks later. Anxiety management training involved sessions of deep-muscle relaxation and imaginal rehearsal of anxiety-producing scenes. Subjects were then taught to use relaxation to counteract the effects of anxiety in their everyday life. The effect of treatment was assessed with respect to blood pressure responses to the Stroop task, which required subjects to respond to conflicting written and color cues under time pressure.

Results indicated, surprisingly, that systolic pressure during the Stroop task declined significantly *less* from pretreatment to posttreatment in the immediate-treatment group than in the delayed-treatment group. Subjects in the latter group also had significantly quicker poststress recovery of systolic and diastolic pressure. Thus, the treatment surprisingly was associated with a relative *increase* of stress response. However, as expected, resting blood pressures declined significantly more in the immediate-treatment group than in the delayed-treatment group. Therefore, the authors speculated that the increase in reactivity to stress in the treatment group might have been related to performance anxiety.

Few studies have been conducted that assessed whether or not treatments would have differential effects on reactivity to different kinds of stressors. Three studies described earlier included two stressors: Lehrer[45] included both reaction time and noise; Lehrer, Schoickett, and coworkers,[50] noise and light; and Lehrer, Woolfolk, and coworkers,[51] noise and an industrial-accident film. In none of these studies was heart rate reactivity affected in differential fashion. English and Baker[56] employed a reaction-time task and the cold pressor test to compare the effects of four weeks of meditation, relaxation, or waiting-list control on heart rate and blood pressure reactivity. The authors found no effect of treatment on heart rate reactivity; however, blood pressure reactivity was differentially affected. The control group had significantly higher tonic blood pressure levels than either the relaxation or meditation group during both stressors. Furthermore, diastolic stress change scores from pretreatment and posttreatment were significantly more reduced in the two treatment groups than in the control group for either stressor. Thus, both treatments resulted in lower blood pressure reactivity in both tasks. Although in general there were no differences between these two treatments, progressive relaxation appeared to be associated with a somewhat smaller response of systolic pressure to the reaction time task.

None of the above studies has examined the effect of relaxation or meditation independent of instruction or expectation effects, defined as the consequences of merely believing that a specific change will occur. Since expectation effects can affect resting levels of blood pressure,[57,58] it is important to sort out whether reduction of cardiovascular reactivity was produced by the treatment technique per se or merely by the subject's believing in the treatment, expecting the treatment to work. A study by Puente and Beiman[59] led to the conclusion that most of the treatment effects associated with meditation or relaxation were attributable to expectation effects. These investigators compared the effects of cognitive restructuring plus progressive relaxation, transcendental meditation, relaxation response meditation, and waiting list control on the cardiovascular response to slides depicting medical surgical scenes. Sixty subjects with complaints of nervous tenseness were employed. The authors assumed that subjects in the relaxation response meditation condition would have a higher expectation that the treatment would reduce cardiovascular reactivity to stress than would subjects in the transcendental meditation condition. The treatments involved between six and seven 1.5-hour sessions extending over 2 to 3.5 weeks. Results showed that only the relaxation response and progressive muscular relaxation/cognitive restructuring lead to an attenuation of heart rate response to the stressful slides. Furthermore, these two techniques were more effective than transcendental meditation and delayed treatment. Thus, this study surprisingly found a difference between the effects of relaxation response and transcendental meditation. According to the authors, these two virtually identical treatments differed mainly in the expectancy for reducing cardiovascular reactivity. Therefore, the authors concluded that the results would be explained best by differences in expectancies induced by the different treatments. However, this interpretation appears to have the benefit of hindsight, because expectancy was not manipulated experimentally.

An experimental study on the effect of expectancy was conducted by Bradley and McCanne,[60] who used the industrial accident film, *It Did Not Have to Happen*. Subjects were assigned to meditation, progressive muscular relaxation, and no treatment; within these groups, subjects were led to expect either a positive or negative outcome with respect to reducing cardiovascular reactivity by providing either a favorable or unfavorable treatment introduction. The experiment extended over four sessions. The investigators found that subjects in the meditation/positive-expectancy group exhibited the lowest heart rates during the accidents in the film. Furthermore, as the film progressed, negative-expectancy subjects had consistently higher heart rates than positive-expectancy subjects, regardless of treatment. There were no differences between meditation and relaxation within positive- or negative-expectancy conditions. Thus, the study strongly pointed toward the importance of expectancy effects in cardiovascular reactivity to stress.

Taken together, the results of the studies described in this section are rather inconsistent. Some studies found that either meditation or relaxation or both reduced cardiovascular reactivity; other studies did not. Studies with positive results often employed abnormal subjects. No study has demonstrated clinically significant differences between relaxation and meditation. Research is only beginning to investigate the specific effects of meditation or relaxation as opposed to the effects of instructions or expectations. In fact, only one study[60] experimentally addressed this question

Since this study indicated that expectation effects may be a highly significant factor, further research should explore whether relaxation or meditation can have specific effects that are independent of the effect of expectation.

Further research is also needed to document the extent to which relaxation-based approaches are operating directly by reducing physiological arousal, as opposed to indirectly by changing cognitive factors. It may be, as the expectancy data suggest, that relaxation provides subjects with the perception that they have a skill that makes them less vulnerable to stress. This perception may alter their appraisal of stimuli as stressful and reduce their anticipation of potential stress and its adverse effects.

BIOFEEDBACK

Biofeedback was developed in the early 1960s to help subjects gain control over specific physiological responses, including cardiovascular parameters.[61-66] Biofeedback involves the measurement of a physiological variable using electrophysiological procedures; the visual, auditory, or tactile display of the current level of or changes in this variable to the subject; and instructions to change the parameter in a desired direction. By means of the amplification and display of the physiological signal by the biofeedback instrument, a subject can detect even small changes, which he or she then can employ to gain increased control.

The application of biofeedback to modify cardiovascular reactivity is based on the assumption that after learning physiological control, subjects can use this skill to reduce their cardiovascular reactivity despite exposure to stressful stimuli. Biofeedback can be employed in two ways to reduce reactivity. First, it can be employed to modify directly a cardiovascular variable, such as heart rate, blood pressure, or pulse transit time. Second, as mentioned earlier, feedback can be employed to facilitate the development of a relaxed state, which then can serve to modify the response to stress. The first approach involves direct feedback of a cardiovascular parameter. The second approach involves feedback of a parameter that covaries with a state of relaxation, such as the electromyogram, the EEG, skin conductance, or finger temperature.

Direct Cardiovascular Feedback

Direct cardiovascular feedback can involve feedback of heart rate, pulse transit time, or blood pressure. Of these modalities, heart rate feedback is by far the most studied, whereas we know of no study concerning the effect of blood pressure feedback on cardiovascular reactivity published in refereed journals. We will first consider studies on heart rate feedback and then proceed to studies on pulse transit time. The heart rate feedback studies can conveniently be subdivided into early and late studies, because of the differences in their complexity and results. Two special applications involve the use of heart rate feedback during exercise and in patients with anxiety disorders.

Early Heart Rate Feedback Studies (1974 to 1977). In 1974 Sirota and coworkers,[67] as well as Williams and Adkins,[68] independently published studies demonstrating the control of heart rate during aversive conditions. In the study by Sirota and coworkers, 20 female subjects received heart rate feedback during one session consisting of 72 15-second trial periods. Half of the subjects received feedback to decrease and half to increase heart rate. At the end of half of the trials, a two-second electric shock was delivered to the forearm. Shock and no-shock trials were signaled by different colored lights. The investigators found that during the course of the experiment, average heart rate levels gradually decreased to a final reduction by 10 to 12 beats per minute in the group receiving feedback to decrease heart rate. This decrease was maintained during the final 24 no-feedback trials. Heart rate increased slightly in the group receiving feedback to increase heart rate, but the increase was less than two beats per minute in most of the trials. In addition to changes in the tonic or average heart rate levels, changes also occurred in the phasic or reactive heart rate responses to the stressor. In the group receiving feedback to decrease heart rate, heart rate fell during both shock and no-shock trials, whereas in the group receiving feedback to increase heart rate, heart rate increased in anticipation of the shock. Thus, the study demonstrated that heart rate response in anticipation of shock could be changed in the direction of feedback. The basic comparison of feedback to increase versus feedback to decrease heart rate was repeated in a second study by Sirota and coworkers,[69] with the main modification that all the subjects were exposed to both feedback to increase and feedback to decrease heart rate. This experiment essentially replicated the results of the earlier study.

The Williams and Adkins study[68] was the other early study assessing the effect of heart rate feedback on heart rate reactivity to stress. Eight male undergraduates first underwent two 20-minute training sessions, during each of which they received feedback alternatively to increase and decrease their heart rates. During a third session they first received anxiety-conditioning trials in which presentation of a red light was paired with electric shock. During subsequent heart rate feedback trials, subjects could prevent the occurrence of electric shock by emitting the appropriate heart rate response. Thus, shock served both as a stressor and as a reinforcer. The investigators found that the heart rate increase due to threat of shock was attentuated when subjects received feedback to decrease heart rate, whereas it was increased even further with feedback to increase heart rate.

DeGood and Adams[70] conducted an experiment comparing the effect of feedback to increase heart rate with progressive muscular relaxation and soothing music, both of the latter procedures being combined with instructions to lower heart rate. The stressor consisted of a stimulus classically conditioned to electric shock, as well as the shock itself. The investigators found that feedback subjects were the most successful in reducing heart rate responses during aversive trials. Furthermore, heart rate levels declined the most from pretraining to posttraining aversive trials in the biofeedback group.

Later Heart Rate Feedback Studies (1978 to 1984). After the publication of the studies described in the preceding section, a number of others were conducted, representing replications with other types of stressors or methodological refinements. As we will see, the later studies have not been able to show strong effects of biofeedback in attenuating cardiovascular reactivity. Magnusson and coworkers[71] assessed the effects of two sessions of training to either increase or decrease heart rate in 20 undergraduate students. They found that during the acquisition or training phase, feedback to decrease heart rate resulted in a reduction of heart rate by approximately five beats per minute; feedback to increase heart rate, however, was not successful. The acquisition phase was followed by a test phase in which the subjects expected and received electric shock. During threat of shock, heart rate levels remained about five beats per minute lower in the decrease condition than in the increase condition. However, there were no differences in stress-induced heart rate changes between the groups. Thus, the study did not show that heart rate reactivity was influenced by the treatments.

Negative results were also obtained in two studies on feedback to decrease heart rate. In the first of these,[72] Malcuit and Beaudry compared the following three treatments in subjects who had completed a mental arithmetic task at the beginning of 10 trials: feedback, instructions only, and self-relaxation (i.e., relaxation without explicit instructions). Results indicated no heart rate differences between the treatment conditions either during the poststress training trials or during the mental arithmetic task itself. Thus, this study did not demonstrate that poststress cardiovascular reactivity could be affected by heart rate feedback.

The second study,[73] conducted by Bouchard and Labelle, included measurements of both heart rate and blood pressure reactivity. Furthermore, the feedback time, a total of 60 minutes distributed over four sessions (i.e., five three-minute trials per session) was longer than in most other studies. Subjects were assigned to groups receiving feedback to decrease heart rate or instructions only. Ischemic arm pain was used as the stressor. Results indicated that during acquisition, no voluntary control was achieved by feedback compared to instructions only. Furthermore, there was no differential response to stress on either heart rate or blood pressure.

Thus, these latter heart rate feedback studies did not confirm the treatment effects found in the earlier studies. In particular, in studies that did not include a condition to increase heart rate as a contrast, the effect of feedback to decrease heart rate appeared not to be reliable.

Another question assessed in later studies was whether the effect demonstrated in the earlier studies was due specifically to the feedback component of treatment or due to the effect of instructions alone. Experiments addressing the effect of feedback as separate from that of instructions only typically involved several groups in which feedback versus no feedback and instructions to increase versus decrease heart rate were manipulated in factorial designs. Victor and others[74] performed one of the first studies of this kind. The stressor in this study involved the cold pressor test. Forty-five young male subjects were assigned to one of five groups: feedback to increase heart rate, feedback to decrease heart rate, instructions to increase heart rate, instructions to decrease heart rate, and habituation control. Members of the feedback groups received 25 30-second training trials to change heart rate in the instructed direction, followed by five control trials in which feedback was withdrawn. Members of the no-feedback groups read magazines during the time corresponding to the 25 conditioning trials and were instructed to increase or decrease their heart rates during the five control trials. Members of the habituation control group also read magazines but received no instructions. The training and control trials were preceded and followed by a 30-second cold pressor test. During the second cold pressor test, no feedback was provided, but the subjects were instructed to increase or decrease heart rate and were rewarded for heart rate changes in the assigned direction. The investigators found that all the members of the feedback-to-increase group increased their heart rates from the first to second cold pressor test, while seven of the nine feedback-to-decrease subjects decreased their heart rates. No consistent trends were seen in the instructions only or habituations groups. No statistical comparisons were reported for the feedback versus instruction conditions within the decrease or increase groups. However, on the whole, the study was somewhat supportive of the conclusion that feedback to decrease heart rate, but not instructions alone, could ameliorate cardiovascular response to stress.

An issue always confronting controlled research designs is to develop control conditions that are as engaging, involving, and plausible as treatments. For example, the no-feedback conditions in the above study by Victor and coworkers may have been less interesting than those that involved feedback and may have provided less involvement or reward for the subjects. A study in which the subjects appeared to have a more nearly equal degree of involvement with treatment was conducted by Reeves and Shapiro.[75] In this study, instructions to increase or decrease heart rate were combined with feedback to increase or decrease heart rate in a factorial design. Thus, in two groups, feedback and instructions were consistent, whereas in two of the groups, instructions and feedback were inconsistent. For example, one inconsistent group received instructions to increase heart rate, while the feedback procedure was arranged such that reward was given for decreasing heart rates. The investigators found that during training, only the group instructed to increase and given veridical feedback to increases in heart rate showed significant changes in the expected direction. However, no reliable effects were obtained for either of the decrease conditions. Thus, during the training phase, subjects were unable to decrease their heart rates. Comparing pretreatment to posttreatment cold pressor responses, instructions to decrease produced an attenuation of the heart rate response, regardless of whether the feedback had been veridical or inconsistent. That is, the subjects that had been instructed to decrease but given feedback to increase their heart rates also showed an attenuation of their heart rate responses. Thus, these experiments did not obtain an effect from feedback that was significantly superior to the effect of instructions alone.

To assess whether instructions are a necessary condition for reduced reactivity, Reeves and Shapiro in a more recent study[76] administered a cold pressor test to subjects who had undergone either biofeedback to increase or biofeedback to decrease their heart rates. However, in contrast to earlier studies, the subjects were given no instructions to change their heart rates during the second cold pressor test. The investigators found no difference in heart rate reactions between the two groups. Thus, when the subjects were not instructed to change their heart rates during the stress tests, no alterations of heart rate occurred, indicating that the effect of biofeedback did not generalize automatically without conscious effort.

The results of a study by McCanne[77] also do not support the notion that feedback per se is the important variable in the control of heart rate reactivity. The design in this study was essentially the same five-group design as in the Victor study,[74] the difference being that the industrial accident film, *It Did Not Have to Happen*, served as a stressor. The surprising finding in this study was that both the subjects who had received feedback to increase their heart rates and those who had received feedback to decrease their heart rates exhibited lower heart rates during the post treatment viewing of the film compared with the pretreatment viewing. The instructions-only group showed no changes, and the control group manifested heart rate increases. To reiterate, heart rate decreased even in subjects who had received feedback to increase their heart rates. There were statistically significant correlations between self-report of ability to control heart rate and decline of heart rate in response to accidents within the posttreatment film. The author concluded that these results were consistent with an interpretation that it was the perception of control and not biofeedback that produced the attenuation of heart rate reactivity to stress.

Besides feedback and instructions, the effects of reward have been considered as possible confounding factors. In a complex factorial design involving 180 subjects, Bennett and coworkers[78] assessed the effects of instructions to increase versus to decrease heart rate, feedback versus no feedback, and reward versus no reward. The reward was money (up to $5) for correct performance. A ninth group, no-treatment control, was also included. It was found that during the training trials, instructions to increase heart rate were associated with significantly higher heart rates than instructions to decrease heart rate or no treatment. However, the decrease instructions and no-treatment control conditions did not seem to differ signficantly. Furthermore, in the increase conditions only, there was a significant reward effect. There was no significant effect, however, of the feedback factor. Thus, during the acquisition phase, instructions and reward to increase heart rate seemed to account for most of the treatment effect. During a second phase of the experiment, those subjects who had received decrease instructions or no treatment received a stress test involving threat of electric shock. The results of this phase were essentially negative: no effect of feedback training or reward was found. Thus, this study did not demonstrate that cardiovascular reactivity could be reduced by any of the feedback conditions studied.

In a final study to be reviewed here, Carroll and Evans[79] evaluated the effects of expectations by adding two false-feedback groups in addition to the usual instructions and feedback to increase or decrease heart rate. The false-feedback procedure was arranged such that subjects in one group were lead to believe that their heart rates increased, and subjects in another group that their heart rates decreased. Subjects in these two groups were not given explicit instructions to change their heart rates. Thus, these false-feedback conditions could serve as controls for expectation effects separate from the effect of instructions. Loud noise was employed as the stressor; this stressor was delivered at each of the 12 trials. The investigators found that in the instructions-to-decrease groups, heart rate declined by 4.2 beats per minute for feedback and 4.9 beats per minute for instructions only. In the instructions-to-increase groups, heart rate increased by 1.8 beats per minute with feedback and decreased by 2.4 beats per minute with instructions only, respectively. With false feedback, the heart rate decreased by 1.6 beats per minute with information that heart rate was increasing and by 2.9 beats per minute with information that the heart rate was decreasing. Only the difference between the two biofeedback groups was statistically significant (i.e., feedback to increase versus feedback to decrease). However, within a given instruction condition, there was no significant difference between feedback and no feedback, with the heart rate changes appearing particularly close in the decrease conditions. Apparently, there was no effect of the expectations induced by false feedback.

Comparing the results of the early heart rate feedback studies described in the preceding section with those of the later studies of this section, an interesting pattern emerges. While the earlier studies showed beneficial effects of feedback, the later studies did not find a positive effect of feedback that was specifically independent of expectations or instructions. Thus, like relaxation, the assumption that biofeedback produces a direct reduction of cardiovascular reactivity is not consistently confirmed by these studies. Rather, biofeedback may in some cases be modifying appraisal stress.

It may also be that certain groups of individuals are particularly responsive to the ameliorative influence of relaxation or biofeedback. Particularly suitable candidates for behavioral treatment may include those individuals who show heightened physiological reactivity or who are characterized by a high level of anxiety. For example, Lott and Gatchel[80] found that high cold pressor reactors could produce larger heart rate changes with feedback than could low cold pressor reactors. In the following section, we describe the use of heart rate feedback in another group of subjects likely to be hyperresponsive to certain stressors: those with anxiety disorders.

Heart Rate Feedback with Anxious Subjects

Two series of studies have been performed in which heart rate feedback was provided either to subjects with various phobias or to subjects with speech anxiety. In the first of these series, Nunes and Marks[81,82] provided heart rate feedback to simple phobics during exposure to feared objects. In the first study, which used 10 female subjects with animal phobias, the investigators found that feedback to decrease heart rate was associated with an average reduction of three beats per minute. However, there was no concomitant change in anxiety levels. In the second study 10 animal phobics received instructions to decrease heart rate either with or without feedback in a complex sequential design. The investigators found that heart rate was significantly reduced with feedback compared to instructions alone, the difference amounting to approximately two beats per minute. Again, this effect was not accompanied by a corresponding reduction in anxiety.

Gatchel and coworkers conducted a series of experiments on subjects with speech anxiety. In each of these studies feedback was provided to decrease heart rate. In the first study[83] the effect of two sessions of heart rate feedback was assessed on the heart rate response to a three-minute speech preceded by five minutes of preparation time. The effect of feedback versus no feedback was evaluated in the context of high versus low expectancy of success. It was found that biofeedback resulted in smaller increases in heart rate than did no feedback, regardless of expectancy. The feedback group also showed a greater reduction in anxiety. High-expectancy instructions tended to augment further the treatment effect on anxiety.

The second study[84] compared the effect of heart rate feedback with that of false feedback, muscular relaxation, and the combination of muscular relaxation and heart rate feedback. During training the heart rate feedback and relaxation groups showed significantly lower heart rates than the false-feedback group. During the speech test, heart rate increased most in the false-feedback group and least in the combined relaxation/feedback group, whereas the muscular relaxation only and biofeedback only groups had intermediate but equivalent results. However, there was no difference between any of the treatments in ratings anxiety.

A third study[85] followed up the puzzling finding of the effectiveness of false heart rate feedback in reducing anxiety ratings of the previous study. The following conditions were evaluated: combined muscular relaxation/-heart rate feedback, "systematic desensitization," and false heart rate feedback. The investigators again found that the greatest heart rate reduction during the posttreatment speech occurred in the feedback group. However, anxiety levels were reduced equally in all three groups.

In a final study[86] McKinney and Gatchel introduced speech skill training as a treatment. This treatment was compared with heart rate feedback and a combination of heart rate feedback and speech skills training. The investigators again found that the two groups involving feedback had the lowest heart rates during the posttreatment test speech. However, the speech skill training groups had the most improvement of overt motor signs of nervousness, as rated by observers.

It appears from these studies that subjects likely to have increased heart rate reactivity due to anxiety may show a more pronounced effect of feedback. However, as has often been found in anxiety research, there was no association between changes in heart rate and changes in anxiety ratings. Nevertheless, it may be that biofeedback studies with subjects identified as "heart rate reactors" might more consistently show effects of biofeedback over mere instructions than might studies with normal subjects.

Modification of Cardiovascular Response to Exercise

The modification of cardiovascular responses to exercise has been suggested to have clinical applications for patients with angina pectoris, although we know of no controlled outcome study assessing the clinical effect of this procedure. In earlier sections we described the effects of relaxation response treatment on cardiovascular response to dynamic exercise[34,49] and static exercise.[36] In a later section on biofeedback-assisted relaxation, we describe two studies using galvanic skin response (GSR) feedback to assist relaxation. However, the greatest number of studies attempting to modify cardiovascular response to exercise have employed heart rate feedback or pulse transit time feedback. Goldstein and coworkers[87] assigned normal volunteers to an immediate- or delayed-treatment group. Subjects in the immediate-treatment group were provided with five weekly 75-minute sessions of feedback to minimize the heart rate increase induced by mild treadmill exercise. Subjects in the delayed-treatment group engaged in five sessions of the same exercise without feedback. After the first five trials, the subjects of the delayed-treatment group were provided with feedback to lower their heart rates for five sessions, while the feedback was withdrawn for members of the immediate-feedback group. Results showed a significant within-session decrease in heart rate reactivity in the feedback group compared with the delayed-treatment control group. Systolic pressure and the heart rate pressure product showed a similar pattern: the reactions of both these variables were lower in the feedback group than in the control group. Surprisingly, the treatment effect was not replicated in the delayed-treatment group.

Perski and Engel[88] performed a similar study employing submaximal bicycle ergometer exercise. They found that during exercise, members of the control group raised their heart rates by 32 beats per minute, while subjects in the feedback group raised their heart rates by only 17 beats per minute. Heart rate and systolic pressure product followed a similar pattern. There was no difference between groups with respect to systolic pressure. During five additional sessions, the control group began biofeedback training. During these sessions, heart rate reactivity was reduced by 13 beats per minute. The original feedback group continued without feedback for two sessions. In this group heart rate increased by only three beats per minute compared with the last two biofeedback sessions. Thus, in this study, unlike the study by Goldstein and coworkers, treatment effects were also observed in the delayed-treatment group. Furthermore, the treatment gains of the immediate-treatment group were maintained during two posttreatment sessions without feedback.

Neither the Goldstein nor the Perski studies separated the effect of feedback from the effect of instructions. In a recent study Lo and Johnston[89] examined this question and also evaluated the effect of feedback of the heart rate and pulse transit time product. As we discuss in the next section, pulse transit time is thought to be related to blood pressure, although the degree to which these two variables are associated can vary. Lo and Johnston assigned 36 normal, healthy volunteers to one of three treatments which were given during bicycle ergometer exercise: feedback of the interbeat interval (IBI), feedback of the product of pulse transit time and IBI, and instructions only. The treatments lasted four sessions and were followed by a final fifth session without feedback. The investigators found that the product feedback group showed a significant lengthening of IBI, that is, slowing of heart rate, across sessions compared with the instructions-only group; the former group also showed a significant change compared with its own initial session. IBI feedback achieved intermediate results that were not significantly different from either instructions only or product feedback.

Because the product feedback condition appeared to have been the most effective, Lo and Johnston, in a second study[90] with the same basic experimental design, examined the effect of feedback of the product of heart rate and pulse transit time compared to no treatment (habituation) and to relaxation training. They found that IBI became significantly longer (heart rate decreased) in the feedback group compared with the relaxation or control group. The same pattern was observed in the group receiving feedback on the product of pulse transit time and IBI.

Taken together, these four studies demonstrated rather convincingly the possibility of controlling heart rate during dynamic exercise. Two studies have examined whether or not the same results can be accomplished in static exercise. In a study by Clemens and Shattock,[91] feedback to increase or decrease heart rate was provided while the subjects engaged in a 10 percent, 30 percent, and 50 percent of maximal static hand grip contraction. It was found that there was a significant difference between the increase and decrease conditions; however, it appears that feedback to decrease was no different from no feedback, except perhaps at the 50 percent contraction level.

In the second study,[92] Riley and Furedy assigned 36 subjects to one of four groups: instructions to increase or decrease heart rate, combined with verbal feedback versus no feedback. The stress task consisted of the subject's pulling a 36-kilo spring weight for 10 seconds. After three practice trials and two baseline trials without instructions, 20 trials were provided in which the assigned treatment was given. Results indicated a significant progressive decline over trials in heart rate responses for the decrease condition, regardless of feedback. There was no change across conditioning trials in the increase condition, although heart rate was higher during the conditioning trials than during the baseline trials for the increase groups. Thus, the two studies on static muscular exercise did not find as convincing an effect of feedback as the ones on dynamic exercise. This conclusion parallels the exercise findings for relaxation response treatments[36,49] discussed in earlier sections.

The studies on heart rate control during dynamic exercise are characterized by the fact that treatment or training consistently occurred during exposure to the stressor. In many studies with other stressors, treatment was implemented during rest, prior to exposure to aversive stimuli. It may be that techniques to modify physiological arousal are more effective when they are acquired in conjunction with exposure to aversive stimuli. Nevertheless, it would be important to evaluate the specific contribution of the technique, in this case, biofeedback. It may be that biofeedback training during stress exposure results in higher expectancies regarding potential control of stress responses than do instructions given under similar conditions.

Pulse Transit Time Feedback

A biofeedback modality besides heart rate that has been studied in the context of cardiovascular reactivity is pulse transit time. Pulse transit time or its inverse, pulse wave velocity, has been considered a correlate of blood pressure, although the degree of this relationship can vary, partly depending on how it is measured (e.g., between the ECG R wave and finger pulse, between the R wave and earlobe, or between two arterial sites).[93–95] One of the investigators most active in studying pulse transit time, Steptoe, conducted three studies evaluating the effect of transit time feedback on reactivity. In the first study,[96] instructions to lower blood pressure were compared with feedback of R wave to radial pulse transit time. In both conditions, subjects were told to reduce their blood pressure during an auditory-choice reaction time task. It was explained to the feedback subjects that changes in blood pressure would be accomplished by changes in pulse transit time. The relationship between pulse transit time and blood pressure was determined by measuring blood pressure changes at the beginning and end of each session. The correlation between pulse transit time and blood pressure was -0.71 for systolic pressure but nonsignificant for diastolic pressure. It was found that subjects who had received only instructions exhibited gradually reduced pulse transit times over minutes within trials over the four minutes of each task, implying an increase in blood pressure. Subjects receiving transit time biofeedback, in addition to lengthening their transit times, also showed the highest heart rates. Thus, this study provided some evidence that the reactivity of pulse transit time and perhaps systolic pressure could be modified by pulse transit time feedback. However, this effect did not generalize to heart rate reactivity.

In the second study Steptoe conducted two experiments comparing pulse transit time feedback with meditation.[97] In the first experiment a reaction time task was again employed as the stressor. In the second experiment both reaction time and a mental arithmetic tasks were used. Results showed that in the first experiment meditation subjects but not biofeedback subjects decreased their pulse transit time during stress, implying an elevation of systolic pressure in the meditation subjects. However, meditation subjects decreased their heart rates more than did the feedback subjects. Thus, as in the earlier study,[96] the heart rate and transit time changes were not parallel. In the second experiment the results depended on which of the two tasks the subjects were engaged in. During the reaction time task there was no difference in transit time response between the feedback and meditation groups. During the mental arithmetic task, however, pulse transit time response increased, implying that blood pressure decreased more rapidly across the three experimental sessions in the feedback group. Furthermore, the feedback group showed a superior generalization to two no-feedback trials held at the end of the experiment.

In the third study Steptoe and Ross[98] improved the design of the earlier studies by including a control group and a test for transfer of training to a task to which the subjects had not been exposed during training. They also modified the feedback procedure by averaging pulse transit time over three-second epochs rather than providing it on a beat-by-beat basis. This alteration resulted in a less confusing feedback display. Furthermore, they provided a somewhat more intensive relaxation intervention by periodically relaying autogenic phases to the subjects while they were engaged in the experimental conditions. Thirty subjects were assigned to a pulse transit group, relaxation group, or control group. Each of the treatment groups underwent four sessions of their assigned training, both during rest and during three tasks presented in counterbalanced order: mental arithmetic, word association, and digit symbol tasks. Transfer of training was assessed in two ways: first, the mental arithmetic task was reimplemented without feedback; and second, a new task, the alphabet task, was provided, to which the subjects had had no prior exposure during their practice trials.

The results indicated, interestingly, that during the trials in which no task was provided, the pulse transit time of the relaxation subjects lengthened relative to that of the feedback or control subjects. During trials involving training concomitantly with one of the tasks, there was a significant treatment effect favoring feedback on interbeat interval reactivity but not on transit time reactivity. On the mental arithmetic transfer task, both treatment groups showed decreased heart rate reactivity, whereas no treatment effect was reported for transit time. On the new task (the alphabet transfer task), the feedback group initially showed the smallest transit time and interbeat interval responses. As the program progressed, however, the relaxation group was able to catch up with the feedback group. Importantly, Steptoe and Ross found that the degree of control obtained over cardiovascular reactivity was the greatest for those subjects who had exhibited the greatest reactivity before treatment. This effect was present even after controlling for the regression effects that were evident in the control group.

A final recent study on transit time feedback was conducted by Benthem and Glaros,[99] who compared the effect of pulse transit time response to mental arithmetic. Forty-eight normal subjects were assigned to one of four groups: transit time feedback plus stress, transit time feedback without stress, false feedback plus stress, and stress-only control. In the pulse transit time plus stress group, subjects first performed a mental arithmetic task and then received pulse transit time feedback after completion of this task. Thus, this treatment involved feedback applied immediately after a stressor. In the no-stress condition, the treatments were provided after a prolonged baseline without stress. During a fourth generalization session, all subjects performed the mental arithmetic task without feedback. It was found that before treatment, pulse transit time decreased during stress in all four groups. After treatment, only the pulse transit time plus stress group showed an attenuation of this response. Thus, consistent with the discussion in the previous section on control of heart rate during dynamic exercise, pulse transit time feedback during stress recovery produced the desired effect, whereas feedback after rest and false feedback did not.

Biofeedback of Relaxation Parameters

As mentioned earlier, biofeedback therapy can be employed either to modify such cardiovascular responses as heart rate, blood pressure, or pulse transit time directly or to facilitate the development of a state of relaxation through feedback of variables thought to mimic the peripheral effects of relaxation. Such variables include finger temperature, skin conductance, EEG alpha wave activity, and electromyographic levels. In most clinical applications, biofeedback and relaxation instructions are given simultaneously, hence the term *biofeedback-assisted relaxation*. In some studies, however, the biofeedback procedure was given in isolation, often with less clinical effect. We first discuss studies that employed biofeedback without concomitant relaxation and then conclude with studies on biofeedback-assisted relaxation.

Electromyographic (EMG) Feedback.   Two studies examined the effect of electromyographic feedback on the responses of various physiological parameters to stress. In the first study Burish and Schwartz[100] compared five conditions: frontalis feedback administered during the stress of anticipated and actual electric shock, frontalis feedback administered without stress, exposure to stress without feedback, and no stress/no feedback. The subjects in these four conditions received a low grade of electric shock after the first training period and were threatened by shock during the second training period. A fifth comparison group that had never been exposed to shock or threat of shock was also included. Results indicated that biofeedback training had no effect on pulse rate response to threat of shock.

In the second study Shirley et al.[101] compared the effects of three sessions of EMG feedback of multiple muscle sites with feedback of only frontalis activity and with no-treatment controls in 36 undergraduate students. The dependent variables were shock-induced reactivity of pulse rate, finger pulse volume, and skin temperature. Results indicated that none of these variables showed a decrease in reactivity to the stress of shock, although all showed lower resting levels during the multiple site feedback condition than during the other two conditions. In conclusion, neither of the two studies using EMG feedback without a program of relaxation showed any effects on cardiovascular reactivity.

Feedback of Peripheral Finger Temperature.   Stouffer et al.[102] assessed the effects of the following treatments on cardiovascular reactivity to the cold pressor test: temperature feedback, yoked feedback, and no feedback. Forty-eight subjects were assigned to one of these treatment, which lasted for five sessions. During the posttreatment cold pressor test, no differences were found between the treatments with respect to reactivity of heart rate or blood pressure. Thus, this study found no evidence that temperature feedback without concomitant relaxation instructions given to normal subjects could reduce cardiovascular reactivity to stress.

Alpha Feedback.   Two studies assessed the effect of EEG feedback to enhance alpha wave density on cardiovascular response to stress. In the first of these, Chisholm et al. assigned 36 volunteers to contingent feedback, noncontingent feedback, or music control groups.[103] Each treatment lasted for 24 minutes. The treatment was preceded and followed by a series of aversive trials in which a tone was followed by shock after a 30-second interval. The investigators found that during the posttreatment test, alpha levels were enhanced in the contingent feedback group only. However, no attenuation of heart rate reactivity was obtained. Thus, similarly to EMG and temperature feedback, alpha feedback alone failed to reduce cardiovascular reactivity to stress.

The second study by Lehrer[45] involved both anxious and normal subjects. The results with the anxious subjects were described earlier in the section on relaxation. The normal subjects were assigned to progressive muscular relaxation, alpha training, or no-treatment control. Results indicated that no treatment effects were found for cardiac accelerations under stress in normal subjects. Taken together, the Chisholm et al. and Lehrer studies indicate that alpha feedback has no effect on reducing cardiovascular stress response.

Biofeedback-Assisted Relaxation.   As mentioned earlier, biofeedback-assisted relaxation involves the combination of relaxation with feedback of a physiological parameter known to change with increasing levels of relaxation, such as finger temperature, skin conductance (GSR), or the electromyogram (EMG). The combination of heart rate feedback and relaxation was assessed by DeGood and Adams[70] and by Gatchel, Hatch, and coworkers.[84,85] These studies were discussed in the section on heart rate feedback.

EMG-feedback-assisted relaxation was assessed in a study by Gatchel, Korman, and coworkers.[104] The investigators assigned 12 undergraduate volunteers to either EMG feedback or false EMG feedback. The feedback group also received one session of relaxation training before the two sessions of EMG feedback. After treatment, subjects were threatened with the stress of electric shock, which was not delivered. The investigators found that during the acquisition trials, heart rate declined in the biofeedback-assisted relaxation group and increased in the group that received false feedback; however, there was no transfer of this effect to the stress trials. Thus, EMG-feedback-assisted relaxation could not produce an attenuation of cardiovascular response to stress in the normal subjects of this study.

GSR-feedback-assisted relaxation was assessed in two studies by Steptoe and coworkers. In the first study, Steptoe and Greer[105] provided 30 minutes of taped relaxation instructions with or without GSR feedback during two sessions to 16 normal subjects in a crossover design. Before and after the training, two mental tasks taken from the Nufferno test and from Raven's Matrices were given. Results indicated that during the treatment itself, heart rate decreased more rapidly with feedback than without. During the posttreatment mental task, heart rate was significantly lower than during the pretreatment task for both groups; however, there was no differential treatment effect. Because of concerns about experimental control, Falkowski and Steptoe[106] conducted a second study, in which 20 normal subjects were assigned to two sessions of relaxation plus skin conduction feedback or to a self-relaxation condition (i.e., relaxation without relaxation instructions). Raven's Matrices and the industrial accident film, *It Did Not Have to Happen*, served as stressors. There was no effect of treatment on the heart rate response to any of the stressors.

The studies discussed so far essentially obtained negative results but involved one-session experiments with normal subjects. Two studies have examined the effect of a longer treatment program of biofeedback-assisted relaxation with clinical subjects. Using both an exercise stressor and the cold pressor test, Patel[107] studied the effects of a six-week program of biofeedback-assisted relaxation compared with attention control in 32 hypertensive subjects, 14 of whom were on antihypertensive medication. On the cold pressor test, the treatment groups exhibited a significant decline of systolic and diastolic maximal rise, as well as an increase of the rate of recovery, whereas the performance of the control group did not change from pre- to post-"treatment." The difference between the treatment and control groups was also significant. On the exercise test the same pattern was found except that the difference between the groups on systolic rise was not significant.

Datey[108] reported a similar study with 20 hypertensive patients on medication. After treatment, the medication would be reduced by 33 percent in the treatment group, whereas no medication reductions was performed in the control group. On the cold pressor test, the treatment group showed a significant decline in average rise of systolic and diastolic pressure and a decrease of recovery time. No corresponding changes were found in the control group. However, the differences between the groups were not tested for significance. On the exercise test, the same pattern emerged, except that the reduction of diastolic rise in the treatment group was not significant.

These last four studies indicate that biofeedback-assisted relaxation reduced cardiovascular reactivity to stress in hypertensive patients but not in normotensive controls. Of special note, the study by Patel[107] demonstrated the significant treatment effects on reactivity in the context of a study designed to evaluate the potential confounding effects of expectancy and other nonspecific treatment factors.

CONCLUSION

The behavioral approaches to the control of cardiovascular reactivity discussed in this chapter were developed as a result of underlying assumptions of the relationship between aversive stimuli, or "stressors," and cardiovascular responses. A general model of these assumptions is shown in Figure 22.1. The model involves three basic elements: (1) an environmental situation, (2) the perception or appraisal of that situation as "aversive," that

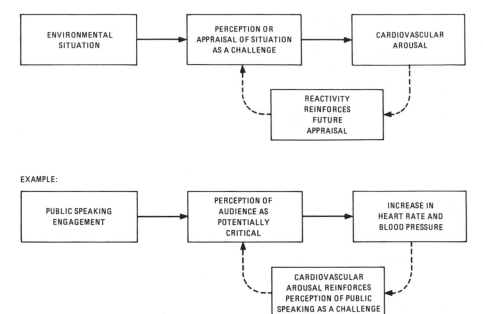

FIGURE 22.1.   A model for the relationship between stressors and cardiovascular reactivity.

is, as a "stressor," and (3) the cardiovascular response elicited by this appraisal. The model, as shown in the figure, is in its simplest form. It becomes more elaborate as secondary elements are considered, such as the reinforcing effect of physiological reactivity on future appraisals of similar stimuli, and the influence of repeated exposure to stimuli and their consequences on the development of anticipatory appraisals of events as stressors. However, even in its most simple form the model provides a framework for the classification of behavioral techniques used to reduce cardiovascular reactivity to stress.

Thus, the behavioral or psychological interventions that have been applied in an effort to modify cardiovascular reactivity can be classified into cognitive restructuring strategies, techniques based on muscular or mental relaxation, and biofeedback approaches, each of which is founded on certain assumptions regarding the nature of cardiovascular responses to stress.

Cognitive approaches assume that cardiovascular responses to stress are influenced by perceptions or appraisal of aversive situations (Figure 22.1). The objective of cognitive approaches is to alter these appraisals and, by doing so, prevent, reduce, or otherwise modify cardiovascular reactivity. Laboratory and clinical studies indicate that such cognitive strategies as detachment, redefinition, diversion, and narrowing attention are capable of modifying the cardiovascular effects of stress. However, the effects of specific strategies have varied across studies. Furthermore, until recently, cognitive techniques have been studied primarily in experimental rather than clinical contexts. In such laboratory or experimental paradigms, cognitive strategies are typically taught with only one training session. That acute effects are obtained with such simple instructional interventions is encouraging but underscores the need for further study of these procedures in the context of a larger time frame.

Approaches based on *relaxation techniques* attempt to modify cardiovascular reactivity by engendering a state of mental and physical deactivation. Progressive muscle relaxation places an emphasis on reducing physical tension, whereas meditation emphasizes mental relaxation. Autogenic training focuses on both mental and physical relaxation. The primary rationale underlying these techniques is that their mental and physical effects are opposite and therefore can counterbalance the physiological changes produced by stress. However, the hemodynamic and endocrinological effects of relaxation strategies are not uniform and, at times, do not always confirm the assumption that the physiological effects of relaxation are the opposite of those of stress. In particular, some forms of meditation may produce cardiovascular and neuroendocrine changes that appear to be in the same rather than opposite directions as those expected from stress.[34,36]

In general, studies examining the effects of relaxation approaches on cardiovascular reactivity have yielded inconsistent results. The studies that report positive findings [e.g.,51-53] often examined effects in subjects reporting anxiety, suggesting that these strategies may be more effective in reducing reactivity in subjects with elevated arousal than in subjects with lower arousal. Besides being an example of the "law of initial values," one explanation that reactivity subjects are more amenable to treatment is that they may have more positive expectations about the efficacy of relaxation to lower their stress response. One study[60] directly investigated the influence of expectancy in these techniques and demonstrated that the subjects' cognitive expectations are highly significant factors in determining treatment effects. These findings point to the need for further study of the specific effects of relaxation or meditation, and of the extent to which these approaches are operating directly by reducing physiological arousal or indirectly through changes in such cognitive factors as expectancy.

In the context of cardiovascular reactivity, *biofeedback strategies* focus on training subjects in the control of physiologic responses either by directly modifying cardiovascular variables or by facilitating a relaxed state, which is thought to reduce stress responses. The assumption underlying the application of these approaches to the modification of cardiovascular reactivity is that the control engendered by the feedback can be used by subjects to reduce their cardiovascular reactivity despite exposure to aversive situations. While early studies of heart rate feedback demonstrated reduction in heart rate responses to stress, most later research demonstrated that these effects did not occur independently from cognitive variables. The results of these later studies indicate that subject's cognitive or instructional set or expectancy play a significant role in determining treatment or training effects, and call into question the concept that biofeedback per se accounts for control of heart rate reactivity. Thus, as with relaxation research, these studies shed doubt on the assumption that these treatments achieve change through a direct reduction of reactivity. On the other hand, they suggest that such cognitive factors involved in biofeedback as expectancy are influencing response to stress, perhaps by modifying the appraisal of stress.

To summarize, cognitive techniques, relaxation and biofeedback all have been able to reduce cardiovascular reactivity, at least in selected subgroups of subjects. It is encouraging that those subgroups that do seem to respond to treatment, that is, those characterized by a comparatively high tendency to react to stress, are the same as those that we suspect might be at increased risk to develop cardiovascular disease. If epidemiological research were to establish elevated cardiovascular reactivity as a cardiovascular risk factor in its own right, then it would be important to further develop behavioral techniques to reduce such reactivity and assess their effects. In particular, techniques would be needed that can result in long-term effects that generalize to extratherapeutic environments. Furthermore, more broadly based interventions, which take into account other known influences on cardiovascular reactivity, might need to be designed. As discussed elsewhere in this book, such influences include psychosocial influences on reactivity as well as substances that stimulate or reduce reactivity. Even more importantly, the final answer to whether or not behavioral techniques can be employed to reduce cardiovascular disease would need to be demonstrated by controlled outcome studies.

REFERENCES

1. Epstein S: Expectancy and magnitude of reaction in a noxious UCS. *Psychophysiology* **10**:100–111, 1974.

2. Thompson SC: Will it hurt less if I can control it? A complex answer to a simple question. *Psychol Bull* **90**:89–101, 1981.

3. Speisman JC, Lazarus RS, et al: Experimental reduction of stress based on ego-defense theory. *J Abnorm Psychol* **68**:367–380, 1964.

4. Lazarus RS, Alfert E: Short-circuiting of threat by experimentally altering cognitive appraisal. *J Abnorm Psychol* **69**:195–205, 1964.

5. Lazarus RS, Opton EM, et al: The principle of short-circuiting of threat: Further evidence. *J Pers* **33**:622–635, 1965.

6. Koriat A, Melkman R, et al: The self-control of emotional reactions to a stressful film. *J Pers* **40**:601–619, 1972.

7. Holmes DS, Houston BK: Effectiveness of situation redefinition and affective isolation in coping with stress. *J Pers Soc Psychol* **29**:212–218, 1974.

8. Bloom LR, Houston B, et al: The effectiveness of attentional diversion and situation redefinition for reducing stress due to an ambiguous threat. *J Res Pers* **11**:83–94, 1977.

9. Houston BK, Holmes D: Effect of avoidant thinking and reappraisal for coping with threat involving temporal uncertainty. *J Pers Soc Psychol* **3**:382–388, 1974.

10. Grimm L, Kanfer FH: Tolerance of aversive stimulation. *Behav Ther* **7**:593–601, 1976.

11. Leventhal H, Brown D, et al: Effects of preparatory information about sensations, threat of pain, and attention on cold pressor distress. *J Pers Soc Psychol* **37**:688–714, 1979.

12. Ahles TA, Blanchard EB, Leventhal H: Cognitive control of pain: Attention to the sensory aspects of the cold pressor stimulus. *Cognitive Ther Res* **7**:159–178, 1983.

13. Ellis A: *Reason and Emotion in Psychotherapy*. New York, Stuart, 1962.

14. Meichenbaum D: *Cognitive-behavior Modification*. New York, Plenum, 1977.

15. Girodo M, Stein SJ: Self-talk and the work of worrying in confronting a stressor. *Cognitive Ther Res* **2**:305–307, 1978.

16. Kaplan RM, Metzger G, Jablecki C: Brief cognitive and relaxation training increases tolerance for a painful clinical electromyographic examination. *Psychosom Med* **45**:155–158, 1983.

17. Jacobson E: *Progressive Relaxation* (2nd ed). Chicago, University of Chicago Press, 1938.

18. Bernstein DA, Borkovec TC: *Progressive Relaxation Training*. Champaign, IL, Research Press, 1973.

19. Beary JF, Benson H: A simple psychophysiologic technique which elicits the hypometabolic changes of relaxation response. *Psychosom Med* **36**:115–120, 1974.

20. Luthe W, Schulz JH: *Autogenic therapy: II. Medical application*. New York, Grune & Stratton, 1969.

21. Lantzsch W, Drunkenmolle C: Kreislaufanalytische Untersuchungen bei Patienten mit essentieller Hypertonie während der ersten und zweiten Standardübung des Autogenen Trainings. *Psychiatr Clin* **8**:223–228, 1975.

22. Davidson DM, Winchester MA, et al: Effects of relaxation therapy on cardiac performance and sympathetic activity in patients with organic heart disease. *Psychosom Med* **41**:303–309, 1979.

23. Messerli FH, Decarvalho JGR, et al: Systematic hemodynamic effects of biofeedback in borderline hypertension. *Clin Sci* **57**:437–439, 1979.

24. DeGood DE, Redgate ES: Interrelationship of plasma cortisol and other activation indices during EMG biofeedback training. *J Behav Med* **5**:213–223, 1982.

25. McGrady AV, Yonker R, et al: The effect of biofeedback assisted relaxation training on blood pressure and selected biochemical parameters in patients with essential hypertension. *Biofeedback Self Regul* **6**:343–353, 1981.

26. Patel C, Marmot MG, Terry DJ: Controlled trial of biofeedback aided behavioral methods in reducing mild hypertension. *Br Med J* **282**:2005–2008, 1981.

27. Jevning R, Wilson AF, et al: Redistribution of blood flow in acute hypometabolic behavior. *Am J Physiol* **235**:9–92, 1978.

28. Jevning R, Wilson AF, Davidson JM: Adrenocortical activity during meditation. *Horm Behav* **10**:54–60, 1978.

29. Michaels RR, Parra J, et al: Renin, cortisol, and aldosterone during transcendental meditation. *Psychosom Med* **41**:50–55, 1979.

30. Stone RA, DeLeo J: Psychotherapeutic control of hypertension. *N Engl J Med* **294**:80–84, 1976.

31. Pollack AA, Weber MA, et al: Limitations of transcendental meditation in the treatment of essential hypertension. *Lancet* **1**:71–72, 1977.

32. Goldstein IB, Shapiro D, et al: Comparison of drug and behavioral treatments of essential hypertension. *Health Psychol* **1**:7–26, 1982.

33. Michaels RR, Huber MJ, McCanne DS: Evaluation of transcendental meditation as a method of reducing stress. *Science* **192**:1242–1244, 1976.

34. Lang R, Dehof K, et al: Sympathetic activity and transcendental meditation. *J Neural Transm* **44**:117–135, 1979.

35. Corby JC, Roth WT, et al: Psychophysiological correlates of the practice of tantric yoga meditation. *Arch Gen Psychiatry* **35**:571–577, 1978.

36. Hoffman JW, Benson H, et al: Reduced sympathetic nervous system responsivity associated with the relaxation response. *Science* **215**:191–192, 1982.

37. Keefe FJ, Surwit RS, Pilon RN: Biofeedback, autogenic training and progressive relaxation in the treatment of Raynaud's disease: A comparative study. *J Appl Behav Anal* **13**:3–11, 1980.

38. Surwit RS, Pilon RN, Fenton CH: Behavioral treatment of Raynaud's disease. *J Behav Med* **1**:323–335, 1978.

39. Folkins CH, Lawson KD, et al: Desensitization and the experimental reduction of threat. *J Abnorm Psychol* **73**:100–113, 1968.

40. Lomont JF, Edwards JE: The role of relaxation in systematic desensitization. *Behav Res Ther* **5**:11–25, 1967.

41. Paul GL: Inhibition of physiological response to stressful imagery by relaxation training and hypnotically suggested relaxation. *Behav Res Ther* **7**:249–256, 1969.

42. Paul GL, Trimble RW: Recorded vs. "live" relaxation training and hypnotic suggestion: Comparative effectiveness for reducing physiological arousal and inhibiting stress response. *Behav Ther* **1**:285–302, 1970.

43. Wolpe J: *Psychotherapy by Reciprocal Inhibition*. Stanford, CA, Stanford University Press, 1958.

44. Lehrer PM: Physiological effects of relaxation in a double-blind analog desensitization. *Behav Ther* **3**:193–208, 1972.

45. Lehrer PM: Psychophysiological effects of progressive relaxation in anxiety neurotic patients and of progressive relaxation and alpha feedback in nonpatients. *J Consult Clin Psychol* **46**:389–404, 1978.

46. Goleman DJ, Schwartz GE: Meditation as an intervention in stress reactivity. *J Consult Clin Psychol* **44**:456–466, 1976.

47. Mills WW, Farrow JT: The transcendental meditation technique and acute experimental pain. *Psychosom Med* **43**:157–163, 1981.

48. Benson H, Dryer T, Hartley LH: Decreased $\dot{V}O_2$ consumption during exercise with elicitation of the relaxation response. *J Human Stress* **4**:38–42, 1978.

49. Gervino EV, Veazey AE: The physiologic effects of Benson's relaxation response during submaximal aerobic exercise. *J Cardiac Rehab* **4**:254–259, 1984.

50. Lehrer PM, Schoickett S, et al: Psychophysiological and cognitive responses to stressful stimuli in subjects practicing progressive relaxation and clinically standardized meditation. *Behav Res Ther* **18**:293–303, 1980.

51. Lehrer PM, Woolfolk RL, et al: Progressive relaxation and meditation: A study of psychophysiological and therapeutic differences between two techniques. *Behav Res Ther* **21**:651–662, 1983.

52. Kirsch I, Henry D: Self-desensitization and meditation in the reduction of public speaking anxiety. *J Consult Clin Psychol* **47**:536–541, 1979.

53. Wilson A, Wilson AS: Psychophysiological and learning correlates of anxiety and induced muscle relaxation. *Psychophysiology* **6**:740–748, 1970.

54. Boswell PC, Murry EJ: Effects of meditation of psychological and physiological measures of anxiety. *J Consult Clin Psychol* **47**:606–607, 1979.

55. Jorgensen RS, Houston BK, Zurawski RM: Anxiety management training in the treatment of essential hypertension. *Behav Res Ther* **19**:467–474, 1981.

56. English EH, Baker TB: Relaxation training and cardiovascular response to experimental stressors. *Health Psychol* **2**:239–259, 1983.

57. Redmond DP, Gaylor MS, et al: Blood pressure and heart-rate response to verbal instruction and relaxation in hypertension. *Psychosom Med* **36**:285–297, 1974.

58. Agras WS, Horne M, Taylor CB: Expectation and the blood pressure lowering effects of relaxation. *Psychosom Med* **44**:389–395, 1982.

59. Puente AE, Beiman I: The effects of behavior therapy, self-relaxation, and transcendental meditation on cardiovascular stress response. *J Clin Psychol* **36**:291–295, 1980.

60. Bradley BW, McCanne TR: Autonomic responses to stress: The effects of progressive relaxation, the relaxation response and expectancy of relief. *Biofeedback Self Regul* **6**:235–251, 1981.

61. Brener J, Hothersall D: Heart rate control under conditions of augmented sensory feedback. *Psychophysiology* **3**:23–28, 1966.

62. Engel BT, Hansen SP: Operant conditioning of heart rate slowing. *Psychophysiology* **3**:176–187, 1966.

63. Hnatiow M, Lang PJ: Learned stabilization of cardiac rate. *Psychophysiology* **1**:330–336, 1965.

64. Miller NE, DiCara L: Instrumental learning of heart rate changes in curarized rats: Shaping and specificity to discriminative stimulus. *J Comp Physiol Psychol* **63**:12–19, 1967.

65. Shapiro D, Tursky B, et al: Effects of feedback and reinforcement on the control of human systolic blood pressure. *Science* **163**:588–590, 1969.

66. Trowill JA: Instrumental conditioning of the heart rate in the curarized rat. *J Comp Physiol Psychol* **63**:7–11, 1967.

67. Sirota AD, Schwartz E, Shapiro D: Voluntary control of human heart rate: Effect on reaction to aversive stimulation. *J Abnorm Psychol* **83**:261–267, 1974.

68. Williams JL, Adkins JR: Voluntary control of heart rate during anxiety and oxygen deprivation. *Psychol Record* **24**:3–16, 1974.

69. Sirota AD, Schwartz GE, Shapiro D: Voluntary control of human heart rate: Effect on reaction to aversive stimulation: A replication and extension. *J Abnorm Psychol* **85**:473–477, 1976.

70. DeGood DE, Adams AS: Control of cardiac response under aversive stimulation. Superiority of a heart-rate feedback condition. *Biofeedback Self Regul* **1**:373–385, 1976.

71. Magnusson E, Hedberg B, Tunved J: Heart rate control and aversive stimulation. *Biol Psychiatry* **12**:211–222, 1981.

72. Malcuit G, Beaudry J: Voluntary heart rate lowering following a cardiovascular arousing task. *Biol Psychiatry* **10**:201–210, 1980.

73. Bouchard MA, Labelle J: Voluntary heart rate deceleration: A critical evaluation. *Biofeedback Self Regul* **7**:121–137, 1982.

74. Victor R, Mainardi A, Shapiro D: Effects of biofeedback and voluntary control procedures on heart rate and perception of pain during the cold pressor test. *Psychosom Med* **40**:216–225, 1978.

75. Reeves JL, Shapiro D: Heart-rate biofeedback and cold pressor pain. *Psychophysiology* **19**:393–403, 1982.

76. Reeves JL, Shapiro D: Heart-rate reactivity to cold pressor stress following biofeedback training. *Beiofeedback Self Regul* **8**:87–99, 1983.

77. McCanne TR: Changes in autonomic responding to stress after practice at controlling heart rate. *Biofeedback Self Regul* **8**:9–24, 1983.

78. Bennett DH, Holmes DS, Frost RO: Effects of instructions, biofeedback, reward and cognitive meditation on the control of heart rate and the application of that control in a stressful situation. *J Res Pers* **12**:416–430, 1978.

79. Carroll D, Evans L: Effects of heart-rate biofeedback and false biofeedback on reactions to stressful stimulation. *Percept Mot Skills* **53**:387–393, 1981.

80. Lott GG, Gatchel RL: A multi-response analysis of learned heart rate control. *Psychophysiology* **15**:576–581, 1978.

81. Nunes JS, Marks IM: Feedback of true heart rate during exposure in vivo. *Arch Gen Psychiatry* **32**:933–936, 1975.

82. Nunes JS, Marks IM: Feedback of true heart rate during exposure in vivo: Partial replication with methodological improvement. *Arch Gen Psychiatry* **33**:1346–1350, 1976.

83. Gatchel RJ, Proctor JD: Effectiveness of voluntary heart rate control in reducing speech anxiety. *J Consult Clin Psychol* **44**:381–389, 1976.

84. Gatchel RJ, Hatch JP, et al: Comparative effectiveness of voluntary heart rate control and muscular relaxation as active coping skills for reducing speech anxiety. *J Consult Clin Psychol* **43**:1093–1100, 1977.

85. Gatchel RJ, Hatch JP, et al: Comparison of heart rate biofeedback, false biofeedback and systematic desensitization in reducing speech anxiety: Short and long-term effectiveness. *J Consult Clin Psychol* **47**:620–622, 1979.

86. McKinney ME, Gatchel RJ: The comparative effectiveness of heart rate biofeedback, speech skills training, and a combination of both in treating public-speaking anxiety. *Biofeedback Self Regul* **7**:71–81, 1982.

87. Goldstein DS, Ross RS, Brady JV: Biofeedback heart rate training during exercise. *Biofeedback Self Regul* **2**:107–125, 1977.

88. Perski A, Engel BT: The role of behavioral conditioning in the cardiovascular adjustment to exercise. *Biofeedback Self Regul* **3**:91–98, 1980.

89. Lo CR, Johnston DW: Cardiovascular feedback during dynamic exercise. *Psychophysiology* **21**:199–211, 1984.

90. Lo CR, Johnston DW: The self-control of the cardiovascular response to exercise using feedback of the product of interbeat interval and pulse transit time. *Psychosom Med* **46**:115–125, 1984.

91. Clemens WJ, Shattock RJ: Voluntary heart rate control during static muscular effort. *Psychophysiology* **16**:327–332, 1979.

92. Riley DM, Furedy JJ: Effects of instructions and contingency of reinforcement on the operant conditioning of human phasic heart rate change. *Psychophysiology* **18**:75–81, 1981.

93. Obrist PA, Light KC, et al: Pulse Transit Time: Relationship to blood pressure and myocardial performance. *Psychophysiology* **16**:292–301, 1979.

94. Jennings JR, Choi S: Methodology: An arterial to peripheral pulse wave velocity measure. *Psychophysiology* **20**:410–418, 1983.

95. Newlin DB: Relationships of pulse transmission times to pre-ejection period and blood pressure. *Psychophysiology* **18**:316–321, 1981.

96. Steptoe A: Voluntary blood pressure reductions measured with pulse transit time: Training conditions and reactions to mental work. *Psychophysiology* **14**:492–498, 1977.

97. Steptoe A: The regulation of blood pressure reactions to taxing conditions using pulse transit time feedback and relaxation. *Psychophysiology* **15**:429–438, 1978.

98. Steptoe A, Ross A: Voluntary control of cardiovascular reactions to demanding tasks. *Biofeedback Self Regul* **7**:149–167, 1982.

99. Benthem JA, Glaros AG: Self-control of stress-induced cardiovascular change using transit-time feedback. *Psychophysiology* **19**:502–505, 1982.

100. Burish TG, Schwartz DP: EMG biofeedback training, transfer of training, and coping with stress. *Psychosom Res* **24**:85–96, 1980.

101. Shirley MC, Burish TG, Rowe C: Effectiveness of multiple-site EMG biofeedback in the reduction of arousal. *Biofeedback Self Regul* **7**:167–184, 1982.

102. Stouffer GR, Jensen JOS, Nesset BL: Effects of contingent versus yoked temperature feedback on voluntary temperature control and cold stress tolerance. *Biofeedback Self Regul* **4**:51–61, 1979.

103. Chisholm RC, DeGood DE, Hartz MA: Effects of alpha feedback training on occipital EEG, heart rate, and experiential reactivity to a laboratory stressor. *Psychophysiology* **14**:157–163, 1977.

104. Gatchel RJ, Korman M, et al: A multiple-response evaluation of EMG biofeedback performance during training and stress-induction conditions. *Psychophysiology* **15**:253–258, 1978.

105. Steptoe A, Greer K: Relaxation and skin conductance feedback in the control of reactions to cognitive tasks. *Biol Psychol* **10**:127–138, 1980.

106. Falkowski J, Steptoe A: Biofeedback-assisted relaxation in the control of reactions to a challenging task and anxiety-provoking film. *Behav Res Ther* **21**:161–167, 1981.

107. Patel CH: Biofeedback-aided relaxation and meditation in the management of hypertension. *Biofeedback Self Regul* **2**:1–41, 1977.

108. Datey KK: Role of biofeedback training in hypertension and stress. *J Postgrad Med* **26**:68–73, 1980.

PART VI

23

Summary, Conclusions, and Implications

KAREN A. MATTHEWS

Having reviewed in great detail accumulating evidence and conceptual and methodological issues relating to stress-induced reactivity and risk for cardiovascular disease, this volume now summarizes the principal findings and highlights key directions for future research in the field. The first two sections of the present chapter consider the data and issues regarding the relationship of stress and reactivity and the relationship of reactivity and cardiovascular disease respectively. The next section notes implications of the data for intervention and for primary and secondary prevention efforts. The chapter concludes by underscoring several arenas of basic research necessary to evaluate adequately the reactivity hypothesis.

STRESS AND REACTIVITY

Reactivity is defined as the deviation of a physiologic response parameter(s) from a comparison or control value that results from an individual's response to a discrete, environmental stimulus. The stimulus can be primarily physical or psychological in nature, for example, strenuous exercise or performing a boring task, respectively. According to this definition, variability of a physiological parameter measured throughout the day—for example, casual blood pressure readings—would not constitute a valid measure of reactivity unless the nature and magnitude of the environmental stimuli to which the individual is responding are specified. Similarly, lability of resting pressure when measured on successive occasions would not be regarded as a measure of reactivity unless a discrete, identifiable environmental elicitor can be identified. This is not to say that measures of variability or lability are unimportant or uninteresting for human physiology or for the pathogenesis of cardiovascular disease. Rather, *reactivity* is the term reserved for those situations in which a physiologic deviation can be attributed to a clear, environmental stimulus over and above ordinary fluctuations.

To be important to the pathogenesis of cardiovascular disease, reactivity must be assumed to be a relatively stable characteristic of the individual. Stated differently, the same persons should repeatedly show heightened physiological responses to stressors in order for those responses to lead to long-term risk. There are two types of evidence pertinent to the stability of reactivity, and the body of evidence is extremely limited and thus only suggestive (see chapters by Buell, Alpert, and McCrory; Krantz, Manuck, and Wing). The first is the extent to which individuals who show heightened responses to a given stressor will be the same individuals who show relatively heightened responses on a subsequent occasion to the same stressor. Several studies do show that heart rate responses to a psychological stressor were reliable over time or reproducible. However, the reproducibility of other cardiovascular or biochemical measures during stress is largely unknown.

The second type of evidence relevant to the notion that reactivity is a stable characteristic concerns the similarity of the magnitude of an individual's physiological responses to similar as well as to diverse stressors. Available data do indicate some modest correspondence in magnitude among responses to tasks. To evaluate this issue properly, however, there must be an a priori way to classify stressor characteristics. It seems naive to expect individuals who are reactive to one task, such as making a speech, to be reactive to all other tasks. Rather, it is more likely that individuals are reactive to a specific class of stressors from a possible taxonomy of stressors.

The latter point brings us to consider an important issue in understanding the relationship of stress and reactivity. What, if any, are the classes of stressors that are important to reactivity? Some investigators believe it is fruitful to classify reactivity according to common characteristics of the stressor. One way to classify stressor characteristics is to partition them into two groups, those that are primarily physical and those that are primarily psychological, and the book devotes two chapters (Buell et al.; Krantz et al.)

to this dichotomy. However, it should be emphasized that considerable data indicate that the physiologic (as well as psychologic and behavioral) effects of many physical stressors depend at least partly on psychological factors. That is, if physical stressors are not viewed or interpreted in the laboratory situation as harmful, threatening, or noxious, they can produce smaller and even opposite physiologic responses. This trend may not apply, however, to those physical tasks that are graded and require individuals to work to their maximal capacity.

The chapters by Buell et al., Krantz et al., and Williams describe different dimensions that can be used to classify stressors. In the case of physical stressors, Buell et al. classify them according to their diagnostic usefulness. The Krantz et al. chapter offers a number of discrete dimensions used to classify characteristics of psychological stressors: challenge, unpredictability or novelty, and task difficulty. It also reviews different dimensions of stressors according to the common physiological responses elicited by them: active versus passive coping, sensory intake versus mental work, specific emotions, and helplessness versus mastery. Krantz et al. conclude that such efforts to classify stressors are extremely useful because they permit a modicum of prediction and point to common response patterns across some stressors. However, they also note that these dimensions are somewhat overlapping and ill-defined. Reviewing the same data, Williams takes a broader perspective. He suggests that many of the dimensions that group stressors according to their common physiological responses are entirely overlapping and that two predominant stress patterns subsume the phenomenon of reactivity.

While efforts to classify reactivity to stressors according to their diagnostic utility, shared stressor characteristics, or common physiological responses have been useful, there are other important issues to consider in understanding the classes of stressors that elicit reactivity. One is simply that stressors can be classified not only by the responses they elicit during exposure but also by the physiologic patterns during the recovery period immediately after exposure. For example, one can imagine that stressors that elicit identical patterns during stress but differ in the duration and quality of the responses during recovery or the cessation of stress may exact a different toll on an individual. In fact, recovery period responses might be the most diagnostic of compromised functioning. Thus, it is interesting to note that, with few exceptions, reactivity studies do not even discuss recovery data.

The acute-chronic nature of the stressors may also be important for classification of stressors. For example, although repeated exposure to a single stressor may eventually lead to habituation, it may also diminish responses to a similar stressor; without information on the chronicity of exposure to the stressor, such diminished responses may be inappropriately interpreted. Another illustration is that repeated exposure to a stressor may lead to a delayed reactivity response; that is, the stressor may have a cumulative effect such that the initial exposure to a stressful event may not co-occur with the peak physiological response. Because reactivity has been largely studied in the laboratory (with the notable exception of the work of Frankenhaeuser and colleagues), relatively little attention has been paid to reactivity induced by chronic stress.

A final consideration is also related to the fact that reactivity has been studied in the laboratory. We do not know the extent to which laboratory challenges elicit responses similar to those exhibited on exposure to naturally occurring, or "field," stress. Stated differently, is reactivity to stressors presented in the laboratory similar in intensity, duration, and pattern to reactivity during naturally occurring stressors in the field? As discussed in the chapter by Manuck and Krantz, at least two models of how laboratory-induced reactivity generalizes to reactivity measured in the field may be suggested. One, called the recurrent activation model, hypothesizes that laboratory-induced reactivity is representative of the individual's peak and repeated responses to discrete challenges throughout the day. A second model, called the prevailing state model, presumes that laboratory-induced reactivity is representative of the prevailing physiological function of the individual and that baseline or resting measures of physiological parameters are only characteristic of limited periods of quiescence, that is, states that occur in the absence of notable behavioral stimuli. Needless to say, we have little data on the viability of these two models or on the more general issue of the relationship between laboratory and field measures of reactivity, despite the advent of exciting technological advances such as ambulatory monitoring of blood pressure, heart rate, and respiration.

REACTIVITY AND CARDIOVASCULAR DISEASE

A crucial question concerns the nature of the relationship between reactivity and cardiovascular disease. Given the absence of human prospective studies designed to address this question, we cannot answer it. Nonetheless, there are important data bearing on the relationship of reactivity and cardiovascular disease, and they do support continued investigation of reactivity as a precursor, precipitant, and consequence of cardiovascular disease. The following two sections highlight the relevant data regarding reactivity as a risk factor for coronary heart disease and hypertension respectively. A third section considers evidence regarding the interaction of stress and risk or protective factors with reactivity and their conjoint impact on cardiovascular disease.

Reactivity and Coronary Heart Disease

Three types of evidence address the relationship between individual differences in reactivity to stress and coronary heart disease (see chapter by Manuck and Krantz). First, data from two studies of cynomolgus monkeys show that male and female monkeys who exhibit elevated heart rates in response to a common laboratory stressor have upon their subsequent sacrifice almost twice the coronary artery atherosclerosis of their low heart rate reactive counterparts (see chapter by Clarkson, Manuck, and Kaplan).

A second line of evidence comes from the findings of case-control studies of reactivity to stress among cardiac patients. For the most part, these investigations demonstrate a heightened reactivity to laboratory stressors in patients with histories of angina or previous infarction, compared with noncoronary patient samples or nonpatient controls. While some of these studies can be faulted on methodological grounds, the reported data do suggest that reactivity is a characteristic of patients suffering from coronary artery disease.

The final source of data concerns the autonomic and neuroendocrine response characteristics of persons at behavioral risk for coronary heart disease—that is, Type A individuals (see chapter by Houston). This line of investigation was encouraged by the observation that influences of Type A behavior on risk for coronary heart disease have been largely independent of the concomitant effects of other major risk factors, such as serum cholesterol, hypertension, smoking, and age. The majority of published studies show that Type A men exhibit larger increases in blood pressure, heart rate, and plasma catecholamines and/or cortisol relative to Type B men, when exposed to appropriately stressful tasks.

Taking these data together, it can be concluded that the preponderance of available evidence, while largely indirect, is consistent with the hypothesis that individual differences in physiologic responses to environmental stress are a risk factor for coronary heart disease. Nonetheless, the key types of evidence to test the reactivity hypothesis have yet to be collected, and the specific mechanisms by which reactivity may promote atherosclerosis underlying coronary heart disease remain unclear.

In regard to the latter, the chapter by Clarkson et al. suggests several hemodynamic mechanisms that might play a role in atherogenesis. The predominant model of the atherogenic process is the endothelial injury model offered by Ross and Glomset and amended by Schwartz: repeated injury to the endothelial cell lining of the artery wall may alter the permeability of the cell membrane to lipoproteins. This altered permeability permits the influx of low-density lipoprotein (LDL) cholesterol into the intima of the artery and a consequent acceleration in the development of atherosclerotic plaque. Clarkson and colleagues speculate that repeated transient elevations of heart rate and/or blood pressure in the individual reactive to environmental stress may represent a hemodynamic stimulus for endothelial injury, particularly at arterial sites subject to acute changes in the strength and direction of pulsatile flow.

Herd, in his chapter, speculates that pronounced neuroendocrine responses to stress may be pathogenic, even when simultaneous cardiovascular adjustments to stress are absent. He notes that plasma levels of cortisol are related to lipid metabolism and that this relationship may be mediated by cortisol effects on insulin sensitivity. High circulating levels of insulin may promote atherogenesis by direct effects on vascular smooth muscle cell proliferation and by elevating circulating levels of triglycerides and LDL.

Reactivity and Hypertension

As in the literature on reactivity and coronary heart disease, three lines of evidence are also pertinent to the relationship between stress-induced reactivity and hypertension (see chapters by Falkner and Light; Manuck and Krantz). First, rats specifically bred for susceptibility to hypertension (spontaneously hypertensive rats: SHR) react to laboratory stressors with greater rises in blood pressure, heart rate, and plasma catecholamines than do normotensive rats; moreover, this hyperresponsivity among SHRs is detectable even prior to the acquisition of hypertension.

Second, case-control studies of hypertensive and normotensive patients reveal distinctive cardiovascular responses of hypertensives to environmental stimuli, particularly those behavioral in nature. In addition, exaggerated neuroendocrine responses are apparent in young, borderline hypertensive individuals.

Third, studies of normotensive offspring of hypertensive parents, who are at high risk for subsequent hypertension, also show exaggerated cardiovascular responses to behavioral stimuli (see chapters by Falkner and Light; Rose).

Like the evidence regarding the relationship between stress-induced reactivity and coronary heart disease, the evidence regarding hypertension is not definitive because it is indirect and is subject to multiple, noncausal interpretations. Although there are several prospective studies of reactivity to the cold pressor test and risk for subsequent hypertension, these studies suffer from several flaws, including the choice of the cold pressor as the elicitor of reactivity. The cold pressor test seldom elicits reactivity differences between hypertensive patients and normotensive persons or between the

normotensive offspring of hypertensive parents and offspring of normotensive parents. Nonetheless, the bulk of available data do support continued
investigation of the relationship between stress-induced reactivity and
hypertension.

Several mechanisms by which reactivity may lead to elevated blood
pressure have been proposed (see chapters by Falkner and Light; Julius,
Weder, and Hinderliter; Manuck and Krantz). Obrist suggests that markedly
increased cardiac output exhibited under stress by highly reactive individuals
may, with sufficient time, lead to increased resistance in the peripheral
vasculature through either of two mechanisms. These include structural
changes in the arterioles as proposed by Folkow and intrinsic autoregulatory
processes acting to prevent an overperfusion of body tissues. Julius suggests
that heightened alertness in individuals having certain behavioral attributes
leads to disruption of centrally integrated cardiovascular autonomic tone,
which leads to an initial increased sympathetic drive on the myocardium
followed eventually by a down-regulation of adrenergic receptors in the
heart and a lowered or normalized cardiac output. Finally, the chapter by
Falkner and Light suggests that reactivity to stress may contribute to
hypertension through disruption of the regulation of blood volume and
control of blood pressure by the kidneys in relatively young, susceptible
individuals.

Although significant progress has been made in testing and elaborating
the above proposed mechanisms, major etiologic questions remain. Julius
and colleagues question whether or not repeated blood pressure elevations
induced by behavioral stressors lead to hypertension because blood pressure
variability (with no specific environmental elicitor) does not predict subsequent hypertensive complications. They also indicate that mild hypertensives
are not necessarily more variable or labile in their casual blood pressures
than are severe hypertensives or normotensives, although mild hypertensives are more responsive to behavioral stimuli. It is also not clear how mild
hypertension influenced by behavioral factors might progress to established
hypertension. Most importantly, no population-based longitudinal data are
yet available that show that normotensives reactive to behavioral stimuli
are more likely than nonreactive normotensives to become hypertensive
later in life.

Reactivity in Interaction with Risk or Protective Factors for Cardiovascular Disease

As the chapter by Dembroski notes, risk and protective factors for
cardiovascular disease are typically measured during a minimum of envir-

onmental stimulation. For example, in epidemiological studies, blood pressure is measured three to nine times after a period of quiescence. Furthermore, the first measure taken by a given technician is typically elevated, because of the well-known anticipatory or novelty response of study participants, and is often discarded in epidemiological investigations. Such measures can be termed static in contrast to risk factors measured during standardized environmental stimuli, which can be termed dynamic. Levels of major risk factors—for example, of blood pressure, cholesterol, and cigarette smoking—are affected by psychological stress. In consequence, dynamic measures of these traditional risk factors may predict significant cardiovascular disease not accounted for by the static measures. (This assertion, of course, assumes that there is little or a modest relationship in individuals between their static and dynamic risk factor levels—a relationship that has not been systematically evaluated.) Stated differently, environmental stress may also interact with risk and protective factors in altering physiologic reactivity, which, in turn, may heighten the risk for a clinical event.

Chapters by Epstein and Jennings and by Dembroski evaluate this hypothesis in regard to the conjoint effect of stress and cigarette smoking, an established risk factor for coronary heart disease, on risk for clinical coronary heart disease. Epstein and Jennings suggest three pathways by which stress and cigarette smoking may interact: (1) stress may cause smokers to increase their consumption of nicotine and place them at higher risk; (2) stress may alter the perception and behavior of smokers in stressful situations in such a way that stress is not adequately coped with and is thus increased; and (3) risk of smoking for coronary heart disease may be in part due to the combined effect of smoking and stress on pathogenic processes responsible for risk of coronary heart disease. Consistent with the third pathway, Dembroski reports data from his own laboratory indicating that exposure to stress combined with cigarette smoking in a sample of habitual smokers leads to elevations in cardiovascular responses over and above the effects of stress and smoking taken separately.

The chapter on caffeine by Shapiro, Lane, and Henry notes the great difficulty in evaluating caffeine consumption as a risk factor for cardiovascular disease because of caffeine's high association with cigarette smoking. Nonetheless, sufficient epidemiological evidence exists to implicate caffeine itself as a possible risk factor. The chapter describes the potent effects of caffeine measured statically and dynamically on physiological function and the strong influence of stress on caffeine consumption. Thus, the chapter provides the rationale and relevant background for investigations of stress-induced reactivity and caffeine consumption on risk for cardiovascular disease and their underlying mechanisms.

Falkner and Light note that consumption of salt in the diet is implicated as a risk factor for hypertension in diverse studies ranging from ecological investigations (comparisons of national prevalence rates of hypertension and salt consumption) to well-controlled experimental studies of animals sensitive to sodium. They also review evidence indicating that high sodium intake augments pressor responses to stress and that behavioral stress can induce retention of sodium and water at least over short time periods, whereas potassium intake may attenuate these responses. Furthermore, the demonstrable variations in pressure and reactivity induced by changes in these environmental factors are more pronounced in persons with borderline hypertension or a family history of hypertension, suggesting that an early susceptibility might be particularly apparent with exposure to certain environmental factors. Thus, it appears that further investigations of the renal and cardiovascular effects of stress exposure under conditions of sodium loading and sodium depletion would be most instructive in understanding biobehavioral mechanisms in risk for hypertension.

In contrast to nicotine, caffeine, and salt consumption, moderate alcohol consumption and vigorous exercise habits can serve as protective factors in risk for cardiovascular disease. The chapter by Levenson provides an overview of alcohol metabolism and the negative effects of alcohol use. Nonetheless, he also presents epidemiological data indicating that moderate consumption of alcohol might be related to low risk for coronary heart disease. The nature of the relationship might be J-shaped with heavy drinkers being at higher levels of risk, followed by abstainers, followed by moderate drinkers. Several reasons for this relationship are considered, including the effects of alcohol on levels of high-density lipoproteins and on neuroendocrine and cardiovascular responses to stress. In regard to the latter, research in Levenson's laboratory consistently shows that alcohol diminishes cardiovascular responses to stressors.

The chapter by Dimsdale, Alpert, and Schneiderman indicates that, in general, individuals reporting high levels of physical activity are protected from coronary heart disease. However, a cautionary note is issued because of methodological problems in existing studies; for example, healthy individuals are more likely to comply with exercise prescriptions than unhealthy ones. Several mechanisms for a possible exercise-disease relationship are suggested: increased aerobic fitness and enhanced mood presumably associated with high levels of exercise may lead to improved efficiency of the myocardium; and most pertinent to this volume, vigorous exercise habits may lead to more efficient ways of handling psychological stress. In regard to the last mechanism, the very little data on the topic do not permit any strong conclusions. Thus, it is important that future research examine the relationships among exercise, aerobic fitness, and physiological responses to stressors in attempting to understand risk for coronary heart disease.

IMPLICATIONS FOR INTERVENTION

To the extent that individual differences in physiologic responses to stressors are implicated in risk for cardiovascular disease, it is important to consider interventions that may be appropriate for altering stress-induced responses. In the previous section, we reviewed some of the factors that may interact with stress in producing highly reactive responses. From this review, it is reasonable to suggest that standard behavioral intervention programs for reducing intake of nicotine, caffeine, salt, and excessive alcohol and for increasing activity level might prove useful in reducing risk for cardiovascular disease in two ways: (1) directly because of their suspected or established associations with cardiovascular disease; and (2) indirectly through their suspected associations with stress-induced reactivity, which, in turn, might be associated with cardiovascular disease. Other techniques to reduce stress responses would involve altering the frequency, duration, and intensity of the stressors themselves. Those interventions, however, are beyond the scope of this volume. Instead, we consider here pharmacological and behavioral interventions for reducing physiological responses to stressors.

The chapter by Surwit introduces us to the pharmacological and behavioral intervention research that the chapter by Shapiro, Krantz, and Grim and by Jacob and Chesney respectively review in greater detail. The Shapiro et al. chapter focuses on those pharmacological compounds that block peripheral receptors, notably the adrenergic blocking agents. These compounds "permit" the central nervous system input and output to occur essentially unchanged but prevent the symptomatic activation of cardiovascular receptors mediating such responses as heart rate and blood pressure changes. After a review of the actions and types of these compounds (known as beta blockers) and their cardiovascular consequences, Shapiro et al. conclude that beta blockers may have positive effects on treatment of patients with cardiovascular disease and on management of anxiety, performance during stressful events, and Type A behavior. In spite of these positive effects, whether or not beta blockers are the treatment of choice raises complex medical, ethical, and social issues, particularly in the case of healthy individuals. For example, beta blockers can have unexpected systemic side effects, which can also be cumulative, and might have abuse potential. Nonetheless, the discovery of beta blocker agents has been a very exciting advance in treatment and control of cardiovascular disease. Because of the impact of beta blockers on cardiovascular responses to stressors, future investigations of the effects of these drugs on health and behavior can also contribute to understanding the relationships among stress, cardiovascular reactivity, and disease.

Jacob and Chesney present a complex picture of the therapeutic efficacy of behavioral interventions for attenuating physiological responses to stressors. They review findings regarding three related types of interventions: cognitive approaches that change the perception or appraisal of the stressor; techniques designed to induce mental and/or physical relaxation; and biofeedback strategies aimed at directly or indirectly modifying cardiovascular parameters. After an exhaustive review, they conclude that all techniques have been able to reduce cardiovascular responses to acute stressors, at least in selected subgroups of participants. Yet, there are a sufficient number of negative studies to warrant a strong, cautionary note about the efficacy of behavioral techniques. Also problematic for drawing firm conclusions are that a single behavioral intervention has been operationalized in a diverse manner across studies; that effects have been studied primarily in experimental, not clinical contexts; and that interventions are often taught in few sessions without the benefit of follow-up sessions to reinforce or maintain use of the newly acquired skills.

DIRECTIONS FOR FUTURE RESEARCH

Throughout this volume, we have identified key questions for future research. It is worthwhile, nonetheless, to highlight here major lines of basic research needed to address the relationships between stress and reactivity, and between reactivity and risk for cardiovascular disease. To advance knowledge of the relationship of stress and reactivity, parametric research is required to identify those stressors, either naturally occurring in the field or presented in the laboratory, that yield reliable, physiological responses in diverse populations of individuals. The same stressor need not and probably cannot be useful for all groups. For example, there may be substantial gender differences in the types of stressors that elicit strong responses (see chapter by Watkins and Eaker). Yet, one can imagine that a battery of stressors could include diverse stimuli known to elicit relevant responses in both men and women. Administering such a battery would take into account the high likelihood that there are somewhat discrete classes of stressors and that these classes may vary in importance for predicting cardiovascular disease in different subpopulations.

In future research, greater emphasis should be placed on understanding patterns of physiological responses to stressors. Current published research on reactivity has focused on blood pressure and heart rate responses to stress. While these investigations have yielded important findings, they cannot identify the mechanisms underlying such responses and do not take advantage of the advances in measurement of cardiovascular function and neuroendocrine responses that can be adapted for laboratory research. In this regard, the chapters by Schneiderman and Pickering and by Goldstein and McDonald provide particularly useful information on specific measures and technological advances for investigators of stress and reactivity.

Further investigation is required to understand those variables affecting the relationship of stress and reactivity. Chapters by Houston, by Watkins and Eaker, and by Rose reveal key attributes already known to characterize the highly reactive individual (e.g., Type A individuals, defensively anxious individuals, males, and offspring of hypertensives) and suggest additional possible attributes for future study. Less known are the health behaviors that affect reactivity. Yet the chapters on caffeine, nicotine, alcohol, salt, and exercise all present data, albeit limited, suggesting that they influence physiological responses to stress. The interplay of these factors and stress holds great promise for understanding physiological function during daily events. At a minimum the data suggest the importance of measuring health behaviors of participants in reactivity studies to identify the systematic variance due to caffeine, nicotine, and other such factors.

Let us now turn our attention to considering what is needed to advance knowledge of the relationship of reactivity and cardiovascular disease. It is vitally important to continue ongoing basic research on identifying the key physiologic parameters for cardiovascular risk that can also be measured dynamically in large-scale studies.

Now that suitable animal models exist for studying atherosclerosis and hypertension, it is important to take advantage of the level of control animal studies allow and study designs not feasible with humans. Not only can animal studies be used to investigate crucial questions regarding the prospective relationship of reactivity and cardiovascular disease, but they can also address the precise interactions among stress-induced reactivity, health behaviors like salt ingestion, and cardiovascular risk. Selective breeding of genetically predisposed animals is particularly informative for understanding the cardiovascular risk associated with stress-induced reactivity.

Although animal studies may prove invaluable, the central questions in this area must ultimately be addressed by prospective, epidemiological studies of humans. Ongoing epidemiological studies may permit opportunistic analyses of the relationship of reactivity and cardiovascular disease, but it is unlikely that any current study can incorporate sufficient sophistication in the measurement of reactivity to allow a "true" test of the reactivity hypothesis. Instead, ongoing studies may provide important hints about the nature of the associations in various populations. It is also possible to ascertain the long-term health status of the many participants in already completed psychophysiological studies of stress and reactivity. Although such efforts may also be informative, they are not likely to provide a definitive test of the reactivity hypothesis for two essential reasons: (1) because the studies tend to overrely on certain types of subject participants and on measurement of only heart rate and blood pressure; and (2) a detailed medical history and comprehensive clinical assessment of initial health status is typically not part of the experimental protocol. Thus, a new, epidemiological investigation specifically designed to evaluate the reactivity hypothesis is necessary.

As noted in the Preface and reiterated in succeeding chapters, this book is not a final accounting of the relationship between stress-induced reactivity and cardiovascular disease; rather, it is a progress report. As summarized here, the book reveals tentative support for the importance of reactivity in cardiovascular disease. It also freely points to methodologic and conceptual gaps in the reactivity hypothesis and to key data as yet unavailable. As such, the book is a primer on what are the major questions for future investigation and how to proceed in addressing these questions. Its chapters detail the current knowledge on measurement of physiological responses in the laboratory and on design of relevant stressors. The book outlines the major attributes now known to characterize persons who are highly reactive to stress and some of the health behaviors that might affect reactivity. We hope that this volume has succeeded in providing a blueprint for addressing the important and challenging research issues in understanding the interrelationships among stress, reactivity, and risk for cardiovascular disease.

Name Index

Subject Index